Make Mine a Mystery

Genreflecting Advisory Series

Diana Tixier Herald, Series Editor

Genreflecting: A Guide to Reading Interests in Genre Fiction, 5th Edition
By Diana Tixier Herald

Teen Genreflecting
By Diana Tixier Herald

Romance Fiction: A Guide to the Genre
By Kristin Ramsdell

Fluent in Fantasy: A Guide to Reading Interests
By Diana Tixier Herald

Now Read This: A Guide to Mainstream Fiction, 1978–1998
By Nancy Pearl with assistance from Martha Knappe and Chris Higashi

Now Read This II: A Guide to Mainstream Fiction, 1990–2001
By Nancy Pearl

Hooked on Horror: A Guide to Reading Interests in Horror Fiction
By Anthony J. Fonseca and June Michele Pulliam

Hooked on Horror: A Guide to Reading Interests in Horror Fiction, 2d Edition
By Anthony J. Fonseca and June Michele Pulliam

Junior Genreflecting: A Guide to Good Reads and Series Fiction for Children
By Bridget Dealy Volz, Lynda Blackburn Welborn, and Cheryl Perkins Scheer

Christian Fiction: A Guide to the Genre
By John Mort

Strictly Science Fiction: A Guide to Reading Interests
By Diana Tixier Herald and Bonnie Kunzel

Make Mine a Mystery: A Reader's Guide to Mystery and Detective Fiction
By Gary Warren Niebuhr

Make Mine a Mystery

A Reader's Guide to Mystery and Detective Fiction

Gary Warren Niebuhr

A Member of the Greenwood Publishing Group
Westport, Connecticut • London

Printed in the United States of America

LIBRARIES UNLIMITED
A Member of Greenwood Publishing Group, Inc.
88 Post Road West
Westport, CT 06881
1-800-225-5800
www.lu.com

Library of Congress Cataloging-in-Publication Data

ISBN 1-56308-784-7

Dedicated with all my love to my parents, Warren and Joyce Niebuhr. Through the magic of parenthood they set this reader on a path of lifelong learning, and for that I will always be grateful.

GWN

Contents

Chapter 4: Amateur Detectives (*cont.*)

Acknowledgments

Reading mystery fiction is my hobby. I have been a lifelong reader, and for that character trait I need to thank my mother and father whose guidance led me to be the reader that I am. As a young man, my parents allowed me access to our public libraries, and that has led to a career as a librarian.

I dabbled in the Hardy Boys and Sherlock Holmes as a developing reader, but my interests in mystery fiction as a hobby did not take off until I took a course as an undergraduate in college. The very first book we read in that survey course was *The Big Sleep* by Raymond Chandler. This book was my epiphany.

I now own about 6,000 private eye novels. I want to acknowledge the efforts of all the mystery writers whom I have encountered, and thank them for their effort on my behalf.

Along this 25-year route that I have taken, many individuals have influenced me. In the mystery field, Mary Ann Grochowski got me started, and Marv Lachman has kept me going. Wonderful editors like Jeff Meyerson, Art Scott, George Easter, Bill Ott, Lynn Kaczmarek, and Chris Aldridge have afforded me the opportunities to test my wings. I especially want to thank all the caring and giving mystery fans who have influenced me since I first entered the mystery fan community. A big thanks to Patti Cheney and her friends on Dorothy-L who helped solidify the authors included in the bibliography. A big thanks to my fellow Noirsketeers, Theodore B. Hertel, Jr. and Sandy Balzo, for their help in previewing this work.

This book could not have been written without the awe-inspiring work by Allen J. Hubin, *Crime Fiction*. There may be no greater single contribution to mystery fiction research than this effort, and it is greatly appreciated.

In the library profession, certain leaders have inspired me to try to write this book and I hope they find it up to their standards. Joyce Saricks has been an inspiration from the first time I heard the words readers' advisory, and Ted Balcom has shown how a love of books can be expressed to our customers. Roberta Johnson and Duncan Smith have shown how electronic resources can be used to promote reading in an era when many think the book is losing its purpose. As a fan, librarian, and mystery mentor, I owe a great debt to Beverly DeWeese for a lifetime of friendship built on a love of books.

However, this book would not exist except for the pioneering work, "Genreflecting," and the work done by Betty Rosenberg and Diana Tixier Herald. This is a debt that can never be paid. I would like to thank Barbara Ittner for the opportunity to produce this work, and thank all the hard-working folks at Libraries Unlimited. A big thank-you to Leslee Pohle, who edited this book with precision, and to Sharon DeJohn for her steady hand on the tiller.

Some of these annotations may have appeared previously in print in one or more of the following sources: *A Reader's Guide to the Private Eye Novel* (G. K. Hall, 1993), *Booklist*, *DAPA-EM*, *Deadly Pleasures*, *Mystery News*, or *The Poisoned Pen*.

Any errors or omissions in this work are unintentional, and in the spirit of maintaining the level of research intended to do a revision, I would appreciate receiving any comments readers may have to improve a later edition. My e-mail address is piesbook@execpc.com.

I would like to thank my wife, Denice, who may be tired of reading the next statement because it is the same statement from the last book I wrote, but it is still true. After 20 years of marriage, she still agrees to live in poverty because of a basement full of books. But she understands, and that is all I need. This book could not have been written without her support.

Introduction

An Overview of This Book

This book is to help readers' advisors, librarians, and others develop a greater understanding of the mystery genre so they can make reading recommendations and successfully answer questions raised by readers who enjoy reading mysteries. The book covers mystery detective novels where a fictional character tries to solve a puzzle concerning a crime to the administration of justice. It does not cover crime, intrigue, thrillers, suspense, adventure novels, or true crime stories.

According to 2001 statistics maintained by the Romance Writers of America from figures provided by several sources, popular fiction sales figures are as follows:

Romance fiction, 37.2 percent

Mystery/Detective/Suspense fiction, 28.1 percent

General Fiction, 12.9 percent

Science Fiction, 7.2 percent

All other types, 14.6 percent

According to the database maintained by *The Drood Review of Mystery* for 2001, there were approximately 900 new mysteries published in the United States during that year, or about three a day. In the same year, there were approximately 700 paperback reprints of previously available titles. At that rate, even the most dedicated mystery reader is going to need some guidance in selecting authors, titles, and series characters to read in the mystery fiction genre. This book serves as an introduction to the mystery, with an emphasis on the mystery series character.

Because I am attempting to represent the entire mystery detective genre, I have included titles from the entire history of the genre. The development of the mystery began in the 1700s. This book covers publications from the late 1800s to 2002. This historical approach, I hope, will deepen the readers' advisor's understanding of the genre and its evolution over time to better understand what appeals to readers of this genre. It also serves mystery readers, who often take interest in the evolution of the genre and of their favorite characters.

Many of the titles listed in this book are in print. However, some titles will only be found by searching a quality collection in a large public library or by haunting specialty mystery or used bookstores. Because of their loyalty to series characters, mystery readers are quite willing to track down older and out of print titles featuring those characters. Readers who are intrigued should not hesitate to use interlibrary loan at their local library, or use the World Wide Web to search for out-of-print book dealers that carry mystery fiction.

The titles listed for each author include all titles in a series. Titles written by the author in other areas of the mystery field (such as suspense or crime) and titles written outside the mystery genre will not be listed. (Sources listed at the end of this work can help you find additional titles by the listed authors.)

Each entry provides complete bibliographic information, listing the first edition first, whether it is the British edition or the American edition. Alternate titles are provided. An asterisk (*) at the beginning of an entry indicates that the title was not located for review in time for this publication. Unfortunately, it can also mean that the title was unavailable from interlibrary loan, a tragedy of loss that bears some contemplation for librarians interested in preserving this literature for the ages.

Although this book is intended for professionals who advise readers, it will also be useful to fans of the genre, mystery bookstore owners, educators who teach literature courses in mystery, mystery publishers, and writers who want to publish in the genre.

Developing an Interest in Readers' Advisory

One of the hardest tasks in readers' advisory service is to determine the appeal of a work of fiction and recommend read-alikes to our customers. For some librarians, this type of question can make their day. For others, it can be the excuse needed to claim it is break time and to flee to the darkest corner of the tech processing area. There is no hope here for the weak of heart, for there are no easy answers in readers' advisory. However, the good news is that there are also no wrong answers—only bad answers.

Librarians have been trained never to give an answer at the information desk without quoting chapter, verse, and source. Although valid for questions dealing with how many home runs Henry Aaron hit, this process does not work in readers' advisory. The customer is really asking for the librarian's opinion. The customer wants to hear what the librarian has to say about a particular part of literature. The customer values the librarian's opinion and is asking the librarian for guidance. Here is a golden opportunity to shine. The customer has validated the librarian as someone whom the customer trusts to consult. Not the reference books, not the databases, not the vertical file, but the librarian. No pressure there—for as everyone knows, not only has the librarian read all the books in the library, but also remembers everything about them including the color of the covers.

Readers' advisory questions are the best and the worst of information work. They combine the challenge of wanting to provide the absolutely correct answer to the reference question with the freedom to equivocate by expressing opinion and conjecture based on the librarian's own knowledge. The process can be especially challenging if the query is in a field of fiction in which the librarian does not read. Each sub-genre of fiction has its intricacies, its specialties, and its appeals. This work attempts to develop the librarian's knowledge of the intricacies and specialties of the mystery field. To speak specifically about mysteries: what make a mystery a mystery, what are the types of mysteries, and what is the general appeal of a mystery to a reader?

The Sub-Genres of Mystery Fiction

Let us take a look at the types of books in the genre to see how the definition of the sub-genres can create an appeal.

What is a *mystery*?

> A mystery is a work of fiction in which the reader is asked to help solve a puzzle. The essential ingredients are an element of crime mixed with an element of detection.

What is a *detective novel*?

> A detective novel is a mystery in which a fictional character tries to solve the puzzle before the reader does. It is an intellectual exercise. The concept is that the author will "play fair" with the reader by providing clues. It is fair for the author to use "red herrings" to distract the reader. The central question is "whodunit?"

What is a *crime novel*?

> A crime novel observes the undertaking of a criminal act, but does not necessarily have a detective who pursues either the criminal or a sense of justice.

What is *intrigue*?

> In a novel of intrigue, the goal is accomplished by devious means.

What is a *thriller*?

> A thriller is fiction designed to keep the reader interested through the use of a high degree of action, intrigue, adventure, and suspense. A thriller involves the reader emotionally.

What is *suspense*?

> A work of suspense keeps the reader waiting for particular outcomes, often by having the narrator in some kind of danger, even if it is a detective. It is also an emotional experience. Suspense poses a threat to a character who is often the primary victim of the evil. The central question is "who is it going to happen to?"

What is *adventure*?

> Dangerous actions or risks are undertaken in an adventure novel.

This book concentrates on the mystery novel with a detective hero. It excludes novels of crime, intrigue, thrillers, suspense, adventure, or true crime stories.

The Appeal of a Series Character

After years of participating in the mystery genre, both as a readers' advisor in my library, as a fan of the mystery genre, and as an educator in the field, I believe that this genre's greatest appeal is the attraction to the detective character featured within a mystery series. The majority of the entries in this book exhibit this appeal. There are a few exceptions, but not too many. The organization of this book reflects this premise, classifying approximately 2,500 titles by lead character type—amateur, public detective, and private detective. Series detectives make up the majority of titles in the genre, and readers' advisors will be able to suggest a series to a reader using the appeal of a series character. Character introductions and annotations throughout the book give brief background sketches of the detectives and offer further glimpses into the content and appeal of the series. If readers' advisors can understand the appeal of the character to the reader, then they can find other series characters with similar jobs, attitudes, styles, or mannerisms. The readers' advisors can then connect readers to a book that will give them a similar and enjoyable reading experience.

In discussing why readers like mysteries, the appeal of the main character cannot be overemphasized. Readers form an emotional attachment to their favorite characters and enjoy reading books in series about the same character. Point of view becomes an important consideration. First-person narration certainly provides a greater opportunity to bond the character to the reader, as the discussion is a direct one. Third-person narration allows authors to further exploit their characters' psyche and offer readers increased objectivity and a broader understanding of the story.

Throughout the history of the mystery, many character types have been allowed into the detective club. Today's mysteries have the freedom to use any type of individual to combat crime. This book is based on the premise that character is mystery's primary appeal and is organized around this love of character. This book's bibliography is organized according to the type of mystery characters featured in series. The basic character types are:

Amateur Detectives

- Traditional classic detectives
- Eccentric detectives
- Amateur detectives

Public Detectives

- Lone wolf police
- Detectives who support the police
- Lawyer detectives

Private Detectives

- Private investigators
- Crime specialist detectives
- Ex-cop detectives
- Rogue detectives

Mystery fans will have a predilection for specific types within these broad ranges—for example, academic amateur detectives, detectives who work in teams, or even detectives who are aided by cats. To find characters with more specific features, users are encouraged to consult the subject index. All users of this book, no matter what their level of expertise, will question the inclusion of certain authors and the exclusion of others. The authors covered in this book represent some aspect of the development and maintenance of the genre. They may be included because they are benchmark authors whose works represent the definition of a style within the genre. They may be included because of their popularity, even if that popularity was only in their own time period. Authors of single titles may be included because their single title is important in the history of the genre. Likewise, some contemporary authors may not be listed because time has not defined their role in the genre. (The sources listed at the end of this work will help you discover the potential significance of contemporary authors and their work.)

Additional Appeals of the Mystery Series

Character is not the only appeal of mystery fiction. Additional appeals include plot, setting, location, theme, and subjects. Access to titles through these features is given through the annotations, the descriptor lines at the end of the annotations, specific icons or symbols that appear throughout the text, and the indexes. Some of these appeals are discussed in Chapter 1, Advising the Mystery Reader.

Hopefully, the annotations for each title, and the indexes that are included in this book, will provide additional clues to the advisors as to what the appeals of a particular series or an individual title are. Each series entry begins with an explanation of how some of these appeals extend over the entire series. Also, each list of detectives is divided into the type of action that is typical with the series, or whether a series can be considered soft-boiled, traditional, or hard-boiled.

Watch for the following symbols in this book (an explanation of these awards is in Chapter 2, Collection Development and Preservation):

AG—The Agatha Awards winners

AN—The Anthony Awards winners

BA—The Barry Award winners

DA—The Dagger Award winners

DI—The Dilys Award winners

ED—The Edgar Award winners

MA—The Macavity Award winners

SH—The Shamus Award winners

Now let's take a closer look at how librarians can serve their readers of mysteries.

Part 1

Introduction to Mystery Fiction

Chapter 1

Advising the Mystery Reader

How Can My Reference Staff Become Readers' Advisory Librarians?

I count myself as fortunate to have had the opportunity to experience the resurgence of interest in readers' advisory service within the library community. It may seem odd that librarians need to be reminded that recommending books is a part of their daily routine. However, emphasis on reference and technology development has led librarians astray from their true path: reading and recommending books to their customers.

Several factors have contributed to this renewed interest in readers' advisory. The concept that libraries could be operated with techniques borrowed from the bookstore business was a refreshing renewal to some librarians in the 1980s. Design strategies were borrowed, including shelving materials face out to take advantage of publisher's covers and display practices that removed materials from their traditional shelves and placed them in more prominent areas. Perhaps the most influential aspect of bookstore operation on libraries was the emphasis on bestsellers and popular new works, and on delivering quantities of materials to the reader rather than quality. These developments produced a renewed awareness in fiction as a marketing tool for libraries, and the interest in promoting fiction grew.

My first introduction to the concepts of readers' advisory came from *Readers' Advisory Service in the Public Library* by Joyce G. Saricks and Nancy Brown, published by the American Library Association (ALA) in 1989. This work was revised and issued in a second edition by the same publisher in 1997. It is a manual for librarians who are interested in providing readers' advisory services in their library or need an outline for training methodologies. Many of the concepts mentioned below are from Saricks and Brown's groundbreaking manual.

Growing interest in readers' advisory encouraged the ALA and the Public Library Association (PLA) to provide workshops and training that continues today through programs at national conventions, as well as the PLA spring symposiums provided in alternate years to its national convention. Opportunities exist there to attend workshops by some of the field's major promoters, such as Joyce G. Saricks, Mary K. Chelton, Diana Tixier Herald, and Duncan Smith.

Some state associations have also taken a proactive interest in readers' advisory. In my home state, the Wisconsin Library Association has a section called the Readers' Advisory Section (READS). The section provides programming at the state annual convention that includes genre studies, author presentations, and breakout sessions for questions and answers. The section produces newsletters, bibliographies, and bookmarks to help promote readers' advisory services.

At the local level, readers' advisory can take many different forms. The first commitment is to the service and an agreement not to avoid the responsibility. This commitment is even more important in the age of electronic communication and the World Wide Web, as will be explained further in this section.

An example of a simple commitment to the service can be found in my own library. Our practice at the reference and information desk is to treat readers' advisory questions with the same care as reference questions. We have two shelves of readers' advisory basic tools to help us answer questions and to provide access to walk-in customers. Useful sites are bookmarked on our reference Internet terminal to help us answer questions. Displays, bibliographies, and bookmarks are prepared and used. We have a monthly reference meeting on a readers' advisory topic.

The next step in commitment is to establish a separate reference desk with dedicated and trained librarians whose responsibility is to answer the library's readers' advisory questions. There are many advantages to having trained librarians who are comfortable and committed to the process of readers' advisory. This dedicated staff can better develop and understand the reference tools in the field and may have the time to create their own. Selecting and retaining materials in the library can be the responsibility of the librarians who know what their customers want within the various genres. Training readers' advisory librarians becomes easier with this level of commitment.

Individual libraries or librarians must decide what level of commitment they can make to readers' advisory services. The following hints will help you develop a basic readers' advisory commitment.

Is There a Readers' Advisory Interview Like the Reference Interview?

All librarians should be trained in the basic concepts of conducting a reference interview to determine their customers' needs. The reference interview helps to determine the real needs of the customer. Any experienced librarian will be able to testify that customers often have difficulty articulating exactly what their needs are. The reference interview draws necessary clues and key words from the customer that allow the librarian to search catalogues and resources to find the information sought by the customer. This process, whether successful or not, can be a very structured process, and tools exist to make the search easier for the librarian.

The protection in a reference interview for the librarian is that the process of finding the information is one of the guarded secrets of the cloistered profession of librarianship. Years of training have provided the librarian a methodology for hunting down specific items of information that provides a comfort in the process. In a sense, by being needed as a vital part of the information-seeking process, the librarian is empowered. The same process for discovering the needs of readers' advisory customers is not always as simple, and this is why librarians often fear readers' advisory questions. When there are no clear methodologies to access the correct answers, librarians may feel threatened and avoid the situation altogether. The good news is that each day more tools are being developed to make readers' advisory questions easier to answer by traditional reference methods.

The readers' advisory experience is very different from the reference interview process. In the reference interview, the customer's needs may be initially vague and undetermined to the librarian, but the needs of a readers' advisory customer are usually clear and are often stated in quite specific terms. The readers' advisory customer often seeks an opinion, and expressing an opinion is a concept absolutely alien to reference service. Readers' advisory work can be incredibly empowering to a librarian if the librarian feels comfortable with the process and is familiar with the tools that are available to help in areas where personal knowledge is absent.

The most common questions in the readers' advisory interview are:

- If I like author X, what else has she or he written?
- If I like author X, who writes like her/him?
- If I like author/book X, what can I read next?
- Have you read any good books lately?

The task of the reader's advisory librarian is to try to determine how to satisfy the clearly stated needs of the customer. Duncan Smith developed an effective staff-training method (based on the work by Saricks and Brown mentioned earlier) for a hands-on workshop. Smith presented a simple statement, "Describe to me a book that you have read and enjoyed," to a series of customers during videotaped interviews. After viewing the videos, workshop attendees are invited to predict the reading interests of the customers. Then the attendees are able to see the reactions of the customers via the videotape. By using the approach to the readers' advisory interview modeled in the training video, librarians have an opening statement to be used for each interview.

In adapting this to the readers' advisory interview, here are some suggestions:

Question: If I like author X, who writes like her/him?

Response: Tell me what you enjoyed about author X's book.

Question: What can I read next?

Response: Describe a book that you have read recently and enjoyed.

Question: Have you read any good books lately?

Response: Describe a book that you have read recently and enjoyed.

By listening to the customer's response, the readers' advisor can identify the most important appeal factors mentioned by the customer. The goal is to understand those appeal factors and provide material to customers that will help them repeat the emotional experience they had with their previous choice of reading material.

What Is It About Mystery Fiction That Appeals to Readers?

Why do readers love mysteries? Mystery fiction has a unique structure that introduces the conventions of the genre to a reader comfortable with the format. The elements of that structure are:

the crime

the search

the resolution

The crime must have some puzzling aspects to it, or the interest and mystery in its solution is lost.

The search must involve more than one suspect for the crime or the work is intended to be another type of literature. Within that search, the author must try to lace clues that could allow the reader to solve the crime before or at the same time as the detective.

The search must be led by a detective interested in discovering the truth. That search must lead to a solution to the crime.

Reading mystery fiction is primarily a recreational activity. Implied within the structure is some exercise of the intellect, but less like a formal learning experience and more along the lines of playing a structured game with specific rules.

Readers' advisors should listen for the stated appeals mentioned by the customer in responding to the statement generated by the readers' advisory interview. These appeals include:

Main Character (and Significant Others)

The premise of this book is that most mystery readers fall in love with a character. With readers who express an interest in a character, the first issue will be whether there are other books featuring that character. The second issue is whether other authors have created similar characters. To satisfy the reader's need, the interview must reveal the characteristics of the character that appeal to the reader. Is the character male or female? What kind of detective is the character: public, private, or amateur? Is the character likeable, or flawed? Is the character soft-boiled, traditional, or hard-boiled? These and other questions will help the librarian determine the character's appeal.

Point of View

Related to the element of character is that of point of view. The difference in appeal between a first-person narration and a third-person narration can be significant to some readers. The author's ability to reveal the intricacies of the plot is dictated by point of view.

Action

Can the way a book is written affect the reader? Does its action, its tone, its very construction create different appeals in different readers? In the mystery field, the answer is a resounding yes. Different levels of action make different requirements of mystery readers, and the affect can be positive or negative depending on the reader's expectations.

What is action? This is the term that I use to describe the tone of mysteries. What level of action is appropriate is debated constantly in the mystery field. It separates and divides fans of the mystery into distinct categories. It is analogous in the readers' advisory field to dealing with the question of the gentle reads. How gentle is too gentle, and how rough is too much?

The most common terms used in the mystery field are "soft-boiled" and "hard-boiled." Even these terms can be contentious. Although hard-boiled seems to be satisfactory to its supporters, the term soft-boiled has been criticized, and substitute words like cozy or traditional are often used. In this book, the terms soft-boiled and cozy are synonymous. By whatever terms we use, these two camps are prominent and vocal within mystery readership.

In a **soft-boiled (or cozy) novel**, the action is low on the description of violence, with little overt sexual content or abusive language. A soft-boiled world is one in which society is viewed as orderly and controlled, and the crime is a failure of the society to function correctly. The society portrayed is often a closed or confined set. The inclusion of a mystery in a soft-boiled world is an intrusion. Most violent action takes place off-stage. The emphasis is on the solution of the crime. Readers anticipate a world where right and wrong are clearly defined. The society depicted in a soft-boiled novel is more moral than in a hard-boiled world, and the reader expects the detective to follow clues left by the perpetrator to an eventual administration of justice. The detective is often an amateur, although not limited to this type of detective. These series will be identified in the literature section with the word **soft-boiled** in bold.

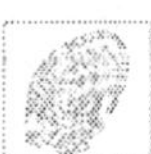

In a **hard-boiled novel**, the action is high on the description of violence, with sexual content and language of the streets. A hard-boiled world is a society where everything is suspect, including established institutions and the people who work for them—even the legal forces. The inclusion of a mystery in a hard-boiled world is inevitable. Most violent action takes place on-stage. The emphasis is on the perpetration of the crime, and characters are often driven to do what they do by circumstances that are often out of their control. Hard-boiled novels can feature protagonists who are not clearly defined as being on either the right or wrong side of the law. The administration of justice is not certain in a hard-boiled novel, and morality may have many definitions in a hard-boiled world. These series will be identified in the literature section with the word **hard-boiled** in bold.

The missing element in this equation is the mystery novel that uses elements from both of these camps. Many contemporary mysteries use elements from either style and are left somewhere outside of each. Therefore, I am choosing to define a middle-ground style that I will call the traditional novel.

In a **traditional novel,** the action uses violence to establish the seriousness of the crime without trivializing its importance or glorifying its horrifying effects. Most violent action takes place on stage but is not graphically described. The emphasis can be equally on the perpetration and solution of the crime. The protagonist's goal is to find a solution to the crime, but not necessarily through the administration of justice by an official court of law. However, the intent of a traditional novel is to restore the balance of right and wrong in a society gone wrong. These series will be identified in the literature section with the word **traditional** in bold.

Historical mysteries are identified in the literature section with the word **historical**.

Action can also involve simple aspects of the mysterythat are easy to overlook. Humor might be a good example of how the tone of the book can affect the reader. Humor can be used to pace a book—to make it light and appealing. Humor can also be used to lighten the darkest aspects of the most hard-boiled novel.

Pace

Pace refers to the time the authors take to develop the elements of their novel, including plot, theme, character development, and the other appeals listed here. Pace can be a difficult appeal to articulate. A fast-paced mystery may appeal because little time is spent on some of the other appeals listed here to concentrate on the case, the clues, and the resolution. Other mysteries are slower paced, concentrating on psychological aspects, or strengthening the involvement of the other appeals listed here. Readers have a different tolerance level for the pace of their mysteries.

Level of Violence

Few readers will ask for a book based on this appeal, but it will be a reason for a reader to reject a title. Therefore, this appeal should be determined from the interview and applied to the other stated appeals. A discussion of the importance of the level of violence can be found in the chapter introductions where the levels of action are defined and discussed. There are few resources to identify novels by their level of violence.

Use of Sexuality

Few readers ask for a book based on this appeal, but it may be a reason for a reader to reject a title. Therefore, this appeal should be determined from the interview and applied to the other stated appeals. Some readers will define sexuality as gratuitous and will reject a book that offends their sensibilities. There are few resources to identify novels by their use of sexuality.

Use of Language

Few readers will ask for a book based on this appeal, but it is sometimes given as a reason for rejecting a title. Therefore, this appeal should be determined from the interview and applied to the other stated appeals. Some readers will find language of the streets offensive and will reject a book that offends their sensibilities. There are few resources to identify novels by their use of language.

Author

Some readers become so enamored with a particular author's work that they want to read everything by that author. Satisfying their needs is relatively easy if the library has access to a large collection internally, or if the library is linked to other libraries to help supplement their own collection. Many resources are available to help the readers' advisor identify all the works by a particular author.

Title

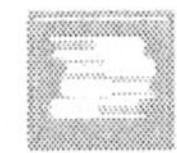

Some readers want to re-experience the satisfactory experience that the previous work just provided them. They are seeking similar titles, but not necessarily by the same author. Chances are other appeals on this list need to be consulted to discover what really provoked the reader to seek another similar experience.

Setting

Some readers enjoy books set in particular settings. The settings can be geographic, or the setting can be a location such as a hospital, a nunnery, or a cruise ship. The interview needs to identify the particular setting of appeal, and then use the available resources to identify additional settings. A good practice for librarians is to recommend books for their setting, but identify other characteristics of the book as well. This avoids disappointing the reader by providing a work that might have other characteristics that do not appeal to him or her.

Time Period

Some readers enjoy books set in particular time periods because that time period has an appeal to the reader that extends beyond the character. After the advisor identifies the particular time period, resources can be used to identify the settings. Advisors suggesting books for a time period should also identify other characteristics of the book to avoid disappointing the reader.

Subject

Some readers like to read books about subjects that they enjoy. The subjects covered by the works within this genre are endless. They can range from authors who use the same subject for each work, such as Simon Brett's use of the entertainment industry, or Diana Mott Davidson's use of cooking. Some authors only touch on a subject for one book. Then the connection is to other authors who have used the same subject matter for a plot device.

Theme

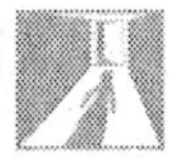

Some readers will want to read mysteries with particular themes. This may be one of the hardest appeals to identify, as there are few resources that deal with theme as a major component. Themes like racism, male/female relationships, or law and order are going to be familiar to the librarian only through genre study or personal knowledge. Reading reviews and being familiar with the genre in general will help identify themes.

Any of the above appeals might be the key feature that makes a particular reading experience unique enough for a reader to approach a readers' advisor and ask for a recommendation. The following chapters attempt to define some of these appeals for key authors in the mystery genre.

Librarians should be comfortable with the concept that opinion is acceptable in readers' advisory service. However, for those questions where opinion is not available, this book provides lists of sources and reference tools that have been developed to support readers' advisory librarians with traditional types of reference tools. Ultimately, it is the librarians' responsibility to understand their customers, understand the genre and its appeals, and understand the collection in order to have a successful readers' advisory experience.

In the traditional reference interview, discussion and participation have been a part of the process of determining the correct path to a source. This is even more vital in readers' advisory. Discussion and participation is open to other customers, other librarians, the clerical staff, and even special consultants in order to reach the goal.

Every library has staff members who read in particular areas of fiction and their expertise should be used. Librarians should not forget that clerical staff also have special areas of interest in their reading that should be considered. A network of librarians or staff in other libraries can also be developed. As librarians do more readers' advisory work, they begin to understand which of their customers or volunteers might be willing to serve as consultants in a particular genre that they enjoy. Librarians should also be aware of bookstores in their area, especially specialty bookstores that specialize in genre fiction. Owners and workers in these specialty stores are an invaluable source of knowledge.

Another difference between reference work and readers' advisory work is the time element. Readers' advisory librarians need to develop a relationship with their customers that allows for the time it takes to consult resources to provide good recommendations. If the customers realize that they will be provided with a good list of titles to read, then they will be willing to wait for a longer period of time than the average reference customer will.

What Is the Goal for a Good Readers' Advisory Contact?

When asked for reading recommendations, the readers' advisor should remember that the customer is not asking for the advisor's opinion of the book as a piece of literature, or whether the advisor enjoyed the book as a reader. Rather, the customer needs to know whether in the advisor's opinion the book's appeal fits the needs of the customer. Recommendations should be based on the wants and desires of the customer.

After customers ask a readers' advisor for suggestions, they should receive a list of titles to read. The list can be in printed form from a catalog, or it can be an armful of books suggested by the advisor. It is advisable to encourage the customer to take a number of selections because, ultimately, the recommendations are based on opinion. If one selection does not meet the reading needs of the customer, the other one might.

Readers' advisors should also be able to booktalk titles to their customers. The goal of a readers' advisory booktalk is a two sentence, non-critical annotation that might consist of the following:

- author
- title
- main character (and significant others)
- setting
- time period
- theme

An example of this is:

> Customer: I am traveling to San Francisco and love old mysteries. Are there any set in that city?
>
> Advisor: You might like Dashiell Hammett's *The Maltese Falcon,* which is a private eye novel set in San Francisco during the 1930s. It features the hunt for a missing art object by Sam Spade, and his love affair with his client, while leaving it up to the reader as to whether Sam is a good man gone bad or a good man caught in a bad situation.

What Reference Tools Are Available to Help a Librarian?

Fortunately for librarians, the renaissance in readers' advisory has been accompanied by a proliferation in reference titles to help librarians with their customers. The Topics appendix of this book lists many sources for librarians in the field of mystery fiction. Mystery fiction is a genre that has about 30 years of concentrated and effective bibliographic research, and this does help librarians in researching their customers' needs.

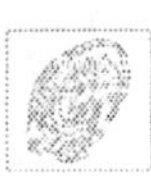

The first guide for readers' advisors was *Genreflecting* (written by Betty Rosenberg in 1982 and now in its 5th edition by Diana Tixier Herald). This guide groups books according to genre, subgenre, and theme, according to reader preferences; and it has spawned the Genreflecting Series, of which this book is a part. Another print source was developed in the 1990s that tried to provide readers' advisory librarians with a source they could quote, or offer to their customers, to help in this field. *What Do I Read Next? A Reader's Guide To Current Genre Fiction*, edited by Neil Barron, and published by Gale, produces a volume each year that provides access to mystery fiction as well as other fiction genre.

What Do I Read Next is now available in an electronic format, as is *NoveList: Electronic Readers' Advisory* from EBSCO. Librarians can use these databases to access information in a variety of formats dictated by the patrons' needs. Keyword searching capabilities help for both the general readers' advisory questions or for specific reference needs. Patrons can do their own research in these databases if access is provided through the library.

Many resources are available on the Web to link readers to books. Some websites, like The Reader's Robot (http://www.tnrdlib.bc.ca/rr.html) are even trying to link readers to the appeal of a particular book.

There are many ways in which a library can help its readers' advisory librarians. Genre stickers on the spines of books are a great way to help librarians and customers who are roaming in the fiction stacks. The fiction stacks could be organized by genre, combining like titles together on the shelves and allowing for readers' advisory browsing. Advances have been made in on-line fiction catalogs that include such helpful items as series titles, series character names, and subject headings for fiction.

How Can a Library Train Its Staff to Be Better Readers' Advisory Librarians?

Staff members need to become comfortable with benchmark authors, style, and theme for all of the subgenres of fiction to be able to make judgments for the customer. To make sure that all staff understand the principles of readers' advisory and the value of providing the services, the training should begin with the following reading list:

Chelton, Mary K. "Read any good books lately? Helping the patrons find what they want." *Library Journal*, May 1, 1993, pp. 33–37.

Herald, Diana Tixier. *Genreflecting: A Guide to Reading Interests in Genre Fiction, 5th ed.* Libraries Unlimited, 2000. $49.00. ISBN 1-563-08638-7.

May, Anne K., et al. "A Look At Reader's Advisory Services." *Library Journal*, September 15, 2000, pp. 40–43.

Ross, Catherine Sheldrick and Mary K. Chelton. "Reader's Advisory: Matching Mood and Material." *Library Journal*, February 1, 2001, pp. 52–55.

Saricks, Joyce G. and Nancy Brown. *Readers' Advisory Service in the Public Library, 2d ed.* ALA, 1997. $22.00. ISBN 0-8389-0711-3.

Smith, Duncan. "Valuing Fiction." *Booklist*, March 1, 1998, pp. 1094–1095.

Perhaps it is overly simplistic to even suggest this, but my experience in the library community requires me to state the obvious. The best method to train in readers' advisory is to

Read!

Although library customers may think that the librarian is familiar with all the titles in the library, knowing the collection is one of the most challenging aspects of readers' advisory work. Most libraries circulate their new materials amongst the staff before putting them out to the public, but how many librarians think in terms of readers' advisory when they are reviewing the titles? When reviewing fiction, staff can try to scan the books in five minutes by reading the blurb, the first chapter, and the last chapter. A staff member can develop some familiarity with the fiction titles that hopefully will be retained for later use in readers' advisory.

Adding readers' advisory training to the schedule can make a significant difference in customer service. One effective way to learn about the various genres is to do a genre study. A genre study can be done in a variety of formats; some involving reading and studying one genre, like mystery fiction, for a year. But genre studies can also be less involved. For example, at my library, we read one book a month from a particular genre, and then have a two-part discussion. The first part is a book discussion on the merits of the title, while the second part is a discussion of how the title could be used in a readers' advisory situation.

Genre studies do not have to be a group activity. Motivated librarians can do individual genre studies. Further exploring a genre of personal interest can make a librarian the local expert on that particular genre. One of the ways to maintain knowledge is to read the genre magazines or visit the Web sites relating to that genre. Belonging to a list serve that is devoted to a particular genre, or readers' advisory in general, is a great way to maintain knowledge in the field.

When learning about genre and readers' advisory, be sure to refer to the section above, "Is there a readers' advisory interview like the reference interview?" The Duncan Smith training methodology is discussed in that section.

Part of the workday can be devoted to activities that relate to readers' advisory and strengthening readers' advisory skills. One of the simplest ways to maintain booklists for customers is to borrow them from other sources. Keeping copies of the booklists in an organized folder makes them accessible to staff and customers, but building a file on a local area network might make them even more accessible. Libraries can enhance their booklists by assigning staff to create their own. Creating a booklist, especially in an area of unfamiliarity, can be a great way to learn about a genre.

Booklists can be made compact to be used as a bookmark. Bookmarks can be used with read-alike lists to attempt to draw readers from one author to a similar author. Compiling the bookmarks is a great way to store readers' advisory knowledge and it can also give the library a favorable public relations boost.

One effective way to influence readers' advisory customers prior to their appearance at the advisory desk is to prepare a booktalk for the community on a particular author or genre. Besides talking about the title(s) selected, be sure to take time to explain the resources available at the library in that particular genre. Book talks create interest in a topic, promote the library's collection, and empower customers with knowledge that can help them locate materials without a librarian's help.

A library staff's commitment to readers' advisory service is key to increasing the individual librarian's understanding of genre fiction and the customer's needs.

Book Discussions

Another similarly effective way to influence readers is to host a book discussion group. Whether done as a single title, drop-in discussion, or a series of titles built around a genre, theme, or author, book discussions can be used to empower the reader.

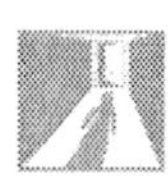

At my library, we have sponsored a mystery-book discussion for years. Each year, we pick a particular topic within the mystery genre to study. Our book discussion is not a drop-in discussion, but requires the participant to enroll for the entire season. This helps maintain numbers in the group over time and leads to a sense of community within the group that helps foster discussion. Following is a list of topics we have used over the past few years:

American Regional Mysteries

Best First Novels

British Mysteries

Classic Mysteries From the Golden Age

Edgar Award Winners

Female Private Eyes

Great Crime Novels Make Great Crime Films

Women Writers of the New Millennium

For a shorter series, try featuring books with the same plot device, as in the following examples.

Reservoir Books

A Likeness in Stone by J. Wallis Martin

On Beulah Height by Reginald Hill

In A Dry Season by Peter Robinson

Flawed Characters

The Sculptress by Minette Walters

Mr. White's Confession by Robert Clark

The Caveman's Valentine by George Dawes Green

Mallory's Oracle by Carol O'Connell

For those libraries that have drop-in book discussions or feel reluctant to have a full series devoted to the mystery, there are many fine titles that would stand on their own for a discussion. These titles will also work well with discussion groups that consider themselves readers of literary fiction and shy away from genre category titles.

Snow Falling On Cedars by David Guterson

The Blind Assassin by Margaret Atwood

A Conspiracy of Paper by David Liss

Wrack by James Bradley

These are just a few of the ways in which readers' advisory service can be improved in your library.

Chapter 2

Collection Development and Preservation

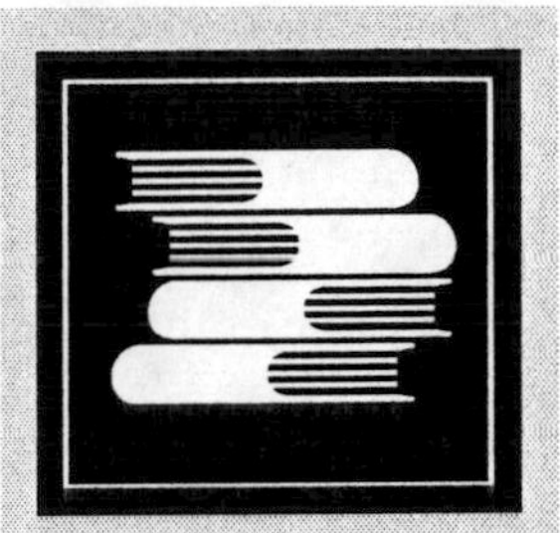

Building the Mystery Collection

In a perfect world, a library would be able to select the best mysteries each year and never have to discard or lose a copy. All the titles of a particular series would be available, in bright, fresh, and attractive copies. Money could be spent on new authors, as well as buying the new titles of the tried and true stalwarts. Paperback originals would be considered the equal of the hardcover, and both would be fully cataloged by author, title, setting, series, character, series title, and type of detective.

A library needs to establish a procedure for selecting fiction that gives fair representation to all the genres. The process should be done with care, as there are many more titles being published than most libraries can afford to buy, catalog, or warehouse. The same principles of the materials-selection policy that govern any other type of material added to the library's collection should be applied to mystery fiction.

Because of the sheer volume of mystery titles published each year, many libraries will find it relatively easy to locate mysteries to select for their collections. By determining a rough estimate of the monthly allotment for mystery fiction, a library can determine how much effort it wants to put into mystery selection. The good news is that mysteries are a popular genre and are well covered by most of the library professional journals. Journals such as *Publishers Weekly*, *Library Journal*, and *Booklist* have special sections marked mystery in each issue, and the sheer number of titles reviewed each month may be more than the average library can purchase.

If relying on reviews from professional journals only, librarians need to focus on the proper cues. Being familiar with the genre and the likes of the local readership will give librarians author-familiarity. This is key in this genre, as there is both loyalty to particular authors within the genre, but more important, the need to have each book in an author's series. If librarians are also familiar with the popular series' characters, they will be ahead of the game.

Librarians who are able to understand the terminology used in the genre will better understand the reviews. Librarians who understand their customers may know whether to have a greater emphasis on soft-boiled cozies, or whether to stock up on all the latest hard-boiled adventures.

If time or the budget allows, non-professional review sources called fanzines are available. These titles are listed in the Topics appendix of this work. Each has a unique approach to reviewing titles within the mystery genre, and when the librarians are done with the selection process, they should be placed in the circulating magazine collection for the customers to use.

Maintaining the Mystery Collection

Perhaps it is true of all genres, but hopefully any popular or significant mystery title can be maintained on the library's shelves. It is especially important to provide all the titles in a particular series. In a perfect world, when normal library use requires that the library seek a replacement for a title, a copy would simply be ordered from a major book jobber, and the book would arrive a few days later.

The sad reality is that many mystery titles have a short life span. Hardcovers are published and go out of print within one year. Paperback issues (assuming that the book is published in paperback) may extend the life of a title by keeping it in print. Certainly all the normal resources available to the library should be explored to determine if needed titles are in print.

Buying and selling out-of-print mysteries is a very large and popular part of the mystery fan community. Most out-of-print bookstores, out-of-print catalogs, and used and antiquarian bookstores have a mystery section. Librarians should become familiar with the resources available in their area. The World Wide Web has several search engines devoted to making the offerings of booksellers readily available. Librarians will need to understand concerns such as condition, edition, and collectibility before venturing into these sites.

Weeding the Mystery Collection

The simple solution to the question of whether to weed a particular mystery is its popularity. Often libraries use circulation as a measure of whether to maintain an item in the collection, and this can be applied to mystery fiction. It would be hard to disagree with the argument that if a popular genre material is not of interest to the local population, then it should be discarded.

Weeding stand-alone mystery novels is easier than dealing with the issue of series. It would make more sense to discard an entire series by an author than to individually discard some of the titles in the series and keep others in an attempt to represent the author's work.

Besides using your own circulation statistics, mystery resources such as those listed in the Topics appendix should be consulted to help determine the value of a particular title or series. Perhaps if a question is raised in the librarian's mind as to the value of a particular title or series, a display could be created to test the interest in the works at the local level.

As a standard, the bibliography presented in this book would ensure a library of a comprehensive and quality overview of this genre. Each library will need to look at the authors listed in the bibliography and decide which series would be best maintained for the reading interests of its customers.

Awards

For those interested in collection development in the genre, one approach is to select award-winning titles. Award lists can be used to do retrospective collection building, even though the issue of availability is often problematic. However, for any librarian who wants to develop a contemporary collection that reflects the recognition offered by these various awards, checking these lists annually would be a wonderful way to develop a collection that includes all the greatest hits of the genre. Including nominated works as well as the winners will equally enhance a library's collection. As with any award given in the humanities, choosing a winner is a very subjective process.

There has been a proliferation of awards in the mystery field in the 1990s. A complete list of the awards given each year can be found on the following websites:

http://www.cluelass.com

http://www.blackbird-mysteries.com/award.cfm

AG The Agatha Awards

These awards, first presented in 1988, are given to mystery fiction material from the previous year that represents the soft-boiled (cozy) literature that is featured at the annual convention called Malice Domestic where the awards are presented each May. The award is named in honor of Agatha Christie and is shaped like a teapot. Malice Domestic attendees create a list of nominees, and the awards are determined by a vote of the convention attendees.

Website: http://users.erols.com/malice/malice5.htm

AN The Anthony Awards

These awards, first presented in 1986, are given to mystery fiction of any type from the previous year at the Bouchercon, the annual world mystery conference held in October. The award and the convention are named in memory of William Anthony Parker White, who wrote mystery fiction and mystery reviews under the pseudonym Anthony Boucher. Each year, the Bouchercon committee designs its own Anthony award. The annual attendees of the Bouchercon create a list of nominees, and the membership of the annual convention votes on which works will win the award.

There does not appear to be a comprehensive list on the Web. Each individual Bouchercon convention maintains its own website and often will list the previous winners of the Anthony Awards.

BA The Barry Awards

These awards, first presented in 1997, are given to any work of mystery material from the previous calendar year at the Bouchercon, the annual world mystery convention held in October. The award is named in memory of Barry Gardner, a reviewer for *Deadly Pleasures* magazine. The readers of *Deadly Pleasures* nominate titles and then vote for a winner from that list.

Website: http://www.deadlypleasures.com/Barry.htm

DA The Dagger Awards

These awards, first presented in 1980, are given to works of mystery fiction from October of the previous year to September of the current year by the Crime Writers Association (CWA), a British professional writing organization, at its annual dinner in December. The awards are gold and silver daggers. Independent committees, created by the CWA chairperson, select the list of nominees and the winners.

Website list and history: http://www.kjm.org/cwa.htm

DI The Dilys Award

This award, first presented in 1992, is given to a work of mystery fiction that the Independent Mystery Booksellers had the most fun selling in the previous year. The award is presented at the Left Coast Crime Conference each year in the spring. The award is named in honor of Dilys Winn, the founder of America's first mystery bookstore, Murder Ink.

Website: http://www.mysterybooksellers.com/dilys.html

ED The Edgar Allan Poe Awards

The Edgar awards, first presented in 1954, are given to mystery fiction from the previous year by the Mystery Writers of America (MWA), a professional organization of writers, at its annual banquet in April. The award is named after the American writer credited with inventing many of the genre's characteristics. Members of the MWA are assigned to committees that read material submitted by publishers. A list of nominees is published, with the committees' choices for the best announced at the annual dinner.

Website: http://www.mysterywriters.org/awards.html

The Arthur Ellis Awards

These awards, first presented in 1984, are given to works of Canadian mystery fiction from October to September of the previous year by the Crime Writers of Canada, a professional writing organization, at its annual dinner in May. The award is named after the official name used to disguise Canada's official hangman. The award is a statuette of a wooden gallows with a puppet suspended from it that dances when you pull the hangman's rope.

Website: http://www.crimewriterscanada.com

The Hammett Awards

These awards, first presented in 1992, are given for a work of literary excellence in the field of crime writing by a U.S. or Canadian author in the previous year and are presented by the North American branch of the International Association of Crime Writers. The award is named after Dashiell Hammett, and the bronze trophy is designed by sculptor Peter Boiger. The winner is chosen by three distinguished judges.

Website: http://www.hycyber.com/MYST/hammetts.html

The Herodotus Awards

These awards, first presented in 1999, are given to the best works of historical mystery fiction by The Historical Mystery Appreciation Society. They are presented each year at Bouchercon. The award is named after Herodotus, the Greek historian of the fifth century.

There appears to be no comprehensive list on the Web.

MA The Macavity Awards

These awards, presented since 1987, are given to mystery fiction material from the previous year at Bouchercon by the members of Mystery Readers International. The award is named for the "mystery cat" of T. S. Eliot (*Old Possum's Book of Practical Cats*). Each year, the members of Mystery Readers International nominate and vote for their favorites.

Website: http://www.mysteryreaders.org/macavity.html

The Ned Kelly Awards

These awards, first presented in 1995, are given for works of Australian crime writing published in the previous year by The Crime Writers' Association of Australia (CWAA). The awards are named after the famous Australian bandit, Ned Kelly.

Website: http://www.thecwaa.net

SH The Shamus Awards

These awards, first presented in 1982, are given to works of private eye fiction from the previous years by The Private Eye Writers of America (PWA). The award's name is a slang term for private eye. The award is a mounted and embossed representation of the work. Members of PWA are assigned to committees that read material submitted by publishers. A list of nominees is published, with the committee's choice for the best announced.

Website: http://my.execpc.com/~piesbook/awardwinners.html

Critics' Choices

Critics' lists are also useful for collection development. The bibliography contained in this book is an example of the kinds of lists that are available in the genre. Many of the other works listed in the Topics appendix contain bibliographies that are helpful resources for collection development.

Some lists are made each year by critics as a guide to the field. Following are some examples.

The following magazines produce excellent lists of mystery. *Booklist* has an annual issue devoted to the mystery. *Publishers Weekly* has an annual issue devoted to current developments in the field. The *New York Times Book Review* section produces various lists throughout the year; some tied to the seasons.

Periodically, independent critics create all-time lists. As the lists age, they can either take on the respect of time, or they can become superceded by time. One of the most interesting lists of all time is the *Queen's Quorum* (Little, Brown, 1951), developed by the two men who made up the writing team of Ellery Queen. Other critics periodically update this list. Two fanzines, *Drood Review* and *Deadly Pleasures*, produce annual lists that can be relied upon for their suggestions because well-respected fan critics in the genre develop the lists.

An example of a contemporary list that will prove helpful to collection development librarians is the list created by the Independent Mystery Booksellers Association. The list of their favorite mysteries of the previous century can be found at http://www.mysterybooksellers.com, or in book form in *100 Favorite Mysteries of the Century* (Crum Creek, 2000).

Chapter 3

The History of the Mystery

The Origins (1845)

Most mystery scholars trace the origins of mystery fiction to the work of Edgar Allan Poe. Many other works have influenced the genre, but no other author's works have had such an impact on developing the conventions of mystery fiction. With his five short stories, Poe established patterns that are the conventions of the mystery genre.

In "Murders in the Rue Morgue," Poe created a story about a murder with confusing details that made the solution to the crime difficult to detect. There is a list of wrongly suspected suspects, and this prevents a police force from finding the correct solution to the crime. Luckily for those suspects, there is an individual—C. Auguste Dupin—willing to be the detective needed to find the correct solution to the crime. And luckily for the reader, there is a faithful chronicler of the detective's great deeds. Thus, the classic template that will define all mystery fiction was established.

This one short story introduced features that would come to define mystery fiction. It is important to note that the police forces in "Murders In the Rue Morgue" are ineffectual. An individual outside the police force must be present to restore order to this society. Also significant is the fact that the individual who is outside the law, but capable of solving this crime, is an eccentric person. The detective's eccentricities not only give that individual the abilities needed to solve the mystery, but also make him or her an interesting fictional character. Poe's plot in "Murders In the Rue Morgue" invented a method of explaining away the mystery that is now known as the locked-room mystery. The concept is that no one has access to or egress from the murder scene, and it becomes the detective's job to not only locate the murderer, but also to explain how the murderer got in and out.

Poe created the series detective when he returned his hero, Dupin, to print in "The Mystery of Marie Roget." Based on a true crime, and using fictionalized newspaper accounts, this story showed how closely fiction could follow fact. But it was with "The Purloined Letter" that Poe further established the importance of plot, and its buried clues, over any other aspect of the short story. This short story established the game, or the concept, that the reader is attempting to solve the crime before the detective reveals the solution.

Poe also provided a cipher story in "The Gold Bug" and used first-person narration in "Thou Art the Man" to continue to propel the development of fiction. His creations established a road map that other authors would use to establish further parameters and define the genre.

The Developmental Years (1887–1920)

After Poe, mystery fiction entered a period where the eccentric detective reigned supreme. The benchmark character is Sherlock Holmes, created by Arthur Conan Doyle. With the publication of *A Study In Scarlet* in 1887, Doyle continued most of the patterns established by Poe. So much has been written about this great detective that a novice fears to tread where the Sherlockians have gone. There were nine novels or collections of short stories published from 1887 to 1927, and since then Holmes has never been out of print. Poe and Doyle's creation spawned many imitators; some good and some bad. Characters like "The Thinking Machine" by Jacques Futrelle or Dr. Thorndyke by R. Austin Freeman were eccentric detectives who relied on their intellect as well as the developing scientific methods of their age to continue to solve crimes.

As a contrast to the eccentric detective, another school of writing was being forged out of a combination of the fledgling mystery and the popular gothic novel. Tagged later as the Had-I-But-Known school of writing, the concept behind these works was a combination of the woman-in-peril and a criminal act. The leader in this field was Mary Roberts Rinehart, whose nurse detective Hilda Adams (Miss Pinkerton) is a hardy example of this type of writing.

The Golden Age of Mystery Fiction (1920–1947)

It is interesting to speculate that the popularity of detective mysteries after the First World War was in direct relationship to the mass destruction of that conflict. In a conflict of that size, the effect of one individual's death is minimized. In trying to restore order to society after a global conflict, one of the healing processes might have involved establishing that the death of an individual does count. An individual's death and its effect on the closed society that is presented in the Golden Age novel is devastating; and it is comforting to know that, even if the established governmental systems fail, there is a heroic individual with the needed skills to solve the crime. Thus, the detective restores order to society and verifies the significance of the individual's death.

Mysteries flourished during the Golden Age, the birth of which can be defined by the publication of Agatha Christie's *The Mysterious Affair At Styles* in 1920, featuring the eccentric retired policeman, Hercule Poirot. Christie continued to press forward with Miss Marple and her other series characters. Christie's use of the Poe/Doyle legacy allowed her to create series characters that were interesting to watch as they solved confusing mysteries that required the author to create plot-driven fiction. The basic concept of most traditional Golden Age novels is that the reader is willing to play a game against the author. The author's job is to create a mystery puzzle with confusing details that the fictional detective will try to unravel. The author must "play fair," or allow the reader to see the detective discover the clues needed to solve the crime, but the author is allowed to lace the book with "red herrings," or false clues, to deceive the reader. A well-written mystery novel from the Golden Age is defined as one that allows the author's fictional detective to reveal the solution to the crime before the reader discovers the correct solution. This revelation usually takes place in some culminating scene in the novel, leading to the creation of the "gathering of the suspects" chapter.

Some of the authors who define the Golden Age in England include Margery Allingham, John Dickson Carr, Ngaio Marsh, Dorothy L. Sayers, and Josephine Tey. Each used some approaches and features of works from the developmental years, and the success of Agatha Christie, to propel their development of the genre. This period is clearly identified by the puzzle novel, and it was by this standard that the period is judged and remembered.

In the United States, the most popular author during the 1920s was S. S. Van Dine, a writer who created a dilettante detective with few pleasing characteristics. However, his ability to solve puzzles in the Poe/Christie tradition ensured his popularity. Other American writers of stature during this period included Ellery Queen and Rex Stout.

During the Golden Age, a school of writing began to develop within the pages of the American pulp magazines, like *Black Mask*, that became known as the hard-boiled school of writing. Influenced by Ernest Hemingway and John Dos Passos, and interested in presenting crime in a more realistic setting, the hard-boiled writers produced massive amounts of short fiction in the pulps, some of which was translated into novel formats. The leaders in the this field were Carroll John Daly, Dashiell Hammett, and Raymond Chandler. Many authors of this period received the training they needed to become novelists of note in the mystery community by writing for the pulps.

The Quiet Years (1947–1970)

The Golden Age, and its emphasis on puzzle novels, came to an end after the Second World War. That conflict had many of the same psychological effects on society as had the First World War but carried an additional effect with the development of weapons of mass destruction that removed the individual's participation. The Second World War seems to be the catalyst for the slow decline of an interest in the plot-driven puzzles of the Golden Age. Part of the reason may be that authors were having more difficulty finding fresh approaches to clue-driven plots. Part of the reason may be that post-conflict readers were expecting their fiction to be more sophisticated in its approach to the reason why crimes were being committed. For whatever reason, characters in mystery novels were developing into complex creatures, and the plots were beginning to find competition from character, theme, and setting in the creation of mystery fiction.

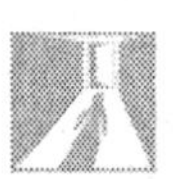

Mickey Spillane's novel, *I, The Jury*, published in 1947, closed the Golden Age and began a new age for the mystery. Based on a comic book character and fashioned after the popular hard-boiled writing of Carroll John Daly, Spillane's emphasis was on action. His appeal was so great that he became the most popular mystery writer of his times in terms of sales, and the majority of his sales came in the relatively new paperback format. Spillane's ability to sell in paperback led to the development of some imitators and their publication in paperback first, bypassing hardcover publication altogether. The paperback original format had several effects on the mystery genre. It created a new market for mysteries by making cheap editions available in non-traditional locations. This may have created new audiences for mysteries. It certainly created a new market for mystery authors, and the importance of paperback originals from this period should not be overlooked. Although published in cheap editions, some paperback originals contain some of the best of the hard-boiled school of writing.

Traditional mysteries continued to be written in this period. Authors like Ngaio Marsh and Rex Stout continued to provide mysteries in the classic traditional style. However, by the late 1960s and the early1970s, the classic clue-driven puzzle as a style is de-emphasized within the mystery community. This period seemed to allow into mainstream fiction some of the hard-boiled characteristics that previously had been the exclusive property of the pulps and the paperback originals. Ever since, there has been a dichotomy in the field between those readers who enjoy the soft-boiled style of their authors versus the readers who enjoy the hard-boiled style of their authors.

The later years of this period are dominated by the espionage genre. Espionage had been a part of the history of mystery from *The Riddle of the Sands* by Erskine Childers (1903) or the works of E. Phillips Oppenheim. Effective contributions by Graeme Greene and Eric Ambler continued to maintain this sub-genre, but it was Ian Fleming and his character, James Bond, in the 1960s that propelled espionage novels to the forefront of the mystery genre. Espionage's popularity was so dominant that traditional mystery novel characters found themselves wrapped up in international conspiracies that bordered on the espionage style. The sub-genre continued with authors like Robert Ludlum, and morphed into a similar style when the techno-thriller debuted with *The Hunt for Red October* by Tom Clancy.

If there is any truism for this period of mysteries, it is that no benchmark style or author defined it. There are many individual authors and titles that will provide enjoyment, but few that will define the period as Agatha Christie defined the Golden Age.

The Second Golden Age (1970–1990)

One might argue that this period represents as flourishing a period for mystery fiction as the original Golden Age. While the first period was defined by the refinement of one style of mystery, the puzzle novel, the Second Golden Age can be defined by its diversity, influenced by support from the publishing industry.

The biggest overall change is in the approach the mystery authors were taking to the creation of their product. While the Golden Age had demanded the puzzle, the Second Golden Age de-emphasized plot for character, setting, and theme. It may be true that the Second Golden Age novels do not have the same quality of mystery in their plots as their early antecedents. And it may be true that the Second Golden Age novels are better contributions to the world of literature and ideas because the scope of their contents has been expanded to include elements that make them better works of literature.

The first indicator that things were different began in the late 1960s, when critical attention began to be paid to mystery fiction. One example is Ross Macdonald, whose front-page review in the *New York Times Book Review* and a cover story in *Newsweek* helped push his books onto the bestseller lists. Throughout this period, novels that can be defined as being a part of the mystery genre continued to have sales figures large enough to create a presence on the bestseller lists.

To its credit, the publishing industry came to some important realizations in this period. Judgments were made in the editorial offices in the major publishing house in four areas:

Regionalism
Inclusion
Specialization
Retrospection

Regionalism moved the setting for mystery novels out of the dominant locations of a few major American urban locations and small English villages. Publishers attempted to create audiences, and readers responded to authors willing to place their detectives in distant and exotic locations. In 1970, Tony Hillerman's first Southwest mystery was published, and it is the benchmark title for the regional mystery. It also represents an example of the inclusion aspect of this period, as well, as the detectives in this series are Native American. *Ask The Right Question* (1971) by Michael Z. Lewin placed a private detective on the mean streets of Indianapolis, and this series helped move P.I. novels into locations previously underused. Yellowthread Street in Hong Kong became William Marshall's location to introduce new and vital police detectives to mystery readers.

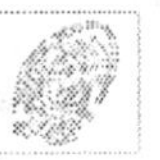

Inclusion means that an awareness of issues on a societal level has allowed a more diverse type of detective to be published. Although there have always been women involved in the private eye field, this is the period that found the early efforts of Maxine O'Callaghan and Marcia Muller rewarded when, in 1982, an interesting alignment occurred. Marcia Muller's second Sharon McCone P.I. novel appeared the same year as *A is for Alibi* by Sue Grafton and *Indemnity Only* by Sara Paretsky. Inclusion of women P.I.s and women authors in the hard-boiled private eye field is a major transition in the genre. The establishment of Sisters in Crime as a powerful force in the industry focused on the issue of including women in all processes of the publishing business and the mystery genre community.

Ethnic and racial representation in the mystery community also improved during this period. Religious issues were brought to the reader through works like the Rabbi David Small series by Harry Kemelman, the Father Koestler series by William X. Kienzle, and the Father Dowling series by Ralph McInerny. Racial issues were explored in the works of James McClure's South African mysteries and in the John Ball novels, featuring the African-American detective, Virgil Tibbs. Howard Fast, under the pseudonym of E. V. Cunningham, explored the Asian-American detective first presented by Earl Derr Biggers and Charlie Chan. Although the inclusion of these characters can

be celebrated, it should be noted that authors of color did not write these novels. Only late in the period did authors of color like Eleanor Taylor Bland, Gar Anthony Haywood, Gary Phillips, Valerie Wilson Wesley, or Paula Woods come into print, giving hope to the concept of diversity in the mystery field.

Specialization was a key to entry into the mystery genre in this period. In a way, both of the areas discussed above, regionalism and inclusion, are variations on this theme. However, where specialization really flourished was in the detectives' occupations. Dick Francis's horse-racing novels may be the benchmarks in this area. Other shining examples are Diane Mott Davidson's catering mysteries, Harlan Coben's sports mysteries, or Patricia Cornwell's forensic mysteries. Each of these specializations adds a flavor to the traditional mystery that extends its interest level to the dedicated mystery reader, and reaches into other interest areas to attract new readers to the mystery. One of the most popular specializations at the end of this period was the historical novel, a form that came to dominate the publisher's lists.

The publishing industry of this period could afford to maintain backlists of author's titles. It was a rich period for readers who wanted to read contemporary writers while exploring past masters. Retrospective reading was relatively easy, as authors' backlists were maintained by paperback publishers. Publishers like Penguin released reprint titles monthly, while reprint houses like Dover made cheap paperback editions of classic works in the field available.

The Money Years (1990–2000)

The decade of the 1990s was a turbulent time for publishers, as mergers shortened the major publisher's lists and their interest in genre fiction. Publishers seemed to be paying a great deal of attention to the sales figures produced by chain bookstores and placed most of their attention on a few authors in an attempt to create bestsellers from a few titles. Authors with contracts and long-standing series found themselves suddenly abandoned. For long-time readers and fans of the genre, it was a period of turnover, and whether new author loyalties were created or not remains to be seen. Long-running series with established characters were becoming truly scarce, and readers who wanted to establish long-term relationships with their fictional characters were abandoned by the publishing industry.

It was unclear whether readers would benefit from this new style of publishing, but new authors certainly did. The number of mysteries being published each year did not seem to diminish, and the diversity of mysteries was being maintained. The danger sign was that many new authors were being given the opportunity to produce three books on the road to bestseller status, and when that status was not achieved, the opportunity to be published was withdrawn. The ability to establish a long-running series and to remain a mystery author seemed to be a new author's greatest challenge. Loyalty to author and series characters has long been a standard in the mystery genre, and it will be interesting to watch how this develops in the new millennium.

The Promise of the Future Is a Third Golden Age (2001 and Beyond)

Recent changes in the major publishing houses may have created a new style of mystery publisher. The closing of the Walker mystery line after many years of introducing and supporting new authors in the field is a depressing way to begin a new century.

In the late 1990s, there was a proliferation of small presses publishing mystery titles, as well as some authors who had taken things into their own hands and began to self-publish. Developments in technology such as on-demand printing and e-books will certainly affect the genre. The question is whether the major houses will continue to provide the rich diversity created in the Second Golden Age, or whether that diversity will come from the smaller publishers using new formats.

It can either be the best of times, or the worst of times. If new technologies make backlist titles available, provide access to contemporary writers, and open new publishing opportunities to the mystery writers of the next millenium, then we may see the emergence of a third Golden Age of mystery fiction.

What we do know is what has happened, so let's take a look at the literature of the series mystery novel and discover its many rich offerings to contemporary readers.

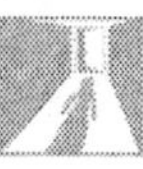

Part 2

The Literature

Chapter 4

Amateur Detectives

Traditional Classic Detectives

With one short story, "Murders in the Rue Morgue," Edgar Allan Poe established many of the parameters that still determine the well-written detective story. Poe created his eccentric detective with superior abilities and placed him in opposition to an ineffectual police force. He created a faithful partner and chronicler for the great detective, so that he would not have to record his own exploits, but ensured that a respectful individual would. He created a murder with confusing details, created a list of wrongly suspected suspects, and he manipulated the story so that the great detective is left alone to deliver the verdict at the end of the story. Poe did one other courageous thing: he brought his detective back for a second adventure and established series fiction as the norm for the detective hero.

From these beginnings, the development of the detective as a fictional hero continued in three directions. The logical extensions into the area of detectives who do investigations as a part of their job, or detectives who do investigations for a profit, make some sense.

If fictional detectives bear any relationship to reality, those furthest from the realities of criminal investigations are the amateurs. Yet, in the history of mystery fiction, the characters of amateur detectives developed more rapidly than those of police or private detectives. This may be partially explained by the rather slow evolution of legitimate police forces and the time it took to develop scientific investigative methods. While private investigations were options for some people in need of a detective, private investigations of murder have always been a fantasy reserved for fiction.

Amateurs have a few advantages over the public and private detective. First, amateurs are independent operators who answer only to themselves. Second, amateurs operate outside any restrictions, including the law, or the cost of an investigation. Third, amateurs have all the time in the world to investigate a case, and can focus all of their attention on it while ignoring the rest of the world.

But the disadvantages are numerous. An amateur would normally never be allowed anywhere near a murder scene, nor would an amateur have access to any of the evidence. An amateur does not have the resources available to a public or private detective, including all the scientific methodologies used in modern investigations, and lacks the resources to conduct an investigation, including the finances to carry it out.

Yet amateurs continue to play major roles in the world of the fictional detective. Their appeal lies strictly in their personalities, which outweigh any doubts the reader might have about their ability or duty to investigate crimes. Also, among all the types of detectives, they create the most reader identification. By being the least-equipped detective to investigate the crime, they are probably most like the average reader. If reading mystery fiction is an escape, perhaps the ability to suspend disbelief is easiest for readers when the detective is an average individual with amateur status who also has uncommon abilities, a pleasing persona, and a continuous access to crime.

The Historical Founding Members

G. K. Chesterton ✍

Father Brown

A Roman Catholic priest may seem an unlikely hero in a detective story, but this quiet churchman approaches his cases from a moral and spiritual angle, echoing the sentiments of his creator. His short stature and rather unimpressive appearance disguises a mind capable of digesting all the facts and the ability to intuitively know the solution to most crimes. He is considered one of the greatest fictional detectives of all time. All of the Father's cases are in the short story form and are masterful examples of the play fair philosophy. See The American Chesterton Society website at http://www.chesterton.org. **Hard-boiled/Traditional**. Series subjects: **Religion · Short stories**.

The Innocence of Father Brown. U.K.: Cassell, 1911 (U.S.: Lane, 1911)
A collection of the following stories: "The Blue Cross," "The Eye of Apollo," "The Flying Stars," "The Hammer of God," "The Honour of Israel Gow," "The Invisible Man," "The Queer Feet," "The Secret Garden," "The Sign of the Broken Sword," "The Sins of Prince Saradine," "The Three Tools of Death," "The Wrong Shape."

The Wisdom of Father Brown. U.K.: Cassell, 1914 (U.S.: Lane, 1915)
A collection of the following stories: "The Absence of Mr. Glass," "The Duel of Dr. Hirsh," "The Fairy Tale of Father Brown," "The God of the Gongs," "The Head of Caesar," "The Man in the Passage," "The Mistake of the Machine," "The Paradise of Thieves," "The Perishing of Pendragons," "The Purple Wig," "The Salad of Colonel Cray," "The Strange Crimes of John Boulnois."

The Incredulity of Father Brown. U.K.: Cassell, 1926 (U.S.: Dodd, 1926)

A collection of the following stories: "The Arrow of Heaven," "The Curse of the Golden Cross," "The Dagger with Wings," "The Doom of the Darnaways," "The Ghost of Gideon Wise," "The Miracle of Moon Crescent," "The Oracle of the Dog," "The Resurrection of Father Brown."

The Secret of Father Brown. U.K.: Cassell, 1927 (U.S.: Harper, 1927)

A collection of the following stories: "The Actor and the Alibi," "The Chief Mourner of Marne," "The Man with Two Beards," "The Mirror of the Magistrate," "The Red Moon of Meru," "The Secret of Father Brown," "The Secret of Flambeau," "The Song of the Flying Fish," "The Vanishing of Vaudrey," "The Worst Crime in the World."

The Scandal of Father Brown. Cassell, 1935

A collection of the following stories: "The Blast of the Book," "The Crime of the Communist," "The Green Man," "The Insoluble Problem," "The Point of a Pin," "The Pursuit of Mr. Blue," "The Quick One," "The Scandal of Father Brown."

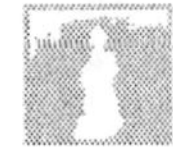

The Father Brown Omnibus. Dodd, 1935

This American edition is a collection of the five Father Brown collections to date. When reissued in 1951, this collection included one more uncollected Father Brown story, "The Vampire of the Village."

Wilkie Collins ✍

Walter Hartright

A friend of Charles Dickens, British author Collins produced two works (see the listing for *Moonstone* under Public Detectives) that help lay the foundation for mystery fiction. Although his output was minimal, the success of his works led to great popularity and financial reward. These works, along with Poe and Dickens, are the true foundations of mystery fiction. See a Wilkie Collins website at http://www.deadline.demon.co.uk/wilkie/wilkie.htm. **Soft-boiled/Traditional**.

The Woman In White. U.K.: Low, 1860 (U.S.: Harper, 1860)

Laura Fairlie is in danger of losing her inheritance when the evil Count Fosco and her equally evil husband, Sir Percival Glyde, hatch a diabolical plot. Laura is left without resources, except the help of Walter Hartright, a drawing student who has fallen in love with her while acting as her tutor, and her faithful half-sister Marian Halcombe. The key to Laura's redemption is a mysterious fugitive from a mental asylum, who dresses in white, resembles Laura, and knows the secret that could set her free.

England · Cumberland · Ghosts

Charles Dickens ✍

It goes without saying that Charles Dickens is a giant of the literary world, but he also produced two works that helped lay a foundation for the development of the mystery genre. His Inspector Bucket, featured in *Bleak House* (see Public Detectives section), is considered one of the first formal police detectives in fiction. *The Mystery of Edwin Drood* is a work that Dickens never finished. Yet it has generated interest over many generations as readers, and a few authors, try to complete the story Dickens never finished. See the Charles Dickens Information Page at http://lang.nagoya-u.ac.jp/~matsuoka/Dickens.html. **Soft-boiled/Traditional**.

The Mystery of Edwin Drood. U.K.: Chapman, 1870 (U.S.: Fields, 1870)

Dickens managed to finish only six chapters of this work before he died, but the chapters were intriguing enough to maintain interest in them to this day. Edwin Drood is an engineer engaged to marry Rosa Budd until his ardor cools. Then, evidence is found near a river indicating that Drood may have gone in, and suspicion falls on Neville Landless, Rosa's lover. He is accused by Jack Jasper, Drood's uncle and guardian, who also had feelings for Rosa. Finished versions of this novel exist by a variety of authors.

England, Cloisterham

Arthur Conan Doyle ✍

Sherlock Holmes/Dr. John H. Watson

So much has been written about Holmes that almost nothing needs to be said here. He was the archetypical classic eccentric detective, and his image dominates mystery fiction. His eccentricities established a pattern for a whole school of detectives with queer habits. Holmes's eccentricities include his deerstalker hat, his affection for cocaine, and his passionate violin playing. This book does not attempt to list the many pastiches written using this famous character. The cases of the greatest detective ever can be recommended to any soft-boiled or traditional mystery reader. See the Sherlockian.net at http://www.sherlockian.net. **Soft-boiled/Traditional**. Series subject: **Team**.

A Study in Scarlet. U.K.: Ward, Lock & Company, 1888 (U.S.: Lippincott, 1890)

Here is the novel that introduces the most famous detective pair in fiction: Sherlock Holmes and his chronicler, Dr. John Watson. Their first case is the Lauriston Gardens mystery in which Holmes solves the murder of two men whose corpses were left in a room with "rache," the German word for revenge, written in blood on the wall.

England, London • Utah

The Sign of Four. U.K.: Blackett, 1890 (U.S.: Lippincott, 1890)

Mary Morstan comes to 221 Baker Street for a detective and ultimately leaves as Mrs. John Watson. In the process, the great detective tries to determine the ultimate fate of her father, a captain in the army serving in India, who has been missing for over 10 years. Holmes will also need to explain who sends Mary a pearl each year.

England, London

The Adventures of Sherlock Holmes. U.K.: Newnes, 1892 (U.S.: Harper, 1892)

A collection of the following stories: “The Adventure of the Beryl Coronet,” “The Adventure of the Blue Carbuncle,” “The Adventure of the Copper Beeches,” “The Adventure of the Engineer’s Thumb,” “The Adventure of the Noble Bachelor,” “The Adventure of the Speckled Band,” “The Boscombe Valley Mystery,” “A Case of Identity,” “The Five Orange Pips,” “The Man with the Twisted Lip,” “The Red-Headed League,” and “A Scandal in Bohemia.”

Short stories

The Memoirs of Sherlock Holmes. U.K.: Newnes, 1894 (U.S.: Harper, 1894)

A collection of the following stories: “The Crooked Man,” “The Final Problem,” “The ‘Gloria Scott’,” “The Greek Interpreter,” “The Musgrave Ritual,” “The Naval Treaty,” “The Reigate Puzzle,” “The Resident Patient,” “Silver Blaze,” “The Stock-Broker’s Clerk,” and “The Yellow Face.”

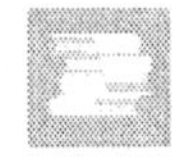

Short stories

The Hound of the Baskervilles. U.K.: Newnes, 1902 (U.S.: McClure, 1902)

The most well known and perhaps best of all the Holmes tales, this novel features the great detective trying to explain the mysterious happenings on the Grimpen Mire. Holmes is absent in the center section of the book, and the good Dr. Watson gets to exercise his detective muscles and try to protect the heir to Baskerville Hall, Sir Henry Baskerville.

England, Devon, Dartmoor

The Return of Sherlock Holmes. U.K.: Newnes, 1905 (U.S.: McClure, 1905)

A collection of the following stories: “The Adventure of Black Peter,” “The Adventure of Charles Augustus Milverton,” “The Adventure of the Abbey Grange,” “The Adventure of the Dancing Men,” “The Adventure of the Empty House,” “The Adventure of the Golden Pince-Nez,” “The Adventure of the Missing Three-Quarter,” “The Adventure of the Norwood Builder,” “The Adventure of the Priory School,” “The Adventure of the Second Stain,” “The Adventure of the Six Napoleans,” “The Adventure of the Solitary Cyclist,” and “The Adventure of the Three Students.”

Short stories

The Valley of Fear. U.K.: Smith Elder, 1915 (U.S.: Doran, 1915)

A coded warning sends the great detective and the good doctor to the country house of the reclusive American, Jack Douglas. Arriving too late to prevent his death by shotgun, the pair is driven to solve the crime.

England, Sussex, Birlstone • Pennsylvania, Vermissa

His Last Bow. U.K.: Murray, 1917 (U.S.: Doran, 1917)

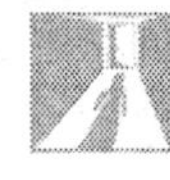

A collection of the following stories: “The Adventure of the Bruce-Partington Plans,” “The Adventure of the Cardboard Box,” “The Adventure of the Devil’s Foot,” “The Adventure of the Dying Detective,” “The Adventure of the Red Circle,” “The Adventure of the Wisteria Lodge,” “The Disappearance of Lady Frances Carfax,” and “His Last Bow.”

Short stories

The Case-book of Sherlock Holmes. U.K.: Murray, 1927 (U.S.: Doran, 1927)

A collection of the following stories: "The Adventure of Shoscombe Old Place," "The Adventure of the Blanched Soldier," "The Adventure of the Creeping Man," "The Adventure of the Illustrious Client," "The Adventure of the Lion's Mane," "The Adventure of the Mazarin Stone," "The Adventure of the Retired Colourman," "The Adventure of the Sussex Vampire," "The Adventure of the Three Gables," "The Adventure of the Three Garridebs," "The Adventure of the Veiled Lodger," and "The Problem of the Thor Bridge."

Short stories

Mary Roberts Rinehart ✍

Miss Pinkerton

Known as Miss Pinkerton by the local police force, which used her as an undercover investigator, Nurse Hilda Adams is the central character in novels that led the way to a writing style that became known as the "Had-I-But-Known" school of writing. In this style, the heroine is at risk, and sooner or later makes the proclamation that had she but known some crucial fact, the case would not have progressed as it did. These tales are often told as reminiscences. Rinehart's choice of a competent nurse/detective may have been influenced by her husband's career as a physician. **Soft-boiled/Traditional**. Series subjects: **Medical**.

Miss Pinkerton. U.S.: Farrar, 1932 (U.K.: *The Double Alibi.* Cassell, 1932)

Old Miss Juliet Mitchell's nephew has committed suicide, and rumor has it he had squandered her money. Inspector Patton of the Homicide Squad calls Nurse Adams onto the case because "we've got a lot of wall-eyed pikes around here calling themselves detectives who could take lessons from her and maybe learn something."

Haunted Lady. Farrar, 1942.

The city's socialite, Eliza Fairbanks, is terrorized by bats, and her caretaker calls in Nurse Adams to solve the mystery. Could the solution have something to do with the divorce of her daughter Marian from the handsome Frank Garrison?

Episode of the Wandering Knife. U.S.: Rinehart, 1950 (U.K.: *The Wandering Knife.* Cassell, 1952).

A collection of the following novelettes: "Episode of the Wandering Knife," "The Man Who Hid His Breakfast," and "The Secret, a Miss Pinkerton Story."

Short stories

Miss Pinkerton: Adventures of a Nurse Detective. Rinehart, 1959.

A collection of the following novelettes: "The Buckled Bag," "Haunted Lady," "Locked Doors," and "Miss Pinkerton."

Short stories

Eccentric Detectives

The most notable attributes of the first detectives may be their personal eccentricities, rather than their detective skills. All the great thinking detectives had the skill necessary to solve the crime, but that ability seemed to handicap them in normal society. Perhaps this can be dismissed as a literary necessity to set one great thinker apart from another, but the model of the detective as an unusual character was established early. During the Golden Age, some authors continued the tradition of giving their characters odd and unusual behaviors. The good news for readers is that as time progressed, odd detectives became more human (during the Golden Age) and that made their stories more readable. Today, authors may still add quirky attributes to their characters, but the better authors handle it in a natural way, adding depth and dimensions to the characters.

The Historical Founding Members

Margery Allingham

Albert Campion

Albert Campion is an eccentric amateur with a royal background and possible covert service in His Majesty's Service. In the early titles, his odd behavior is used to his advantage as a detective, placing him outside the normal sphere and thus able to carry out investigations without interference. In later titles, as with many eccentrics and dilettantes, he matures into a more humane character, and he allies himself with Scotland Yard Inspectors Oates, Yeo, and Luke. The series features a love story between Campion and Lady Amanda Fitton. Campion does not appear in some of the later cases until very late in the book. After Allingham's death, her husband, Philip Youngman Carter, helped finish one novel and wrote two on his own. See The Margery Allingham Archives at http://www.idir.net/~nedblake/allingham_01.html. **Soft-boiled/Traditional**.

The Crime at Black Dudley. U.K.: Jarrolds, 1929 (U.S.: *The Black Dudley Murder.* Doubleday, 1929)

A weekend party at Black Dudley Manor turns deadly when the host, Colonel Gordon Coombe, is murdered. Luckily, Campion is a guest for the weekend and he is driven to find the murderer.

England, Suffolk • Locked room

Mystery Mile. U.K.: Jarrolds, 1930 (U.S.: Doubleday, 1930)

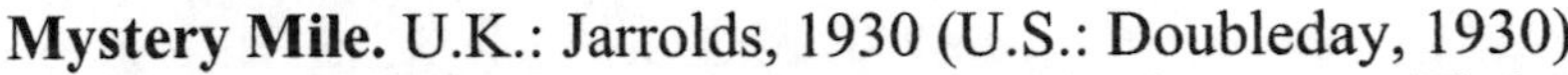

Being near Judge Crowdy Lobbett can be dangerous. His butler drinks poisoned Scotch, his chauffeur is killed in an accident, and his walking companion is killed by a falling stone. When the Judge seeks solace in England, it falls to Campion to try and discover the truth behind the failed attempts.

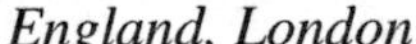

England, London

Look to the Lady. U.K.: Jarrolds, 1931 (U.S.: *The Gyrth Chalice Mystery.* Doubleday, 1931)

For generations, the Gryth family has held The Chalice as a prized possession, but the rare artifact is also desirable to collectors, one of whom is not afraid to commit murder to possess it. Campion has insider knowledge that helps him protect the family and the chalice.

Antiquities · England, Suffolk, Santuary

Police at the Funeral. U.K.: Heinemann, 1931 (U.S.: Doubleday, 1932)

Caroline Faraday runs an old Cambridge household as a Victorian boarding house for her relatives until a strange disappearance leads her to write requesting Campion's services. The death of Andrew Seeley and, eventually, other relatives, leads Campion to try and unravel the mysteries of this dysfunctional family.

England, Cambridge

Sweet Danger. U.K.: Heinemann, 1933 (U.S.: *Kingdom of Death.* Doubleday, 1933; also published as *The Fear Sign.* Macfadden, 1961)

In the case that first brings Campion and Amanda together, the detective finds himself involved in a fake treasure hunt that has real consequences. The challenge of an ancient riddle may prove that the Pontisbright family legacy is real.

France, French Riviera

Death of a Ghost. U.K.: Heinemann, 1934 (U.S.: Doubleday, 1934)

At the annual unveiling of a painting by John Sebastian Lafcadio, held each year as an anniversary celebration of the artist's death, the lights go out and Tommy Dacre is found stabbed. The patrons of the arts are thankful that Campion is a witness to the crime.

Art · England, London

Flowers for the Judge. U.K.: Heinemann, 1936 (U.S.: Doubleday, 1936; also published as *Legacy in Blood.* Mercury, 1949)

Twenty years separates the disappearance of Tom Barnabas and the murder of his cousin Paul Brande. What connects the two incidents is the Barnabas and Company book publishing company. It becomes Campion's task to explain the connection.

England, London · Publishing

The Case of the Late Pig. U.K.: Hodder, 1937 (U.S.: *Mr. Campion: Criminologist.* Doubleday, 1937)

The British edition is the novelette "The Case of the Late Pig." The American edition has that novelette as well as the following stories: "The Borderline Case," "The Case of the Man with the Sack," "The Case of the Old Man in the Window," "The Case of the Pro and the Con," "The Case of the White Elephant," and "The Case of the Widow."

Short stories

Dancers in Mourning. U.K.: Heinemann, 1937 (U.S.: Doubleday, 1937; also published as *Who Killed Chloe?* Avon. 1943)

Dancer Jimmy Sutane is the star of London's Argosy Theatre, but jealousies are creating a dangerous situation for him. He retreats to a country estate, and Campion wants to find the prankster and prevent murder.

England, London · Theater

The Fashion in Shrouds. U.K.: Heinemann, 1938 (U.S.: Doubleday, 1938)

Georgia Wells is deadly to the male: her fiancé, missing for two years, has turned up dead, and then her husband dies as well. While struggling with his relationship with the lovely Amanda, Campion needs to find the truth behind the deaths before Georgia's attentions turn to another male.

England, London

Mr. Campion and Others. U.K.: Heinemann, 1939 (U.S.: Penguin, 1950)

The British and American editions are a collection of the following stories: "The Borderline Case," "The Case of the Frenchman's Gloves," "The Case of the Hat Trick," "The Case of the Longer View," "The Case of the Name on the Wrapper," "The Case of the Old Man in the Window," "The Case of the Question Mark," "The Case of the White Elephant," and "The Case of the Widow." The British and American editions also include different non- Campion stories.

Short stories

Traitor's Purse. U.K.: Heinemann, 1941 (U.S.: *The Sabotage Murder Mystery.* Avon Books, 1942)

The great detective struggles on this case as he has lost his memory. He knows he has assaulted a policeman, and he knows the number 15 has importance, but he knows he must solve this case of the mysterious Anscombe's death to save himself. Luckily, he has the plucky Amanda on his side.

Amnesia • *England, London*

Coroner's Pidgin. U.K.: Heinemann, 1945 (U.S.: *Pearls Before Swine.* Doubleday, 1945)

In wartime London, Campion has returned from serving his country to discover his servant Lugg putting a body in his bed. To his surprise, the chief suspect is a good friend. Campion's investigation takes place across the backdrop of a nation at war.

England, London • *World War II*

***The Case Book of Mr. Campion.** Mercury, 1947

More Work for the Undertaker. U.K.: Heinemann, 1948 (U.S.: Doubleday, 1949)

A writer of poison pen letters is taken serious by Campion when a few people are actually poisoned in the household of two famous literary artists. Someone has it in for the surviving Palindoe siblings, and it will take everything Campion has to discover the murderer.

England, London

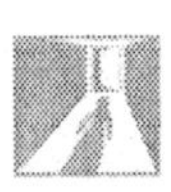

The Tiger in the Smoke. U.K.: Chatto 1952 (U.S.: Doubleday, 1952)

Widow Meg Elginbrodde's greatest happiness is her second marriage to Geoffrey Levett until she is shown a photograph of her late husband alive and well in London. She hires Campion to discover the truth and free her from her past. Campion finds himself battling his greatest and most mysterious enemy, The Tiger.

England, London

The Beckoning Lady. U.K.: Chatto, 1955 (U.S.: *The Estate of the Beckoning Lady.* Doubleday, 1955)

The weekend parties in Suffolk hardly stop for the corpse that lays for days in a field, or when William Faraday dies at The Beckoning Lady. But Campion is on the alert to discover the murderer while the parties continue.

England, Suffolk, Pontisbright

Hide My Eyes. U.K.: Chatto 1958 (U.S.: *Tether's End.* Doubleday, 1958; also published as *Ten Were Missing.* Dell, 1961)

On a rainy night in London, a corpse is found near the theaters, and the police know they have two mysterious witnesses who rode into town on the country bus. Campion helps his police friends tie this crime to old unresolved cases and bring some criminals to justice.

England, London

The China Governess. U.K.: Chatto, 1962 (U.S.: Doubleday, 1962)

In the East End area rebuilt by a London government trying to move forward, there is a plague. The residents of the new homes are being terrorized by a mysterious vandal. Campion must uncover secrets from the past to allow the new residents to stay.

England, London

The Mind Readers. U.K.: Chatto, 1965 (U.S.: Morrow, 1965)

When some businessmen and some scientists team up to try and produce a new form of communication, it leads to murder.

England, London

Cargo of Eagles. U.K.: Chatto, 1968 (U.S.: Morrow, 1968)

This novel was completed by Philip Youngman Carter and posthumously published. Campion is called upon to investigate the mysterious goings on in Saltey, a town with a historical reputation for housing pirates. A new resident, Dr. Dido Jones, has been receiving poison-pen letters, and he needs Campion's help.

England, Essex, Saltey

The Allingham Casebook. U.K.: Chatto, 1969 (U.S.: Morrow, 1969)

A collection of the following stories: "The Border-Line Case," "Face Value," "Joke Over," "Little Miss Know-All," "Mum Knows Best," "One Morning They'll Hang Him," "The Snapdragon and the C. I. D.," "Tall Story," "The Pro and the Con," and "The Villa Marie Celeste." The collection also includes eight non-Campion stories.

Short stories

Mr. Campion's Farthing (by Philip Youngman Carter). U.K.: Heinemann, 1969 (U.S.: Morrow, 1969)

The historic estate of Lottie Cambric is the last place that a Russian scientist was seen before he went missing. It is up to Campion to renew his acquaintance with government activities and try to help his government get its answers.

Carter, Philip Youngman • England, London • Espionage

Mr. Campion's Falcon (by Philip Youngman Carter). U.K.: Heinemann, 1970 (U.S.: *Mr. Campion's Quarry*. Morrow, 1971)

This novel involves an archaeologist whose exploration of a fourth-century Roman ship leads to his disappearance.

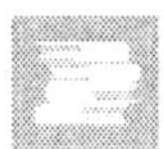

Archeology • Carter, Philip Youngman • England, London

The Allingham Minibus. U.K.: Chatto, 1973 (U.S.: Morrow, 1973; also published as *Mr. Campion's Lucky Day and Other Stories.* Penguin, 1992)

A collection of the following stories: "The Man with the Sack," "Mr. Campion's Lucky Day," and "The Unseen Door." The other stories are not Campion tales.

Short stories

H. C. Bailey ✍

Reggie Fortune

As a physician, Reggie Fortune acts as an advisor to Scotland Yard in the books created by British writer Bailey. His odd mannerisms, one of which is his odd phraseology, endear him to readers with their quirkiness. He is a large man, as are quite a few of the eccentrics, and he is often taken lightly because of his romantic attitudes about life, even by the police he aides. However, he is deadly serious about crime. Sources list Fortune as onc of the most popular British mystery characters in the period between the two world wars. **Soft-boiled/Traditional**.

Call Mr. Fortune. U.K.: Methuen, 1919 (U.S.: Dutton, 1921)

A collection of the following stories: "The Archduke's Tea," "The Business Minister," "The Efficient Assassin," "The Hottentot Venus," "The Nice Girl," and "The Sleeping Companion."

Short stories

Mr. Fortune's Practice. U.K.: Methuen, 1923 (U.S.: Dutton, 1924)

A collection of the following stories: "The Ascot Tragedy," "The Leading Lady," "The Magic Stone," "The President of San Jacinto," "The Snowball Burglary," "The Unknown Murderer," and "The Young Doctor."

Short stories

Mr. Fortune's Trials. U.K.: Methuen, 1925 (U.S.: Dutton, 1926)

A collection of the following stories: "The Furnished Cottage," "The Hermit Crab," "The Long Barrow," "The Only Son," "The Profiteers," and "The Young God."

Short stories

Mr. Fortune, Please. U.K.: Methuen, 1928 (U.S.: Dutton, 1928)

A collection of the following stories: "The Cat Burglar," "The Lion Party," "The Little House," "The Missing Husband," "The Quiet Lady," and "The Violet Farm."

Short stories

Mr. Fortune Speaking. U.K.: Ward, 1929 (U.S.: Dutton, 1931)

A collection of the following stories: "The Cat's Milk," "The German Song," "The Hazel Ice," "The Lion Fish," "The Painted Pebbles," "The Pink Macaw," "The Woman in Wood," and "Zodiacs."

Short stories

Mr. Fortune Explains. U.K.: Ward, 1930 (U.S.: Dutton, 1931)

A collection of the following stories: "The Bicycle Lamp," "The Face in the Picture," "The Football Photograph," "The Little Milliner," "The Picnic," "The Rock Garden," "The Silver Cross," and "The Wedding Ring."

Short stories

Case for Mr. Fortune. U.K.: Ward, 1932 (U.S.: Doubleday, 1932)

A collection of the following stories: "The Bunch of Grapes," The Greek Play," "The Little Dog," "The Mountain Meadow," "The Oak Gall," "The Pair of Spectacles," "The Spotted Oak," and "The Walrus Ivory."

Short stories

Mr. Fortune Wonders. U.K.: Ward, 1933 (U.S.: Doubleday, 1933)

A collection of the following stories: "The Cigarette Case," "The Fairy Cycle," "The Gypsy Moth," "The Lilies of St. Gabriel's," "The Love Bird," "The Old Bible," "The Oleander Flowers," and "The Yellow Diamonds."

Short stories

Shadow on the Wall. U.K.: Gollancz, 1934 (U.S.: Doubleday, 1934)

Roger Poyntz's aeroplane has crashed in a manner that suggests suicide, and the reason may be Lady Poyntz's recent suicide. As Fortune begins an investigation among London society, a few other strange occurrences happen that lead to the deaths of Mrs. Harley and Mrs. Darett.

England, London

Mr. Fortune Objects. U.K.: Gollancz, 1935 (U.S.: Doubleday, 1935)

A collection of the following stories: "The Angel's Eye," "The Broken Toad," "The Little Finger," "The Long Dinner," "The Three Bears," and "The Yellow Slugs."

Short stories

A Clue for Mr. Fortune. U.K.: Gollancz, 1936 (U.S.: Doubleday, 1936)

A collection of the following stories: "The Dead Leaves," "The Hole in the Parchment," "The Holy Well," "The Swimming Hole," "The Torn Stocking," and "The Wistful Goddess."

Short stories

Black Land, White Land. U.K.: Gollancz, 1937 (U.S.: Doubleday, 1937)

General Duddon has a theory that the Bible tells us giants roamed the earth, and he believes he has the bones to prove it. Out of curiosity, Fortune makes an investigation, and discovers that some of the bones may belong to Tracy's son, who went missing ten years prior to the start of this book.

Anthropology · England, Durshire

This Is Mr. Fortune. U.K.: Gollancz, 1938 (U.S.: Doubleday, 1938)

A collection of the following stories: "The Burnt Tout," "The Children's Home," "The Cowslip Ball," "The Key of the Door," "The Lizard's Tail," and "The Yellow Cloth."

Short stories

The Great Game. U.K.: Gollancz, 1939 (U.S.: Doubleday, 1939)

Someone is sounding the Mary bell in the Hurst church tower, and the sound signifies death. In this case, however, it is not the parson's death that the bells signify; instead it is the death of Mrs. Carson. Fortune realizes that until he knows why Mrs. Carson went to church when there was no service, he will not be able to catch a murderer.

England, Hurst · Religion

The Bishop's Crime. U.K.: Gollancz, 1940 (U.S.: Doubleday, 1941)

Peggy and Bobby Rankin, the children of the Bishop of Badon Cathedral, are a handful for the widower to raise. But they will not be his only problem when Fortune is called in to investigate a corpse found on a roadside, and the body leads him right back to the Bishop's church.

England, St. Albans · Religion

Mr. Fortune Here. U.K.: Gollancz, 1940 (U.S.: Doubleday, 1940)

A collection of the following stories: "The Bird in the Cellar," "The Blue Paint," "The Bottle Party," "The Brown Paper," "The Fight for the Crown," "The Gilded Girls," "The Point of the Knife," "The Primrose Petals," and "The Spider's Web."

Short stories

No Murder. U.K.: Gollancz, 1942 (U.S.: *The Apprehensive Dog.* Doubleday, 1942)

A boy named Bony is playing with his friends when he stumbles upon the body of a woman who is both a stranger to his community and quite dead. Identified as Nell Marcle, gone 12 years from the village of Marstow, her death is but the beginning of a series of deaths and assaults that are laid at the footsteps of the Ambury family and might have something to do with Miss Corve's will.

England, Marstow • Wills

Meet Mr. Fortune. Doubleday, 1942

A collection of the following stories: *The Bishop's Crime* (novel), "The Broken Toad," "The Brown Paper," "The Gypsy Moth," "The Greek Play," "The Hole in the Parchment," "The Holy Well," "The Little Finger," "The Point of the Knife," "The Wistful Goddess," "The Yellow Cloth," "The Yellow Diamonds," and "The Yellow Slugs."

Short stories

Mr. Fortune Finds a Pig. U.K.: Gollancz, 1943 (U.S.: Doubleday, 1943)

Mr. Fortune is insistent that a pig is involved in the outbreak of typhus that strikes a small Welsh village. With the help of an American intelligence officer, the two detectives trace a deadly killer.

Medical • England, Wales, Westbrook

Dead Man's Effects. U.K.: Macdonald, 1945 (U.S.: *The Cat's Whisker.* Doubleday, 1944)

Fortune is called in by Scotland Yard when two bodies are found in conjunction with each other: a man who has been burnt to death in a haystack and a woman who drowned in a nearby river. The Germans had bombed this area during the night, and Fortune finds himself caught between British, Canadian, and American troops who are less allied than they should be.

England, Radbury • World War II

The Life Sentence. U.K.: Macdonald, 1946 (U.S.: Doubleday, 1946)

The plight of Rosalind Bruce is brought to Fortune's attention.Taking pity on the depressed young girl, he goes down to the coast to save her life. Another murder, this time of an old man, draws Fortune's attention, and then he finds that the two cases may be related.

England, Manningham

Saving a Rope. U.K.: Macdonald, 1948 (U.S: *Save a Rope.* Doubleday, 1948)

Nancy and Bill Butler discover the skeleton of a woman who has been dead some time, and it is Fortune who is asked to travel at Christmas time and try to discover the truth. When it is apparent that the village holds some secrets, and that the queer Kemp family may hold some clues to the strange occurrences in the village, Fortune knows he needs to dig into the local culture to understand the crime.

England, Ribland City

Anthony Berkeley (pseud. of A. B. Cox) ✍

Roger Sheringham

British novelist Berkeley must have had some fun creating the obnoxious British novelist Sheringham. Becoming a best-selling author on a lark, the Oxford graduate holds great contempt for his own writing and the people who read him. His disdain is not reserved for his readers, but extends to anyone who comes within his range. Sheringham's redeeming feature is that he is able to solve crimes, although often incorrectly, and that is his charm. One of his cases, *The Poisoned Chocolates Case,* is considered a classic golden age novel. He is often included in investigations by his friend Chief Inspector Moresby, and he is also an active member of the Crimes Circle, a spoof of the famous Detection Club. **Soft-boiled/Traditional**.

The Layton Court Mystery. U.K.: Jenkins, 1925 (U.S.: Doubleday, 1929)

While puttering in a rose garden at Layton Court, Sheringham witnesses Barbara Shannon's dramatic announcement to her intended, Alec, that she cannot marry him. Victor Stanworth, the host, and the others gathered at his country home, are shocked when Alec commits suicide. Sheringham doubts some of the evidence, and launches his first investigation.

England, Hertfordshire

***The Wychford Poisoning Case.** U.K.: Collins, 1926 (U.S.: Doubleday, 1930)

Roger Sheringham and the Vane Mystery. U.K.: Collins, 1927 (U.S.: *The Mystery at Lover's Cave.* Simon, 1927).

Sheringham is asked by the Courier to go to Hampshire where a woman named Vane has fallen from the cliffs of Ludmouth Bay. Accompanied by his cousin, Anthony Walton, the young man ends up falling in love with Margaret Cross, the dead woman's companion. Inspector Moresby proves to be a worthy opponent for Sheringham as they race to reach a solution to the crime.

England, Hampshire, Ludmouth

The Silk Stocking Murders. U.K.: Collins, 1928 (U.S.: Doubleday, 1928)

When Sheringham receives a plea from A. E. Manners in Dorset asking the great detective to search for his missing daughter, Janet, the detective is surprised when she is identified as Unity Ransome, the actress who recently hung herself with her own stockings. Sheringham sets off to discover the truth behind a hidden identity and the name of a murderer.

England, London

The Poisoned Chocolates Case. U.K.: Collins, 1929 (U.S.: Doubleday, 1929)

The intriguing premise of this work is that a man receives a sampler box of candies that he gives to a friend who gives it to his wife. When she dies of poisoning, the members of the Crimes Circle, including Sheringham and another Berkeley series character named Ambrose Chitterwick, are given the challenge of solving the murder. Their series of solutions plays with the methods and madness of this genre.

England, London

The Second Shot. U.K.: Hodder, 1930 (U.S.: Doubleday, 1931)

At a house party held by detective storywriter John Hillyard, a game of detective is to be played among several famous mystery writers. The body is to be Eric

Scott-Davies, renowned man about town, and everyone is having a grand time until Scott-Davies's body is discovered in the woods on Hillyard's farm. When the writers need help, they turn to Sheringham.

England, Devon, Budeford • Mystery games

Top Storey Murder. U.K.: Hodder, 1931 (U.S.: Doubleday, 1931)

Inspector Moresby brings Sheringham along to the scene of the murder of Miss Barnett, who appears to have been strangled by a burglar. Trying to stay close to the investigation when he feels things cannot so easily be dismissed, he hires the dead woman's niece as his secretary. Together the two press on with the private investigation.

England, London

Murder in the Basement. U.K.: Hodder, 1932 (U.S.: Doubleday, 1932)

Reginald Dane and his lovely new wife Molly have just moved into their new home when he discovers the body of a woman buried in their cellar. Called to the scene is Chief Inspector Moresby, and that means that Sherringham cannot be far behind. Could the death have anything to do with Miss Staples, the elderly spinster who had occupied the house prior to the newlyweds?

England, Middlesex, Lewisham

Jumping Jenny. U.K.: Hodder, 1933 (U.S: *Dead Mrs. Stratton.* Doubleday, 1933)

A party where all the guests are dressed like murderers or victims may seem like fun, until Mrs. Stratton really does end up dead, hung from a mock gallows. When the police feel Sherringham may be their best suspect, he needs to move quickly to clear himself and find the real murderer.

England, Westerford • Mystery games

Panic Party. U.K.: Hodder, 1934 (U.S.: *Mr. Pidgeon's Island.* Doubleday, 1934)

Guy Pidgeon has inherited so much money he can be eccentric, and his idea of fun is to get stranded on an island full of strangers. Deciding to make the most of it, he tells them that one of them may be a murderer. Little does he know his joke will prove to be true.

Islands

***The Roger Sheringham Stories.** Carnacki, 1994

Ernest Bramah ✍

Max Carrados

Eccentricity often sets amateur detectives apart, but nothing can be more separating than a physical handicap that would seem to prevent the detective from carrying out his or her duties. When Bramah introduced the blind Carrados, he created the first physically handicapped detective in mystery fiction. Having become blind as an adult, Carrados is able to adjust and maintain his life, including his abilities to detect. His blindness does not weaken his zest for life. He works side by side with his friend Louis Carlyle, a private investigator who is a disbarred lawyer. The key to the books is the way a sighted man is blind to the clues that Carrados can detect. See the Ernest Bramah Bibliography site at http://www.ernestbramah.com. **Soft-boiled/Traditional**. Series subject: **Blind**.

Max Carrados. U.K.: Methuen, 1914 (U.S.: Garland, 1976)

A collection of the following stories: "The Clever Mrs. Straithwaite," "The Coin of Dionysius," "The Comedy at Fountain Cottage," "The Game Played in the Dark," "The Knight's Cross Signal Problem," "The Last Exploit of Harry the Actor," "The Tilling Shaw Mystery," and "The Tragedy at Brookbend Cottage."

Short stories

The Eyes of Max Carrados. U.K.: Grant Richards, 1923 (U.S.: Doran, 1924)

A collection of the following stories: "The Disappearance of Marie Severe," "The Eastern Mystery," "The Ghost at Massingham Mansions," "The Ingenious Mr. Spinola," "The Kingsmouth Spy Case," "The Missing Actress Sensation," "The Mystery of the Poisoned Dish of Mushrooms," "The Secret of Dunstan's Tower," and "The Virginiola Fraud."

Short stories

***Max Carrados Mysteries.** U.K.: Hodder, 1927 (U.S.: Penguin, 1964)

The Bravo of London. Cassell, 1934

Tapsfield is the home of the company that manufactures the paper for the Bank of England, and that makes it of special interest to the nefarious Julian Joolby. Carrados and Inspector Beedel match wits against the master criminal and his network to prevent a crime.

England, Tapsfield

Best Max Carrados Detective Stories. Dover, 1972

A collection of the following stories: "The Coin of Dionysius," "The Disappearance of Marie Severe," "The Ghost at Massingham Mansions," "The Holloway Flat Tragedy," "The Ingenious Mr. Spinola," "The Knight's Cross Signal Problem," "The Last Exploit of Harry the Actor," "The Mystery of the Poisoned Dish of Mushrooms," "The Mystery of the Vanished Petition Crown," and "The Tragedy of Brookbend Cottage."

Short stories

John Dickson Carr ✍

Dr. Gideon Fell

Carr modeled Gideon Fell after G. K. Chesterton, the creator of the Father Brown short stories. He is a large man who loves to build houses of cards and tell jokes. A slightly mad detective, Fell's real passion is crimes of the locked room and impossible methods. His education and training as a schoolmaster and lexicographer add to his abilities and help establish him as a perfect eccentric detective. His cases can be recommended to any soft-boiled or traditional mystery reader. See a site for John Dickson Carr Collectors at http://www.jdcarr.com. **Soft-boiled/Traditional.** Series subject: **Locked room.**

Hag's Nook. Harper, 1933

While visiting Dr. Fell at Yew Cottage, Tad Rampole develops an interest in the ruins of Chatterham Prison on Hag's Nook. The land belongs to the Starberth family, and the family's heir must spend an hour in the old prison in order to inherit, an act to which Fell and Rampole agree to be witnesses.

England, Chatterham

***The Mad Hatter Mystery.** Harper, 1933

The Blind Barber. Harper, 1934.

When the Queen Victoria sails from New York to Southhampton, on board is mystery writer Henry Morgan. He will be witness to a strange series of events that lead to a death. It will be up to Fell, given the facts in his armchair in London, to decide whether or not it was murder.

Shipboard

The Eight of Swords. Harper, 1934

Septimus Depping is found shot in the head with the tarot card, The Eight of Swords, near his hand. Fell is intrigued by a murderer who knows his tarot, but in the course of bringing him to justice, he must explain why the murderer ate the dead man's last meal.

England, Gloucestershire

Death-Watch. Harper, 1935

Fell is visiting his friend Melson and is on the spot when a body is discovered murdered with a clock hand. Fell is able to clear the name of Eleanor Smith Carver, ward of clockmaker Johannus Carver, when it becomes obvious to him he is dealing with a massive conspiracy to falsely convict her of the crime.

England, London

The Three Coffins. U.S.: Harper, 1935 (U.K.: *The Hollow Man.* H. Hamilton, 1935)

When Professor Charles Grimaud is found dead, the blame falls on a murderer who seemed capable of doing the crime and disappearing from the scene. Then, Pierre Fley dies in a snowstorm with no footprints in the snow, and the two mysterious deaths need to be solved by Fell. This novel includes the famous locked-room lecture by Fell and helps explain how this great detective solves his cases.

England, London

The Arabian Nights Murder. Harper, 1936

Fell only appears to introduce the beginning and close the end of this case. The body of the text is made up of the statements of the police officers that investigated the death of the actor Raymond Penderel. The actor was found in a museum, dressed to confuse, and stabbed with an ornamental knife. Fell solves the case by outthinking the actual detectives who worked the case.

England, London

The Crooked Hinge. Harper, 1938

John Farnleigh is saved the night the Titanic sinks, but when the estate to which he can make a claim comes due, two Farnleigh's show up to place a claim. It falls to Fell to figure which claimant is the real heir when one is killed.

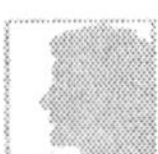

England, Kent, Mallingford

To Wake the Dead. Harper, 1938

Christopher Kent, South African mystery writer, arrives in London in time to be accused of strangling his two cousins. First, his cousin's wife Jenny Kent is found strangled and beaten in his hotel room; and then he is informed his cousin Rod has died by the same method. Dr. Fell is interested in proving him innocent, and sets out to find the evidence necessary to convince others of his theory.

Authors • England, London

The Problem of the Green Capsule. U.S.: Harper, 1939 (U.K.: *The Black Spectacles.* H. Hamilton, 1939)

Inspector Andrew Elliot is asked to investigate the troubles at Bellegarde, the country house of Marcus Chesney. As the case appears to be one of child poisoning, he is disturbed to find himself falling in love with Marjorie Wills, the niece of Chesney. When Chesney is murdered, Elliot is happy to seek aid from Fell to catch the real murderer.

England, Sodbury Cross

The Problem of the Wire Cage. Harper, 1939

Frank Dorrance was strangled on a tennis court, but only one set of footprints can be found on the clay court, and they are the dead man's own. Fell has six suspects to pursue as he tries to solve this strange case.

England

The Man Who Could Not Shudder. Harper, 1940

Fell has to explain how three witnesses at Longwood House could testify that they saw the pistol taken down from the wall and used to commit murder. Yet, no hand held the gun.

England, Essex • Ghosts

The Case of the Constant Suicides. Harper, 1941

On the Highland in Scotland, two distant cousins, Allan and Kathryn Campbell, arrive on the same train. Their new-found love for each other will be challenged when the legend of the death in the Case of Shira tower leads to someone's fall from its 60-foot tower. A drink called the Doom of the Campbells is one of the clues that Fell will use to find a murderer.

Scotland

Death Turns the Tables. U.S.: Harper, 1941 (U.K.: *The Seat of the Scornful.* H. Hamilton, 1942)

When Judge Horace Ireton is found with the murder weapon next to the dead man, his case looks bleak. The dead man was Ireton's daughter's fiancé, and the case against Ireton looks firm until he turns to his friend Fell for help.

England, Tawnish

Till Death Do Us Part. Harper, 1944

Sir Harvey Gilman is poisoned, and suspicion falls on Lesley Grant. Gilman, the Home Office pathologist, believed she had committed a prior crime and tried to warn her fiancé, Dick Markham, the playwright. Fell's job is to prove that the lovely Lesley is innocent so that she can marry Dick.

England, Six Ashes

He Who Whispers. Harper, 1946

Mike Hammond enters the Beltring's Restaurant in Soho to attend a dinner with The Murder Club. There he hears the story of the unsolved swordstick murder of Howard Brooke at the top of a tower near Chartres. Fell has to hunt a vicious killer many years after the actual murder was committed.

England, London · France, Chartres

Dr. Fell, Detective, and Other Stories. Mercury, 1947 (Also published as *The Third Bullet and Other Stories.* Harper, 1954)

A collection of the following stories: "A Guest in the House," "The Locked Room," "The Proverbial Murder," and "The Wrong Problem." The collection also includes "Strictly Diplomatic," a non-Fell story. *The Third Bullet and Other Stories (*Harper, 1954) contains all of the above except "A Guest in the House."

Short stories

The Sleeping Sphinx. Harper, 1947

Donald Holden, a language master at Lupton, rashly became engaged to Celia Devereux before going off to war. Declared dead during the conflict, he has now returned to civilization only to discover that he is Sir Donald Holden and has buckets of cash. Within this personal conflict, a costume party in which all the guests must come dressed as a famous murderer from the past is thrown, and someone kills Celia's sister Margot.

England, London · Mystery games

Below Suspicion. Harper, 1949

Patrick Butler is The Great Defender, and his favorite cases occur when his clients are guilty and he is able to free them. Joyce Ellis, charged with a poisoning, seems the perfect client, until another similar murder occurs while she is locked up. Butler now needs to defend Lucia Renshaw from the same charge, and Fell finds a series of clues that lead him to the truth.

England, London

The Dead Man's Knock. Harper & Row, 1958

Rose Lestrange is found with a letter opener in her heart, and the most likely reason is her tormenting of the Queen's College campus in Virginia. The police rule that her death is a suicide, but Fell, visiting the campus, discovers clues that lead to a charge of murder.

Academia · Virginia, Queenshaven

In Spite of Thunder. Harper & Row, 1960

Brian Innes's job is to prevent Audrey Page from visiting the villa of actress Eve Eden. Eve is haunted by the death of Hector Matthews in 1939 near Hitler's Berchtesgaden. Audrey's arrival is the catalyst for murder when Eve falls to her death like Hector.

Switzerland, Geneva

The Man Who Explained Miracles. Harper & Row, 1963

A collection of the following stories: "The Incautious Burglar," and "The Invisible Hands." The remaining five stories are non-Fell stories.

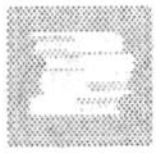

Short stories

The House at Satan's Elbow. Harper & Row, 1965

Could a ghost be a murderer? It seems possible when Pennington Barclay believes the long-dead Horace Wildfare tried to murder him at the house at Satan's Elbow. This case proves to be another locked-room case for Fell.

England, Hampshire · Ghosts

Panic in Box C. Harper & Row, 1966

A crossbow is not a usual murder weapon of choice in the 1960s, but when Fell is in the United States and attends a dress rehearsal of *Romeo and Juliet*, death by such a weapon occurs.

New York, New York · Shakespeare, William · Theater

Dark of the Moon. Harper & Row, 1967

Shifting his detecting to the United States, Fell is on hand at the Maynard Hall weekend party when a 300-year-old murder is re-created. A modern murder occurs with a tomahawk as the weapon, and Fell must put together the clues to solve the crime.

South Carolina, Charleston

Jacques Futrelle ✍

The Thinking Machine (Professor Augustus S. F. X. Van Dusen)

Jacques Futrelle died on the Titanic when it sank. His eccentric detective, nicknamed appropriately, used his incredible intellect to solve crimes. Professor Augustus S. F. X. Van Dusen practices the same type of prestigious miracles as the great one, Sherlock Holmes. So smart that he was removed from his academic position for his ideas, only to be restored when they proved true, he astounds everyone with his application of pure logic to all the puzzles that are brought to him. Like many of the eccentrics, he is ill tempered, and his large head makes him look odd. His cases can be recommended to any soft-boiled or traditional mystery reader. See the Jacques Futrelle website at http://www.futrelle.com. **Soft-boiled/Traditional**.

The Chase of the Golden Plate. Dodd, 1906

Van Dusen makes an appearance in the last third of this novel to help solve the crime. It begins when a man named Dick appears at a costume party dressed as The Burglar, and plots to boldly separate the millionaire, Stuyvesant Randolph, from the plate in his gold service. His campaign is successful, and he escapes with an accomplice, a woman dressed as a cowgirl. What Van Dusen is able to deduct is that an old alliance, coupled with some mistaken identities, has confused the police, but he is able to see the path to the truth.

The Thinking Machine. Dodd, 1907 (also published as *The Problem of Cell 13.* Dodd, 1918)

A collection of the following stories: "The Flaming Phantom"; "The Great Auto Mystery"; "The Man Who was Lost," "The Mystery of a Studio," "The Problem of Cell 13," "The Ralston Bank Burglary," and "The Scarlet Thread."

Short stories

The Thinking Machine on the Case. U.S.: Appleton, 1908 (U.K.: *The Professor on the Case.* Nelson, 1909)

This novel appears to be a collection of short stories strung together to give the appearance of a novel. All the cases are the typical puzzles brought to The Thinking Machine, and his Solomon-like pronouncements bring each case to a conclusion.

Short stories

Best Thinking Machine Detective Stories. Dover, 1973

A collection of the following stories: "The Brown Coat," "The Crystal Gazer," "The Fatal Cipher," "The Flaming Phantom," "His Perfect Alibi," "Kidnapped Baby Blake, Millionaire," "The Lost Radium," "The Missing Necklace," "The Phantom Motor," "The Problem of Cell 13," "The Problem of the Stolen Rubens," and "The Scarlet Thread."

Short stories

Great Cases of the Thinking Machine. Dover, 1977

A collection of the following stories: "The Haunted Bell," "The Interrupted Wireless," "The Motor Boat," "The Problem of the Auto Cab," "The Problem of the Broken Bracelet," "The Problem of the Cross Mark," "The Problem of the Hidden Million," "The Problem of the Souvenir Cards," "The Problem of the Vanishing Man," "The Roswell Tiara," "The Silver Box," "The Superfluous Finger," and "The Three Overcoats."

Short stories

S. S. Van Dine (pseud. of Willard Huntington Wright) ✍

Philo Vance

One of the most obnoxious dilettantes, Philo Vance (a non-de-plume for a man who wished to remain anonymous) worked in concert with New York District Attorney John F. X. Markham to solve crimes. He has the distinction of being the most popular American detective of the 1920s. Vance's arrogance does not prevent him from being a great detective, although his cases are virtually unreadable by today's reader (except those reading them for historical purposes). Each novel is littered with footnotes in a fashion similar to Dorothy L.

Sayers, and often asides are made to Chinese antiquities, rare books, and the other esoteric interests of the great detective. **Traditional**. Series subject: **New York, New York**.

The Benson Murder Case. Scribner, 1926

The death of Wall Street broker Alvin Benson draws Philo Vance into his first investigation. Having asked his acquaintance, D.A. Markham, to allow him to aid in an investigation, Vance proves an unusual but effective detective.

The Canary Murder Case. Scribner, 1927

Broadway star "Canary" Margaret Odell has been brutally strangled, and once again D.A. Markham asks Vance to help with the investigation.

Theater

The Greene Murder Case. Scribner, 1928

Someone is trying to eliminate all the residents of the Greene mansion, a wealthy but dysfunctional family. Vance is able to solve these baffling crimes, which occur right in front of the police.

The Bishop Murder Case. Scribner, 1929

The Bishop is an alias used by a clever murderer who sends codes to the police to taunt them about his murders committed with a bow and arrow. The codes are based on Mother Goose rhymes and the first victim is named Joseph Cochrane Robin. It takes Vance's intellect to divine the meaning behind the messages and to capture the criminal.

4

The Scarab Murder Case. Scribner, 1930

In Gramercy Park's private Egyptian museum, patron Benjamin H. Kyle is killed with the statue of Sekhmet, the Egyptian goddess of vengeance. Vance focuses on the only clue at the scene, a small lapis scarab left beneath the body.

Museums

The Dragon Murder Case. Scribner, 1933

Tropical fish are the focus when Rudolph Stamm, one of the foremost aquarists in the United States, has an accident in his swimming pool. Sandford Montague, fiancé to Stamm's sister Bernice, has disappeared from the pool. When his body is discovered, it has the mark of the dragon.

Tropical fish

The Kennel Murder Case. Scribner, 1933

Archie Coe, unpopular dog breeder, is found murdered in his townhouse. When the chief suspect is murdered as well, it becomes Vance's job to use his knowledge of dog breeds and Chinese ceramics to solve the case.

Antiquities · Dogs

The Casino Murder Case. Scribner, 1934

Vance is warned that tragedy will strike the casino owned by Richard Kincaid, brother of a prominent social worker, Mrs. Anthony Llewellyn. The warning was timely as a person dies of poison, and Vance finds himself on the trail of a murderer.

Gambling

The Garden Murder Case. Scribner, 1935

Ephraim Garden, a chemist, is murdered at a party in his penthouse while his guests are listening to a horse race. Vance's ability to absorb arcane knowledge, from radioactivity to the Aeneid, helps him solve this case.

The Kidnap Murder Case. Scribner, 1936

The letter "K" is the key when Karl K. Kenting's son Kaspar is kidnapped, possibly by Kenyon, Karl's kin. Vance is not kidding when he tries to solve this case.

The Gracie Allen Murder Case. Scribner, 1938 (Also published as *The Smell of Murder*. Bantam, 1950)

The idea for this novel was an attempt by Van Dine to create a vehicle for his friend, Gracie Allen, and her comedy partner, George Burns, that could be translated to film. Although Burns never made it to the screen, Allen did, starring as a perfume factory worker whose firm may have manufactured a new poison.

The Winter Murder Case. Scribner, 1939

A trip to the Berkshires should be relaxing for Vance, but when the crumpled body of Lief Wallen is found at the base of a cliff, he finds himself in competition with Winewood's Lieutenant O'Leary. Vance's challenge is to find out who is after the priceless emerald collection Wallen was supposed to be guarding. This novel was published posthumously in this form and was never completed by Van Dine.

New York, Winewood (Berkshires)

The Golden Agers and Beyond

Ellery Queen (pseud. of Manfred B. Lee and Frederic Dannay) ✍

Ellery Queen

Two cousins, interested in winning a mystery fiction contest, created an American dilettante with obnoxious characteristics equal to those of other eccentric detectives. Fortunately for mystery fiction, this character grew in stature and, over time, became an interesting and fulfilled character. Ellery Queen (the character) has access to many crimes because his father is an Inspector for the New York police. Ellery Queen (the author) served the mystery community well by founding *Ellery Queen Mystery Magazine* and by contributing scholarship to the field. The strength of this series over time is its wonderful puzzle plots. However, it should be noted that after 1958, other authors wrote the novels from outlines provided by Dannay. A fan site about the authors of this series can be found at http://meltingpot.fortunecity.com/kirkland/266/eq/eqnovs.htm. **Soft-boiled/Traditional**.

The Roman Hat Mystery. Stokes, 1929

During a performance of *Gunplay*, Monte Field, lawyer and blackmailer, is found sitting in his seat at the Roman Theater, dead and missing his top hat. Only a detective like Ellery Queen would be able to use that clue to find a murderer.

New York, New York · Theater

The French Powder Mystery. Stokes, 1930

French's Department store is demonstrating its wares in one of its windows, when a wall-bed is unfolded and out falls the owner's wife's dead body. Winnifred French was a likely candidate to be murdered, having left behind a trail of husbands and lovers.

New York, New York

The Dutch Shoe Mystery. Stokes, 1931

When Abby Doorn is brought to the operating room, it is already too late. She has been strangled with wire and the only one with access to her was her doctor. Queen works with his father to find the correct suspect among a hospital full of suspects.

Medical · New York, New York

The Greek Coffin Mystery. Stokes, 1932

Blind art dealer Georg Khalkis dies of natural causes, but his will is missing. When Queen deduces that the only place it can be is buried with the art dealer, he discovers that a second corpse has joined Khalkis in his casket.

New York, New York · Wills

The Egyptian Cross Mystery. Stokes, 1932

Andrew Van, schoolmaster, is the first victim of a serial killer, crucified on Christmas Day. The clues all form around the letter "T," and it is Queen who points toward an ancient Egyptian tau religious symbol. Additional deaths occur and clues lead to an international complication before Queen can tumble to the reason behind the killings.

New York, New York · Serial killer · West Virginia, Arroyo

The American Gun Mystery. Stokes, 1933 (Also published as *Death at the Rodeo*. Mercury, 1951)

In front of many witnesses, silent film cowboy Buck Horne is murdered during a Wild West Show. The cast had been assigned blanks, but one fatal bullet was either fired from the cast or from the audience. Another killing occurs, and Queen assists his father in solving this bizarre crime.

New York, New York · Theater

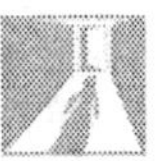

The Siamese Twin Mystery. Stokes, 1933

Using the Tepees mountaintop as a locked room, this mystery isolates a group of travelers when a forest fire cuts them off and strands them at the home of Dr. John Xavier. Unfortunately, one of their party commits murder. Fortunately, Queen and his father are part of the group, and despite the danger, Queen decides to solve the murder.

Locked room · Mountains

The Adventures of Ellery Queen. Stokes, 1934

A collection of the following stories: "The Adventure of the African Traveler," "The Adventure of the Bearded Lady," "The Adventure of the Glass-Domed Clock," "The Adventure of the Hanging Acrobat," "The Adventure of the Invisible Lover," "The Adventure of the Mad Tea-Party," "The Adventure of the One-Penny Black," "The Adventure of the Seven Black Cats," "The Adventure of the Teakwood Case," "The Adventure of the Three Lame Men," and "The Adventure of 'The Two-Headed Dog'."

Short stories

The Chinese Orange Mystery. Stokes, 1934

A corpse with his clothes on backwards is the puzzle presented to Queen. Found in the offices of Mandarin Press owner, Donald Kirk, this case leads to other backwards clues that puzzle the great detective.

New York, New York

The Spanish Cape Mystery. Stokes, 1935

Handsome leading man John Marco is found naked and dead beneath his flowing cloak. He was the rival for the hand of the married Stella Godfrey, and for the woman's 18-year-old daughter, Rosa. Queen needs to discover who is the guilty party at the Godfrey summer estate in Spanish Cape.

Halfway House. Stokes, 1936

William Angell is Queen's friend, and Queen jumps to help him when Angell's sister is accused of murdering her husband, Joe Wilson. The case takes Queen between three cities as he hunts for the clues to free the falsely accused woman.

New Jersey, Trenton · New York, New York · Pennsylvania, Philadelphia

The Door Between. Stokes, 1937

Queen does not believe that Karen Leith has committed suicide, and he is right. Terry Ring, private eye, tries to help publisher Eva MacClure when her fingerprints are found on the murder weapon used against her prize-winning author, Karen Leith. Eva thought she loved another, but her attentions turn to Terry as he fights for her cause.

New York, New York

The Devil to Pay. Stokes, 1938

While working on a film in Hollywood, Queen is asked to solve a murder resulting from a feud between two Hollywood millionaires.

California, Los Angeles · Film

The Four of Hearts. Stokes, 1938

Queen has a writing job for a major studio in Hollywood, and that job brings him into contact with some of Hollywood's biggest stars. When Jack Royle and Blythe Stuart decide to set aside their family's differences and marry, their honeymoon ends abruptly when they are poisoned while in flight.

California, Los Angeles · Film

The Dragon's Teeth. Stokes, 1939 (Also published as *The Virgin Heiress.* Pocket Books, 1954)

Beau Rummell and Queen have decided to start a detective agency together, and their first job is to discover which of two nieces may have murdered the millionaire Cadmus Cole to inherit his money.

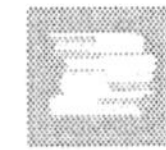

New York, New York • Wills

The New Adventures of Ellery Queen. Stokes, 1940

A collection of the following stories: "The Adventure of the Bleeding Portrait," "The Adventure of the Hollow Dragon," "The Adventure of the House of Darkness," "The Adventure of the Treasure Hunt," "The Lamp of God," "Long Shot," "Man Bites Dog," "Mind Over Matter," and "Trojan Horse."

Short stories

Calamity Town. Little, 1942

Ellery Queen needs to get away to write, so he chooses the small New England town of Wrightsville to hide from the limelight. He is not in town very long before his identity is revealed, and that is important when death strikes the town and one of its finest is accused of murder. Is Jim Haight trying to poison Pat Wright, daughter of the town banker? This novel is as much about the town as it is about the mystery, and it is a classic in the field.

New England, Wrightsville

There Was an Old Woman. Little, 1943 (Also published as *The Quick and the Dead.* Pocket Books, 1956)

Cordelia Potts, head of a shoe manufacturing giant, is making her family's life miserable. Queen thinks it would be a great idea to let her brothers Thurlow and Robert have the duel they want, if they use the blanks Ellery substituted in the guns. The problem: someone substitutes real bullets for blanks, and a death occurs.

New York, New York

The Murderer Is a Fox. Little, 1945

Captain Davy Fox has returned from WWII haunted by the decades-old murder of his mother. Queen, knowing that events in the present may turn horrible if he fails, reopens the murder investigation of Davy's mother, Jessica.

New England, Wrightsville

Ten Days' Wonder. Little, 1948

Howard Van Horn has a missing 19 days to account for, and Ellery returns him to his home in Wrightsville to get the answers. Ellery finds himself battling the family head, tycoon Dietrich Van Horn, and Howard's jealous brother Wolfert, to try and get answers. Sally Van Horn is Howard's stepmother, but young and attractive enough to upset the father-son relationship.

New England, Wrightsville

Cat of Many Tails. Little, 1949

During a summer heat wave in the Big Apple, a mass murderer strikes. Queen, despite almost giving up detecting after his previous case, is drawn into the battle against a killer who seems to pick his victims at random and strangle them with cords of India silk.

New York, New York • Serial killer

Double, Double. Little, 1950 (Also published as *The Case of the Seven Murders.* Pocket Books, 1958)

Why would a rich man die broke and a poor man die rich? That is the puzzle that intrigues Queen when he returns to his safehaven, Wrightsville, to solve this conundrum, which seems to be based on a child's verse.

New England, Wrightsville

The Origin of Evil. Little, 1951

Queen is out west researching a novel when he is asked by Laurel Hill to investigate why someone sent a dead dog to her father and caused him to die of fright. Hill's partner, Roger Priam, may also be a target, and something in the past of these two men is causing a person to seek murder.

California, Los Angeles

Calendar of Crime. Little, 1952

A collection of the following stories: "The Dauphin's Doll," "The Dead Cat," "The Emperor's Dice," "The Fallen Angel," "The Gettysburg Bugle," "The Ides of Michael Magoon," "The Inner Circle," "The Medical Finger," "The Needle's Eye," "The President's Half Disme," "The Telltale Bottle," and "The Three R's."

Short stories

The King Is Dead. Little, 1952

King Bendigo, head of one of the biggest military-industrial giants, needs to live on an isolated island in the Atlantic Ocean to protect his assets and his life. Needing a great detective, he kidnaps Queen and his father and brings them to the island, where the two detectives match wits against an isolated group of people who wish to murder King.

Locked room

The Scarlet Letters. Little, 1953

Alphabetical clues lead Queen on a wild chase when he agrees to investigate the adultery and blackmail associated with Nicki Porter's childhood friend, Martha Lawrence. Dick Lawrence has the history of adultery in his family, but Martha may be the one who is straying. Nicki and Ellery trail their friends to try to prevent a tragedy.

New York, New York

QBI: Queen's Bureau of Investigation. Little, 1954

A collection of the following stories: "The Black Ledger," "Child Missing!" "Cold Money," "Double Your Money," "Driver's Seat," "The Gambler's Club," "GI Story," "A Lump of Sugar," "A Matter of Seconds," "Miser's Gold," "Money Talks," "My Queer Dean!" "The Myna Birds," "A Question of Honor," "The Robber of Wrightsville," "Snowball in July," "The Three Widows," and "The Witch of Times Square."

Short stories

Inspector Queen's Own Case. Simon, 1956

Listed here because of the character's long association with Queen, this book features a retired and restless Inspector Richard Queen on the hunt. Jessie Sherwood, a registered nurse who ministers to the millionaires on Nair Island, is sure a child was murdered and she asks the Inspector to investigate.

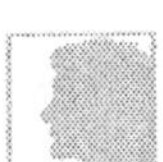

Connecticut, Nair Island

The Finishing Stroke. Simon, 1958

Retrospectively, Queen looks back to the time of the publication of *The Roman Hat Mystery* and the night he was invited to the home of Arthur B. Craig. Housebound by a snowstorm, the guests are baffled by the case of the missing Santa Claus with clues coming from the 12 days of Christmas, all indicating a murder will take place.

Christmas · Holidays · New York, New York

The Player on the Other Side. Random House, 1963

Using a new device, the authors reveal early who the murderer is in this novel. The puzzle is who is using a murderer to orchestrate the murders when four cousins, each living at one of the corners of York Square, are threatened with death, and then die.

New York, New York · Serial killer

And on the Eighth Day. Random House, 1964

Told as a flashback to 1944, Queen recounts a tale of his adventures in Death Valley. After his car breaks down, Queen finds a prophet wandering in the desert, and becomes involved in an isolated religious community where his presence triggers a murder.

Nevada, Death Valley · Religion

The Fourth Side of the Triangle. Random House, 1965

Dane McKell has fallen in love with his father's mistress Shelia Grey, and the complex nature of the emotions involved does lead to murder. Queen solves the case of Shelia's murder from his hospital bed, where he is confined by a skiing accident.

New York, New York

Queens Full. Random House, 1965

A collection of the following stories: "The Case Against Carroll," "The Death of Don Juan," "Diamonds in Paradise," "E = Murder," and "The Wrightsville Heir."

Short stories

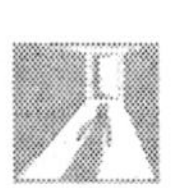

A Study in Terror. U.S.: Lancer, 1966 (U.K.: *Sherlock Holmes vs. Jack the Ripper*. Gollancz, 1967)

The authors of the Ellery Queen series offer a pastiche in which Sherlock Holmes takes on the Jack the Ripper case. When the solution leaves something to be desired, it is Queen who ends the narrative with an explanation to this great puzzle. The Queen section was written by Queen, but the Holmes section was written by Paul W. Fairman.

England, London • Fairman, Paul W. • Holmes, Sherlock • Jack the Ripper

Face to Face. New American Library, 1967

"Face" is the dying clue left by former singing sensation Gloria Guild. The widowed Count Carlos Armando and British agent Harry Burke are part of the ensemble that Queen and his father need to sort through to find out why this canary was silenced.

Music • New York, New York

The House of Brass. New American Library, 1968

Inspector Queen, now retired and married again, is invited to the estate of Hendrik Brass, a renowned jeweler. This gathering is to determine who will inherit from the millionaire, and this is a recipe destined to produce a murder. This novel was written by Avram Davidson from an outline provided by Frederic Dannay.

Davidson, Avram • New York, Phillipskill • Wills

QED: Queen's Experiments in Detection. New American Library, 1968

A collection of the following stories: "Abraham Lincoln's Clue," "The Broken T," "Dead Ringer," "Eve of the Wedding," "Half a Clue," "Last Man to Die," "The Little Spy," "The Lonely Bride," "Miracles do Happen," "Mum is the Word," "Mystery at the Library of Congress," "No Parking," "No Place to Live," "Object Lesson," "Payoff," and "The President Regrets."

Short stories

The Last Woman in His Life. World, 1969

John Benedict III is Queen's old friend now residing in Wrightsville. His three ex-wives are all in town when John dies before he can change his will. Ellery's friendship drives him to solve the murder where the clues include various articles of clothing belonging to the women.

New England, Wrightsville • Wills

A Fine and Private Place. World, 1971

Nino Importuna is obsessed with the number nine. With his two brothers, he runs the Importuna Industries and lives with them in an apartment on the Upper East Side. When Julio, the youngest, is found dead, the Inspector asks Queen to take a look at this strange case where the evidence points to brother Marco.

New York, New York

Dorothy L. Sayers ✍

Lord Peter Wimsey

The first of the charming dilettantes, Lord Peter is the second son of a Duke. Damaged by his WWI experience, Lord Peter becomes a competent detective-hobbyist who grows as a character, enhanced by a love life that develops within the series. Accompanied by Bunter, his gentleman's gentleman, Wimsey is a delight to watch in action. Sayers was a brilliant writer, and she included many literary allusions within the text, managing to create interesting plots, great characters, and wonderful settings. In 1998, Jill Paton Walsh completed one manuscript left unfinished by Sayers. See the website for the Dorothy L. Sayers Society at http://www.sayers.org.uk. **Soft-boiled/Traditional**.

Whose Body? U.K.: Unwin, 1923 (U.S.: Boni, 1923)

Lord Peter's first case begins when he is informed that a well-known financier, wearing only a pince-nez, has been found dead in a bathtub. Intrigued by the mysterious death, Lord Peter begins his detective career by having doubts about the identity of the corpse.

England, Battersea

Clouds of Witness. U.K.: Unwin, 1926 (U.S.: Dial, 1927)

While on vacation in France, Lord Peter hears that his brother has been charged with the murder of their sister's fiancé, Captain Denis Cathcart. Lord Peter returns to England to defend his brother and to explain who used the Duke's pistol to commit the crime.

England, Riddlesdale

Unnatural Death. U.K.: Benn, 1927 (U.S.: *The Dawson Pedigree.* Dial, 1928)

Cancer will kill but the premature death of an elderly cancer patient leads to an accusation against her nurse. A chance-overheard remark in a restaurant is enough to set Lord Peter on the trail of a killer.

England, Hampshire · Medical

The Unpleasantness at the Bellona Club. U.K.: Benn, 1928 (U.S.: Payson, 1928)

General Fentiman is thought to be sleeping in the club one night, until it is discovered that he is dead. After his burial, it is discovered that his exact time of death may influence the distribution of his estate. Lord Peter's investigation leads to the evidence for a murder charge.

England, London · Wills

Lord Peter Views the Body. U.K.: Gollancz, 1928 (U.S.: Brewer, 1929)

A collection of the following stories: "The Abominable History of the Man with Copper Fingers," "The Adventurous Exploit of the Cave of Ali Baba," "The Bibulous Business of a Matter of Taste," "The Entertaining Episode of the Article in Question," "The Fantastic Horror of the Cat in the Bag," "The Fascinating Problems of Uncle Meleager's Will," "The Learned Adventure of the Dragon's Head," "The Piscatorial Farce of the Stolen Stomach," "The Undignified Melodrama of the Bone of Contention," "The Unprincipled Affair of the Practical Joker," "The Unsolved Puzzle of the Man with No Face," and "The Vindictive Story of the Footsteps That Ran."

Short stories

Strong Poison. U.K.: Gollancz, 1930 (U.S.: Brewer, 1930)

Mystery writer Harriet Vane is accused of murdering her lover, Philip Boyes. When Lord Peter takes up her case, little does he know the ultimate outcome this case will have on his future.

Authors • England, London

The Five Red Herrings. U.K.: Gollancz, 1931 (U.S.: *Suspicious Characters.* Brewer, 1931)

Campbell, the landscape painter, was not this small Scottish town's favorite son since his recent arrival. When his body is found in the water at the edge of a cliff, most assume it was an accident until Lord Peter thinks it is murder.

Artists • Scotland, Kirkcudbright

Have His Carcase. U.K.: Gollancz, 1932 (U.S.: Brewer, 1932)

Harriet finds herself a suspect in a murder for the second time. This time, while walking on the beach to find an idea for her next mystery novel, she sees a man, with his throat cut, lying on a rock and disappearing into the rising tide. Luckily, she knows that Lord Peter is her biggest ally when the corpse proves to be a gigolo who had intentions to marry for money.

England, Wilvercombe

Murder Must Advertise. U.K.: Gollancz, 1933 (U.S.: Harcourt, 1933)

Using her own background in the advertising business, Sayers creates a mystery around the Pym's Publicity advertising firm. The previous copywriter, Victor Dean, had fallen to his death at work, and the new copywriter, Bredon, finds himself in mysterious circumstances as he follows in Dean's footsteps.

Advertising • England, London

Hangman's Holiday. U.K.: Gollancz, 1933 (U.S.: Harcourt, 1933)

A collection of the following stories: "The Image in the Mirror," "The Incredible Elopement of Lord Peter Wimsey," "The Necklace of Pearls," "The Poisoned Dow '08," and "The Queen's Square." Also contains seven non-Wimsey stories.

Short stories

The Nine Tailors. U.K.: Gollancz, 1934 (U.S.: Harcourt, 1934)

The village in East Anglia loves its bells, but the bells are causing some trouble, and it is all detailed for the reader. When Sir Henry Thorpe's death and burial reveals an additional body, Wimsey decides to investigate.

England, East Anglia • Religion

Gaudy Night. U.K.: Gollancz, 1935 (U.S.: Harcourt, 1936)

Harriet Vane, having twice been accused of murder herself, finally gets her own case to solve as a detective. Returning to Shrewsbury College, Oxford, she becomes embroiled in personal attacks on others at the college.

Academia • England, Oxford

Busman's Honeymoon. U.K.: Gollancz, 1937 (U.S.: Harcourt, 1937)

Finally united as a couple, Lord Peter and Harriet head off to an isolated cottage to celebrate their union. The problem is that Miss Twitterton's uncle, who has disappeared, is located by the happy couple in the cellar of their honeymoon retreat, very dead.

England, Broxford

In the Teeth of the Evidence. U.K.: Gollancz, 1939 (U.S.: Harcourt, 1940)

A collection of the following stories: "Absolutely Elsewhere," and "In the Teeth of the Evidence." A later edition, issued in 1972, adds "The Haunted Policeman," "Striding Folly," and "Talboys." All editions also include 15 non-Wimsey stories.

Short stories

Lord Peter. Harper, 1972

A collection of the following stories: "Absolutely Elsewhere," "The Abominable History of the Man with Copper Fingers," "The Adventurous Exploit of the Cave of Ali Baba," "The Bibulous Business of a Matter of Taste," "The Entertaining Episode of the Article in Question," "The Fantastic Horror of the Cat in the Bag," "The Fascinating Problems of Uncle Meleager's Will," "The Haunted Policeman," "The Image in the Mirror," "In the Teeth of the Evidence," "The Incredible Elopement of Lord Peter Wimsey," "The Learned Adventure of the Dragon's Head," "The Necklace of Pearls," "The Piscatorial Farce of the Stolen Stomach," "The Queen's Square," "Striding Folly," "Talboys," "The Undignified Melodrama of the Bone of Contention," "The Unprincipled Affair of the Practical Joker," "The Unsolved Puzzle of the Man with No Face," and "The Vindictive Story of the Footsteps that Ran."

Short stories

Thrones, Dominations (by Jill Paton Walsh). St. Martin's Press, 1998

When Sayers died, a manuscript with this title was left behind, tantalizingly close to showing us the married relationship of Wimsey and Harriet. Commissioned to complete the manuscript, Walsh completed the task in 1998. Wimsey and Harriet meet Lawrence and Rosamund Harwell in Paris in 1936, and are reunited with the couple when Rosamund is strangled at their cottage in Hampton. Laurence produces an alibi, and Peter must investigate the death of a friend.

England, Hampton • Walsh, Jill Paton

Amateur Detectives

Why would reasonable people who are not professional detectives investigate a crime? Perhaps it is because there is no better person for a reader to identify with than another member of society with the courage to act when others are standing by. Perhaps it is the need to believe that individuals can still matter, and that society is not completely dependent on organizations, but rather on the courage and tenacity of its individual members. Perhaps it is because reading about the amateur is more fun.

The Historical Founding Members

E. C. Bentley ✍

Philip Trent

British writer Bentley played with the genre when he created his artist detective Philip Trent. Readers of these novels will find that not only is the character interesting, but so are the structure of the stories. Written as parodies of the genre, the books can still be enjoyed for their gentle poke in the ribs. Although Trent was intended as a spoof of the genre, readers took his first case to heart and welcomed him into the ranks of the genre. The reason may lie within Trent's basic humanity and fallibility, traits not commonly found in the eccentrics. The middle book in the series was co-written with Warner Allen. **Soft-boiled/Traditional**.

Trent's Last Case. U.K.: Nelson, 1913 (U.S: *The Woman in Black.* Century, 1913)
The repercussions of the murder of financier Sigsbee Manderson do not compare to the difficulties endured by the Trent is he tries to find the correct solution to this baffling murder.

England

Trent's Own Case (with Warner Allen). U.K.: Constable, 1936 (U.S.: Knopf, 1936)
Trent finds himself a suspect when James Randolph, famous philanthropist financier, is found shot to death after meeting with Trent at the Cactus Club. This time the great detective needs to save himself.

Allen, Warner • England, London

Trent Intervenes. U.K.: Nelson, 1938 (U.S.: Knopf, 1938)
A collection of the following stories: "The Clever Cockatoo," "The Genuine Tabard," "The Inoffensive Captain," "The Little Mystery," "The Old-Fashioned Apache," "The Ordinary Hairpins," "The Public Benefactor," "The Sweet Shot," "Trent and the Bad Dog," "Trent and the Fool-Proof Lift," "The Unknown Peer," and "The Vanished Lawyer."

Short stories

Nicholas Blake (pseud. of Cecil Day-Lewis) ✍

Nigel Strangeways

Britain's Poet Laureate developed a mystery series whose hallmark is its ability to present cases in the classic tradition of fair play. Strangeways is well educated, but has rejected the world of academia to set himself up as an investigator. Offering his skills to his clients, he is able to consult with Scotland Yard through his uncle, an investigator. Strangeway's personal life is filled with tragedy, and these challenges enhance him as a character. **Soft-boiled/Traditional.**

A Question of Proof. U.K.: Collins, 1935 (U.S.: Harper, 1935)

It is Sports Day at Sudeley Hall prep school, and Algernon Wyvern-Wemyss, the bullying nephew of the headmaster, has been found strangled. When English instructor Michael Evan's pen is found with the body, only he knows he dropped it while meeting with the headmaster's wife. He calls his friend Strangeways to get him off the hook.

Academia • England, Staverton

Thou Shell of Death. U.K.: Collins, 1936 (U.S.: *Shell of Death.* Harper, 1936)

WWI flying ace Fergus O'Brien is planning a party at Christmas. He needs Strangeways's aid when he believes that one of the invited guests is planning his murder. When Fergus is found dead in his office with his own gun, the only valuable clues are an old photograph and some footprints in the snow.

England, Chatcombe

There's Trouble Brewing. U.K.: Collins, 1937 (U.S.: Harper, 1937)

Strangeways is on the lecture circuit when he is asked by the unliked brewer, Eustace Bunnett, to look into the mystery of how his pet dog ended up in one of his vats. Truffles the terrier was only the first victim, for when Strangeways arrives on the scene, another body is floating in the vat, and this time it is human.

Brewers • England, Dorset, Maiden Astbury

The Beast Must Die. U.K.: Collins, 1938 (U.S.: Harper, 1938)

When Martin Cairnes is killed by a hit-and-run driver, his grieving father, Frank, plans foul things for the driver, George Rattery. When the hunter and the hunted meet, Rattery disappears, but Cairnes claims he is innocent. Strangeways is called into this case to try and resolve if revenge was gained, or if the father should go free.

England, Gloucestershire

The Smiler with the Knife. U.K.: Collins, 1939 (U.S.: Harper, 1939)

Strangeways and his wife Georgia are trimming their hedges when they discover a mysterious locket. The locket belongs to their neighbor Major Keston, and the initials on the locket stand for English Banner, a clandestine group eager to take over the government and the wealth of Great Britain. In a sense, this is Strangeways's *Gaudy Night*, as he takes a backseat to Georgia on this case.

England, Devonshire

Malice in Wonderland. U.K.: Collins, 1940 (U.S.: *The Summer Camp Mystery.* Harper, 1940; also published as *Murder With Malice.* Pyramid, 1964)

In the British vacation camp of Wonderland, a practical joker calling himself The Mad Hatter is ruining everyone's good time with his sabotaged tennis balls, ruined talent shows, and attempted drownings. Strangeways's vacation is no paradise when the jokes turn to murder.

Amusement parks · England, Wonderland

The Case of the Abominable Snowman. U.K.: Collins, 1941 (U.S.: *The Corpse in the Snowman.* Harper, 1941)

Having some fun by pretending to be an expert in psychic phenomena, all Strangeways wished to do was investigate the strange behavior of a cat. But when he arrives at the Restorick's Easterham Manor, he discovers the daughter Elizabeth is dead, an apparent suicide.

England, Easterham

Minute for Murder. U.K.: Collins, 1947 (U.S.: Harper, 1948)

Strangeways has been serving his country in the Ministry of Morale, but when V-E Day arrives, he finds himself back on a murder case. Nita Prince, the director's personal secretary and mistress, is murdered with cyanide. Her fiancé, thought killed in the war, is the top suspect.

England, London

Head of a Traveler. U.K.: Collins, 1949 (U.S.: Harper, 1949)

Renowned poet Robert Seaton has been unable to produce his prose. Is he troubled by the long disappearance of his older brother? The answer may come when a headless corpse is found in the river near his estate, and the mute dwarf, Finny Black, produces its head in a string bag. Strangeways and Inspector Blount of the Yard must try and piece this puzzle together.

England, Oxford, Hinton Lacey

The Dreadful Hollow. U.K.: Collins, 1953 (U.S.: Harper, 1953)

Sir Archibald Blick wants to put a factory in the normally quiet village of Priors Umborne. His financial plans are disrupted when the resident's secrets are revealed in poisoned pen letters, leading some to commit suicide. Blick asks Strangeways to investigate, so the detective finds himself looking for someone who wants to ruin a village.

England, Prior's Umborne

The Whisper in the Gloom. U.K.: Collins, 1954 (U.S.: Harper, 1954; also published as *Catch and Kill.* Bestseller, 1955)

Bert "the Brain" Hale is the leader of a gang of small boys, and when the boys are handed a crumpled message by a dying man named Dai Williams, it starts them on a grand adventure. When things turn dangerous, the boys turn to Strangeways for help.

England, London

End of Chapter. U.K.: Collins, 1957 (U.S.: Harper, 1957)

The publishing firm of Wenham & Geraldine feels it is thc target when it has troubles with an autobiography of General Richard Thoresby. Certain passages in the work have been deemed libelous, and three separate times the material has been removed, yet copies released to the public still had the offending content intact. It becomes Strangeways's job to find the person out to the sabotage the project, especially when it turns to murder.

Bibliomystery • England, London

The Widow's Cruise. U.K.: Collins, 1959 (U.S.: Harper, 1959)

Strangeways and Clare Massinger were sailing on the S. S. Menelaos to Athens when they notice two women. One, a schoolteacher, is plain while the other is known as The Merry Widow. Late one night someone dies in the ship's swimming pool, and Strangeways finds himself on the track of a killer, with the two women as chief suspects.

Aegean • Shipboard

The Worm of Death. U.K.: Collins, 1961 (U.S.: Harper, 1961)

Strangeways and Clare's neighbor is the venerable Dr. Peirs Loudron, and his family becomes very concerned when the old man disappears. When his body is pulled from the Thames with his wrists cut, Strangeways must decide if this is suicide, or if he should be concerned about the doctor's family.

England, Greenwich

The Sad Variety. U.K.: Collins, 1964 (U.S.: Harper, 1964)

Sent by the Security Department, Strangeways is ostensibly holidaying with Clare Massinger, but in reality he is protecting professor Alfred Wragby from the Russians. When the professor's eight-year-old daughter, Lucy, is kidnapped, Strangeways pursues the truth of out a sense of guilt over his failure to do his job.

England, Downcombe • Espionage • Kidnapping

The Morning After Death. U.K.: Collins, 1966 (U.S.: Harper, 1966)

Strangeways finds himself in America working a case when he is in residence as a poet at Cabot University. Josiah Ahlberg of the Classics Department is not liked, so there is no shortage of suspects on campus when he is murdered.

Academia • Massachusetts, Boston

Agatha Christie ✍

Jane Marple

Miss Jane Marple is the archetype of the little old lady detective. Besides setting the standard for that subgroup of amateurs, Christie's use of the English village as a setting established another convention for the genre. Marple's interest in gardening, knitting, and sketching brings her into contact with a circle within the isolated community that provides her a network for solving crimes. Each case is a great puzzle, a trademark of all of Christie's writing. See the Agatha Christie Society website at http://fly.cc.fer.hr/~shlede/my/society.html. **Soft-boiled/Traditional**.

The Murder at the Vicarage. U.K.: Collins, 1930 (U.S.: Dodd, Mead, 1930)

The quiet village of St. Mary Mead is disturbed by the death of Colonel Protheroe. The question for its resident detective is which of the seven people who wanted him dead actually did the deed.

England, St. Mary Mead

The Thirteen Problems. U.K.: Collins, 1932 (U.S.: *The Tuesday Club Murders.* Dodd, Mead, 1933; also published as *Miss Marple and the Thirteen Problems.* Penguin, 1953)

A collection of the following stories: "The Affair at the Bungalow," "The Blood-Stained Pavement," "The Blue Geranium," "A Christmas Tragedy," "The Companion," "Death by Drowning," "The Four Suspects," "The Herb of Death," "The Idol House of Astarte," "Ingots of Gold," "Motive v. Opportunity," "The Thumbmark of St. Peter," and "The Tuesday Night Club."

Short stories

The Body in the Library. U.K.: Collins, 1942 (U.S.: Dodd, Mead, 1942)

Dolly Bantry calls on her friend Jane Marple when a dance-hall girl's death occurs in her home at Gossington Hall. Ruby Keene had been making a conquest that will only complicate Miss Marple's case.

England, St. Mary Mead

The Moving Finger. Dodd, Mead, 1942 (Also published as *The Case of the Moving Finger.* Avon Books, 1948)

The first part of this novel is the tale of Jerry Burton, who is recovering from an accident, and his sister Joanna, and their life in Lymson. It is disturbed by a letter sent to them alleging illicit activity. In the second half of the book, Miss Marple takes the lead.

England, Lymson

A Murder Is Announced. U.K.: Collins, 1950 (U.S.: Dodd, Mead, 1950)

Someone has placed an announcement in the local paper declaring the day, date, location, and time of a murder. Unbelievably, driven by curiosity, some of the residents of Chipping Cleghorn go, and when the lights go out, one is murdered. The man killed had placed demands on one of the residents, and Miss Marple's job is to see if this led to murder.

England, Chipping Cleghorn

They Do It with Mirrors. U.K.: Collins, 1952 (U.S.: *Murder With Mirrors.* Dodd, Mead, 1952)

When a murder occurs at Stoneygates, a juvenile detention facility with over 200 incarcerated, Inspector Curry of the Yard relies on Miss Marple to help him solve the crime. Does an attempting poisoning lead to a murderer?

England, St. Mary Mead

A Pocket Full of Rye. U.K.: Collins, 1953 (U.S.: Dodd, Mead, 1954)

A nursery rhyme, "Sing a Song of Sixpence," may hold the clue to this mysterious poisoning. Miss Marple wants to know why the wealthy Rex Fortescue drank his last cup of tea and died, with a pocket full of rye.

England, London • Nursery rhymes

4.50 from Paddington. U.K.: Collins, 1957 (U.S.: *What Mrs. McGillicuddy Saw!* Dodd, Mead, 1957; also published as *Murder, She Said.* Cardinal, 1961)

Miss Marple's friend, Elspeth McGillicuddy, reports being on one train and seeing a murder in another. Only the astute amateur detective believes her story and begins an investigation.

England, Brackhampton • Film: Meet Miss Marple (1961) • Railroads

The Mirror Crack'd from Side to Side. U.K.: Collins, 1962 (U.S.: *The Mirror Crack'd.* Dodd, Mead, 1963)

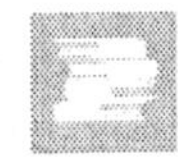

Marian Gregg has moved to St. Mary Mead and into Gossington Hall, but the fading film star still needs the public's attention. She holds a féte at the Hall, and one of the guests, Heather Badcock, is murdered.

England, St. Mary Mead

A Caribbean Mystery. U.K.: Collins, 1964 (U.S.: Dodd, Mead, 1965)

Major Palgrave carries the photograph of a murderer in his pocket. When he uses it to illustrate one of his long stories, he is finished before he can complete his tale. Despite the fact that she is resting after a bout of pneumonia, Miss Marple is driven to solve the murder of her new acquaintance.

Caribbean, St. Honore

At Bertram's Hotel. U.K.: Collins, 1965 (U.S.: Dodd, Mead, 1966)

Bertram's has a distinct clientele, but when murder occurs, the doors swing wide open to admit the spinster sleuth Miss Marple.

England, London • Hotels

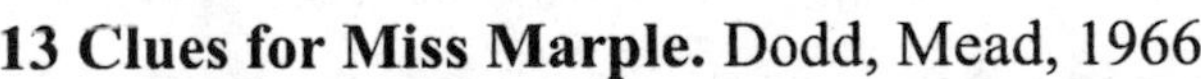

13 Clues for Miss Marple. Dodd, Mead, 1966

A collection of the following stories: "The Bloodstained Pavement," "The Blue Geranium," "The Case of the Caretaker," "The Case of the Perfect Maid," "The Companion," "The Four Suspects," "Greenshaw's Folly," "The Herb of Death," "Motive v. Opportunity," "Sanctuary," "Strange Jest," "Tape-Measure Murder," and "The Thumbmark of St. Peter."

Short stories

Nemesis. U.K.: Collins, 1971 (U.S.: Dodd, Mead, 1971)

A letter from the grave to Miss Marple sends her on a quest for a killer. Her only hope to solving the mysterious death of the financier Rafiel is to join a bus tour and investigate among her fellow travelers.

England

Sleeping Murder. U.K.: Collins, 1976 (U.S.: Dodd, Mead, 1976)

A newlywed is sent by her husband to find a suitable house, and when she finds a charming Victorian villa called Hillside, she thinks it is perfect. Until it is haunted. Lucky for her, she can call upon the unbelieving detective, Miss Marple, who helps her remember an old murder.

England, Plymouth • Ghosts

Miss Marple. Dodd, Mead, 1985

A collection of the following stories: "The Affair at the Bungalow," "The Bloodstained Pavement," "The Blue Geranium," "The Case of the Caretaker," "The Case of the Perfect Maid," "A Christmas Tragedy," "The Companion," "Death by Drowning," "The Four Suspects," "Greenshaw's Folly," "The Herb of Death," "The Idol House of Astarte," "Ingots of Gold," "Miss Marple Tells a Story," "Motive vs. Opportunity," "Sanctuary," "Strange Jest," "Tape-Measure Murder," "The Thumbmark of St. Peter," and "The Tuesday Night Club."

Short stories

R. Austin Freeman ✍

Dr. John Thorndyke

Many of the classic detective's methods were developed during the time when major scientific advances were changing the way people dealt with everyday life. One of the detectives who took advantage of that was Dr. Thorndyke. His application of scientific methods to detective work made him an interesting new kind of detective, and a direct descendant of Sherlock Holmes, albeit without the eccentricities. Dr. Thorndyke was a scientist and followed clues rather than human nature to the source of a crime. The last two titles listed were produced by other authors. **Soft-boiled/Traditional**.

The Red Thumb Mark. U.K.: Collingwood, 1907 (U.S.: Newton, 1911)

When someone manages to open the safe, steal a fortune in diamonds, and close it again, the only clue left is a bloody thumbprint. Scotland Yard matches the print to Reuben Hornby, but the young man protests himself as innocent. It is up to the remarkable Dr. Thorndyke to break the case.

England, London • Jewels

John Thorndyke's Cases. U.K.: Chatto, 1909 (U.S.: *Dr. Thorndyke's Cases.* Dodd, 1931)

A collection of the following stories: "The Aluminium Dagger," "The Anthropologist at Large," "The Blue Sequin," "The Man with the Nailed Shoes," "The Mandarin's Pearl," "A Message from the Deep Sea," "The Moabite Cipher,;" and "The Stranger's Latchkey."

Short stories

The Eye of Osiris. U.K.: Hodder, 1911 (U.S.: *The Vanishing Man.* Dodd, 1912)

John Bellingham, well known in archeological circles, has disappeared from the home of his relative, Hurst. This endangers the collection of Egyptian antiquities that had been in his care. But it will take Dr. Thorndyke to investigate the mysterious disappearance of Bellingham and keep a young man falsely accused of the crime out of jeopardy.

Antiquities • England, London

The Singing Bone. U.K.: Hodder, 1912 (U.S.: Dodd, 1923; also published as *The Adventures of Dr. Thorndyke.* Popular Library, 1947)

A collection of the following stories: "The Case of Oscar Brodski," "A Case of Premeditation," "The Echo of a Mutiny," "The Old Lag," and "A Wastrel's Romance."

Short stories

The Mystery of 31, New Inn. U.K.: Hodder, 1912 (U.S.: Winston, 1913)

Dr. Jervis agrees to treat a man who wishes to remain anonymous. Suspecting morphine poisoning, the doctor is unable to treat his patient, but soon after reads that a prominent man has died from morphine poisoning. With Dr. Thorndyke by his side, Jervis tries to unravel the case of conflicting wills when Jeffrey Blackmore dies.

England, London · Wills

A Silent Witness. U.K.: Hodder, 1914 (U.S.: Winston, 1915)

Dr. Jervis discovers the body of a man on a lonely road, but when he returns with a constable, the body has disappeared. When the incident has to be set aside because of the missing evidence, Jervis finds himself suddenly the victim. He turns to Thorndyke for the answers to this puzzle, and the great detective's inquiries begin to unravel the mystery.

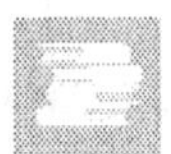

England, Hampstead

***Helen Vardon's Confession.** U.K.: Hodder, 1922

Dr. Thorndyke's Case-Book. U.K.: Hodder, 1923 (U.S.: *The Blue Scarab.* Dodd, 1924).

A collection of the following stories: "The Blue Scarab," "The Case of the White Footprints," "A Fisher of Men," "The Funeral Pyre," "The New Jersey Sphinx," "The Stolen Ingots," and "The Touchstone."

Short stories

The Cat's Eye. U.K.: Hodder, 1923 (U.S.: Dodd, 1927)

Thorndyke's counsel Robert Anstey, is on the spot when Sir Lawrence Drayton's brother is murdered at Rowan Lodge. This case involves a missing pendant called The Cat's Eye, and needs testimony from the past to explain a murder in the present.

England, London · Jewels

***The Mystery of Angelina Frood.** U.K.: Hodder, 1924 (U.S.: Dodd, 1925)

The Puzzle Lock. U.K.: Hodder, 1925 (U.S.: Dodd, 1926)

A collection of the following stories: "The Apparition of Burling Court," "The Green Check Jacket," "The Mysterious Visitor," "A Mystery of the Sand-Hills," "Phyllis Annesley's Peril," "The Puzzle Lock," "Rex v. Burnaby," "The Seal of Nebuchadnezzar," and "A Sower of Pestilence."

Short stories

The Shadow of the Wolf. U.K.: Hodder, 1925 (U.S.: Dodd, 1925)

Margaret Purcell consults Dr. Thorndyke when her husband goes missing. Mr. Purcell had gone sailing with a Mr. Varney, and it is upon his testimony that the disappearance hinges.

England, Sennen · Shipboard

The D'Arblay Mystery. U.K.: Hodder, 1926 (U.S.: Dodd, 1926)

Gray is out on holiday looking for a spot to paint when he comes across Marion D'Arblay searching for her missing father, Julius. Then he comes across the father's body. Knowing that his hospital has Dr. Thorndyke as its chair of medical jurisprudence means that Gray does not mind playing detective.

England, Highgate · Medical

The Magic Casket. U.K.: Hodder, 1927 (U.S.: Dodd, 1927)

A collection of the following stories: "The Contents of a Mare's Nest," "Gleanings from the Wreckage," "The Magic Casket," "Mr. Ponting's Alibi," "The Naturalist at Law," "Pandora's Box," "The Pathologist to the Rescue," "The Stalking Horse," and "The Trail of Behemoth."

Short stories

A Certain Dr. Thorndyke. U.K.: Hodder, 1927 (U.S.: Dodd, 1928)

Osmond is a fugitive from justice who lands in West Africa and within two weeks, he is reported dead of blackwater fever. This is reported by his friend, the trader Larkin, the only white man in the village. The circumstances appeal to the analytical mind of Dr. Thorndyke, and he pursues an investigation beginning with the original theft that caused Osmond's flight.

Africa, Adaffia

As a Thief in the Night. U.K.: Hodder, 1928 (U.S.: Dodd, 1928)

Mayfield knows that the whole case began with the arrival of the Reverend Amos Monkhouse from his Yorkshire parish because he finds his brother Harold very ill and Harold's wife Barbara away on holiday. When Monkhouse dies, and others follow, it is up to Dr. Thorndyke to trace the links between the deaths.

England, London

The Famous Cases of Dr. Thorndyke. U.K.: Hodder, 1929 (U.S.: *The Dr. Thorndyke Omnibus.* Dodd, 1932)

A collection of the following stories from the American edition: "The Aluminium Dagger," "The Anthropologist at Large," "The Apparition of Burling Court," "The Blue Scarab," "The Blue Sequin," "The Case of Oscar Brodski," "A Case of Premeditation," "The Case of the White Foot-Prints," "The Contents of a Mare's Nest," "The Echo of a Mutiny," "A Fisher of Men," "The Funeral Pyre," "Gleanings from the Wreckage," "The Green Check Jacket," "The Magic Casket," "The Man with the Nailed Shoes," "The Mandarin's Pearl," "A Message from the Deep Sea," "Mr. Ponting's Alibi," "The Moabite Cipher," "The Mysterious Visitor," "A Mystery of the Sand-Hills," "The Naturalist at Law," "The New Jersey Sphinx," "The Old Lag," "Pandora's Box," "The Pathologist to the Rescue," "Phyllis Annesley's Peril," "The Puzzle Lock," "Rex v. Burnaby," "The Seal of Nebuchadnezzar," "A Sower of Pestilence," "The Stalking Horse," "The Stolen Ingots," "The Stranger's Latchkey," "The Touchstone," "The Trail of Behemoth," and "A Wastrel's Romance."

Short stories

Mr. Pottermack's Oversight. U.K.: Hodder, 1930 (U.S.: Dodd, 1930)

Mr. Pottermack is the victim of a blackmailer. Dr. Thorndyke's duty is to decide how this ties in to a missing bank manager named James Lewson.

Blackmail • England, Borley

***Dr. Thorndyke Investigates.** University of London Press, 1930

Pontifex, Son & Thorndyke. U.K.: Hodder, 1931 (U.S.: Dodd, 1931)

Dr. Jervis tells Thorndyke of a strange occurrence in which the wrong letter is sealed in an envelope. This discovery leads to another: Sir Edward Hardcastle is missing. His death will unseal a long-held secret and lead Thorndyke to a tragic and powerful motive for murder.

England, Stratford

When Rogues Fall Out. U.K.: Hodder, 1932 (U.S.: *Dr. Thorndyke's Discovery.* Dodd, 1932)

The murder of Didbury Toke, criminal, leads to the murder of Inspector Badger, and soon Dr. Thorndyke is asked to investigate. Not knowing the two cases are connected until his investigation opens the path, he proceeds down it to the thrilling capture of a murdering criminal.

England, Greenhithe

Dr. Thorndyke Intervenes. U.K.: Hodder, 1933 (U.S.: Dodd, 1933)

Dobson arrives at Fenchurch Station to claim his bag, and although he recognizes his bag, the head inside is not familiar, so he bolts. Meanwhile, two witnesses discover that they have a mutual interest: proving that the young American can lay claim to the estate of the Earl of Winsborough. Eventually, it is Dr. Thorndyke who can explain the lineage of the head and the estate.

England, London

For the Defense: Dr. Thorndyke. U.K.: Hodder, 1934 (U.S.: Dodd, 1934)

Andrew Barton has been disfigured by a cricket ball, and he is desperate to spare his wife Molly from further pretenses of love. When circumstances place him in connection with a nefarious cousin who is nearly a twin, an armed robbery, and the opportunity to make drastic changes, he makes his choice and a death occurs.

England, Bunsford

The Penrose Mystery. U.K.: Hodder, 1936 (U.S.: Dodd, 1936)

Daniel Penrose has established an enormous collection of gems, but he catalogs and houses them with indifference. When he disappears, his home is burglarized, and this attracts the attention of Dr. Thorndyke.

England, London • Jewels

The Dr. Thorndyke Omnibus: 38 of his criminal investigations as set down by R. Austin Freeman. Dodd, 1936

A collection of the following short stories: this collection reprints the contents of *The Singing Bone, Dr. Thorndyke's Cases, The Magic Casket, The Puzzle Lock,* and *The Blue Scarab.*

Short stories

Felo De Se? U.K.: Hodder, 1937 (U.S.: *Death at the Inn.* Dodd, 1937)

John Gillum's death is ruled a suicide, and the case is put aside. The evidence that pointed to the end of his life is gambling debts to blackmailers. When the evidence seems suspect to Dr. Thorndyke, he is enticed into opening a new investigation.

England, London

The Stoneware Monkey. U.K.: Hodder, 1938 (U.S.: Dodd, 1939)

Diamond merchant Arthur Kempster has left his diamonds unguarded in his home, called The Hawthorns, and when they disappear, the pursuit of the criminal leads to the death of a constable. Later, James Oldfield has a client named Peter Gannet who he diagnosed as suffering from arsenic poisoning, and when the patient is cured, he disappears. It takes Dr. Thorndyke to connect these two incidents and find a murderer.

England, Newingstead • Jewels

Mr. Polton Explains. U.K.: Hodder, 1940 (U.S.: Dodd, 1940)

Cecil Moxdale is killed in a fire, but was the fire deliberately set? This question is key to the investigation when Dr. Thorndyke is asked to take the case. When a will's legacy is the key to the crime, the death must be examined with all due care.

Arson • England, Bloomsbury • Wills

The Jacob Street Mystery. U.K.: Hodder, 1942 (U.S.: *The Unconscious Witness.* Dodd, 1942)

Thomas Pedley is painting one day when he witnesses two men being followed by a woman. His interest is drawn to them by the woman's surreptitious behavior, and when she returns with only one of the men, he notes the significance of this. When a murder is announced, he realizes he might have seen the beginning and the end of the conspiracy to commit it, and he has committed the perpetrators to his canvas.

Artists • England, Linton Green

The Best Dr. Thorndyke Detective Stories. Dover, 1973

A collection of the following stories: "The Aluminium Dagger," "The Blue Sequin," "The Case of Oscar Brodski," "A Case of Premeditation," "The Echo of a Mutiny," "The Mandarin's Pearl," "The Moabite Cipher," and "31 New Inn."

Short stories

Goodbye, Dr. Thorndyke. Norris, 1972

This chapbook contains one short story featuring the classic detective penned by the author of a non-fiction book about Thorndyke and Freeman.

Donaldson, Norman

Dr. Thorndyke's Dilemma. Aspen, 1974

This novelette, written by a devotee of Freeman's style, resurrects the great detective. Narrated by Jervis, it begins with the discovery of a drowning victim during a picnic, and leads to the discovery of a murderer.

Dirckx, J. H. • England, Gravesend

Philip MacDonald

Anthony Gethryn

Like many men of his generation, Colonel Anthony Gethryn was affected by his service in WWI. This service also gave him the characteristics he needed to become an effective investigator. After his years of service as a soldier and then as an operative, he lived in the countryside and wrote a novel. As the series develops, he grows as a character and even finds romance. His urbane intelligence makes him an effective detective very much in the style of the other great thinking detectives. **Soft-boiled/Traditional.**

The Rasp. U.K.: Collins, 1924 (U.S.: Dial, 1925)

When John Hoode, Minister of Imperial Finance, is murdered, Gethryn is called onto the case by his newspaper friend Hastings. Despite the fact that the murder took place in front of witnesses, no one can offer an explanation to the detective.

England, Marling, Abbotshall

***The White Crow.** U.K.: Collins, 1928 (U.S.: Dial, 1928)

The Noose. U.K.: Collins, 1930 (U.S.: Dial, 1930)

The noose is tightening around the neck of Daniel Bronson, accused of murdering a man named Blackatter. When Gethryn's wife Lucia takes sympathy upon Selma Bronson, the man's wife, her husband begins to work to free the man from the accusations.

England, London

The Link. U.K.: Collins, 1930 (U.S.: Doubleday, 1930)

Lord Grenville is married to the beautiful Shelia, a woman who casts spells over the men around her. One man who is affected by her is Lawless, the local vet, and it is he who is accused of Grenville's murder when he admits to having had a rifle in his possession at just the wrong time.

England, Samsford

Persons Unknown. Doubleday, 1930 (U.K.: *The Maze.* U.K.: Collins, 1932)

When Maxwell Brunton's body is found lying on his hearthrug, pierced through the eye with a chunk of mineral quartz, the police begin an investigation. This novels allows the reader to hear the evidence presented in court just as the Gethryn did, and to try and solve the case along with the great detective.

England, London • Trials

The Wraith. U.K.: Collins, 1931 (U.S.: Doubleday, 1931)

The faithful chronicler Toller, needing some fodder for Gethryn's fans, demands that the great detective recount his investigation of a case that took place in 1920. Attempting to write a book, Gethryn had settled into a small village wherein a dinner party leaves the host dead. The most likely suspect is a man who accused the dead host of experimenting on cats.

Cats · England, High Fen

The Choice. U.K.: Collins, 1931 (U.S.: *The Polferry Riddle.* Doubleday, 1931; also published as *The Polferry Mystery*. Collins, 1932

The Wessex Police ask for help when the wife of Dr. Hale-Stoeford is discovered with her head chopped off. It proves to be an intriguing case when Gethryn is confronted by a locked-room puzzle.

England, Wessex · Locked room

The Crime Conductor. Doubleday, 1931

Inspector Meridew of Scotland Yard needs Gethryn's help when producer Willington Sigsbee is found dead in his bathtub. While the police suspected accident or suicide, Gethryn suspects murder. The producer has just made an unpopular choice in selecting Lars Kristania for his next production, and the resulting conflict may have caused someone to act.

England, London · Theater

Rope to Spare. U.K.: Collins, 1932 (U.S.: Doubleday, 1932)

Convalescence is the order for Gethryn after a particularly brutal investigation, and he finds himself resting in a small hamlet when he receives communications that throw him right back into the violent world of crime. His presence in the hamlet makes people nervous, and they assume he is there to investigate a case he knows nothing about.

England, North Greyne, Ford-under-Stapleton

Death on My Left. U.K.: Collins, 1933 (U.S.: Doubleday, 1932)

Just prior to challenging for the world heavyweight championship, boxer Kim Kinnarid is found murdered in a gymnasium. It falls to Gethryn to discover why.

Boxing · England, Perry Down

The Nursemaid Who Disappeared. U.K.: Collins, 1938 (U.S.: *Warrant for X.* Doubleday, 1938)

A visiting American playwright, Sheldon Garrett, overhears two women in a tea shop plotting murder, and only Gethryn takes him seriously enough to launch an investigation.

England, London

The List of Adrian Messenger. Doubleday, 1959

Adrian Messenger delivers a list of ten names and addresses to Scotland Yard, asking for verification and location. When he dies in a plane crash the next day, the examination of the members of the list leads to the unraveling of a strange and dangerous association.

England, London

The Golden Agers and Beyond

Caudwell, Sarah (pseud. of Sarah Cockburn)

Hilary Tamar

When readers tackle this series, they not only have to guess who the murderer is, but also the sex of the main character. What readers do know is that Tamar is a medieval law specialist at Oxford, and is the mentor for the young lawyers practicing at 62 New Square in London. The team at the Bar includes Cantrip, Selena, Timothy, Ragwort, and Julia. Readers may also enjoy Colin Dexter. **Traditional**. Series subjects: **Law · Teams**.

Thus Was Adonis Murdered. U.K.: Collins, 1981 (U.S.: Scribner, 1981)

On holiday in Venice, barrister Julia Larwood takes a gorgeous young male to her bed for a fling. When she wakes, he is a corpse. Her friends back in London at 62 New Square need to come to her rescue, and they turn to their former instructor at Oxford for guidance in the matter.

England, London · Italy, Venice

The Shortest Way to Hades. U.K.: Collins, 1984 (U.S.: Scribner, 1985)

The team is assigned the job of changing Camilla Galloway's trust when the simple step would save a huge tax payment. All in the family agree except for cousin Deirdre, who tries to hold the family up for a large payoff. When she suffers a fatal accident, the subject of murder is raised with Tamar.

England, London · Wills

The Sirens Sang of Murder. U.K.: Collins, 1989 (U.S.: Delacorte, 1989)

Michael Cantrip is off to Monaco and the Cayman Islands to aid the Daffodil Settlement, when death strikes. He calls upon his office mates, and eventually Tamar, for help in solving this riddle in tax law and murder.

Caribbean, Cayman Islands · England, London · Monaco

The Sibyl in Her Grave. Delacorte, 2000

When Julia Larwood's aunt needs help with her huge capital gains made on an investment in equities, the team jumps to her aid. But when a local psychic counselor is found dead, the team turns onto the path of a murderer.

England, Sussex, Parsons Haven

Edmund Crispin (pseud. of Robert Bruce Montgomery)

Gervase Fen

The University of Oxford's professor of English Language and Literature, Gervase Fen, is the creation of British writer Edmund Crispin. These novels feature classic golden age puzzles in novels that still entertain. For despite his academic background, Fen is a barrel of laughs, and the cases often take on a screwball comedy atmosphere. At times, Fen may seem more properly placed with the Golden Age eccentrics, but his down days make him a bit more human. **Soft-boiled/Traditional**.

The Case of the Gilded Fly. U.K.: Gollancz, 1944 (U.S.: *Obsequies at Oxford.* Lippincott, 1945)

Yseut Haskell has given everyone in her production a reason to hate her. Does one person in the company hate her enough to commit murder? That is the question that Fen must answer on his first case when a death occurs in a repertory theater in Oxford.

Academia • England, Oxford • Theater

Holy Disorders. U.K.: Gollancz, 1945 (U.S.: Lippincott, 1946)

On vacation in Tolnbridge, Fen finds himself embroiled in the murder of a cathedral organist. Geoffrey Vintner, composer and keyboardist, thought the quiet village would provide him with a refuge as well, until threatening letters warn of murder.

England, Tolnbridge • Music • Religion

The Moving Toyshop. Gollancz 1946 (U.S.: Lippincott, 1946)

Poet Richard Cadogan finds an old woman murdered in an Oxford toyshop whereupon he is attacked as well. Escaping, he returns, only to find that the toyshop has been replaced by a grocery store and no one will believe he witnessed what he did. Fortunately, he has the eccentric detective Fen as a friend and an investigator.

England, Oxford

Swan Song. U.K.: Gollancz, 1947 (U.S.: *Dead and Dumb.* Lippincott, 1947)

Edwin Shorthouse dies while in rehearsal for a production of Wagner's Die Meistersinger. He was the company's bass, and he was much hated, giving Fen plenty of suspects from which to uncover the murderer.

England, Oxford • Opera • Theater

Buried for Pleasure. U.K.: Gollancz, 1948 (U.S.: Lippincott, 1949)

Fen decides to run for office, and his campaign takes place in the town of Sanford Angelorum. Not surprising, the town has more to offer than an election: the murder of Bussy.

Elections • England, Sanford Angelorum

Love Lies Bleeding. U.K.: Gollancz, 1948 (U.S.: Lippincott, 1948)

It's Speech Day at Casterevenford School, but the headmaster is distracted by the report from his counterpart at the Casterevenford High School for Girls that one of her charges is behaving oddly. Eventually the girl disappears, someone burglarizes the chemistry department, and two teachers are murdered. Fen, on the campus, is in place to deliver a speech and a murderer.

Academia • England, Casterevenford

Frequent Hearses. U.K.: Gollancz, 1950 (U.S.: *Sudden Vengeance*. Dodd, 1950)

Who could guess that a film about Alexander Pope could generate such excitement? First a young actress commits suicide, and then a cameraman dies. Fen is on hand to find out what secrets lay both in front of and behind the camera.

England, Long Fulton · Film

The Long Divorce. U.K.: Gollancz, 1951 (U.S.: Dodd, 1951; also published as *A Noose for Her*. Mercury, 1952)

A series of poisoned-pen letters leads to two tragedies in a small village. Fen is on board to discover the motive behind telling embarrassing secrets by letter, and the motive for sending obscene messages as well.

England, Cotton Abbas

The Glimpses of the Moon. U.K.: Gollancz, 1977 (U.S.: Walker, 1978)

After a 25-year absence, Fen returns in a case that involves everyone in a small English village in the murder investigation of Routh's death. The Rector, the Major, and even old Gobbo, the town's eccentric, take a hand at playing detective in a story that involves a herd of cows, a motorcycle chase, and a very confused local constable.

England, Burraford

Fen Country. U.K.: Gollancz, 1979 (U.S.: Walker, 1980)

A collection of the following stories: "A Country to Sell," "Death and Aunt Fancy," "Dog in the Night-Time," "Gladstone's Candlestick," "The Hunchback Cat," "The Lion's Tooth," "Man Overboard," "The Man Who Lost His Head," "Merry-Go-Round," "The Mischief Done," "Occupational Risk," "Outrage in Stepney," "Shot in the Dark," "The Two Sisters," "The Undraped Torso," and "Wolf!" Also includes 10 non-Fen stories.

Short stories

Lillian de la Torre (pseud. of Lillian de la Torre Bueno McCue) ✍

Dr. Sam: Johnson/James Boswell

Using an actual historical figure can be a challenge, but it was well met by de la Torre. The cases of the eighteenth-century literary giant, Dr. Sam: Johnson, are narrated by James Boswell, who was Johnson's biographer. Echoing the relationship of Holmes and Watson, these two detectives take on the challenges of the criminal mind and put their mental capabilities to use. de la Torre's two collections of short stories are considered well worth finding for their historical style and great mystery cases. **Soft-boiled/Traditional/Historical**. Series subjects: **Historical (1700–1799) · Short stories · Teams**.

Dr. Sam: Johnson, Detector. Knopf, 1946

A collection of the following stories: "The Conveyance of Emelina Grange," "The Flying Highwayman," "The Great Seal of England," "The Manifestations in Mincing Lane," "The Monboddo Ape Boy," "Prince Charlie's Ruby," "The Second Sight of Dr. Sam: Johnson," "The Stolen Christmas Box," and "The Wax-Work Cadaver."

The Detections of Dr. Sam: Johnson. Doubleday, 1960

A collection of the following stories: "The Black Stone of Dr. Dee," "The Frantick Rebel," "The Missing Shakespeare Manuscript," "Saint-Germain the Deathless," "The Stroke of Thirteen," "The Tontine Curse," "The Triple-Lock'd Room," and "The Viotti Stradivarius."

The Return of Dr. Sam: Johnson, Detector. International Polygonics, 1984

A collection of the following stories: "The Bedlam Bam," "The Blackamoor Unchain'd," "The Disappearing Servant Wench," "The Lost Heir," "Milady Bigamy," "Murder Lock'd In," and "The Resurrection Man."

***The Exploits of Dr. Sam: Johnson.** International Polygonics, 1987

Harry Kemelman ✍

Rabbi David Small

Often downtrodden by his congregation, but never defeated by crime, Rabbi Small is one of several religious detectives who developed in this period. A combination of the inner workings of the Barnard's Crossing congregation and the complex nature of the crimes presented to Rabbi Small is what makes these novels so enjoyable. Small is an introspective detective and carries on in the tradition of Father Brown and Sherlock Holmes. After getting over the first case in which Rabbi Small is a suspect, Barnard's Crossing's Chief of Police, Hugh Lanigan, becomes the Rabbi's best friend. **Traditional**. Series subjects: **Massachusetts, Barnard's Crossing · Religion**.

Friday the Rabbi Slept Late. Crown, 1964

Chief of Police Hugh Lanigan is surprised to have a rabbi as a suspect. Rabbi Small is about to have his contract terminated by his congregation when the body of a young girl is discovered in his car on the day he fails to arrive for services. ED

Saturday the Rabbi Went Hungry. Crown, 1966

It takes a Talmudic scholar like Rabbi Small to deliberate on the relationship between a man who refuses to take his medicine on Yom Kippur and the death of a drunken man found in his garage with the car motor running.

Sunday the Rabbi Stayed Home. Putnam, 1969

At Passover, Rabbi Small has time to spend with the younger, and in some cases, more radical members of his congregation. When one is smothered, he helps Chief Lanigan catch a murderer.

Monday the Rabbi Took Off. Putnam, 1972

Leaving the challenges of Barnard's Crossing behind him, Rabbi Small has embarked on a sabbatical to the Holy Land. Replaced at home by the more acceptable

Rabbi Deutsch, Rabbi Small ironically finds himself coming to the aid of the new rabbi's Israeli relative.

Israel, Jerusalem

Tuesday the Rabbi Saw Red. Fields, 1974

Widemere Christian College may have seemed like a refuge to Rabbi Small, but when he arrives on the campus, he discovers murder. When the head of the English Department is murdered with a bust of Homer, Rabbi Small is on the case.

Academia · Massachusetts, Boston

Wednesday the Rabbi Got Wet. Morrow, 1976

The mysterious death of old man Kestler from a prescription he picked up from the local pharmacist, Marcus Aptaker, proves baffling to the Rabbi and his police chief pal. Could the cause be Marcus's son Arthur of whom Marcus is so proud?

Pharmacies

Thursday the Rabbi Walked Out. Morrow, 1978

When an anti-Semite dies in the community, suspicions fall on members of Rabbi Small's congregation. Meanwhile the congregation is in turmoil as its female members are beginning to demand inclusion in some religious ceremonies previously open only to men.

Someday the Rabbi Will Leave. Morrow, 1985

Rabbi Small gets exposure to enough political maneuverings dealing with his own congregation, but when underhanded campaign tactics and blackmail lead to murder, he steps in to save the integrity of a political campaign gone mad.

4

Politics

One Fine Day the Rabbi Bought a Cross. Morrow, 1987

For the second time, the Rabbi visits Israel, this time on vacation with his wife Miriam. When an innocent American from Barnard's Crossing dies, the Rabbi cannot rest until a murderer is charged.

Israel, Jerusalem

The Day the Rabbi Resigned. Fawcett Columbine, 1992

The battles that Rabbi Small has had with his congregation are nearly over, as he prepares for his resignation after 25 years of service. Before he can go, Chief Lanigan asks for his help on a case. The renegade professor, Victor Joyce, has been killed in a drunk-driving accident, but one of the witnesses insists that the man was alive after the accident.

That Day the Rabbi Left Town. Fawcett Columbine, 1996

Rabbi Small, resigned from Barnard's Crossing's congregation, is returning to Widermere Christian College to teach. But, as the last time on the campus, murder occurs. On Thanksgiving, when English Professor Kent goes missing, no one expects to find his body in a snowbank.

Academia · Massachusetts, Boston

Emma Lathen (pseud. of Mary Jane Latsis and Martha Hennissart) ✍

John Putnam Thatcher

The banking community is nearest to one of the cardinal rules of detecting: follow the money. Thatcher is the senior vice-president of the Sloan Guaranty Trust Company. His business instincts also work well when it comes to being a detective. Working with an ensemble cast from the company, Thatcher's cases all involve convoluted business deals and practices that eventually lead to a crime. **Traditional**. Series subject: **Banking**.

Banking on Death. Macmillan. 1961

John Putnam Thatcher decides to teach his new co-worker, Kenneth Nichols, the methods of finding a missing heir. What he does not expect is that Robert Schneider, the heir, will be dead when he is found.

Massachusetts, Boston • New York, New York

A Place for Murder. Macmillan, 1963

Going to Shaftsbury for the weekend to mix business and pleasure should be fun for Thatcher, but not when it brings him in close proximity with Olivia Austin. Recently abandoned by her husband, her ill feelings for him distract from the weekend dog show and may lead to the murder of Peggy Lindsay.

Connecticut, Shaftsbury

Accounting for Murder. Macmillan, 1964

If fraud is occurring at the National Calculating Company, it will be Thatcher's job to prove it. When the accountant hired by the stockholders is found strangled by an adding machine's cord, it falls upon Thatcher to investigate.

New York, New York

Murder Makes the Wheels Go 'Round. Macmillan, 1966

Thatcher is sent to Detroit to check out the recovering Michigan Motors, a car business trying to bounce back after three top executives were sent to prison for price fixing. Despite soaring sales, Thatcher believes something is not right in the Motor City. He is right, as a dead body falls out of the newest line's model in the middle of an auto show.

Automobiles • Michigan, Detroit

Death Shall Overcome. Macmillan, 1966

Thatcher must deal with a case of bigotry and murder on the New York Stock Exchange when someone feels the Exchange should not elect it's first African-American member.

African-Americans • New York, New York • Race • Stock Exchange

Murder Against the Grain. Macmillan, 1968

When scandal erupts within the international grain futures market, Thatcher must be both detective and diplomat. His own company is missing a million dollars, intended as a downpayment by the Russians for a shipment of American wheat.

New York, New York

A Stitch in Time. Macmillan, 1968

Thatcher is pressing to prove that a suicide is actually a murder when seven homeostatic clips are found sewn inside the victim, Pemberton Freebody, and scandal rocks Southport Memorial Hospital. The $100,000 life insurance policy on Freebody will be invalidated if Thatcher fails, but another murder occurs at the hospital as Thatcher's investigation proceeds.

Medical • New York, New York

Come to Dust. Simon & Schuster, 1968

It is believed that Elliot Patterson has stolen a $50,000 bearer bond, and Thatcher is set on his trail. The beneficiary of the bond was to be Brunswick College, and it is on that campus that Thatcher launches his investigation. When a student dies, Thatcher knows he is closing in on the answer to the mysterious disappearance.

Academia • New Hampshire, Brunswick

When in Greece. Simon & Schuster, 1969

Ken Nicolls of Sloan is kidnapped in Greece when a military coup topples the government and threatens a $30 million dollar investment in a hydroelectric plant. It becomes Thatcher's job to decide which side in the conflict has his colleague, and why senior archivist Dr. Elias Ziros was murdered.

Greece, Salonika • Kidnapping

Murder to Go. Simon & Schuster, 1969

Sloan's $12 million dollar investment in Chicken Tonight is threatened when they are suspected of being the source for a food poisoning epidemic on the East Coast. Thatcher is sent to the test kitchens of the company to prevent panic when it is discovered that the poisonings may have been deliberate.

Food • New Jersey, Willoughby

Pick Up Sticks. Simon & Schuster, 1970

Vacationing on the Appalachian Trail with friend and hiking companion Henry Morland seems like a pleasant enough diversion until the two discover the corpse of Stephen Lester, murdered with a hammer. Two ex-wives prove to be likely suspects, and Thatcher is just the man to sort out the reasons for this unlikely murder, especially when the cause could be linked to a real estate development.

New Hampshire, Fiord Haven

Ashes to Ashes. Simon & Schuster, 1971

Thatcher will need to balance the needs of a tiny Catholic school versus the Sloan's investment in Unger Realty and their plans to build a 20-story complex on the land they wish to purchase from the church. When Francis Omara, leader of the school's parent group, which has launched a suit to stop the project, is found murdered, the Queens neighborhood is radically changed.

Academia • New York, New York

The Longer the Thread. Simon & Schuster, 1971

Slax Unlimited, owned by Harry Zimmerman, has opened a Sloan-backed plant in Puerto Rico, and it has operated for two years despite some sabotage. When Benito Dominguez is murdered, Zimmerman loses his number one suspect for the acts, and Thatcher is dispatched to resolve the conflict, solve a murder, and save the bank's investment.

Puerto Rico, Bayamon

Murder Without Icing. Simon & Schuster, 1972

Sloan decides to shift its sponsorship from the symphony to a losing hockey team called the New York Huskies. When the Huskies rocket to contention, they also create two murders, one of which takes place in the penalty box at Madison Square Garden.

Hockey · New York, New York · Sports

Sweet and Low. Simon & Schuster, 1974

Dreyer Company is dependent on the cocoa trade from Ghana, and when its commodity expert, Dick Frohlich, returns to America only to be murdered in a motel swimming pool, Sloan asks its resident detective banker to solve the crime.

Food · New York, New York

By Hook or By Crook. Simon & Schuster, 1975

A violent rivalry in the Parajian family threatens the solvency of the Oriental rug business that Sloan has an interest in; and when two murders occur, it falls to Thatcher to catch a murderer.

New York, New York

Double, Double, Oil and Trouble. Simon & Schuster, 1978

Thatcher is in Zurich when the bank pays a huge ransom to Black Tuesday, a terrorist group that has captured Davidson Wylie, chief negotiator for the Macklin Company, a drilling company that wants to start offshore drilling in Scotland. While Wylie is held in Istanbul, Thatcher travels the globe to try and gain his release and recover the ransom money put up by Sloan.

Switzerland, Zurich · Terrorism · Turkey, Istanbul

Going for the Gold. Simon & Schuster, 1981

Yves Bisson is France's skiing wonder, and when he dies on the slopes at the Lake Placid Olympics, Thatcher is a witness. A series of incidents from bad checks, drugs, and a blizzard complicate the banker's investigation into murder.

New York, Lake Placid · Olympics · Skiing · Sports

Green Grow the Dollars. Simon & Schuster, 1982

Controversy rages in the commercial nursery business when the venerable mail-order firm of Vandam Nursery and Seed is accused of stealing the Numero Uno tomato from Wisconsin Seedman. Standard Foods, a client of Sloan's has just purchased Vandam, and Thatcher is given the job of rescuing the bank's interests. When the investigation needs to also solve the murder of the woman accused of stealing the plant, it tests Thatcher's skills.

Gardening · Illinois, Chicago · New York, New York

Something in the Air. Simon & Schuster, 1988

When the airline Sparrow Flyways wishes to expand and become a national carrier, it turns to Sloan for the financial backing. However, some of the employees and stockholders oppose the move, and when one of Sparrow's pilots, an outspoken critic of the plan, is found murdered in Boston Harbor, Thatcher is dispatched to the scene.

Airlines · Massachusetts, Boston

East Is East. Simon & Schuster, 1991

Sloan needs to face the facts that there may be a takeover, so Thatcher is sent to Japan to negotiate a deal with Japanese banks to save the company. Meanwhile, the president of Lackawanna Electric Industries is in Japan to strike his own deal, and when the negotiations turn to murder, Thatcher is in place to solve the crime.

England, London · Japan, Tokyo

Right on the Money. Simon & Schuster, 1993

A large kitchen-fixture manufacturer named Aqua Supplies Inc. wants to absorb Ecker, a small, family-owned business, to advance its position in the market. At first Ecker accepts the idea, but when murder occurs, the merger becomes a disaster.

Connecticut, Bridgeport · New Jersey, Princeton

Brewing Up a Storm. St. Martin's Press, 1996

Madeline Underwood is angry because she believes Quax, a non-alcoholic beer, is teaching young people to drink and has led to the death of a 19-year-old boy. Kischel Brewery had created the beer with the best intentions, but when Underwood is murdered, the company needs the help of an experienced investigator like Thatcher.

New York, New York

A Shark Out Of Water. St. Martin's Press, 1997

Baltic businessman Stefan Zabriski believes he can rebuild a canal and help Poland's decaying economy if he can prevent the fraud surrounding the project. Thatcher is drawn into the controversy when Zabriski is killed, and he is dragged into an international conspiracy when Sloan shows an interest in financing the project.

Poland, Gdansk

Frances and Richard Lockridge ✍

Pamela North/Jerry North

Jerry North, a publisher, is half of a plucky couple that includes his wife Pamela, a woman doomed to continually find herself immersed in a murder mystery. Echoing Dashiell Hammett's book about Nick and Nora Charles, *The Thin Man*, this series uses humor as well as interesting plots to entertain its readers. Pamela's uncanny ability to be around murder and to help solve them has led to their police friend, Lt. Bill Weigand, using her as an unofficial consultant. **Soft-boiled/Traditional.** Series subjects: **Humor · New York, New York · Teams.**

The Norths Meet Murder. U.K.: Stokes, 1940 (U.S.: *Mr. & Mrs. North Meet Murder.* Avon Books, 1952)

Death first introduces itself to the Norths when they explore their own house and discover a corpse in a bathtub in a long-unused top floor apartment. Lt. Bill Weigand of the NYPD suspects the Norths, but soon Pam helps Weigand's investigation when even the identity of the corpse proves to be difficult.

Murder Out of Turn. Stokes, 1941

When the Norths invited their police friend, Bill Weigand, to vacation in their summer cottage, little did they know that both parties would find murder. When one woman has her throat cut and another is burned to death, the cop and Pam combine their efforts to solve the case.

New York, Brewster

A Pinch of Poison. Stokes, 1941

Pam and Lois Winston share an interest in the Placement Foundation, which places children for adoption. When Lt. Weigand becomes involved in an investigation of Lois's death, Pam once again helps the NYPD detective solve the case.

Death on the Aisle. Lippincott, 1942

Dr. Carney Bolton is the backer for the Broadway-bound *Two in the Bush*, but he is murdered with an icepick during a rehearsal. When the playwright is one of Jerry's authors, and a chief suspect, Pam needs to use her detective skills to chase a murderer.

Theater

Hanged for a Sheep. Lippincott, 1942

Pam is drawn into a serial killing when someone tries to poison her Aunt Flora but fails. When two more attempts are made, one successful, Pam helps Lt. Weigand find a murderer.

Serial killer

Death Takes a Bow. Lippincott, 1943

When Jerry is finished introducing one of his authors to a New York book discussion club, he is stunned to discover that Victor Sproul is now a corpse. Audience members Pam and Lt. Weigand rise from their seats to become investigators.

Authors

Killing the Goose. Lippincott, 1944

A circle of New Yorkers, including socialite Ann Lawrence, radio commentator Dan Beck, writer John Elliot, investment secretary Frances McCalley, and her boyfriend Franklin Martinelli, are surrounded by murder. A series of strange clues, including a baked apple and a dress at the cleaners, leads Pam to a murderer.

Payoff for the Banker. Lippincott, 1945

Mary Hunter arrives home to find the body of wealthy banker George Merle seated in her living room. She becomes suspect number one when the police discover that Merle was the father of a man whom Mary loved but had not been allowed to marry, and she needs Pam North to investigate on her behalf.

Murder Within Murder. Lippincott, 1946

Jerry is publishing a true crime work by Amelia Gipson. When the author, while doing research, is poisoned from a drinking fountain at the New York Public Library, Pam takes a hand in the investigation.

Authors · Publishing

Death of a Tall Man. Lippincott, 1946

Eye doctor Andrew Gordon normally does his visitations on Monday, but this day he is discovered in his office, murdered. Weigand is so baffled that he needs the help of the amateur sleuth Pam North to discover the truth.

Untidy Murder. Lippincott, 1947

When Dorian Hunt visits the offices of the magazine *Esprit* to deliver her drawings, she does not expect to become involved in the death of the art editor, who has fallen through a window. Dorian's husband is Lt. Bill Weigand of the NYPD, and they ask the Norths for help.

Murder Is Served. Lippincott, 1948 (Also published as *A Taste For Murder*. Phantom, 1954)

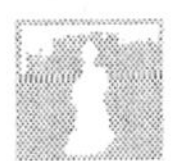

One of Jerry's authors has a problem: he loves a student of his, and when she turns in a monstrous essay dealing with murder, he fears for her. Her former marriage to playboy Tony Mott proves a trap when Tony is found murdered. Pam knows that there are plenty of others who would have wished Tony dead.

Academia

The Dishonest Murderer. Lippincott, 1949

Senator Bruce Kirkhill fails to appear for a New Year's Eve party at the home of his fiancée's father. The Norths are guests of the party, and are surprised later to discover that the body is found in a strange neighborhood wearing the wrong clothes.

Holidays · New Year's Eve

Murder in a Hurry. Lippincott, 1950

Millionaire eccentric J. K. Halder loved animals, but no one expected to find his elderly body in one of his own cages in his Greenwich Village pet shop. When Lt. Bill Weigand investigates, he needs to rely on his old pal Pam to help him with the case.

Pets

Murder Comes First. Lippincott, 1951

Pam's three maiden aunts, Thelma, Lucinda, and Pennina Whitsett, have their vacation plans upset when they visit a childhood friend, Grace Logan, and find her dead from poison. Did an old grudge lead one of Pam's relatives to commit murder?

Dead As a Dinosaur. Lippincott, 1952

Jerry publishes the works of mammalogist Dr. Orestes Preson, and when the doctor is harassed, he turns to the Norths for help. Someone drugs the doctor's sister, and the Norths know they have a serious case when harassment turns to murder. Why would someone kill the dear doctor with a caveman's ax?

Death Has a Small Voice. Lippincott, 1953

Pam is sent a recording of a murder. When novelist Hilda Godwin is discovered missing and her dictating machine is found in the possession of Harry Eaton, a small-time burglar, Lt. Weigand finds himself dependent on Pam for help. Why did the blackmailer Eaton record his own murder?

Authors · Blackmail

Curtain for a Jester. Lippincott, 1953

Perhaps the practical jokes that party-giver Byron Wilmot provided his guests were more than someone could take. The day after his April Fool's party, attended by Jerry and Pam, the man is found dead. Pam finds the body and helps her pal Lt. Weigand solve the crime.

April Fool's Day · Holidays

A Key to Death. Lippincott, 1954

When Forbes Ingraham, lawyer, is murdered, Pam's big clue is a passkey to the offices of the law firm he ran. The North's friendship with the dead man drives them to discover his murderer.

Death of an Angel. Lippincott, 1955 (Also published as *Mr. & Mrs. North and the Poisoned Playboy.* Avon Books, 1957)

When Bradley Fitch announces that he is marrying Naomi Shaw, the star of the hit Broadway play *Around the Corner* that he financed, thus ending its run, someone poisons him to maintain the status quo. Pam and Jerry are small investors and investigate to protect their interests.

Theater

Voyage Into Violence. Lippincott, 1956

Detectives can never take a vacation, and that proves true when the Norths sail on the S.S. Carib Queen and one of their fellow passengers, retired P.I. J. Orville Marsh, is murdered. When the corpse is skewered with a ceremonial sword, Pam decides to determine which of the many ceremonial swords used in an encampment reenactment will show the truth.

Caribbean · Cuba, Havana · Shipboard

The Long Skeleton. Lippincott, 1958

The Norths need to move out of their place while it is being painted but when they enter their hotel room, they discover a corpse. The case leads the Norths to uncover the link between a brilliant journalist and a recent best seller when the corpse proves to be talk show host Amanda Towne.

Hotels

Murder Is Suggested. Lippincott, 1959

A psychologist whose specialty was hypnosis is murdered, and the Norths find themselves investigating. Perhaps it was not wise for Professor Jameson Elwell to try and discover if people under hypnosis are capable of murder?

The Judge Is Reversed. Lippincott, 1960

John Blanchard, wealthy lawyer, tennis judge, and cat show judge, is murdered. Pam, who just wanted to add a pet to her family, instead finds herself investigating the world of cats and tennis to locate a murderer.

Cats · Sports · Tennis

Murder Has Its Points. Lippincott, 1961

After a fight between the two novelists Anthony Payne and Gardner Willings, a corpse is found. Did the Hemingway-like Willings cause Payne's death, or can the cause be found among the lovers and ex-wives that pepper Payne's life?

Authors

Murder By the Book. Lippincott, 1963

A fishing vacation is shattered when Pam reels in the body of Dr. Edmund Piersal, medical examiner for the city of New York. Even the local police find themselves fascinated by the investigative methods of the always-ablc Pam.

Florida, Key West

Ellis Peters (pseud. of Edith Pargeter) ✍

Brother Cadfael

This historical series of novels, set at Shrewsbury Abbey in England, features the detective work of the herbalist monk, Brother Cadfael. His quietly charming character, hiding a bloody past as a soldier of fortune, makes him a fascinating character. Combined with the historical accuracy of the series, these novels are great examples of the power of the historical novel. Their popularity helped spawned an interest in historical mystery novels that extended into the next millennium and opened up the field to new eras previously unexplored in mystery fiction. See the Cadfael Compendium at http://www.iw.net/~csonne. **Traditional/Historical**. Series subjects: **England, Shrewsbury · Historical (1100–1199) · Medieval England · Religion**.

A Morbid Taste for Bones. U.K.: Macmillan, 1977 (U.S.: Morrow, 1978)

Brother Cadfael travels to the remote Welsh mountain village of Gwytherin to acquire the relics of St. Winifred for the ambitious head of Shrewbury Abbey. He finds himself in the middle of a bizarre mystery when the leading opponent to moving the bones is murdered.

England, Gwytherin

One Corpse Too Many. U.K.: Macmillan, 1979 (U.S.: Morrow, 1980)

When Stephen captures Shrewsbury in his battles with his royal cousin, he orders the monks to provide last rites to the hanged prisoners. It is Brother Cadfael who discovers that there is one too many bodies, and that an extra man has been murdered.

Monk's Hood. U.K.: Macmillan, 1980 (U.S.: Morrow, 1981)

Monk's Hood is a deadly poison, and when it appears to have been administered to Gervase Bonel, a guest at the abbey, the source may lay among Brother Cadfael's stock. Mistress Bonel is a woman the good brother once loved, and his investigation must balance his personal feelings against the truth. DA

The Leper of Saint Giles. U.K.: Macmillan, 1981 (U.S.: Morrow, 1982)

Brother Cadfael's sympathies lie with the young lovers when they are thwarted in their relationship by an arranged marriage. However, when the potential bridegroom is murdered, the good brother must suspect the young lovers as he investigates the death.

England

Saint Peter's Fair. U.K.: Macmillan, 1981 (U.S.: Morrow, 1981)

What should be a joyous celebration is marred when Thomas of Bristol is found stabbed and dumped in the river Severn during an annual event. The merchant's niece, Emma, asks Brother Cadfael for help, but before the investigation can proceed, two more deaths occur.

England

The Virgin in the Ice. U.K.: Macmillan, 1982 (U.S.: Morrow, 1983)

King Stephen's battles with the Empress Maud have driven two orphans to the Abbey for protection. Their nearest kinsman is unable to enter the king's territory to save them, as he is an ally of the Empress, so the children travel with a nun. Cadfael travels to the priory at Bromfield to practice his medicinal skills, but once again is asked to solve a murder when the nun is killed.

England, Ludlow

The Devil's Novice. U.K.: Macmillan, 1983 (U.S.: Morrow, 1984)

Two travelers seek refuge in Shrewsbury: a new novice named Meriet Aspley, and a political envoy named Peter Clemence. When Clemence is murdered, the good brother Cadfael is asked to solve the crime and protect the young novice from attack.

The Sanctuary Sparrow. U.K.: Macmillan, 1983 (U.S.: Morrow, 1983)

The abbey must provide sanctuary to an itinerant acrobat named Liliwin when an angry mob, accusing him of robbery and murder, chases him to the abbey walls. Brother Cadfael believes the boy is innocent, and begins an exploration for the truth to free both the boy and the abbey from the mob's wrath.

Dead Man's Ransom. U.K.: Macmillan, 1984 (U.S.: Morrow, 1985)

An exchange is arranged between the two camps of the Empress and the King, when the sheriff of Shropshire is taken prisoner. He is to be exchanged for Elis, a young Welshman, but the sheriff is murdered. Elis is accused of the crime and appeals to Brother Cadfael for help.

The Pilgrim of Hate. U.K.: Macmillan, 1984 (U.S.: Morrow, 1984)

Four years prior to this day, the Abbey received the sacred remains of St. Winifred, and now there is to be a celebration in their honor. When two celebrants prove to have ties to a murder in Winchester, Brother Cadfael begins an investigation.

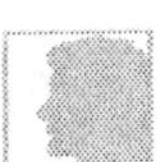

England

An Excellent Mystery. U.K.: Macmillan, 1985 (U.S.: Morrow, 1986)

Two mysteries encourage Brother Cadfael to use his investigative skills. When Julian Cruce disappears, suspicion falls on the newly arrived Nicholas Harnage. Meanwhile, two brothers arrive seeking sanctuary at the abbey, and one proves to be a mysterious mute named Fidelis who is devoted to the very ill Brother Humilis.

The Raven in the Foregate. U.K.: Macmillan, 1986 (U.S.: Morrow, 1986)

Alinoth is the new priest of Foregate, but he is a zealot, and ends up murdered in the millpond on Christmas morning. A long list of suspects makes Brother Cadfael's task more difficult.

Christmas · Holidays

The Rose Rent. U.K.: Macmillan, 1986 (U.S.: Morrow, 1987)

Judith Perle has an arrangement to rent her garden and cottage to the Abbey for the price of a single rose per year. When Brother Eluric tries to deliver the annual rent, he is found murdered in the garden. Could the death of the brother mean someone wanted the abbey's contract null and void so they could assume Judith's patrimony?

The Hermit of Eyton Forest. U.K.: Headline, 1987 (U.S.: Mysterious, 1988)

When Richard Ludel, Lord of Eaton, dies, his legacy passes to his son, also named Richard, who is a student at the Abbey. When the hermit Cythred, under the protection of Richard's grandmother Dionisia, arrives at the abbey in the company of the beautiful Hyacinth, their interests in the young Richard prove deadly when he disappears.

The Confession of Brother Haluin. U.K.: Headline, 1988 (U.S.: Mysterious, 1989)

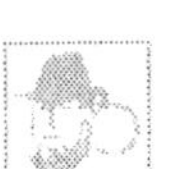

Brother Haluin feels driven to make a journey of expiation, and his sole companion on the journey is Brother Cadfael. On the journey, the companions discover thwarted lovers whose plans lead to murder.

England

A Rare Benedictine. U.K.: Headline, 1988 (U.S.: Mysterious, 1989)

A collection of the following stories: "Eye Witness," "A Light on the Road to Woodstock," and "The Price of Light."

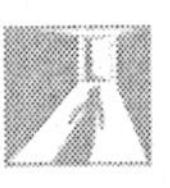

Short stories

The Heretic's Apprentice. U.K.: Headline, 1989 (U.S.: Mysterious, 1990)

William of Lythwood has been reproved for heretical views, but upon his death, his attendant Elave has returned his body to the abbey for burial. Prelate

Gerbert has also arrived at the abbey, and the accompanying pomp and circumstance confuses the issue of William and Elave and leads to murder.

The Potter's Field. U.K.: Headline, 1989 (U.S.: Mysterious, 1990)

The abbey accepts a field previously owned by a potter named Ruald, but when the field is plowed for planting, a dead body is found. Could the body be that of Ruald's long-lost wife Genery, who everyone thought had run off with her lover? It will be up to Brother Cadfael to discover how the past affects the present.

The Summer of the Danes. U.K.: Headline, 1991 (U.S.: Mysterious, 1991)

Cadfael is asked to carry out a diplomatic mission to his native country of Wales. Accompanied by Brother Mark, he discovers a dangerous disagreement exists between two Welsh princes. When Cadfael is captured by one of the Dane allies of the renegade prince Cadwaladr, he needs to solve a crime to save his life.

England, Wales

The Holy Thief. U.K.: Headline, 1992 (U.S.: Mysterious, 1992)

The abbey at Ramsey can be returned to its holy business when the business of war removes the evil Geoffrey de Mandeville as its overseer. Brothers Herluin and Tutilo are raising funds to restore the abbey, and they are present at Shrewsbury when a flood threatens the precious bones of St. Winifred. When murder occurs, suspicion falls on Tutilo, but equally important, the bones of the saint disappear as well.

Brother Cadfael's Penance. U.K.: Headline, 1994 (U.S.: Mysterious, 1994)

Brother Cadfael's son, Olivier de Bretagne, is missing during the conflicts between Stephen and the Empress. Breaking his cloister, Cadfael acts as a father rather than a monk, until a murder interferes with his search and requires him to solve a crime.

England, Coventry

The Modern Practitioners

Donna Andrews ✍

Meg Langslow

Amateur investigator Meg Langslow cannot seem to distance herself from her extended family, and they cannot seem to distance themselves from murder. A sculptor/blacksmith by trade, Meg spends little time working her craft and most of her time investigating crimes. The series blends a mixture of romance and crime and should appeal to readers of M. C. Beaton and Carolyn G. Hart. The author's website can be found at http://www.donnaandrews.com. **Soft-boiled**. Series subject: **Humor**.

Murder with Peacocks. St. Martin's Press, 1999

Langslow finds herself the reluctant wedding planner for not one, but three, weddings. When a meddling out-of-town visitor is murdered, Langslow's father decides to play detective. Soon, it is a case of like father like daughter. AG AN BA

Virginia, Yorktown • Weddings

Murder with Puffins. St. Martin's Press, 2000

Aunt Phoebe has lent Langslow and her boyfriend Michael an isolated cottage in Maine for a romantic getaway. They are surprised to discover upon arrival that most of Langslow's relatives will be staying in the cottage as well, while a hurricane brews offshore. When Langslow's father is accused of murdering a hated artist named Victor Resnick, it is up to the blacksmith to play detective.

Hurricanes · Maine, Monhegan Island

Revenge of the Wrought-Iron Flamingos. St. Martin's Minotaur, 2001

Langslow has a battle when her man Michael's mother is the fiercest defender of the faith in a re-enactment of the battle of Yorktown. But when local businessman Roger Benson is found murdered with a dagger she created, Langslow must defend herself against a murder charge.

Reenactments · United States–Revolutionary War · Virginia, Yorktown

M. C. Beaton (pseud. of Marion Chesney) ✍

Agatha Raisin

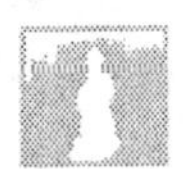

British novelist Beaton retires her businesswoman detective Raisin to the Cotswolds, where dead bodies are never in short supply. Being a Londoner initially sets Agatha outside the society she wishes to enter, but her acumen as a detective earns her grudging respect. Written in a cozy style, these novels use humor as well as the traditional plots, and have a touch of romance between Agatha and her neighbor, James Lacey. Readers who enjoy Beaton's work may also enjoy Donna Andrews, Agatha Christie (Jane Marple), Diane Mott Davidson, Carolyn G. Hart (Annie Darling), Joan Hess (Claire Malloy), Katherine Hall Page, or Valerie Wolzien. See a website about this author at http://www.booksnbytes.com/authors/beaton_mc.html. **Soft-boiled**. Series subject: **Humor**.

Agatha Raisin and the Quiche of Death. St. Martin's Press, 1992

Retirement to the quiet village of Carsley is the plan for the former public relations firm owner when she sells her firm. Finding the small village a little standoffish, she decides to enter a quiche for the local competition. To her surprise, her store-bought entry loses the competition, and it is her sample that poisons the judge.

Cooking · England, Cotswold, Carsley

Agatha Raisin and the Vicious Vet. St. Martin's Press, 1993

Although Agatha would prefer to have a relationship with her next door neighbor James Lacey, she is not above flirting with the new veterinarian in Cotswold. However, when he stands her up, and treats everyone's pets poorly, it leads to his murder. Raisin asks James to help her solve the crime.

England, Cotswold, Carsley · Pets

Agatha Raisin and the Potted Gardener. St. Martin's Press, 1994

By taking up gardening, Raisin hopes to win the heart of bachelor Jimmy Lacey. But when she finds herself in competition with the beautiful Mary Fortune for both flowers and Jimmy, it leads to death.

England, Cotswold, Carsley · Gardening

Agatha Raisin and the Walkers of Dembley. St. Martin's Press, 1995

The Dembley Walkers Association is under attack for using the public footpaths, and their president Charles Fraith is under personal attack from the feisty Jessica Tartinck. When her protest march leads to her murder, Raisin takes up the cause, especially when it allows her to work side by side with her beloved James.

England, Gloucestershire, Dembley

Agatha Raisin and the Murderous Marriage. St. Martin's Press, 1996

After waiting years for the date of her second marriage, Raisin ends up with an unsightly rash, and a miraculously returned first husband who then ends up dead. Will she be able to retain true love, get married, and solve the crime?

England, Cotswold, Carsley · Weddings

Agatha Raisin and the Terrible Tourist. St. Martin's Press, 1997

Raisin's marriage to James has fallen through, and James has left for Cyprus, the planned site of their aborted honeymoon. Raisin wants him back, and she hunts him down, moving into his rented house. They meet an odd mix of tourists, and when Rose Wilcox is murdered after a night on the town, they find themselves involved in murder again.

Cyprus

Agatha Raisin and the Wellspring of Death. St. Martin's Press, 1998

When a company seeks to tap into the village spring in Ancombe to sell mineral water, the local community is divided into two camps. Raisin has taken the job of PR representative for the Ancombe Water Company, and when the Ancombe council chairman is murdered, she needs to play detective.

England, Cotswold, Ancombe

Agatha Raisin and the Witch of Wyckhadden. St. Martin's Minotaur, 1999

Raisin has taken off to hide and repair damages from her last case. After consulting a local witch, named Francie Juddle, she regains her hair and the fancies of the local police inspector. When Francie is murdered, the police inspector thanks his stars he has an experienced amateur like Raisin to help.

England, Wyckhadden

Agatha Raisin and the Wizard of Evesham. St. Martin's Press, 1999

Mr. John saves Raisin's hair, and she falls under his charming spell. But rumors have it that he could be a blackmailer, and when he is murdered, it is Raisin's job to sort out the facts.

England, Cotswold, Evesham

Agatha Raisin and the Fairies of Fryfam. St. Martin's Minotaur, 2000

Moving to Norfolk when she follows the advice of a fortuneteller, Raisin discovers she has moved to a community haunted by the fairies. But when Tolly Trumpington-James is murdered, she realizes that, fairies or not, there is a murderer also at work.

England, Norfolk, Fryfam

Agatha Raisin and the Love from Hell. St. Martin's Minotaur, 2001

Raisin finally marries her love, James Lacey, but she finds that her marriage is shaken when each partner believes the other may be unfaithful. When James disappears, and then James's mistress, Melissa Sheppard, is murdered, Raisin needs to ally herself with her old friend Sir Charles Fraith to solve the crime and locate her husband.

England, Cotswold, Carsley · England, London · Weddings

Agatha Raisin and the Day the Floods Came. St. Martin's Minotaur, 2002

When her husband survives a brain tumor but retires to a French monastery, Raisin takes a hiatus in the South Pacific. Upon her return to England, she discovers that a bride who had honeymooned on the same trip has committed suicide. Suspicious, Raisin begins an investigation that focuses on the woman's fiancé and leads Raisin toward a new love in her life.

England, Costwold Hills, Evesham · Pacific Ocean, Robinson Crusoe Island

Lilian Jackson Braun ✍

Jim Qwilleran/Koko/Yum Yum

No one can question the power of cats and crime in the 1990s, and the leader in this field is Braun. Her human detective, Qwilleran, may not be as popular as his two Siamese cats, Koko and Yum Yum. Qwilleran's skills as a detective are developed when he is a crime reporter, a job he is eventually forced to give up by his life's circumstances. When he recovers from these traumas, and as the series begins, he is able to land a job as a reporter with the *Daily Fluxton* in a city vaguely defined as down there. Qwilleran is a throwback to the dilettante detectives, because after he inherits a large sum of money, he eventually leaves the rat race of the big city and moves somewhere north to Pickax in Moose County. Readers may also enjoy Carole Nelson Douglas. See a fan site for this author at http://home.att.net/~RACapowski. **Soft-boiled**. Series subjects: **Cats · Teams**.

The Cat Who Could Read Backwards. Dutton, 1966

Qwilleran is asked by the *Daily Fluxton* to cover the art beat. The assignment sounds easy until there is a series of vandalized paintings, a stabbing in an art gallery, and finally a homicide he needs to investigate. The first death is discovered by Zoe Lambreth when she finds her husband dead in his gallery. The second homicide is Qwilleran's landlord, George Mountclemen, who leaves him Koko, a cat capable of aiding the detective in his investigation.

Art

The Cat Who Ate Danish Modern. Dutton, 1967

Jim Qwilleran is not exactly thrilled by his new assignment for the *Daily Fluxion*—a weekly magazine on interior design called *Gracious Abodes*. Qwilleran is embarrassed when the exclusive residence featured on the cover of the first issue is burglarized and the resident murdered, so he and Koko investigate.

Interior design

The Cat Who Turned On and Off. Dutton, 1968

When Qwilleran decides to do a feature on Junktown, the antiques section of town, it leads to murder. One of the antique dealers dies in a mysterious fall, and Qwilleran and Koko suspect murder.

Antiquities

The Cat Who Saw Red. Jove, 1986

Qwilleran moves into Maus Haus, an old mansion with an old mystery surrounding a suicide, to do a cooking assignment featuring Robert Maus, gourmet cook. When strange things begin to happen around the old house, Qwilleran is forced to begin an investigation, especially when his old girlfriend disappears.

Cooking

The Cat Who Played Brahms. Jove, 1987

Qwilleran needs a break, so he heads for a cabin owned by Aunt Fanny in Mooseville. He receives no break from crime when several deaths occur in the area. But when death strikes Aunt Fanny, Qwilleran decides to investigate in Moose County.

The Cat Who Played Post Office. Jove, 1987

Qwilleran inherits millions of dollars, and the trio moves into a mansion. After Qwilleran staffs the mansion, a housemaid goes missing and then murder occurs. Life in the fast lane is not going to be any easier for Qwilleran until he can solve this crime.

The Cat Who Knew Shakespeare. Jove, 1988

The Pickax police believe that an accident has claimed the life of the local paper's eccentric publisher, but to Qwilleran it seems like murder. The revelation of a town secret may hold the key, but Koko thinks an edition of Shakespeare may hold the real solution.

The Cat Who Had 14 Tales. Jove, 1988

A collection of the following stories: "A Cat named Conscience," "A Cat Too Small for His Whiskers," "The Dark One," "East Side Story," "The Fluppie Phenomenon," "The Hero of Drummond Street," "The Mad Museum Mouser," "Phut Phat Concentrates," "The Sin of Madame Phloi," "Stanley and Spook," "SuSu and the 8:30 Ghost," "Tipsy and the Board of Health," "Tragedy on New Year's Eve," and "Weekend of the Big Puddle."

Short stories

The Cat Who Sniffed Glue. Putnam, 1988

Qwilleran is settling into life in Pickax as the town's richest man when the son of the town's banker and his wife are murdered. The police have written this off as a burglary, but it is when Qwilleran notices that Koko is addicted to glue that it all comes clear.

The Cat Who Went Underground. Putnam, 1989

Its summertime and that means Jim Qwilleran and his two Siamese cats are heading for his log cabin in Moose County. Their vacation starts off ominously with the disappearance of a handyman hired to patch up Qwilleran's cabins. Then it becomes clear that all the carpenters keep disappearing or dying. It takes Qwilleran and the two cats to solve this small-town mystery.

The Cat Who Lived High. Putnam, 1990

Qwilleran decides he wants to refurbish the Casablanca Apartment building, but the powers to be want to tear it down. He moves in to save the building and discovers that in his apartment a famous art dealer met his death.

The Cat Who Talked to Ghosts. Putnam, 1990

When Mrs. Cobb hears strange sounds in her antique-filled farmhouse, she asks Qwilleran for help. Qwilleran is too late to prevent Mrs. Cobb's death, but he does not believe that she died of fright. So, he and the cats move into the farmhouse to try and figure out what happened.

The Cat Who Knew a Cardinal. Putnam, 1991

The Theater Club has just closed *The Famous History of the Life of King Henry the Eighth,* and Qwilleran has offered to have the cast out to his farmhouse after their final production. Hilary VanBrook, the director, is much disliked, and after the cast party he is found dead. Once again, Qwilleran has to investigate a death in his small town.

Theater

The Cat Who Moved a Mountain. Putnam, 1992

Qwilleran rents a house on top of Big Potato Mountain built by J. J. Hawkinfeld, a real estate developer. Not everyone was pleased with the changes brought to Big Potato by the development, and J. J. was pushed from a mountain cliff by Forest Beechum. But after spending time on the mountain, Qwilleran becomes more and more convinced that the wrong person is behind bars.

The Cat Who Wasn't There. Putnam, 1992

Qwilleran is talked into spending time in Scotland by Polly Duncan, but the trip does not go smoothly. In one day someone swipes a suitcase, Bruce the bus driver disappears, and Irma Hasselrich is murdered.

Scotland

The Cat Who Went into the Closet. Putnam, 1993

Moving into the Gage mansion, the cats are adjusting to their new home. Meanwhile, two deaths have captured Qwilleran's attention: the mansion's former occupant and a local potato farmer. Euphonia Gage's suicide in Florida seems awfully suspicious to the well-practiced detective.

The Cat Who Blew the Whistle. Putnam, 1994

Why would the owner of a steam locomotive embezzle millions of dollars from Lumberton Credit Union investors? Does the train wreck and the body in the railroad tavern mean something else is occurring? It will take Qwilleran's investigative skills, and the cats, to solve this one.

Railroads

The Cat Who Came to Breakfast. Putnam, 1994

Visiting Breakfast Island, Qwilleran is struck by the number of incidents that have occurred in this isolated community. The topper comes when a cabin cruiser explodes in the marina, and once again Qwilleran launches an investigation.

The Cat Who Said Cheese. Putnam, 1996

Qwilleran's foundation has created a huge new promotional event to promote Pickax: the Great Food Explo. The Explo was arranged to bring new restaurants, inns, and food specialty shops to the area. The great event is only a week away when a bomb goes off in the only hotel in town, killing a housekeeper. Staying at the hotel is a mystery woman that has the whole town gossiping. To save his big event, Qwilleran must once again play detective.

The Cat Who Tailed a Thief. Putnam, 1997

Willard Carmichael has upset Pickax with his plans to remodel the Victorian houses on Pleasant Street into a new real estate development called Gingerbread Alley. Since his arrival, the crime rate has rocketed, but no one expects the news that Carmichael has been killed in a mugging while in the cities. Qwilleran doubts the guilt of the petty thief arrested by the police, and wonders if there is just too much eagerness being shown by some folks in renewing the Gingerbread project.

The Cat Who Sang for the Birds. Putnam, 1998

Recluse Maude Coggin dies in an accidental fire after selling her 100-acre farm to Northern Land Improvement. Local acts of vandalism including a break-in and a theft at the art center fluster the whole town. When all of this climaxes with a body being discovered in Bloody Creek, it becomes time for the cats to help Qwilleran discover the truth behind all these terrible occurrences.

The Cat Who Saw Stars. Putnam, 1998

Once again a peaceful vacation to Mooseville is ruined when UFOs and a backpacker's disappearance disturb the locals. Then the hiker's body is found on the shore of the lake, and Qwilleran must discover who committed this crime.

UFOs

The Cat Who Robbed a Bank. Putnam, 1999

Pickax is about to reopen its grand hotel, have its Highland Games, and receive the annual visit of the jeweler Delacamp. When the visitor is a victim found dead in the presidential suite of the hotel, Qwilleran and the cats spring into action. Will blame fall on the missing "niece" who accompanied the jeweler and has seemed to escape with all the jewels?

Jewels

The Cat Who Smelled a Rat. G. P. Putnam's Sons, 2001

Moose County is under the threat of forest fires while it waits for the first big snow of the season, but a fire that sweeps across the Big B minesite is deemed to be arson. As

Qwilleran casts about for the reasons, it is Koko who discovers the clue needed to solve this case.

Arson

The Cat Who Went up the Creek. Putnam, 2002

Qwilleran is investigating the odd doings at the Nutcracker Inn in Black Creek when the body of a guest at the inn is discovered drowned in a nearby creek. The reason for the murder may lie in the potential for gold in the Black Forest Conservancy, and Qwilleran finds himself relying on his allies, Koko and Yum Yum, to solve this mystery.

Gold

Simon Brett ✍

Charles Paris

Being an unlucky actor does not keep Charles Paris from being a lucky detective in this humorous series of books from the British author, Simon Brett. Plied with Bell's Whiskey and always with an eye out for the ladies, Paris manages to exude charm while maintaining a little of the rascal temperament. His long non-relationship with his wife Frances is a constant struggle. Trust that no matter how good his casting call sounds, trouble will follow any production that Paris nears. Brett fans may also enjoy Lawrence Block (Bernie Rhodenbarr), Harlan Coben, or Jonathan Gash. **Traditional**. Series subject: **Humor**.

Cast, in Order of Disappearance. U.K.: Gollancz, 1975 (U.S.: Scribner, 1976)

Mauris Steen is murdered, and the London theater loses one of its big producers. Does his death have anything to do with his mistress Jacqui, or the Sally Nash prostitution case? While stumbling around in this case, Paris becomes involved with a blackmailer, named William Sweet, and the blackmailer's wife. Assuming the role of McWhirter of the Yard helps the actor detective get to the bottom of these two crimes.

England, London · Theater

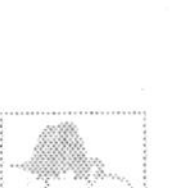

So Much Blood. U.K.: Gollancz, 1976 (U.S.: Scribner, 1977)

Paris has had the good fortune to do a one-man show at the Edinburgh Festival called *So Much Comic, So Much Blood*. Meanwhile, in another play in the series called *Mary Queen of Sots*, cast member Willy Mariello is stabbed to death when a prop knife is switched with a real one. Once again, Paris cannot resist playing detective.

Scotland, Edinburgh · Theater

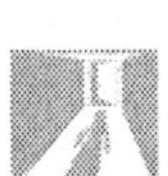

Star Trap. U.K.: Gollancz, 1977 (U.S.: Scribner, 1978)

Paris is in a West End musical version of *She Stoops to Conquer* when two deaths occur. Having been placed in the cast specifically to prevent disorder, he needs to be an amateur detective once again to save the show and his part in it.

England, London · Theater

An Amateur Corpse. U.K.: Gollancz, 1978 (U.S.: Scribner, 1978)

Paris agrees to critique an amateur dramatic society called the Breckton Backstagers. But when his boyhood friend, Hugo Mecken, is accused of murdering his wife Charlotte, Paris feels he needs to investigate to free his friend.

England, Breckton · Theater

A Comedian Dies. U.K.: Gollancz, 1979 (U.S.: Scribner, 1979)

Bill Peaky may be becoming a successful comedian, but he is not succeeding as a human being. When he is electrocuted during a performance at a seaside resort, Paris has plenty of suspects with good motives for eliminating the jokester.

England, Hunstanton · Theater

The Dead Side of the Mike. U.K.: Gollancz, 1980 (U.S.: Scribner, 1980)

Hired to write a radio program about Swinburne for a show called *Who Reads Them Now?*, Paris is shocked when a young studio manager is found dead with her wrists slashed. When the crooked American record producer she was involved with also dies and the death is ruled a suicide, Paris decides to investigate.

England, London · Radio

Situation Tragedy. U.K.: Gollancz, 1981 (U.S.: Scribner, 1982)

Paris has landed the part of a golf club barman in *The Strutters*, a new BBC situation comedy. But someone is killing the members of the show's production crew, and Charles soon finds himself in the role of detective.

England, London · Television

Murder Unprompted. U.K.: Gollancz, 1982 (U.S.: Scribner, 1982)

Paris has labored for 30 years in minor parts, and when the Taunton show, *The Hooded Owl*, is picked to move to the West End, he and the rest of the cast are thrilled. But when the producers force the cast to understudy the big names brought in to replace them, Paris finds that other cast members may not be so willing to step aside.

England, London · Theater

Murder in the Title. U.K.: Gollancz, 1983 (U.S.: Scribner, 1983)

Paris's sole role in the play, *The Message is Murder,* is to fall down dead, but he must act in his own defense when he begins to think that someone in the cast wants his performance to be more realistic.

England, London · Theater

Not Dead, Only Resting. U.K.: Gollancz, 1984 (U.S.: Scribner, 1984)

Too long out of work to care, Paris accepts an offer from Stan Fogden to redecorate the flat of Tristram Gowers, the owner of Trysts, a fashionable restaurant where theatrical types often hang about. To Paris's surprise, they discover the mutilated corpse of Yves Lafeu, Tristram's protégé.

England, London · Food

Dead Giveaway. U.K.: Gollancz, 1985 (U.S.: Scribner, 1986)

A one-day job on a game show called *If The Cap Fits* would be no problem for anyone else but the actor detective Paris. Famous celebrities try to guess his occupation. The show is hosted by the much-hated Barrett Doran, and the host's death leads to another investigation job for Paris.

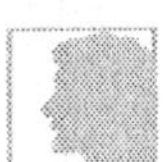

England, London • Television

What Bloody Man Is That? U.K.: Gollancz, 1987 (U.S.: Scribner, 1987)

The most cursed play in history is *Macbeth*, but Paris is desperate enough to accept the roles of Bleeding Sergeant and Drunken Porter in a provincial repertory production at the Pinero Theatre in Warminster just to get on the boards. He regrets his decision when he learns that the lead is George Birkitt, television actor. But the roles of Lady Macbeth and Duncan are given to other actors with equal flaws, and soon Paris finds himself in the role of detective.

England, Warminster • Theater

A Series of Murders. U.K.: Gollancz, 1989 (U.S.: Scribner, 1989)

What better role for Paris than Sergeant Clump of the Little Beckington Police Station? This a character created in a series of 1930s mystery novels to play the Watson to the great thinking detective, Stanislas Braid, now played by Russell Bentley. The weakest link in the cast is Sippy Stokes, who is assigned the role of the naïve young daughter. Her bad acting is no longer a problem when murder ends her career, but Paris must play a detective both in front of and behind the cameras to solve this one.

England, London • Television

Corporate Bodies. U.K.: Gollancz, 1991 (U.S.: Scribner, 1992)

Delmoleen Company has developed a snack food that is going to save the company because it is nutritious and its packaging is biodegradable. When Paris is hired to portray a forklift operator in a corporate video, his character speaks of the happy family at Delmoleen. But while he is on the company grounds, Paris needs to deal with the jealous forklift operator he has replaced, and also deal with the situation when his forklift is used to commit murder.

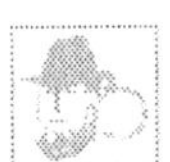

England, Bedford

A Reconstructed Corpse. U.K.: Gollancz, 1993 (U.S.: Scribner, 1994)

Because he bears a startling resemblance to Martin Earnshaw, Paris is asked to portray the missing property developer on a television re-enactment show called *Public Enemies*. He finds himself playing detective when he is fascinated by the case and some startling clues begin to appear.

England, London • Television

Sicken and So Die. U.K.: Gollancz, 1995 (U.S.: Scribner, 1995)

How good can things get for poor old Paris: he is living again with Frances, his ex-wife, and he is acting as Sir Toby Belch in a festival production of *Twelfth Night*. Paris's work received the approval of Gavin Scholes, the original director, but when he dies from food poisoning, the new Romanian director feels Paris is wrong

for the part. When another mysterious death occurs, Paris begins to think someone may want him permanently out of the cast.

England, Great Wensham · Theater

Dead Room Farce. U.K.: Gollancz, 1998 (U.S.: St. Martin's Press, 1998)

Cast in a role in the bedroom farce *Not On Your Wife!*, Paris sets sail with the cast, taking his role so seriously he is caught with two different women. Then, a man for whom Paris is recording an audio book is murdered, and Paris finds himself behind the eight ball again.

England, London · Theater

Jill Churchill (pseud. of Janice Young Brooks) ✍

Jane Jeffry

Jane Jeffry is a single mother with three kids living in the Chicago area. The amazing thing about her life is that despite all of her domestic and social entanglements, she still has time to investigate an occasional crime. Eventually, she develops a relationship with Mel VanDyne, a detective on the local police force, which will keep her close to crime. Churchill's fans may also enjoy Katharine Hall Page and Valerie Wolzien. See the author's website at http://www.jillchurchill.com. **Soft-boiled**.

Grime and Punishment. Avon Books, 1989

Everyone needs Ramona Thrugood, the Happy Helper, but no one is really happy with her work. Yet, who would strangle the cleaning person with the chord of a vacuum cleaner? That becomes the first case for the new detective, Jane Jeffry. AG MA

Illinois, Chicago

A Farewell to Yarns. Avon Books, 1991

Phyllis Wagner is murdered while visiting with Jeffry, and the case throws the single mom in close contact with Detective Mel VanDyne. Because it is the Christmas season, Jeffry tries to maintain her family's schedule while trying to discover the reason for the murder of her acquaintance.

Christmas · Illinois, Chicago

A Quiche Before Dying. Avon Books, 1993

Jeffry has enrolled in a summer writing class while her kids are at summer camp. To her surprise, a fellow student dies when poisoned by a snack from a buffet provided by other students. Jeffry cannot help herself and plunges into an investigation of the crime.

Illinois, Chicago

The Class Menagerie. Avon Books, 1994

Jeffry has agreed to set aside her busy schedule to help her good friend, Shelley Nowack, handle a gathering of Shelley's high school friends. The event will open the new bed and breakfast in the old Francisco mansion. Despite the time that has gone by, the women are quite willing to gossip about each other, and one is willing to murder another.

Illinois, Chicago · Reunions

A Knife to Remember. Avon Books, 1994

Jeffry invites a Hollywood movie company into her backyard to film its new movie. The bickering between the cast leads to controversy, but a blackmailing prop man is the one who is killed. To her surprise, Jeffry finds herself a suspect, and she must launch an investigation in order to save herself from the law.

Film · Illinois, Chicago

From Here to Paternity. Avon Books, 1995

Jeffry, with her friends Shelley Nowack and Mel VanDyne, and all the kids are spending a vacation at a Colorado ski resort. They find themselves at a resort whose ownership is controversial, and the charismatic Hawk Hunter is present to add to the stress. When one of those contesting the ownership is found murdered, VanDyne tries to stay out of the investigation while Jeffry gladly gives up her vacation to play detective.

Colorado · Native Americans

Silence of the Hams. Avon Books, 1996

A rack of hams falls on the obnoxious attorney, Robert Stonecipher, at the deli where Jeffry's son works. When a second victim falls to the same murder method, Jeffry decides to help VanDyne investigate the crime.

Illinois, Chicago

War and Peas. Avon Books, 1996

The Auguste Caspar Snellen Museum is dedicated to preserving the heritage of peas, but it is also hosting a Civil War reenactment at its annual festival. After all the shots have stopped, it is discovered that one of the reenactors is dead. Jeffry, a museum volunteer, feels compelled to investigate when the corpse proves to be the museum director, Regina Price Palmer.

Reenactments · Illinois, Chicago · Museums

Fear of Frying. Avon Books, 1997

Jeffry and Shelley visit the north woods of Wisconsin and Camp Sunshine to judge its suitability as a summer camp for urban kids. What they discover is a dead Sam Claypool, murdered with a frying pan. When they report the murder, and the victim is not dead, things heat up for the two amateur detectives.

Wisconsin

The Merchant of Menace. Avon Books, 1998

It is Christmas, and Jeffry is expecting her late husband's mother, VanDyne's mother, and her usual brood. She also has to host two Christmas celebrations in her neighborhood, one of which is to be covered by television. When a scandal-seeking action reporter plunges off a neighboring roof and is speared by some Christmas decorations, Jeffry needs to defend her turf.

Christmas · Holidays · Illinois, Chicago

A Groom with a View. Avon Books, 1999

Livvy Thatcher is too busy running her father's business to plan her own wedding, so she hires Jeffry to do the event. She chooses to hold the event in the old Titus place, now owned by the Thatcher family. The building, described as a cross between a monastery and a hunting lodge, soon houses many quarreling relatives and hangers-on. When murder enters the picture, Jeffry needs to stop planning and start detecting.

Illinois, Chicago · Weddings

Mulch Ado About Nothing. Morrow, 2000

Jeffry has a broken foot, but that does not keep her from attending a gardening class with her friend Shelley. However, the teacher is beaten before the class can get started, and the new instructor proves very boring. Then, while visiting the homes of the class members, the new instructor is found dead, and Jeffry must set aside her crutches and investigate the murder.

Gardening · Illinois, Chicago

The House of Seven Mables. Avon Books, 2002

Bitsy Burnside has purchased an old Victorian house and is in need of an all-female crew to restore the mansion to its previous glory. With only one child left at home, Jeffry takes the plunge and joins in the fun with her pal Shelley Nowack. But when a series of pranks on the worksite suddenly turn deadly, she finds herself investigating again.

Architecture

Harlan Coben ✍

Myron Bolitar

A combination of detective work, sports, and humor is featured in the early paperback originals about the sports agent Bolitar. These books were well received, but as the series migrated to hardcover, the themes got darker and dealt less with sports. The character of Win Horne, the psychotic sidekick, may be one of the more disturbing allies a detective has ever had, but his choice of morality lends depth to the themes chosen by Coben. Bolitar's office team includes Esperanza and Big Cindy, two wonderful female characters, each with her own definite sense of self. Readers who enjoy Coben's work may also enjoy Simon Brett (Charlie Paris), Robert Crais, or Laura Lippman. See the Official Harlan Coben website at http://www.harlancoben.com. **Traditional/Hard-boiled**.

Deal Breaker. Dell, 1995

Bolitar is about to cut the deal of his life when his client, Christian Steele, is poised to sign a huge contract with the New York Titans. But when Christian is accused of murdering his missing girlfriend, Kathy Culver, the deal begins to go south unless Bolitar can play detective.

Football · New York, New York · Sports

Dropshot. Dell, 1996

Valerie Simpson is shot dead at the U.S. Open tennis tournament, and her troubled past is going to affect Myron and his client, Duane Richwood. Duane is poised to take his first grand slam tournament, but the police find his phone number in Valerie's black book, and he is suspect number one. A six-year-old murder may hold the clue to breaking the case and rescuing his client's career, so once again sports agent Bolitar turns detective.

New York, New York • Sports • Tennis

Fade Away. Dell, 1996

Bolitar's old basketball injury kept him from professional sports and turned him to a career as a sports agent. Having shown some skills as a detective, the New Jersey Dragons basketball team are interested in adding Bolitar to their squad if he will search for missing star player, Greg Downing. Mixing playing time with detection leads Bolitar down a dark path through the underbelly of professional sports.

Basketball • New Jersey • Sports

Backspin. Dell, 1997

At the height of the U.S. Open golf championships, someone kidnaps the son of superstar golfer Linda Coldren and her aging pro husband Jack. Bolitar steps in to try and resolve the situation, but everyone is taken aback when Jack is found dead in a sand trap. Does his death relate to the championship he should have won but did not? BA

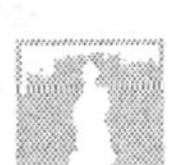

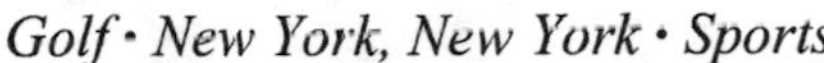

One False Move. Delacorte Press, 1998

While his girlfriend Jessica is off in Hollywood working on a movie, Bolitar's eye falls on the lovely and talented Brenda Slaughter, the star player of the Women's Professional Basketball Association. She is brought into his life when she is the target of threatening phone calls and Norm Zuckerman, owner of the league, convinces Bolitar to protect her. But Brenda wants Bolitar to find her missing father, Horace, who is also Bolitar's old coach; by the time this case winds down, Bolitar is tested on a detecting and a personal level.

Basketball • New York, New York • Sports

The Final Detail. Delacorte Press, 1999

Bolitar is resting in the Caribbean from the wounds he suffered on his last case when word reaches him that Esperanza has been accused of murdering New York Yankees baseball star, Clu Haid. Rushing back to aid her, Bolitar finds that Esperanza is silent and does not want his help. Helping anyway, Bolitar relies on Win and Big Cindy to probe into his friend's life, a case that leads him to discover truths about himself as well.

New York, New York

Darkest Fear. Delacorte Press, 2000

Bolitar's life is turned upside-down when his old girlfriend, Emily Downing, arrives on his doorstep to inform him that her son needs a bone marrow transplant. She also informs him that the boy is his son. His assignment is to find the one proper donor who has disappeared, which sets him on the trail of a serial killer.

New York, New York • Serial killer

Amanda Cross (pseud. of Carolyn Heilbrun) ✍

Kate Fansler

English professor Kate Fansler solves mystery cases with a literary style. It is often noted that Cross's books may be the modern equivalent of Dorothy L. Sayers in that they are witty yet crisp in their social commentary. Her thoroughly modern feminist heroine is not shy about expressing opinions or solving crimes. Readers may also enjoy Colin Dexter, Terence Faherty, Antonia Fraser, Reginald Hill, Nancy Pickard, or Dorothy L. Sayers. **Traditional.**

In the Last Analysis. Macmillan, 1964

When a beautiful young student named Janet Harrison asks Fansler for help, she recommends a session on the couch with a prominent psychiatrist named Emanuel Bauer. The student ends up dead on that couch, and Fansler feels compelled to investigate.

Medical · New York, New York

The James Joyce Murder. Macmillan, 1967

Fansler is resting over the summer break by sorting through a valuable private collection of James Joyce's papers left in the estate of publisher, Sam Lingerwell. But a farmer's wife is killed nearby, and the murder weapon comes from the household hosting Fansler, so she feels compelled to investigate.

Massachusetts, Berkshire Hills

Poetic Justice. Knopf, 1970

Fansler is placed in an odd position when her fiancé, Reed Amhearst of the New York District Attorney's Office, is assigned to investigate the death of Fansler's colleague, Jeremiah Cudlipp. Fansler's rivalry with the dead man makes her a suspect from the beginning, but then incriminating evidence begins to mount up.

Academia · New York, New York

The Theban Mysteries. Knopf, 1971

Alumnus Fansler is a guest lecturer at Theban, a woman's college where there are some violent student protests against the war in Vietnam. When a mother of one of the students is murdered, Fansler wrestles with the crime and her feelings about the conflict overseas and how it affects her old school.

Academia · New York, New York · Vietnamese Conflict

The Question of Max. Knopf, 1976

Max Reston is Fansler's colleague at her university, and he is just one of the things she sought to escape by retreating to the woods on a vacation. She is surprised when Max ends up on her doorstep, and more surprised when the reason for a murder seems to hinge on the estate of a famous English novelist, Cecily Hutchins.

Authors · England, Oxford · Maine, Berkshires

Death in a Tenured Position. U.S.: Dutton, 1981 (U.K.: *A Death in the Faculty*)

Janet Mandelbaum has just become the first woman professor in the English Department at Harvard University. Not everyone is happy with her appointment, and when someone slips her a mickey during an afternoon tea, she asks her friend Fansler to investigate. Unfortunately, the harassment turns serious and Janet is murdered.

Academia • Massachusetts, Boston

Sweet Death, Kind Death. Dutton, 1984

Patrice Umphelby had a reputation at Clare College that ranged from respect as a renowned historian and novelist to rejection for her eccentricities. When she drowns in the campus lake, the verdict is suicide. However, doubts in the mind of the college president lead him to ask Fansler to investigate her death.

Academia • Massachusetts, Boston

No Word from Winifred. Dutton, 1986

Winifred Ashby disappeared while she was on a mission to get Charlie appointed as British novelist Charlotte Stanton's official biographer. Fansler is asked to investigate and must use Winifred's journal, and Stanton's novels, to trail the young girl and solve the mystery.

Authors • New York, New York

A Trap for Fools. Dutton, 1989

Just after Thanksgiving, the body of Professor of Middle Eastern Culture, Dr. Canfield Adams, is found at the base of the building outside his officc window. Knowing that someone may have pushed Adams, the Vice-President of Internal Affairs wants Fansler to investigate the death. Her role is to save the university from an embarrassing lawsuit and to find a murderer.

Academia • New York, New York

The Players Come Again. Random House, 1990

Fansler is between projects when she is offered the opportunity to become the biographer of Gabrielle Foxx. Wife of the modernist author, Emmanuel Foxx, speculation is that Gabrielle was the power behind the throne, and the truth may lie with three friends from Gabrielle's past.

Authors • New York, New York

An Imperfect Spy. Ballantine, 1995

Fansler is guest lecturing at Schuyler Law School, where she has been asked to teach a course on literature and the law. Harriet Furst is a secretary at the school, and she is helpful to Fansler's research when the detective decides to investigate the suspicious death of a former female professor at the school. Finding herself up against the school's old-boy network, Fansler needs to watch her back as she investigates.

Academia • New York, New York

The Collected Stories. Ballantine, 1997

A collection of the following stories: "Arrie and Jasper," "The Disappearance of Great Aunt Flavia," "The George Eliot Play," "Murder without Text," "Once Upon a Time," "The Proposition," "Tania's Nowhere," and "Who Shot Mrs. Byron Boyd." Contains one non-Fansler short story.

Short stories

The Puzzled Heart. Ballantine, 1998

Fansler's feminism has always been a part of her life, but now it is an issue as her husband Reed has been kidnapped. The ransom demand requires Fansler to abandon her personal philosophy, but instead she rescues her husband. However, when an unexpected death occurs, Fansler finds herself on a related murder investigation.

Kidnapping · New York, New York

Honest Doubt. Ballantine, 2000

Fansler takes a back seat to a new character named Woody Woodhaven. This P.I. is hired to discover who murdered the woman-hating Professor Charles Haycock. When the investigation bogs down, the P.I. turns to the resident amateur expert, Fansler.

Academia · New Jersey

Diane Mott Davidson ✍

Goldy Bear Schulz

Cooking was the hook that brought Davidson's heroine to the attention of readers, and her books contain recipes for those readers who want to challenge themselves in the kitchen. However, the books do a good job of blending humor with suspense. Based in Colorado's fictional town of Aspen Meadow, this caterer never finds herself too far from a mysterious death. It also helps that Goldy's husband, Tom Schulz, is a police detective. Readers may also enjoy Katherine Hall Page or Valerie Wolzien. **Soft-boiled/Traditional**. Series subjects: **Colorado, Aspen Meadow · Food · Humor**.

Catering to Nobody. St. Martin's Press, 1990

Catering a wake for her son's favorite teacher turns to disaster when Schulz's former father-in-law passes out from rat poison in the coffee she's serving. She needs to become a detective to free herself from suspicion and to restore her business.

Catering

Dying for Chocolate. Bantam Books, 1992

To get away from the unwanted attentions of her ex-husband, Dr. John Richard Korman, aka The Jerk, Schulz takes a job as a live-in cook at the Aspen Meadows Country Club mansion. Courted by Philip Miller, a handsome local psychiatrist, Schulz is shocked to be a witness at the auto accident that kills him. Convinced that the accident was caused by suspicious means, Schulz decides to investigate.

The Cereal Murders. Bantam Books, 1993

Asked to cater the first College Advisory Dinner for Seniors and Parents at the exclusive Elk Park Preparatory School seems like an honor for her until Schulz discovers the body of Keith Andrews, the school's valedictorian. Both her boys are students there, so Schulz feels driven to discover the truth.

Academia · Catering

The Last Suppers. Bantam Books, 1994

Schulz's lucky day is here as she is about to marry Tom Schulz, the county homicide detective who has won her heart. But on their wedding day, as Tom is dropping by to pick up the Reverend Theodore Olson, he discovers the good man has been shot. When the other detectives arrive to investigate, Tom has disappeared, and Schulz needs to investigate to keep her man.

Weddings

Killer Pancake. Bantam Books, 1995

Mignon Cosmetic's low-fat luncheon is the latest assignment for Goldilock's Catering, but on the day of the lunch she finds herself part of the target for the protests staged by Spare the Hares, folks who want to stop Mignon's animal testing. When one of their employees is murdered, Schulz feels the need to investigate.

Animal rights · Catering

The Main Corpse. Bantam Books, 1996

Business comes Schulz's way because her friend Marla Korman is having an affair with one of the owners of Prospect Financial Partners. Tony Royce and Albert Lipscombe are partners. They have plans to reopen the Eurydice Gold Mine, and they want a big party to celebrate. But when Albert is missing with the company funds and the police think Marla has murdered Tony, Schulz needs to investigate.

Catering

The Grilling Season. Bantam Books, 1997

Schulz's friend, Patricia McCracken, is suing Schulz's ex-husband over the loss of her baby. But John Richard Korman's troubles are just starting, because he is arrested for murdering his girlfriend Suz Craig. Schulz decides to put her personal feelings aside and investigate this murder.

Prime Cut. Bantam Books, 1998

Schulz's business, always on the edge, is now being pressured by a rival business while her own kitchen is in ruins from a bad contractor. When Schulz discovers the body of a missing contractor, her friend and president of the local historical society, George Eliot, is arrested for the murder by the new DA, who is feuding with her policeman husband Tom.

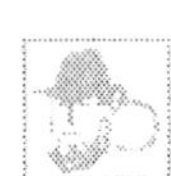

Catering

Tough Cookie. Bantam Books, 2000

Schulz would like to concentrate on her new job as a host on the PBS cooking show, but when death occurs at the ski resort used for a taping backdrop, she must become an investigator.

Colorado, Killdeer · Television

Sticks & Scones. Bantam Books, 2001

After someone takes a shot at her, Schulz decides it would be easier to move into the English castle where she is going to be catering some Elizabethan meals to celebrate the castle's restoration in Colorado. However, her husband Tom is shot and Schulz discovers a dead thief on the castle's grounds. As if this is not enough, her ex-husband is released from jail while Tom seems to have connected with an old flame.

Catering

Chopping Spree. Bantam Books, 2002

Schulz is hired to cater a reception for high-end shoppers at the Westside Mall, managed by Schulz's friend Barry Dean. When Dean is found murdered with one of Schulz's carving knives, she has to launch an investigation to prove that her own helper, Julian Teller, is innocent of murder. Schulz finds that her best clues are the ones left by the dead man.

Carole Nelson Douglas ✍

Temple Barr/Midnight Louie

Along with Lilian Jackson Braun, Douglas uses the popularity of cats and mysteries by creating the sleuthing feline Midnight Louie, a 19-pound black cat capable of telling his own side of the story. Teamed with Temple Barr, a Las Vegas freelance publicist, the two follow the clues to the solution. These cases can be recommended to soft-boiled mystery readers. Douglas's fans may also enjoy Lilian Jackson Braun. See the author's website at http://www.fastlane.net/cdouglas. **Soft-boiled**. Series subjects: **Cats · Nevada, Las Vegas · Teams**.

Crystal Days. Bantam, 1990 (Also published as *The Cat and the King of Clubs.* Five Star, 1999; *The Cat and the Queen of Hearts.* Five Star, 1999)

A collection of the following novels: *The Cat and the King of Clubs* and *The Cat and the Queen of Hearts.*

Crystal Nights. Bantam, 1990 (Also published as *Jill of Diamonds.* Five Star, 2000; *The Cat and the Jack of Spades).*

A collection of the following novels: *Jill of Diamonds* and *Solitaire.*

Catnap. Tor, 1992

At the American Booksellers Association convention in Las Vegas, publishing jobber Baker and Taylor loses the two feline mascots who bear its name. When the founder of Pennyroyal Press, a paperback house specializing in medial thrillers, is found murdered on the convention floor, the two detectives decide to investigate.

Publishing

Pussyfoot. Tor, 1993

A striptease contest turns deadly when one of the contestants is found strangled with her own G-string. Meanwhile, Barr gets involved in the disappearance of her old magician boyfriend.

Cat on a Blue Monday. Forge, 1994

While Barr tries to understand her relationship with Matt Devine, the hotline counselor who has moved into her life, Midnight Louis is trying to discover who is stalking the prize-winning purebreds from the Las Vegas Cat Show.

Cat in a Crimson Haze. Forge, 1995

The manager of the Crystal Palace has hired Barr to restore the hotel's reputation. But when the job places her in danger and some treasure goes missing, Barr needs the help of Midnight Louie to solve this case.

Cat in a Diamond Dazzle. Forge, 1996

Barr decides to attend a romance writers' convention called G.R.O.W.L., Great Readers of Wonderful Literature. She and Midnight Louie are on the spot to investigate the murder of a male model at the Incredible Hulk pageant.

Authors

Cat with an Emerald Eye. Forge, 1996

Attending a séance on Halloween Eve should be a lot of fun, so Barr goes along with her landlord Electra Lark to try and resurrect the spirit of Harry Houdini. But the séance leaves the psychic dead, and Barr starts an investigation.

Halloween · Holidays

Cat in a Flamingo Fedora. Forge, 1997

Midnight Louie is going to star in another cat food commercial, but Barr cannot enjoy the experience because famous comic Darren Cooke is shot to death. Cooke had asked Barr to protect him from a stalker who might be his long-lost daughter.

Cat in a Golden Garland. Forge, 1997

A murder occurs on Madison Avenue when Barr and Midnight Louie are in New York to check on his advertising campaign. The head of the agency was to be in the Santa Claus suit, but it is the substitute who is murdered in his place.

Advertising · Christmas · Holidays · New York, New York

Cat On a Hyacinth Hunt. Forge, 1998

One of the typical stunts that occur in Las Vegas goes very wrong when two battling Egyptian barges outside the Oasis hotel actually create a dead body. Barr's two boyfriends are both suspects when the victim turns out to be someone they might have liked to see out of the way.

Hotels

Cat in an Indigo Mood. Forge, 1999

Carmen Molina, the tough homicide lieutenant, relaxes by singing torch songs in the Blue Dahlia, a forties-style club in Vegas. One night she discovers a dead body in the parking lot of the club, and she needs to rely on Barr and Midnight Louie to help her cause.

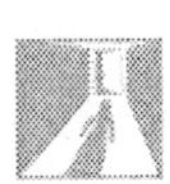

Cat in a Jeweled Jumpsuit. Forge, 1999

The Crystal Phoenix Hotel's construction is being delayed by the ghost of Elvis Presley. Barr has the hotel as a client, and she is driven to investigate when her competitor's daughter, who looks like Priscilla Presley, is viciously attacked.

Hotels

Cat in a Kiwi Con. Forge, 2000

Las Vegas is host to TitaniCon, the world's largest science fiction and fantasy convention. When the crew stumbles upon the dead body of one of the conventioneers, they launch an investigation that will require them to interview science fiction characters to finds a murderer.

Science fiction

Cat in a Leopard Spot. Forge, 2001

Osiris, a famous performing leopard, is kidnapped and found with the dead body of Cyrus Van Burkleo. Burkleo had been running a ranch for big game hunters outside of Las Vegas, and as the two detectives investigate the mystery around his death, they are challenged by animal rights activists.

Hunting

Cat in a Midnight Choir. Forge, 2002

Cop friend C. R. Molina is still on the case of the stripper murder, while Barr investigates the murderous tendencies of a special group of magicians called The Synth. Louie helps in the investigation as all the detectives, human and non-human, find themselves battling black magic.

Magic

Aaron Elkins ✍

Gideon Oliver

Proving that the past has many secrets, Elkins created a forensic physical anthropologist named Gideon Oliver, who helps solve current mysteries by unraveling their histories. To add spice to the series, Oliver is a travelling consultant, visiting many foreign locations in his searches, echoing the career of Elkins. As the series progresses, Oliver's wife Julie helps give a plucky-couple feeling to the cases. The series has drawn praise for its accuracy in presenting the anthropological aspects of the cases without taking anything away from the character development. Readers who enjoy Elkins may also enjoy Patricia Cornwell, Sharyn McCrumb (Elizabeth MacPherson), and Elizabeth Peters (Jacqueline Kirby/Amelia Peabody). **Traditional**. Series subject: **Forensics**.

Fellowship of Fear. Walker, 1982

Oliver likes the idea of being a visiting fellow until someone tries to kill him. John Lau, the Army Intelligence officer assigned to protect him, does not understand Oliver's skills: he can identify his assailants by their speech patterns. But when a dead body turns up, Oliver can use its charred bones and teeth to identify it.

Academia · Germany, Heidelberg · Italy, Sicily

The Dark Place. Walker, 1983

When the body of Norris Eckert is discovered in the rain forests of the Northwest, the murder weapon appears to be an ancient spear. Oliver teams with forest ranger Julie Tendler to explore for a murderer.

Antiquities · Washington, Quinault

Murder in the Queen's Armes. Walker, 1985

Having married the lovely park ranger Julie Tendler, the couple is in England on their honeymoon. Oliver stops by a dig being run by his former classmate, Nate Marcus, but he finds himself put to work when he finds the dig is under suspicion. When a student dies before he can give information to Oliver, the amateur detective must catch a killer.

Archeology • England, Wessex

Old Bones. Mysterious Press, 1987

Guillaume de Rocher, patriarch of the Breton family, is drowned near the family chateau. When a human skeleton is discovered under the stone flooring of the old family home, they turn to Oliver for an explanation of these strange happenings. ED

France, St. Malo

Curses! Mysterious Press, 1989

Bored with his academic career, Oliver travels to the Yucatan Peninsula to inspect a skeleton in a Mayan archaeological dig that was recently reopened. But when people begin to die and a set of hieroglyphs describe the consequences, Oliver must play detective.

Archeology • Mexico, Yucatan

Icy Clutches. Mysterious Press, 1990

Accompanying his wife Julie on a trip to Alaska, Oliver finds himself in conflict with M. Audley Tremaine, television's popular science spokesperson. Tremaine is on site to review the consequences of a 30-year-old expedition that killed three people, and when bones are discovered, it is considered expedient to ask the Skeleton Detective to take a look.

Alaska, Glacier Bay

Dead Men's Hearts. Mysterious Press, 1994

Visiting the Nile Valley to take part in a documentary film with his wife Julie, Oliver expects no special events. But when a skeleton is found in the garbage at the Egyptological Institute, the Skeleton Detective is asked to investigate. Returned to storage by Oliver, the bones are released again and a murder occurs, thus changing the definition of this investigation.

Archeology • Egypt

Twenty Blue Devils. Mysterious Press, 1997

Brian Scott has been tossed off a cliff, and when two other deaths occur, FBI agent John Lau calls on his friend Oliver for help on the case. Although his expertise is things dead, Oliver discovers that the secrets held by the living members of the family-run Paradise Coffee Company may be more relevant.

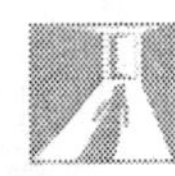

Pacific Ocean, Tahiti

Make No Bones. Mysterious Press, 1999

The ultimate contribution by a scientist is to will his bones to science, but after Professor Alber Evan Jasper does so, it takes 10 years to decide what to do with them. When a decision is made to display them at the Museum of Natural History in Bend, everyone is surprised when someone steals them. Oliver is forced to detect again when two murders occur.

Oregon, Bend

Skeleton Dance. Morrow, 2000

The Institut de Prehistoire is France's most prestigious institute for prehistoric study. It is located in an area of many sites, so when a dog drags a few bones into its backyard, no one thinks twice until a death occurs. The local inspector knows of Oliver's reputation, so he is asked to investigate.

Archeology • France, Les Eyzies-de-Tayac

Terence Faherty ✍

Owen Keane

Owen Keane, a failed seminarian, is hiding from life in a series of odd jobs, all of which seem to lead him to a murder. Keane would probably also see himself as a failed detective, as he is reluctant to admit he has a talent for the craft. His cases are often hauntings from the past, and the author's ability to be introspective with both the characters and the plot make this series a literary treat. Readers may also enjoy Walter Mosley and Don Winslow. See the author's website at http://www.terencefaherty.com. **Traditional**.

Deadstick. St. Martin's Press, 1991

Keane is working as a researcher for a New York law firm when he is asked to investigate a 40-year-old airplane crash. Fascinated by the details of a plane crash that took the life of William Carteret and his fiancée in 1941, the rather bored young man suddenly finds himself energized by the hunt.

Airplanes • New Jersey, Pine Barrens • New York, New York

Live to Regret. St. Martin's Press, 1992

Keane is asked to be a guardian over his old friend Harry Ohlman, a man still grieving over the death of his wife Mary. Mary was killed in an auto accident, and she was Keane's college girlfriend, so his attachment to the case is personal. When he gets involved with a woman obsessed with death, he finds his control beginning to unravel.

New Jersey, Spring Lake

The Lost Keats. St. Martin's Press, 1993

Reverting to a time when Keane was still a seminarian, but on the verge of being expelled, he is asked to locate the missing seminarian, Michael Crosley. Teamed with his girlfriend Mary Fitzgerald, he becomes obsessed with the idea that a lost sonnet by Keats is the essential clue to the missing man.

Academia • Indiana, Huber • Religion

Die Dreaming. St. Martin's Press, 1994

Keane attends his tenth high school reunion at Our Lady of Sorrows, where he discovers that his former classmates, The Sorrowersby clique, have a dark secret he is sent to uncover when he professes to be a private investigator. To his surprise, it takes him 10 years, and attendance at his twentieth reunion, to find the truth.

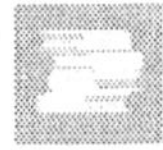

Massachusetts, Boston

Prove the Nameless. St. Martin's Press, 1996

Barbara Lambert wants to know why, when her family was murdered, she was spared. She turns to Keane for the answers. He is now working as a reporter for a newspaper and launches a probe into her family's 20-year-old murder. His ability to dig into the past does not save him from having to confront some dangerous things in the present, including Barbara's death.

New Jersey, Atlantic City · Pennsylvania, Lake Trevlac · Reporters

The Ordained. St. Martin's Press, 1997

Twenty years prior to the start of this tale, Keane had helped put Curtis Morell in prison for murder, and left the seminary. Now he has returned to Indiana to testify at the man's parole hearing, but finds himself distracted when people in the small town of Rapture begin to disappear.

Indiana, Rapture

Orion Rising. St. Martin's Press, 1999

In 1969, Keane and his circle of friends came under suspicion when a nurse was raped and murdered. Years later he returns to Boston when his old friend, James Courtney Murray, is accused of the crime through the magic of DNA testing.

4

Massachusetts, Boston

Anne George ✍

Patricia Anne Hollowell/Mary Alice Crane

A pair of Southern sisters is featured in this humorous series. While Hollowell (Mouse) appears to be the more stable sister, Crane (Sister) challenges her sister's preconceived notions of approved Southern female behavior. Like all good amateurs, they cannot seem to go anywhere without running into murder, to the frustration of Sheriff Reuse. The cases are narrated from Hollowell's rather narrow first-person point of view. This series can be recommended to readers of the soft-boiled mystery. George fans may also enjoy Carolyn G. Hart (Annie Laurance/Max Darling) and Joan Hess (Claire Malloy). See a fan website about this author at http://welcome.to/annegeorge. **Soft-boiled**. Series subjects: **Alabama, Birmingham · Humor · Teams.**

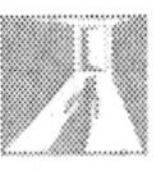

Murder on a Girl's Night Out. Avon Books, 1996

Crane has decided to purchase the Skoot 'n' Boot, and her sister Hollowell is doing all she can to discourage the thought. But while the contracts are being negotiated, the previous owner is found murdered in the wishing well in the club. It does not help that the sisters may be the last people to have seen the victim. AG

Music

Murder on a Bad Hair Day. Avon Books, 1996

The sisters cannot agree on the merits of some local folk artists on display at Mercy Armistead's gallery. When Armistead is murdered, the two barely manage to agree on the course of the investigation.

Art

Murder Runs in the Family. Avon Books, 1997

Crane's daughter Debbie is getting married to Henry Lamont, and the subject of family histories comes up with genealogist Meg Bryan. When Meg's session with the sister is interrupted by a call from a local judge, the sisters are startled by the results. Meg has plunged from the ninth floor of the courthouse, supposedly a suicide, but the sisters have decided it could be a murder.

Genealogy

Murder Makes Waves. Avon Books, 1997

Hollowell decides to vacation with her sister in Florida, where Crane knows everybody. She also knows the body when one washes ashore on the beach. The sisters launch an investigation into the death that leads them to some slightly shady real estate dealings.

Florida, Destin

Murder Gets a Life. Avon Books, 1998

Crane's son Ray has just married Sunshine Dabbs, and she is determined to investigate her new extended family. When invited to the family compound of Sunshine's grandmother, Meemaw Turkett, the sisters are shocked to discover a corpse in the woman's trailer.

Alabama, Locust Fork

Murder Shoots the Bull. Avon Books, 1999

The sisters have joined with their good friend Mitzi Phizer in an investment club. The club is distracted by the philandering behavior of Mitzi's husband, Arthur, and shocked when Arthur is accused of murdering her. The sisters rise to the occasion and launch an investigation.

Murder Carries a Torch. Avon Books , 2000

Cousin Pukey Lukey's wife of 40 years has run off with a house painter and preacher named Monk Crawford, and the sisters agree to set out on her trail. On the top of Chandler Mountain, in a church where snake handling is common practice, the sisters discover their cousin injured, with a dead redhead as his companion.

Alabama, Chandler Mountain

Murder Boogies with Elvis. Avon Books, 2001

The civic-minded sisters are in attendance at the fundraiser to restore the glory of a statue of the god Vulcan. The finale is a display of 30 Elvis imitators, one of whom dies on stage. Crane's future husband was standing next to the victim at the time of his death, so the sisters decide to investigate.

Carolyn G. Hart ✍

Annie Laurance/Max Darling

Death on Demand is the mystery bookstore owned by Laurance, located on the island of Broward's Rock off the coast of South Carolina. Part of the fun of reading Hart's books is that readers can follow clues about other great mystery novels while reading these cases. As Hart makes reference to the greats who preceded her in the field, she also creates two separate levels of enjoyment in her books. This series includes a plucky-couple relationship with Annie's eventual husband, Max Darling, the dilettante private eye, playing an equal role as detective. Readers may also enjoy Anne George, Frances and Richard Lockridge, Joan Hess, or Katherine Hall Page. See the author's website at http://www.carolynhart.com. **Soft-boiled.** Series subject: **Teams**.

Death on Demand. Bantam Books, 1987

When author Elliot Morgan dies during a weekly gathering of the Sunday Night Regulars, killed by a poisoned dart, it lands Laurance in the hot seat as suspect number one. Teamed with her rich boyfriend Darling, the two amateurs try to solve the mystery and save Laurance's reputation and her store.

Bibliomystery · South Carolina, Broward's Rock

Design for Murder. Bantam Books, 1988

The Historical Preservation Society's annual house tour is going to include a mystery night designed by Laurance. When the unpopular Corinne Webster, Grande Dame of Chastain, is murdered, the evidence points to Laurance and she must launch an investigation to protect herself.

Mystery games · South Carolina, Chastain · Theater

Something Wicked. Bantam Books, 1988

Arsenic and Old Lace is a fine old mystery play, but in the version that is being produced on the island, there are as many nefarious happenings backstage among the cast, including Laurance and Darling, as there are on stage during the play. When the bad feelings eventually lead to murder, Laurance decides to investigate because this time the evidence points at Darling. AG AN

South Carolina, Broward's Rock · Theater

Honeymoon with Murder. Bantam Books, 1989

No plucky couple can ever enjoy their wedding day, and Laurance and Darling are no exception. When their honeymoon is just about to begin, the two discover that bookstore assistant Ingrid Jones has disappeared and the dead body of the island's peeping tom, Jessie Penrick, is on her living room floor. Wedding or no wedding, this couple never hesitates in launching a rescue of their employee. AN

South Carolina, Broward's Rock · Weddings

A Little Class on Murder. Doubleday, 1989

Invited to teach a class on the three great female mystery writers at Chastain Community College, Laurance is present when a series of exposés in the college paper leads to a suicide. She finds many motives among the school population, but two more deaths occur before she can discover the truth with the help of some students who try to use the methods of the old masters. MA

Academia · South Carolina, Chastain

Deadly Valentine. Doubleday, 1990

Laurance's marriage to Darling is tested when a Valentine's Day celebration is spoiled by the attentions directed at Darling by her next-door neighbor, Sydney Cahill, wife of a shipping magnate. The arrival of Darling's mother Laurel unexpectedly finds her implicated in murder when Sydney's body is discovered in a gazebo.

Holidays · South Carolina, Broward's Rock · Valentine's Day

The Christie Caper. Bantam Books, 1991

To celebrate the one hundredth anniversary of Agatha Christie's birth, Laurance decides to host an international Christie convention on the island. Many of the attendees are taking things too seriously when Neil Bledson, despised book critic, finds his life threatened twice during the Christie Treasure Hunt. Is it because he revealed he is about to write a scandalous biography of Christie?

Authors · Bibliomystery · South Carolina, Broward's Rock

Southern Ghost. Bantam Books, 1992

Once again finding another woman's attention being focused on Darling, Laurance flies to his rescue when the beautiful, blonde Courtney Kimball disappears and Darling has to be bailed out of jail. The mystery seems to center on the Tarrant family and a 40-year-old murder.

South Carolina, Chastain

Mint Julep Murder. Bantam Books, 1995

When Laurance agrees to attend the Dixie Book Festival as the author liaison to those nominated for the coveted Dixie Book Festival Medallion, she does not expect trouble. However, the egos swirling around the nominees create tension, which is ratcheted up when publisher Kenneth Hazlitt arrives on the island toting a novel of tell-all secrets of those same Southern writers. When a poisoning occurs and Laurance's fingerprints are on the glass, she is in deep trouble again.

Authors · South Carolina, Hilton Head Island · Publishing

Yankee Doodle Dead. Avon Books, 1998

Northerner and retired Brigadier General, Charlton "Bud" Hatch, is so unacceptable to the island community that he is about to get tossed off the Library Board. His control over the Fourth of July celebration has angered so many people that he ends up shot during the festivities. Despite the fact that she could not stand the man, Laurance decides to do her civic duty and investigate.

Fourth of July · Holidays · South Carolina, Broward's Rock

White Elephant Dead. Avon Books, 1999

A blackmailer has convinced prominent citizens to make valuable donations to the island's annual Women's Club White Elephant Sale, or certain bits of information will be made public. When a storm hits the island and a volunteer for the sale is killed trying to make a pickup of some donations, Laurance feels driven to investigate.

Blackmail · South Carolina, Broward's Rock

Sugar Plum Death. Morrow, 2000

Marguerite Dumaney, an aging movie star, has gathered a list of guests for her annual Christmas and birthday bash, one of whom is Darling's long-estranged father. Dumaney has also fallen under the spell of the new age preaching of Dr. Emory Swanson, and when she alters her will, a death occurs that leaves Darling defending his long-lost father.

Christmas · Holidays · South Carolina, Broward's Rock · Wills

April Fool Dead. Morrow, 2002

A simple promotion for her mystery bookstore on April Fool's Day is intended to promote the visit of mystery author Emma Clyde. When a counterfeit flyer ruins the store's reputation and makes some serious accusations, Darling has to scramble to restore Laurence's. Then the accusations lead to murder.

April Fool's Day · Holidays · South Carolina, Broward's Rock

Carolyn G. Hart ✍

Henrie O

Henrietta O'Dwyer is a retired newspaper reporter whose cases take her all over the American landscape. This series is darker than the series featuring Laurance and Darling that is listed above. Readers may also enjoy Sujata Massey or Nancy Pickard. See the author's website at http://www.carolynhart.com. **Traditional**.

Dead Man's Island. Bantam Books, 1993

An attempted poisoning in New York so angers media tycoon Chase Prescott that he defies his murderer to follow him to an isolated island. There, with a hurricane in progress, a group gathers that includes Prescott's old flame, Henrie O. She is unable to prevent his death, but she is able to investigate it. AG

South Carolina, Dead Man's Island

Scandal in Fair Haven. Bantam Books, 1994

Relaxing in her friend Margaret Frazier's mountain cabin, the last thing Henrie O. expects is death. But when Margaret's nephew is accused of murdering his wife, Patty Fay, Henrie O. helps an old friend's family.

Tennessee, Fair Haven

Death in Lover's Lane. Avon Books, 1997

Teaching journalism at Thorndyke University in Missouri, Henrie O. is challenged by one of students. Maggie Winslow wants to investigate three unrelated and unsolved local crimes, and Henrie O. encourages her. But when Maggie is killed, Henrie O. finds she needs to step out of the classroom and onto the case.

Academia · Missouri, Derry Hills

Death in Paradise. Avon Books, 1998

A mysterious communication arrives at Henrie O.'s doorstep hinting that her husband's death on a Hawaiian island six years prior may not have been an accident. Richard had fallen off an island cliff, but Henrie O. packs up and goes to the island paradise to discover if he was pushed.

Hawaii, Kattai

Death on the River Walk. Avon Books, 1999

Iris Chavez had a job on the famed River Walk in San Antonio at the Tesoros Gallery, and when she goes missing, Henrie O. flies to the Texas town to conduct an investigation. When the gallery's employees and owner, Maria Elena Garza, seem disinterested in the case, Henrie O.'s investigative radar begins to operate.

Texas, San Antonio

Resort to Murder. Morrow, 2001

A woman in her seventies and one who is also recovering from pneumonia is not inclinded to travel to Bermuda for the wedding of her grandchildren's father. A re-marriage can be tough on a family, and when Henry O.'s son-in-law, Lloyd Drake, decides to marry the beautiful Connor Bailey, it upsets certain members of the family to the point where it may have roused the spirit of the dead.

Caribbean, Bermuda · Weddings

Joan Hess ✍

Claire Malloy

One of two Arkansas series that Hess writes (see also the Police Chief Arly Hanks series), this one features a bookstore owner named Claire Malloy. One of the appeals to the series is Malloy's troubled relationship with her teenaged daughter, Caron. Light but not entirely cozy, the stories take advantage of the unique landscape and the secondary characters to create the proper atmosphere within The Book Depot. Using humor and humorous situations is this series' strength. The cases can be recommended to soft-boiled and traditional mystery readers. Readers may also enjoy M. C. Beaton (Agatha Raisin), Anne George, or Carolyn G. Hart (Annie Laurance/Max Darling). See the author's website at http://www.joanhess.com. **Soft-boiled/Traditional**. Series subjects: **Arkansas, Farberville · Humor**.

Strangled Prose. St. Martin's Press, 1986

The Book Depot is hosting romance author Azalea Twilight and launching the publication of *Professor of Passion*. Azalea is really Malloy's friend Mildred Twiller, or at least Malloy thought she was her friend until feminist protestor Maggie reads out loud from the book at the signing, and Malloy discovers her own life is a part of the story. When Mildred is murdered, it looks like Malloy may be one of the suspects.

Academia · Authors · Bibliomystery

The Murder at the Murder at the Mimosa Inn. St. Martin's Press, 1986

Malloy thought it would be fun to dress as her favorite detective and take part in the mystery play being held at the Mimosa Inn, so she even brought along her daughter Caron. But when the pretend turns to real and organizer Harmon Crundall is killed, Malloy must practice the same skills as the fictional detectives she so admires.

Mystery games · Theater

Dear Miss Demeanor. St. Martin's Press, 1987

Why Malloy would agree to be the substitute teacher at Faberville High School, especially the high school attended by her own daughter Caron, is up for question. But it turns out Caron wants her detective mom on the premises to discover who has embezzled from the school journalism accounts. Who knew the principal would fall down dead from a poisoning?

Academia

A Really Cute Corpse. St. Martin's Press, 1988

Malloy finds herself the director of Farberville's Miss Thurberfest beauty pageant. She thinks her problems are the contestants, until someone sabotages the stage and tries to kill the queen. When murder does occur, the amateur detective knows she needs to find the truth.

Beauty pageants

A Diet to Die For. St. Martin's Press, 1989

Maribeth Galleston is the heiress to the Farber fortune, but she is not happy with the way she looks. To shed pounds, she enrolls at the Ultima Diet Center. Maribeth looks great, but begins to act erratic, and when she loses control of her car and kills someone, Malloy decides to step in and see if she can figure out what is happening.

Roll Over and Play Dead. St. Martin's Press, 1991

Malloy has agreed to watch Emily Parchester's two basset hounds, Nick and Nora, while Emily takes a trip. But when Caron is left in charge and the two dogs are dognapped, Malloy finds herself on the trail of animal suppliers for labs and men like Newton Churls. When Churls is killed by one of his own pit bulls, Malloy continues to investigate to rescue her charges.

Dogs

Death by the Light of the Moon. St. Martin's Press, 1992

Invited to Malloy Manor, the ancestral home of her father, Caron discover that she and her mother Malloy have walked into a gothic novel. Before Grandmother Justicia can distribute her estate to her gathered relatives, she is found drowned in the local bayou.

Louisiana · Wills

Poisoned Pins. Dutton, 1993

The Kappa Theta Eta house is next door to the Malloys, and it is a source of never-ending irritation to Malloy. When Caron is recruited by one of the sorority sisters to be a My Beautiful Self sales consultant, Malloy has a reason to worry when one sales girl is found dead in an alley.

Tickled to Death. Dutton, 1994

Malloy is concerned that her friend Luanne's affair may be with a man who has killed his two previous wives. Dick Cissel is a dentist and may be dangerous, but Luanne asks Malloy to clear her man of all suspicions.

Arkansas, Turnstone Lake

Busy Bodies. Dutton, 1995

The neighbors are worried when interactive artist Zeno Gorgias moves onto their block and sets up a nearly nude model in a coffin in his frontyard. Hope arrives in the form of the artist's ex-wife, who comes to town intent on having him committed. However, when the artist's house burns and the body in the coffin is a real body, Malloy finds herself searching for the answers to this strange behavior.

Art

Closely Akin to Murder. Dutton, 1996

Malloy receives a phone call from a long-lost cousin she thought had been dead for 30 years. Instead, Ronnie Landonwood has been on the run from a murder charge, accused of killing a man who tried to rape her in Mexico. Now that Ronnie is about to be nominated for the Nobel Prize, she is deathly afraid her past will come back to haunt her. Despite misgivings, Malloy finds herself in Acapulco investigating an old murder and dodging current danger.

Mexico, Acapulco

A Holly, Jolly Murder. Dutton, 1997

Malloy finds her customer in search of New Age titles is none other than Malthea Hendlerson, the self-proclaimed Arch Druid of the Sacred Grove of Keltria. Invited to attend the winter solstice, Malloy instead finds that the wealthy supporter of the Druids has been killed.

Christmas · Holidays

A Conventional Corpse. St. Martin's Minotaur, 1999

When the local organizer of the "Murder Come to Campus" mystery convention is too ill to run the event, Malloy is drafted to take charge of the five mystery authors in attendance. When the hated editor Roxanne Small, makes an unscheduled appearance, the event turns from a fun time about murder to a real case for Malloy and her cop boyfriend, Peter Rosen. A suspicious accident, a missing person, and a missing cat complicate the bookstore owner's life.

Authors

***Out On a Limb.** St. Martin's Minotaur, 2002

Laurie King ✍

Mary Russell/Sherlock Holmes

It is dangerous to play with a legend, but King has proven herself worthy of tackling the best. Her creation, Mary Russell, is a protégé and accomplice to the legend, Sherlock Holmes. Beginning as a teenage waif and maturing into a full partner, the relationship that develops between the two characters is almost as important as the mystery cases that attract their detective skills. Less pastiche and more historical, these novels can be recommended to readers who are not particularly Holmesian by nature. They can be also be recommended to traditional mystery readers. Readers may also enjoy Arthur Conan Doyle, Sharyn Newman, and Anne Perry. See the author's website at http://www.laurierking.com. **Traditional/Historical**. Series subjects: **Historical (1800–1899) · Holmes, Sherlock · Teams · Victorian England**.

The Beekeeper's Apprentice. St. Martin's Press, 1994

Fifteen-year-old Russell is living with her aunt when she encounters the master lying in a field, studying bees. Despite his being semi-retired, he tutors the girl in his ways. When they both become victims of a bombing attempt, she is a capable detective able to stand side-by-side with a legend.

England, Sussex Downs

A Monstrous Regiment of Women. St. Martin's Press, 1995

Russell finds a friend from her Oxford days in London who provides the introduction to Margery Childe, the leader of the sect called The New Temple of God. When deaths begin to occur within the circle of the sect, Russell uses her detective skills, and her mentor Holmes, to solve the crimes.

Cults · England, London

A Letter of Mary. St. Martin's Press, 1997

Russell and Holmes are enjoying their private pursuits in Sussex when an archeologist named Dorothy Ruskin brings them a relic from the Holy Land. When Dorothy dies in an accident, the dynamic pair decides to investigate.

Antiquities · England, Sussex

The Moor. St. Martin's Press, 1998

Invited by the Reverend Baring-Gould to return to the moors and the scene of one of his great adventures, Holmes finds himself on the trail of a sighting of a phantom coach that haunts the lonely landscape. When Holmes asks for Russell's help, the young detective leaves Oxford and walks the same landscape that Dr. Watson had tread those many years ago.

England, Dartmoor

O Jerusalem. Bantam Books, 1999

Mycroft summons Holmes to Palestine, where the detective and his ward find themselves greeted by two mysterious Arabs who put them through a series of tests.

The next rite of passage finds the pair disguised as Bedouins so that they can investigate the deaths caused by tensions between the various ethnic groups struggling for power in this land.

Palestine

Justice Hall. Bantam Books, 2002

Two characters from *O Jerusalem* return to the lives of this detective couple when they request an investigation into the combat-related execution of a British soldier, which affects who is heir to Justice Hall.

England, London · France · World War I

Sharyn McCrumb ✍

Elizabeth MacPherson

Forensic anthropology provides the door to solving mysteries in this series by Sharyn McCrumb. However, its real strength may be its use of the lore of the Appalachian territory, and the insight that McCrumb received from her own relatives' years of preaching on the Appalachian circuit. These novels have elements of the cozy, and provide an interesting love life for MacPherson. MacPherson's family also plays a big part in these novels. However, these books should not be dismissed by traditional mystery readers, to whom they may also be recommended. McCrumb fans may also enjoy Patricia Cornwell, Aaron Elkins, and Nancy Pickard. See the author's website at http://www.sharynmccrumb.com/. **Soft-boiled/ Traditional.**

Sick of Shadows. Avon Books, 1984

Eileen Chandler is about to marry the man of her dreams, but many in the family feel he is a nightmare. When cousin MacPherson is present at the wedding, she is able to step in when murder occurs.

Georgia, Chandler Grove · Weddings

Lovely in Her Bones. Avon Books, 1985

To determine if an Indian tribe has a legal claim to the land they want, MacPherson joins an archaeological dig to prove their origins. When the leader of the dig, Professor Lerche, is murdered and the town proves very hostile to the project, MacPherson turns detective.

Archeology · Forensics · Virginia, Sarvice Valley

Highland Laddie Gone. Avon Books, 1986

Colin Campbell spoils the revels when he is murdered during the annual Glencoe Mountain Games, just part of his family legacy of ill will amongst the Scots. MacPherson is on hand to launch an investigation, and a second death places a greater emphasis on the job.

Virginia, Meadow Creek

Paying the Piper. Ballantine, 1988

Joining an expedition to Scotland, MacPherson is part of a crew that does not mix well. An American is murdered, and MacPherson has begun an investigation to find out why when a second death places her life in danger.

Archeology · Scotland, Edinburgh

The Windsor Knot. Ballantine, 1990

MacPherson's fiancé, Cameron Dawson, is invited to meet the Queen. Only a spouse can accompany him, so MacPherson pushes up their wedding date. Their plans are set aside though when widow Clorine Mason is informed her husband was killed in a car accident. Then who died in the car accident five years prior, and who is in the urn holding her husband's ashes?

Forensics · Scotland, Edinburgh · Virginia, Chandler Grove

Missing Susan. Ballantine, 1991

Visiting England's most famous murder sites with a group of American tourists, MacPherson never expects to need to investigate a new one. But when the desperate tour guide agrees to eliminate Susan Cohen for an American businessman named Aaron Kosminski, there is hell to pay on the tour.

England

MacPherson's Lament. Ballantine, 1992

Personal family problems bring MacPherson back to Virginia where her lawyer-brother is in jail for fraud, and her parents are ending a 25-year marriage. Her brother Bill has sold an antebellum mansion that his seller did not own, and MacPherson needs to discover if this ties in with the long-missing Confederate treasury rumored to be buried in Danville.

Virginia, Danville

If I Killed Him When I Met Him. Ballantine, 1995

Teamed with her brother Bill's law firm as their investigator, MacPherson finds herself working two cases. The first involves the shooting by Eleanor Royden of her ex-husband and his new wife. The second case finds Donna Jean Morgan suspected when her bigamist husband dies under mysterious circumstances. 

Virginia, Danville

The PMS Outlaws. Ballantine, 2000

MacPherson has checked into a psychiatric hospital to battle the depression brought on by the death of her husband. Meanwhile, her brother Bill has bought a permanent residence for his law firm with one catch: someone is still living there. Bill's partner A. P. Powell is chasing a gang of two, known as the PMS Outlaws, who steal men's money and leave them in compromising positions.

Virginia, Danville

Sujata Massey ✍

Rei Shimura

Rei Shimura, an English teacher living in Tokyo, is trying to understand the conflicts between her American and Japanese backgrounds. Rei's other skills lie in the area of antiques, and her cases often involve the complex relationships of a piece of antiquity to a modern drama. To her surprise, she finds herself constantly challenged by death, as well as the culture she lives in. Readers may also enjoy Carolyn G. Hart (Henrie O.), Nancy Pickard, and S. J. Rozan. See the author's website at http://interbridge.com/sujata. **Traditional.**

The Salaryman's Wife. HarperPaperbacks, 1997

Shimura is determined to make it in Tokyo, even though she struggles on her small salary as an English teacher. Able to travel to the town of Shiroyama where there is an ancient castle, she is the one who discovers the dead body of the wife of a very powerful businessman. Her attitude towards the police called to investigate leads her deeper into this strange case of murder in the snow. AG

Japan, Shiroyama

Zen Attitude. HarperPaperbacks, 1998

Back in Tokyo with her new boyfriend, Shimura makes a decision to purchase a chest of drawers. When the chest leads her to the death of the con man that sold it to her, she finds herself required to investigate a murder again.

Antiquities • Japan, Tokyo

The Flower Master. HarperCollins, 1999

Ikebana is the art of flower arranging in Japan, and Shimura is taking this class in a vain attempt to forget that her antiques business is floundering and so is her love life. When her instructor, Sakura Sato, is murdered with ikebana scissors, it is Shimura who discovers the body and discovers herself in trouble again. MA

Flower arranging • Japan, Tokyo

The Floating Girl. HarperCollins, 2000

Shimura is now writing for the *Gaijin Times*, an English-language magazine published in Tokyo. When assigned to write about manga, or Japanese animation, she discovers a comic book that piques her interest. When one of the three creators is murdered, Shimura starts an investigation to find out why.

Animation • Comic books • Japan, Tokyo

The Bride's Kimono. HarperCollins, 2001

Sent to Washington, D.C., to deliver some antique kimonos to the museum of Asian Arts, Shimura is shocked to find one stolen. Then, one of the women who accompanied her is murdered, and Shimura's passport is found with the dead body. When her ex-boyfriend Hugh Glendinning appears to help, things really get complicated for the antiques dealer.

Antiquities • Washington, D.C.

Walter Mosley ✍

Easy Rawlings

Revealing the African-American experience in America through a set of historical novels, Mosley recounts the travails of Easy Rawlings as he tries to make a spot for himself in America. Mosley takes cases to make money or as favors to friends, and occassionally out of a sense of outrage for justice. His friend Mouse is one of the most interesting and dangerous sidekicks ever created for a detective. These novels should be recommended to hardboiled mystery readers. Readers may also enjoy Terence Faherty and Don Winslow. See the author's website at http://www.twbookmark.com/features/waltermosley/index.html. **Hard-boiled/Historical**. Series subjects: **African-American · California, Los Angeles · Historical (1900–1999) · Race**.

Devil in a Blue Dress. Norton, 1990

Rawlings has just been laid off at the defense plant, and he needs some money. Hired by a connected white man named Dewitt Albright, Rawlings is told to find a blonde named Daphne Monet, who likes to frequent the black jazz joints of L.A.

A Red Death. Norton, 1991

When the IRS pressures Rawlings, he finds himself infiltrating the First African Baptist Church on behalf of the FBI. They think a former Polish resistance fighter has stolen some defense plans, and Rawlings is the man to figure out how.

White Butterfly. Norton, 1992

In 1956 L.A., no one cares when three black barflies are murdered, but when the fourth is The White Butterfly, a stripper and the daughter of a powerful lawyer, L.A.P.D. detective Quinten Naylor asks for Rawlings's help in his investigation. Rawlings is uneasy because the chief suspect seems to be his acquaintance Mouse.

Black Betty. Norton, 1994

On the edge of the dream in 1961, but deeply in debt, Rawlings accepts money from a white private eye to locate Elizabeth "Black Betty" Eady. The woman's beauty has left a trail of hurt and angry people, and while Rawlings deals with this, he must also worry about Mouse's imminent release from jail.

Bad Boy Brawly Brown. Little, Brown, 2002

Rawlins is asked by Alva Torres to persuade her son, Brawly Brown, to leave the radical black movement Urban Revolutionary Party. When Rawlins is the one who discovers Torres's dead ex-husband, he finds himself trying to separate politics from murder during America's turbulent mid-sixties.

Sharan Newman ✍

Catherine LeVendeur

The Middle Ages provides a rich tapestry for Newman, as her historically accurate mysteries try to dispel some of the myths of women's roles during this period. Set in twelfth-century France, this series follows LeVendeur from her days as a young novice in a convent into womanhood. They can be recommended to traditional mystery readers. Readers may also enjoy Laurie King (Mary Russell/Sherlock Holmes), Ellis Peters, and Steven Saylor. See the author's website at http://www.hevanet.com/sharan/Levendeur.html. **Traditional/Historical**. Series subjects: **Historical (1100–1199) · Religion**.

Death Comes As Epiphany. Tor, 1993

LeVendeur is a young novice-scholar in the Convent of the Paraclete, where she has come to conquer her sin of pride. She is asked by the abbess to uncover a Psalter that falsely accused theologian Ablard in a heresy plot. When she travels to the Abby of St. Denis, she becomes embroiled in a the death of an old sculptor and meets his apprentice, Edgar. MA

France, Paris

The Devil's Door. Forge, 1994

When a wealthy countess is beaten by unknown assailants, she seeks refuge at the Convent of the Paraclete. Her dying wish is to join the order, but LeVendeur wishes only to discover the truth behind this awful crime, even if it means delaying her rendezvous with her beloved Edgar.

France, Paris

The Wandering Arm. Forge, 1995

The mummified arm of St. Aldhelm has been stolen from Salisbury Cathedral in England and is now in Paris, where murder and treachery surround it. When Edgar, now married to LeVendeur, is asked to find the relic, he needs to fight the anti-Semitism of the day when suspicions fall on the Jewish community.

France, Paris

Strong As Death. Forge, 1996

Their loving marriage has only produced miscarriages and a stillborn, so LeVendeur and Edgar decide to make a pilgrimage to the monastery at Compostela to petition St. James for a healthy birth. When other pilgrims are murdered along the route, LeVendeur practices her passion for detection.

Spain

Cursed in the Blood. Forge, 1998

Edgar's two oldest brothers have been murdered in Scotland, and the family now travels to that far-off, war-torn land. When his Scottish family proves unloving, LeVendeur becomes separated from Edgar and falls out of their protection. To protect her son, she must be brave.

Scotland, Wedderlie, Berwickshire

The Difficult Saint. Forge, 1999

LeVendeur's estranged sister Agnes comes to Paris seeking no love, only money, for she is to be married to a German lord. When news reaches Paris that Agnes's husband has been murdered, LeVendeur sails for another foreign land to try and solve a murder.

Germany, Trier

To Wear the White Cloak. Forge, 2000

When LeVendeur returns from France, her life is disturbed because a Knight Templar has been discovered murdered in her home. The investigation puts her family in the spotlight and threatens to reveal a long-held family secret that could threaten their health and well being.

France, Paris • Knight Templars

***Heresy.** Forge, 2002

Katherine Hall Page ✍

Faith Sibley Fairchild

Having given up a career as a caterer and moved to a small Massachusetts town to marry her clergyman lover, Fairchild finds that in a small town setting murder still occurs. This series manages to combine an interest in food with an interest in crime, and each book comes with recipes. It can be recommended to soft-boiled or traditional mystery readers. Readers may also enjoy Jill Churchill, Diane Mott Davidson, and Valerie Wolzien. **Soft-boiled/Traditional.**

The Body in the Belfry. St. Martin's Press, 1990

Fairchild thinks life in a small town is boring until she discovers the body of Cindy Shepherd in the church belfry. Shepherd had a reputation as a tramp, but she was also the president of the church's Young People's Club. So, Fairchild decides a little amateur sleuthing may clear the name of her husband's church. AG

Massachusetts, Aleford • Religion

The Body in the Kelp. St. Martin's Press, 1991

On the island of Sanpere, while her husband is in New Hampshire at a religious retreat, Fairchild becomes involved in a treasure hunt whose clues are found in a patchwork quilt created by Matilda Prescott. When the hunt leads to the death of one of the island's residents, Fairchild decides to play detective again.

Maine, Sanpere Island • Quilts

The Body in the Bouillon. St. Martin's Press, 1991

Fairchild's aunt has an old friend named Howard Perkins, and in his last communication before his death in Hubbard House, he had implied he needed the help of a detective. As a volunteer Pink Lady, Fairchild has access to the death house, so she decides to investigate this murder and help set her relative's mind at ease.

Massachusetts, Aleford

The Body in the Vestibule. St. Martin's Press, 1992

Off on a holiday to write a cookbook on the French provinces, Fairchild decides to throw a dinner party. After the guests leave, she is shocked to discover a corpse. When she calls the local cops, they arrive only to discover one thing: no body.

Bibliomystery · Cooking · France, Lyon

The Body in the Cast. St. Martin's Press, 1993

Aleford is all agog as an updated version of *The Scarlet Letter* is to be filmed in their hometown. Having decided to jump back into catering, Fairchild is crushed when one of the film company's crew gets food poisoning. To protect her reputation, she needs to prove that the poisoning was deliberate.

Cooking · Film · Massachusetts, Aleford

The Body in the Basement. St. Martin's Press, 1994

When a contractor fails to pour the concrete on time, Pix Miller, Fairchild's friend and neighbor, is quick to spot the body buried in the basement of the Fairchild's new summer cottage. With Fairchild stuck in Aleford, Pix decides to play amateur detective and help her friend in the process.

Maine, Sanpere Island

The Body in the Bog. Morrow, 1996

Miss Lora, Ben's nursery-school teacher, has been receiving threatening phone calls, and Reverend Tom thinks his wife would make a great detective. When the church is also swept up in the controversial sale of Beecher's Bog because it lies directly behind the church, Fairchild's job is to see if the two cases are directly related.

Massachusetts, Aleford · Religion

The Body in the Fjord. Morrow, 1997

Pix Miller is at it again when she travels to Norway to investigate the disappearance of a family friend. When her investigation gets to close to the truth, she finds herself nearing victim status.

Norway

The Body in the Bookcase. Morrow, 1998

To take a break from her catering, Fairchild makes some parish calls only to discover the bound and gagged body of Sarah Winslow. When her friend dies, Fairchild is determined to catch the thieves and murderers.

Massachusetts, Aleford

The Body in the Big Apple. Morrow, 1999

As a prequel to her life in Aleford, this book reveals how Fairchild first got into detecting. Emma Stanstead, an old classmate of Fairchild's, tells her that she is being blackmailed. If the truth were revealed, Emma's politically ambitious husband's career would be ruined.

Blackmail · New York, New York

The Body in the Moonlight. Morrow, 2001

Fairchild has been asked to take a catering job when the First Parish asks her to create a Murder Mystery Game to kick off the fundraiser for the restoration of the historic Ballou House. When Gwen Lord, one of the guests, topples over after being poisoned by the amaretto topping of Fairchild's dessert, she finds herself embroiled in another murder mystery.

Cooking · Massachusetts, Aleford · Mystery games

The Body in the Bonfire. Morrow, 2002

Fairchild is asked to teach a course called Cooking for Idiots during Mansfield Academy's upcoming Winter Project Term. While at the prestigious prep school, she learns of the racial harassment of African-American Daryl Martin. As she tries to teach and investigate, a body is found in a bonfire, and the amateur detective is now chasing a murderer.

Academia · Catering · Cooking · Massachusetts · Race

Elizabeth Peters ✍

Vicky Bliss

Art history is Bliss's specialty, and also her entrée into the world of murder. Her Ph.D in Medieval European history adds some interesting aspects to her career in crime, as does the author's use of humor. Mostly it is the detective's plucky spirit that appeals to the reader. Readers may also enjoy Aaron Elkins or Nancy Pickard. See the author's website at http://www.mpmbooks.com. **Soft-boiled/Traditional.** Series subject: **Antiquities.**

Borrower of the Night. Dodd, Mead, 1973

On the search in Germany for a centuries-old artifact carved by the Gothic artisan, Tilman Riemenschneider, Bliss is challenging an arrogant young man in her party. But what she discovers is that an old castle can hold many mysteries, and one of them is a threat to her.

Germany, Rothenburg

Street of the Five Moons. Dodd, Mead, 1978

A crumpled scrap of paper found in a dead man's pocket leads Bliss to Rome in search of the source for some forged jewels that are appearing on the market.

Italy, Rome

Silhouette in Scarlet. Congdon, 1983

Bliss is off again in search of an ancient artifact, the Karlsohm Chalice. Her trip to Sweden leads her on a merry adventure.

Sweden, Stockholm

Trojan Gold. Atheneum, 1987

Sir John Smythe has tantalized Bliss with clues in the past, but this time he may need her talents as a detective when the whereabouts of the gold of Troy is sought. Not having been seen since it disappeared in 1945, Bliss discovers that her knowledge may be deadly.

Germany, Munich

Night Train to Memphis. Warner, 1994

Asked by an intelligence agency to investigate on the river Nile, Bliss is expected to anticipate and prevent the theft of some Egyptian artifacts. What worries Bliss the most is that she may be on the trail of her sometime lover, Sir John Symthe.

Egypt

Elizabeth Peters ✍

Jacqueline Kirby

No librarian mystery lover should fail to read the series of books featuring the heroine Kirby. As time goes by, Kirby shifts careers, and she becomes a romance writer. Feisty by nature, she also has some humorous characteristics that make her a slightly daffy detective. Readers may also enjoy Carolyn G. Hart (Annie Laurance/Max Darling) and Joan Hess (Claire Malloy). See the author's website at http://www.mpmbooks.com. **Soft-boiled/Traditional.**

The Seventh Sinner. Dodd, Mead, 1972

Jean Suttman considers herself the luckiest girl in the world to have a fellowship to study in Rome. She makes the acquaintance of a fellow traveler named Kirby, and that is fortunate when Jean discovers the body of her fellow student Albert, a pushy boy no one had liked.

Italy, Rome

The Murders of Richard III. Dodd, Mead, 1974

When Kirby is invited to an English country estate to join a group of Richard III supporters, it sounds like a fun trip. That is, until someone decides to re-create the famous fifteenth-century crimes.

England, Yorkshire

Die for Love. Congdon, 1984

Kirby is attending a romance writer's conference in the Big Apple. She meets author Valerie Valentine, who asks for her help as a detective while inscribing Kirby's copy of *Slave of Lust*. A gossip columnist is already dead, and Val does not want to be next.

Authors • Bibliomystery • New York, New York

Naked Once More. Warner, 1989

Having given up librarianship to become a best-selling novelist, Kirby is not quite ready to abandon detective work. Asked to write the sequel to the national bestseller *Naked in the Ice*, she must first determine the cause of the original author's suicide. AG

Authors • Bibliomystery • West Virginia, Pine Grove

Elizabeth Peters ✍

Amelia Peabody

Dilettante spinster Peabody is free to roam the late-Victorian world as an explorer of Egyptology, and her match with archaeologist Radcliffe Emerson makes for an interesting mystery duo. Eventually Peabody and Radcliffe have a son named Ramses, and as more time goes by, the minor characters begin to take major places on the mystery stage in this series. As historicals, these cases also provide a canvas for the changing world picture as the world prepares for war. Readers may also enjoy Aaron Elkins, Sharyn McCrumb (Elizabeth MacPherson), and Anne Perry. See the author's website at http://www.mpmbooks.com. **Soft-boiled/Traditional/ Historical.** Series subjects: **Archeology · Historical (1900–1999)**

Crocodile on the Sandbank. Dodd, Mead, 1975

Having inherited her father's money, Peabody decides to travel to Egypt. Her interest in archeology brings her into contact with Radcliffe Emerson, and she is able to save his life, win his heart, and solve the case of the walking mummy.

Egypt, Cairo

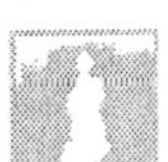

The Curse of the Pharaohs. Dodd, Mead, 1981

Now married to Radcliffe, Peabody finds herself uncovering the tomb at Luxor on behalf of the widow of Sir Henry Baskerville. A curse may lay over the expedition as the natives and the workers are falling prey to strange occurrences.

Egypt, Luxor

The Mummy Case. Congdon, 1985

Returning to Egypt to fulfill her lifelong ambition to open a pyramid, Peabody instead finds herself looking into the death of an antiquities dealer who may have been operating illegally.

Egypt, Cairo

Lion in the Valley. Atheneum, 1986

The Black Pyramid at Dahshoor may be Peabody's dream, but when Prince Kalenischeff is murdered, she must put aside her work to solve a crime. She protects the young woman sought as the most likely suspect, and finds herself battling an evil enemy she calls the Master Criminal.

Egypt, Dahshoor

The Deeds of the Disturber. Atheneum, 1988

Back home in Britain, Peabody becomes involved in a highly publicized case of death by fright when a nightwatchman in the British Museum is found dead on the floor before a mummy case. Peabody must show that a ghost cannot commit a crime.

England, London · Museums

The Last Camel Died at Noon. Warner, 1991

Setting out for the Sudan, Emerson and Peabody wish to explore the unexplored lost city of Napata. As the British fight a colonial war, the pair is asked to search for a missing explorer, Willoughby Forth, whose father has waited 14 years for his return.

Sudan

The Snake, the Crocodile and the Dog. Warner, 1992

Returning to the location where they first fell in love, Peabody is hoping to rekindle a little romance. She does not heed the warning contained in the fairytale she has translated from the ancient Egyptian, and she finds a snake, a crocodile, and a dog a danger to her, as once again she must face down the Master Criminal.

Egypt, Amarna

The Hippopotamus Pool. Warner, 1996

A masked stranger offers the location of a secret tomb, so Peabody and husband Emerson set sail for Thebes to find the tomb of Queen Tetisheri.

Egypt, Thebes

Seeing a Large Cat. Warner, 1997

A warning to stay away from the Valley of the Kings is not heeded by Peabody and Emerson, as they begin a new season of digs. Her son David is now old enough to be a lovestruck teenager, while her adopted daughter Nephret has designs on her own expedition. When Peabody's exploration of the mysterious site 20-A reveals the modern corpse of the fourth wife of Colonel Bellingham, she has another mystery to solve.

Egypt, Cairo

The Ape Who Guards the Balance. Avon Books, 1998

While attending a suffragettes' rally outside the home of Geoffrey Romer, one of the few remaining private collectors of Egyptian antiquities, a series of bizarre events at the protest soon embroil Peabody in grave personal danger. Departing for Egypt anyway with her beloved Emerson, she finds herself in the Valley of Kings where they soon acquire a papyrus of the Book of the Dead, and a woman's dead body is found in the Nile.

Egypt, Valley of the Kings

The Falcon at the Portal. Avon Books, 1999

Ramses's best friend David has married his cousin Lia, but then he is accused of selling ancient Egyptian artifacts that in reality are very good fakes. While Peabody is trying to lend aid there, a dead American appears in Emerson's excavation, and the summer dig season is in full swing.

Egypt

He Shall Thunder in the Sky. Morrow, 2000

As World War I approaches, Peabody and Emerson return to Egypt to begin another season of archeological digs. With war fervor in the air, their son Ramses's pacifist stand is not popular, and the nationalist fervor in Cairo is running rampant. As the political dangers cloud the air, Peabody discovers an artifact that may mean her archenemy, Sethos, has reemerged.

Egypt

Lord of the Silent. Morrow, 2001

It is 1915, and the entourage surrounding Peabody has sailed for Cairo to get back to digging and get away from further attempts to recruit her son Ramses into the Secret Service. But not even the sanctuary of a remote dig can keep the war's effects away from them, as tomb robbers are boldly destroying sacred sites. When a body is discovered at Luxor, the family is once again threatened by dangerous rivalries.

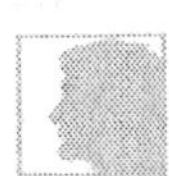

Egypt, Luxor

The Golden One. Morrow, 2002

Upon returning to Egypt for a new season of digging, the enterprise is interrupted when a tomb robber's corpse is found in the dig. Meanwhile, British intelligence sends Ramses to Gaza where he finds himself up against the ghost of the family's old enemy, Sethos.

Egypt, Gaza • Egypt, Luxor • World War I

Nancy Pickard ✍

Jenny Cain

As if running a philanthropic foundation were not enough, Cain finds herself involved in murder. Set in the small Massachusetts town of Port Frederick, thcsc traditional mysteries portray a modern career woman with a troubled family life. Readers who enjoy Pickard may also enjoy Laura Lippman or Sujata Massey. **Soft-boiled/Traditional**. Series subject: **Massachusetts, Port Frederick**.

Generous Death. Avon Books, 1984

Cain is director of the Port Frederick Civic Foundation, recipient of the charitable intentions of the town's wealthiest citizens. A body is discovered in the antique bed housed in the Oriental Wing of the Foundation's museum. When some more citizens end up murdered, Cain must find the killer—especially since a rhyme placed at the crime scene states that Cain will be the next victim.

Museums

Say No to Murder. Avon Books, 1985

The Liberty Harbor Restoration project should be a boon to the town with its new shops, museums, and restaurants. However, when someone uses a runaway truck to scare the Harbor committee, Cain is frustrated when the police's suspect is the one person she wishes to keep out of jail. AN

No Body. Scribner, 1986

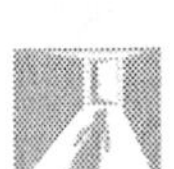

Port Frederick's cemetery is found to have nothing but empty graves, a fact so curious that Cain feels she must investigate. When a funeral home worker is killed, the focus on death moves to the present rather than the past.

Marriage Is Murder. Scribner, 1987

Marriage is in the making for Cain to her longtime friend, policeman Geof Bushfield, but only if she can get him over his depression regarding the high number of husbands killed by their battered wives in Port Frederick. The two work these cases from their own ends, with none of the women confessing to their crimes and no murder weapons found. MA

Dead Crazy. Scribner, 1988

MaryDell Paine wants the foundation's help to build a recreation hall for released mental patients, a cause Cain can support because her own mom is a psychiatric patient who will never recover. Finding herself in competition for the same land that a development company wants does not help her cause. When a released patient is accused of murder, she must work to save the man and her cause.

Mentally challenged

Bum Steer. Pocket, 1990

In Kansas to collect a $4 million dollar cattle ranch, Cain needs to talk to the donor, Cat Benet, but by the time she gets to the hospital, the donor is dead. While some suspicion falls on her, the more likely candidates are Cat's four ex-wives. AG

Kansas, Kansas City

I.O.U. Pocket, 1991

Cain's mom has died after years of care in a psychiatric hospital, but in her grief Cain is unable to remember who says to her, "Forgive me. It was an accident." For the first time, Cain begins to ask why her mother was the way she was, and who was responsible. AG MA

But I Wouldn't Want to Die There. Pocket, 1993

Cain's good friend Carol Margolis has just been killed, and Cain rushes off to New York to replace her at the Hart Foundation. When she discovers a cryptic message on Carol's answering machine, Cain begins to doubt the police version of the mugging that killed Carol.

New York, New York

Confession. Pocket, 1994

Cain is shocked the day a young stranger appears on her door claiming to be Geof's son. David Mayer wants nothing from his biological father except an investigation into the death of the man and woman who raised him.

Twilight. Pocket, 1995

Halloween has brought the Autumn Festival, sponsored by Cain's foundation. It is ill timed when Melissa Barney tells Cain her sad story: three weeks prior her husband had been killed hiking by a hit and run driver. Cain knows that a little girl had also died under the same circumstances in the same spot, and her investigation is started to prove that enough is enough.

Halloween · Holidays

Stephen White ✍

Alan Gregory

As a Boulder clinical psychologist, Dr. Alan Gregory uses his professional talents to profile the murderers who cross his path. Paired with his girlfriend, Lauren Crowder, a deputy D.A., he explores the reason behind the crimes that occur within his purview. His cases can be recommended to traditional and hardboiled mystery readers. Readers may also enjoy Jonathan Kellerman. See the author's website at http://www.authorstephenwhite.com. **Traditional/Hard-boiled**. Series subjects: **Colorado, Boulder · Psychology**.

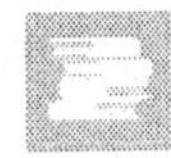

Privileged Information. Viking, 1991

When a female patient of his commits suicide, a newspaper campaign starts accusing the doctor of improper sexual conduct. How can he defend himself without violating the client privilege that is the basis of his treatment? When other patients of his begin to die, Gregory knows there has been breach somewhere in his office security and he needs to act.

Private Practices. Viking, 1993

Two witnesses scheduled to appear before a grand jury have died mysterious deaths, and detective Sam Purdy finds himself teamed with Gregory to try and find out why. As a second story, Gregory must care for a young man who is the sole survivor of an airplane crash that killed his family.

Higher Authority. Viking, 1994

Comedian Teresa Crowder has filed sexual harassment charges against Blythe Oaks, chief clerk for U.S. Supreme Court Justice Lester Horner. Teresa asks her sister Lauren Crowder, a deputy D.A. and Gregory's girlfriend, for help. When Oaks is killed, Lauren asks Gregory for help in bringing a killer to justice.

Utah, Salt Lake City

Harm's Way. Signet, 1996

Gregory's good friend Peter Arvin is found dying on the stage of a road production of *Miss Saigon*, the second victim in the company. The police want a profile and Peter's widow wants a perpetrator.

Colorado · Theater · Wyoming, Jackson Hole

Remote Control. Dutton, 1997

Lauren is jailed on charges that she killed the stalker menacing Emma Spire, the beautiful daughter of the assassinated Surgeon General of the United States. Gregory can work outside the legal system to explore, and when he discovers a connection between a biotech genius and Emma, he wonders if Lauren is being railroaded.

Critical Conditions. Dutton, 1998

Merritt Strait is a 15 year old who has tried to commit suicide, but when Gregory is called to administer to her, he discovers she is no ordinary person. Her family includes an investigative reporter, a psychologist, and another girl named Chaney, who is at the center of a medical tragedy.

Manner of Death. Dutton, 1999

A mass murderer has targeted Gregory and his long-lost love, Sawyer Sackett. Arnie Dresser is dead, and the connection between the three people is their years together at the University of Colorado Health Science Center. As Gregory works with Sawyer to save his life, he must also work to save his marriage.

Cold Case. Dutton, 2000

Gregory is asked by a private club of criminologists to look at a 10-year-old case involving the disappearance of two teenaged girls after they had visited the ranch of talk show host, Raymond Welle. Welle has covered a lot of ground since that day, and the land he owns could be very valuable, but an assassination attempt shows he may have made mistakes along the way.

The Program. Doubleday, 2001

In this book, Gregory is a secondary character involved in the life of the featured player, a New Orleans prosecutor named Kirsten Lord. Lord is in the witness protection program because her husband has been killed, and she wishes to protect her daughter from the same possibility. When things get tough, she is sent to Gregory for therapy, and eventually she finds herself placing her self in danger in order to save herself.

Warning Signs. Delacorte, 2002

D.A. Royal Peterson has been murdered with a blunt object in his own home, and suspicion falls on Boulder homicide cop, Lucy Tanner, the partner of Gregory's best friend, Sam Purdy. By coincidence, Gregory has heard some testimony from his client Naomi Bigg that might be the clue the police need to point out the murderer.

Valerie Wolzien ✍

Susan Henshaw

An upscale member of Hancock, Connecticut, Henshaw is in position to help out when murder affects her community. With the same precision as any golden age traditional, each player in these books assumes a position in the community that is being disturbed, and the fun is in knocking down each suspect to get to the criminal. Readers may also enjoy Jill Churchill, Diane Mott Davidson, Joan Hess, and Katherine Hall Page. See the author's website at http://www.nmomysteries.com. **Soft-boiled/Traditional**. Series subject: **Connecticut, Hancock**.

Murder at the PTA Luncheon. St. Martin's Press, 1988

The elementary school spring luncheon is destroyed when the PTA president downs a cyanide-laced canapé. Between car-pooling and running her household, vice-president Henshaw finds herself helping two cops investigate the murder.

Academia

The Fortieth Birthday Party. St. Martin's Press, 1989

The lovely Dawn Elliot, rumored to have had a lot of Hancock's men, returns to the town just as Henshaw turns 40. When her husband throws her a surprise party, Dawn ends up the biggest surprise: dead.

We Wish You a Merry Murder. Gold Medal, 1991

At Christmas time, Kelly Knowlson gets what she wanted: her husband has returned to her. Unfortunately, he is dead, and she is the prime suspect. Henshaw balances her holiday preparations with a little investigation.

Christmas • Holidays

All Hallow's Evil. Gold Medal, 1992

When a body is found in the public library and someone kills the morning talk-show host, Jason Armstrong, Henshaw realizes the small town of Hancock has a serial killer for Halloween.

Halloween • Holidays • Serial killer

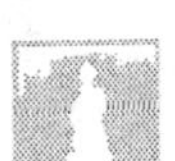

An Old Faithful Murder. Gold Medal, 1992

A family reunion at Yellowstone sounds like the perfect family getaway. When a friend of the family, George Ericksen, is murdered near Old Faithful, Henshaw needs to solve this one so everyone can go home.

Wyoming, Yellowstone

A Star-Spangled Murder. Gold Medal, 1993

Vacation is no time to relax for Henshaw when the family makes its trek to their summer home. Their neighbor, Humphrey Taylor, is found bludgeoned in their living room, and Henshaw must help the small town police solve a crime.

Maine

A Good Year for a Corpse. Gold Medal, 1994

All the wealth in the world cannot protect Horace Harvey from one of those courting his money. They leave him strangled with his own money in the wine cellar of the Hancock Inn. Henshaw finds herself spearheading an investigation when the source of Harvey's money and his need to give it away seem like solid clues.

'Tis the Season to Be Murdered. Gold Medal, 1994

Too tired after Christmas to do it herself, Henshaw has hired The Holly and Mrs. Ivy caterers to do her annual New Year's Eve party. But when Z Holly, the ladies man of Hancock, is found strangled in a van full of balloons, Henshaw needs to put aside her party plans and get to work.

Holidays • New Year's Eve

Remodeled to Death. Gold Medal, 1995

Summertime seems like a great time for relaxing, until the pipes in an upstairs bathroom burst and water inundates the floors below. Coincidentally, the town's building inspector Simon Fairweather has just been murdered, and Henshaw finds herself thinking that one of her contractors could also be a murderer.

Elected for Death. Gold Medal, 1996

Ivan Deakin was part of a three-way race for mayor in Hancock when someone kills him with cyanide-laced water. He was the dark horse, so why would anyone bother? Henshaw needs to solve this one to restore order and the reputation of her husband, who has decided to run for town council.

Politics

Weddings Are Murder. Fawcett, 1998

Henshaw learns the good news that her daughter Chrissy is going to get married, and she plans to create a spectacular wedding for her. When the wedding dress is ordered from Italy, a corpse is shipped instead.

Weddings

The Student Body. Fawcett, 1999

Having put her kids through college, Henshaw decides that now she can go as well. But when her backpack is used to murder her lab partner, she wishes she had stayed home.

Academia

Death at a Discount. Ballantine, 2000

Hancock is about to get a new outlet mall called Once In A Blue Moon, and everyone is anxious to shop there. The woman voted least likely to shop there is Amanda Worth, known throughout the community as a connoisseur of fine clothes. So everyone is shocked when she is found strangled on the floor of a dressing room at the mall, and Henshaw launches her own private investigation.

An Anniversary to Die For. Fawcett, 2002

For their thirtieth anniversary, Susan and Jed Henshaw decide to party in the same spot where they honeymooned. Doug and Ashley Marks are also celebrating together, and when Ashley's dead body is found among the Henshaw's anniversary presents in their room at the Landing Inn, the amateur detective must launch an investigation.

Connecticut, Oxford Landing · Hotels

Chapter 5

Public Detectives

The concept of a publicly supported police force is only about 200 years old. The French must receive some credit for beginning a police force with the work of Francois Eugene Vidocq. Figuring it was best to send a thief to catch a thief, Napolean hired the former criminal as his first chief of police. Vidocq was eventually forced from office and opened one of the first private detective businesses. His adventures and reputation proved so great that several Honoré de Balzac novels featured a character named Vautrin based on Vidocq, and Vidocq himself authored several reminiscences that were sensationalized accounts of his own career.

In most of the early great thinking detective series, where the hero stood outside the formal police departments, the policeperson was a figure of ridicule. The policeperson as hero was slow to develop. Following the success of the eccentric private detective or amateur detective, the first police series found their heroes functioning within the system for their access to the cases, but often outside the system in the methods they used to solve them.

Ed McBain is credited with having created the contemporary police procedural when he developed his 87th Precinct novels in the 1950s. Besides basing their case work on actual police procedure, his books feature more than one case that more accurately reflects the actual workload of a police department. Avoiding the lone wolf concept, McBain established a vigorous and vibrant crew of cops working out of the same department.

Since McBain's work, the police detective has evolved into a full-fledged hero whose evolution includes all types of police officers in all types of police forces. Cases can now be found in cities as wide spread as Hong Kong and Maggody, Arkansas. The inclusion of women and minority characters throughout the 1960s and 1970s broadened the palette on which these cases can be drawn.

Of the three main directions that mystery fiction took for the development of its detectives, this category is the closest it gets to reality. This may be one of its strongest appeals. Unlike the amateur and private detectives, who are cut off from all the legitimate resources for an investigation, the public detectives are fully vested in institutions that can provide the necessary resources to conduct an investigation. All the functionaries whose jobs are created to support them as they investigate also aid these detectives. This subgenre also has the appeal of watching a team work together to solve a crime, with plenty of social interaction, sometimes supportive and sometimes challenging, to go with it. All this effort lends an air of legitimacy to the process that validates these fictional characters as capable and believable detectives.

Police Detectives

Police often functioned as buffoons in the great detective's cases. The establishment of police procedure parallels the establishment of the policeman as the hero. Using scientific methods, once the sole purview of the great thinking detective, moves from the great detective to the police force as the procedures become more complex and the methodologies become too difficult to be replicated by a detective outside the police department.

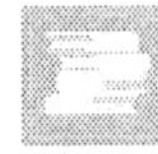

The characters listed in this section basically follow standard procedures within a fairly well-functioning institution. They may, on occasion, act independently of their departments, but usually they are dependent on the department and their fellow officers to help them solve the crimes. These officers stand in contrast to the Lone Wolf Police, who function more independently than a standard police officer.

The Historical Founding Members

Wilkie Collins ✍

Sergeant Cuff

A friend of Charles Dickens, British author Collins produced two works (see the listing for *The Woman In White* in the Amateur section) that helped lay the foundation for mystery fiction. The success of his works led to great popularity and financial reward, but his output was minimal. These two works, along with Poe and Dickens, are the foundations of mystery fiction. In this work, Cuff is not a major player, but he does serve a useful and important role in the resolution. See a website about the author at http://www.rightword.com.au/writers/wilkie. **Soft-boiled/ Traditional.**

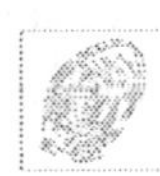

The Moonstone. U.K.: Tinsley, 1868 (U.S.: Harper, 1868)

One of the earliest English-language detective novels, *The Moonstone* involves a theft, not a murder. It introduces Sergeant Cuff, often considered the first fictional detective. The Moonstone diamond, stolen from India, proves fateful to Rachel Verinder, who should have inherited it when it was delivered by solicitor Franklin Blake.

England, Yorkshire · India

Charles Dickens ✍

Inspector Bucket

Charles Dickens stands as a giant in any discussion of the development of fiction as literature. Dickens produced two works that helped lay the foundation for mystery fiction. In *The Mystery of Edwin Drood* (see listing in the Amateur section), he managed to create an effect with a work he never had the opportunity to finish. His Inspector Bucket, featured in *Bleak House*, is considered one of the first formal police detectives in fiction. See a website about the author at http://lang.nagoya-u.ac.jp/~matsuoka/Dickens.html. **Softboiled/Traditional**.

Bleak House. U.K.: Bradbury, 1853 (U.S.: Harper, 1953)

The seemingly never-ending litigation in the case of Jarndyce vs. Jarndyce condemms the existing judicial system in Victorian England, while providing one of the earliest detectives in fiction, Inspector Bucket. His bulldogged determination makes him an archtype of the forthcoming great detectives.

England, London • Law

Anna Katharine Green ✍

Ebenezer Gryce

With a few novels of distinction, Green introduced some concepts from other styles of fiction into the mystery community and strengthened its approach to the classic pattern. Her New York policeman, the elderly Gryce, is almost unique in this time period as he is not an eccentric, but rather a competent detective doing his job. Some modern readers may have difficulty with Green's works because they are dependent on melodrama. **Soft-boiled/ Traditional.** See a fan website at http://www.law.utexas.edu/lpop/green.htm. Series subject: **New York, New York**

The Leavenworth Case. Putnam, 1878

Perhaps with a nod to Dicken's *Bleak House,* Green introduced her policemen Gryce in this legal melodrama. Horatio Leavenworth is shot to death in his library with his own gun, and his two beautiful nieces, Mary and Eleanore, are suspected because they are the heirs. The family lawyer, Everett Raymond, is the Watson to Gryce's detecting as he battles the legal system. This novel is considered the first full-length mystery novel by a woman.

Law

A Strange Disappearance. Putnam, 1880

A young servant girl named Emily has gone missing from the Blake house, and during the investigation, Gryce finds himself battling New York society as well as a murderer.

Hand and Ring. Putnam, 1883

Widow Clemmens has been struck on the head and left for dead in her own dining-room in the quiet town of Sibley. Orcott, the criminal lawyer, feels he needs to pursue the clues, especially when they appear to threaten his fiancee, Imogene Dare. But it will be Gryce who is the real detective on this case, and who ultimately brings a desperate criminal to justice.

New York, Sibley

Behind Closed Doors. Putnam, 1888

It may be Dr. Cameron's wedding day, but Gryce has come to inform him that his bride-to-be, Genevieve Gretorex, has abandoned her family and secluded herself in a hotel. It will take the good detective's best investigative skills to explain the strange behavior of the bride-to-be.

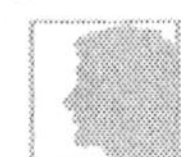

A Matter of Millions. Bonner's, 1890

Artist Hamilton Degraw is summonded to perform a commissioned work featuring Selina Valdi, the musical debutante, but is shocked to discover her laid out in a coffin when he arrives. Does his fortuitous arrival on the scene have anything to do with the mysterious Andrea Montelli who commissioned the work?

The Doctor, His Wife, and the Clock. Putnam, 1895

In the summer of 1851, a younger Gryce is assigned the murder case that took place in the Hasbrouck household. When Hasbrouck's wife hears a cry in the night, it indicates someone has murdered the wrong person.

That Affair Next Door. Putnam, 1897

Miss Amelia Butterworth, next-door neighbor to the Van Burnam household, is nosey enough to see a young man let himself and a woman in with a key one dark night when the Van Burnam house was closed. The next day, when a mysterious cleaning woman opens the house, as ordered by the eldest son Franklin, a dead body is found.

Lost Man's Lane. Putnam, 1898

Ninety miles from New York City is a small village where people have been disappearing, and that troubles Inspector Gryce. He turns for solace, and help, to his friend from his previous adventure, Miss Amelia Butterworth, and hopefully she will be able to discover the secret of Lost Man's Lane.

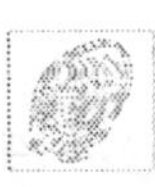

New York

The Circular Study. McClure. 1900

Gryce is called upon to solve the mystery of the strange death in the circular study of an old New York mansion.

One of My Sons. Putnam, 1901

When a grandfather dies in the arms of a passing stranger, the lawyer Arthur Outhwaite, Outhwaite also comes into possession of the dying man's last communication. The lawyer's first-person perspective will provide the venue to display the investigative skills of Gryce while he tries to sort out the differences between the brothers George, Leighton, and Alfred.

Initials Only. Dodd, 1911

The beautiful Miss Edith Challoner, a millionairess daughter of the well-known Moses Challoner, has been murdered at the Hotel Clermont. Is Oswald Brotherson, the eccentric inventor, the reason for or the cause of the murder, and what role does an airship play in the death?

The Mystery of the Hasty Arrow. Dodd, 1917

A young woman is found dead with an arrow in her torso in the galley of a famous museum. Director Roberts and Curator Jewett need to clear the reputation of the museum, while it will be up to Gryce to explain how a body can be pierced by an arrow when there is no bow.

Museums

Fergus Hume ✍

One of the early arrivals to mystery fiction, Hume had the distinction of producing the most popular novel in this field in the nineteenth century, and that is why this standalone title is listed here. Hume was an Englishman, living in Australia, who decided he would write a bestseller, and he did. In contrast to most of the writers of this period, he focused on a legitimate police investigation. **Soft-boiled/Traditional**.

The Mystery of a Hansom Cab. U.K.: Hume, 1886 (U.S.: Munro, 1888)

Late one night, a drunken man is placed in a hanson cab, but upon reaching his destination he is discovered to be dead. The murder allows this author to present a mystery as well as the dark underside of Melbourne.

Australia, Melbourne

The Golden Agers and Beyond

Catherine Aird (pseud. of Kinn Hamilton McIntosh) ✍

Christopher Sloan

Aird's works features CID Inspector Sloan, sardonic and brash, who works his cases in the mythical town of Berebury in the county of Calleshire. His world includes his wife Margaret, his companion on his cases, Constable William Crosby, and his boss, Superintendent Leeyes. Rehashing the typical British whodunit format, these novels can be recommended to readers looking for that type of mystery. **Soft-boiled/Traditional**. Series subject: **England, Calleshire, Berebury.**

The Religious Body. U.K.: Macdonald, 1966 (U.S.: Doubleday, 1966)

Inspector Sloan is asked to isolate a suspect from a cloistered group of 50 nuns when Sister Anne is found murdered at the base of the cellar stairs. The Convent of St. Anselm will prove a challenging hunting ground to the detective, especially when he every nun looks the same to him.

England, Calleshire, Cullingoak • Religion

Henrietta Who? U.K.: Macdonald, 1968 (U.S.: Doubleday, 1968)

Henrietta is surprised to discover that an autopsy on her mother, killed in a hit-and-run accident, reveals that her mother has never given birth. Inspector Sloan is also intrigued that her mother died just before the girl's twenty-first birthday.

England, Calleshire, Larking

The Complete Steel. U.K.: Macdonald, 1969 (U.S.: *The Stately Home Murder.* Doubleday, 1970).

Henry Cremond Cremond, thirteenth Earl of Ornum, opens his home to tours, but did not expect to open his suit of 1595 armor and discover the body of Osbourne Meredith. Meredith's problem was discovering something in the family's past, and it may connect to their notorious ancestor, Bad Betty.

England, Calleshire

A Late Phoenix. U.K.: Collins, 1970 (U.S.: Doubleday, 1971)

When a small pile of bones in Lamb Lane is discovered to contain a bullet, Inspector Sloan is called. What should have stayed buried in the past reveals that a murderer still stalks this town and will strike again.

Archeology

His Burial Too. U.K.: Collins, 1973 (U.S.: Doubleday, 1973)

The Fitton Bequest, a marble statue, lies in ruins and bars access or egress to a Saxon church tower. So how did the body of research engineer end up in the tower, and how did the murderer escape?

Locked room

Slight Mourning. U.K.: Collins, 1975 (U.S.: Doubleday, 1976)

Bill Fent, the owner of the manor in Constance Parva, dies in an automobile accident, and the town is in turmoil when it is revealed the accident was murder. All the friends and family members who attended his last meal are suspects for Inspector Sloan.

England, Calleshire, Constance Parva

Parting Breath. U.K.: Collins, 1977 (U.S.: Doubleday, 1978)

The University of Calleshire is experiencing unrest, but not the kind it will receive from Inspector Sloan when he is called in to discover the killer of student Henry Moleyns.

Academia

Some Die Eloquent. U.K.: Collins, 1979 (U.S.: Doubleday, 1980)

Death in a coma from a lack of insulin is a sad way for Beatrice Gwendoline Wansdyke to die. The maidenly chemistry teacher's tragic death turns suspicious when it is discovered that she had a quarter of a million pounds in a secret bank account.

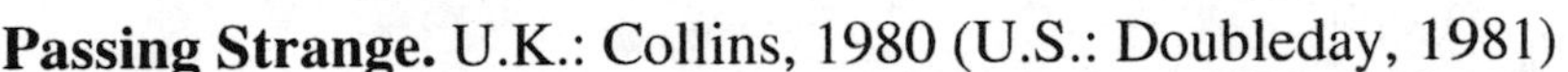

Passing Strange. U.K.: Collins, 1980 (U.S.: Doubleday, 1981)

Every year the famed Almstone Flower Show and Horticulture Fair is held on the Priory Estates, but that event is spoiled when a midwife named Joyce Cooper is murdered with florist's wire behind the fortuneteller's tent. Some people think a far worse thing is the claim made against the estates by a young woman that threatens to end the annual tradition.

England, Calleshire, Almstone · Gardening

Last Respects. U.K.: Collins, 1982 (U.S.: Doubleday, 1982)

A dinghy overturns at sea and a body is found floating in the sea; when the coroner reports to Sloan that it is murder, he begins to investigate. Then while spring cleaning, Elizabeth Busby discovers another body, and the sleepy little coastal town is rocked.

England, Calleshire, Edsway

Harm's Way. U.K.: Collins, 1984 (U.S.: Doubleday, 1984)

Gordon Briggs and Wendy Lamport of the Berebury County Footpaths Society are out walking when a crow delivers to them a human finger. Sloan is assigned the job of finding the body, which turns up on the roof of the Mellot barn, owned by a family who had been feuding with the missing financier, Ivor Haberton.

A Dead Liberty. U.K.: Collins, 1986 (U.S.: Doubleday, 1987)

Lucy Durmast is speechless, literally, when her former boyfriend engineer, recently fired from her father's company, is found dead after eating some chili. When the girl cannot defend herself, it is up to Sloan to investigate and decide if she is a murderer.

Food

The Body Politic. U.K.: Macmillan, 1990 (U.S.: Doubleday, 1991)

MP Peter Corbishley has two problems: the country of Lasserta is demanding he return to that country and face the consequences of an automobile accident that killed Alan Ottershaw. Then, while campaigning in East Berebury, someone calls for his death while death stalks a military re-enactment.

Politicians

A Going Concern. Macmillan, 1993

Amelia Kennerly is not thrilled to be the executrix of Octavia Garamond's estate, a woman so worried about her future that she asked for a police presence at her funeral and a thorough examination of her body for evidence of foul play. After her funeral, her home is burgled, and Sloan begins to think that perhaps there was something legitimate behind the woman's request.

Injury Time. U.K.: Macmillan,1994 (U.S.: St. Martin's Press, 1995)

A collection of the following stories: "Bare Essentials," "Double Jeopardy," "A Fair Cop," "The Hard Sell," "Her Indoors," "Home is the Hunter," "Lord Peter's Touch," "Memory Corner," "One Under the Eight," and "Steady as She Goes." Also contains six non-Sloan stories.

Short stories

After Effects. U.K.: Macmillan, 1996 (U.S.: St. Martin's Press, 1996)

Dr. Paul Meggie is trying a new drug trial called the Cardigan Protocol. When Muriel Galloway passes away, her son is not satisfied with the explanation and asks for an investigation. Sloan is called in when the doctor dies, and he learns that all is not well within the walls of the Berebury Hospital.

Medical

Stiff News. U.K.: Macmillan, 1998 (U.S.: St. Martin's Press, 1999)

The military regiment Fearnshires and their families have the comfort of knowing that the Manor at Almstone is there for their old age and comfort. The peace is disturbed when, after Gertrude Powell's death, her son Lionel receives a letter from her that declares someone was trying to kill her.

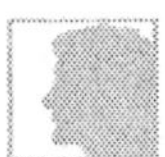

England, Calleshire, Almstone

Little Knell. U.K.: Macmillan, 2000 (U.S.: St. Martin's Minotaur, 2001)

The Greatorex Museum in Berebury has received a donation from the estate of Colonel Caversham, a former colonial serviceman. His mummy case, when opened, contains the body of a young woman, recently murdered. While Inspector Sloan tries to solve this baffling case, a local drug conduit is discovered, and he finds himself trying to balance both investigations.

Antiquies • Museums

Earl Derr Biggers ✍

Charlie Chan

Punchbowl Hill may have been home for Honolulu's detective Charlie Chan, but many of his cases took him far afield of his Hawaii home. Much could be made of whether Chan's creation is an example of inclusion or a continuation of racial stereotypes, but it can also be said that he is a great detective, a lovable father figure, and well-respected by his peers. Created as an attempt to counter the use of Asian characters as the sinister stereotype common in the literature and films of the times, it is ironic that Chan is now considered a stereotype as well. See a website about the author at http://www.charliechan.net. **Soft-boiled/Traditional**. Series subject: **Asian-American**.

The House Without a Key. Bobbs, 1925

Who has murdered the richest man in Hawaii is the question for Chan in his first case. A knife is stuck in the victim's chest, and a lizard has left a clue as well, but suspicion falls on two siblings who have feuded most of their life.

Hawaii, Honolulu

The Chinese Parrot. Bobbs, 1926

Even though Chan can't find the body, he is convinced that a murder has been committed. Disguised as the help on a ranch in the desert, he is free to investigate the clue left by the talking parrot.

California, Eldorado

Behind That Curtain. Bobbs, 1928

Asked by Inspector Duff of the Yard, Chan stays in California to try and solve two crimes, committed many years apart, in which the victims both wore slippers. Scotland Yard is grateful to Chan when his investigation of Sir Frederic's murder leads to the solution of a decades-old crime.

California, San Francisco

The Black Camel. Bobbs, 1929

When she dies on Waikiki Beach, the solution to silent screen star Shelah Fane's murder solves an old Hollywood crime. It takes the skills of the master detective Charlie Chan to link the two.

Actors · Film · Hawaii, Waikiki

Charlie Chan Carries On. Bobbs, 1930

Chan's old acquaintance, Inspector Duff, has been trailing the murderer of auto tycoon Hugh Drake on a worldwide cruise. He is shot in Chan's office when the tour reaches Honolulu. Chan jumps on ship to take the inspector's place, and is challenged to find a murderer before the ship docks in San Francisco.

Shipboard

Keeper of the Keys. Bobbs, 1932

Chan has four ex-husbands to sort out when their ex-wife Madame Ellen Landini, an opera singer, is murdered. Or could the current husband be the guilty one?

California, Lake Tahoe · Opera

Charlie Chan Returns. Bantam, 1974

Facing a death threat head on, New York philanthropist Victor Cosmo invites everyone capable of having sent him the death threat to his home. He also invites Charlie Chan. This novel was written by Dennis Lynds from a movie script that was never produced.

Lynds, Dennis · New York, New York

Charlie Chan and the Curse of the Dragon Queen. Pinnacle, 1981

The novel was written by Michael Avallone as a movie novelization. Chan must deal with the Dragon Queen, a murderer he once put away, who has returned to San Francisco in 1980 to plague society again.

Avallone, Michael · California, San Francisco

Christianna Brand
(pseud. of Mary Christianna Milne Lewis) ✍

Cockrill

British writer Brand created her diminutive detective and placed him in the English-village setting of the Kent County Constabulary typically so popular with American readers. His personality is such that people believe him to be a curmudgeon, but he can display occasional glimpses of compassion. One of Brand's novels, *Green For Danger,* is considered a classic in the field, and also includes enough medical detail to engage readers of that type of mystery. Considered a worthy successor to Dorothy L. Sayers, her novels can be recommended for their literary treatments and their strong Golden Age plots. **Traditional**.

Heads You Lose. U.K.: Lane, 1941 (U.S.: Dodd, Mead, 1942)

While discussing the death of a kitchen-maid, poor old Grace Morland declares she would not be caught dead in Francesca Hart's hat, but she will be proven wrong. It falls to Cockrill to investigate among this closed set of villagers to find a murderer.

England, Kent, Pigeonsford

Green for Danger. Dodd, Mead, 1944

During the Blitz, in a military hospital, a patient dies under anesthetic. When the nurse is murdered, Inspector Cockrill must decide which of the three nurses or three doctors might have done it.

England, Kent, Hersonsford • Medical

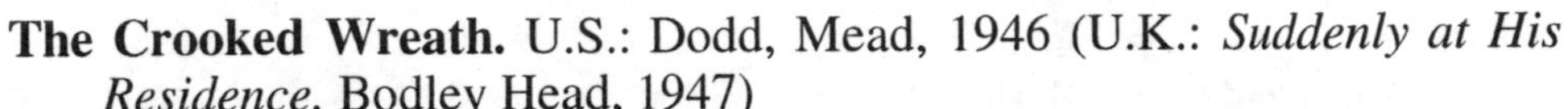

The Crooked Wreath. U.S.: Dodd, Mead, 1946 (U.K.: *Suddenly at His Residence.* Bodley Head, 1947)

Sir Richard March loves to challenge his children by threatening to change his will every year at the annual gathering to honor the memory of their mother and his first wife. When someone takes him too seriously, it may have led to murder.

England, Kent, Heronsford • Wills

Death of Jezebel. Dodd, Mead, 1948

When Johnny Wise comes to London from Malaya in 1940, only to kill himself over his unfaithful girlfriend, it leads to revenge seven years later. During a pageant, one of the 11 visored knights seems to have murdered the woman in the tower, and it is up to Cockrill to show how and why.

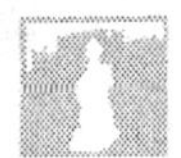

England, London • Theater

London Particular. U.K.: Joseph, 1952 (U.S.: *Fog of Doubt.* Scribner, 1952)

Is the mad grandmother the best suspect in the murder of the foreign visitor Raoul Vernet at Dr. Thomas Evans's house? And why would someone use a mastoid mallet as a murder weapon?

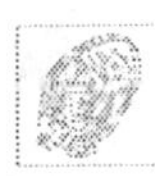

England, Maida Vale

Tour de Force. U.K.: Joseph, 1955 (U.S.: Scribner, 1955)

Vacationing is never restful for fictional detectives, and that proves true when one of Cockrill's fellow travelers is stabbed to death. When the local police cannot find a murderer, it falls to Cockrill to resume his role of detective.

Mediterranean, San Juan el Pirata Island

John Dickson Carr ✍

Henri Bencolin

Early practitioners of police mysteries were not opposed to giving their characters the eccentric characteristics of the classic detective, and Carr, with his Bencolin of the Paris Police, is no exception. Bencolin acts in a manner not unlike the great thinking detectives, and it is his eccentricities that provide his charm and his ability to solve crimes. He is reputed to look like the devil, and on occasion he enjoys the wilder side of the Parisian life. His cases are mainly narrated by a young American novelist named Jeff Marle, and some of the cases involve gothic elements as well as classic deduction. See a site for John Dickson Carr Collectors at http://www.jdcarr.com. **Soft-boiled/Traditional**.

It Walks by Night. Harper, 1930

The question for Bencolin is whether Louise Laurent's first husband, an escaped mental patient incarcerated for attacking for her with a razor, decapitated Louise's second husband.

France, Paris • Mentally challenged

Castle Skull. Harper, 1931

Schloss Schadel is a castle shaped like a skull and is the perfect setting for a murder as it looms above the Rhine River. But who can explain how Myron Alison could be shot three times yet die of burns? The answer is Bencolin, who travels to the Rhine to seek the clues necessary to solve this puzzle.

Germany, Coblenz

The Lost Gallows. Harper, 1931

An Egyptian's chauffeur has his throat cut on the streets of London, and Bencolin is asked to investigate the crime. The chauffeur's boss, El Moulk, had been receiving threats regarding an ancient curse from his homeland, and the notes are signed by the famous seventeenth-century English hangman, Jack Ketch.

England, London

The Corpse in the Waxworks. U.S.: Harper, 1932 (U.K.: *The Waxworks Murder.* H. Hamilton, 1932)

When a young woman is found dead in the arms of a wax replica of a famous womanizer in Paris's Musee Augustin wax museum, it leads Bencolin to the nightclub behind the museum. Therein the rich and famous rendezvous for pleasure, but when a dead woman is found floating in the Seine, he knows something has gone terribly wrong.

France, Paris

The Four False Weapons. Harper, 1937

Now retired, and rather bored, Bencolin is pleased to be asked to investigate a murder. His Paris neighbor Rose Klonec has been killed, her corpse discovered by her former lover, Ralph Douglas. The odd clues include four separate murder weapons left at the scene of the crime.

France, Paris

Vera Caspary ✍

Mark McPherson

Vera Caspary had a long career as a novelist and Hollywood screenwriter. With this particular novel, Caspary created a wonderful blend of police work and romance, doing for the police procedural what Daphne DuMaurier did for the gothic with *Rebecca*. The multiple points of view executed within the novel translated well to the big screen, and this film, its cast, and the musical score, did much to make the book a classic. The novel can be recommended to any mystery reader, as its noirish love story could appeal to the hard-boiled reader, while its romantic plot and twisted clues will appeal to the soft-boiled and traditional reader as well. Although a standalone effort, this novel is listed here because of its impact on the developing police procedural. **Soft-boiled/Traditional/Hard-boiled**.

Laura. Houghton Mifflin, 1943

When Mark McPherson, the investigating officer who tries to solve the murder of Laura Hunt, falls in love with her portrait, he discovers two other men who also loved the woman when she was alive.

New York, New York

Freeman Wills Crofts ✍

Joseph French

British author Crofts created his Scotland Yard detective around cases that require the detective to defeat the unbreakable alibi. His meticulous examination of railway timetables, a standard in these books, is the clue that these adventures are to be recommended to readers of the Golden Age plot novel, as well as the softboiled mystery reader. French is a rather plodding, normal man, yet one of his appeals is his unrelenting drive to solve these cases. **Soft-boiled/Traditional.**

Inspector French's Greatest Case. U.K.: Collins, 1924 (U.S.: Seltzer, 1925)

William Orchard, clerk at Duke & Peabody's diamond merchants, discovers the dead body of Gething laying in front of the open safe. When Inspector French is called onto the case, he must follow a series of clues that create his first and typically meticulous case.

England, London • Jewels

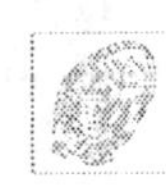

Inspector French and the Cheyne Mystery. U.K.: Collins, 1926 (U.S.: *The Cheyne Mystery.* Boni, 1926)

Maxwell Cheyne is at first honored when he is recognized while lunching at the Edgecomb Hotel. However, after his luncheon companion drugs him into a stupor, and his house is burglarized, he turns to Inspector French for the reasons and the culprit behind these strange activities.

England, Plymouth

Inspector French and the Starvel Tragedy. U.K.: Collins, 1927 (U.S.: *The Starvel Hollow Tragedy.* Harper, 1927)

Ruth Averill is away from her uncle Simon's house for the first time since being orphaned when the home burns to the ground, killing Simon along with John and Flora Roper. Oddly, the neighboring entomologist, Markham Giles, is found dead on the same night. How these crimes tie together, and how they tie Ruth into a conspiracy, provides Inspector French the opportunity to show his skills.

England, Yorkshire, Hellifeld

The Sea Mystery. U.K.: Collins, 1928 (U.S.: Harper, 1928)

When a corpse is discovered floating in a crate, the Inspector is able to begin a careful investigation that leads right back to the murderer.

England, Burry Inlet

The Box Office Murders. U.K.: Collins, 1929 (U.S: *The Purple Sickle Murders.* Harper, 1929)

Two drowning deaths occur, and it is discovered that the dead women had one thing in common: they worked the box office stations for various forms of entertainment.

England, London

Sir John Magill's Last Journey. U.K.: Collins, 1930 (U.S.: Harper, 1930).

Sir John Magill is the head of an Ulster family who made its millions in linens, but at the advanced age of 72, his linen-silk invention may not be welcomed by all members of his family. When Sir John travels to Ireland and then disappears, Inspector French is put on the trail of a missing man and a potential case of patricide.

England, London • Ireland (Northern), Belfast • Scotland, Glasgow

Mystery in the Channel. U.K.: Collins, 1931 (U.S.: *Mystery in the English Channel.* Harper, 1931)

The Chichester is crossing the channel when it discovers a drifting yacht containing two bodies, shot dead. When its captain brings the yacht to Newhaven, Chief Constable Turnbull turns to Inspector French for help on this baffling murder at sea.

England, Newhaven • Shipboard

***Death on the Way.** U.K.: Collins, 1932 (U.S.: *Double Death.* Harper, 1932)

Sudden Death. U.K.: Collins, 1932 (U.S.: Harper, 1932)

The death of Reverend Latimer Day has left his daughter Anne alone in the world to take jobs like companion and scullery maid, until she becomes the housemaid for Severus Grinsmead's wife, Sybil. When Sybil is killed by gas, it is not readily apparent who is the culprit as Inspector French begins to suspect murder.

England, London

The Hog's Back Mystery. U.K.: Hodder, 1933 (U.S.: *The Strange Case of Dr. Earle.* Dodd, Mead, 1953)

Julia Earle has two visitors to her remote village: her old school friend Ursula Stone and her unmarried sister Marjorie Lawes. As Ursula begins to observe some strange and disturbing ripples in the calm of St. Kilda's ideal setting, her sense of foreboding is heightened. Then, Julia's husband, Dr. Earle, disappears under extraordinary circumstances, and Inspector French arrives to investigate.

England, Surrey, Farnham

The 12:30 from Croydon. U.K.: Hodder, 1934 (U.S.: *Wilful and Premeditated.* Dodd, Mead, 1934)

When a flight from London to Paris lands, it is assumed that Andrew Crowther, retired manufacturer and quite wealthy, has been dozing on the flight over. When it is discovered that he has been poisoned and died in route, Inspector French is asked to discover whether Crowther's nephew, Charles Swinburn, is a murderer.

Airplanes • England

***Mystery on Southampton Water.** U.K.: Hodder, 1934 (U.S.: *Crime on the Solent.* Dodd, Mead, 1934)

Crime at Guildford. U.K.: Collins, 1935 (U.S.: *The Crime at Nornes.* Dodd, Mead, 1935)

It is agreed that all parties concerned with the potential failure of a London jeweler should meet at the country home of its managing director, Claude Willington Norne. When Charles Minter, their accountant, dies at the estate, the investigation into his death falls into the hands of the Guildford police. When the firm itself is robbed, that investigation falls into the hands of Inspector French.

England, Guildford · Jewels

The Loss of the Jane Vosper. U.K.: Collins, 1936 (U.S.: Dodd, 1936)

When the Jane Vosper is lost at sea after a series of mysterious explosions, suspicion begins to fall on the actual cargo that the ship was carrying. With the outcome of the investigation deciding the fate of her owners, the men who crewed the ship, and the insurance company who will have to pay out the money, Inspector French finds himself under pressure to render a fair decision.

England, London · Shipboard

Man Overboard! U.K.: Collins, 1936 (U.S.: Dodd, Mead, 1936; also published as *Cold-Blooded Murder.* Avon, 1947)

Jack Penrose, solicitor, and Pamela Grey, his fiancée, are hoping to cash in on a scheme put together by Edward M'Morris and Fred Ferris surrounding a chemical formula. When an investor's agent, Reginald Platt, is dispatched to examine the evidence of the claims of M'Morris, his return from Belfast to Liverpool leads to his death.

Ireland (Northern), Down, Hillsborough

Found Floating. U.K.: Hodder, 1937 (U.S.: Dodd, Mead, 1937)

Mant Carrington, a long-lost cousin from Australia, has alienated himself from his English cousins, Jim Musgrave and Katherine Shirley. The fault lies with the passing of the torch from Uncle William Carrington to the Australian, and the first symptom occurs when the entire family falls victim to arsenic poisoning. To try to save themselves, the entire family embarks on a Mediterranean cruise, only to sail into more danger.

England, Birmingham, Bromsley · Shipboard

Antidote to Venom. U.K.: Hodder, 1938 (U.S.: Dodd, Mead, 1939)

George Surridge is master at the zoo, but not master of his own life. Ruined by an ambitious wife and his own gambling debts, his world begins to fall apart. Eventually, as things begin spinning out of control, one of his employees falls victim to a snake poisoning, and Inspector French is on the hunt for a murderer.

England, Birmingham · Zoo

The End of Andrew Harrison. U.K.: Hodder, 1938 (U.S.: *The Futile Alibi.* Dodd, Mead, 1938)

Andrew Harrison may be a millionaire financier, but money does not buy happiness, especially among his unhappy family. Then, while sailing with his family on his yacht, the Cygnet, he is murdered, and French is sent to investigate.

England, London • Shipboard

Fatal Venture. U.K.: Hodder, 1939 (U.S.: *Tragedy in the Hollow.* Dodd, Mead, 1939)

Harry Morrison and Charles Bristow are partners in Bristow's idea to run a gambling ship up and down the coast of England. As they battle to retain their rights to the idea and to launch their ship, their dealings lead them into a partnership with John A. Stott. Stott is rich but hated, and when his body is discovered, the path leads back to the two gamblers.

England • Gambling

Golden Ashes. U.K.: Hodder, 1940 (U.S.: Dodd, Mead, 1940)

American George Butler is happy to inherit Forde Manor, but not happy to be rejected by English society. When he flees to the Continent to escape his unhappiness, his estate burns to the ground. Inspector French wants to know the whereabouts of Charles Barke, an art expert who had visited the art collection at Forde Manor just before the disaster.

Art • England, Surrey, Ockham

***James Tarrant, Adventurer.** U.K.: Hodder, 1941 (U.S.: *Circumstantial Evidence.* Dodd, Mead, 1941)

The Losing Game. U.K.: Hodder, 1941 (U.S.: *A Losing Game.* Dodd, Mead, 1941)

Albert Reeve is a moneylender and blackmailer. When he makes the decision to put himself between Marjorie Gale and Howard Broad, he uses evidence provided by the scheming Tony Cullen. As this spider's web of deceit begins to weave itself around the participants, it is not long before Inspector French's talents are needed.

England, London

Fear Comes to Chalfont. U.K.: Hodder, 1942 (U.S.: Dodd, Mead, 1942)

Julia Elton's marriage to Richard is one based on convenience. He married her to gain social status, while she was provided with the needed income to raise her daughter Mollie, a child produced from a previous marriage. As the marriage takes its inevitable path towards destruction, Julia finds affection for yet another man. When Richard is dispatched, Inspector French must decide who has taken this tragic step to change the arrangement.

England, Surrey, Dorkford

The Affair at Little Wokeham. U.K.: Hodder, 1943 (U.S.: *Double Tragedy.* Dodd, Mead, 1943)

Dr. Anthony Mallaby has lent Hurst Lodge to new tenants, and the village of Little Wokeham is intrigued to discover the ins and outs of the Winningtons. The old man, Clarence Winnington, has struck an arrangement with his younger relatives, Bernard and Christina. As the spiral begins, it leads to Clarence's death and the appearance of Inspector French, looking for a murderer.

England, Surrey, Little Wokeham

Enemy Unseen. U.K.: Hodder, 1945 (U.S.: Dodd, Mead, 1945)

Even as a nation finds itself at war, an Inspector finds there are those who still need to deal with their personal interests. In the village of St. Pols, someone has broken into the store of arms waiting to be used against the enemy. When Joshua Radlett, an elderly gentleman, is blown up on the beach, the initial investigation falls to Captain Arthur Rollo, French's former assistant at Scotland Yard.

England, Cornwall, St. Pols • World War II

Death of a Train. U.K.: Hodder, 1946 (U.S.: Dodd, Mead, 1947)

When the government creates a special train to carry war supplies, it is sabotaged, and they know they have a spy in the highest levels of government. When Colonel Trevor of the Ministry of War Transport is killed, the Yard is able to send French in to solve both problems.

England, Pullover • Espionage • World War II

Murderers Make Mistakes. Hodder, 1947

A collection of the following stories: "The Case of the Army Truck," "The Case of the Avaricious Moneylender," "The Case of the Burning Barn," "The Case of the Cliff Path," "The Case of the Enthusiastic Rabbit-Breeder," "The Case of the Evening Visitor," "The Case of the Fireside Mountaineer," "The Case of the Hidden Sten Gun," "The Case of the Home Guard Trench," "The Case of the Hunt Ball," "The Case of the Invalid Colonel," "The Case of the L-Shaped Room," "The Case of the Limestone Quarry," "The Case of the Lower Flat," "The Case of the Old Gun," "The Case of the Playwright's Manuscript," "The Case of the Relief Signature," "The Case of the Retired Wine Merchant," "The Case of the Solicitor's Holiday," "The Case of the Stolen Hand Grenade," "The Case of the Swinging Boom," "The Case of the Telephone Call," and "The Case of the Waiting Car."

Short stories

Silence for the Murderer. Dodd, 1948

Frank Roscoe has just completed his six years of service in World War II, and his friend Dulcie Heath has patiently waited his return. Rather than a celebration, their reunion descends into a series of petty crimes. When Frank takes a position as secretary for Sir Roland Chatterton, his new employer ends up dead, and the noose begins to tighten around a desperate man.

England, London

Dark Journey. U.S.: Dodd, Mead, 1951 (U.K.: *French Strikes Oil.* U.K.: Hodder, 1952)

The discovery of oil should bring joy and wealth to Brigadier Rodney Vale's family, but instead it brings death to the one son, Maurice, who wished to preserve the family estate and ignore the oil.

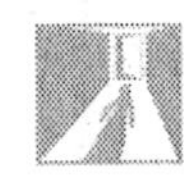

England, Radbury

Many a Slip. Hodder, 1955

A collection of the following stories: "The Aspirins," "Boomerang," "The Broken Windscreen," "The Brothers Bing," "Crime on the Footplate," "The 8:12

from Waterloo," "The Flowing Tide," "The Footbridge," "Gull Rock," "The Icy Torrent," "The Medicine Bottle," "The Mountain Ledge," "Mushroom Patties," "The New Cement," "The Photograph," "The Ruined Tower," "The Sign Manual," "The Suitcase," "Tea at Four," "The Unseen Observer," and "The Upper Flat."

Short stories

The Mystery of the Sleeping Car Express and Other Stories. Hodder, 1956

A collection of the following stories: "The Affair at Saltover Priory," "East Wind," "The Landing Ticket," "Mr. Pemberton's Commission," and "The Raincoat." Also includes five non-French stories.

Short stories

Anything to Declare? Hodder, 1957

Peter Edgley, ex-commando, has found civilian life difficult, and now he finds himself out of work. When he is propositioned into a smuggling operation involving secret forays into the waterways of Europe, he little suspects that soon he will have Inspector French on his trail.

Shipboard

Peter Dickinson ✍

James Pibble

British writer Dickinson has a wonderful way with words, and his non-series novels should be sought as well by readers who enjoy his playful style. His series books about the older Superintendent Pibble, who actually leaves the force in the middle of the series, have clue-driven plots. Readers should be aware that those plots are a bit different from your run-of-the-mill police procedure. Dickinson is recognized by his peers as having the ability to balance the traditional mystery puzzle with a modern sense of humor and some non-traditional style. **Traditional.**

Skin Deep. U.K.: Hodder, 1968 (U.S.: *The Glass-sided Ants' Nest.* Harper & Row, 1968)

When WWII ended, the New Guinea tribe known as the Ku are moved to London. Then Pibble is handed the case of the dead Ku chief, and he finds that all the suspects and witnesses are Ku as well, in name as well as tribe.

England, London • New Guineans

A Pride of Heroes. U.K.: Hodder, 1969 (U.S.: *The Old English Peep Show.* Harper & Row, 1969)

Pibble is sent to Herryngs, the home of Sir Ralph Claverly, a general, and Sir Richard Claverly, an admiral, when the Admiral's ex-coxswain commits suicide. Herryngs is a spectacular estate, including a lion park, but the two lions that rule the roost may be the most dangerous.

England, Herryngs

The Seals. U.K.: Hodder, 1970 (U.S.: *The Sinful Stones.* Harper & Row, 1970)

Sir Francis Francis is 92 years old, has twice won the Nobel Prize, but is now retired on the islands of the Herbrides. He insists that Pribble is the only person who can help him when he suspects that someone has stolen his autobiography.

England, Hebrides Island

Sleep and His Brother. U.K.: Hodder, 1971 (U.S.: Harper & Row, 1971)

The McNair Foundation administers to children with special needs, and its popularity has made it so successful that it has more money than it knows what to do with. The money attracts attention, and the foundation is of interest to ex-Inspector Pibble, especially when his contact, Mrs. Dixon-Jones, is murdered.

England, London

The Lizard in the Cup. U.K.: Hodder, 1972 (U.S.: Harper & Row, 1972)

Mary and Pibble are vacationing in Greece, but it is a working vacation for the retired inspector. He is asked to prevent the assassination of Thanassi Thanatos, who brings the couple to the island at his expense. Unfortunately, he has brought others to the island as well, and everyone knows what is at stake as Pibble tries to develop a line of defense against a murderer.

Greece, Corfu

One Foot in the Grave. U.K.: Hodder, 1979 (U.S.: Pantheon, 1980)

Pibble is now living out his life in the Flycatchers nursing home, and he has decided to commit suicide. Unfortunately for him, but fortunately for the readers, he discovers a dead body when he goes to commit the act, and decides to mount one more attack as a detective.

England

Chester Himes ✍

Grave Digger Jones/Coffin Ed Johnson

Chester Himes moved from the United States to France in the 1950s to escape America's racism. As a novelist, he created works in other styles, but these two detective partners are perhaps his most famous creations. Hard-boiled action is the ticket when these two Harlem detectives hit the streets. Perhaps less mystery and more thriller, these novels should be noted for the fact that they are written by an African-American about African-American characters. See a website about the author at http://www.math.buffalo.edu/~sww/HIMES/himes-chester_LINKS.html. **Hard-boiled**. Series subjects: **African-American · New York, New York · Teams**

For Love of Imabelle. Gold Medal, 1957 (Also published as *A Rage in Harlem.* Avon, 1965)

The issue of counterfeiting is the main thrust of this novel that features a bumbling man named Jackson who is caught red-handed with the goods. Needing to buy off the cop who would arrest him, he steals real money from a funeral parlor safe, and gets the two Harlem police detectives on his case.

The Crazy Kill. Avon, 1959

During a robbery of a grocery store, the Reverend Short leans out his window to watch and falls into a basket. Saved from death, he has a vision of a dead man, while in the basket below his window lies the corpse of Valentine Haines. The case of the basketed body falls to Grave Digger and Coffin Ed.

The Real Cool Killers. Avon, 1959

Grave Digger and Coffin Ed have no problems taking in Sonny Pickens, who they catch standing over the body of the Big Greek, Ulysses Galen. However, the gun in Sonny's hands is loaded with blanks. Plenty of other suspects make themselves known to the two cops, who discover that Coffin Ed's daughter may be involved as well.

All Shot Up. Avon, 1960

Three men dressed as police officers rob a man and start a major gun battle that kills two in Harlem. Grave Digger and Coffin Ed find themselves on the trail of a stolen gold Cadillac that will lead them to the killers.

The Big Gold Dream. Avon, 1960

Grave Digger and Coffin Ed find themselves on the trail of more money when a revival meeting kills the converted Alberta Wright. Everyone is after her money, and even her old furniture becomes a part of the treasure hunt as the two cops try to figure out who's money it is and who has it now.

Cotton Comes to Harlem. Putnam, 1965

Deke O'Hare has the ultimate scam going: his Back-to-Africa movement has collected thousands of dollars and he plans to take off with the money. He never expects to be ripped off by a white man, and Grave Digger and Coffin Ed find themselves chasing the money one more time.

The Heat's On. Putnam, 1966 (Also published as *Come Back, Charleston Blue.* Berkley, 1970)

An albino black man tries to save his father's life, but gets shot for his reward. As expected, a lot of money is missing, and Grave Digger and Coffin Ed are on the trail. But this time they are suspended for brutality, and Grave Digger's death is announced.

Blind Man with a Pistol. Morrow, 1969 (Also published as *Hot Day Hot Night.* Dell, 1970)

Two separate cases are keeping Grave Digger and Coffin Ed on the run. First, a white man has his throat cut on the streets of Harlem. Then a preacher seeking another wife is asked to account for the ones found buried in his basement.

Peter Lovesey ✍

Cribb/Thackery

These historical mysteries feature Sergeant Cribb and his long-suffering assistant, Constable Thackery. Lovesey's research into the Victorian period has allowed him to feature a particular aspect of that life in each of his titles, with an emphasis on the sport of the period. Rich in historical details, the series also deals with the class difficulties in England as Cribb struggles for respectability. **Traditional/Historical.** Series subjects: **England, London · Historical (1800–1899) · Teams**

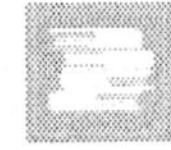

Wobble to Death. U.K.: Macmillan, 1970 (U.S.: Dodd, Mead, 1970)

A "wobble" is an illegal sporting event in Victorian London, where people gather to bet on a brutal marathon walking race. When the leading competitor is taken out by poison, the promoters are force to turn to the police.

Sports

The Detective Wore Silk Drawers. U.K.: Macmillan, 1971 (U.S.: Dodd, Mead, 1971)

Cribb feels that a death he is asked to investigate can be blamed on the illegal sport of pugilism. Suspecting the boxing academy run by a young widow, Cribb sends a police officer into training as an undercover spy, and the case becomes a chase to prevent another death.

Boxing · Sports

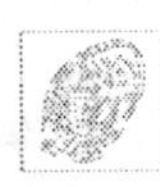

Abracadaver. U.K.: Macmillan, 1972 (U.S.: Dodd, Mead, 1972)

Performance hall artists are falling victim to various pranks that at first seem to be innocent attempts to publicly embarrass them. When the pranks accelerate and eventually lead to murder, Cribb and Thackery find themselves chasing a serial prankster.

Theater

Mad Hatter's Holiday. U.K.: Macmillan, 1973 (U.S.: Dodd, Mead, 1973)

Albert Moscrop is in Brighton when he becomes enamored with a beautiful woman viewed through his binoculars. His voyeuristic tendencies lead him to discover more about her, and when she disappears from his view, he finds Cribb and Thackery involved in his search.

England, Brighton

Invitation to a Dynamite Party. U.K.: Macmillan, 1974 (U.S.: *The Tick of Death.* Dodd, Mead, 1974)

Terrorism plagues Victorian England, and the blame lies with a free Ireland movement. When Scotland Yard itself is threatened and Thackery finds himself under suspicion, Cribb goes underground to catch the terrorists.

Terrorism

A Case of Spirits. U.K.: Macmillan, 1975 (U.S.: Dodd, Mead, 1975)

Seances are the rage, and may be the medium used by a burglar who specializes in taking unique objects from former séance participants. Cribb and Thackery need to investigate this world of prediction to decide who to arrest.

Swing, Swing Together. U.K.: Macmillan, 1976 (U.S.: Dodd, Mead, 1976)

Harriet Shaw's nude midnight swim finds her pinned in the light from a passing boat containing three men. Harriet's testimony could mean these men are the murderers of a tramp. Cribb gets his own skiff and takes to the river to hunt some killers who seem to be using a current bestseller to plot their evil deeds.

Waxwork. U.K.: Macmillan, 1978 (U.S.: Pantheon, 1978)

Scotland Yard is perfectly happy with the conviction of Miriam Cromer. She confessed to the murder of her husband's assistant, but new evidence has surfaced to cast doubt on her guilt. It becomes Cribb's job to discover why this woman would calmly go to her death for a crime she did not commit.

Ed McBain (pseud. of Evan Hunter) ✍

The 87th Precinct/Steve Carella

Ed McBain is credited with putting the procedure in the police procedural. His long-running series about the cops who work with Steve Carella in the 87th Precinct of Isola (read: Manhattan) are considered the best examples of integrating real police procedure into the mystery. One of the strengths of these novels is the ensemble cast used to populate the stories. **Soft-boiled/Traditional/Hard-boiled**. Series subjects: **Isola · Teams**

Cop Hater. Permabooks, 1956

The 87th Precinct is energized when cop Mike Reardon is shot in the head on the way to work. Then Reardon's partner, David Foster, is killed, and a third cop goes down. Steve Carella and the gang start with one small clue and begin to build an investigation to catch a cop killer.

The Mugger. Permabooks, 1956

A mugger, whose signature is to say "Clifford thanks you, madam," is terrorizing the precinct until his fifteenth victim is also murdered. Officer Bert Kling knows the murdered girl, so this time it is personal.

The Pusher. Permabooks, 1956

A young boy who pushes dope is found hung, an apparent suicide. But when the preliminary investigation raises some questions, and the boy's sister is murdered, the cops know there is something hidden in the background on this case.

The Con Man. Permabooks, 1957

The cops know a con man is running his scams on the streets of the precinct, and he is linked to the death of a young girl with an unusual tattoo who is found in the river. When the cause of death is listed as arsenic poisoning and another woman dies, the cops realize they have a serial killer on their hands.

Serial killer

Killer's Choice. Permabooks, 1958

Annie Boone is an enigma: a woman who has led two different lives, but has just lost the one she had. Cotton Hawes comes on board at the precinct, while one of the other cops is killed trying to find a murderer from one of Annie's lives.

Killer's Payoff. Permabooks, 1958

The blackmailer Sy Kramer takes a bullet in the head, and the precinct's cops must shift through his victims to find one desperate enough to kill.

Blackmail

Lady Killer. Permabooks, 1958

The precinct's detectives have 12 hours to consider the message contained in a killer's warning. He will kill The Lady, but there are three women in the district who might qualify to be his intended victim.

Killer's Wedge. Simon & Schuster, 1959

Virginia Dodge has a reason to seek vengeance against Carella. She takes the precinct house captive and is willing to sit with her bottle of nitro until Carella shows up.

'Til Death. Simon & Schuster, 1959

Steve Carella's sister Angela is about to get married when the groom receives an unwanted gift: a black widow spider in a box. Other attempts occur until finally one of the wedding guests is murdered, and Steve must hunt among jealous ex-lovers and those who would financially benefit from Tommy's death so that his sister can be a bride.

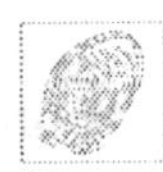

Weddings

King's Ransom. Simon & Schuster, 1959

A series of unexplained robberies at radio parts supply houses confuses the detectives in the precinct. When Bobby King is kidnapped and Doug King seems unwilling to make the payoff, the detectives have two cases that will merge into one explanation.

Give the Boys a Great Big Hand. Simon & Schuster, 1960

The 87th Precinct detectives think they have a killer who wants it to be personal between him and them when he begins to deliver body parts around the precinct.

The Heckler. Simon & Schuster, 1960

Many local businessmen are complaining that they are receiving phone calls from a man threatening them with various and dire consequences. The businessmen claim the threats are coming from someone named the Deaf Man, and this is the first time the precinct will face this deadly enemy.

See Them Die. Simon & Schuster, 1960

The gangs of the 87th Precinct honor the reputation of Pepe Miranda, and when he returns to Isola to hide out, the cops try to hunt him down. While the gangs try to enhance their territory by threatening to kill a young boy, the cops keep their focus on arresting Miranda.

Gangs

Lady, Lady, I Did It! Simon & Schuster, 1961

Officer Bert Kling's fiancée, Claire Townsend, is massacred in a bookstore with three other people. Bert knows whose killer he wishes to catch, but the other cops need to ask themselves, who of the four was the intended victim?

Like Love. Simon & Schuster, 1962

The detectives discover a clear case of suicide when two lovers die naked together in bed with the gas on. Or is it? The detectives find that the mother had an insurance policy on the dead girl, the cuckolded husband is upset about his wife's lover, and the dead man's brother claims it is murder.

The Empty Hours. Simon & Schuster, 1962

A collection of the following stories: "The Empty Hours," "J," and "Storm."

Short stories

Ten Plus One. Simon & Schuster, 1963

A sniper becomes active in the precinct, and his first victim is Anthony Forrest, followed by Randolph Horden. The cops of the 87th are nervous about finding a link, until a third death leads them to Ramsey University.

Ax. Simon & Schuster, 1964

Eighty-seven-year-old George Lasser is the superintendent of his apartment building, and it is there in the basement that he is discovered killed with an ax. His rather eccentric family may provide a suspect, but they are provided with alibis. The detectives know they must increase their efforts when the ax murderer strikes again.

He Who Hesitates. Delacorte, 1965

Roger Broome is a country boy on his first visit to the big city of Isola, there to sell the woodenwares his family creates upstate. As Valentine's Day nears, he has met a few women to his liking, but one dead woman puts him under the examination of the 87th Precinct's detectives.

Doll. Delacorte, 1965

Tenka Sachs, fashion model, is brutally murdered while her five-year-old daughter sits listening in the next room. Shaken by the brutality of the case, Bert King and Steve Carella separate, and soon the detectives are searching for one of their own as well as a killer.

Eighty Million Eyes. Delacorte, 1966

Comedian Stan Gifford wanted to end his television career with a bang on his last live show, but the nation watches in horror as he dies on camera. The 87th's detectives believe that the murderer lies amongst the famous actor's entourage.

Television

Fuzz. Doubleday, 1968

The Deaf Man returns to the precinct, and this time he is extorting money against a threat to murder certain public officials.

Shotgun. Doubleday, 1969

Andrew Leyden and his wife are slain with a shotgun, and the job of the 87th is to locate the owner once they know who he is. Meanwhile, Meyer Meyer has a case involving the stabbing of an old woman.

Jigsaw. Doubleday, 1970

Irving Krutch, insurance investigator, delivers two pieces of a photo jigsaw puzzle to the squad, pieces that match the one found in the hands of a dead man. The pieces hold the key to the Bonamico gang's stash stolen from a savings and loan six years prior to the start of this work.

Hail, Hail, the Gang's All Here! Doubleday, 1971

The precinct goes crazy when a bigot bombs a church, a young boy may have been pushed from a building, and Detective Andy Parker is shot on duty. Carella's case involves a dead actress, remembered for playing a stripteaser, who was threatened with a misspelled death threat.

Sadie When She Died. Doubleday, 1972

Gerald Fletcher expresses delight at his wife's death but also his innocence of the crime, and the case falls to Steve Carella. When a burglar confesses, Gerald walks, but Carella has his doubts.

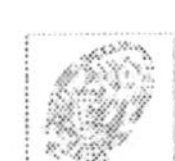

Let's Hear It for the Deaf Man. Doubleday, 1973

Once again their nemesis returns, this time to tantalize Steve Carella into unwillingly helping the Deaf Man rob a bank.

Hail to the Chief. Random House, 1973

Six bodies are discovered brutally murdered as a part of the continuing war between the black gang, the Scarlet Avengers, and the white gang, Clique.

Gangs

Bread. Random House, 1974

Roger Grimm's warehouse has been burnt by an arsonist, and Carella and Hawes find themselves unwillingly teamed with an obnoxious cop named Fat Ollie from the 83rd. When Grimm's house is burnt as well, the cops find themselves exploring a black gang and the company's employees.

Arson

Blood Relatives. Random House, 1975

A battered and bloody victim stumbles into the stationhouse to tell the cops a man with a knife has attacked her and her cousin. When Muriel Sparks is found dead at the scene, the cops begin to hunt an anonymous street person for the crime of murder.

So Long As You Both Shall Live. Random House, 1976

Detective Bert Kling finds happiness with his new bride, Augusta Blair, short-lived when she disappears on their wedding night. All the precinct's cop feel the personal nature of this crime and begin a massive hunt for Blair.

Long Time No See. Random House, 1977

A blind black man is killed, and when the cops go to bring his white and blind widow in to identify the body, she is found killed in the same manner. Is this a hate crime, or does their insurance policy have something to do with it?

Calypso. Viking, 1979

Meyer Meyer and Steve Carella have two dead bodies shot within a few hours of each other, both with the same gun, and the dead people share no characteristics. Will there be another death or can the cops solve this one fast enough to prevent another murder?

Ghosts. Viking, 1980

Gregory Craig, famous ghostwriter, has been found murdered inside a building where the cops had been called because a woman was dead outside. With some missing jewelry to trace, Carella finds himself drawn into the strange and terrifying world of the supernatural.

Ghosts

Heat. Viking, 1981

Bert Kling's world begins to come apart during a heatwave when his wife appears unfaithful and an ex-con is stalking him for sending him up. Meanwhile, he is teamed with Carella on a suicide case that bothers the two because the man's air conditioner was turned off.

Ice. Arbor House, 1983

A dancer and a cocaine pusher are shot with the same gun in different locales, and the 87th's detectives catch both cases.

Lightning. Arbor House, 1984

Lightning does strike twice in the 87th when the same women are raped by a madman. Then, female track stars are being found hung in the 87th, and the detectives realize they have two madmen on the loose.

Eight Black Horses. Arbor House, 1985

Women are dying in the precinct, and the clues are coming from The Deaf Man. Worse, he is impersonating Steve Carella, and the murderous clues are leading right back to the station house.

And All Through the House. Mystery Guild, 1986

This novelette reveals what life is like on Christmas in the 87th precinct.

Christmas · Holidays

Poison. Arbor House, 1987

When various men are being poisoned in the precinct, the unifying commonality is their relationship with the beautiful Marilyn Hollis. Is she a femme fatale, or is she being set up? And how does one cop handle this case when he falls under her spell?

Tricks. Arbor House, 1987

It's Halloween in the precinct, and four different cases explode. One involves a tag team of costumed children who are sticking up liquor stores, while other cops deal with corpses found without all their parts.

Halloween · Holidays

Lullaby. Morrow, 1989

A babysitter and her charge have been found brutally murdered, and the crime occurs on New Year's Eve. The new year does not keep the gangs from killing each other, as well, so the cops in the 87th have their hands full.

Holidays · New Year's Eve

Vespers. Morrow, 1990

A Catholic church and a Satanic cult practice their craft a few blocks from each other, and when one of the Catholic priests is found murdered in his garden, surrounded by Satanic signs, the obvious is suggested.

Religion

Widows. Morrow, 1991

A penthouse apartment reveals the brutally stabbed body of Susan Brauer, mistress to a rich old man. When he is also found murdered, the cops begin an investigation that will dig into his family to find the perpetrator in this case.

Kiss. Morrow, 1992

Martin Bowles's concern for his wife Emma leads him to hire her a bodyguard. After two near successful attempts, she turns to the 87th for protection. Meanwhile, Carella must watch the trial of the men accused of murdering his father.

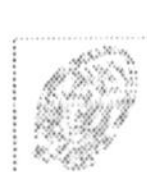

Mischief. Morrow, 1993

While some of the squad is investigating the death of taggers in the precinct, Steve Carella's old nemesis, The Deaf Man, returns to challenge him with clues to a million-dollar caper.

Romance. Warner, 1995

An actress in the play *Romance* is attacked, and then fatally attacked again. The cops are divided on whom to suspect, and once again their personal lives threaten to upset the investigation.

Theater

Nocturne. Warner, 1997

Svetlana Dyalovich, world-famous Russian pianist, dies an old and forgotten woman in the 87th, forgotten by everyone except the murderer who shot her twice in the chest. Following the missing money may be the most promising lead the detectives are going to be offered.

The Big Bad City. Simon & Schuster, 1999

Cute is not popular with the 87th's detectives, so they are not enjoying being taunted by The Cook Boy, a professional thief who leaves treats for his victims.

Others in the precinct need to trace the murderer of a young girl found dead in a park, a girl whose past proves to be unusual.

The Last Dance. Simon & Schuster, 2000

The death of an old man leads the detectives on a hunt from the strip clubs of Isola to the theater district where a forthcoming project may have ties to the highly profitable drug business.

Theater

Money, Money, Money. Simon & Schuster, 2001

Cass Ridley was a pilot, but she was also a drug courier who might have been paid off in phony money. When she is mauled to death at the zoo by a lion, the cops from the 87th are on the trail of a murderer. The cops find themselves investigating a publishing house when one of its salesmen is connected to Ridley.

Drugs • Publishing

James McClure ✍

Tromp Kramer/Mickey Zondi

Set in South Africa prior to the contemporary changes, this dramatic series draws its strengths from the plots and the description of a country in turmoil. When a white detective who supports apartheid teams up with a Bantu investigator, their dramatic adventures play out across the landscape of this troubled land. **Traditional/Hard-boiled.** Series subject: **Teams.**

The Steam Pig. U.K.: Gollancz, 1971 (U.S.: Harper & Row, 1972)

When two bodies are switched in the morgue, an autopsy is performed on Theresa Le Roux, a quiet and unassuming piano teacher. It is discovered that she was killed with a bicycle spoke, a method that leads the two investigators to the South African natives who use this method.

South Africa, Trekkersburg

The Caterpillar Cop. U.K.: Gollancz, 1972 (U.S.: Harper & Row, 1973)

A twelve-year-old white boy's body is found emasculated on the grounds of a country club. The case seems like a sex crime until an American teenager dies as well.

South Africa, Trekkersburg

The Gooseberry Fool. U.K.: Gollancz, 1974 (U.S.: Harper & Row, 1974)

Hugo Swart was killed by multiple stab wounds in his own kitchen, and the two detectives are assigned the case. The investigation begins at his church, where he was last seen by the priest, and eventually leads to the big city where Swart's fiancée lived.

South Africa, Cape Town

Snake. U.K.: Gollancz, 1975 (U.S.: Harper & Row, 1976)

Eve dances each night on the stage of her club, and she uses her snakes to charm the audience. But when she is strangled by her own snake named Clint, the two detectives are assigned to the case. At the same time, a candy store owner named Lucky, who is not, is murdered, and the detectives must explore the countryside to solve the riddle of his death.

South Africa, Trekkersburg

The Sunday Hangman. U.K.: Macmillan, 1977 (U.S.: Harper & Row, 1977)

When Tollie Erasmus hangs himself, the detective pair has no sorrow, because it was Erasmus who shot Zondi and left him with a long recovery that threatened his career. Yet, when it appears that Erasmus's crimes against others may be the cause of his fake suicide, they are forced to investigate.

South Africa, Trekkersburg

The Blood of an Englishman. U.K.: Macmillan, 1980 (U.S.: Harper & Row, 1981)

Bonzo Hookham is the brother of the dignified Mrs. Lillian Digby-Smith, and she is as surprised as anyone when his body is found by her mechanic, bound within the trunk of her car. He was not the most honorable or popular man locally, and his death may tie in to an assault the two cops are investigating.

South Africa, Trekkersburg

The Artful Egg. U.K.: Macmillan, 1984 (U.S.: Pantheon, 1985)

Naomi Stride has exposed the evils of apartheid through her novel *The Last Magnolia*, and someone has murdered her to silence her. Or could the reason for this death be found in the riches she received from abroad despite having her books banned at home?

Authors • Publishing • South Africa, Trekkersburg

The Song Dog. Mysterious Press, 1991

This historical novel looks at 1962, the year that sent a young Kramer to the small community where a Bantu Detective named Mickey Zondi worked. Each has their own case to solve, but when their paths cross, a bond is formed and a team is made.

Historical (1900–1999) • South Africa, Jafini

J. J. Marric (pseud. of John Creasey) ✍

George Gideon

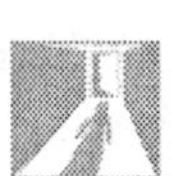

Considered by some experts to be the British equivalent of Ed McBain in terms of developing the contemporary police procedural, prolific author Creasey, under his Marric pseudonym, wrote these novels about his deceptively slow Scotland Yard Commander Gideon. As with McBain, one of the key elements to this series is the ensemble cast who work each case. The series was continued by William Vivian Butler after Creasey's death. **Traditional**. Series subject: **England, London**.

Gideon's Day. U.K.: Hodder, 1955 (U.S.: Harper & Row, 1955; also published as *Gideon of Scotland Yard.* Berkley, 1958)

Detective Sergeant Eric Foster is accused of conduct unbecoming, and Gideon's day starts with the accusations. As the day wears on, New Scotland Yard must deal with the death of a seven-year-old girl, a gang of drug dealers, and the desperate acts of a gunman.

Children at risk

Gideon's Week. U.K.: Hodder 1956 (U.S.: Harper & Row, 1956; also published as *Seven Days to Death.* Pyramid, 1958)

Ruby thought she had done the right thing by setting up Sid Benson and letting the cops take him out of her life. But his escape from jail threatens her, and she turns to Gideon for help.

Gideon's Night. U.K.: Hodder, 1957 (U.S.: Harper & Row, 1957)

Gideon takes the night shift, and that includes The Prowler's attempts to terrorize London. Meanwhile, a series of baby kidnappings and a gang rumble in the East End add to the stew.

Gangs · Kidnapping

Gideon's Month. Hodder 1958 (U.S.: Harper & Row, 1958)

Gideon's work stretches over 30 days as he tries to balance three separate cases: a woman taken prisoner by her unstable husband, a missing child, and a murder that someone tried to make look accidental.

Gideon's Staff. U.K.: Hodder, 1959 (U.S.: Harper & Row, 1959)

Staff reductions have cut the police's ability to keep track of criminals like George Arthur Smith, who likes to follow little girls. Meanwhile, bank robber Keith Ryman accelerates his activities, and Gideon is forced to stretch his limited resources to bag these criminals.

Gideon's Risk. U.K.: Hodder, 1960 (U.S.: Harper & Row, 1960)

Gideon finds himself up against two sets of crimes. The first involves the Carter brothers, noted car thieves, kidnappers, and maybe cop killers. Then Gideon's suspicions fall on the wealthy tycoon, John Borgman, whose first wife's death provided the wealth, who seems to be preparing to do in number two.

Gideon's Fire. U.K.: Hodder, 1961 (U.S.: Harper & Row, 1961)

Gideon is challenged by the work of an arsonist in a tenement that has led to the death of eight people, including a policeman. Then, a 14-year-old child is murdered, and someone has murdered three women and allowed them to share the same grave. ED

Arson

Gideon's March. U.K.: Hodder, 1962 (U.S.: Harper & Row, 1962)

A four-nation conference in London has drawn two sets of problems for Gideon. The first are those who would prey on the crowds gathered to witness the event. Even worse are those who would end the participants' lives.

Gideon's Ride. U.K.: Hodder, 1963 (U.S.: Harper & Row, 1963)

Riding public transportation becomes deadly when Robert Dean is attacked and robbed by some hoods, and the bus driver risks her life to be a witness. Meanwhile, in the tube, someone is pushing people in front of trains.

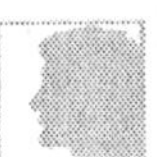

Gideon's Vote. U.K.: Hodder, 1964 (U.S.: Harper & Row, 1964)

Fight For Peace, despite its name, intends to blow up Parliament if the congress does not ban the bomb. Gideon is asked to take time off, but he knows that with the streets full of protesters and someone with some deadly intentions, he needs to be on the job.

Gideon's Lot. Harper & Row, 1964

Importing criminals from America is not what Gideon needs, but it is discovered that three different troublemakers have come from abroad. One is a safecracker, another a confidence man, but the worst of the lot is a murdering rapist.

Gideon's Badge. Harper & Row, 1965

Gideon is hesitant to leave the big poisoning case in the hands of his assistant Lemaitre, but he sails to New York anyway with his wife Kate to attend a conference. When murder follows him overseas, Gideon learns he can never leave his work at the office.

New York, New York • Shipboard

Gideon's Wrath. U.K.: Hodder, 1967 (U.S.: Harper & Row, 1967)

A murderer, while leaving the scene of the crime at St. Ludd's Church, does his civic duty and reports a burglary in progress. When the troops arrive, neither burglar nor murderer is around. Gideon is on the spot because there have been a rash of church vandalisms, and the Commissioner wants them stopped. As always, Gideon's other cases, including some missing girls who had posed for a photographer, keep him busy.

Churches

Gideon's River. U.K.: Hodder, 1968 (U.S.: Harper & Row, 1968)

Sir Jeremy Pilkington has formed a flotilla to sail down the Thames to display fashions from Paris, and the police have to deal with the criminal interest. As always, their attention must also stray to the case of a missing woman and a man who has been savagely beaten.

Shipboard

Gideon's Power. U.K.: Hodder, 1969 (U.S.: Harper & Row, 1969)

Industrial crime hits the CID when an old furniture factory burns to the ground and the city's power plants are threatened with sabotage.

Gideon's Sport. U.K.: Hodder, 1970 (U.S.: Harper & Row, 1970)

The prediction of cheating at the annual London Derby may prove true when the stoolie that came forward is found drowned in the Thames. Meanwhile, a visiting South African cricket team is being threatened, and Gideon finds himself focused on sports.

Sports

Gideon's Art. U.K.: Hodder, 1971 (U.S.: Harper & Row, 1971)

A Velazquez painting has been stolen from the National Gallery, and Gideon's suspects that any of five men currently loose have the capability to have stolen the piece. He may be proven right as someone begins to kill these men, and the daughter of a famous collector is kidnapped.

Art

Gideon's Men. U.K.: Hodder, 1972 (U.S.: Harper & Row, 1972)

The murder of Rosamund Lee has haunting similarities to a killing from three years past, one for which that woman's husband is serving time.

Gideon's Press. U.K.: Hodder, 1973 (U.S.: Harper & Row, 1973)

When the city is threatened by violence during a dock strike, the newspapers also go on strike, and communication in the city is disrupted. Meanwhile, the police must deal with the issue of continuing urban strife in the poorer immigrant areas of London.

Gideon's Fog. Harper && Row, 1974

Fog has encompassed London, and Gideon himself is almost a victim of some quick-thinking criminals guiding people into danger instead of away. When the fog clears on the crime scene, the police are left with a series of crimes that test their skills at finding the bad guys.

Gideon's Drive. U.K.: Hodder, 1976 (U.S.: Harper & Row, 1976)

Gideon's favorite restaurant is the victim of some tainted food, but when he tries to discreetly solve the case, the main suspect is murdered. Meanwhile, other food is being hijacked around the city, and Gideon realizes he has a conspiracy on his hands.

Cooking

Gideon's Force (by William Vivian Butler). U.K.: Hodder, 1978 (U.S.: Stein, 1985)

Three separate cases embroil Gideon in the world of crime: Wellesley Estate is suffering a crime wave, a gangland style murder of a restaurant owner's two brothers, and a kidnapping that involves a clairvoyant.

Butler, William Vivian • England

Gideon's Law (by William Vivian Butler). U.K.: Hodder, 1981 (U.S.: Stein, 1985)

Gideon is overwhelmed when three of his officers all fall under suspicions of illicit behavior.

Butler, William Vivian • England

Gideon's Way (by William Vivian Butler). U.K.: Hodder, 1983 (U.S.: Stein, 1986)

Three cases are handed to Gideon, but the one that strikes terror into his family is the kidnapping of his own grandson. Gideon, the old veteran, finds himself pressured by his son-in-law and Assistant Commissioner Alec Hobbs to try new methods for catching the criminals.

Butler, William Vivian

***Gideon's Raid** (by William Vivian Butler). U.K.: Hodder, 1986 (U.S.: Stein, 1986)

Butler, William Vivian

Gideon's Fear (by William Vivian Butler). U.K.: Hodder, 1990

Gideon needs to clear the name of his own long-lost son, Matthew, when drugs are connected to his family and threaten his career.

Butler, William Vivian

William Marshall ✍

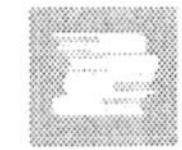

Yellowthread Street Police

Marshall used his familiarity with Southeast Asia to set a series in the wild and crazy streets of Hong Kong. Led by Chief Inspector Harry Feiffer, this Ed McBain-like crew of cops finds itself battling the bizarre on a regular basis. Yellowthread Street cases are a little unusual, with great stress on the action, and probably should be recommended to the reader who enjoys an elevated level of action. **Hard-boiled**. Series subjects: **Hong Kong · Teams**.

Yellowthread Street. U.K.: H. Hamilton, 1975 (U.S.: Holt, 1976)

The dancehall district of Hong Bay produces three separate cases for the Yellowthread Street cops: Chen has axed his wife and her lover; a New Jersey tourist has lost track of his wife; and The Mongolian, an independent mobster, is terrorizing the local shopkeepers.

The Hatchet Man. U.K.: H. Hamilton, 1976 (U.S.: Holt, 1977)

The Hatchet Man is loose and killing people in the old run-down theaters of Hong Kong, and the cops have no clues or physical description to aid them in the hunt.

Gelignite. U.K.: H. Hamilton, 1976 (U.S.: Holt, 1977)

This time the district is being threatened by a letter bomber, who has twice been successful in eliminating some local people. The Yellowstreet Station personnel are as divided in their personal lives as they are on the solution to this case.

Thin Air. U.K.: H. Hamilton, 1977 (U. S: Holt, 1978)

A plane departs from Hong Kong, and a threatening phone call is received at the station about the fate of the plane. Recalled, it is discovered that all the passengers aboard are dead. Now it falls to Feiffer and his crew to prevent this from happening again.

Airplanes

Skulduggery. U.K.: H. Hamilton, 1979 (U.S.: Holt, 1980)

A raft floats ashore containing a skeleton and some other odd clues. When Feiffer investigates, he discovers that dental records lead him to a man who is very much alive.

Sci Fi. U.K.: H. Hamilton, 1981 (U.S.: Holt, 1981)

The All-Asia Science Fiction and Horror Movie festival has arrived in Hong Kong, and the attendees prove troublesome for the Yellowthread Street cops. However, none are prepared when The Spaceman's ray gun really works.

Science fiction

Perfect End. U.K.: H. Hamilton, 1981 (U.S.: Holt, 1983)

Determined to discover who killed six officers in a neighboring police district, Feiffer and his cops must also battle a typhoon.

War Machine. U.K.: H. Hamilton, 1982 (U.S.: Mysterious Press, 1988)

World War II has returned to Hong Kong as a mysterious battle breaks out that threatens the station itself. Help may lie with the elderly Fireworks Man, who may have served in the Japanese version of the Gestapo.

World War II

The Far Away Man. U.K.: Secker, 1984 (U.S.: Holt, 1985)

The Far Away Man is a cold-blooded killer who seems to remorsefully choose his victims and terminate them without cause. The only common link between the victims is a yellow cholera vaccination certificate.

Roadshow. U.K.: Secker, 1985 (U.S.: Holt, 1985)

A random series of bombings terrorizes Hong Kong, and the Yellowthread Street officers think they are dealing with a meaningless danger. Then a pattern is recognized, and they realize that unless the clues can be followed, the last bomb will be the worst.

Head First. U.K.: Secker, 1986 (U.S.: Holt, 1986)

An elaborate coffin is found floating in Hong Kong's bay, and in it is a decapitated body. This proves to be only the first in a series of bodies shipped back from China, each with a missing body part.

Frogmouth. U.K.: Secker, 1987 (U.S.: Mysterious Press, 1987)

Their own station is haunted by The Terror That Has No Name, so all the officers are glad to be on the streets until they come up against two strange cases. Someone is terrorizing the animals at Yak's Animal and Bird Life Park and Children's Zoo, while a Tibetan mountain climber has unique skills that allow him to rip off the Russo Harbin Hong Kong Trading Bank.

Zoos

Out of Nowhere. Mysterious Press, 1988

Four disparate people in a van crash head-on into a truck while driving the wrong way on the freeway. The van is full of plate glass and the detective's job becomes figuring out what was the commonality in this incident, and is it possible that one passenger killed another just before the crash?

Inches. Mysterious Press, 1994

Inside a bank, nine dead bodies lay, killed mysteriously. An undercover cop is on a strange mission to leave a code word in chalk on the city's sidewalks. The Institute of Inner

Yu's clients have been committing suicide. Just another day in the life of the Yellowthread Street station cops.

Nightmare Syndrome. Mysterious Press, 1997

Just weeks before the Chinese will reclaim Hong Kong, the Yellowthread Street Station has a series of wealthy, but now dead, industrialists who have clawed out their own eyes before their death.

To the End. Mysterious Press, 1998

Feiffer's friend, the Australian Charlie Porter, has been shotgunned to death, and Feiffer fears for his sanity as change overwhelms him. O'Yee feels the same way as he desperately hates the arrival of the Communists. Meanwhile, two other officers probe the Geomancer's Union castle with results that may affect all of Hong Kong.

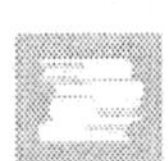

Jennie Melville (pseud. of Gwendoline Butler) ✍

Charmian Daniels

Melville is credited with writing one of the earliest female police procedurals. Her creation, a transplanted Scot, works the village of Deerham Hills. Daniels begins her career as a Sergeant, and ends up a Chief Superintendent. Feminism is an aspect of Daniels's life, and she is a competent and interesting detective to watch follow the clues. **Traditional**.

Come Home and Be Killed. U.K.: Joseph, 1962 (U.S.: London House, 1964)

When Mumsy and Janet go missing from their home with their stepdaughter and sister Kathy, the focus of the investigation is on the men in their lives. But, everyone keeps wondering what Kathy's role could have been in all of this drama.

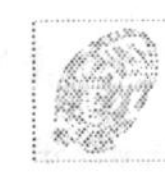

England, Deerham Hills

Burning Is a Substitute for Loving. U.K.: Joseph, 1963

The petty crime in the small village of Deerham Hills is being tracked by Daniels, when things become serious. She finds herself needing to identify the victim before she can begin to track a killer.

England, Deerham Hills

Murderers' Houses. Joseph, 1964

A woman floats into Deerham Hills by river, her death a disruption in the sleepy little town. But what is worse, it appears that the police have four suspects who could be the woman-hating murderer who finished her off.

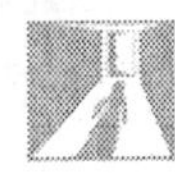

England, Deerham Hills

There Lies Your Love. Joseph, 1965

Sleepy little Deerham Hills has a crime wave when a girl goes missing. At the same time, an elderly woman is found dead, and the question for Daniels is whether she was murdered or committed suicide. The last case she has to juggle involves the death of a Peeping Tom, tortured by poison-pen letters.

England, Deerham Hills

A Different Kind of Summer. Hodder, 1967

The pathology department at Deerham Hills Hospital has been sent a body, except nobody knows it is coming or wants it when it arrives. When time finally allows the hospital to retrieve the body, it is headless, and someone has left the woman's possessions in its place.

England, Deerham Hills

A New Kind of Killer, an Old Kind of Death. U.K.: Hodder, 1970 (U.S.: *A New Kind of Killer.* McKay, 1971)

Alda Fearon is Daniels's old colleague, and as the Lodging Officer for the University of Midport, she is concerned about some activities on the campus. When she dies, Daniels is on the campus taking criminology courses, so she takes on student groups and other campus personnel to try and find some answers.

Academia • England, Midport

Murder Has a Pretty Face. U.K.: Macmillan, 1981 (U.S.: St. Martin's Press, 1989)

A corpse is found in Deerham Hills with Daniels's name and telephone number on a card in his pocket. While this murder is being investigated, the village has some fur and jewelry robberies, and then a strange woman comes to town and makes everyone nervous. It is Daniels who begins to believe that all of these occurrences may tie together.

England, Deerham Hills

***Death in the Garden.** U.K.: Macmillan, 1987 (U. S.: *Murder in the Garden.* St. Martin's Press, 1987)

Windsor Red. U.K.: Macmillan, 1988 (U.S.: St. Martin's Press, 1988)

Daniels has taken a sabbatical to study feminist crime at Brunnel University. Her rooms in Wellington Yards are nice, but it is not nice when a dismembered body is discovered in a rubbish sack. Other crimes occur, and Daniels begins a personal investigation.

Academia • England, Windsor

A Cure for Dying. Macmillan, 1989

While she is attacked one night with little consequences, the night proves to be fatal to a horse whose throat is cut. Then, women begin to die by the same method. Faced with an investigation of a Jack the Ripper style killer, Daniels finds herself personally involved.

England, Windsor

Making Good Blood. U.K.: Macmillan, 1989 (U. S.: St. Martin's Press, 1990)

After earning her diploma, Daniels decides to settle down in Windsor, buying a house and traveling to work in London each day. In one night, she is attacked walking home, a horse is killed, and another woman has her throat slashed.

England, Windsor

Footsteps in the Blood. U.K.: Macmillan, 1990 (U. S.: St. Martin's Press, 1993)

When Nella Fisher tries to bribe some potential witness to testify against a dangerous man, she places herself in danger. Daniels finds herself investigating Fisher's murder and finds that two of her suspects are personal friends. Then she suspects the murderer is after her.

England, Windsor

Witching Murder. U.K.: Macmillan, 1990 (U.S.: St. Martin's Press, 1991)

Home on sick leave, Daniels has her first chance to meet her neighbor in Windsor, Winifred Eagle, who is rumored to be the leader of a coven of witches. When one of the women in the group is murdered, the rituals of witchcraft are displayed at the murder scene, and Daniels finds herself investigating women who will not talk.

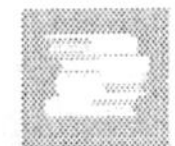

England, Windsor • Witchcraft

Dead Set. U.K.: Macmillan, 1992 (U.S.: St. Martin's Press, 1993)

Ted Gray finds himself a suspect when he is unlucky enough to discover the dead body of a strangled schoolgirl. When he goes missing, Daniels begins an investigation that runs up against the man's wife who is reluctant to talk.

Academia • England, Merrywick

Whoever Has the Heart. U.K.: Macmillan, 1993 (St. Martin's Press, 1994)

Daniels decides to buy a cottage in the small village of Brideswell where some recent deaths have disturbed the community. When part of a young woman's body is found near her new domicile, she launches an investigation among her new neighbors.

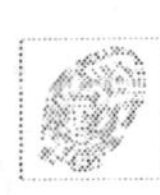

England, Brideswell

Baby Drop. U.K.: Macmillan, 1994 (U. S.: *A Death in the Family.* St. Martin's Press, 1995)

Eight-year-old Sarah Holt has gone missing, and it falls to Daniels to lead the hunt for the child. Depressed by the idea that she does not know if she is searching for a missing, or dead, child, Daniels is not surprised when a body is found. However, it proves to be another young child, just gone missing, and the case begins to spiral out of control.

Children at risk • England, Windsor

The Morbid Kitchen. U.K.: Macmillan, 1995 (U.S.: St. Martin's Press, 1996)

Miss Bailey's school is closed now because ten years prior a student was murdered. When the original owner's half-sister inherits and tries to sell the school, another corpse is found and Daniels, a friend of Emily Bailey, decides to investigate.

Academia • England, Windsor

***The Woman Who Was Not There.** Macmillan, 1996

***Revengeful Death.** Macmillan, 1997

***Stone Dead.** Macmillan, 1998

Dead Again. Macmillan, 2000

Daniels's job is to keep a serial murderer, Joan Dingham, safe while she lives for a month in Merrywick upon her release from prison before she goes on to the university for a degree. Joan had been part of a gang of five woman who ran wild together, but now Diana King is dead and the others have settled down. Or have they? Before Joan can be released in the public, someone starts to commit murders using her style.

Children at risk • England, South Downs • Serial killer

***Loving Murder.** U.K.: Severn House, 2001 (U.S.: Chivers, 2001)

***Loving Money.** Severn, 2001

Lillian O'Donnell ✍

Norah Mulcahaney

One of the first female police officers, Mulcahaney is a member of the New York City force. A strength of this series is that Mulcahaney is forced to climb the ladder of success as the series progresses. She often shares her cases with Joseph Capretto, and later shares her life with him when they marry. **Traditional/Hard-boiled**. Series subject: **New York, New York**.

The Phone Calls. Putnam, 1972

Ruth Emerson gets obscene phone calls after her husband dies. Victoria Neumann gets them after her husband dies in Vietnam. Arabella Broome gets them after her husband commits suicide. When the phone company changes all their numbers, the calls keep coming.

Don't Wear Your Wedding Ring. Putnam, 1973

Diane Vance's mutilated body is found in the Apex Hotel. Evidently she and her suburban housewife friends thought it would be fun to be call girls instead of forming a bridge club. When another member of the group is murdered after confessing her part in the operation, Mulcahaney and Carpetto investigate.

Dial 577 R-A-P-E. Putnam, 1974

When her neighbor's daughter is raped, Mulcahaney investigates, but eventually is reassigned. Launching her own personal investigation leads Mulcahaney to a rapist who is also a murderer.

The Baby Merchants. Putnam, 1975

Mulcahaney and Capretto are considering adopting a child, and the legal ramifications lead her to an underground process where children are available for a price. While Capretto is investigating an organized crime family, Mulcahaney is investigating an organization that will provide a family.

Leisure Dying. Putnam, 1976

When Mulcahaney cracks a case of young hoods preying on the elderly, one of the boys confesses to the murders of several elderly people living in an Upper West Side hotel. These cases had been ruled natural deaths, and Capretto was in charge of the unit that failed to notice the homicides. When he is disciplined, he leaves their home, and Mulcahaney must decide between the truth and her family.

No Business Being a Cop. Putnam, 1978

A cop killer is bad enough, but this killer is targeting the female officers on the New York police force. Recently promoted, Mulcahaney is handed the case and forced to save her fellow officers and herself.

The Children's Zoo. Putnam, 1981

A series of murders in the Belmode Towers and the death of the animals in the petting zoo in Central Park are two cases that confound Mulcahaney. When the clues begin to point to a prestigious school, Mulcahaney begins to think that the crimes could be traced to the children.

Zoos

Cop Without a Shield. Putnam, 1983

Needing a change for personal reasons, Mucahaney moves to a small town to hide out. But she learns that a cop cannot hide from death, and when she is the witness to an abduction that turns to murder, she launches a private investigation.

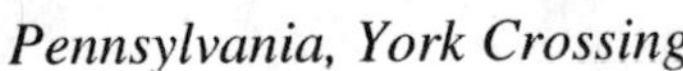

Pennsylvania, York Crossing

Ladykiller. Putnam, 1984

Mulcahaney is assigned the case of a young girl found brutally murdered in Central Park. When other deaths occur, she realizes she is chasing a man who uses women's vulnerability to commit the ultimate act.

Casual Affairs. Putnam, 1985

Recently promoted to Lieutenant, Mulcahaney is given the case of the wealthy socialite Christina Isserman, found comatose after an all-night binge. As Mulcahaney investigates, she begins to wonder if someone is also using her to promote their interests.

***Shadow in Red.** Putnam, 1986

The Other Side of the Door. Putnam, 1987

When a convicted child molester is released from prison, he is the most likely suspect when the woman whose testimony sent him to prison is found murdered. The lead detective, Gary Reissig, asks Lieutenant Mulcahaney for help when the case does not progress smoothly.

A Good Night to Kill. Putnam, 1989

Mulcahaney is handed two difficult cases. The first involves a mugging in which Stefanie Altman, the victim, becomes the aggressor by shooting her assailant. When the witnesses disappear, the case gets complicated. Meanwhile, Mulcahaney is also investigating the death of a Mafia don's wife.

A Private Crime. Putnam, 1991

When an assailant uses a weapon like an AK-47 in a crowded open-air flea market, why does he only shoot one unwed teenager and her little son? Mulcahaney is given the assignment to discover why, and must investigate against the background of a media frenzy.

Pushover. Putnam, 1992

Multiple cases again perplex Mulcahaney when she must investigate the death of a silent screen star and the kidnapping of her ten-year-old grandson. Meanwhile, someone is pushing women onto the subway tracks with fatal consequences.

Lockout. Putnam, 1994

The Earth Shakers have just lost Bo Russell to a murder in the isolation booth in a recording studio, but the band, and Bo's brother, are reluctant to cooperate with the police. Distracted by having to defend herself against a charge of excessive force for shooting an unarmed mugger, Mulcahaney finds this a difficult case to investigate.

Music

Blue Death. Putnam, 1998

Mulcahaney reaches two of her goals when she makes Captain and adopts a baby boy. Things do not go smoothly for her as she tries to arrange care for her son, but that pales in comparison to a rash of cop suicides that leads Mulcahaney down a dark path that tests her loyalty and friendships with her comrades.

Dell Shannon (pseud. of Elizabeth Linnington) ✍

Luis Mendoza

Linnington was one of the few politically conservative mystery writers of her period. Mendoza was born in the Hispanic slums of Los Angeles. Proving it was possible to have a dilettante detective in the police force, Shannon created Mendoza as a cop with a taste for the finer things in life, which he developed after he inherited his wealth. His Los Angeles beat proves an interesting scene for this unique character, but the series has the feel of Queen and Sayers more than a contemporary procedural. **Soft-boiled/Traditional**. Series subject: **California, Los Angeles**.

Case Pending. Harper & Row, 1960

Two murders six months apart have the cops chasing their own tails. The only clue is a stolen doll, and their witness is a frightened schoolboy. Mendoza meets Alison Weir for the first time on this case.

The Ace of Spades. Morrow, 1961

A murder dismissed as a junkie's death becomes complicated when the autopsy shows the victim was not a drug user. Alison Weir brings Mendoza a special case when she finds a rare coin in the backseat of her car when it is returned to her after being stolen.

Extra Kill. Morrow, 1962

A con man's death may be connected to a recent cop killing. The case gets complicated when one of the officers get personally involved with a suspect.

Knave of Hearts. Morrow, 1962

The cops are on the hot seat when it is shown that a man they arrested, tried, convicted, and executed may be innocent of the charges. Worse, the guilty man may have committed five more acts of outrage while the cops were looking the other way. Meanwhile, Mendoza must deal with the breakup of his relationship with Alison.

Death of a Busybody. Morrow, 1963

Margaret Chadwick is famous for being a busybody, but now she is a dead one when she is found murdered in a freight yard. Her history of turning people against each other made her a prime target for so many suspects, and the killing leaves Mendoza no clues.

Double Bluff. Morrow, 1963

Mendoza's case begins when a man claims his sister has been murdered, but there is no body. A cursory examination proves her missing, and eventually she does turn up dead. The autopsy reveals that she was dead before the car accident that ostensibly killed her, and now Mendoza must look at who profits from the two million dollar inheritance.

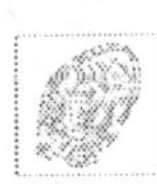

Wills

Mark of Murder. Morrow, 1964

While on vacation in Bermuda, Mendoza receives a call that his Sergeant, Art Hackett, has been in a suspicious automobile accident while investigating two separate murders. He gets back to L.A. just in time to investigate a serial killer's deadly efforts.

Serial killer

Root of All Evil. Morrow, 1964

After her rich parents died, Valerie Ellis fell in with the wrong crowd and turned to drugs. Her body is found on a schoolyard playground, and Mendoza must probe her drug connections to find a murderer. Soon his attentions are turned back to the rich and powerful.

The Death-Bringers. Morrow, 1965

Mendoza's men are frustrated by a series of bank robberies, but they are horrified when one of their own is killed during one. While they try to keep their focus, a young girl named Carol Coffey is murdered and they must balance their time.

Death by Inches. Morrow, 1965

In the L.A. slums, in a rundown rooming house, Marion Stromberg has been murdered. The method of death seems overly violent to Mendoza, and he keeps that in mind as he probes to find out what caused this old pensioner's death.

Coffin Corner. Morrow, 1966

While the officers are busy with the death of a poisoned shopkeeper, one of their own is run over by an automobile and the witnesses say it was murder.

With a Vengeance. Morrow, 1966

Mendoza has a corpse left with the message: "The vengeance is just." Seven more murders follow, and it takes all the police resources to find a clue to the connections so that they can bring down a murderer.

Serial killer

Chance to Kill. Morrow, 1967

While they have to search for two men wanted for a double homicide and find a young man dead in an alley, the cops are informed that one of their own, a policewoman, has been found dead in a dry riverbed.

Rain with Violence. Morrow, 1967

A series of murders test the mettle of the cops, one striking close to home for Mendoza. The victims include a young mother, a prostitute, two elderly women, and two men who may have been rolled in a bar notorious for its drug dealing.

Kill with Kindness. Morrow, 1968

Downtown, the cops are on their own when Mendoza calls in sick, and the list of their cases includes a rape, the death of a minister, and a man who was tied to the railroad tracks. Left to his own devices when he catches the measles, Mendoza practices his craft from home when his housekeeper brings him a strange tale.

Crime on Their Hands. Morrow, 1969

Mendoza's squad faces a series of bizarre crimes: a woman is found strangled and a sheep's heart is left as a clue; the police academy's janitor and his wife are murdered; and a car is brought to California by a dead man.

Schooled to Kill. Morrow, 1969

A lethal sex offender, still at large after the last case, may be the reason why two schoolmates have gone missing. Meanwhile, a young man comes to the police to confess he has been offered money to murder a woman.

Unexpected Death. Morrow, 1970

Separate cases confuse the officers under Mendoza: a blind man found dead where he should not be, a victim found in her nightgown, and a murdered mother-in-law.

The Ringer. Morrow, 1971

Detective Tom Landers is accused of heading an automobile theft ring, and while distracted by this accusation, Mendoza's men must solve their usual caseload of crimes and murders.

Whim to Kill. Morrow, 1971

The cops in Mendoza's crew have 12 different murder cases to work. Further complications arise when three escaped cons capture a sergeant and hold him hostage.

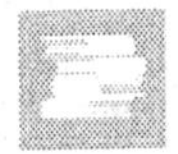

Murder with Love. Morrow, 1972

A major earthquake strikes Los Angeles, and while the population lives in fear of the aftershocks, their neighbors are bent on taking advantage of the opportunities. The cases for the cops include a man who shoots his wife's lover, the murder of a renowned doctor, and the murder of one of their own.

With Intent to Kill. Morrow, 1972

A series of homicides baffles Mendoza and his men. They range from the death of three hippies, to the death of a rich man, and the shooting of one of their motorcycle officers.

No Holiday for Crime. Morrow, 1973

Christmas offers the police no rest as they battle the usual list of crimes in their division including murder, rape, and robbery.

California, Los Angeles · *Christmas* · *Holidays*

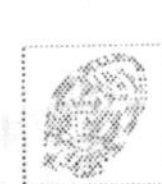

Spring of Violence. Morrow, 1973

Robbery and Homicide have been merged into one department, and as the new operation begins, a 10-year-old boy is killed in a hit-and-run, a power company employee is stabbed, a bank is held up, and some tropical fish are stolen. In addition, an old woman that has disappeared is given to the department as a homicide without a corpse.

Crime File. Morrow, 1974

An elderly woman, once a woman in much demand with the boys, is murdered and the suspicion is that her past has finally caught up with her. Meanwhile, someone is robbing the best restaurants in town, and Mendoza's officers are again balancing many cases.

Deuces Wild. Morrow, 1975

When his own twins are kidnapped, Mendoza must retain his sanity and use his detective skills to find his own children.

Streets of Death. Morrow, 1976

How could a man in a wheelchair disappear? Can you trust a busybody when he tries to tell the police his neighbor is plotting a murder? Why would three boys rob the elderly if there is no profit? These questions must be answered by Mendoza's squad as they do their jobs.

Appearances of Death. Morrow, 1977

The squad is faced with a series of crimes that include a death by overdose of a boy who does not seem the type and a senior citizen that robs a store at gunpoint.

Cold Trail. Morrow, 1978

Mendoza's workload includes an unidentified female body found under a condemned house, a rapist and child molester who may be a murderer, and the usual robberies and street crimes.

Felony at Random. Morrow, 1979

The usual list of crimes perplex Mendoza: a diplomat's daughter is kidnapped while on a school outing; a murder includes a three-year-old child, and a reason is sought for a cop killing.

Felony File. Morrow, 1980

Bullock's Department store loses a half-a-million dollars, a nine-year-old girl is raped and beaten, and another series of robberies keeps the cops busy.

Murder Most Strange. Morrow, 1981

A man uses his good looks to get close to his victims, and the cops want him for several unsolved crimes. Additional open cases include a murder and suicide that has some strange features, a series of robberies that have the cops baffled, and the death of a senator that may cause the squad to investigate.

The Motive on Record. Morrow, 1982

A child rapist haunts Mendoza's district, while the officers also hunt for the murderer of an elderly fortune hunter, some theater robbers, and a murdered mailman.

Exploit of Death. Morrow, 1983

Mendoza knows the murdered Frenchwoman, Julliette Martin, from his trip to Paris with his wife Alison. He allows his personal feelings to outweigh his common sense, and even travels to Paris to try and solve the case. Meanwhile, in L.A., the crew has numerous investigations to balance.

France, Paris

Destiny of Death. Morrow, 1984

As always, Mendoza's detectives need to have a sense of humor as well as a sense of duty: how about a robber who takes the money and the clothes of the gas station attendants he robs. That is balanced against cases without humor: a 12-year-old girl imprisoned by her foster mother, or a mugger who preys on senior citizens.

Chaos of Crime. Morrow. 1985

A psychotic sex killer is preying on the city's prostitutes in a fashion reminiscent of Jack the Ripper. A gorgeous redhead is sticking up liquor stores, and other cases continue to keep the detectives busy.

Serial killer

Blood Count. Morrow, 1986

Keeping busy, the detectives have to deal with a couple who may have murdered an unwanted child, a string of hit-and-run accidents caused by a Model A Ford, and a mugger who takes the cash and shoes of his victims.

Murder by the Tale. Morrow, 1987

A collection of stories including the following: "Accident," "The Bronze Cat," "The Cat," "The Clue," "The Long Chance," "The Motive," "Novelties," and "The Ring." Also includes seven non-Mendoza stories.

Short stories

Maj Sjowall and Per Wahloo ✍

Martin Beck

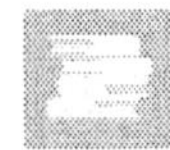

This Swedish husband and wife team created a unique detective for audiences when they introduced Martin Beck. His introspective attitude and laid-back style of investigation brought a European atmosphere to the procedural in combination with a political perspective that can be characterized as left of center. **Traditional/Hard-boiled**.

Roseanna. Pantheon, 1967

A dredging machine working below the locks at Borenshult scoops up the nude body of a woman in its bucket. When the local police are unable to identify her, and lack the skills to investigate, they call Stockholm and Martin Beck is sent to investigate.

Sweden, Motala

The Man on the Balcony. Pantheon, 1968

A killer is preying on young women in the city, and the only witness to the man's identity is another criminal. That mugger is not willing to come forward to identify the killer as that will compromise his freedom.

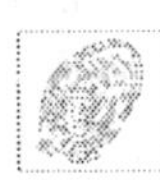

Sweden, Stockholm

The Man Who Went Up in Smoke. Pantheon, 1969

Pulled back to work from his holiday, Beck is sent to Hungary to find Swedish journalist Alf Matsson, who has gone missing. Forced to investigate on strange grounds among the Eastern European underworld, Beck is trying to discover how involved Matsson was in an international racket.

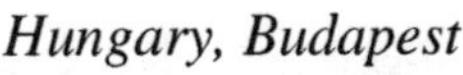

Hungary, Budapest

The Laughing Policeman. Pantheon, 1970

Why would someone shoot all eight passengers on a city bus, and what do you do when one of the dead is your colleague, Ake Stenstrom? That is the puzzle that faces Beck when he is assigned the task of finding the assassin. (ED)

Sweden, Stockholm

The Fire Engine That Disappeared. Pantheon. 1971

When Ernst Sigurd Karlsson kills himself, he leaves a brief suicide note: Martin Beck's name. Beck does not know Karlsson, nor can he imagine a connection to the other big incident of the day: an apartment house is blown up, causing the death of the 11 occupants, and the fire department cannot respond because someone has stolen their ladder truck.

Sweden, Stockholm

Murder at the Savoy. Pantheon, 1971

While giving a post-dinner speech, industrialist Viktor Palmgren is shot by an assassin. Beck is asked to identify a killer that the witnesses cannot.

Sweden, Malmo

The Abominable Man. Pantheon, 1972

Beck is given the politically sensitive case of a police captain's death when the man is murdered in his hospital bed. Hunting the assassin, who used a rifle to commit the crime, Beck also battles the media and his personal contempt for the man.

Sweden, Stockholm

The Locked Room. Pantheon, 1973

A very nervous woman robs a branch of one of Sweden's major banks, and then shoots a customer who foolishly feels he can stop the crime. Beck returns from his medical leave to begin an investigation.

Sweden, Stockholm

Cop Killer. Pantheon, 1975

When the body of a woman is pulled from a swamp, suspicions fall on a former prisoner convicted of sex crimes. Beck travels to the small town of Malmo to try and prove who is responsible.

Sweden, Malmo

The Terrorists. Pantheon, 1976

As foreign dignitaries are visiting Sweden, they are threatened by terrorists. At the same time, Beck must deal with the death of a pornographic filmmaker.

Sweden, Stockholm

Josephine Tey (pseud. of Elizabeth MacKintosh) ✍

Alan Grant

Scottish mystery writer Josephine Tey created a Scotland Yard Investigator named Grant who is best remembered for his ability to solve a case from his hospital bed. Grant is, in a sense, a dilettante detective, having enough money to choose to do police work. The first title in the series appeared under the pseudonym of Gordon Daviot. Grant's adventures can be recommended to traditional mystery readers, as his fallibility as a detective makes him a more developed character than many of the Golden Age types, and his cases can also be recommended to the Golden Age plot novel fans. **Soft-boiled/Traditional.**

The Man in the Queue. U.K.: Methuen, 1929 (Originally published under the pseud. of Gordon Daviot and later reprinted as by Josephine Tey). (U.S.: Dutton, 1929; also published as *Killer in the Crowd.* Mercury, 1954)

A stabbing takes place in a line outside the Woffington Theater in London. Assigned to the case is Grant of the Yard. He must discover how a murder could take place in front of numerous people queuing up for a show, and yet no one saw anything.

Daviot, Gordon · England, London · Theater

A Shilling for Candles. U.K.: Methuen, 1936 (U.S.: Macmillan, 1954)

At first, the death of movie actress Christine Clay on the beach is dismissed as a swimming accident, until an important clue is found. Inspector Grant is distressed to discover that many people wished her ill, and that he may have too many clues to sort through to discover a murderer.

Actors · England, Westover

To Love and Be Wise. U.K.: Davies, 1950 (U.S.: Macmillan, 1951)

Alan Grant first meets handsome young American photographer, Leslie Searle, when he arrives at author Lavinia Fitch's place to date actress Marta Hallard. When Grant next hears of Searle, it is because he has disappeared.

England, London

The Daughter of Time. U.K.: Davies, 1951 (U.S.: Macmillan, 1952)

Using her detective as an armchair detective, Tey confines Grant to bed and then lets him use research tools to investigate the case of Richard III. By the time this work is over, her detective will be healed and his version of the past will be displayed.

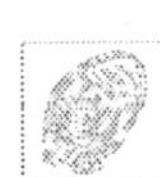

England, London · Medical

The Singing Sands. U.K.: Davies, 1952 (U.S.: Macmillan, 1953)

Taking the night train to Scotland while on a recreational holiday for overwork and mental fatigue, Grant is surprised to discover a dead man and a poem scribbled on a newspaper . Hoping a leisurely investigation away from home will mend his mind, Grant finds the pace quickens as he gets closer to a murderer.

Scotland

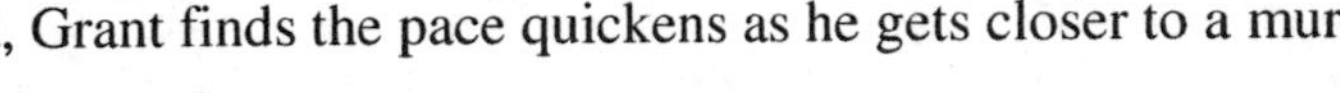

Arthur W. Upfield ✍

Napoleon Bonaparte

The Queensland Police Department in Australia is lucky to have the half-Aborigine detective Bonaparte on its staff. His use of his native skills, blended with his university education, make him a formidable detective. The unique Australian settings make these novels fascinating reading. The last novel in the series was completed by J. L. Price and Dorothy Strange. These novels can be recommended to readers looking for non-traditional detectives or detectives from non-European descent. **Traditional**. Series subject: **Aborigine-Australian**.

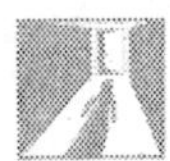

The Barrakee Mystery. U.K.: Hutchinson, 1929 (U.S.: *The Lure of the Bush.* Doubleday, 1965)

When the leader of the aborigines in the Darling River basin, King Henry, has been murdered, a hired hand investigates. In reality, that hired hand is the undercover detective, Bony, on the job.

Australia, Barrakee Station

The Sands of Windee. Hutchinson, 1931

Once again Bony is undercover, strolling the bush tracks in New South Wales. He is on loan to locate the missing Luke Marks, but before he is done, he will track down a murderer.

Australia, Windee Station

Wings Above the Diamantina. U.K.: Angus, 1936 (U.S.: *Wings Above the Claypan.* Doubleday, 1943; also published as *Winged Mystery.* Hamilton, 1937)

When a plane lands in Queensland, the passenger is found but not the pilot. It becomes Bony's job to locate the pilot while he waits for the female passenger to revive from her coma and provide the witness he needs to explain this mystery.

Australia, Queensland

Mr. Jelly's Business. U.K.: Angus, 1937 (U.S.: *Murder Down Under.* Doubleday, 1943)

Bony is on holiday in Western Australia when he finds himself drawn into a case by Sergeant Muir. A local farmer named George Loftus has disappeared, and the clues all indicate that Leonard Wallace, owner of the local hotel, might know why.

Australia, Burracoppin

Winds of Evil. U.K.: Angus, 1937 (U.S.: Doubleday, 1944)

The Strangler has caught a half-caste girl one year prior to the start of this novel, and more recently a young man named Marsh. Bony is sent in country to try and discover the secret behind these killings when a third murder, the lovely Mabel Storrie, points its clues at a young man who claims his innocence.

Australia, Carie • Serial killer

The Bone Is Pointed. U.K.: Angus, 1938 (U.S.: Doubleday, 1947)

Jeff Anderson, on the stallion Black Emperor, was to ride the fences, but he never reports back to his boss. Could his disappearance have anything to do with the Gordons, who lost their father 12 years prior in a similar circumstance? Bony follows an old and new trail on this adventure that unites him with his roots.

Australia, Opal Town

The Mystery of Swordfish Reef. U.K.: Angus, 1939 (U.S.: Doubleday, 1943)

Three men launch the Marlin to do some fishing off the town of Bermaguee and never return. Bony is called in when another fisherman catches one of their heads—and it has a bullet hole in the temple.

Australia, Bermaguee • Shipboard

Bushranger of the Skies. U.K.: Angus, 1940 (U.S.: *No Footprints in the Bush*. Doubleday, 1944)

Two stockmen are murdered on the ranch of wealthy cattleman Donald McPherson, and Sergeant Errey, sent to investigate, is killed by a bombing. Bony is almost a victim of the same incident, and now must hunt a murderer and a cop killer.

Australia, Diamantina

Death of a Swagman. Doubleday, 1945

George Kendall, a stockman, is found dead in the outback town of Merino. Six weeks later, after the local police have made no progress, a stockman comes to town looking for work. It is Bony, undercover, and before he has completed his investigation, he finds himself jailed like the men he hunts.

Australia, Merino

The Devil's Steps. Doubleday, 1946

The orderly life of Eleanor Jade, proprietress of Wideview Chalet, is about to be shattered when her help discovers the body of Grumman, one of her guests, near her place. Bony needs to connect that death with the murder of First Constable Rice, which was his first assignment in the area.

Australia, Melbourne • Hotels

An Author Bites the Dust. U.K.: Angus, 1948 (U.S.: Doubleday, 1948)

Mervyn Black, author and critic, is found murdered in his writing room at the foot of the garden during a houseparty. Assigned to help the local police, Bony is like a fish out of water among the literary clique who surrounded the famous man.

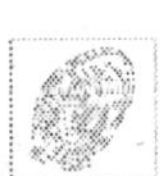

Authors • Australia, Yarrabo

The Mountains Have a Secret. Doubleday, 1948

Two hikers have disappeared into the mountains of New South Wales, and the police detective sent to find them has been murdered. Bony's tracking skills are tested again as he is asked to complete the assignment by investigating the strange Baden Park Hotel and its owner.

Australia, New South Wales • Hotels

The Widows of Broome. Doubleday, 1950

Two widows have been brutally strangled and the local police need an inside man to discover the truth. So Bony is assigned to Dickenson, the former rich man now turned town drunk, and is on the spot when a third widow is killed.

Australia, Broome • Serial killer

The Bachelors of Broken Hill. Doubleday, 1950

Two elderly men have been poisoned with cyanide in the small town of Broken Hill. Bony is dispatched to the town two months later, on the trail of a mysterious woman who was present at both killings. With little progress being made in his investigation, the detective feels he is waiting for a killer to strike again.

Australia, Broken Hill

The New Shoe. Doubleday, 1951 (Also published as *The Clue of the New Shoe.* Thorpe, 1974)

On a routine inspection, a body is found entombed in a thick wall of the Split Point Lighthouse, and when the local police are baffled, they ask Bony to do an undercover investigation.

Australia, Melbourne • Lighthouses

Venom House. Doubleday, 1952

In Edison, the Answerth place is known to the locals as The Venom House. Set islolated in the center of a lake, it houses two sisters and their brother, a man with limited capabilities. It is Bony's job to explain the drownings that have occurred near the odd manor house.

Australia, Edison

Murder Must Wait. U.K.: Heinemann, 1953 (U.S.: Doubleday, 1953)

Four children must disappear from Mitford before they realize help is needed from the outside. When Bony arrives, he finds Mrs. Rockcliff has been murdered, and the most likely suspect is the baby thief.

Australia, Mitford • Children at risk

Death of a Lake. U.K.: Heinemann, 1954 (U.S.: Doubleday, 1954)

The sheep station residents huddled around Lake Otway have two problems. A drought has lowered their lake and threatens the sheep that provide their livelihood. Even worse, the slowly lowering lake may also reveal the body of Ray Gillen, who disappeared in the lake one night. Bony is there to see who might find the body and the large amount of money that disappeared with the corpse.

Australia, Lake Otway

Sinister Stones. U.S.: Doubleday, 1954 (U.K.: *Cake in the Hat Box.* Heinemann 1955)

In the wild territory around Agar's Lagoon, Bony finds himself on the spot when Constable Stenhouse is murdered. Bony feels pressed to investigate when the suspicions fall on the tracker assigned to the policeman.

Australia, Agar's Lagoon

The Battling Prophet. Heinemann, 1956

Ben Wickham was a meteorologist with a stormy temperament, and his career was marked by controversy. His death brings an investigation, and his system that attempted to predict the weather one year in advance is the key for Bonaparte.

Australia, Mount Marlo • Weather

The Man of Two Tribes. U.K.: Heinemann, 1956 (U.S.: Doubleday, 1956)

Using his tracking skills, two camels, and a dog, Bonaparte hunts for a missing woman on the desolate Nullarbor Plain. Myra Thomas, wife of the Railways Commissioner, has either walked, jumped, or been pushed from one of the trains, and no one can find her.

Australia, Nullarbor Plain

Bony Buys a Woman. U.K.: Heinemann, 1957 (U.S.: *The Bushman Who Came Back.* Doubleday, 1957)

When someone kills her mother, seven-year-old Linda Bell disappears. The local trackers do their best, but eventually they need to turn to Bonaparte and his special skills to begin to locate the clues needed to find the child.

Australia, Mount Eden • Children at risk

Bony and the Black Virgin. U.K.: Heinemann, 1959 (U.S.: *The Torn Branch.* Scribner, 1986)

Eric Downer's elderly father, John, is a handful, but the young man has more problems when a man unknown to them is found murdered in their hired hand Carl Brandt's quarters. While they search for the dead man's identity, enough time goes by to uncover Brandt's corpse. Now confused, the local constable calls in Bonaparte who begins to find some answers to the many questions.

Australia, Fort Deakin

Bony and the Mouse. U.K.: Heinemann, 1959 (U.S.: *Journey to the Hangman.* Doubleday, 1959)

Sent incognito to try to find a connection between the death of a young aborigine girl, the wife of a cattleman, and a young garage apprentice, Bony rides into the small town of Daybreak. Melody Sam is the boss of Daybreak, and it is Bony's job to work within his fiefdom to catch a murderer.

Australia, Daybreak

Bony and the Kelly Gang. U.K.: Heinemann, 1960 (U.S.: *Valley of Smugglers.* Doubleday, 1960

Disguised as a nefarious horse thief, Bony has entered the Cork Valley to try to sort out the murder of an Excise Officer named Eric Torby. The blame for this one can most likely be laid between the hard-drinking and constantly feuding Conway and Kelly clans, known bootleggers.

Australia, Cork Valley

Bony and the White Savage. U.K.: Heinemann, 1961 (U.S.: *The White Savage.* Doubleday, 1961; also published as *Boney and the White Savage.* Pan, 1987)

Bony's tracking skills are put to the test when he must travel into the cave country of Western Australia in search of Marvin Rhudder—thief, rapist, and murderer.

Australia, Rhudder's Inlet

The Will of the Tribe. U.K.: Heinemann, 1962 (U.S.: Doubleday, 1962)

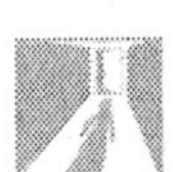

Bony does not have to track this victim, just explain how the body of a white man could be found in the middle of a meteor crater in the Australian desert. Bony is frustrated when it becomes evident the aborigines are hiding as much evidence as the white family involved in the case.

Australia, Hall's Creek

Madman's Bend. U.K.: Heinemann, 1963 (U.S.: *The Body at Madman's Bend.* Doubleday, 1963)

After the death of her father, Jill Madden's mother marries her hired hand, William Lush. His abuse of the women leads the girl to take matters into her own hands, and it becomes Bony's job to find William Lush when Jill's mother dies.

Australia, White Bend

The Lake Frome Monster (by J. L. Price and Dorothy Strange). Heinemann, 1966

This book was left unfinished by Upfield, and it was completed by Price and Strange. Eric Maidstone, a guest at the Quinambie Station, fails to return from an expedition in the wild. When a new hand, Edward Bonnay, arrives three weeks after the death, the reader knows that Bony is on the job again.

Australia, Lake Frome • Price, J. L. • Strange, Dorothy

The Modern Practitioners

Thomas Adcock ✍

Neil Hockaday

The tough streets of New York are the hunting ground for this cop who works in the Street Crimes Unit Manhattan. Readers may also enjoy Lawrence Block (Matthew Scudder), Michael Connelly, J. A. Jance (J. P. Beaumont), and Ian Rankin. See a website about the author at http://www.uni.edu/kollasch/darkmaze. **Hard-boiled**.

Sea of Green. Mysterious Press, 1989

Originally assigned to investigate some death threats against a Harlem minister, Hockaday soon finds that case connected to some deaths in Hell's Kitchen, his old neighborhood. The case will pit two factions against each other: the people who need a place to live and the people who want to develop the city right on top of them.

New York, New York

Dark Maze. Pocket, 1991

When the old man named Picasso spoke to Hockaday about murder, Hockaday should not have dismissed him as another example of the mentally challenged living in the streets. He should have accepted him as the key to a series of killings that expresses the depression of big city life.

New York, New York • Serial killer

Drown All the Dogs. Pocket, 1994

Aidan Hockaday, Neil's father, disappeared during WWII, and a trip to Ireland to find his roots seems like a good idea to Hockaday. A murder in Dublin puts Hockaday on the hot seat, and his Uncle Liam is of little help. Meanwhile, back in New York, Father Tim Kelly, who had given Hockaday a medallion that set him on his journey, is brutally murdered and Hockaday's friend, Police Captain Davy Mogaill, disappears.

Ireland, Dublin • New York, New York

Devil's Heaven. Pocket, 1995

Hockaday's overseas pilgrimage, new marriage, and days off booze have made him into a new man. However, crime can change that, and when his wife's partner in the ad agency is found dead in a sexual bondage costume, he is forced to investigate.

New York, New York

Thrown-Away Child. Pocket, 1996

Having married black actress Ruby Flagg, Hockaday travels to his wife's hometown when he witnesses two racist cops hunting for Ruby's cousin, Perry Duciat. Hockaday unofficially joins the New Orleans police in their hunt for a boy wanted for murder.

Louisiana, New Orleans

Grief Street. Pocket, 1997

On the outside of the force because of a complaint he lodged against a fellow officer for brutality, Hockaday is distracted by the upcoming birth of his first child. When a series of murders plagues the Hell's Kitchen area of his birth, the clues lie in a death play sent to Ruby.

New York, New York · Theater

M. C. Beaton (pseud. of Marion Chesney)

Hamish Macbeth

Scotland provides the backdrop for Hamish Macbeth, village constable of the Scottish Highlands. Charmer that he may be, Macbeth seems to have a dark cloud following him around, now matter how hard he tries. These police novels are written with a decidedly light feel, and Macbeth's need to support his family as a prime motivator adds depth to this character's motivations. Readers may also enjoy Joan Hess (Arly Hanks) and H. R. F. Keating. See a website about this author at http://www.booksnbytes.com/authors/beaton_mc.html. **Soft-boiled.** Series subjects: **Humor · Scotland, Lochdubh**.

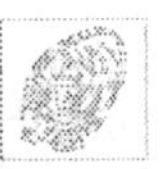

Death of a Gossip. St. Martin's Press, 1985

The Lochdubh School of Casting: Salmon and Trout Fishing has just lost a student when the unpopular Lady Jane is drowned while casting. Being the weekly topic of gossip for the town means the list of possible suspects is very long. Macbeth dives into his first case with all the vigor of a fledgling detective.

Fishing

Death of a Cad. St. Martin's Press, 1987

Henry Sutherland is a successful playwright and the fiancée of Priscilla Halburton-Smythe, to the disappointment of Macbeth as he had once dated the fair Priscilla. When one of the houseguests at their engagement party is shot on the grouse moor, Macbeth is called to investigate.

Death of an Outsider. St. Martin's Press, 1988

Reassigned to Cnothan, Macbeth finds the residents resent him only a little less than the abrasive Englishman, William Mainwaring, another newcomer to the village. Macbeth had laughed off the witchcraft charges Mainwaring had made against some residents until his body is found on a high cliff at the outskirts of the village.

Scotland, Cnothan · Witchcraft

Death of a Perfect Wife. St. Martin's Press, 1988

Trixie Thomas arrives in Lochdubh, married, unemployed, and English. When she begins to organize the small village, resentment builds until Macbeth has a case of murder to solve.

Death of a Hussy. St. Martin's Press, 1990

Maggie Baird is a bit randy for the village, and she is murdered when her car is torched with her in it. Macbeth is left with Maggie's timid niece named Alison Kerr, and Maggie's four former lovers, one of whom was to be Maggie's next husband, and all of whom were guests in her Highland cottage.

Death of a Snob. St. Martin's Press, 1991

Macbeth is brought to the island of Eileencraig at Christmas to protect Jane Wetherby, owner of The Happy Wanderer Health Farm, and a woman fearful of her own death. When Morag Todd, one of her guests, dies instead, Macbeth finds hostility both inside and outside the health farm, and plenty of suspects for an investigation.

Christmas · Holidays · Scotland, Eileencraig

Death of a Prankster. St. Martin's Press, 1992

Arthur Trent once pulled Macbeth's leg with a fake death at Arrat House, but this time when the call comes through it is to investigate the death of the owner. At the house, he finds a group of suspects interested in Trent's will, and a clue that involves his former love, Priscilla.

Scotland, Arrat · Wills

Death of a Glutton. St. Martin's Press, 1993

Priscilla's Tommel Castle Hotel is hosting Britain's exclusive Checkmate Singles Club, where potential matches are made by its director, Maria Worth. To Maria's dismay, the four couples who arranged to meet in Lochdubh dislike each other, and her obnoxious partner Peta's arrival does not help. Nor does Peta's murder.

Hotels

Death of a Travelling Man. St. Martin's Press, 1993

Promoted to Sergeant and given an assistant constable named Willie Lamont, Macbeth is ready for a crime wave. Disturbed by a wanderer with an evil way, Macbeth keeps his eye on the trailer parked next to the Lochdubh Hotel, until the wanderer's body is discover within.

Death of a Charming Man. Mysterious Press, 1994

Macbeth visits Drim to check out the villager's complaints about the newcomer, handsome Englishman Peter Hynd. When death strikes, Macbeth is in place to launch an investigation.

Scotland, Drim

Death of a Nag. Mysterious Press, 1995

Macbeth and his faithful dog, Trowser, are on holiday in Skag as he is trying to forget the breakup of his engagement and his demotion. Checking into Friendly House proves just the opposite, and the death of the unpopular nag, Bob Harris, creates a busman's holiday for the constable.

Scotland, Skag

Death of a Macho Man. Mysterious Press, 1996

The sleepy village is awakened by the arrival of The Macho Man, a professional wrestler prone to buying drinks in the pub and brawling with all comers. Challenged to a bout, Macbeth accepts, but the bout is called off when someone shoots The Macho Man.

Wrestling

Death of a Dentist. Mysterious Press, 1997

Macbeth needs to visit Dr. Frederick Gilchrist, famous for his strange technique in the dentist chair and perhaps with some of the village ladies. But when Macbeth arrives at the dentist's office, he finds someone has poisoned the dear doctor.

Dentists · Medical · Scotland, Braikie

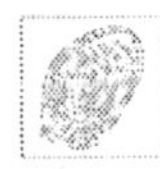

Death of a Scriptwriter. Mysterious Press, 1998

Macbeth offers a little romance to spinsterish author Patricia Martyn-Broyd, who has been unable to write a follow-up to her successful 1965 mystery novel. News that a film is going to be made of her old character brings little joy, as a porn star has been hired to play the female detective, and the film company plans nude scenes. When the cameras start rolling in Drim, it leads to murder.

Authors · Film · Scotland, Drim

Death of an Addict. Mysterious Press, 1999

A sea monster has been reported near Drim, and Macbeth is distracted by that adventure and unable to prevent Tommy Jarret's recurring drug use. When the drugs lead to his death, Macbeth decides to infiltrate the drug scene and end the source.

Scotland, Stathbane

Death of a Dustman. Mysterious Press, 2001

Strathbane Councilperson Fred Fleming wishes to green Lochdubh, so she appoints dustman (garbage man) Fergus MacLeod to the position of environment officer over the new recycling center. Already living under the cloud of his violent personality, Fleming's appointment leads to his murder. The quest to solve this crime falls to Macbeth, a task made difficult by the community's relief at losing one of its local bullies.

Environment

Death of a Celebrity. Mysterious Press, 2002

The village of Lochdubh is thrown into turmoil when the scandal-raking television journalist, Crystal French, arrives with her production crew. The investigation of her death is left to others, but Macbeth cannot keep himself from probing into her murder, allied with the local astrologer, Elsbeth Grant.

Scotland, Lochdubh · Television

Eleanor Taylor Bland ✍

Marti MacAlister

Lincoln Prairie, Illinois, is the home of African-American female cop Marti MacAlister, who is often partnered with Vik Jessenovik. As a single mother of two children, she struggles to maintain a homelife and a professional career. The crimes in Lincoln Prairie are as serious as in the neighboring city of Chicago, and MacAlister needs to call on all her skills, and the skills of her support organization, to solve the cases. Readers may also enjoy J. A. Jance (Joanna Brady), Laurie King (Kate Martinelli), and Margaret Marton (Sigrid Harald). See the author's website at http://home.earthlink.net/~etbland. **Traditional.** Series subjects: **African-American · Illinois, Lincoln Prairie**.

Dead Time. St. Martin's Press, 1992

Lauretta Dorsey is murdered in her room at the Cramer Hotel, and the other residents of the hotel are unable to provide much help to MacAlister and her partner, Vik Jessenovik. But when it appears that two children living on the streets may provide the clues necessary to solve the crime, MacAlister uses her streetwise ways to locate the children.

Slow Burn. St. Martin's Press, 1993

Two deaths at a women's clinic may be tied to a right-to-life group, or could just be an arson-for-profit scheme. The connected death of a young man, found in a ravine in Lincoln Prairie, leads MacAlister and Jeesenovik to young girls with secrets.

Gone Quiet. St. Martin's Press, 1994

Henry Hamilton's death by suffocation is complicated, as he is the stepfather of Denise Stevens, a juvenile probation officer in the department. Trying to protect Denise, who proves unhelpful and protective of her family, MacAlister also probes the Mount Gethsemane Baptist Church, where Hamilton was a deacon.

Done Wrong. St. Martin's Press, 1995

MacAlister left Chicago behind when her husband Johnny MacAlister, a narcotics detective, was killed in action. Now, another officer has died, and the suggestion is made that she could discover the reason for Johnny's death by investigating this new lead.

Illinois, Chicago

Keep Still. St. Martin's Press, 1996

Sophia Admunds is sent tumbling down her basement stairs, and the cops focus their investigation on her two grown sons. MacAlister also has to investigate the death of an elderly woman in a motel pool. The second case proves the crack needed to see the connection between some old events and the current deaths.

See No Evil. St. Martin's Press, 1998

A dead woman from Chicago is found on the shores of Lake Michigan in Lincoln Prairie, and MacAlister and Jessenovik suspect her drug-dealer boyfriend. Meanwhile, death is stalking MacAlister and her family, and she needs to use all her resources to protect her children.

Tell No Tales. St. Martin's Press, 1999

MacAlister's new-found love and honeymoon are interrupted when Lincoln Prairie's slums reveal the body of the mentally ill son of one of Chicago's wealthiest families. Another case gives them a mummy in a movie theater, and MacAlister finds little time for her new husband, Ben.

Scream in Silence. St. Martin's Minotaur, 2000

Virginia McCroft may have been a busybody and the town gadfly, but she did not deserve to be shot in her own home, with her body left in the rubble of an arson attempt to hide the murder. When MacAlister and Jessenovick are assigned the case, they fear it may have been caused by blackmail, and two bomb explosions in the town add fuel to the fire.

Whispers in the Dark. St. Martin's Minotaur, 2001

MacAlister and her partner Jessenovik are set on the trail of a serial killer when a severed arm is discovered buried in a field, the beckoning hand a taunt to the detectives to find the killer. At the same time, her concern for her friend Sharon finds MacAlister in the Bahamas as a hurricane bears down on the island.

Caribbean, Bahamas • Hurricanes • Illinois, Chicago • Serial killer

***Windy City Dying.** St. Martin's Minotaur, 2002

K. C. Constantine (pseud. of Carl Kosak) ✍

Mario Balzic/Ruggiero Carlucci

Small-town America can still provide a decent amount of work for a cop. Balzic's Rocksburg, Pennsylvania, is a churning caldron of complications, especially because of its own version of the mob. When Balzic retires, the series shifts to the acting chief, Balzic's long-suffering aide, Ruggiero Carlucci. These novels can be read both for their procedural cases, and for the social history of small-town America. Readers may also enjoy Eleanor Taylor Bland, Reginald Hill, Tony Hillerman, Sharyn McCrumb (Spencer Arrowood), and Alan Robinson. **Traditional/ Hard-boiled**. Series subject: **Pennsylvania, Rocksburg**.

The Rocksburg Railroad Murders. Saturday Review Press, 1972

John Andrasko is murdered in the small town of Rocksburg, riding the train to his job at Knox Steel. Before the police are done with their investigation, their inquiries will affect the town's social structure and raise the specter of organized crime.

The Man Who Liked to Look at Himself. Saturday Review Press, 1973

Balzic thought the worst that could happen to him on the first day of hunting is being bit by a hunting dog, but when the beast also unearths a human bone, he must not only try to find a murderer, he must first find a victim.

The Blank Page. Saturday Review Press, 1974

Janet Pisula is found dead in the rooming house for college students run by Cynthia Summer. A blank piece of typing paper is found on the victim's stomach, and her background is blank as well. With nothing to go on, Balzic and his officers struggle to find a murderer.

Academia

A Fix Like This. Saturday Review Press, 1975

Armand Manditti has been hauled into the hospital, stabbed, and left there for Balzic to explain that when you are the victim, you do not need a lawyer. Debating whether he needs to involve his shadow-figure Muscotti, he plunges into an investigation that eventually leads to a much more involved and dangerous case than originally assumed.

The Man Who Liked Slow Tomatoes. Godine, 1982

In a small town like Rocksburg, it is not easy for Balzic to work some cases. When Jimmy Romanelli is murdered, Balzic finds the investigation difficult, and the man's passion for tomatoes is an odd and compelling reason to commit a murder.

Always a Body to Trade. Godine, 1983

The new mayor of Rocksburg wants results when some crimes in the city can be traced to the drug subculture. His pressure on Balzic is intense, and Balzic must turn to the Reverend Rutherford Rufee as his contact with the black underworld.

Upon Some Midnights Clear. Godine, 1985

It is Christmas in Rocksburg, but that offers no rest for Balzic and his forces. Mrs. Garbin claims she has lost her Christmas funds to Billy Lum, there is a shooting in the town, and some dissatisfied Vietnam Vets are still warring back home.

Christmas • Holidays

Joey's Case. Mysterious Press, 1988

Albert Castelucci's son was shot in neighboring Westfield Township five months prior, while Balzic was out of Rocksburg. Not satisfied with the investigation provided by the state police, Castelucci wants Balzic to launch a new investigation and find his son's killer.

Pennsylvania, Westfield Township

Sunshine Enemies. Mysterious Press, 1990

Balzic thinks his problems with a newly established pornography shop will come from the campaign against it launched by Reverend P. Shaner Weier. However, the discovery of a murder at the shop yields a corpse with two names that has been repeatedly stabbed.

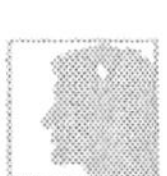

Pornography

Bottom Liner Blues. Mysterious Press, 1993

Balzic is warned in a rather cryptic fashion that a Farley Gruenwald is in danger from Boomer, the husband of a woman who thinks her association with both men is going to endanger her child. His inability to get a handle on both the case and his own personal life is complicated by the unwanted help of Nick Myushkin, a Russian writer with insight.

Cranks and Shadows. Mysterious Press, 1995

Balzic is forced by the mayor to lay off five of his officers, and the chief is beginning to see the end of his career. But worse, he must deal with the Conemaugh Foundation, a secret organization out to seize control of the town.

Good Sons. Mysterious Press, 1996

Detective Ruggerio Carlucci is the acting chief of Rocksburg now that Balzic has retired, and he is waiting for the mayor to appoint a new chief, a job he could use but for which he may not be qualified. The rape and beating of a local businesswoman puts Carlucci on a hunt that will take him to Pittsburgh and up against the organized crime family that operates in Rocksburg.

Family Values. Mysterious Press, 1997

Bored in his retirement, Balzic is almost happy when Deputy Attorney General Warren Livingood asks him to become a Special Investigator for the state and probe a 17-year-old murder. What makes this old case of a double homicide around a drug deal so messy is that it may lead to another police officer.

Pennsylvania

Brushback. Mysterious Press, 1998

Bobby Blasco is a local hero, having earned the nickname of Brushback for his hard style as a Boston Red Sox pitcher. After a mysterious accident, he was forced back to Rocksburg where he runs an illegal gambling den. His unsavory local history may be the reason he is beaten to death with a Louisville Slugger, and is the newest case for acting-chief Ruggerio.

Baseball

Blood Mud. Mysterious Press, 1999

Balzic cannot sit still so he accepts an assignment from lawyer Panagios Valcanas to determine if a recent gun shop burglary is legit or an insurance scam. Told the case will rap up in a few short days, Balzic's radar should have told him there was more to this story than a few missing guns.

Grievance. Mysterious Press, 2000

Steel magnate James Deford Lyon, whose company has moved to Brazil causing massive layoffs in Rocksburg, is found murdered. Detective Carlucci finds himself with hundreds of unemployed suspects, while his own personal life begins to spin out of control.

Saving Room for Dessert. Mysterious Press, 2002

The focus of this series has shifted before, and here the light shines on three beat officers named William Rayford, Robert Canoza, and James Reseta. The story focuses on one evening shift and the professional and personal demons that haunt The Flats of Rocksburg.

Deborah Crombie ✍

Duncan Kincaid/Gemma James

In contemporary times, it is not unusual to find American authors writing about English detectives. Deborah Crombie lived in England and Scotland for a time, but now lives in Texas. Detective Superintendent Kincaid comes from the upper class, and within the series he develops a professional and personal relationship with Sergeant James, who is not from his class. See the author's website at http://www.deborahcrombie.com/welcome/welcome.html. Readers may also enjoy Martha Grimes, Elizabeth George, and Anne Perry. **Traditional**. Series subject: **Teams**.

A Share in Death. Scribner, 1993

Kincaid is vacationing in the Yorkshire Moors in autumn when he meets Sebastian Wade, only to have the man's body found bobbing in the jacuzzi at Followdale. Forced to ask for help from his sergeant, Gemma James, he must abandon his holiday and become an inspector, unfortunately not swiftly enough to prevent another murder.

England, Woolsey-Under-Bank

All Shall Be Well. Scribner, 1994

Kincaid finds that trouble follows his footsteps again when he is forced to investigate the death of his neighbor Jasmine Dent, a cancer victim who is thought to have passed away from her disease. When Jasmine's young friend Margaret Bellamy tells Kincaid she had been asked to assist in Jasmine's death and had refused, the detective and his sergeant must discover who might have helped things along.

England, Hampstead

Leave the Grave Green. Scribner, 1995.

The operatic family of Sir Gerald Asherton, conductor, and Dame Caroline Stowe, soprano, finds itself in the news when their son-in-law, Connor Swann, is found dead in the Thames. The exploration of the present murder leads Kincaid and James to the past, where they must confront some family secrets, and their feelings for each other.

England, High Wycombe

Mourn Not Your Dead. Scribner, 1996

No officer likes to investigate the death of another officer and especially not when it appears the reasons may be domestic. Kincaid and James are assigned the case of Alastair

Gilbert, a London commander, found knifed in his own kitchen with no signs of forced entry.

England, Surrey

Dreaming of the Bones. Scribner, 1997

Kincaid risks his current happiness with James when he agrees to investigate a historical case after being prompted by his ex-wife, Victoria McClellan. Vic believes that when poet Lydia Brooke committed suicide five years prior, the case should have been investigated as a murder. MA

England, Grantchester

Kissed a Sad Goodbye. Bantam, 1999

Kincaid is trying to forge a relationship with his son Kit when he is called away by the murder of Annabelle Hammond, the director of an old family firm of tea merchants. Hammond's abrasive personality and lifestyle leaves Kincaid and James with plenty of suspects, and their personalities leave them in a stew about their relationship.

England, London

A Finer End. Bantam, 2001

The legends of England still haunt the countryside, and when Glastonbury's legends dealing with King Arthur draw New Age followers to the town, the tensions are high. When Kincaid's cousin, Jack Montfort, receives an ancient communication from a dead monk, it stirs up the townsfolk. When death occurs, it stirs up Kincaid and James, who despite being drawn apart professionally, are drawn to solve this case.

Antiquities • England, Glastonbury • Religion

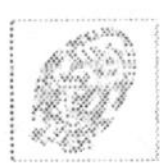

And Justice There Is None. Bantam, 2002

James's life is changing rapidly, as she is pregnant with Kincaid's child and she has just made the decision to move in with her fellow detective. As her impending promotion to Inspector is dangling in front of her, she is given the case of the murder of Dawn Arrowood. Dawn was also pregnant, and the focus for solving her murder is on the missing antique porcelain dealer Alex Dunn, with whom she was having an affair.

Antiquities • England, London • Pregnancy

Colin Dexter ✍

Chief Inspector Morse

The cult of personality dominates many contemporary mysteries, and one of the most interesting ones is Chief Inspector Morse. His intriguing personal complications and his relationship with the supporting cast in these novels make Dexter's work some of the best of the contemporary procedurals. As an intellectual in a community of intellectuals, Morse has a tendency to distance himself from the very people he is supposed to protect, and from the community of officers who should be his safety net. These novels can be recommended to anyone who likes a traditional approach, plus those who like novels with psychological motivations. Readers may also enjoy Sarah Caudwell, Amanda Cross, Antonia Fraser, Reginald Hill, and Alan Robinson. **Traditional**.

Last Bus to Woodstock. U.K.: Macmillan, 1975 (U.S.: St. Martin's Press, 1975)

Sylvia Kaye and another secretary are hitchhiking on a road near Oxford. Later Sylvia's body is found outside a pub in Woodstock. When Morse and Lewis track down the most likely companion for the dead woman, she proves uncooperative. As Morse pushes the investigation, he discovers some disturbing facts within what outwardly appears a calm and quiet existence amongst Sylvia's friends.

England, Woodstock

Last Seen Wearing. U.K.: Macmillan, 1976 (U.S.: St. Martin's Press, 1976)

Two years prior to the start of this novel, Valerie Taylor disappeared from the Roger Bacon School near Oxford. Her parents have just received a letter from her, but Morse is suspicious of the letter from the beginning.

England, Oxford

The Silent World of Nicholas Quinn. U.K.: Macmillan, 1977 (U.S.: St. Martin's Press, 1977)

Being deaf proves no handicap to Nicholas Quinn when he gets appointed to the Foreign Examinations Syndicate at Oxford, until someone puts cyanide in his sherry. The case forces Morse inside the cloistered walls of the university.

Academia · England, Oxford

Service of All the Dead. U.K.: Macmillan, 1979 (U.S.: St. Martin's Press, 1980)

In sleepy little St. Frideswide, things are not well, as the churchwarden H. A. Joseph has been stabbed to death in the vestry during the service. Morse arrives and begins an investigation that uncovers other church members who are behaving badly, and that leads to another murder.

England · Religion

The Dead of Jericho. U.K.: Macmillan, 1981 (U.S.: St. Martin's Press, 1982)

Morse had known Anne Scott briefly, so when he finds himself in Jericho, he stops to see her. She never came to the door, but she was present. When the verdict is that Anne had committed suicide, Morse's personal knowledge makes him doubt the verdict. DA

England, Jericho

The Riddle of the Third Mile. U.K.: Macmillan, 1983 (U.S.: St. Martin's Press, 1984)

Oliver Maximilian Alexander Browne-Smith has led a long life, some of which involves a rather sordid and hidden personal life kept secret from his Oxford companions. When his body is found dumped in the Oxford canal, Morse finds himself probing into the life of this elderly Oxford don.

Academia · England, Oxford

The Secret of Annexe 3. U.K.: Macmillan, 1986 (U.S.: St. Martin's Press, 1987)

Morse and Lewis are awakened early on New Year's Day and summoned to the Haworth Hotel. The winner of their New Year's Eve costume party contest is dead, while his female companion and the other guests have all checked out.

England, Oxford · Holidays · New Year's Eve

The Wench Is Dead. U.K.: Macmillan, 1989 (U.S.: St. Martin's Press, 1990)

In a tribute to *The Daughter Of Time* (Josephine Tey), Morse is hospital-bound as he recovers from an ulcer attack. Reading *Murder on the Oxford Canal*, he becomes enamored with the case of Joanna Franks, murdered aboard the canal boat Barbara Bray. Believing the verdict in the case was incorrect, he begins an investigation on a case over 100 years old. DA

England, Oxford · Medical

The Jewel That Was Ours. U.K.: Macmillan, 1991 (U.S.: Crown, 1991)

Laura Stratton is staying at the Randolph Hotel with her American tour group, preparing to donate the Wolvercote Jewel to the Ashmolean Museum. When she dies in her bathtub, and the jewel is missing, Morse and Lewis are asked to investigate.

Antiquities · England, Oxford · Jewels

The Way Through the Woods. U.K.: Macmillan, 1992 (U.S.: Crown, 1993)

For a year Morse had tried to tell everyone that the girl who disappeared was murdered, but it is not until an anonymous letter arrives at the station, containing a cryptic poem, that an investigation is launched. Morse, on holiday in Dorset, reads of the poem in the paper, and begins to contemplate the solution to a crime. DA

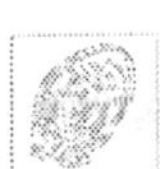

England, Dorset

Morse's Greatest Mystery and Other Stories. U.K.: Macmillan, 1993 (U.S.: Crown, 1995)

A collection of the following stories: "As Good as Gold," "At the Lulu-Bar Motel," "The Carpet-Bagger," "A Case of Mis-Identity," "Dead as a Dodo," "Evans Tries an O-Level," "The Inside Story," "Last Call," "Monty's Revolver," "Morse's Greatest Mystery," and "Neighbourhood Watch."

Short stories

The Daughters of Cain. U.K.: Macmillan, 1994 (U.S.: Crown, 1994)

Dr. Felix McClure, formerly of Oxford University, is found stabbed to death in his home. Morse follows the clues to Edward Brooks, a college handyman who disappears when the attention focuses on him and his possible drug dealing.

Academia · England, Oxford

Death Is Now My Neighbour. U.K.: Macmillan, 1996 (U.S.: *Death is Now My Neighbor.* Crown, 1996)

Morse and Lewis are investigating the shooting of a woman in her North Oxford home that leads them to the strip joints of Soho. Meanwhile, the Master of

Lonsdale College has retired, and two senior dons are left competing for the single spot while their wives compete as well.

Academia · England, Oxford

The Remorseful Day. Crown, 2000

Yvonne Harrison's death has never been officially explained, and there are hints surfacing that new evidence may help the police with their inquiries. However, Morse is refusing to look a second time at the case, despite the fact that he has some personal connection to the victim. While Lewis does his duty, he finds his mentor keeping a close eye on the case, maybe to the point of launching an unofficial investigation.

England, Costwold, Lower Swinstead

Elizabeth George ✍

Thomas Lynley/Barbara Havers

An American writing about English detectives, George has created an ensemble of characters in a similar fashion to McBain. Scotland Yard Inspector Lynley is another aristocratic detective a la Roderick Alleyn, being the Earl of Asherton. His team, which includes Sergeant Barbara Havers, pathologist Simon Allcourt-St. James, and Lady Helen Clyde, provides an interesting ensemble. Readers may also enjoy Deborah Crombie and Martha Grimes. See the author's website at http://www.elizabethgeorgeonline.com. **Traditional**. Series subject: **Teams**.

A Great Deliverance. Bantam, 1989

A 300-year-old legend talks of the death of an infant, sacrificed when it cried and almost revealed that the villagers were using the Keldale Abbey as a refuge from Cromwell's raiders. In the present, Lynley and Havers are arriving in the village because Roberta Teys has chopped off her father's head. AG AN

England, Yorkshire

Payment in Blood. Bantam, 1989

A controversial play has caused a London theatrical company to come to Scotland, and its playwright, Joy Sinclair, is murdered on an isolated estate in the Scottish Highlands. Asked to investigate where they have no authority, Lynley and his partner, Havers, search for a murderer among four promising suspects, one of whom is personally connected to Lynley.

Scotland, Strathclyde · Theater

Well-Schooled in Murder. Bantam, 1990

As boys, John Corntel and Lynley went to school together at Eton, and when Corntel has a boy named Matthew Whateley missing from his Bredgar Chambers school located in West Sussex, he calls upon his friend at New Scotland Yard. Operating outside his jurisdiction with the help of Havers and Allcourt-St. James, he finds himself hunting for a child murderer.

Academia · England, West Sussex

A Suitable Vengeance. Bantam, 1991

Lynley has brought his fiancée, Deborah Cotter, to the family home at Howenstow for an engagement party, but the personal tensions in the air among friends and family spoil the atmosphere. Then a journalist is murdered in Nanrunnel, and the officers must return to work.

England, Cornwall, Howenstow

For the Sake of Elena. Bantam, 1992

Elena Weaver is a student at St. Stephen's College at Cambridge, and on one of her usual early-morning runs, she is beaten to death. The young woman had many troubling and intense relationships with individuals that give Lynley plenty of suspects, including the fact that her father's mistress was the person who found her body.

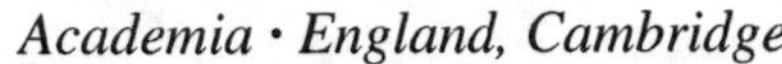

Academia • England, Cambridge

Missing Joseph. Bantam, 1993

Deborah and Simon St. James have taken a vacation in Lancastershire when they discover the dead body of the vicar of Winslough. When the local police rule the death an accidental poisoning, Simon asks Lynley to pursue an investigation focusing on the man's last meal.

England, Lancastershire

Playing for the Ashes. Bantam, 1994

In an old cottage in Kent occupied by Gabriella Patten, a fire is set to hide the body of a national cricket star named Kenneth Fleming. Patten's far-reaching relationship is disturbing, but Fleming's family and personal life are equally disturbed, providing Lynley and Havers with a disturbing case to conduct.

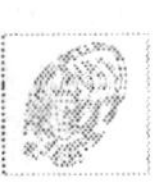

England, Kent

In the Presence of the Enemy. Bantam, 1996

Dennis Luxford, editor of the scandal-mongering newspaper *The Source*, finds himself on the other end of the problem when a letter informs him that his child, Charlotte Bowen, has been kidnapped. Born after a liaison with Eve Bowen, who is now a Conservative Party candidate, the child will be killed if Luxford does not publicly admit to the affair. When Luxford fails to act, and the child is killed, Lynley and Havers pursue a blackmailer and murderer.

England, London • Journalism • Kidnapping

Deception on His Mind. Bantam, 1997

In a pillbox on the shore of Balford-le-Nez, a Pakistani man named Haytham Querashi, who has just arrived from the home country, is found murdered. Havers's neighbor Khalidah Hadiyyah is related to the man, and she asks to be assigned to the case, thus conducting her own investigation while Lynley is on his honeymoon.

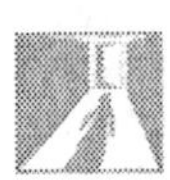

England, Balford

In Pursuit of the Proper Sinner. Bantam, 1999

At the feet of the Nine Sisters Henge, two bodies, each killed in a different fashion, are discovered and turned over to Inspector Lynley. When one of the victims proves to be the daughter of a former police officer who was his mentor, it sets him on a path that includes trying to save the career of the disgraced Havers.

England, Derbyshire, Calder Moor

A Traitor to Memory. Bantam, 2001

A hit-and-run accident leaves Eugenie Davies dead on a London street, and the crime lands in the lap of Lynley and Havers. The clues left at the scene point to mysteries from the past, including some that swirl around the woman's dead child. The most mysterious may be the reason behind her surviving child-prodigy son's inability to perform on his violin.

England, London

Martha Grimes ✍

Richard Jury/Melrose Plant

Written by an American, these English mysteries are reminiscent of Dorothy L. Sayers. Named for English pubs, each title features Grimes's well-developed supporting cast. Inspector Jury is supported by two major cohorts: the slightly potty professor, Melrose Plant, and Jury's intrusive Aunt Agatha. Grimes's breezy tone, and use of humor, adds a lightness to the books that will appeal to readers who enjoy this kind of mystery. Her style echoes the traditional Golden Age writers. Readers may also enjoy Deborah Crombie and Elizabeth George. See the author's website at http://www.marthagrimes.com. **Soft-boiled/Traditional**. Series subject: **Teams.**

The Man with a Load of Mischief. Little, Brown, 1981

When two strangers arrive in Long Piddleton and are each murdered in a strange and unusual way on consecutive nights, the murders ignite this sleepy village. Because they occurred during the village's Christmas revelries and many of the village's major players find themselves suspects, Inspector Jury is called to investigate.

Christmas • England, Northants, Long Piddleton • Holidays

The Old Fox Deceiv'd. Little, Brown, 1982

Gemma Temple arrives in the little fishing village of Rackmoor, claiming to be Dillys March, the long-lost heir of Colonel Titus Carel. When she is murdered soon after her arrival, it falls to Jury to sort out the underlying politics in the small village.

England, Yorkshire, Rackmoor

The Anodyne Necklace. Little, Brown, 1983

Littlebourne seems to be creating its own trouble: a severed finger reveals that there is a dead body to deal with, while one of its residents is mugged and left in a coma in the underground in East London. Jury must put together the clues to restore order to the small village.

England, Littlebourne

The Dirty Duck. Little, Brown, 1984

A visiting group of American tourists have their trip disrupted when Gwendolyn Bracegirdle is murdered after a performance of *As You Like It*. When two lines of an unknown poem are left on her body as a clue, Jury worries that he may not find the killer before he strikes again.

England, Stratford

Jerusalem Inn. Little, Brown, 1984

While on holiday, Jury meets a woman in a graveyard, but when she is murdered, he is driven to discover the truth behind her death. Meanwhile, Melrose has also found a woman, equally dead. The detectives' job is to link the deaths and restore the season to its right path.

Christmas · England, Newcastle · Holidays

The Deer Leap. Little, Brown, 1985

Polly Pread has asked Jury to the small village of Ashdown Down after a series of pets have been murdered, but her call leads to a dead human. Questions lead in the direction of the Rumford Laboratories, and the answers may be held by a 15-year-old girl proficient at healing strays.

England, Ashdown Dean · Pets

Help the Poor Struggler. Little, Brown, 1985

Sam Waterhouse has been released after 20 years in prison, but three murders occur almost simultaneously with his release, so the police focus on him. Jury feels compelled to solve the case that sent Waterhouse to prison to solve the deaths in the present.

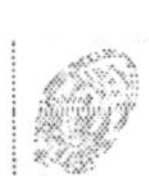

England, Dartmoor

I Am the Only Running Footman. Little, Brown, 1986

Revisiting the same territory as the previous book, and working again with Devon policeman Brian Macalvie, Jury is handed a case of two dead bodies, murdered one year apart. It is Macalvie's insistence that keeps the fires lit under this investigation.

England, Devon

The Five Bells and Bladebone. Little, Brown, 1987

Marshall Trueblood buys more than he bargained for when the antique piece of furniture also contains a corpse. The victim is Simon Lean, the nephew of Lady Summerston, and Jury is able to make a connection to another murder that may help him trap a killer.

England, Limehouse

The Old Silent. Little, Brown, 1989

A stay at a Yorkshire inn leads Jury to discover three separate murders. Nell Healey's silence does not help her case, and Jury finds his personal feelings interfering in the investigation.

England, Yorkshire

The Old Contemptibles. Little, Brown, 1991

Jane Holdsworth's attractiveness draws Jury into her world, and before things stop spinning, he finds himself a suspect. Forced to use Melrose to a greater extent, Jury sends him out undercover as a librarian. Can these two prove Jane did not murder Crabbe, and neither did Jury?

England, Lake District

The Horse You Came in On. Knopf, 1993

Jury is in Baltimore in the States, with his usual crew, to investigate the murder of Philip Calvert, a relative of a friend. Ellen Taylor reappears in Jury's life, and the clues lead to an undiscovered Edgar Allan Poe story.

Authors • Maryland, Baltimore

Rainbow's End. Knopf, 1995

When three women die in England, Jury becomes convinced that clues lie in the United States. One of the victims lived in Santa Fe, and the other two had recently visited there, so leaving his crew to investigate at home, Jury heads back to the States.

New Mexico, Santa Fe

The Case Has Altered. Henry Holt, 1997

A notorious actress and a servant girl have been killed on the fens of Lincolnshire, and Jury is interested in the case because his friend Jenny Kennington has been accused. However, Jury finds the locals a closed society, and the help he needs to solve this one must come from his friends .

England, Lincolnshire

Stargazey. Henry Holt, 1998

Jury has no problems identifying the beautiful blonde with whom he rode the bus when, one week later, he is looking at her corpse. His only clue to her identity is her fur coat, and that clue leads him to the owner, a Russian immigrant now running a top-flight art gallery with a missing painting.

Art • England, London

The Lamorna Wink. Viking, 1999

Plant thinks he is on his own when he tries to vacation in Bletchley, but he cannot escape Aunt Agatha, who arrives unexpectedly and upsets his good time. Meeting waiter Johnny Wells intrigues him when the man's aunt has disappeared, so Plant moves into the Seabourne house of American millionaire Morris Bletchley to have a base for his investigation. When a local woman, who had left to make porn, turns up dead in the neighborhood, Plant begins to wish that all his usual investigating team was around to lend a hand.

England, Cornwall, Lamorna

The Blue Last. Viking, 2001

DCI Mickey Haggerty has found two old skeletons in an excavation that lead him to believe the heir to brewery magnate Oliver Tyncdale's estate may be a phony. When a modern murder occurs and Haggerty's research on the old estate disappears, he asks Jury for help. Jury knows that only Plant can infiltrate Tynedle Lodge to get the information Jury needs to solve this old crime.

England, London · World War II

The Grave Maurice. Viking, 2002

Jury is hospitalized in the Royal London Hospital under the care of Dr. Roger Ryder. Melrose Plant is spending time across the street in the Grave Maurice, where he overhears a discussion of the two-year-old disappearance of the doctor's daughter Nell. Plant begins the investigation into the world of horse racing, but it is Jury who finishes it.

England, London · Horses

Joan Hess ✍

Arly Hanks

Maggody, Arkansas, is the location of this series of novels about female Police Chief Arly Hanks. Arly's adventures in rural Arkansas have a soft-boiled approach to crime. Hess has surrounded her detective with a nutty supporting cast, making these regional cop novels very enjoyable. They can be recommended to readers who enjoy the soft-boiled and traditional style. Readers may also enjoy M. C. Beaton (Hamish Macbeth) and H. R. F. Keating. See the author's website at http://www.maggody.com. **Soft-boiled/Traditional**. Series subjects: **Arkansas, Maggody · Humor**.

Malice in Maggody. St. Martin's Press, 1987

Having resigned her position in New York, Hanks moves to Maggody to assume a new assignment as the local chief of police. Thinking a town of less than 1000 will not provide much action, she is not initially troubled when an EPA representative disappears, even though his report would allow the favorite local fishing hole to be used as a garbage dump.

Environment

Mischief in Maggody. St. Martin's Press, 1988

Hanks returns from a vacation to find a few changes in the small town of Maggody from the psychic who has set up shop, the new health store run by hippies, and the disappearance of the town prostitute, Robin Buchanon. When Hanks discovers her body near a booby-trapped marijuana field, she finds herself on the hunt for a killer.

Much Ado in Maggody. St. Martin's Press, 1989

Johanna Mae Nookim's failed attempt to file sex discrimination charges against the bank leads her to invite WAACO, a women's rights group, to town to organize the locals. While the group is holding its first protest, the local bank goes up in flames, and the new head teller is found dead inside.

Madness in Maggody. St. Martin's Press, 1991

Everyone in the town of Maggody is afraid that the new superstore soon to be opened by Mayor Jim Bob Buchanon and his partner Lamont Petrel may have some negative aspects. When 23 folks are sent to the hospital by food poisoning after eating the tamales at the grand opening, Hanks realizes someone is serious about sabotaging the new store.

Food

Mortal Remains in Maggody. Dutton, 1991

A film crew has arrived in Maggody, promising roles to the locals, and promising trouble for Hanks, especially when it appears to be an adult film. The first death is Kitty Kave, one of the actresses in the company, who is found stabbed in the hotel room she shared with her actor husband, Buddy Meredith. He has disappeared, and so has a cameraman, and then the film's director, Hal Desmond, is killed as well. What was to be a boon for the town has turned into a nightmare, and Hanks needs to act fast to stop the bleeding.

Film

Maggody in Manhattan. Dutton, 1992

As a finalist in the KoKo Nut Cooking Contest, Ruby Bee will leave Maggody and head to the Big Apple. Little does Hanks realize that she will soon be flying to New York to rescue Ruby and Estelle when they are accused of murder.

New York, New York

O Little Town of Maggody. Dutton, 1993

Local boy done good and country-western singer, Matt Montana, decides to return home to Maggody at Christmas to use the good press to cover up his problems with alcohol. The town turns out in style, but when Matt's aunt disappears, Hanks has to investigate. Could this have anything to do with the aunt's ability to listen to space aliens on her hearing aid?

Christmas • Holidays • Music

Martians in Maggody. Dutton, 1994

Hanks is suspicious when Raz Buchanan starts charging folks to look at the UFO circles in his cornfield, but is dismayed when the press arrives and the whole town begins to recount strange occurrences, from Bigfoot to insemination by aliens. When one of the UFO enthusiasts is found dead in Boone Creek, she has a real case to ground herself.

UFOs

Miracles in Maggody. Dutton, 1995

Twice before visitors have promised great things for Maggody, so Hanks is not impressed when the Reverend Malachi Hope and his faith healer circus arrive, ready to build a 2,000-acre theme park called "The City of Hope." Is there a connection between the girls' high school basketball coach's death and the fact that the former coach is selling his land to the Reverend?

Religion

The Maggody Militia. Dutton, 1997

Things might stay calm if everyone left Maggody alone, but this time the town is invaded by survivalists who want to use the newly purchased farm of Kayleen Smeltner to teach its ways. The problem is that paintball players are in the woods with the hunters on the first weekend of that sport, and trouble is going to follow.

Hunting

Misery Loves Maggody. Simon & Schuster, 1999

Hanks believes that some of her locals will be out of her hair when Ruby Bee and Estelle go to Graceland. But she receives a call from Farberville, that Ruby Bee is in the hospital, and Mayor Jim Bob Buchanon has been arrested for murder.

Arkansas, Farberville

Murder@maggody.com. Simon & Schuster, 2000

Computers come to Maggody, and not everyone supports the choice of Mayor Buchanon to get Maggody on line. When the computers cause some families to split, some additional local drama turns up the tension in the small town until it turns to the murder of a young unwed mother.

Computers

Maggody and the Moonbeams. Simon & Schuster, 2001

At Camp Pearly Gates, a disgruntled Hanks is chaperoning a church youth group when the body of a mysterious woman is found on the grounds. The dead woman is a member of a local commune that requires her to wear white robes and shave her head. Once again the small community of Maggody has enough strange and bizarre characters to complicate this mystery and entertain the reader.

Cults

Reginald Hill ✍

Andy Dalziel/Peter Pascoe

Yorkshire, England, is the setting for British writer Hill's long running series. Dalziel's acerbic personality contrasts with Pascoe's brooding moodiness. The two cops' personalities are the yin and yang of these books, but as the series progresses, the novels become rich in the depth of their plots and the increased reliance on psychological insight. Readers may also enjoy Colin Dexter and Peter Robinson. See the author's website at http://www.randomhouse.com/features/reghill. **Traditional/Hard-boiled**. Series subjects: **England, Yorkshire · Teams**.

A Clubbable Woman. U.K.: Collins, 1970 (U.S.: Foul Play, 1984)

Sam Connon is sleeping off an injury from a local rugby match, when he goes downstairs to discover his wife Mary has been murdered. When Dalziel and Pascoe investigate, some letters surface making accusations of adultery.

An Advancement of Learning. U.K.: Collins, 1971 (U.S.: Foul Play, 1985)

The grounds of Holm Coutram College is more the territory of Pascoe than Dalziel. So when a five-year-old corpse is found buried beneath a statute, Dalziel is uncomfortable and Pascoe is pleased to discover a long-lost love. Thinking this old case will be easy, the pair are disconcerted when a sex scandal erupts on campus when a lecturer is accused of giving out preferential grades.

Academia

Ruling Passion. U.K.: Collins, 1973 (U.S.: Harper, 1977)

Pascoe and his girlfriend, Ellie Soper, have been asked to spend the weekend at the cottage of their friends, Colin and Rose Hopkins, with his other friends, Timothy Mansfield and Charles Rushford. But when they arrive, three are dead and one is on the run, and although Pascoe is out of his area, he wants desperately to help in the investigation.

England, Thornton Lacey

An April Shroud. U.K.: Collins, 1975 (U.S.: Foul Play, 1986)

While on holiday during Pascoe's honeymoon, Dalziel's downtime is disturbed by a flood that puts him in contact with the widow Bonnie Fielding. As interested in her as in her husband's recent death, Dalziel finds his professional senses are humming once he finds himself at Lake House.

England, Lincolnshire

A Pinch of Snuff. U.K.: Collins, 1978 (U.S.: Harper & Row, 1978)

The Calliope Kinema Club offers its membership access to pornography, but one night dentist Shorter believes he may have seen a film that was too real. The investigation into the movie proves fruitless, but someone eliminates the Calliope's owner, and Dalziel and Pascoe's interest shifts into high gear.

Pornography

A Killing Kindness. U.K.: Collins, 1980 (U.S.: Pantheon, 1981)

Mary Dinwoodie is found strangled in a ditch, the first victim of the Yorkshire Strangler. The Strangler's signature is to call the police and quote Shakespeare, an act committed two more times. Meanwhile, Dalziel and Pascoe know they have to move fast to make sure this serial killer's list stops at three.

Serial killer

Deadheads. U.K.: Collins, 1983 (U.S.: U.K.: Macmillan, 1984)

Patrick Aldermann either has remarkable luck or great timing. When his Great Aunt Florence dies, he inherits Rosemont House and can pursue his hobby of rose growing. His accounting career also takes a positive turn when a timely death allows his promotion, and he soon comes to the attention of Dalziel, Pascoe, and the newest member of the team, police cadet Singh.

Exit Lines. U.K.: Collins, 1984 (U.S.: U.K.: Macmillan, 1985)

One stormy November night, in three separate incidents, three old men die from violent causes. When Pascoe discovers that one man's dying words indicate he was struck by an automobile driven by Dalziel, he knows that this case will not be easy.

Child's Play. U.K.: Collins, 1987 (U.S.: U.K.: Macmillan, 1987)

Whenever a will is read in a mystery, death will shortly follow, and when Geraldine Lomas's will is read, that is indeed what happens. Geraldine's son died in WWII in Italy, but she always believed that he was alive. Everyone is surprised when at her funeral, a man claims to be the long lost son, Alexander Huby.

Wills

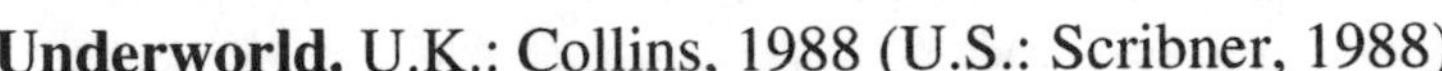

Underworld. U.K.: Collins, 1988 (U.S.: Scribner, 1988)

The mining community of Yorkshire has one old case that bothers them: although a pedophile had confessed to killing Tracey Pedley, the locals felt the last man who was with her, Billy Farr, might make a far better candidate. Years later, his son Colin, a friend of Ellie Pascoe's, returns to the community, and the reminder of the old murder begins to stir the community to violent action.

Children at risk

Bones and Silence. U.K.: Collins 1990 (U.S.: Delacorte, 1990)

A very inebriated Dalziel witnesses a crime that some want to classify as an accident, but that he considers a murder. Pascoe knows that a woman will commit suicide as she has written the police to tell them of her plans. As each cop works the boundaries of his case, he discovers the deep psychological motivations for these actions. DA

One Small Step. Collins, 1990

This novella is set on the moon in the year 2010, when Emile Lemarque dies as he steps from the lunar lander Europa. The incident was witnessed live by 27 million television viewers, and the crime is such an international event that Peter Pascoe, Commissioner of the Eurofed Justice Department is sent to investigate. Knowing the importance of this case, Pascoe turns to his old mentor, Andy Dalziel, and brings him out of retirement to help solve the baffling case.

Moon · Science fiction

Recalled to Life. U.K.: Collins, 1992 (U.S.: Delacorte, 1992)

In 1963, the Mickledore Hall Murder took place, and the killings were laid at the doorstep of Cissy Kohler, a nanny. When new evidence surfaces in the killing of Pam Westropp, Kohler receives a new trial. The process is painful for Dalziel as he was the protégé of the original investigator, and now he must retrace that man's steps to prove an injustice was done. But when Cissy begins to act reluctant to take advantage of the situation, the cops are confused.

Asking for the Moon. U.K.: Collins, 1994 (U.S.: Norton, 1996)

A collection of the following stories: "Dalziel's Ghost," "The Last National Service Man," "One Small Step," and "Pascoe's Ghost."

Short stories

Pictures of Perfection. U.K.: Collins, 1994 (U.S.: Delacorte, 1994)

The Green, in Enscombe, has survived all of England's rich history until now, when it faces the developers' desire to change everything. The detective pair are there hunting one of their own who has gone missing, but Dalziel believes everyone is overreacting. Then, after two days, the case comes to a head with tragic results.

England, Yorkshire, Enscombe

The Wood Beyond. U.K.: Collins, 1996 (U.S.: Delacorte, 1996)

This book takes Dalziel and Pascoe in two different directions. Dalziel must deal with the death of a security officer at a pharmaceuticals headquarters where some animal activists have just discovered some human remains. Meanwhile, while mourning his dead grandmother, Pascoe finds some communication regarding his grandfather's court-martial and execution for cowardice at Passchendaele in 1917 that prompts him to probe his own family history.

World War I

On Beulah Height. U.K.: Collins, 1998 (U.S.: Delacorte, 1998)

When Dendale was flooded by the government to create a new reservoir, the water buried a landscape that had suffered the loss of three kidnapped children. Fifteen years later, in Danby village, where most of the Dendale residents moved, a girl goes missing, and the residents believe that Benny Lightfoot, the man most likely to have struck 15 years earlier, may be stalking them again. BA

Children at risk • England, Yorkshire, Danby • Serial killer

Arms and the Women. U.K.: Collins, 1999 (U.S.: Delacorte, 1999)

Ellie was shaken by the recent illness of their daughter, and she has taken to novel writing to relax, only to just avoid a kidnapping by a mysterious couple. Then a neighbor is beaten when she disturbs a stalker outside the Pascoe home. While Peter searches his old cases for a cause, constable Shirley Novello, assigned to guard Ellie, becomes convinced this has more to do with Ellie than Peter.

Dialogues of the Dead. U.K.: Collins, 2001 (U.S.: Delacorte, 2002)

There has been a series of deaths in the territory of the Yorkshire police, but it is not until a local librarian stumbles across a short story submitted to a competition that the clues are presented to the police indicating they have a serial killer on the loose. It becomes the task of the cops to chase the Wordman and bring him to justice before another of his literary word clues leads to another murder.

Serial killer

***Death's Jest Book.** Collins, 2002

Tony Hillerman

Joe Leaphorn/Jim Chee

Originally started as two separate series, these two Native American detectives eventually find themselves working together in the same books as the series progresses. Joe Leaphorn is the experienced detective who has established his way in the world. Jim Chee is the brash young detective who tries to maintain his contact with his spirituality while acting as a detective. Besides creating great characters and plots, Hillerman's strength is his ability to sympathetically depict the Navajo culture without distracting from the pace of the mystery, creating works that are as much literature as genre writing. Readers may also enjoy Nevada Barr, Jean Hager, J. A. Jance (Joanna Brady), Reginald Hill, and Abigail Padgett. See a fan's website at http://www.umsl.edu/~smueller. **Traditional/Hard-boiled**. Series subjects: **Native Americans · New Mexico · Teams**.

The Blessing Way. Harper & Row, 1970

Lt. Leaphorn is searching the reservation for Luis Horseman, accused of shooting a man. Meanwhile, Jeremy Canfield is spending his summer with anthropologist Bergen McKee investigating rumors of Navajo sorcery. When McKee's probing begins to unearth Navajo legends, Leaphorn finds his concentration is focused in two directions because he finds Horseman dead in a ritualistic and meaningful fashion.

Anthropology · New Mexico, Lukachukai Mountains

Dance Hall of the Dead. Harper & Row, 1973

A Zuni Indian boy named Ernesto Cato dies in a ritual slaying, and his best friend, a Navajo youth named George Bowlegs, is missing. Leaphorn must decide if an archaeology dig that had interested the boys has anything to do with their plight. ED

Archeology · New Mexico, Zuni

Listening Woman. Harper & Row, 1978

Leaphorn is handed a variety of assignments including the murder of an old man and a teenage girl. He encounters Maragret Cigaret who is a Listening Woman, or a speaker with the ghosts. His attachment to a contingent of Boy Scouts on an exploration places him in danger, and he must use all of his skills to save their lives and his own.

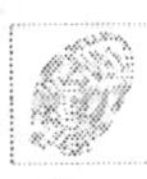

Arizona

People of Darkness. Harper & Row, 1980

Chee has to answer these baffling questions: who would steal a box of rocks and why would a rich man's wife buy them back? Exploring this question will place Chee in the path of a hunter, with himself as the prey.

The Dark Wind. Harper & Row, 1982

Chee is guarding a windmill against vandalism on land once used by the Navajo but soon to be given to the Hopi. He hears a plane crash and a gunshot in the nighttime and stumbles into the middle of a drug sting that will leave a corpse whose palms and soles have been scalped.

The Ghostway. Harper & Row, 1984

Old Joseph Joe witnesses a killing at the Shiprock Wash-O-Mat, and the perpetrator shows him the photo of his next victim. That evidence sends Chee after a killer, and into the mystical world on the reservation.

Skinwalkers. Harper & Row, 1987

Leaphorn has three unsolved murders in his jurisdiction, and then he has to add an attempted murder when someone puts three shotgun blasts into Chee's trailer. For the first time, these two Native American detectives unite on a case, trying to decide if a "skinwalker," or someone with the power of witchcraft, is stalking the reservation. AN

Witchcraft

A Thief of Time. Harper & Row, 1988

At first sympathy falls on Dr. Eleanor Friedman-Bernal when she discovers that her Anasazi site dig has been ruined, until Leaphorn's suspicions fall on her as the thief who is reporting the items as lost to cover her work. Then Chee, investigating a similar complaint at a different site, discovers two corpses. MA

Archeology

Talking God. Harper & Row, 1989

Leaphorn has a dead body whose identifying characteristics have been carefully removed. Chee is waiting to arrest an anthropologist who has taken it upon himself to return ancestral bones from the Smithsonian to the reservation. As the cases proceed, they begin to merge, and the officers find themselves in the nation's capital.

Anthropology • Washington, D.C.

Coyote Waits. Harper & Row, 1990

When Navajo Tribal Policeman Delbert Nez is murdered, Chee is badly burnt trying to save his life. The arrest of Navajo shaman Ashie Pinto is relatively easy as he is on the scene and holding the murder weapon. But doubts begin to build about the man's guilt, Chee works from his recovery bed while Leaphorn handles the official investigation.

Sacred Clowns. Harper & Row, 1993

Officially teamed for the first time, Leaphorn has assigned Chee to a special investigation regarding the missing student, Delmar Kanitewa. At a tribal ceremony involving the ancient Kachina rituals, a second murder occurs, and the two officers must search for the connection.

The Fallen Man. HarperCollins, 1996

Leaphorn has retired, but finds himself intrigued with the discovery of the 11-year-old corpse of Hal Breedlove, found at the foot of Ship Rock Mountain. In pondering the old murder, Leaphorn makes a connection to a current crime, and Chee finds himself drawn into the case

The First Eagle. HarperCollins, 1998

Officer Benny Kinsman is found murdered by Chee, with a Hopi poacher named Robert Jano standing over the corpse. Thinking he has an open-and-shut case, he is disturbed by Leaphorn, who is looking for a missing woman named Catherine Pollard, who disappeared on the same day as Kinsman's death, and who was a subject of Kinsman's attentions.

Hunting Badger. HarperCollins, 1999

Officer Dale Claxton paid with his life when he stopped some heavily armed survivalists in a stolen truck in 1998. Despite a massive manhunt, and the suicide of one member, the cops and the FBI were unable to locate the men. Then, in the present, three men rob a Ute tribe gambling casino, and the memories of the first case bring Leaphorn out of retirement and Chee to the forefront of a second-chance investigation.

The Wailing Wind. HarperCollins, 2002

The myth surrounding the Golden Calf Mine has Sergeant Jim Chee wondering whether the murder of a swindler by Wiley Denton could connect to a new murder involving a corpse in an abandoned pickup truck. When Officer Bernadette Manuelito fails to handle the crime scene correctly, Chee calls upon the retired Joe Leaphorn to bail out his department.

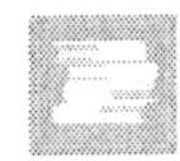

Mining

P. D. James ✍

Adam Dalgliesh

British writer James's series about Inspector (later Chief Superintendent) Dagliesh combines dramatic stories, literate writing, and most of the classic traditional elements from the best of the Golden Age. With a subdued personality that separates him from the Great Thinking or Eccentric Detectives, Dalgliesh brings a solemn dignity to his investigations that places him in the forefront of the books yet keeps his personality distant even from the reader. Dalgliesh can also claim to be a published poet! Readers may also enjoy Ngaio Marsh, Colin Dexter, Ruth Rendell, and Peter Robinson. **Traditional**.

Cover Her Face. U.K.: Faber & Faber, 1962 (U.S.: Scribner, 1966)

Eleanor Maxie has hired the unwed mother, Sally Jupp, as household help. Sally causes a few disturbances, someone murders her, and it becomes Dalgliesh's assignment to discover who felt strongly enough about the woman's conduct to commit murder.

England, Chadfleet

A Mind to Murder. U.K.: Faber & Faber, 1963 (U.S.: Scribner, 1967)

When the administrative head of the Steen Psychiatric Clinic is found stabbed to dead with a chisel, the clinical efficiency of the institution begins to unravel. Dalgliesh must decide if the staff is as disturbed as the patients, and whether this killing was a singular statement or a symptom of a larger problem.

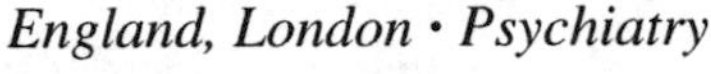

England, London • Psychiatry

Unnatural Causes. U.K.: Faber & Faber, 1967 (U.S.: Scribner, 1967)

A 10-day holiday on the Suffolk coast with his spinster aunt is disturbed when Dalgliesh finds himself drawn into a murder investigation. Crime writer Maurice Seton's body has been found drifting in a dinghy, and the cast of characters who surround this author's private life provide plenty of suspects for his murder.

Authors • England, Suffolk, Monksmere

Shroud for a Nightingale. U.K.: Faber & Faber, 1971 (U.S.: Scribner, 1971)

Nightingale House is a nursing school with a scandal when two young student nurses are murdered using different methods. Dalgliesh finds he must solves crimes that are being committed in full view of the witnesses.

Academia • England, Heatheringfield • Medical

The Black Tower. U.K.: Faber & Faber, 1975 (U.S.: Scribner, 1975)

Too ill to respond instantly to the request of Father Michael Francis Badderly, Dalgliesh finds that when he finally reaches the village of Toynton, the priest is dead. By nature an inquisitive, Dalgliesh putters about in the priest's life, and begins to discover some disturbing things that will lead to additional deaths.

England, Toynton • Religion

Death of an Expert Witness. U.K.: Faber & Faber, 1977 (U.S.: Scribner, 1977)

Dr. Lorrimer, Principle Scientific Officer in the Biology Department of the Hoggatt's Forensic Science Laboratory, used by the police for their own needs, has been murdered. Dalgliesh discovers that the man was not liked, and the politics within the lab provides enough kindling to light the fire of murder.

England, Chevisham • Medical

A Taste for Death. U.K.: Faber & Faber, 1986 (U.S.: Knopf, 1986)

A Baronet and Minister of the Crown has had his throat cut and his body left in the Little Vestry of St. Matthew's Church. For Dalgliesh, the intriguing question is why an equally dead neighborhood derelict is left next to the Baronet's body. DA MA

England, London

Devices and Desires. U.K.: Faber & Faber, 1989 (U.S.: Knopf, 1990)

Relaxing in his inherited windmill in Larksoken after the publication of his latest book of poetry, Dalgliesh finds himself drawn into a local case involving a serial killer. Clues seem to draw attention to the Larksoken Nuclear Power Station and the unhappy staff who work within.

England, Norfolk, Larksoken • Serial killer

Original Sin. U.K.: Faber & Faber, 1994 (U.S.: Knopf, 1995)

Peverell Press, a London publisher, is rocked by the death of managing director Gerard Etienne, who may have created enemies as he tried to restore the firm to financial health. Now Dalgliesh needs to restore order in the firm when the killer decides to strike again.

England, London • Publishing

A Certain Justice. U.K.: Faber & Faber, 1997 (U.S.: Knopf, 1997)

Barrister Venetia Aldridge is successful in the courtroom, but someone murders her in her chambers, and the case is given to Dalgliesh. Teamed with Kate Miskin, the detective probes within and without the legal community to find a motive for murder.

England, London • Law

Death in Holy Orders. U.K.: Faber & Faber, 2001 (U.S.: Knopf, 2001)

When the body of a student from the theological college of St. Anselm is found on the coast, Dalgliesh is asked to determine the cause of the death. Dalgliesh investigates, and is reminded of pleasant memories of childhood visits to this site. However, he and his team are overwhelmed when a second death, this time of a priest, leaves no doubt that a murderer is at work in this holy setting.

England, Suffolk, East Anglia • Religion

J. A. Jance ✍

J. P. Beaumont

Beaumont is a heroic figure in the Seattle Police force with a reputation for being a wild card. His battles with alcohol and the demons in his personal life add richness to the texture of modern Seattle, a city with its own troubles. Readers may also enjoy Thomas Adcock, Lawrence Block (Matthew Scudder), Michael Connelly, and John Sandford. **Traditional/Hard-boiled**. Series subject: **Washington, Seattle**.

Until Proven Guilty. Avon, 1985

When a five-year-old girl is strangled with her own nightgown, the case goes to Beaumont. He discovers the family are members of Faith Tabernacle, and his suspicions are drawn towards the zealous members of that faith. Meanwhile, his attention is drawn to a woman who appeared at the funeral, and his personal feelings interfere with the investigation.

Religion

Injustice for All. Avon, 1986

Beaumont is supposed to be relaxing on vacation when the screams of beautiful Ginger Watkin draw his attention to the dead body of the State Parole Board member laying at her feet. Only wanting to help the woman, Beaumont finds himself accused of the crime, and he must scramble to save his own reputation and catch a murderer.

Trial by Fury. Avon, 1986

Darwin Ridley's high school basketball team lost in the first round of the championships, and he has been missing since that game. This fact is not reported to the police by his pregnant wife Joanna, so it is Beaumont who has to tell her that her husband was lynched and dumped in a dumpster. Then it becomes his job to find out why and by who.

Basketball

Taking the Fifth. Avon, 1987

A member of the Starlight Productions theater crew is found murdered with strange puncture marks. The method is explained when a shoe with a five-inch stiletto heel is found, and Beaumont must follow that clue, plus a pay stub and a matchbook, to the reason for the killing.

Theater

Improbable Cause. Avon, 1988

Dr. Frederick Nielsen was a dentist who was a pain, to his wife, his dental assistant, and even his patients. When he is found murdered in his own dental chair, Beaumont looks at all the suspects, including the ex-con that was previous person in the hot seat.

Dentist • Medical

A More Perfect Union. Avon, 1988

Assigned the cushy job of liaison to a film crew, Beaumont is disturbed when a body is found floating in a nearby lake. When a second body is found, and the word "ironworker" appears on each corpse, Beaumont finds himself investigating a case that places him in opposition to an ironworker's union.

Unions

Dismissed with Prejudice. Avon, 1989

Software magnate Tadeo Kurobashi commits hara-kiri, perhaps tying into his fascination with all things involving the samurai. But when Beaumont investigates, he decides that the man's wealth and his knowledge of the industry may have made him a target for murder.

Computers

Minor in Possession. Avon, 1990

Finally forced to confront his own drinking problem, Beaumont finds himself in Ironwood Ranch to dry out. His roommate is Joey Rothman, a teenage drug dealer, who is murdered with Beaumont's service weapon, and the detective finds himself on the defensive.

Alcoholism • Arizona, Phoenix

Payment in Kind. Avon, 1991

Two corpses are found in a custodial closet at the Seattle School District building. Beaumont gets the call and knows that the entwined lovers were left to send a message, but the question is to whom and why.

Without Due Process. Morrow, 1992

Junior Weston was hiding in the closet when his family was murdered, and that leaves Beaumont with a very frightened five-year-old witness. The fact that the boy's father was a cop adds fuel to this fire, and the detective finds himself fighting a gang war to get his answers.

Failure to Appear. Morrow, 1993

Intending to return his wayward daughter Kelly to the fold, Beaumont travels to Oregon in pursuit. However, once there, he finds himself embroiled in two murders that take place backstage at the famed Shakespeare Festival in Ashland.

Oregon, Ashland • Theater

Lying in Wait. Morrow, 1994

Beaumont has a new partner named Sue Danielson, and the two detectives draw a strange case when a fishing-boat captain is killed and set afire aboard his boat after each of his fingers and toes has been removed. To make matters worse, the wife of the captain is an old flame of Beaumont's, and the crime ties to the horrible legacy of the Holocaust.

Holocaust • World War II

Name Withheld. Morrow, 1996

Beaumont's New Year begins with a biotech executive's body floating in the bay, dead from a gunshot wound. While he tries to solve that case and additional killings in the industry, his personal life disintegrates when his ex-wife is diagnosed with cancer and he is accused of being a pedophile.

Breach of Duty. Avon, 1999

At the age where he can be reflective, Beaumont finds himself contemplating his own life and the life of his partner, Danielson. Two cases keep the detective hopping: the first involves the elderly Agnes Ferman, burned to death in her own bed, but able to leave behind a huge sum of money as a possible motive. The second case involves the death of a Native American, a case that may have the cops involved in a hate crime.

Birds of Prey. Morrow, 2001

Beaumont has decided to retire. With the time available, he sails on the Starfire Breeze with his grandmother, who is celebrating the start of a new marriage. When one of the passengers falls overboard, and it was someone Beaumont had taken a shine to, he feels compelled to investigate.

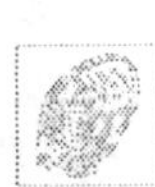

Alaska • Shipboard

Partner in Crime. Morrow, 2002

This case combines the talents of J. P. Beaumont with those of Joanna Brady. When artist Rochelle Baxter is murdered and Brady's investigation shows she was in the witness protection program, help is sent from the state of Washington in the form of Beaumont.

Arizona, Bisbee • Witness Protection Program

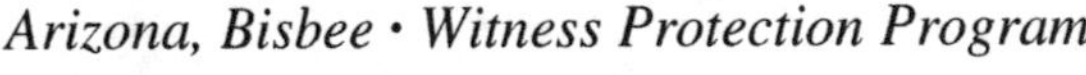

J. A. Jance ✍

Joanna Brady

So successful in performing as an investigator on her first case, Brady becomes the sheriff of Cochise County in Arizona. As the widow of the previous sheriff, she finds herself on a mission to educate herself in the ways of crime, and to face down all opposition to her attempts to prove herself worthy. Although not quite as troubled as Jance's previously-created character, Beaumont, Brady is still a troubled woman making a challenging career change. These novels can be recommended to traditional mystery readers. Readers may also enjoy Nevada Barr, Jean

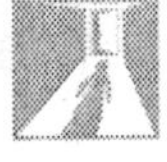

Hager, Tony Hillerman, and Abigail Padgett. **Traditional**. Series subject: **Arizona, Cochise County**.

Desert Heat. Avon, 1993

When Andy Brady is killed on the eve of his wedding anniversary to his wife Joanna, that tragedy would seem to be enough for one woman to deal with. But an accusation of drug running quickly follows, and Joanna decides to clear the name of the sheriff she loved for her daughter's sake.

Tombstone Courage. Morrow, 1994

Having accomplished what she wanted for her husband, Brady is elected the new sheriff of Cochise County. Faced with a hostile work environment, she also finds herself confronted by a double homicide that has deep-rooted connections to the victim's families.

Shoot, Don't Shoot. Morrow, 1995

Just elected as the new sheriff of Cochise County, Brady decides to enroll in a police academy in Phoenix. The community is under the threat of a serial killer that preys on women, and the only other female in her class falls victim to the stalker. Brady decides to hunt for the man when her daughter comes to Phoenix for Thanksgiving.

Arizona, Phoenix • Serial killer

Dead to Rights. Avon, 1996

For a year, the grieving and complaining widower of Bonnie Morgan had let everyone know he did not appreciate the light sentence given to the drunk driver who killed his wife. So Hal Morgan is on the hot seat when the driver is found torched to death, and Sheriff Brady must decide if he is the only logical suspect in the case.

Skeleton Canyon. Avon, 199

Brianna O'Brien's love for the forbidden Ignacio Ybarra leads to tragedy when she is discovered murdered in Skeleton Canyon. Her family blames the Hispanic boy, but he can only proclaim his love for Bree. It falls to Sheriff Brady to determine the truth in her death and what happened between these star-crossed lovers.

Rattlesnake Crossing. Avon, 1998

When a gun dealer dies and his stock disappears, suspicion falls on separatist Alton Hosfield. Brady feels there may be more to this case than the cut-and-dried, and she discover clues that point to a New Age resort with some strange practices.

Outlaw Mountain. Avon, 1999

Alice Rogers was a free-spirited widow with a wild streak, and her murder seems easy to lay at the feet of the teens caught riding in her stolen car. But because of her vast wealth, Brady feels a member of her family might have tried to help themselves by helping her out of this life.

Devil's Claw. Morrow, 2000

The neighborhood handyman Clayton Rhodes dies, and Sheriff Brady finds herself accused by the man's family of covering up a murder for her personal profit. Distracted by her own wedding plans, she is overwhelmed by a second murder that takes place at the Cochise

Stronghold, the murder of an Indian woman just released from prison for killing her husband.

Native Americans

Paradise Lost. Morrow, 2001

Jennifer Brady, young daughter of the sheriff, finds a body while on a Girl Scout outing. Her mother's job is to hunt for a killer and be concerned for her own daughter, while trying to hold together her new marriage. But then the girl who was with Jennifer is murdered, and Brady knows her family is threatened by a murderer.

Children at risk

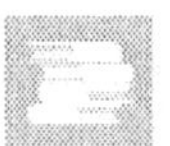

Partner in Crime. Morrow, 2002

This case combines the talents of J. P. Beaumont with those of Joanna Brady. When artist Rochelle Baxter is murdered and Brady's investigation shows she was in the witness protection program, help is sent from the state of Washington in the form of Beaumont.

Arizona, Bisbee • Witness Protection Program

Stuart Kaminsky ✍

Porfiry Rostnikov

American writer Kaminsky started his series set in the Soviet Union about the time that things were beginning to unravel. The books reveal what life was like under the Communists, and then how life has changed for the Russian citizens. Rostnikov has his political problems, but he manages to keep a solid team around him, consisting of Sasha Tkach and Emil Krapo. Readers may also enjoy H. R. F. Keating, William Marshall, and Janwillem Van de Wetering. **Traditional/ Hard-boiled**.

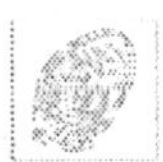

Death of a Dissident. U.S.: Charter, 1981 (U.K.: *Rostnikov's Corpse*. Macmillan, 1981)

Inspector Rostnikov is asked to save the KGB's face. They had dissident Aleksander Granovsky under house arrest when he is murdered, and the detective is given this locked-room puzzle to solve so that the world-famous rebel's death will not viewed as a state crime.

Locked room • Soviet Union, Moscow

Black Knight in Red Square. Charter, 1984

To the embarrassment of the Russian hosts, four attendees at an international film festival are killed by drinking poisoned vodka. Rostnikov is given the case, and discovers that an international group of terrorists wants to take credit for the deaths.

Film • Soviet Union, Moscow

Red Chameleon. Scribner, 1985

Three cases keep Rostnikov and his assistants busy: first, an old man is murdered in his bathtub; second, auto thieves are plaguing Moscow; and third, an assassin has murdered a police officer.

Soviet Union, Moscow

A Fine Red Rain. Scribner, 1987

Demoted, Rostnikov finds himself assigned to less important crimes in the national police force. However, when a trapeze artist dives into a net rigged to fail at its job, he is reunited with his old team during the investigation.

Circus • Soviet Union, Moscow

A Cold Red Sunrise. Scribner, 1988

Rostnikov is sent to Siberia when a dissident's daughter is murdered, and the Commissar sent to solve her case is also killed. Crippled by the constant vigilance of the KGB, and orders not to investigate the girl's death, he finds himself frozen out of clues. ED

Soviet Union, Siberia, Tumsk

The Man Who Walked Like a Bear. Scribner, 1990

While his beloved wife Sarah lies ill in the hospital of a brain tumor, Rostnikov is accosted by a man who claims the devil has come to his factory. While he chooses to investigate, Rostnikov's team also has to hunt for a missing Moscow bus and a man who wants to kidnap a Politburo member.

Soviet Union, Moscow

Rostnikov's Vacation. Scribner, 1991

Tkach and Karpo are left alone when Rostnikov is ordered to take a vacation. Going undercover to try and discover who is stealing computer components, they need their mentor to speak up despite being officially off duty. Meanwhile, the vacationing Rostnikov looks into the murder of Georgi Vasilievich, an old friend from the force.

Soviet Union, Moscow • Soviet Union, Yalta

Death of a Russian Priest. Columbine, 1992

Rostnikov and Karpo are sent to Arkush to solve the murder of Father Merhum, and the dying words of the priest may point away from a political reason and towards a personal one. Meanwhile, Tkach and her new partner, Timofeyeva, are searching the Moscow night life for a woman they want to save from a killer.

Soviet Union, Arkush • Soviet Union, Moscow

Hard Currency. Fawcett Columbine, 1995

After the fall of communism, Rostnikov is surprised to be sent to Cuba on a diplomatic assignment. A Cuban woman has been murdered, and the Cubans want to convict a Russian advisor for the deed. Meanwhile, back in Moscow, Karpo is tracking down a vicious serial killer in Moscow.

Cuba, Havana • Serial killer • Soviet Union, Moscow

Blood and Rubles. Fawcett Columbine, 1996

As crime increases in the new Russia, the metropolitan police find themselves chasing three phantoms. The first case finds Tkach hunting for thieves in a depressed neighborhood, while Timofeyeva is raiding a house full of Czarist treasures. Karpo's case is personal: he is hunting the killers of the woman he loves, shot dead in a drive-by.

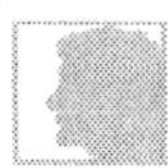

Russia, Moscow

Tarnished Icons. Ivy, 1997

People of the Jewish faith are being killed in Moscow, and it falls to Rostnikov to find the reason and the perpetrator. At the same time, he must hunt for a rapist named the Shy One, and an antinuclear advocate who wants to be explosive.

Russia, Moscow

The Dog Who Bit a Policeman. Mysterious Press, 1998

Illegal dogfights have sprung up as a new form of sport, and Tkach and Timofeyeva are asked to go undercover to try and find the sponsor. This may be a dangerous assignment, as the crew's new boss is Igor Yaklovev, and he seems to like the dogs. Meanwhile, Rostnikov and Karpo find themselves in the middle of a Russian Mafia war.

Organized crime · Russia, Moscow

Fall of a Cosmonaut. Mysterious Press, 2000

This novel finds Rostnikov working on three different cases. The first involves cosmonaut Tsimion Vladovka, whose last words on the space station Mir were instructions to contact Rostnikov if something went wrong with its mission. Now Vladovka could have defected, gone mad, or gone missing. The second case involves a chess fanatic who has stolen the print of a film detailing the life of Tolstoy. The last case involves the murder of Dr. Andrei Vanga, leader of a center for the paranormal.

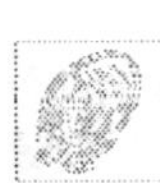

Astronauts · Chess · Film · Russia, Moscow

Murder on the Trans-Siberian Express. Mysterious Press, 2001

Now working out of the Moscow Office of Special Investigation, Rostnikov finds himself aboard the Trans-Siberian Express in pursuit of an extortionist. Meanwhile, his son, also a cop, and Elena Timofeyeya are trying to catch a female murderer lose in the Moscow Metro. The final case finds Detectives Karpo and Zelach trying to locate the kidnapped heavy-metal rocker who is the son of a powerful Jewish businessman.

Railroads · Russia, Moscow · Subways

H. R. F. Keating ✍

Ganesh Ghote

Taking advantage of the widening horizons of mystery fiction, Keating chose to create a series of novels featuring a Bombay Criminal Investigation Division officer. Ganesh Ghote, naïve by nature but not to be underestimated, provides a fascinating look at a fresh location for the mystery. It would be easy to compare Ghote to Charlie Chan, but these novels are less dependent on the traditional than those by Biggers. Readers may also enjoy Stuart Kaminsky, William Marshall, and Janwillem Van de Wetering. **Soft-boiled/Traditional.**

The Perfect Murder. U.K.: Collins, 1964 (U.S.: Dutton, 1965)

The papers called it The Perfect Murder, because the victim was named Perfect, although the reality for Inspector Ghote is that the victim survived. The fact that the assault took place in the home of tycoon Arun Varde only complicates the case. With his plate full, Ghote also has to host a UNESCO tour observing third-world police methods, and investigate the theft of one rupee from the Minister for Police Affairs and the Arts.

India, Bombay

Inspector Ghote's Good Crusade. U.K.: Collins, 1966 (U.S.: Dutton, 1966)

Frank Masters is the founder of the Masters Foundation for the Care of Juvenile Vagrants, and he is venerated for his efforts on behalf of the poor. When he is poisoned with arsenic, the case is assigned to Inspector Ghote, who finds himself under the unique pressure applied by the Western leaders of the foundation.

India, Bombay

Inspector Ghote Caught in Meshes. U.K.: Collins, 1967 (U.S.: Dutton, 1968)

Highway robbers have murdered the brother of world-famous scientist Gregory Strongbow, an American working in India. Ghote's investigation begins to show that, rather than being a random incident, this may have been a rather well-planned murder.

India, Poona

Inspector Ghote Hunts the Peacock. U.K.: Collins, 1968 (U.S.: Dutton, 1968)

Ghote has been sent to England to make an address to the Emergency Conference on the Smuggling of Dangerous Drugs as a stand-in for his boss. His wife's cousin's husband asks him to search for a missing niece, and the Inspector finds himself trying to uphold the dignity of his superiors while solving a personal case for his family.

England, London

Inspector Ghote Plays a Joker. U.K.: Collins, 1969 (U.S.: Dutton, 1969)

Politics between America and India place Ghote on guard duty at the zoo, protecting the last of four flamingos presented by the U.S. Consul. When he fails to save the animal, he finds himself on the track of someone who either finds it funny to perpetrate the acts, or someone who has politics as a motive. When the perpetrator is murdered, Ghote needs to shift gears one more time on this case.

India, Bombay

Inspector Ghote Breaks an Egg. U.K.: Collins, 1970 (U.S.: Doubleday, 1971)

Accepting an assignment from an "eminent figure in our public life," Ghote finds himself disguised as a chicken feed salesman. His assignment is to investigate a 15-year-old murder of a politician's first wife, now that the politician's shift in loyalties has laid him open to investigation.

India

Inspector Ghote Goes by Train. U.K.: Collins, 1971 (U.S.: Doubleday, 1972)

Ghote is on the Calcutta Mail train taking a 1200-mile journey to Calcutta to bring back the notorious antiques fraud artist, A. K. Bhattacharya. But the journey proves to be more arduous than he would have predicted, and his travelling companions prove more a mystery than he expected.

India · Trains

Inspector Ghote Trusts the Heart. U.K.: Collins, 1972 (U.S.: Doubleday, 1973)

Manibhai Desai has received a ransom demand from kidnappers. The problem is that the kidnappers have taken the tailor's son, not the rich man's son. Ghote finds himself in a dilemma when he wants to believe that a poor man's son is equal to a rich man's son.

India, Bombay · Kidnapping

Bats Fly Up for Inspector Ghote. U.K.: Collins, 1974 (U.S.: Doubleday, 1974)

The force has an anti-fraud crew known as The Bats. Ghote is assigned to the Black-Money and Allied Transactions Squad as a spy, to find out who in this elite police force is a turncoat to the organization.

India, Bombay

Filmi, Filmi, Inspector Ghote. U.K.: Collins, 1976 (U.S.: Doubleday, 1977)

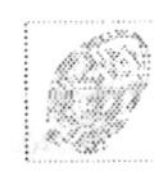

India's world-famous film industry is shaken by the real-life murder of the movie star villain, Dhartiraj. Ghote finds that his suspects are the stars revered by the people, and he struggles to find a murderer.

Film · India, Bombay

Inspector Ghote Draws a Line. U.K.: Collins, 1979 (U.S.: Doubleday, 1979)

Disguised as the literary help Judge Asif Ibrahim will need to write his memoirs, Ghote is in a remote part of India trying to prevent the judge's death. The judge refuses to believe that someone within his own family could prove a threat, but Ghote knows he must be vigilant to prevent a crime.

India

Go West, Inspector Ghote. U.K.: Collins, 1981 (U.S.: Doubleday, 1981)

Nirmala Shahani was sent to America by her rich father, but when she drops out of college and joins an ashram in Los Angeles, her father sends Ghote to America to straighten her out. Faced with a locked-room puzzle and The Swami With No Name, Ghote finds America to be a challenge.

California, Los Angeles · Locked room

The Sheriff of Bombay. U.K.: Collins, 1984 (U.S.: Doubleday, 1984)

While escorting a famous personage in one of Bombay's brothels, Ghote witnesses the Sheriff of Bombay leaving just prior to the discovery of a dead prostitute. Unable to find a way to convince anyone of the guilty party's identity, Ghote is startled when another woman is murdered.

India, Bombay

Under a Monsoon Cloud. U.K.: Hutchinson, 1986 (U.S.: Viking, 1986)

Newly assigned to the remote police station of Vigatpore, Ghote finds himself being inspected by Additional Deputy Inspector-General Tiger Kelkar. When things go terribly wrong, and Ghote finds himself under the cloud of suspicion, he finds he must used all his skills to save his own reputation.

India, Vigatpore

The Body in the Billiard Room. U.K.: Hutchinson, 1987 (U.S.: Viking, 1987)

In the remote station area of Ootacamund, too many of the old colonial things still exist. One of the servants in the famous Ooty Club, where snooker was invented, is found dead on a billiard table, and Ghote finds himself the detective needed to solve the crime.

India, Ootacamund

Dead on Time. U.K.: Hutchinson, 1988 (U.S.: Mysterious Press, 1989)

While visiting Bombay, Ramrao Pendke is murdered in the Tick Tock Watchworks, and the police arrest the owner, Rustom Fardoomji, for the crime. Ghote has his doubts, and he has 24 hours to prove that a businessman would never murder his best customer.

India, Dharbani

Inspector Ghote. His Life and Crimes. Hutchinson, 1989

A collection of the following stories: "The All-Bad Hat," "The Cruel Inspector Ghote," "Hello, Hello, Inspector Ghote," "Inspector Ghote and the Noted British Author," "Light Coming," "The Miracle Baby," "Murder Must Not at All Advertise, Isn't It?," "Nil by Mouth," "The Not So Fly Fisherman," "A Present for Santa Sahib," "The Purloined Parvati and Other Artifacts," "The River Man," "The Test," and "The Wicked Lady."

Short stories

The Iciest Sin. U.K.: Hutchinson, 1990 (U.S.: Mysterious Press, 1990)

Ghote is set on the trail of the infamous blackmailer Dolly Daruwala, and he is surprised to stumble onto a murder and additional blackmailers. Torn between his duties and his profession, he is stunned to find himself a victim of extortion.

India, Bombay

Cheating Death. U.K.: Hutchinson, 1992 (U.S.: Mysterious Press, 1994)

Bombay's Oceanic College has a scandal when student Bala Chambhar overdoses on sleeping pills after stealing an exam paper. Ghote's assignment includes determining how the exam was stolen from a locked room, but his biggest challenge is chasing the institutionalized cheating that exists in the system.

Academia • India, Bombay

Doing Wrong. U.K.: Macmillan, 1994 (U.S.: Otto Penzler, 1994)

Mrs. Shoba Popatkar has been murdered, and her status as a national figurehead causes Ghote to be extra careful in his investigation. When clues indicate the murderer came from the holy city of Banares, Ghote travels there only to discover that the mysterious nature of that city, and its religious population, can be as complicated to understand as a murder investigation.

India, Banares · Religion

Asking Questions. St. Martin's Press, 1997

Ghote finds himself investigating the film industry again when film star Asha Rani provides an experimental drug called ACE-I to a film director, only to have the man die. The source of the drug is the Mira Behn Institute for Medical Research, and it is there that Ghote finds that his most likely suspect, snake handler and drug supplier Chandra Chagoo, is dead as well.

Film · India, Bombay

Bribery, Corruption Also. St. Martin's Press, 1999

Wife Protima has inherited an estate in Calcutta, and she wants her husband Ghote to move to that city. He is not ready to retire, and the home proves to be a handful when an eager buyer pressures for a sale and squatters have taken occupation.

India, Calcutta

Breaking and Entering. U.K.: Macmillan, 2000 (U.S.: St. Martin's Minotaur, 2001)

When millionaire Anil Ajmani is murdered in his secured mansion in Bombay, Ghote is frustrated to be assigned to a different case. While he is searching for a cat burglar nicknamed Yeshwant, he keeps a private investigation going on the murder case. Hosting his Swedish friend, Alex Svensson, provides a distraction to the Inspector from the Crime Branch of the newly named Mumbai Police.

India, Bombay

Faye Kellerman ✍

Peter Decker/Rina Lazarus

Faye Kellerman is the wife of mystery writer Jonathan Kellerman. The two writers began their writing careers at roughly the same time. Working for the Los Angeles Police Department, Peter Decker goes on a path of discovery that leads back to his Jewish roots. Along the way, he begins a relationship with Rina Lazarus, adding depth to the series as she explores their Jewish heritage and beliefs. Readers may also enjoy Deborah Crombie, Elizabeth George, and Anne Perry. **Traditional**. Series subjects: **California, Los Angeles · Teams**.

The Ritual Bath. Arbor House, 1986

Decker is disturbed when he is asked to investigate the brutal rape of a woman on a remote yeshiva community. She had been returning to the community from a mikvah, or bathhouse, where the cleansing ritual is performed. When the community itself proves closed to the investigator, it only makes Decker's job harder.

Judaism • Religion

Sacred and Profane. Arbor House, 1987

Taking Sammy and Jake, Rina's children, on a camping trip turns to disaster when the kids discover two charred skeletons. The trail from these bodies leads Decker to the seamier side of Hollywood, and a community that uses its children and discards them when they are finished.

Children at risk

Milk and Honey. Morrow, 1990

Decker stumbles on a blood-covered child, and when it is discovered that her family has been slaughtered, Decker needs to know if this young girl was a witness to the tragedy. At the same time, Decker needs to deal with an old friend from Vietnam who is now accused of raping a prostitute.

Children at risk

Day of Atonement. Morrow, 1991

Decker and Rita are honeymooning in Brooklyn, celebrating the High Holidays, and meeting long-lost relatives. Then Noam, an Orthodox teenager, really becomes lost, and Decker uses his professional skills on unfamiliar territory to try and solve a family crisis. Discovering that he needs to return home to find the solution, Decker is happy to receive help from Rita.

Judaism • New York, New York

False Prophet. Morrow, 1992

Lilah Brecht is the child of Hollywood legends, and her Valley Canyon Spa Resort represents Hollywood at its best, until someone beats, robs, and rapes her. Decker takes the case, but he passes the baton to his partner Margie when Lilah proves too much of a femme fatale for his liking. After becoming convinced that the original case may be false, and after a few more deaths, Decker knows he has a tough one to solve.

Grievous Sin. Morrow, 1993

The birth of their own child is a source of joy for Decker and Rita, but at their hospital, suffering from the burdens of budget cuts, Rita finds herself in emergency surgery for complications. Even more complications occur when a nurse disappears with a baby from the ward, and Decker finds himself well-motivated to search for the missing child.

Children at risk

Sanctuary. Headline, 1994

Honey Klein has moved into the Decker household to escape her diamond-merchant husband. Then, she and her children disappear, and Decker finds he has a murder case that involves a different diamond-merchant's family. When Honey's husband is murdered as well, the trail leads the Deckers to Israel as they desperately search for the truth to their friend's disappearance.

Diamonds • Israel • Jewels

Justice. Morrow, 1995

Decker is assigned the case of a murdered high school prom queen, and the trail leads him to a disturbed young man who seems to want to be the killer. But Decker has his doubts, and as he probes into the underworld of teenage angst in L.A., he finds a deeper cause for the crime.

Prayers for the Dead. Morrow, 1996

Heart surgeon Azor Sparks has been murdered, and the reason may lie within his family and the eagerness for his large inheritance. However, Decker discovers that Sparks's colleagues were also jealous, and there may be more to Sparks's background when a biker gang shows up at his funeral.

A Serpent's Tooth. Morrow, 1997

A gunman destroys Estelle's, a trendy L.A. restaurant, and Decker is not satisfied when former bartender, Harlan Manz, is arrested. Evidence shows that there may have been a second gunman, but the owner files a sexual harassment suit against Decker and gets him removed from the case. Troubles at work, troubles at home, and Decker finds himself twisted in new directions during the course of this case.

Jupiter's Bones. Morrow, 1999

The Order of the Rings of God is lead by the cult leader Jupiter, and his death from a combination of alcohol and drugs could be accidental or intentional. Decker finds the cult uncooperative, and his investigation must follow a careful path to avoid the kind of confrontations that occur with violent and isolated fringe cults.

Cults

Stalker. Morrow, 2000

This novel features Peter Decker's daughter, Cynthia, now a Los Angeles police officer. Her personal life is thrown into turmoil when it becomes obvious to her that she is being stalked. Unable by her nature to ask her father for help, she plots to catch her tormentor.

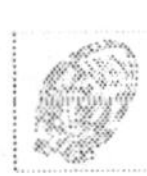

The Forgotten. Morrow, 2001

Lazarus is the caretaker for a storefront synagogue that is vandalized by Ernest Golding. When the young boy and his therapist are murdered, the case falls to Decker to solve. It becomes complicated when Rina's son knows the victim and a hidden connection to Nazism is discovered.

Religion

Stone Kiss. Warner, 2002

Decker's half-brother Jonathan Levin is a rabbi in New York, and he asks for help when Jonathan's brother-in-law Ephraim Leiber is murdered and a young girl disappears. The girl, Shayndie, becomes the key as she links Decker to a man from Decker's past who is connected to the pornography industry and who will end up threatening Decker's and Lazarus's lives.

Judaism · New York, New York · New York, Quinton · Religion

Laurie King ✍

Kate Martinelli

San Francisco homicide detective Martinelli has a complex personal life that adds layers to this series. As a lesbian and a woman in a man's world, she struggles to maintain her status in both areas. Partnered with an equally complex veteran investigator, Alonzo Hawkin, these two capture cases that force them to look at the psychological nature of life as well as the criminal. Readers may also enjoy Eleanor Taylor Bland, J. A. Jance (Joanna Brady), and Margaret Maron (Sigrid Harald). See the author's website at http://www.laurierking.com. **Traditional**. Series subjects: **California, Los Angeles · Homosexuality · Lesbian detectives**.

A Grave Talent. St. Martin's Press, 1993

New to homicide, Martinelli is tested when she and her partner Hawkin are asked to investigate three deaths of young girls in the vicinity of a remote art colony. The presence of an artist who has served time for murdering a child only adds spice to the complex stew that develops before Martinelli begins to see the pattern within the pattern. ED

Artists · Children at risk

To Play the Fool. St. Martin's Press, 1995

A homeless man is killed in the park that also provides a home for Brother Erasmus, a man who speaks in quotations and who may hold the key to the crime for Martinelli. The question becomes: is he a Holy Fool, or is Martinelli a fool to rely so much on this man to solve the crime?

With Child. St. Martin's Press, 1996

Still trying to deal with the tragic effects of her first case on her life partner Lee, Martinelli feels crushed when Lee asks for some time away from their relationship. Seeking solace in a trip to Washington with a 12-year-old named Jules, Martinelli finds herself missing the girl in a territory where a serial killer has worked.

Children at risk · Washington

Night Work. Bantam, 2000

The first corpse is baggage handler James Larsen, dead with candy in his pocket. The second corpse is software salesman Matthew Banderas, also adorned with a piece of candy. Each man has some relationship to an abuse case, and Martinelli and Hawkin battle media pressure to try and find a murderer.

Margaret Maron ✍

Sigrid Harald

As a homicide detective in the New York Police Department, Sigrid Harald is a competent investigator, but in her personal life, she struggles to make connections. Although much time passes in the publication history of this series, the character only ages one year. The combination of the two aspects of her life is what makes this series interesting. Readers may also enjoy Eleanor Taylor Bland, J. A. Jance (Joanna Brady), and Laurie King (Kate Martinelli). See the author's website at http://www.margaretmaron.com. **Traditional**.

One Coffee With. Raven, 1981

Eight suspects stand out in the art department of Vanderlyn College when Professor Ripley Quinn topples over from poison in his coffee. Motivation could have come from his potentially damaging new book of criticism, or from his love life, and it takes Harald's talents to sift through the suspects to find the right motive.

Academia • New York, New York

Death of a Butterfly. Doubleday, 1984

A divorcee with a young child seems an unlikely blackmailer, but when Julie Redmond's body is found and her murder is assigned to Harald, the detective quickly learns that the woman had many enemies. Her ex-husband is a prime suspect, as he is unable to marry while she is alive, and the woman's brother seems as criminal as the victim. With the help of a precocious teen, Harald is able to peel away the layers of deception and discover a murderer.

New York, New York

Death in Blue Folders. Doubleday, 1985

Attorney Clayton Gladwell may have been using his insider information to blackmail his own clients, and that may explain why he is dead and folders full of client information were burnt in his office wastebasket. While probing among Gladwell's client list for likely suspects, Harald discovers several that could have been Gladwell's victims, including a millionaire with a kidnapped grandson, an aging screen star, or a member of the Algonquin Round Table.

New York, New York

The Right Jack. Bantam, 1987

When a bomb goes off in a prestigious Manhattan hotel, it injures Harald's partner Tildon. Her investigation is focused on discovering the intended victim of the bomb. Was it aimed at the radical college professor, the millionaire banker, or the beautiful naval intelligence officer?

New York, New York

Baby Doll Games. Bantam, 1988

Emmy Mion is murdered during a dance performance on Halloween, and the outrage of her death is only equaled by the mystifying method used to kill her. Harald finds herself chasing a clever killer willing to kill in a public setting and a motive that may include an earlier murder of a child on the way home from dance class.

Halloween • Holidays • New York, New York • Theater

Corpus Christmas. Doubleday, 1989

Oscar Nauman's exhibition at Bruel House was to save the museum and its unique collection, not to bring the tragedy of murder. But when one of the museum's trustees is found dead, Harald launches an investigation because she was a guest at the opening, and she could see personally the damaged caused by the caustic trustee.

Christmas · Holidays · New York, New York

Past Imperfect. Doubleday, 1992

Harald's father was killed in the line of duty, and years later Mick Cluett, who served with her father, is murdered just two months short of his retirement. As Harald investigates, she finds the murder weapon connects to another murder, and the murdered officer may have held secrets about her father's death that will force her to confront her own heritage.

New York, New York

Fugitive Colors. Mysterious Press, 1995

Harald is devastated by two losses: a fellow officer is killed on duty and her lover, artist Oscar Nauman, is killed in an automobile accident. Trying to put her life back together, she can barely deal with the paintings left to her by her lover. When a gallery owner is murdered in Oscar's apartment, Harald knows she must get back in the saddle and return to being a cop.

Art · New York, New York

Sharyn McCrumb ✍

Spencer Arrowood

Set in the rural areas of the Appalachian Mountains of Tennessee, McCrumb's novels, which all take their titles from folk ballads, are dark and humorless looks at the effects of crime on this rural community. Based on her own family history and the stories she heard as a child, McCrumb weaves a tapestry that includes character, setting, and plot. Readers may also enjoy K. C. Constantine. See the author's website at http://www.sharynmccrumb.com. **Traditional**.

If Ever I Return, Pretty Peggy-O. Scribner, 1990

Hamelin High School's reunion will return people and their emotions to this rural Appalachian community. Included is folk singer Peggy Muryan, a recently returned expatriate whose fame leads to veiled threats against her safety. When another woman disappears and things turn violent, Arrowood finds himself concentrating on murder rather than the reunion. MA

Music · Tennessee, Hamelin

The Hangman's Beautiful Daughter. Scribner, 1992

Nora Bonesteel is an elderly mountain woman whose abilities to see into the future have predicted death in the community. But the community is suffering from several compelling crimes that range from the murder of an entire family by their son Joshua, to the deaths caused by the careless attitudes and policies of a local company that is polluting the community and killing its residents.

Tennessee, Dark Hollow

She Walks These Hills. Scribner, 1994

In a previous time, Katie Wyler was kidnapped by the Shawnee, and her tragic story of escape and return to her family has haunted the Appalachian Trail ever since. Three people have decided to retrace her steps for different reasons, including a historian, an escaped con, and a young woman on a personal crusade. When Martha Ayres wants to be deputy, she takes off after the con to prove her worth, and Arrowood finds himself drawn onto the paths in the mountains to find the trail to the truth. AG AN MA

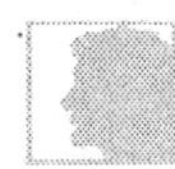

Tennessee, Hamelin

The Rosewood Casket. Dutton, 1996

Randal Stargill's death has brought his four sons to the mountain to bury him in the rosewood casket he requested. A real estate developer sees the death as an opportunity to gain the Stargill's land, but when local seer, Nora Bonesteel, Stargill's former lover, arrives at the funeral with a small casket filled with a child's bones, the family is unable to quietly settle its affairs.

Tennessee, Hamelin

The Ballad of Frankie Silver. Dutton, 1998

Fate Harkryder is about to be executed for a 20-year-old double homicide, convicted on the testimony of a young Arrowood. Not as convinced of Fate's guilt as he once was, Arrowood is haunted by a case from 1832 that contains parallels and lessons about Fate's case.

Tennessee, Hamelin

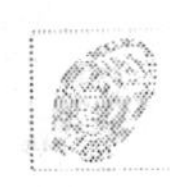

Michael McGarrity ✍

Kevin Kerney

The Southwest has become an increasingly popular place for mystery stories, and McGarrity's New Mexico settings certainly are one of the significant attractions to this series. When Kerney is forced to step aside as Chief of Detectives in Santa Fe, his desire to provide a sense of justice to the cases that cross his path keep him coming back for more. Eventually he returns to the force as the Deputy Chief of the State Police. This series can be recommended to traditional and hard-boiled mystery novel readers. Readers may also enjoy Tony Hillerman. See the author's website at http://michaelmcgarrity.tripod.com/default.htm. **Traditional/Hard-boiled**.

Tularosa. Norton, 1996

An injury forces Kerney to step away from his job as Chief of Detectives in Santa Fe, but he does not retire from investigations. That is because the man who caused his career-ending injury, his ex-partner Terry Yazzi, asks Kerney to investigation the disappearance of Yazzi's son. The disappearance is tied to the White Sands Missile Range, and Kerney finds he must cooperate with a female officer named Sara Bannon who is also investigating the disappearance.

Native Americans • New Mexico, Santa Fe • White Sands Missile Range

Mexican Hat. Norton, 1997

Kerney is working as a seasonal forest ranger in the Gila Wilderness when the body of a Mexican tourist is found in an area where poachers may be at work. Working with a fish and game officer named Jim Stiles, Kerney begins an investigation that pits him against the new Assistant District Attorney Karen Cox and her father and uncle, who are powerful landowners in the area.

New Mexico, Gila Wilderness · Poachers

Serpent Gate. Scribner, 1998

Assuming the role of Deputy Chief of the State Police, Kerney finds himself struggling with a six-month-old murder case. A policeman named Paul Gillespie had been murdered after the local town rodeo, and the clue to finding his killer may rest with a schizophrenic man named Robert Cordova. Then, some precious art disappears from the governor's office, and Kerney finds himself up against an old nemesis.

Art · New Mexico, Mountainair

Hermit's Peak. Scribner, 1999

After Kerney inherits 6,400 acres of land, he finds his life-long dream to own a ranch is spoiled when a stray dog brings him a shoe. The dead body from which the shoe came is only the first of two discovered on his new ranch. The case reunites Kerney with investigator Sara Bannon and the sparks fly.

New Mexico, Las Vegas

The Judas Judge. Dutton, 2000

Six people have been murdered in a campground at the Oliver Lee State Park, and Kerney has a feeling that five of the murders may have been committed to cover up the reason for the murder of Vernon Langford, a wealthy retired judge. His recent marriage, and his desire to retire to his ranch, do not keep him from perusing an investigation that threatens his reputation as an investigator.

New Mexico, Tularosa

Under the Color of the Law. Dutton, 2001

Opting for the job of Police Chief in Santa Fe, Kerney finds himself embroiled in a messy case when a United States Ambassador's estranged wife is found murdered. Forced out of the picture when the FBI assumes the investigative lead, Kerney is forced to investigate from the sidelines when he is suspicious of the federal officer's intent.

Federal Bureau of Investigation · New Mexico, Santa Fe

The Big Gamble. Dutton, 2002

Eleven years after Kerney failed to find her killer, the corpse of Anna Maria Montoya is discovered in Lincoln County next to the remains of a victim of a new crime. Forced to run a parallel investigation with his son, Deputy Sheriff Clayton Istee, Police Chief Kerney discovers things about his victim and himself.

New Mexico, Lincoln County · New Mexico, Santa Fe

Anne Perry

Thomas Pitt/Charlotte Pitt

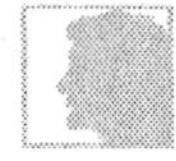

Perry's command of the Victorian period is evident in this series. Thomas Pitt struggles with the fact that he is often unable to deal with the upper classes. His contact in that world becomes Charlotte Ellison. As the series progresses, Pitt marries Charlotte, their love allowing her to marry outside her class. The novels not only provide fine mysteries, but they also dissect the ills of Victorian society. They can be recommended to traditional mystery readers. Readers may also enjoy Elizabeth Peters (Amelia Peabody), Deborah Crombie, Elizabeth George, and Martha Grimes. See the author's website at http://www.anneperry.net. **Traditional/Historical**. Series subjects: **England, London · Historical (1800–1899) · Teams · Victorian England**.

The Cater Street Hangman. U.K.: Hale, 1979 (U.S.: St. Martin's Press, 1979)

London in 1881 is not a place where policeman can question the residents of an area where Charlotte and Emily Ellison live, even if someone is strangling young women in their neighborhood. When the plain daughter, Charlotte, begins to attend to the young policeman named Pitt who keeps pressing his investigation, the family reacts in horror.

Serial killer

Callander Square. U.K.: Hale, 1980 (U.S.: St. Martin's Press, 1980).

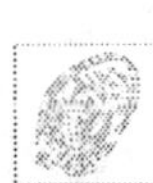

Charlotte Ellison Pitt is now married to Inspector Thomas Pitt, and when two children's bodies are discovered in her old neighborhood, she returns to her old haunts. With the aid of her sister Emily, she follows rumors that the children may be those of a wayward servant, while Pitt follows police procedure to lead him to a murderer.

Paragon Walk. St. Martin's Press, 1981

Fanny Nash has been raped and murdered, and this crime shocks the upper-class Paragon Walk area where her family lives. Pitt tries to work the case from the streets, but Charlotte has access to the inside information because her sister Emily has married and moved to the Walk.

Resurrection Row. St. Martin's Press, 1981

After a performance of Gilbert and Sullivan, Pitt and Charlotte are present when two of their fellow theater goers discover that the cab they have raised has a dead occupant. When the corpse is discovered to be Lord Augustus Fitzroy-Hammond, all are shocked, as he was buried two weeks prior to his resurrection in the cab. When he is buried again, and is resurrected one more time, Pitt feels that someone has something against the survivors.

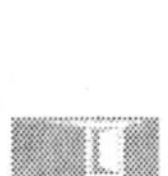

Rutland Place. St. Martin's Press, 1983

Fashionable Rutland Place wants to keep their petty thefts under wraps, but Charlotte's mother knows her daughter's talents and also wants her stolen locket returned. As Charlotte presses her discreet investigation, a death occurs at Rutland Place, and Pitt must exercise his talents to help his mother-in-law and catch a murderer.

Bluegate Fields. St. Martin's Press, 1984

Bluegate Fields is one of London's worst slums, and the police are shocked to discover the body of a young boy in a sewer. The boy is a part of the Waybourne family, and the family is determined to find out who has drowned their son. Pitt finds himself working against the family's public respectability, so Charlotte uses her talents to probe behind the scenes.

Death in the Devil's Acre. St. Martin's Press, 1985

Pitt finds himself chasing a serial killer when bodies are found in the Devil's Acre. Each corpse has been stabbed in the back and mutilated in the same way, and once again London finds itself in the grip of a serial killer. Pitt's aid comes from Charlotte, whose instincts lead her into the better neighborhoods to solve the murders in the slums.

Serial killer

Cardington Crescent. St. Martin's Press, 1987

A scandal in a prominent family is often kept a secret, but when George March is killed with digitalis in his morning coffee, the affair he is having with Sybilla, his wife Emily's cousin, is considered the cause. However, this family includes Charlotte Pitt, and her skills as a detective are put to use for a personal purpose this time with the help of her policeman husband.

Silence in Hanover Close. St. Martin's Press, 1988

Feeling pressure from his superiors, Pitt is asked to reopen the three-year-old murder case of Foreign Office official Robert York, which took place in the fashionable Hanover Close. When he discovers his inquiries are to be made among people who feel he is not worthy of having his questions answered, a maid reveals a little too much to him and dies for her good deed. Charlotte's help is provided when she can penetrate into a society closed to her husband.

Bethlehem Road. St. Martin's Press, 1990

Pitt is assigned the case of a murdered member of Parliament, but when two more deaths of MPs quickly follow, he realizes he has a case that focuses national attention on his skills as a policeman. Meanwhile, Charlotte makes the acquaintance of suffragette Florence Ivory, a woman who is one of Pitt's main suspects in the deaths of the politicians.

Highgate Rise. Fawcett Columbine, 1991

Clemency Shaw, the wife of a prominent doctor, has died in a tragic fire in the suburb of Highgate. An arsonist may have wanted the doctor, or could the doctor have set the fire himself? While Pitt explores among Clemency's family, Charlotte tries to understand the woman who died and what might have caused her death.

Arson

Belgrave Square. Fawcett Columbine, 1992

If Lord Sholto Byam had not come forward to ask for the police's help, they would have never connected him to the death of a minor moneylender named William Weems. But when Pitt learns that Byam was a victim of blackmail, he also discovers that other officials have felt the long arm of Weems's illegal schemes. While he must tread carefully, Charlotte mancuvers within London society to try and find out which blackmail victim made Weems the victim of a murderer.

Blackmail

Farrier's Lane. Fawcett Columbine, 1993

Pitt and Charlotte are enjoying a rare evening on the town at the theater when Court of Appeals Judge Samuel Stafford dies in his box at the theater of opium poisoning. His death revives the case of Kingsley Blaine, found crucified in Farrier's Lane five years earlier, and the conviction of Jewish actor Aaron Godman for the crime. Once again, Pitt is foiled by status, whereas Charlotte is able to penetrate to the right places and begin to get the information needed to solve this long-standing question.

Theater

The Hyde Park Headsman. Fawcett Columbine, 1994

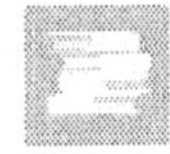

London is once again terrorized by a maniac, this time a murderer that leaves beheaded corpses in prominent places in the city. Pitt is given the case, but he can find no commonality between the victims except that they appeared not to have resisted their killer.

Serial killer

Traitor's Gate. Fawcett Columbine, 1995

A spy in the Colonial Office is aiding Germany in its struggles with England in Africa, and Pitt has the assignment to find the treasonous son of England. At the same time, his mentor, Sir Arthur Desmond, has died of an overdose of laudanum. Ruled a suicide, Pitt believes it may have been murder and it may tie to his other investigation. Pitt's procedure and Charlotte's probing may point to the Inner Circle, a closed society of highly influential men who move behind the scenes to rule the land.

Espionage

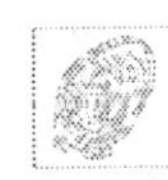

Pentecost Alley. Fawcett Columbine, 1996

Finlay Fitzjames, son of a prominent and influential member of London's society, is suspected of murder when his Hellfire Club badge is found under the body of the murdered prostitute, Ada McKinley. Pressured to look elsewhere for a suspect, Pitt finds himself needing Charlotte's help to penetrate a strata of society closed to his investigation.

Ashworth Hall. Fawcett, 1997

Pitt is assigned guard duty to some politicians meeting to solve the Irish Problem. The difficulty lies in the fact that the meeting is taking place in the country at the estate where Pitt grew up as the son of the servants. However, when murder occurs, the past and the problem are put aside to try and solve the current crime.

England, Ashworth Hall

Brunswick Gardens. Fawcett, 1998

When Unity Bellwood is found at the base of a staircase in a Brunswick Gardens mansion, it is also discovered that she was three months pregnant. Pitt is assigned to the case, and his suspicions fall on three devout men who live there, and who were in conflict with the young woman over her belief in the new science of Darwinism.

Bedford Square. Ballantine, 1999

General Brandon Balantyne's doorstep holds a body, and the distinguished gentleman denies all knowledge of the man. Yet Pitt is intrigued by the fact that the general's snuffbox is in the pocket of the tramp. Using Charlotte's abilities to aid him in his investigation of this sensitive household, he is able to probe towards an answer.

Half Moon Street. Ballantine, 2000

Pitt is handed a strange case when a body is found floating in a punt on the Thames, wearing a green gown, manacled to the punt, and covered with flowers. When the dead man is identified as Delbert Cathcart, photographer, the question becomes who would need to kill this man in this fashion.

The Whitechapel Conspiracy. Ballantine, 2001

Pitt's duty is to testify against the respected soldier John Adinett and send him to his death for the murder of Martin Fetters. The fabled Inner Circle is not pleased, and Pitt finds himself exiled to the slums of Spitalfields as an undercover agent. Cut off from Pitt, Charlotte uses her methods and allies to restore her husband's reputation and save him from an anarchist's plot.

Southampton Row. Ballantine, 2002

The Inner Circle suffered a setback in the last book, but their leader, Charles Voisey, is now running for Parliament as a Tory candidate. Pitt, now working for the Special Branch, is charged with bringing the man down, a task made difficult when the Liberal candidate for the seat in Parliament, Aubrey Serracold, is tied to the murder of a spiritualist named Maude Lamont.

Ruth Rendell ✍

Reginald Wexford

A master of psychological suspense, Rendell applies her talents to a series about Reginald Wexford, the police inspector for the town of Kingmarkham. Partnered with Mike Burden, Wexford's cases often follow the patterns of the Golden Age but are enhanced with modern sensibilities and themes that enrich that books in comparison to those that came before her. These novels can be recommended to readers of the traditional mystery. Readers may also enjoy Colin Dexter, Reginald Hill, and P. D. James (Adam Dalgliesh). **Traditional**. Series subject: **England, Sussex, Kingmarkham**.

From Doon with Death. U.K.: Long, 1964 (U.S.: Doubleday, 1965)

Wexford and Burden work a case brought to them by a worried husband named Parson, who is missing his wife Margaret. Assured by Burden not to worry, because the police believe she may have run off with another man, Parsons is distraught when Margaret's body is found strangled in a nearby woods. When the police investigation gets serious, the clues reveal that there may have been more to Margaret than even her husband understood.

A New Lease of Death. U.K.: Long, 1967 (U.S.: Doubleday, 1967; also published as *Sins of the Fathers.* Ballantine, 1970)

Reverend Henry Archery has revived interest in a 16-year-old axe murder, although Wexford is convinced the right man hung for the crime. The Reverend wants to be certain, as his son is about to marry the daughter of the murderer. As the past unravels, Wexford discovers that there may be something to the suspicions of the worried father.

Wolf to the Slaughter. U.K.: Long, 1967 (U.S.: Doubleday, 1968)

Wexford's introduction to a crime comes when Rupert Margolis, complains that his missing sister, Ann, is not available to manage his household. When an anonymous note informs the inspector that a woman named Ann was murdered by a man named Geoff Smith, he may have an explanation for a blood-soaked hotel room.

The Best Man to Die. U.K.: Long, 1969 (U.S.: Doubleday, 1970)

Charlie Hatton was heading home from the Dragon Pub when someone killed him and dumped his body in the Kingsbrook River, making him unavailable to be the best man at the wedding scheduled for the next day. Wexford's job is to tie this murder into a fatal auto accident involving the stockbroker Fanshawe, and to show who would murder the likeable and well-heeled Hatton.

A Guilty Thing Surprised. U.K.: Hutchinson, 1970 (U.S.: Doubleday, 1970)

Myfleet Manor is the peaceful home of Elizabeth and Quentin Nightingale whose tranquility is shattered when, on one of her normal walks through the woods, Elizabeth is murdered. It falls to Wexford to decide who would ruin this fairytale life.

No More Dying Then. U.K.: Hutchinson, 1971 (U.S.: Doubleday, 1972)

For the second time in eight months, a child has been kidnapped in the Kingmarkham area, and Wexford finds that the only thing in common among the clues are the useless and the crank contributions. When his sergeant, Mike Burden, relives his feelings for his dead wife by getting involved with the missing child's mother, it only complicates a difficult case.

Children at risk

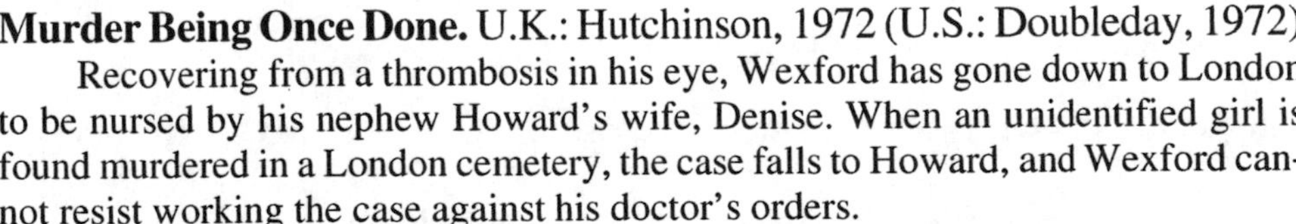

Murder Being Once Done. U.K.: Hutchinson, 1972 (U.S.: Doubleday, 1972)

Recovering from a thrombosis in his eye, Wexford has gone down to London to be nursed by his nephew Howard's wife, Denise. When an unidentified girl is found murdered in a London cemetery, the case falls to Howard, and Wexford cannot resist working the case against his doctor's orders.

England, London

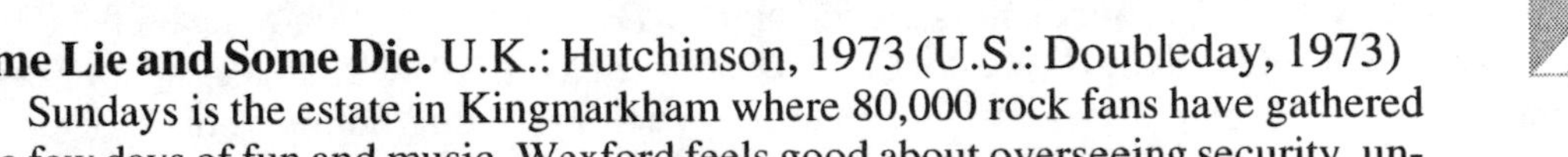

Some Lie and Some Die. U.K.: Hutchinson, 1973 (U.S.: Doubleday, 1973)

Sundays is the estate in Kingmarkham where 80,000 rock fans have gathered for a few days of fun and music. Wexford feels good about overseeing security, until a pair of lovers discover a body in a quarry and the peace dissipates.

Music

Shake Hands for Ever. U.K.: Hutchinson, 1975 (U.S.: Doubleday, 1975)

Angela Hathall has been strangled, discovered in her bed by her mother-in-law. Wexford feels that whoever committed this murder covered their tracks well, and that kind of care points Wexford's interest in the direction of her husband, Robert.

A Sleeping Life. U.K.: Hutchinson, 1978 (U.S.: Doubleday, 1978)

Rhoda Comfrey is murdered in the village of Kingsmarkham, but she had lived her last 20 years in London. Wexford's investigation will focus on her life there, but he finds himself struggling for any clue as to who would want to kill this woman.

England, London

Put On by Cunning. U.K.: Hutchinson, 1981 (U.S.: *Death Notes.* Pantheon, 1981)

Flautist Sir Manuel Camargue has surprised the world by announcing his intentions to marry a woman 50 years younger. Three days before the wedding, he is found floating in the lake near his English country house, and his death is ruled an accident. Wexford discovers that there is something wrong both with the young fiancée, and Natalie, Camargue's daughter, who arrives to collect her inheritance.

California, San Diego

The Speaker of Mandarin. U.K.: Hutchinson, 1983 (U.S.: Pantheon, 1983)

After returning from China where he had the dreamlike experience of being followed by a woman with bound feet, Wexford finds himself assigned to the murder of Adela Knighton, a fellow tourist from the trip. His quest to find out who shot her will also lead him down a path of discovery about his own experiences.

People's Republic of China

An Unkindness of Ravens. U.K.: Hutchinson, 1985 (U.S.: Pantheon, 1985)

Rodney Williams travels so much that quite a bit of time goes by before he is missed. When his neighbor, Wexford, is asked to search for him, Wexford uncovers secrets that lead him into Williams's financial and social life.

The Veiled One. U.K.: Hutchinson, 1988 (U.S.: Pantheon, 1988)

A bomb blows up Wexford's home, his daughter's car, and places him in the hospital, leaving Mike Burden in charge of a murder. Evidence points to Clifford Sanders as the murderer of a middle-aged housewife whose body was left in the parking garage of a suburban shopping mall. Then the question becomes, who wanted to kill Wexford?

Kissing the Gunner's Daughter. U.K.: Hutchinson, 1992 (U.S.: Mysterious Press, 1992)

Davina Flory is an elderly novelist whose peaceful life at Tancred House is shattered by a robbery that leaves her, her husband Harvey Copeland, and her daughter Naomi dead. The only survivor of the incident is granddaughter Daisy, left bleeding to death but somehow able to survive. Wexford believes there is more to this crime than a simple burglary gone mad, and his empathetic connection to Daisy acts as a balm for him as his own daughter, Shelia, has become estranged from her father.

Simisola. U.K.: Hutchinson, 1994 (U.S.: Crown, 1995)

Dr. Akande is trying to locate his daughter, Melanie, and he turns to Wexford for help. As Wexford continues to press his search, three women's bodies are revealed, each that he hopes will not be Melanie. His hope is honored, but each of the dead women has a connection to the missing Melanie, and one of the connections is race. As Wexford deals with the unhappy parents, he must also deal with a nation torn by racial problems.

Race • Serial killer

Road Rage. U.K.: Hutchinson, 1997 (U.S.: Crown, 1997)

Farmhurst Great Wood is about to be torn apart by a highway construction project, and Wexford is sadden by the loss. However, when the eco-terrorist group Sacred Globe kidnaps his wife Dora and others, he is galvanized into action against their cause. Able to concentrate despite the personal involvement, Wexford moves forward in his dogged determination to save his wife.

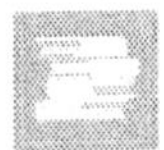

Harm Done. U.K.: Hutchinson, 1999 (U.S.: Crown, 1999)

Lizzie, a disabled young girl, has been missing for three days, and when she reappears, she is incapable of telling anyone what happened to her. Shortly after, a convicted pedophile is released into the community, a second girl goes missing, and a suspect for the kidnappings is murdered. Wexford must pick through the curious happenings in his town to restore order to a community torn apart by its emotions.

Children at risk

Peter Robinson ✍

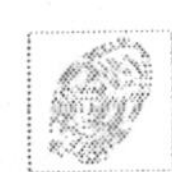

Alan Banks

Canadian writer Robinson has a series of novels set in Yorkshire, England, where he grew up. Banks, a displaced big city cop, incorporates some big-city sensibilities when he works the more genteel countryside murders of this area. He is often teamed with Constable Susan Gay. The vistas and themes of Robinson's books have drawn award nominations to his works. Readers may also enjoy Colin Dexter and Reginald Hill. See the author's website at http://www.inspectorbanks.com/index.html. **Traditional/Hard-boiled**.

Gallows View. Canada: Viking, 1987 (U.S.: Scribner, 1990)

Banks and his family have made the decision to leave London and settle in the Yorkshire area. As Chief Inspector, he is handed the case of a peeping Tom, and the local women are up in arms. Equally disturbing is the gang of thugs terrorizing the elderly in the area. Banks finds himself busy enough with his new assignment, but when the violence begins to threaten his own family, he feels his new location may be as dangerous as his old.

England, Yorkshire, Eastvale

A Dedicated Man. U.K.: Viking, 1989 (U.S.: Scribner, 1991)

Harry Steadman has been killed, and the only one in Gratly who seems to have a clue as to why is the 16-year-old Sally Lumb. Steadman was interested in the archaeology of the local ruins, and had plans to write a history of the village. For Banks, the question becomes was something discovered in the past a reason for a murder in the present?

Archeology • England, Yorkshire, Gratly

The Hanging Valley. Canada: Penguin, 1989 (U.S.: Scribner, 1992)

Banks is given the case of a faceless corpse found weeks after the murder, and he becomes obsessed with the case when it echoes a similar murder that had taken place five years earlier. He has plenty of suspects in the town of Swainshead, but when someone interferes with his investigation, it appears that a big clue may lie in Canada.

Canada, Toronto • England, Yorkshire, Swainshead

A Necessary End. U.K.: Viking, 1989 (U.S.: Scribner, 1992)

When a policeman is killed during a nuclear power protest, the police are baffled by the number of suspects and the lack of a motive. Normally Banks would be in charge of the investigation, but instead he finds himself working under a former London colleague, Richard "Dirty Duck" Burgess.

England, Yorkshire, Eastvale

Past Reason Hated. U.K.: Viking, 1991 (U.S.: Scribner, 1993)

Susan Gay pulls her first homicide case three days before Christmas when Caroline Hartley is murdered and left on her sofa. Managing a trendy café and keeping her sex life a secret, this woman also acted in the Eastvale Amateur Dramatic Society, and each aspect of her life adds more suspects for Banks and Gay. Sorting through the clues proves challenging to the detectives, and teaches each of them something about themselves.

England, Yorkshire • Theater

Wednesday's Child. U.K.: Viking, 1992 (U.S.: Scribner, 1994)

When Brenda Scupham is approached by two representatives from social services, she unwillingly is intimidated into handing over her seven-year-old daughter, Gemma. When no one knows where the child has been taken, the case is handed over to Banks. His quest is desperate, driven by the need to know if the child is still alive.

Children at risk • England, Yorkshire, Eastvale

Final Account. U.K.: Viking, 1994 (U.S.: Berkley, 1995)

The Yorkshire police are troubled by the death of accountant, Keith Rothwell, who was murdered in front of his family. Banks, with his assistant constable Gay, investigates the man's life, which had presented itself as normal until a former lover steps forward and reveals his secret life. Equally troubling, he seems to have been skimming from a drug-dealing client, and this may be what really put his family in danger.

England, Yorkshire, Eastvale

Innocent Graves. Berkley Prime Crime, 1996

A teenaged girl named Deborah Harrison has been found strangled with the strap of her school satchel, her body dumped in the St. Mary's churchyard. The secrets she hinted about may have led to her death, but as Banks pursues his investigation, it leads him back to the church itself, where things are not as they seem.

England, Yorkshire, Eastvale • Religion

Blood at the Root. Avon, 1997

Banks is suffering on all fronts when his wife Sandra asks for a separation and he has been suspended at work. His investigation of the death of Jason Fox, beaten outside a rustic pub in Eastvale, has led him into a sensitive racial area, and he is set aside by his superiors. Investigating anyway, he discovers that some people are trying to return England to a state of racial purity, and his drive to find the truth is putting him in danger.

England, Yorkshire, Eastvale • Race

Not Safe After Dark & Other Stories. Crippen & Landru, 1998

A collection of the following stories: "Anna Said," "The Good Partner," and "Summer Rain." Also includes 10 non-Banks stories.

Short stories

In a Dry Season. Avon, 1999

Stuck on desk duty for his insubordination, Banks is called back into action when a particularly dry summer lowers Thornfield Reservoir. Uncovered by the drought is Hobb's End, a village buried by the water after WWII, and which now reveals a corpse dead for almost 50 years. AN BA

England, Yorkshire, Hobb's End

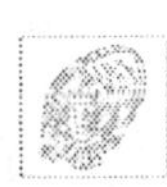

Cold Is the Grave. Morrow, 2000

Banks has often been in conflict with his supervisor, Chief Constable Jimmy Riddle. So he is surprised to find himself helping Riddle when the man's daughter is featured on a pornographic website. Venturing to London in search of clues, Banks finds himself battling the gangster who controls Emily Riddle. When he restores order, it is only for a brief moment, and then tragedy places him on the trail of a murderer.

England, London • England, Yorkshire, Eastvale • Pornography

Aftermath. Morrow, 2001

When a popular teacher named Terence Payne is accused of abuse, it leads to an even more startling discovery. Payne has killed a policeman to try and protect the secrets in his basement. When the case falls to Banks to investigate, he finds himself in the spotlight of the media and an angry community suffering from the loss of some of its children.

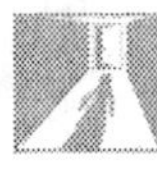

Children at risk • England, Yorkshire

John Sandford (pseud. of John Camp) ✍

Lucas Davenport

At times it is difficult to distinguish between the thriller and the detective novel. Davenport's constant battles against serial killers could be categorized as thrillers because we know who is committing the murders, but he is a hard-working Minneapolis cop either way. These novels can be recommended to readers who like hard-boiled detectives. Readers may also enjoy Lawrence Block (Matthew Scudder) and J. A. Jance (Joanna Brady). See the author's website at http://www.johnsandford.org. **Hard-boiled**. Series subjects · **Minnesota, Minneapolis** · **Serial killer**.

Rules of Prey. Putnam, 1989

Davenport is challenged when a serial killer leaves him no clues to his random attacks. Maddog Vullion is a lawyer, and he knows he is mad, but his drive to kill intensifies and the intervals between his kills narrows.

Shadow Prey. Putnam, 1990

Davenport has a strange case when a slum landlord and a probation officer have their throats slashed by an Indian ceremonial knife. He believes the case is his to solve, but then he is informed that a politician in New York and a judge in Oklahoma City were murdered the same way. Without an way to probe into the Native American community, and with the FBI involved in his case, Davenport finds himself overwhelmed by the task.

Native-Americans

Eyes of Prey. Putnam, 1991

Davenport has another serial killer case when a series of mutilation murders rocks the Twin Cities. As the case begins to shape up, it becomes obvious that there is more than one hand involved in these crimes.

Silent Prey. Putnam, 1992

Michael Bekker, on trial for his deeds in *Eyes of Prey*, escapes from a Minneapolis courthouse, and flees to New York. Lily Rothenbery, Davenport's old flame, is a police detective there who wants Davenport's help in capturing Bekker. She believes that some of New York's finest may be taking the law into their own hands.

New York, New York

Winter Prey. Putnam, 1993

The Iceman needs to retrieve an incriminating photo and begins his retrieval by killing three people in a desperate attempt to regain it. Recuperating, Davenport reluctantly agrees to help the outmanned police force, cut off from resources by the brutal weather. Knowing that an evil exists that can even bother him, Davenport suffers as he tries to bring a madman to justice.

Wisconsin, Ojibway County

Night Prey. Putnam, 1994

State investigator Megan Connell is disturbed by something she sees in the murder victim found frozen on the Carlos Avery game reserve. With the police are reluctant to listen to her and the new female police chief distracted, she ends up with Davenport as her only hope. When a second victim appears, the same feelings that Megan had occur to Davenport, and he begins to put the case together.

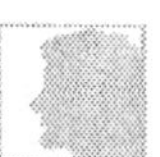

Mind Prey. Putnam, 1995

Andi Manette has been kidnapped with her two children, and she must use all her skills as a psychiatrist to slow down her captor. Meanwhile, Davenport intuitively knows that he is up against a monster when he is shown the evidence of their abduction and realizes the clock is ticking.

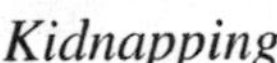

Kidnapping

Sudden Prey. Putnam, 1996

Two woman bank robbers are gunned down when the police try to stop one of their robberies, and the mourning Dick LaChaise, husband to one and brother to the other, escapes from prison to revenge their deaths. His method is to hunt down the officers who shot his women and kill their families. One of those cops is Davenport, and he must use all his skills to hunt this madman before more innocents die.

Secret Prey. Putnam, 1998

Still suffering depression from the emotional lows of his last case and the breakup of his relationship, Davenport is assigned the murder of banking executive Daniel Kresge. Murdered in a hunting lodge north of the city, Kresge's four fellow hunters, all employees in his bank, and the murdered man's ex-wife all have motives for the kill.

Certain Prey. Putnam, 1999

Clara Rinker has been called north to the Twin Cities to take out attorney Hale Allen's wife, Barbara, on behalf of attorney Carmel Loan. As a professional hitwoman, she is used to things going smoothly, but in this case, most things are going wrong. Loan's contact has a tape of her deal, and Rinker kills a witness to her crime that just happens to be a cop. With Davenport on her tail, she decides the easiest thing might be to take him out as well.

Hit men

Easy Prey. Putnam, 2000

Everyone involved in a fashion shoot with supermodel Alie'e Maison went to Silly Hanson's house to party upon completion. Two people did not walk away. The first is Alie'e herself, whose murder brings Davenport to Hanson's house, where he discovers a second body. The possible involvement of a fellow officer has Davenport scrambling to find a killer before the department suffers.

Chosen Prey. Putnam, 2001

Davenport is on the quest to discover who has dumped a young woman's body in a remote wilderness when clues inspire him to have the area searched for more victims. He then finds himself on the trail of a serial killer who has been using his victims in pornographic drawings.

Pornography

Mortal Prey. Putnam, 2002

Clara Rinker, who escaped from Davenport in *Certain Prey*, is still at large, and the detective is drafted by the F.B.I. to take up the chase. Rinker is seeking revenge for some old injuries, and while the team assembles seeks to stop her, it is the work of Davenport that will lead to the final confrontation.

Hit men · Missouri, St. Louis

Janwillem Van de Wetering ✍

Henk Grijpstra/Rinus de Gier

This long-running series has gone through some changes, but the initial titles feature an Amsterdam setting and much philosophical discourse. The two detectives work the streets as members of the Amsterdam Municipal Police under the wise leadership of the Commissaris. As the series progresses, the officers face retirement and solve their problems by retiring in comfort. Not all readers will take to this series because of its philosophical diversions and its European style. The series should be recommended to traditional mystery readers looking for a challenge. Readers may also enjoy Stuart Kaminsky, H. R. F. Keating, and William Marshall. See the author's website at http://www.dpbooks.com/vandewet.htm. **Traditional**. Series subject: **Teams**.

Outsider in Amsterdam. Houghton Mifflin, 1975

The two detectives are asked to investigate the suicide of Piet Verboom, who was found hanging from a beam in the Hindist Society restaurant commune that he ran in Amsterdam. As the probe continues, questions begin to arise as to whether Verboom was a spiritual leader or a drug dealer.

Netherlands, Amsterdam · Religion

The Corpse on the Dike. Houghton Mifflin, 1976

While on routine assignment, the two detectives discover the corpse of Wernekink, an inoffensive man who lived alone in a house on the dike. They discover that the man had a visitor named The Cat, a mysterious middleman who might hold the key to the murder.

Netherlands, Amsterdam

Tumbleweed. Houghton Mifflin, 1976

A houseboat on the Amersterdam canal reveals the corpse of a high-class prostitute named Maria van Buren. As the detectives investigate, they find that her clients have alibis, so they must turn to other sources for a potential perpetrator.

Caribbean, Curacao · Netherlands, Amsterdam · Prostitution

Death of a Hawker. Houghton Mifflin, 1977

While the city tries to evict longtime residents from an area ready for urban renewal and a riot ensues, the two detectives are sent into the area to verify the reported death of Abe Rogge. Grijpstra and de Gier discover that this death will be hard to explain, as they have a classic locked-room puzzle to solve.

Locked room · Netherlands, Amsterdam

The Japanese Corpse. Houghton Mifflin, 1977

A simple missing person's report by a waitress in a Japanese restaurant leads to the discovery that the Japanese Mafia, or Yakusa, is actively dealing in stolen art and smuggling drugs into the country. Asked for their help by the Japanese government, de Gier and the Commissaris travel to Japan to try and draw the criminals out into the open.

Japan, Kyoto • Netherlands, Amsterdam

The Blond Baboon. Houghton Mifflin, 1978

Elaine Carnet has had a checkered life as a former nightclub singer, owner of a furniture company, and an alcoholic. When her body is found at the base of her garden steps, the question for the two detectives is: Who pushed her? The suspects are her daughter, her business partner, and a salesman in her company.

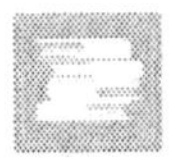

Netherlands, Amsterdam

The Maine Massacre. Houghton Mifflin, 1979

When the commissar's brother dies, he travels to America to help settle the estate. The town of Jameson has had some murders, and de Gier is sent over to work in conjunction with his American police brothers and help them solve their murders.

Maine, Jameson

The Mind Murders. Houghton Mifflin, 1981

The two detectives have two cases to work on in the streets of Amsterdam. A unidentified man has been found in the trunk of a stolen Mercedes. Meanwhile, the detectives attention is drawn to a man whose wife is missing and may be murdered.

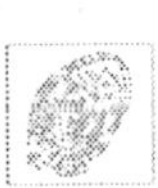

Netherlands, Amsterdam

The Streetbird. Putnam, 1983

No one mourns the loss of a pimp, so when the notorious Luku Obrian is murdered, the two detectives are not all that inspired to find his killer. But nothing is ever simple for these two, and when De Gier sees a vulture in the red-light district, and he knows the country has no vultures, he realizes he is involved in another complex case.

Netherlands, Amsterdam

The Rattle-Rat. Pantheon, 1985

Returning to his parent's homeland of Friesland, Grijpstra is the lead and de Gier the follower in this land where language and customs are different. Brought there because Friesland native, Douwe Scherjoen, has been murdered in Amsterdam, it is a surprised de Gier who begins to pick up the clues needed to find the murderer of this land's native son.

Netherlands, Friesland

Hard Rain. Pantheon, 1986

The Commissaris takes a personal interest in the case of a murdered banker when he knows the man has some secrets. The death of three junkies on a houseboat ties in, but the whole unit is called off the investigation when their efforts focus on a man named Fernandus. Fernandus is the leader of the Society of Help Abroad, and the cops work off-duty to prove their belief that the organization is a front for a vice gang.

Netherlands, Amsterdam

Just a Corpse at Twilight. Soho, 1994

Grijpstra has retired from the force, but he gets a frantic phone call from his former partner, de Gier, who is now living in isolation in Maine. De Gier is the subject of blackmail, having a fear that one night, while drunk, he may have killed his missing girlfriend Lorraine. Grijpstra initially believes that Lorraine is alive, but he runs afoul of the local law when a body is found.

Maine, Squid Island

The Hollow-Eyed Angel. Soho, 1996

Now it is the commissar's turn to retire, but he has been invited to New York to speak to a police conference. So when Jo Termeer, fellow officer, asks the Commissaris to help investigate the death of Bert Termeer, a New York bookseller whose body was found in Central Park, De Gier finds himself called to New York to help his boss solve this international crime.

Netherlands, Amsterdam • New York, New York

The Perfidious Parrot. Soho, 1997

All of the detectives are now happily retired on someone else's money. The Commissaris is in Aruba, managing their money, while the two detectives are avoiding work while ostensibly functioning as private detectives. Reluctantly, they are forced to search for a missing cargo of oil bound for Cuba that leads them on an international chase.

Caribbean, Aruba • Caribbean, St. Eustatius • Florida, Key West

The Amsterdam Cops. Soho, 1999

A collection of the following stories: "The Bongo Bungler," "The Deadly Egg," "Heron Island," "Holiday Patrol," "Houseful of Mussels," "Hup Three," "The Letter in the Peppermint Jar," "Letter Present," "The Machine Gun and the Mannequin," "The Sergeant's Egg," "Six This, Six That," "Sure, Blue, and Dead, Too," and "There Goes Ravelaar."

Short stories

Lone Wolf Police

The police who are categorized as Lone Wolf Police are actually holdovers from the great detective style. Through circumstances often out of their control, they are forced to live within the institution but act without. The appeal of their solo act can be their heroism as the loner steps outside the safety net that an institution can provide. The Lone Wolf Police are very similar to the detectives found in the Private Detectives section, where it is standard that the detective is a lone wolf, and the exception are detectives who work within an institution. Readers who are attracted to the Private Detectives should find these Lone Wolf Police appealing as well.

The Historical Founding Members

Ngaio Marsh

Roderick Alleyn

Inspector (and later Superintendent) Roderick Alleyn of Scotland Yard is the creation of this New Zealand author. Her love of theater and mysteries is often combined in her works. She created a detective who walked in the world of police investigation but was not reliant on police procedure to solve his cases. His upper-class heritage and his marriage to Agatha Troy, a painter, placed him outside the normal realm of police detectives in England. This social dichotomy is what makes him a fascinating character, as does his association with his partner, Inspector Fox. A website about the author can be found at http://www.kirjasto.sci.fi/nmarsh.htm. **Traditional**.

A Man Lay Dead. U.K.: Bles, 1934 (U.S.: Sheridan, 1942)

Sir Hubert Handesley is a master at throwing unique house parties, and this weekend his plans include the parlor game "Murders." When the victim is selected to die, the guest's job is to find the murderer. It becomes Chief Detective Alleyn's job this time, because the corpse is really dead.

England, Frantock • Mystery games

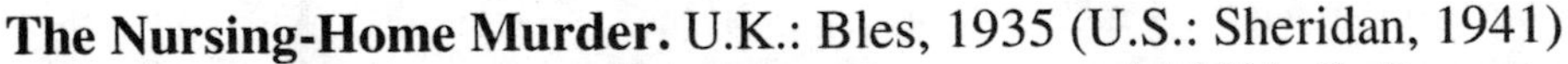

The Nursing-Home Murder. U.K.: Bles, 1935 (U.S.: Sheridan, 1941)

Sir Derek O'Callaghan is the author of a controversial bill in Parliament and a man balancing a wife and a mistress who is a nurse. When he takes ill while speaking in Parliament, he is operated on by the doctor who is in love with his nurse, and she is assisting in the operating room. So, when O'Callaghan dies, his wife, who knew of the affair, insists that it was murder.

England • Jellett, Dr. H. • Medical

Enter a Murderer. U.K.: Bles, 1935 (U.S.: Pocket, 1941)

In the play called *The Rat and the Beaver*, the rat and the beaver hate each other. But from the look at rat Felix Gardener's face, he did not expect the stage gun he used to really kill the beaver, Arthur Surbonadier. Watching from the audience is Alleyn, so he inherits a strange case where reality and the theatrical have mixed.

England, London · Theater

Death in Ecstasy. U.K.: Bles, 1936 (U.S.: Sheridan, 1941)

The House of the Sacred Flame is conducting its weekly religious rites when Cara Quayne drinks the ritual wine and drops dead. Poisoned by cyanide, her death confuses Alleyn, as he must decide who would choose this method to kill her, and whether she was the real target.

England, London · Religion

Vintage Murder. U.K.: Bles, 1937 (U.S.: Sheridan, 1940)

The Carolyn Dacres English Comedy Company is on a tour of New Zealand, and the company is feeling the aches and pains suffered when people are confined together for too long. When an elaborate opening night stage party goes terribly wrong, and a prop kills Alfred Meyer, Carolyn's husband, Alleyn is on the scene to begin an investigation.

New Zealand, Middleton · Theater

Artists in Crime. U.K.: Bles, 1938 (U.S.: Furman, 1938)

Agatha Troy's drawing class has a model who is enacting a crime scene, but when the scene proves too real and the model, Sonia Gluck, is murdered, the case is turned over to Alleyn. Although the students are suspected, so is the woman that Alleyn loves, and that adds a difficult dimension to a confusing case.

Artists · England, Bucks., Bossicote

Death in a White Tie. U.K.: Bles, 1938 (U.S.: Furman, 1938)

Alleyn knows that someone is blackmailing some of the most prominent women in London, and his man on the inside is the popular Lord "Bunchy" Gospell. When Gospell is found asphyxiated in a taxi cab, Alleyn needs to figure out why this case has turned to murder.

England, London

Overture to Death. U.K.: Collins, 1939 (U.S.: Furman, 1939)

In the village of Pen Cuckoo, a charity production finds the residents sparring for their roles, with none more invigorated by the excitement than Idris Campanula, the local gossip. When she is dispatched, Alleyn finds the case more difficult than he thought when it appears the wrong woman may have been murdered.

England, Pen Cuckoo · Theater

Death at the Bar. U.K.: Collins, 1940 (U.S.: Little, Brown, 1940)

Luke Watchman is travelling to meet his cousin Sebastian Parrish and artist Norman Cubitt at the Plume of Feathers in Devonshire when he has a car accident. When he finally arrives at his destination, he finds himself surrounded by his friends, the man with whom he had the accident, and the local and colorful characters. These same folks will become the suspects when Watchman is hit by a dart during a friendly game and collapses in death.

England, Devonshire

Surfeit of Lampreys. U.K.: Collins, 1941 (U.S.: *Death of a Peer.* Little, Brown, 1940)

Gabriel Lamprey was always kind enough to bail out his family, but when a bill collector comes calling, he refuses for the first time. Soon after, Lamprey meets his death, and the family inherits his fortune. Alleyn needs to figure out if someone in the family was tired of asking for money, or if the cause of this death lies outside the family.

England, London

Death and the Dancing Footman. U.K.: Collins, 1942 (U.S.: Little, Brown, 1942)

Jonathan Royal is a bored millionaire, and his idea of fun is to invite sets of people to his house party who hate each other. When all the guests are stranded by a snowstorm, and someone dies, the plan is to have Alleyn solve the crime.

England, Dorset, Cloudyfold

Colour Scheme. U.K.: Collins, 1943 (U.S.: Little, Brown, 1943)

Alleyn is in New Zealand hunting down leaks to the enemy when he is notified of some suspicious activities at a decaying resort by some British expatriates. When conflict develops with the neighboring Maori tribesman, the combination proves fatal.

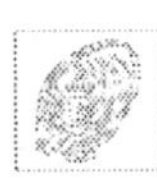

New Zealand, Auckland • World War II

Died in the Wool. U.K.: Collins, 1945 (U.S.: Little, Brown, 1945)

The wool-raising community has moved on after the disappearance of the prominent Parliament member, Florence Rubrick. When her body is discovered pressed to death in a bale of wool, Alleyn is on the scene looking for a motive in a country still torn by war but also torn by the personal emotions tied to the wool industry.

New Zealand, Mount Moon

Final Curtain. U.K.: Collins, 1947 (U.S.: Little, Brown, 1947)

Troy Alleyn has been commissioned to paint the portrait of Shakespearean actor, Sir Henry Ancred. She is disturbed by the acrimonious household she has entered, with events occurring under the guise of practical jokes and irritating vandalism. Then, the actor dies at a birthday party, and Alleyn is called in to sort out the practical jokes from the lethal act.

Art • England, Bucks., Bossicote • Theater

Swing, Brother, Swing. U.K.: Collins, 1949 (U.S.: *A Wreath For Rivera.* Little, Brown, 1949)

George Settinger, the Marquis of Pastern and Bagott, is going to play the drums during his own song, "Hot Guy Hot Gunner." The gag in the song is that he will kill the accordion player Carlos Rivera, who will be carted off stage. Unfortunately, the gag works too well, and Alleyn is a witness to the accidental death, creating a case for the detective to solve.

England, London • Music

Opening Night. U.K.: Collins, 1951 (U.S.: *Night at the Vulcan.* Little, Brown, 1951)

The Vulcan Theater is about to mount a play entitled *Thus To Revisit*, but there is turmoil among the cast members. Some of it is caused by the mysterious new dresser, but things are so bad that on opening night leading lady Helen Hamilton's husband, Clark Bennington, is murdered, and Alleyn must step in.

England, London • Theater

Spinsters in Jeopardy. U.K.: Collins, 1954 (U.S.: Little, Brown, 1953; also published as *The Bride of Death.* Mercury, 1955)

Alleyn and family are ostensibly on vacation in the French Riviera, but the detective is really on a secret assignment for the government. But when his attention is focused on a chateau where mysterious and deadly games are being played, his own son Ricky is kidnapped.

France, Roqueville • Kidnapping

Scales of Justice. U.K.: Collins, 1955 (U.S.: Little, Brown, 1955)

Sir Harold Lacklander passes away in the village of Swevenings, and all is well until the publication of his memoirs. There are those who would have preferred their secrets stay secret, and when one of the residents is beaten to death, Alleyn must step in and discover who has the most guilty secret of all.

England, Swevenings

Off with His Head. U.K.: Collins, 1957 (U.S.: *Death of a Fool.* Little, Brown, 1956)

Mrs. Bunz is too interested in the ritual dance performed at the winter solstice in Mardian for the taste of the locals who perform the pageant. But when someone is actually decapitated during the folklore celebration, the attention of Scotland Yard and Alleyn focuses on the ceremony.

England, Mardian

Singing in the Shrouds. U.K.: Collins, 1959 (U.S.: Little, Brown, 1958)

A serial killer is strangling women in London, but his last victim is found clutching a clue that indicates the murderer is sailing on the Cape Farewell. Getting Alleyn on board as an undercover detective is the easy part. The hard part is sorting through all the passengers to find the murderer before he can strike again.

Serial killer • Shipboard

False Scent. Little, Brown, 1959

Used to the homage of her entourage, actress May Bellamy is distressed to discover that at her fiftieth birthday party everyone is destined to disappoint her. Her writer, Richard Dakers, has a new play with no role for her, and she takes out her anger on her husband and her dresser. Very shortly she is dead, and Alleyn is left with this conflicted life as his first clue when searching for her killer.

England, London • Theater

Hand in Glove. U.K.: Collins, 1962 (U.S.: Little, Brown, 1962)

On the night of a wild treasure hunt, all manner of people stopped at an open sewer line searching for a hidden clue. The next morning, the only thing uncovered is the dead body of Harry Cartell, found in that very same sewer. As Alleyn and Fox investigate, they find that all things were not normal in the village of Little Codling, especially with Cartell's rival, Percival Pyke Period, and within the dead man's family.

England, Little Codling

Dead Water. Little, Brown, 1963

Alleyn's old friend, Emily Pride, has inherited 14 acres connected to the mainland by a narrow causeway that has been developed in reaction to the presence of the healing waters of Pixie Falls. When Pride makes a journey to the area to shut down the springs and set free the land, she is met with local resistance. When murder occurs, Alleyn and Fox are forced to step in and settle the issues.

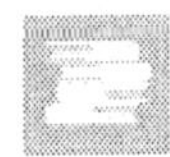

England, Portcarrow

Killer Dolphin. U.S.: Little, Brown, 1966 (U.K.: *Death at the Dolphin.* Collins, 1967)

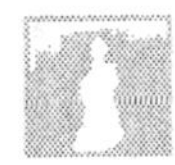

Vassily Conducis, a Greek millionaire, has supported the efforts of director and playwright Peregrine Jay to restore the Dolphin Theater. Jay's decision to write a play around a glove found in a Victorian desk leads to a death within the company, and solving the case may require Alleyn to determine if the glove can be connected to Shakespeare himself.

England, London • Shakespeare, William • Theater

Clutch of Constables. U.K.: Collins, 1968 (U.S.: Little, Brown, 1969)

Troy Alleyn takes advantage of a last-minute opening on the cruise ship Zodiac, and little does she know the opening was caused by a murder. Once onboard, her fellow passengers feud, and she finds herself in the middle of a case involving a missing jewel. When Alleyn and Fox work their way onboard, murder cannot be far behind.

Shipboard

When in Rome. U.K.: Collins, 1970 (U.S.: Little, Brown, 1971)

Barnaby Grant, author, is in Rome when his manuscript is taken. Alleyn is in Rome as an undercover agent looking into the illegal drug trade, and he finds himself connected to a guided tour of Rome that includes Grant. When their guide disappears and a murder occurs, Alleyn finds himself acting as policeman and spy.

Authors • Italy, Rome

Tied Up in Tinsel. U.K.: Collins, 1972 (U.S.: Little, Brown, 1972)

Hilary Bill-Tasman believes he has restored Halberds Manor to its previous glory, and he celebrates with a Christmas party to which a number of eclectic individuals are invited, including Troy. When Hilary's uncle's manservant is missing and later found dead, the celebration turns sour. Perhaps all this could have been predicted when Hilary hired five ex-murderers to staff his manor.

Christmas • England, Halberds • Holidays

Black As He's Painted. U.K.: Collins, 1974 (U.S.: Little, Brown, 1974)

Bartholomew Opala is an old schoolchum of Alleyn, and his friend is now the president of the nation of Ng'ombwana. As Opala journeys to England, there is a threat of assassination that he will not take seriously, so the Special Branch asks Alleyn to help them protect the world leader.

England, London

Last Ditch. U.K.: Collins, 1977 (U.S.: Little, Brown, 1977)

Son Ricky has rented rooms on an island to work on his novel, and he finds himself involved in murder when a pregnant woman named Dulcie Harkness, who refused to name the father of her child, is murdered. While trying to think like his father, Ricky finds himself overwhelmed and is happy to see his father arrive to help.

Authors • England, Montjoy

Grave Mistake. U.K.: Collins, 1978 (U.S.: Little, Brown, 1978)

Hypochondriac Sybil Foster commits suicide and her death is investigated by Alleyn and Sybil's friend, Verity Preston. The introduction of a surprise will seems out of character for Sybil, and Alleyn finds himself hunting for a motive for what could be a murder.

England, Upper Quintern

Photo-Finish. U.K.: Collins, 1980 (U.S.: Little, Brown, 1980)

Troy has been asked to paint the portrait of Isabella Sommita, an internationally famous opera star who has been harassed by the paparazzi. The portrait is commissioned by Montague V. Reece, and the job is to be done on the estate of the opera patron in New Zealand during the gathering of an international assemblage brought to hear the debut of a new piece. When the piece proves unbearable, and the diva is murdered, Troy is glad that her husband Alleyn is along for the trip.

New Zealand, Rivermouth • Opera • Theater

Light Thickens. U.K.: Collins, 1982 (U.S.: Little, Brown, 1982)

Macbeth is the cursed play, and when the Dolphin Theatre decides to mount a production, the play is plagued with problems. Alleyn is in the audience for a rehearsal when a climatic battle scene proves too real and a real casualty of war is left on the stage.

England, London • Theater

The Collected Short Fiction of Ngaio Marsh. International Polygonics, 1989

A collection of the following stories: "Chapter and Verse," "Death on the Air," "I Can Find My Way Out," and "The Little Copplestone Mystery." Also includes four non-Alleyn short stories, two essays, and a telescript.

Short stories

Georges Simenon ✍

Jules Maigret

With a European sensibility, this French detective combines psychological insight into the criminal mind with an introspective character. Commissaire Maigret may not be as isolated as other dectectives, but his dependence on the internal makes him a fascinating lone wolf detective. His method is to absorb the clues in the cases and do his deduction from the facts without much interaction with the case. Most of Maigret's cases were either short stories or novellettes. Because of the extensive (75 novellettes and 28 short stories) and sometimes confusing bibliography of French, British, and American editions of the many Maigret works, only the first and last title are listed here. However, every library and every reader should have some Maigret novels in their collections. A website about the author, and a complete list of all the Maigret titles, can be found at http://www.trussel.com/maig/maibib.htm. **Traditional**.

***Pietr-le-Leton.** France: Fayard, 1931 (U.S.: *The Strange Case of Peter the Lett.* Covici, Friede, 1933)
The first appearance of Commissaire Maigret.

***Maigret et Monsieur Charles.** France: Presses de la Cite, 1972 (U.K.: *Maigret and Monsieur Charles.* Hamish Hamilton, 1973).
The last appearance of Commissaire Maigret.

Beyond the Golden Agers

John Ball ✍

Virgil Tibbs

Although created by a white writer, black detective Virgil Tibbs was a forerunner of minority inclusion in the mystery fiction field. His race was used as an issue to isolate him from his safety nets in the first title, and that story has become a classic in the literature. Later novels would find Tibbs performing his duties in his normal surroundings. **Traditional**. Series subject: **African-Americans**.

In the Heat of the Night. Harper & Row, 1965

The town of Wells pins its resurrection on a concert to be conducted by Enrico Mantoli, but its hopes are shattered when Deputy Sam Wood finds Mantoli mugged and murdered on the streets late one night. Doing a sweep of likely suspects, Wood arrests a black man found loitering in the railroad station. To Police Chief Bill Gillespie's distress, the black man is Virgil Tibbs, a Pasadena homicide detective and Gillespie's unwanted ally in trying to solve the crime. ED

South Carolina, Wells

The Cool Cottontail. Harper & Row, 1966

The Sun Valley Lodge is a nudist colony, and its pastoral nature is disturbed when an unidentified man is found floating in the pool. The sheriff's department needs a homicide investigator, so once again Tibbs finds himself on loan to solve a mysterious and delicate murder case.

California · Nudists

Johnny Get Your Gun. Little, Brown, 1969 (Also published as *Death For a Playmate.* Bantam, 1972)

There is racial conflict in Pasadena, and it is a time when small things can mean a lot. When nine-year-old Johnny McGuire receives a transistor radio from his parents to help him adjust to his new environment, he is crushed when a bully takes it away. So, Johnny borrows his Dad's .38 Colt revolver and decides to settle the issue.

California, Pasadena

Five Pieces of Jade. Little, Brown, 1972

Tibbs is given the case of a ritualistic murder of jade importer Wang Fu-sen, found with a Ya-Chang ritual knife buried in his chest and four pieces of jade displayed around his head. Tibbs has a few suspects from the dealer's personal life, but the involvement of drugs and the Red Chinese adds an international flair to the case.

California, Pasadena · Gems

The Eyes of Buddha. Little, Brown, 1976

The Pasadena Police need to find the missing heiress Doris Friedkin, so when a decomposed woman's body is found, they fear the worst. But, when it is not Doris, Tibbs has to identify the new body and still locate the missing woman.

California, Pasadena

Then Came Violence. Doubleday, 1980

Tibbs is confused to find himself in possession of a new home, which also includes a family. The switch in his personal life is arranged by the department when they are asked to protect some citizens of Bakara from their pursuers. Still expected to go to work, Tibbs is asked to explain a series of robberies and several deaths that are plaguing the Pasadena area.

California, Los Angeles

Singapore. Dodd, Mead, 1986

Tibbs is sent to Singapore to protect the interests of the United States when the widow of President Motamboru of Bakara is falsely accused of murder. Unfortunately, all the evidence points to her guilt, and she is scheduled to be hanged unless Tibbs can unravel this puzzle.

Singapore

William McIlvanney ✍

Jack Laidlaw

Scottish writer McIlvanney's series is one of the shining examples of the rogue and isolated cop, and influenced other writers such as Ian Rankin. Laidlaw is a disturbed cop, but McIlvanney shows the society that made him so in a descriptive and literary style. His novels can be recommended to hard-boiled readers. **Hard-boiled**. Series subject: **Scotland, Glasgow**.

Laidlaw. U.K.: Hodder, 1977 (U.S.: Pantheon, 1977)

Bud Lawson once stood accused by the police, but now he is asking the police for help in finding his missing daughter, Jennifer. When she is discovered raped and murdered, the case falls to Laidlaw.

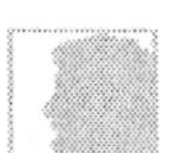

The Papers of Tony Veitch. U.K.: Hodder, 1983 (U.S.: Pantheon, 1983

Only Laidlaw seems to care when an old tramp named Eck Adamson is murdered, and he uses the three clues left by the dead man to hunt for his murderer. One clue leads to a pub, another to a rich and beautiful woman, while the last takes Laidlaw into the underworld of modern Glasgow. DA

Strange Loyalties. U.K.: Hodder, 1991 (U.S.: Morrow, 1991)

Laidlaw takes a week's leave to investigate the strange occurrences around his brother Scott's death. Discovering that Scott's wife is missing and that his brother had been acting oddly motivates him to bring closure to this family crisis.

Scotland, Ayrshire

The Modern Practitioners

Kent Anderson ✍

Hanson

The character of Hanson first appeared in Anderson's Vietnam War novel, *Sympathy For the Devil.* Anderson, a former police officer, then used his own experiences to move Hanson to the police force in Portland, Oregon. Although only one novel in this two-book series is a mystery, it is such a powerful example of the hard-boiled police detective that it is included for readers who enjoy a tough edge to their reading. Readers may also enjoy James Lee Burke and Michael Connelly. **Hard-boiled.**

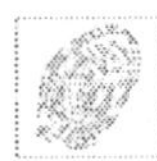

Night Dogs. Dennis McMillan, 1996

When Hanson returns from Vietnam, he establishes a career in the North Precinct of Portland, where his life becomes an extension of the street crimes he battles. Then, a campaign begins that threatens Hanson, and he finds himself dependent on a killer from his past who may hold the key to his survival on the force.

Oregon, Portland · Vietnamese Conflict

James Lee Burke ✍

Dave Robicheaux

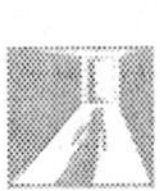

Former homicide cop Robicheaux has retired to his bait shop in New Iberia, Louisiana, where he tries to repair a life ripped open by violence and alcoholism. In the tradition of Travis McGee, Robicheaux is motivated the most when people close to him are in danger. Eventually, he joins the New Iberia sheriff's staff and returns to the saddle as a professional. Among Burke's many talents are his use of words, making his novels read like fine literature. The books will also appeal to readers looking for a unique setting. Readers may also enjoy Kent Anderson, Lawrence Block (Matthew Scudder), Michael Connelly, and James Crumley. See a fan's website at http://www.palmersguide.com/jamesburke. **Hard-boiled**.

The Neon Rain. Holt, 1987

Detective Robicheaux is called out to the Angola penitentiary where he hears from a killer about to be executed that there is a contract out on the detective's life. As he proceeds to hunt for the man hunting him, he is beaten and left for dead. His rambling, drunken story sounds too unbelievable to be true and leaves him suspended from the force.

Louisiana, New Orleans

Heaven's Prisoners. Holt, 1988

Robicheaux and his wife witness the crash of a small plane into the swamp near their bait shop. Diving on the wreck, Robicheaux finds four dead bodies and a little girl saved by an air pocket. But when the authorities raise the plane, there are only three bodies aboard. The reason for the flight, the reason for the crash, and the reason for an interest in keeping Robicheaux from the truth about both leads to a desperate search for the truth.

Louisiana, New Iberia

Black Cherry Blues. Little, Brown, 1989

Dixie Lee Pugh, a former singing star, asks Robicheaux for help. As a leaseman for the Star Drilling Company, he is having trouble securing land in Montana for drilling. Robicheaux takes a trip to Montana to help, and finds himself confronted by angry Native Americans and some greedy Mafioso. ED

Louisiana, New Iberia • Montana, Blackfeet Indian Reservation • Native Americans • Organized crime

A Morning for Flamingos. Little, Brown, 1990

Forced by his financial situation, Robicheaux joins the New Iberia police, and is given the job of transporting Jimmie Lee Boggs and Tee Beau Latiolais to New Orleans for their scheduled executions. When they escape, they leave Robicheaux wounded and his partner dead. Robicheaux infiltrates the New Orleans mob to try and hunt down the prisoners, and has to face his own dangerous past on the quest.

Louisiana, New Orleans • Organized crime

A Stained White Radiance. Hyperion, 1992

Weldon Sonnier is a successful oilman and a childhood friend of Robicheaux. When someone shoots out one of the windows in his antebellum home, plainclothes detective Robicheaux is dispatched and enters a world of power, violence, money, and a sad family history.

Louisiana, New Iberia

In the Electric Mist with Confederate Dead. Hyperion, 1993

When a film crew comes to New Iberia to shoot a civil war epic, the star, Elrod Sykes, cannot stop being a public menace. When he is pulled over for drunk driving, he tells Robicheaux about the skeleton of a black man in the Atchafalaya Swamp, the remains of a murder that Robicheaux witnessed when he was a young man. Partnered with Rosie Gomez from the FBI, the two finds themselves grappling with the old case while Robicheaux also has a dead hooker's murder to solve. He wants to tag mobster Baby Fee Balboni for the crime and receives some clues from the vision of an old civil war general he meets in the magical swamps near his home.

Civil War · Ghosts · Louisiana, New Iberia

Dixie City Jam. Hyperion, 1994

As a college student, Robicheaux discovered the remains of a German sub used to sink American tankers leaving New Orleans during WWII. Now, years later, he is confronted by Will Buchalter, a man who believes the holocaust was a hoax, and a threat because of Robicheaux's knowledge of the sub's location.

Louisiana, New Iberia · Submarines · World War II

Burning Angel. Hyperion, 1995

Robicheaux has two cases to balance in this adventure. The first involves a man named Sonny Boy Marsallus who once worked the mob-covered areas of New Orleans, but who has returned from an exile in Central America with some secrets. The second case involves the Fonetnot family, whose claim to the land they have lived on for over 100 years, is now in jeopardy.

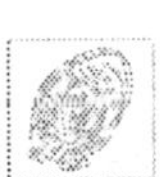

Louisiana, New Iberia

Cadillac Jukebox. Hyperion, 1996

Aaron Crown is poor white trash and a perfect suspect in the assassination of black civil rights leader, Ely Dixon, in the 1960s. But after years in prison, Crown has escaped, still pleading that he is innocent of the charges. Despite his misgivings, Robicheaux believes that Crown's conviction might be a set up. Even the governor, Buford LaRose, who wrote a book on the case, has a stake in the matter, as does the Mafia man who warns Robicheaux away from Crown's cause.

Louisiana, New Iberia

Sunset Limited. Doubleday, 1998

Forty years have passed since photojournalist Megan Flynn's father, a labor organizer, was crucified against a barn wall in New Iberia. She has returned to her home with her filmmaker brother Cisco to document their father's death, and their insistence on finding the truth opens a new case for Robicheaux. DA

Louisiana, New Iberia

Purple Cane Road. Bantam, 2000

Robicheaux's upbringing never included a mother, but when he arrests Zipper Chum, a New Orleans pimp, the man reveals some secrets about the death of Robicheaux's mother. Seeking the truth about his heritage, and the truth behind the murder of his mother, Robicheaux goes on a journey that will test him as a man.

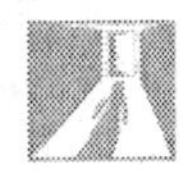

Louisiana, New Orleans

Jolie Blon's Bounce. Simon & Schuster, 2002

Musician Tee Bobby Hulin has been accused of the murder of a prostitute and a teen-aged girl, but Robicheaux believes he is innocent. When he sets out to prove it, Robicheaux finds he must confront his deepest fears to battle an old plantation overseer named Legion Guidry.

Louisiana, New Iberia

Michael Connelly ✍

Harry Bosch

In a contemporary Los Angeles that echoes Raymond Chandler, Harry Bosch struggles against a system that places him outside its safety net. Bosch, a Vietnam veteran, is haunted by his sad childhood. He is also a dedicated cop, but his contrary nature means he can be his own worst enemy when dealing with the system. Complex plots and a noirish atmosphere highlight these rogue cop tales in which the past has as great an effect on the characters as the present. Readers may also enjoy Kent Anderson, Lawrence Block (Matthew Scudder), Robert Crais, and Ian Rankin. See the author's website at http://www.michaelconnelly.com. **Hard-boiled**. Series subject: **California, Los Angeles**.

The Black Echo. Little, Brown, 1992

Echoes of his Vietnam experiences are raised when Bosch investigates the death of Billy Meadows, a fellow tunnel rat. As Bosch pursues his investigation, he finds ties to a safety vault robbery that used tunneling expertise, and he finds himself in an uneasy alliance with an FBI agent named Eleanor Wish. ED

Vietnamese Conflict

The Black Ice. Little, Brown, 1993

Black ice is a new drug coming across the border from Mexico, and when Bosch has a murder case taken away from him, it is because the dead man may be a narcotics officer who went bad. Driven to investigate despite the fact that the official ruling is suicide, Bosch finds himself working against the system to try and solve this case.

The Concrete Blonde. Little, Brown, 1994

Bosch is convinced that he killed the Dollmaker, a serial killer, in a justifiable action although the man was reaching for his wig, not a gun. Years later, he is sued by the widow of the Dollmaker, and during the trial a shocking discovery is made: another body killed in an identical fashion to the work of the Dollmaker. While his trial occurs by day, Bosch is working the new case by night to prove the serial killer is really dead.

Serial killer

The Last Coyote. Little, Brown, 1995

Set aside for attacking his superior, and living in a home condemned because of earthquake damage, Bosch is ready to resign. But the realization that he has never come to terms with his mother's murder in 1961 leads him to decide to use his free time to investigate her death. DI

Trunk Music. Little, Brown, 1997

A Hollywood producer is found shot to death in the trunk of a car, and Bosch gets the case. Convinced that this is a mob hit, he finds the organized crime unit disinterested. Clues that lead him to Las Vegas confirm some of his suspicions, but as the case progresses and his love life disintegrates, Bosch finds himself on the outside looking in again. BA

Nevada, Las Vegas

Angels Flight. Little, Brown, 1999

Howard Elias has been challenging the LAPD with his lawsuits built around its racist nature, and when his body is found on the inclined railway called Angels Flight in Los Angeles, the high profile case is given to Bosch. Knowing the world is watching, and that he may have a cop as a suspect, Bosch moves carefully through the minefield of race and politics that defines the LAPD.

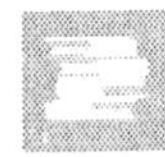

Race

A Darkness More Than Night. Little, Brown, 2001

Terry McCaleb, a retired FBI agent who starred in *Blood Work*, is pulled from retirement one more time when two bizzarre clues draw his interest to a case. Things get complicated when the cop who questioned the victim on the night he died is Harry Bosch.

City of Bones. Little, Brown, 2002

Bosch and partner Jerry Edgar draw the assignment to identify the 20-year-old bones of a small child and then find his killer. When the case dredges up personal and painful memories for Bosch, he refuses to let go, even when his dogged determination threatens his love life with rookie cop Julia Brasher.

Children at risk

John Harvey

Charlie Resnick

Divorced and lonely, Charlie Resnick has all the classic symptoms of the loner cop. British author Harvey sets his series in Nottingham and features jazz as one of the underlying themes. The themes of these novels are very dark. Readers may also enjoy Bill James, Ian Rankin, and Peter Robinson. See a website about this author at http://www.mellotone.co.uk. **Hard-boiled**. Series subject: **England, Nottingham**.

Lonely Hearts. U.K.: Viking, 1989 (U.S.: Henry Holt, 1989)

Resnick's life is in turmoil; besides his cats and his jazz, he now has a new girlfriend. The problem is his main case has him looking for a serial killer of lonely women, and his girlfriend Rachel may be on the killer's list.

Serial killer

Rough Treatment. U.K.: Viking, 1990 (U.S.: Henry Holt, 1990)

Paired as burglars but not in temperament, kind-hearted Jerry Grabianski finds himself matched with his more aggressive partner, Trevor Grice. Resnick is looking for the evidence to shut these two down and has them on his list of suspects for a burglary that left a corpse behind. When Grice falls for the wife of one of his victims, things begin to get really complicated, especially when her husband will not cooperate with Resnick.

Cutting Edge. U.K.: Viking, 1991 (U.S.: Henry Holt, 1991)

Someone is using a knife to cut his victims in the vicinity of the city's major hospital with the intent of ending their ability to practice medicine again. As the panic increases, the case falls to Resnick, who must search for a motive for the attacks when one turns fatal.

Medical

Off Minor. U.K.: Viking, 1992 (U.S.: Henry Holt, 1992)

Two little girls go missing, each from a different environment. The first, Gloria Summers, was snatched from the swings in a playground six weeks prior to the second disappearance. The second child, Emily Morrison, is stolen out of the garden of her parent's home. When one of the children is found dead, Resnick is driven to find the second before another death.

Children at risk

Wasted Years. U.K.: Viking, 1993 (U.S.: Henry Holt, 1993)

Resnick finds the present echoes the past when a series of robberies reminds him of an investigation he conducted when just a beat cop. Working the robberies that haunted his town while it suffered a series of urban riots, Resnick came face to face with his adversary and nearly lost his life. He did lose his wife, and 10 years later the memories still haunt him.

Cold Light. U.K.: Heinemann, 1994 (U.S.: Henry Holt, 1994)

Dana Matthieson has reported that her roommate, Nancy Phelan, has disappeared from her work Christmas party. The reason for her disappearance may lie in her work as a caseworker for the Welfare Department, and the two men who were pursuing her affections. While Resnick fights a Christmas crime wave, he devotes some time to searching for Nancy until clues begin to develop that indicate he is searching for a psychopath.

Christmas • Holidays

Living Proof. U.K.: Heinemann, 1995 (U.S.: Henry Holt, 1995)

Cathy Jordan is a best-selling mystery author from America, and her arrival at the annual Shots in the Dark mystery convention means Resnick has to protect her from the stalker whose poison-pen letters have threatened her with harm. Meanwhile, a mad slasher is attacking men in the red light district, and the Nottingham police find their resources stretched thin.

Authors

Easy Meat. U.K.: Heinemann, 1996 (U.S.: Henry Holt, 1996)

Nicky Snape is one of those youths lost to society at an early age, and when his crimes accelerate to murder, he is sent to the children's home to await trial. When he is found hanging from the shower, Resnick is convinced someone has murdered the young man.

Still Waters. U.K.: Heinemann, 1997 (Henry Holt, 1997)

A series of women's deaths is plaguing Nottingham, but when Resnick's girlfriend becomes convinced her friend's death was caused by her abusive husband and not the serial killer, she convinces Resnick to investigate.

Last Rites. U.K.: Heinemann, 1998 (U.S.: Henry Holt, 1999

Ten years ago the police put away Michael Preston for murdering his father. While out of prison on leave for his mother's funeral, the man escapes. Resnick and his fellow cops are too busy combating a drug war, but when it seems that an old killer may be up to his old tricks, Resnick's attention is drawn to the escapee.

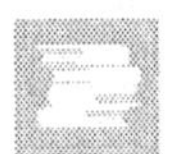

Bill James (pseud. of James Tucker) ✍

Desmond Iles/Colin Harpur

Paired together, these two British cops are world weary and cynical. With Colin Harpur leading the investigations under the scrutiny of his boss Desmond Iles, their cases combine police procedure with suspense. Their personal lives are equally dysfunctional, and the triumphs and tragedies within their families also make up a significant part of the books. These novels can be recommended to hard-boiled readers. Readers may also like John Harvey and Ian Rankin. **Hard-boiled**. Series subjects: **England · Organized crime · Teams**.

You'd Better Believe It. U.K.: Constable, 1985 (U.S.: St. Martin's Press, 1986)

Associating with criminals is a necessity in the tough underworld where crimes are committed. Harpur is deeply indebted for the information passed on to him by his narcs, or snitches. When a tip about a bank robbery proves unreliable, the police begin to question their own, and Harpur finds himself caught between the bad and the good.

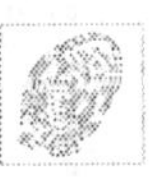

The Lolita Man. U.K.: Constable, 1986 (U.S.: Foul Play, 1991)

Harpur has the task of hunting down the Lolita Man, suspected of raping and murdering five teenage girls. His interest in the case is accelerated when he believes the daughter of his friend may be the next victim, and he feels compelled to run his own investigation.

Serial killer

Halo Parade. U.K.: Constable, 1987 (U.S.: Foul Play, 1992)

Harpur is responsible for placing a young policeman named Ray Street into a drug lord's gang. Street is murdered, and Harpur tries to maneuver the case around to convict the leader of the gang.

Protection. U.K.: Constable, 1988 (U.S.: Foul Play, 1992)

An underworld war is brewing when Bernie "Tenderness" Mellick maims Ivor Wright with a blowtorch and Wright reacts by kidnapping Mellick's 11-year-old grandson. While the department has to deal with the wait for the ransom demand, it finds one of its own officers is under investigation for improper conduct with none other than Tenderness.

Kidnapping

Come Clean. U.K.: Constable, 1989 (U.S.: Foul Play Press, 1993)

Iles has wrestled with his wife's unfaithfulness, but when she and her latest lover, Ian Aston, frequent an underworld nightclub and are witnesses to a knifing, they are threatened for what they know. Harpur finds himself a part of his boss's need for revenge, and he must balance the personal needs of Iles while conducting his investigation.

Take. U.K.: Macmillan, 1990 (U.S.: Countryman Press, 1994)

Ron "Planner" Preston plans to hit a payroll van when suddenly his plans are changed by shifts in the van's schedule. When Iles and Harpur become aware of the attention in the underworld being focused on Planner's plan, they try to stay one step ahead of the crooks.

Club. U.K.: Macmillan, 1991 (U.S.: Countryman Press, 1995)

"Panicking Ralph" Ember runs a club that is frequented by members of the underworld, and he is tapped to replace a dead man on a bank heist team. The dead man is Ian Aston, lover of Iles's wife, and the two policeman have a special interest in solving his death as some suspicion points to Iles himself. While the bank heist goes forward, the murder investigation keeps the cops distracted.

Astride a Grave. U.K.: Macmillan, 1991 (U.S.: Foul Play Press, 1996)

"Panicking Ralph" Ember is still up to his neck in the remnants of a bank heist, and things get nasty when the group begins to splinter and the big question becomes: Where is the money? Harpur is especially determined to run the crooks to ground, and his focus is the bar owner who may be the one to break.

Gospel. U.K.: Macmillan, 1992 (U.S.: Foul Play Press, 1997)

Harpur may be married, but he is dallying with a college student named Denise, a woman who happens to be acquainted with Harpur's snitch, Jack Lamb. Lamb's tip on Martin Webb leads to the death of Webb's son, and Webb uses Denise to get to Harpur.

Roses, Roses. U.K.: Macmillan, 1993 (U.S.: Foul Play Press, 1998)

Megan Harpur has finally taken a lover in an act of revenge against her husband's infidelity. But when she is returning from London to tell him, she is murdered. While dealing with his daughters who feel the betrayal of a mother's death, Harpur tries to solve Megan's death before Iles does.

In Good Hands. U.K.: Macmillan, 1994 (U.S.: Norton, 2000)

With Iles suspected in the death of two criminals who may have murdered Iles's mistress and a detective, Harpur finds himself assigned the job of reining in his own boss. When two more deaths occur in the underworld mimicking the same pattern, Harpur must decide if he should chase Iles or look at Panicking Ralph as a suspect.

The Detective Is Dead. U.K.: Macmillan, 1995 (U.S.: Norton, 2001)

While the underworld works hard to carve up the drug empire of the now-deceased Kenward Knapp, a trial begins. Harpur refuses to name his informant. Because Harpur's hands are dirty with the involvement of his snitch, Keith Vine, he finds himself in conflict with Iles, who wants even more from Vine.

Top Banana. U.K.: Macmillan, 1996 (U.S.: Foul Play, 1999)

Thirteen-year-old Mandy Walsh is murdered when she is caught between two warring drug gangs. Mansel Shale, drug boss, is willing to deal with Iles and the police, while Harpur discovers that evidence may show the girl was the actual target.

Lovely Mover. U.K.: Macmillan, 1998 (U.S.: Foul Play Press, 1999)

Up and coming drug lord, Keith Vine, murders one of his pushers when she gets out of line, setting off a struggle for control of the drug trade. Meanwhile, he is unaware that Harpur has infiltrated his organization, but now the cop finds himself at risk. Harpur wonders if he can trust his superior, Iles, to help him out of this situation.

Panicking Ralph. U.K.: Macmillan, 1998 (U.S.: Norton, 2001)

"Panicking" Ralph Ember wants to be his own master, and plans to expand and control his own drug distribution network. However, when he takes a few minutes to relax with his mistress, Christine Tranter, it turns to murder, and the drug dealer finds himself beholden to Harpur, and suspicious of him as well.

Eton Crop. U.K.: Macmillan, 1999 (U.S.: Foul Play Press, 1999)

"Panicking" Ralph Ember and drug lord Mansel Shale are wary allies in opposition to the London crime syndicates moving into their city. The prize this time is the floating restaurant Eton Boating Song. Trying to out maneuver everyone, the police send in officer Naomi Anstruther, but she is a known pawn in this struggle, and soon Harpur and Iles are as interested in saving her as they are in stopping the gangs.

Kill Me. U.K.: Macmillan, 2000 (U.S.: Norton, 2000)

The undercover sting operation with Naomi Anstruther has led to the death of her ex-boyfriend, Donald McWater, and her new lover, Lyndon Evans, and placed her in an uneasy alliance with a woman named Esme, who wishes to reap revenge for those deaths. The personal nature of this leaves Harpur's sting in jeopardy, and puts officers in danger of losing their own lives.

Pay Days. U.K.: Constable Robinson, 2001 (U.S.: Norton, 2001)

Harpur has worked both sides of the street in his investigations, so he is now quick to condemn a fellow officer named Nivette when evidence indicates the officer may be working for the criminals Panicking Ralph or Top Banana. As the investigation proceeds within the department, a pusher's body is found murdered in a spectacular fashion, and the underworld moves to hide the trail that leads back to them.

***Naked at the Window.** U.K.: Constable Robinson, 2002 (U.S.: Norton, 2002)

Peter Lovesey ✍

Peter Diamond

British writer Lovesey's Peter Diamond faces the ultimate lone wolf punishment: exclusion. Booted from the force, he needs to redeem himself in the eyes of the very authority he fails to understand or respect. Whether inside or outside, Diamond is not a team player, and his cases test his personal abilities to carry out his mission. Readers may also enjoy John Harvey and Ian Rankin. **Traditional/Hard-boiled**.

The Last Detective. U.K.: Scribner, 1991 (U.S.: Doubleday, 1991)

Superintendent Peter Diamond is assigned the case of a nude female body found in a reservoir. His techniques in trying to find the killer of Geraldin Jackman irritate his colleagues and the press, and he finally resigns his position. However, he does not resign his determination to find a killer. AN

England, Bristol

Diamond Solitaire. U.K.: Little, 1992 (U.S.: Mysterious Press, 1993)

Fired for failing to clear Harrod's department store at the end of his day as a security guard, Diamond decides to discover the secret behind the abandoned child found in the store. She is Japanese, and that nation's top sumo wrestler takes an interest in her fate. Soon Diamond discovers he has a truly international case on his hands, and that some evil people are now interested in him.

Children at risk • England, Kensington

The Summons. U.K.: Little, 1995 (U.S.: Mysterious Press, 1995)

Diamond may be unwanted by most employers, but when John Mountjoy takes a hostage, he wants the officer who arrested him to come to the scene. Diamond listens to his old adversary, and begins to believe that he may have arrested the wrong man. Probing an old crime, he discovers the things he needs to keep another victim from falling to Mountjoy.

England, Bath

Bloodhounds. U.K.: Little, 1996 (U.S.: Mysterious Press, 1996)

Diamond is handed a locked-room mystery when a corpse is discovered on a locked houseboat and the only key is in the possession of someone with an airtight alibi. Complicating the matter is the fact that everyone connected to the murder is a member of the mystery lover's group, The Bloodhounds. BA MA

England, Bath

Upon a Dark Night. U.K.: Little, 1997 (U.S.: Mysterious Press, 1997)

Needing a homicide to investigate, Diamond pursues what initially looks like two separate suicides. The first involves a woman who leaps off the roof of the Royal Crescent, while the second is a farmer who dies from a head shot. While others have doubts, Diamond plunges ahead, and discovers that the two cases may be strangely related.

England, Bath

The Vault. U.K.: Little, 1999 (U.S.: Soho, 2000)

Diamond's latest case is unsettling when a hand is discovered amongst the renovations being done in Bath's Pump Room. When the assumption that this is an artifact is disproved, and the hand proves contemporary, Diamond must deal with the fact that the hand was discovered in proximity to Mary Shelley's house where *Frankenstein* was finished.

England, Bath

Diamond Dust. U.K.: Little, Brown, 2002 (U.S.: Soho, 2002)

Diamond faces a transfer to Bristol, but before he can be shoved aside a murder is reported in Bath's Victoria Park. He will not be the investigating officer because the victim is his wife.

England, Bath

Carol O'Connell ✍

Kathleen Mallory

Mentored by an experienced police officer, Mallory is saved from a life on the streets. However, the compelling question in this series is can she be saved from herself. Her abilities with a computer save her from the streets and give her a place on the police force, but can she find a place for herself in society? Readers may also enjoy Abigail Padgett. **Traditional/Hard-boiled**. Series subject: **New York, New York**.

Mallory's Oracle. Putnam, 1994

Mallory owes her whole redemption to Louis Markowitz, an NYPD police detective who, along with his late wife, Helen, adopted her and let her grow up in his family. When Markowitz's body is found in a tenement with a Gramercy Park woman, their deaths tie into two other deaths that Markowitz had been working. His death energizes Mallory, who makes it her mission to hunt down his killer.

The Man Who Cast Two Shadows. Putnam, 1995

The television informs New York that Kathleen Mallory has been murdered, but when she sees the broadcast, Mallory understands that a mistake has been made. With the murder occurring only a few blocks from her house, and with the victim wearing her jacket, Mallory has the motivation to hunt for a killer.

Killing Critics. Putnam, 1996

Dean Starr has died, and in a fashion that suggests performance art. It also suggestions a connection to the 12-year-old murder of an artist and a dancer that was blamed on Oren Watt. Mallory's interest is piqued because it was her adoptive father, Louis Markowitz, who put Watt away, and she needs to find the truth to settle an old and current score.

Stone Angel. Putnam, 1997

At the age of 10, Mallory appeared on the streets of New York, where she was rescued by her mentor Markowitz. Some of the answers to the question of what

Mallory's young life was like can be found here when Mallory journeys to Louisiana where her mother died, stoned to death by a mob. Current crimes land Mallory in jail, but it is the past that will prove the most threatening when all is said and done.

Louisiana, Dayborn

Judas Child. Putnam, 1998

Rouge Kendall's twin sister was murdered long ago, and although a policeman, he is still haunted by the past crime. When forensic psychologist Ali Cray connects the disappearance of two young girls to Susan Kendall's death, the force wrestles with the complications of having possibly convicted the wrong man many years ago. Mallory rallies to find the truth so that her friend can finally be at peace.

Shell Game. Putnam, 1999

While performing for a national television audience, magician Oliver Tree dies when his trick involving four crossbows goes awry. The only one convinced that this tragedy is actually murder is Mallory, who also predicts that whoever set up this crime will strike again. Her suspects lie among the talented magicians who could be Tree's equal, including the gifted Malakhia. The clue seems to lie with an occurrence from World War II, and it becomes Mallory's goal to out-trick these famous prestidigitators.

Magic

Crime School. Putnam, 2002

Part of Mallory's past is explained when the murder of a prostitute named Sparrow reveals Mallory's upbringing before she was rescued from the streets. As she pursues a copycat killer through the Special Crimes Unit, she must deal with her emotional attachment to the dead woman and the continuing legacy of her own past.

Prostitution • Serial killer

Anne Perry ✍

William Monk

As if solving crimes in Victorian England were not tough enough, Perry handicaps her detective by taking away his memory. Struggling with his own fate, and the various crimes of the times, Monk is a searcher after the truth on many fronts. He receives aid and comfort from his nurse, Hester Latterly, and their alliance helps him patch his life back together. Later, his connection to the crimes comes through counsel for the defense, Oliver Rathbone, and Monk becomes a private inquiry agent. Readers may also enjoy Elizabeth Peters (Amelia Peabody) and Charles Todd. See the author's website at http://www.anneperry.net. **Traditional/Historical**. Series subjects: **England, London • Historical (1800–1899) • Victorian England**.

The Face of a Stranger. Fawcett Columbine, 1990

Monk awakens in a hospital with amnesia, the victim of a bad hansom cab accident. He is told that he is a London police detective, and when he is well enough, he returns to work, masking his illness. Assigned an old case involving the murder of a Crimean War hero, he has no clue how to investigate a crime. His ability to mask his lack of understanding does not prevent some of the old instincts from rising and allowing him to pursue a criminal, while his boss Runcorn appears to want him to fail.

A Dangerous Mourning. Fawcett Columbine, 1991

Still suffering some memory loss and a serious lack of confidence, Monk is assigned the murder investigation involving Octavia Haslett. She is the daughter of Sir Basil Moidore, and she was found stabbed to death in her own bed. When Monk's investigation focuses on the family, Runcorn fires Monk from the force. Determined to find the truth, he receives help from Hester and proceeds to investigate the crime independent of the police.

Defend and Betray. Fawcett Columbine, 1992

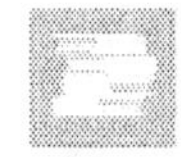

Monk, Hester, and Rathbone are convinced that Alexandra Carlyon did not push her husband over a banister to his death. General Thaddeus Carlyon may have given his wife a reason, but her sister believes it may be one to keep her sister from the gallows as a murderer. Through Hester, she is able to gather the detectives to her case and rally them for Alexandra's cause.

A Sudden, Fearful Death. Fawcett Columbine, 1993

Monk, now a private inquiry agent, is hired by Lady Callandra Daviot to work the case of a murdered nurse. Prudence Barrymore had served in the Crimean War, and was working at Royal Free Hospital when she was strangled. With Hester's help as an undercover agent inside the hospital, Monk proceeds to hunt a killer.

Medical

The Sins of the Wolf. Fawcett Columbine, 1994

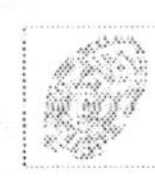

Hester is hired to escort Mary Farraline in London and to make sure the woman's digitalis is properly administered. When the woman dies of an overdose, Hester is accused of murder. Monk and Rathbone travel to Scotland looking for clues, convinced the real murderer hides within this Scottish family.

Scotland, Edinburgh

Cain His Brother. Fawcett Columbine, 1995

Monk is asked by Genevieve Stonefield to find her husband, Angus. Angus was visiting his brother Caleb and is now missing. With Angus viewed as the saintly brother and Caleb perceived as the devil himself, logically suspicion for the evil deed falls on the ruffian brother. Now all Monk has to do is find the body.

Weighed in the Balance. Fawcett Columbine, 1996

Countess Zorah Rostova is in exile, and she hires Rathbone to discover the truth behind the murder of Prince Friedrich. Friedrich renounced his crown to marry Princess Gisela, but Zorah is convinced that it is the Princess who murdered her prince, and her accusation has led to a charge of slander. Monk is sent abroad to investigate, while Hester may be able to provide a clue given to her by a young patient.

Germany, Felzburg • Italy, Venice

The Silent Cry. Fawcett Columbine, 1997

The dead body of solicitor Leighton Duff is found in the slums of London, with his son Rhys beaten and left for dead next to his father. With Rhys being Hester's patient, and Monk asked to investigate some brutal rapes in the St. Giles area, the two cases begin to merge. When the police begin to suspect Rhys of the crimes, the pair rises to his defense.

A Breach of Promise. Fawcett Columbine, 1998

Rathbone is the defense for architect Killian Melville when he is sued for breach of contract by the Lambert family. Killian now refuses to marry Zillah Lambert, and when he refuses to say why, Monk is brought into the case to seek the truth from a reluctant client.

The Twisted Root. Ballantine, 1999

Miriam Gardner went missing during a party at her fiancée Lucius Stourbridge's family's estate, and now he wants to hire Monk to find her. Sympathetic because he is himself a newly married man, Monk accepts the case, and when the family servant who helped Miriam escape is found murdered, Monk finds himself with a client whose bride is the most likely suspect.

Slaves of Obsession. Ballantine, 2000

As the American Civil War rages across the seas, arms dealer Daniel Alberton is entertaining two Americans. Philo Trace wants arms for the South, while Lyman Breedlove wants them for the North. When this international conflict leads to a murder in London, Monk and Hester shift from guests to detectives.

Funeral in Blue. Ballantine, 2001

Dr. Kristian Beck, a friend of Hester, is accused of murdering his wife and an artist's model. Monk finds he must develop his investigation with the knowledge that their family friend, Lady Callandra, is in love with the accused.

Ian Rankin ✍

John Rebus

Following the tradition established by fellow Scotsman McIlvanney, Rankin created a masterfully crafted and very disturbed police officer in John Rebus. His drive to solve crimes is balanced against his personal struggles to remain in touch with the human spirit. This series displays the underbelly of Scotland, and these hard-boiled stories can be recommended to readers who enjoy a tough, gritty story. Readers may also enjoy John Harvey and Bill James. See the author's website at http://www.ianrankin.com. **Hard-boiled**. Series subject: **Scotland, Edinburgh**.

Knots and Crosses. U.K.: Bodley Head, 1987 (U.S.: Doubleday, 1987)

Detective Sergeant Rebus is one of many cops assigned to the case of the Edinburgh Strangler, a menace to all young girls, including Rebus's own daughter. His role is accelerated when the someone begins to provide Rebus with his own personal clues to the identity of the perpetrator.

Serial killer

Hide and Seek. U.K.: Barrie & Jenkins, 1991 (U.S.: Otto Penzler, 1994)

Detective Inspector Rebus is not impressed with a city that makes its advances over the people who live there, including the people who live in the squats. When a junkie is murdered in a ritualistic manner, it is only Rebus who takes the time to find out why.

Wolfman. Century, 1992

Rebus is sent as a liason to London when a serial killer named the Wolfman has left behind four mutilated corpses.

England, London · Serial killer

A Good Hanging and Other Stories. U.K.: Century, 1992 (U.S.: St. Martin's Press, 2002)

A collection of the following short stories: "Auld Lang Syne," "Being Frank," "Concrete Evidence," "The Dean Curse," "The Gentlemen's Club," "A Good Hanging," "Monstrous Trumpet," "Not Proven," "Playback," "Seeing Things," "Sunday," and "Tit for Tat."

Short stories

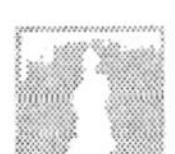

Strip Jack. U.K.: Orion, 1992 (U.S.: St. Martin's Press, 1994)

Some people refuse to withdraw their support for the young and popular MP Gregor Jack when he is caught in a brothel and the media displays his shortcomings on the front page. When Jack's wife disappears, Rebus is drawn into the case.

The Black Book. U.K.: Orion, 1993 (U.S.: Otto Penzler, 1994)

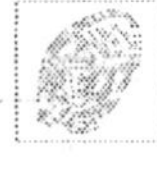

Five years prior to this novel, the seedy Central Hotel burned to the ground and left the Edinburgh police with an unidentified body with a bullet in its brain. In the present, when Detective Sergeant Brian Holmes is ambushed and left in a coma, a cryptic message in the officer's notebook refers back to the old crime. Now both cases belong to Rebus, who must connect the present to the past.

Mortal Causes. Orion, 1994

It is the time of The Festival in Edinburgh, and the city is filled with tourists. In Mary King's Close, where people once died of the plague, a young man has been hung, and the ill-timed case falls to Inspector Rebus.

Let It Bleed. U.K.: Orion, 1995 (U.S.: Simon & Schuster, 1996)

Rebus has an embezzlement case, but the case escalates to include the death of two dropouts who fall from the Forth Bridge in Edinburgh. How does a fake kidnapping relate to the death of a corrupt politician, and why is everyone trying to drive Rebus from the case?

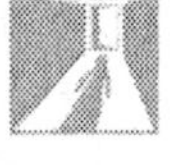

Black and Blue. U.K.: Orion, 1997 (U.S.: St. Martin's Press, 1997)

In the 1960s and 1970s, Scotland was terrorized by a serial killer named Bible John. Now, a copycat killer nicknamed Bible Johnny has emerged as the latest media star. Left out of the loop while assigned to the murder of an off-shore oilworker, Rebus finds himself drawn to the old case. DA

Serial killer

The Hanging Garden. U.K.: Orion, 1998. (U.S.: St. Martin's Press, 1998)

Thinking they have Rebus safely working on a war criminal case, his supervisors are not prepared when he becomes personally involved with a callgirl sent to Scotland from war-torn Bosnia. His affections place him in the middle of a turf war between two mobsters, and when his own daughter becomes a victim, he decides to turn on gangster Tommy Telford with a vengeance.

Dead Souls. U.K.: Orion, 1999 (U.S.: St. Martin's Minotaur, 1999)

Rebus is trying to balance all the aspects of his life that are spinning out of control: his guilt over his injured daughter, his drinking, a former sweetheart whose son is missing, and the suicide of a fellow officer. Then he is assigned watchguard duty to Cary Oakes, a convicted murderer deported from the United States to Edinburgh, and the psychological pressure applied by a master manipulator pushes Rebus to the edge.

Death Is Not the End. U.K.: Orion, 1998 (U.S.: St. Martin's Minotaur, 2000)

This novella expands a subplot from *Dead Souls* as Rebus agrees to track down the missing son of his high school sweetheart.

Set in Darkness. U.K.: Orion, 2000 (U.S.: St. Martin's Minotaur, 2000)

Queensbury House is about to host the first Scottish parliament in 300 years when a dead body is discovered in the bricked-up fireplace. Two contemporary deaths further muddy the waters when a homeless man jumps from a bridge, and a prominent politician is murdered. These political hot potatoes fall into Rebus's lap as he has been assigned to the Policing of Parliament Liaison Committee.

The Falls. U.K.: Orion, 2000 (U.S.: St. Martin's Minotaur, 2001)

Rebus is assigned the disturbing case of a missing university student named Philippa Balfour that he ties to a role-playing game on the Internet. Teamed with DC Siobhan Clarke, Rebus finds himself dragged into a dark subculture that may have ties to some older crimes.

Internet

***Resurrection Man.** U.K.: Orion, 2001 (U.S.: TimeWarner, 2003)

Charles Todd (pseud. of Caroline and Charles Todd) ✍

Ian Rutledge

Ian Rutledge has returned from the First World War a damaged man, haunted by the voice of a Scotsman he had to execute on the battlefield. A brilliant investigator prior to the war, he now struggles to regain his skills and his sanity as an Inspector for Scotland Yard. These novels are written by a mother-son team. Readers may also enjoy Anne Perry. **Traditional/Historical**. Series subject: **Historical (1900–1999)**.

A Test of Wills. St. Martin's Press, 1996

Damaged by the war, and under the suspicions of his supervisors, Inspector Ian Rutledge is sent to a small village to handle a very political murder case. Colonel Charles Harris has been shot out of his saddle, and the suspicion has fallen on his ward, Lettice

Wood's, fiancé, Captain Mark Wilton. While battling his own personal demons, Rutledge must slowly peel back the layers of deception in this sleepy English village. BA

England, Warwick, Upper Streetham • World War I

Wings of Fire. St. Martin's Press, 1998

O. A. Manning is the author of the book of poetry, *Wings of Fire*, that helped Rutledge deal with his wartime trauma. When Olivia Marlowe commits suicide, Rutledge is assigned to the case. Unraveling how her death, and the death of her brother, relates to previous deaths in the family and to the current surviving members, will test the skills of the recovering detective.

Authors • England, Cornwall, Borcombe • Poetry

Search the Dark. St. Martin's Press, 1999

Bert Mowbray looks out a train window one day and sees his family, who he thought had died in a bombing during the war. When his desperate chase of these phantoms places him in proximity to a murder, his arrest brings him in contact with Rutledge, a man who can understand being haunted by the war.

England, Dorset, Singleton Magna

Legacy of the Dead. Bantam, 2000

Sent to the homeland of Hamish MacLeod, the soldier who haunts him, Rutledge is asked to handle another delicate case. This time, some human remains have been unearthed, and the suspicion is that they are the remains of Eleanor Gray. The current Lady Maude Gray is a handful, and Rutledge feels compelled to defend the most likely suspect, Fiona MacDonald.

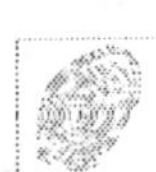

Scotland, Durham, Duncarrick

Watchers of Time. Bantam, 2001

Rutledge is handed a puzzling case in which a dying Anglican named Herbert Baker makes his last confession to the local Catholic priest. Within a few weeks, the priest, Father James, is also dead, and the Scotland Yard detective has a tangled case on his hands when the local authorities want an easy solution.

England, Norfolk, Osterley • Religion

A Fearsome Doubt. Bantam, 2002

Rutledge has always been torn by his war experiences, but now his judgment as a police officer prior to his combat experience is called into question. Rutledge had been responsible for the apprehension and execution of Ben Shaw, a man accused of the murder of a number of elderly victims. Now Nell, Shaw's widow, has proof he might have been innocent. In addition, Rutledge must solve the mystery of who is killing ex-soldiers.

England, Kent, Marling • Serial killer

Detectives Who Support the Police

As the police forces developed as legitimate practitioners of police procedure, they became surrounded by support forces geared to making their lives easier or by businesses willing to help the police for a profit. To aid in the administration of justice, the police forces find themselves allied with the judicial system. From the ranks of each of these support groups, authors have selected detectives with particular skills to act as detectives on their own. The appeal of this type of detective is that they sometimes can function like the professional, the private, or the amateur, thus giving the reader a choice of a broad style of character to read.

The Historical Founding Members

As police systems themselves do not have a long and rich history, their supporters do not either. This example, translated from the folk tales of a culture by a modern writer, does serve as a representative sample.

Robert Van Gulik ✍

Judge Dee

Beginning his series with translated Chinese folktales, Van Gulik eventually began to create his own mysteries featuring this character, Judge Dee, who served in the dynasty of Kao-tsung, Tang Emperor. Judge Dee is essentially Solomon, traveling around the Chinese countryside and making his proclamations to solve the mysteries he discovers. The first book, published in Tokyo in 1949, was the translation of a folktale. Some of the titles that followed were published first in other lands, but the bibliography below only lists the British and American first editions. The last book on the list was written by two authors as a continuation of the character. See a website about the author at http://hjem.get2net.dk/bnielsen/gulik.html. **Soft-boiled/Traditional/Historical**. Series subjects: **Historical (0000–1000) · Law**.

Dee Goong An: Three Murder Cases Solved by Judge Dee. Japan: The Author, 1949 (U.S.: *Celebrated Cases of Judge Dee*. Dover, 1976)

This translation of Chinese tales tells the story of a double murder among travelling merchants, the poisoning of a bride on her wedding day, and a small town murder, all of which are solved by the travelling Judge Dee.

China, Chang-ping

The Chinese Bell Murders. U.K.: Joseph, 1958 (U.S.: Harper & Row, 1959)

The Judge must adjudicate the case of Pure Jade, who has been raped, and her lover who stands accused of the crime. The Judge must also investigate the Buddhist Temple of Boundless Mercy, where rumors claim the monks may not be as virtuous as their order requires. A third case complicates the overworked magistrate's life.

China, Poo-Yang

The Chinese Gold Murders. U.K.: Joseph, 1959 (U.S.: Harper & Row, 1961)

Judge Dee finds himself trying to solve the death of the judge who preceded him. Two other cases, one involving a bride and the other a bully, further involve the magistrate in detective work.

China, Poo-Yang

The Chinese Lake Murders. U.K.: Joseph, 1960 (U.S.: Harper & Row, 1960)

The judge has three cases to solve. The first involves a murdered courtesan. The second finds a bride's corpse replaced in her coffin. Lastly, the dreaded White Lotus sect is active.

China, Han-yuan

The Chinese Nail Murders. U.K.: Joseph, 1961 (U.S.: Harper & Row, 1962)

Three cases confront the Judge in Pei-Chow. The first involves a headless corpse, the second a boxing champion, and the third a murdered cotton merchant.

China, Pei-chow

The Haunted Monastery. U.K.: Art Printing Works, 1961 (U.S.: Scribner, 1969)

At the Monastery of the Morning Clouds in Han-yuan, the judge is given three murders to solve. One involves an abbot named Jade Mirror, one involves a maid, and the last one involves a monk.

China, Han-yuan

The Red Pavilion. U.K.: Art Printing Works, 1961 (U.S.: Scribner, 1968)

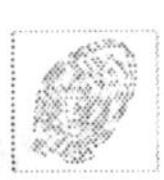

During the Festival of the Dead, at the amusement resort of Paradise Island, the magistrate finds himself dealing with the death of a courtesan, an academician, and a pair of star-crossed lovers.

China, Paradise Island

The Chinese Maze Murders. U.K.: Joseph, 1962 (U.S.: Dover, 1977)

A retired general found murdered in his locked library, a murdered ex-Governor, and a decapitated corpse all provide interesting cases for Judge Dee.

China, Lan-Fang

The Lacquer Screen. U.K.: Art Printing Works, 1962 (U.S.: Scribner, 1970)

While staying a few days in the district of Wei-ping, the magistrate finds himself involved in cases featuring the magistrate of Wei-ping, a wealthy silk merchant, and a banker.

China, Wei-ping

The Emperor's Pearl. U.K.: Heinemann, 1963 (U.S.: Scribner, 1964)

The judge is puzzled when the drummer of the favorite boat in the annual dragon-boat races dies in the saddle. The death of a young woman murdered in a country mansion may be connected to the first death and to the missing Emperor's Pearl.

China, Poo-yang

The Willow Pattern. Heinemann, 1965

Judge Dee is now serving as the President of the Metropolitan Court in the Imperial City, where he must deal with a murdered merchant, an accidental death that may be murder, and the death of a servant girl whipped to death by her master.

China, Imperial City

The Monkey and the Tiger. U.K.: Heinemann, 1965 (U.S.: Scribner, 1966)

Two novelettes make up this work. "The Morning of the Monkey" finds the judge taking his clues from a gibbon. In "The Night of the Tiger," a journey forces the magistrate to stay in a haunted house and introduces him to a murdered girl.

China, Han-yuan · China, Pei-chow

The Phantom of the Temple. U.K.: Heinemann, 1966 (U.S.: Scribner, 1966)

While in the Western provinces of the Tang dynasty, the judge must deal with a series of murders that center around a centuries-old Buddhist temple.

China, Lan-fang

Murder in Canton. U.K.: Heinemann, 1966 (U.S.: Scribner, 1967)

Visiting the South of China, the magistrate is confounded by a mysterious belly-dancer, confused by an arsonist intent on burning down the city, and confronted by the case of a blind girl who is rescued from a rape.

China, Canton

Judge Dee at Work. U.K.: Heinemann, 1967 (U.S.: Scribner, 1973)

A collection of the following stories: "The Coffins of the Emperor," "Five Auspicious Clouds," "He Came with the Rain," "Murder on New Year's Eve," "The Murder on the Lotus Pond," "The Red Tape Murder," "The Two Beggars," and "The Wrong Sword."

Short stories

Necklace and Calabash. U.K.: Heinemann, 1967 (U.S.: Scribner, 1971)

While on a fishing trip, the judge discovers that the Kingfisher Inn keeper has been murdered. Meanwhile, the Third Princess's necklace is stolen, and the judge leaps into action.

China, Rivertown

Poets and Murder. U.K.: Heinemann, 1968 (U.S.: Scribner, 1972 · also published as *The Fox-Magic Murders.* Panther, 1973)

Judge Dee is visiting Chin-hwa for the Mid-autumn festival when a student is murdered. Then the maid of a beautiful woman is whipped to death. The clues to solving these crimes may lay in the Shrine of the Black Fox.

China, Chin-hwa

Deception (by Daniel Altieri). Morrow, 1993

To highlight the rise to power of China's only female emperor, Empress Wu, these two authors brought Judge Dee back to life. This case baffles him because the only clue to the deaths of four families in Ch'ang-an are the bloody hoofprints left on their wooden floors.

Altieri, Daniel · China · Cooney, Eleanor

The Modern Practitioners

Working hand-in-hand with police departments that need their support, or working at odds with a police department that fears what they will discover, the detectives in this section all play a valuable role in helping to seek the truth.

Caleb Carr ✍

Dr. Laszlo Kreizler/John Schuyler Moore/Sara Howard

As the science of psychology developed, practioners like Kreizler were known as alienists, practicing their craft in relative obscurity because of skepticism about its veracity. With police science also in the developmental stages at this time, investigators were reluctant to accept the theories of behavior behind the crimes, but Kreizler proves a worthy ally to the police. Teamed with reporter Schuyler and police secretary Howard, this trio investigates disturbing crimes at the end of the nineteenth century with the help of an extended motley crew. These novels can be recommended to traditional and hard-boiled mystery readers. See the publisher's website for this author at http://www.randomhouse.com/features/calebcarr. **Traditional/ Hard-boiled/Historical.** Series subjects: **Historical (1800–1899) · New York, New York · Psychology · Roosevelt, Theodore · Teams**

The Alienist. Random House, 1994

Police Commissioner Theodore Roosevelt calls on the alienist, Dr. Kreizler, after Kreizler and his newspaper reporter friend Moore discover the body of a teenage male prostitute near the East River. A series of transvestite murders takes place, and the search for a killer covers all the areas of this fabled city and displays cameos by some of its more famous former residents. This story is told from the perspective of reporter Moore.

Prostitution · Serial killer

The Angel of Darkness. Random House, 1997

Told from the perspective of the street urchin, Steve Taggert, this tale involves the kidnapping of a Spanish diplomat's infant child. With Spain and the United States about to go to war, Roosevelt feels compelled to solve this case quickly, and calls upon the team to help restore the child to its parents.

Kidnapping

Patricia Cornwell ✍

Kay Scarpetta

Virginia's Chief Medical Examiner, Dr. Kay Scarpetta, working out of Richmond, Virginia, proved to be one of the best-selling mystery characters in the 1990s. Often working with her niece Lucy, an FBI agent, and police captain Peter Marino, Scarpetta uses her medical skills to play detective. Her cases can be recommended to hard-boiled mystery readers. Readers may also enjoy Aaron Elkins,

Sharyn McCrumb (Elizabeth MacPherson), and John Sandford. See the author's website at http://www.patriciacornwell.com. **Hard-boiled**. Series subjects: **Forensics · Medical · Virginia, Richmond**.

Postmortem. Scribner, 1990

Three women have been strangled in the city of Richmond on Saturday mornings, and when Scarpetta receives a call early one Saturday, she knows it will be for victim number four. As she probes into the area of detection, Scarpetta uncovers clues that place her own life in jeopardy. AN ED MA

Serial killer

Body of Evidence. Scribner, 1991

Novelist Beryl Madison is being stalked, yet she appears to have opened her door to a killer who nearly decapitates her. Scarpetta becomes intrigued by the case when the woman's revealing memoirs are missing, and Scarpetta's office receives political pressures to close the examination. Soon the case places Scarpetta in danger again.

Authors

All That Remains. Scribner, 1992

When Fred Cheney and Deborah Harvey are found dead in their car while travelling, they are another in a series of couples killed by an anonymous and random murderer. This case is especially visible because Deborah is the daughter of national drug-czar Pat Harvey, and the political pressure is on Scarpetta to determine a cause of death and help find the killer.

Serial killer

Cruel and Unusual. Scribner, 1993

On the same night that convicted murderer Ronnie Joe Waddell is executed, the body of 13-year-old Eddie Heath is found. What is puzzling is that Eddie appears to have been killed by the same method Waddell used, and this death calls into question the validity of the execution. DA

The Body Farm. Scribner, 1994

Scarpetta receives a phone call from North Carolina telling her an old nemesis, serial killer Temple Brooks Gault, has struck again. A child named Emily Steiner is murdered, but the investigation raises more questions than it solves. The trail leads to the Body Farm in Tennessee, a research facility that will provide the answers Scarpetta needs.

Children at risk · North Carolina, Asheville

From Potter's Field. Scribner, 1995

Temple Brooks Gault strikes again, this time using New York's subway system as a hiding place. His first victim is a bald female, left nude in the snow of Central Park at Christmas. As Scarpetta rushes to New York with some of her allies, she begins to think the killer is as interested in her as he is in any of his victims.

New York, New York · Serial killer

Cause of Death. Putnam, 1996

Scarpetta receives notification of the death of investigative reporter Ted Eddings, who died diving into ruins at the Inactive Ship Yard. The problem is the call came before the police knew there was a problem. When a second death exposes a pathway, Scarpetta, Marino, and Lucy try to discover the reason for the reporter's dive to death.

Diving

Unnatural Exposure. Putnam, 1997

Scarpetta has been investigating a murder victim in Dublin, Ireland, and has just returned to Virginia when a similar murder is discovered on her home territory. When the killer sends her a direct challenge via the Internet, Scarpetta is driven to bring him to justice.

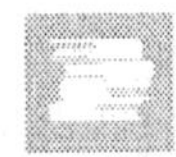

Serial killer

Point of Origin. Putnam, 1998

Scarpetta's old nemesis from *Body Farm* sends her a cryptic note challenging her with a riddle. When someone burns a horseranch to the ground and leaves a body, Scarpetta suspects this action may relate to the note she has received.

Horses

Black Notice. Putnam, 1999

When a cargo ship arrives in Richmond containing the body of a stowaway, Scarpetta's exam fails to identify a cause of death. Scarpetta finds her only link from the first body on a second, and that leads her overseas. Interpol in Paris is helpful, and their information leads Scarpetta into an international conspiracy.

France, Paris

Scarpetta's Winter Table. Wyrick and Company, 1998

This novelette features a glimpse into Scarpetta's private life. Along with Pete Marino and Lucy Farinelli, she gets involved with a lonely boy who needs her help. Along the way, Scarpetta shows the way around her kitchen.

Cooking

The Last Precinct. Putnam, 2000

Still suffering the consequences from her battles against the Werewolf murderer in *Black Notice*, Scarpetta finds herself needing to clear her own name. She is again on the track of Jean-Baptiste Chandonne, and the extent of his influence threatens her life and the safety of her supporters.

Serial killer

Jeffrey Deaver ✍

Lincoln Rhyme

Lincoln Rhyme was NYPD's head of forensics, but an accident has left him a quadriplegic, only able to lift one finger. But what he lacks in physical movement is made up for by his mental facilities and his determination to continue apprehending criminals. Aided by Amelia Sachs, Rhyme continues to work from his bedside. His cases can be recommended to hard-boiled mystery readers. Readers may also enjoy John Sandford and Mary Willis Walker. **Hard-boiled**. Series subjects: **New York, New York · Physically challenged**.

The Bone Collector. Viking, 1997

Hearing about a body buried on the West Side of New York, Rhyme's investigative drive is re-awakened, and he begins to pursue a criminal with the help of Amelia Sachs. They find themselves chasing a man named The Bone Collector, who is obsessed with old New York and the murders he commits.

The Coffin Dancer. Simon & Schuster, 1998

The Coffin Dancer is a hit man with a tattoo on his arm: the Grim Reaper dancing with a woman in front of a casket. He is so adept at changing his appearance that no one can catch him, until Rhyme and Sachs combine their talents to begin the hunt.

The Empty Chair. Simon & Schuster, 2000

Rhyme has traveled to North Carolina to prepare for an experimental surgical procedure when he is approached by a relative of one of his New York colleagues. Jim Bell of the Paquenoke County Sheriff's Department needs Rhyme and Sachs to help him apprehend The Insect Boy, Garrett Hanlon. The detectives agree to take the case, but their investigation will divide them on the cause and on Hanlon's guilt.

North Caroline, Tanner's Corner

The Stone Monkey. Simon & Schuster, 2002

The Ghost, who has murdered a ship full of illegal Chinese immigrants to avoid capture for smuggling them into America, is chasing the few families who managed to swim to shore. In a race against time, Rhyme and Sachs must use their allies to penetrate New York City's Chinatown and stop the slaughter.

Immigration

Jonathan Kellerman ✍

Alex Delaware

Jonathan Kellerman is the husband of mystery writer Faye Kellerman. As a child psychologist, Alex Delaware is not afraid to consult with the Los Angeles Police Department on cases that involve children placed at risk. Often given access to the cases by his friend, Detective Milo Sturgis, Delaware finds himself drawn into cases that disturb and distress. These novels can be recommended to readers of the hard-boiled mystery. Readers may also enjoy Stephen White. See a website about the author at http://mysterynet.com/jkellerman/main. **Hard-boiled**. Series subjects: **California, Los Angeles · Children at risk · Psychology**.

When the Bough Breaks. Atheneum, 1985

It is up to a seven-year-old child to reveal the perpetrator in a double homicide, and Delaware is assigned the job of getting the child to open up. Because it seems his work is underappreciated by the police, he begins to conduct a personal investigation into the case that places him on the trail of a murderer. AN ED

Washington, Bellevue

Blood Test. Atheneum, 1986

Multimodal chemotherapy may be the key to saving the life of Heywood Swope, a five year old suffering from non-Hodgkin's lymphoma. Because his parent's religious beliefs do not allow treatment, Delaware is involved in the case. When the child is kidnapped and two people are murdered, he finds himself in the middle of the case.

Kidnapping

Over the Edge. Atheneum, 1987

Jamey Cadmus was Delaware's patient when he was 12, a genius but withdrawn child who needed the psychologist's help. Five years later, Cadmus is accused of killing male prostitutes, and he needs Delaware's help again.

Serial killer

Silent Partner. Bantam, 1989

Delaware is at a party held by a controversial sex therapist when he meets his old lover, Sharon Ramsom. When she asks for his help, and ends up an apparent suicide the next day, he begins to explore her life and discovers the seamier side of the sexual activities of the ultrarich.

Time Bomb. Bantam, 1990

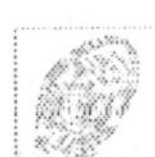

When a sniper fires on a schoolyard, Delaware is called in to deal with the trauma left in the childrens' lives. However, when it is revealed that the shooter was Holly Lynn Burden, his attention shifts to her. While he tries to help the shooter's father explain his daughter, the staff at the school searches for its answers with another psychologist.

Private Eyes. Bantam, 1992

Melissa Dickinson was Delaware's patient when she was seven; now it is ten years later and she needs his help once again. She lives in San Labrador, a gated community for the rich that cannot protect her from her deepest fear. Her mother, who had been stalked in the past, is about to fall victim to her tormentor, who has been released.

Devil's Waltz. Bantam, 1993

Dr. Stephanie Eves has a 21-month-old child whose repeated visits to the emergency room at her pediatrics hospital trouble her. She asks for help from her friend Delaware, who believes the problems may be at home. But as his investigation moves forward, to his horror, he begins to believe something may be wrong at the hospital.

Medical

Bad Love. Bantam, 1994

When Delaware receives a series of messages that scare him, he turns to his friend, detective Milo Sturgis, for help. As the two of them probe, they discover a connection to Dr. Andres de Bosch, a child psychologist whose use of bad love may be the cause of the messages.

Self-Defense. Bantam, 1995

Lucy Lowell has survived her testimony at the trial of a serial killer, but she needs Delaware's counseling when a recurring dream about a child in a forest is disturbing her life. As Delaware probes backwards into Lucy's life, an alarming story is revealed.

The Web. Bantam, 1996

Delaware accepts the assignment to work with Dr. Woodrow Wilson Moreland on the island of Aruk, organizing the papers of the great scientist and philanthropist. But as his work progresses, Delaware begins to wonder why he has been chosen, and what the real reason is behind the invitation.

Pacific Ocean, Aruk

The Clinic. Bantam, 1997

Detective Sturgis needs Delaware's help when pop psychologist and author, Hope Devane, is murdered and three months pass without any progress. As the two men probe her life, they discover that Devane left many suspects in her wake as she progressed in her career.

Survival of the Fittest. Bantam, 1997

Milo has a murder case featuring the 15-year-old retarded daughter of a diplomat, and he turns to Delaware for help. Before the investigation can even get going, another girl with a similar situation is found in a similar way. Besides the two similar murders, each girl was found with a piece of paper with the initials DVLL, and this investigation will take them into the world of eugenics and ally them with an Israeli detective.

Monster. Randon House, 1999

Murder victims are being found in places and ways predicted by Ardis "Monster" Peake, a man in a hospital for the criminally insane. One of the victims was Ardis's psychologist, Claire Argent, and Milo asks Delaware to replace her. His job is to explain how a man who is incarcerated can see the victims in their plight.

Dr. Death. Random House, 2000

Dr. Eldon Mate is a proponent of euthanasia, and a killer has decided that the ultimate irony will be to hook the doctor up to his own "Humanitron" device and snuff out his life. When Milo Sturgis asks Delaware to help, the secret held by Delaware may influence the outcome of the investigation.

Euthanasia

Flesh and Blood. Random House, 2001

When Lauren Teague is the entertainment at a stag party attended by Delaware, he recognizes her as one of the failures in his practice. When her body is found in a dumpster, he takes on the challenge of probing her past to find the clues that lead to her murderer.

The Murder Book. Ballantine, 2002

Someone has sent Delaware a police murder book with photos and details about more than 40 cases. When he takes it to his cop friend Milo Sturgis, Milo focuses on the photos detailing the death of a high school-aged girl named Janie Ingalls. Milo had been a rookie detective when the murder occurred, and he and his partner Pierce Schwinn were pulled from the case before they could find a killer.

Virginia Lanier ✍

Jo Beth Sidden

Sidden owns a business called Bloodhounds, Inc. Her specialty is raising and training bloodhounds for search and rescue missions in the Okefenokee Swamp. Her challenges come both from her cases and from the men in her life, who do not trust her skills. This series can be recommended to traditional mystery readers. Readers may also enjoy Nevada Barr. **Traditional**. Series subjects: **Dogs · Georgia, Okefenokee Swamp · Okefenokee Swamp**.

Death in Bloodhound Red. Pineapple Press, 1995

When she finds herself under suspicion for attempted murder, Sidden uses her hounds to prove that she is not only innocent of the charges, but a talented dog handler with good detectivc skills.

The House on Bloodhound Lane. HarperCollins, 1996

Sidden has to teach her first law enforcement seminar, has just turned 30, and has just learned her ex-husband is out of prison and stalking her. Then she is handed the assignment of finding a long-lost kidnapping victim.

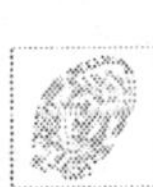

Kidnapping

A Brace of Bloodhounds. HarperCollins, 1997

Gilly Ainsley shows Sidden a letter from her mother, written just before her mother's death. The letter claims that a superior court judge with whom she is living will murder Gilly's mother. It will take all of Sidden's skills as a dog handler and a detective to bring a murderer to justice when the secret lies in the swamps near her home.

Blind Bloodhound Justice. HarperCollins, 1998

Samuel Debbs has just been released after serving 30 years for a crime he claims he did not commit. He was accused of kidnapping two children, one of whom was recovered and the other who was never accounted for. The old case, and a contemporary kidnapping, keep Sidden guessing and send her into the swamps again.

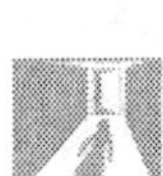

Kidnapping

Ten Little Bloodhounds. HarperCollins, 1999

Sidden has had many adventures in her search-and-rescue business, but searching for a missing cat does not appear to be much of a challenge. However, when its owner, the very rich Alyce Cancannon, is murdered, Sidden finds herself assigned a role in finding her murderer.

Margaret Maron ✍

Deborah Knott

This is the second series started by this author, being a change from her Sigrid Harald cop novels. Beginning her career as a lawyer in North Carolina, Knott is surrounded by all of her family members. Knowing her territory and her family, Knott's cases explore both as the character grows in stature and gets elected judge of Colleton County. These novels can be recommended to soft-boiled and traditional mystery readers. Readers may also enjoy Frances Fyfield, Lia Matera, and Julie Smith. See the author's website at http://www.margaretmaron.com. **Soft-boiled/Traditional**. Series subjects: **Law · North Carolina, Colleton County**.

Bootlegger's Daughter. Mysterious Press, 1992

Eighteen years prior to this story, Janie Whitehead was murdered and her young daughter, Gayle, was left next to her body. Now, Gayle wants her mother's murder solved. As Knott campaigns to be elected judge in Colleton County, she begins to ask the residents questions that may lead her to the answers needed by Gayle. AG AN ED MA

Southern Discomfort. Mysterious Press, 1993

After losing the election, Knott finds herself appointed when the incumbent dies. Forced to fulfill one of her campaign promises, she begins to organize an effort to build a home for needy mothers. However, when the all-female crew is harassed, and the electrician is murdered, she finds herself in the middle of a murder investigation.

Shooting at Loons. Mysterious Press, 1994

Hoping to spend a week on her cousin's Harkers Island cottage, the judge is on hand when a local fisherman's corpse is found. Knott soon discovers that the cause may lie within the battle between the locals and the new-found wealth brought in by the weekend residents.

North Carolina, Beaufort

Up Jumps the Devil. Mysterious Press, 1996

Knott's childhood neighbor, Dallis Stancil, has been murdered, and Knott is suspicious that the value of the land he owned may have been the cause of his death. She is disturbed by the fact that, as she probes into the case, Stancil's connection to her own family may be one of the causes. AG

Killer Market. Mysterious Press, 1997

Substituting for a judge in High Point while the International Home Furnishings Market is being conducted, Knott seeks refuge with an eccentric old lady named Mrs. Jernigan. When the woman disappears and a dead man is left behind, Judge Knott finds herself out of her territory and out of her league.

North Carolina, High Point

Home Fires. Mysterious Press, 1998

Race relations are disturbed in her district when teens begin to vandalize a local cemetery where African-Americans are buried. When one of the teens is her nephew A. K., she realizes that campaign promises are not enough to restore the order in her county. When someone begins to burn African-American-based churches, she finds herself in the midst of a burgeoning race disturbance.

Race

Storm Track. Mysterious Press, 2000

Hurricane Fran grows in intensity as Knott's district is challenged by the strangulation of Lynn Bullock at the Orchid Motel. She was the wife of Jason Bullock, lawyer on the rise and not Knott's favorite person to see in her courtroom. When one of her own family is suspected in the killing, Knott finds herself battling the storm within the community as nature's storm bears down. AG

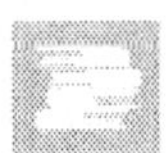

Uncommon Clay. Mysterious Press, 2001

The pottery industry is explored when Judge Knott is asked to adjudicate the divorce proceedings of Sandra Kay and James Lucas Nordan. When James is murdered in a kiln, Knott discovers that this is just another step in a tragedy that has patriarch Amos Nordan wounded and silent. A second death means Knott has to move fast to catch a murderer out to end this family's dynasty.

Pottery

Slow Dollar. Mysterious Press, 2002

It is the time of year when the carnival comes to town, and this should be a festive time for Knott and all her relatives. When a concessionaire from the midway is murdered, his body left with a mouth full of coins, the cause appears to be blackmail. The reason may be that the dead man is related to her family, so the judge must investigate to clear their good name.

Carnivals

Abigail Padgett ✍

Bo Bradley

Bradley is a child abuse investigator for the Juvenile Court of San Diego. It may come as no surprise that she also suffers from and battles against manic depression, or bi-polar disorder. Combined with this look at mental illness are issues such as the status of Native Americans and the state of California's environment, all of which strengthen the novels in this series. Her cases can be recommended to traditional and hard-boiled mystery readers. Readers may also enjoy Eleanor Taylor Bland, Jean Hager, Laurie King (Kate Martinelli), and Margaret Maron. **Traditional/ Hard-boiled**. Series subjects: **California, San Diego · Children at risk**.

Child of Silence. Mysterious Press, 1993

Bradley becomes responsible for a small child found on the Barona Ranch Indian Reservation. While others think Weppo is retarded, Bradley knows he is deaf.

What she does not know is that he may be the key to an investigation when someone tries to harm the boy.

Deaf · Native Americans

Strawgirl. Mysterious Press, 1994

Bradley becomes involved in investigating the rape and death of a three-year-old child, left mutilated by the killer. Suspicions fall on Paul Massieu, the child's stepfather and a member of a cult. Bradley finds her investigation takes her to the cult's home state and to the belief that she may be on the trail of the wrong person.

Cults · New York

Turtle Baby. Mysterious Press, 1995

The workers have nicknamed the eight-month-old Mayan baby Acito, or little turtle, for his toughness at surviving an attempted poisoning. It falls to Bradley to decide who took the time to cultivate the rare herb used as a murder device, and why it was used on such a young child.

Mexico, Tijuana

Moonbird Boy. Mysterious, 1996

Bradley has sought the innovative practices of the psychiatric healing center at the Ghost Flower Lodge on the Neji Indian Reservation. One of her fellow patients, comic Mort Wagman, is murdered on the reservation, and Bradley finds herself involved in his murder investigation and the fate of his young son, Bird.

Native Americans

The Dollmaker's Daughters. Mysterious, 1997

Flanna is a 15 year old with a host of problems that lead her to an eerie nightclub for teen vampires. She becomes Bradley's problem when she is found in a catatonic state, hiding in fear from things she knows, including the reality behind an old dollmaker.

Lawyer Detectives

Most courtroom thrillers will not qualify to be listed here as they often have other intentions than to tell a straight mystery. However, sometimes those who work in the legal profession cannot resist the opportunity to leave the courtroom and get out in the streets to hunt for the perpetrators.

The Historical Founding Members

Cyril Hare (pseud. of Alfred Alexander Gordon Clark) ✍

Francis Pettigrew

After a promising beginning, this British lawyer faces difficulties that turn his career in a different direction, and he spends time as a circuit judge. However, when faced with a crime to solve, he is an intelligent and determined investigator. In his early adventures, he is teamed with another Hare creation: Inspector Mallett. These cases are for traditional mystery readers. See a website about the author at http://www.twbooks.co.uk/authors/chare.html. **Traditional**. Series subject: **Law**.

Tragedy at Law. U.K.: Faber & Faber, 1942 (U.S.: Harcourt Brace, 1943)

The judges of the Southern circuit are under various irritating threats, and everyone is puzzled as to whether these incidents should be taken seriously. Judge William Barber's auto accident brings his old friend Pettigrew into the mix, as along with Inspector Mallett. Can a practical joke turn to murder?

England • World War II

With a Bare Bodkin. U.K.: Faber & Faber, 1946 (U.S.: HarperPerennial, 1991)

When the war forces Pettigrew into the Ministry of Pin Control, he is relocated to the remote northern community of Marsett Bay. There, to pass the time, a fellow worker and mystery writer decides to play a mystery game. When the results lead to a real death, Pettigrew finds himself acting in the role of detective.

England, Marsett Bay • Mystery games • World War II

When the Wind Blows. U.K.: Faber & Faber, 1949 (U.S.: *The Wind Blows Death.* Little, Brown, 1950)

When his WWII government service is completed, Pettigrew longs to retire to the quiet village of Markshire. There, as the treasurer of the Markshire Orchestral Society, an amateur musical organization in which his wife plays the violin, he once again is touched by a murder.

England, Markshire • Music

That Yew Tree's Shade. U.K.: Faber & Faber, 1954 (U.S.: *Death Walks the Woods.* Little, Brown, 1954)

Assuming the role of judge for Markshire has pleased Pettigrew. But trouble brews in the small village when a newly released criminal relocates to his home town.

England, Markshire

He Should Have Died Hereafter. U.K.: Faber & Faber, 1957 (U.S.: *Untimely Death.* Macmillan, 1957)

Pettigrew's wife has talked him into vacationing in the Exmoor region. He is haunted by the vision of a body on the moors that he saw 50 years ago, and he decides to confront his fears by visiting the spot, only to find another body. When he returns with some help, the body is no longer there.

England, Exmoor

The Golden Agers and Beyond

Erle Stanley Gardner ✍

Perry Mason

Using his own personal knowledge of the law, and his enormous ability to produce literary works at incredible speeds, Gardner managed to create 84 novels about the greatest lawyer-adventurer of all time. Helped by private detective Paul Drake and his faithful secretary, Della Street, Mason managed to win all of his cases. Thomas Chastain produced Mason novels after Gardner's death. These novels can be recommended to all traditional mystery readers. See a website about the author at http://www.grooviespad.com/esg. **Traditional**. Series subjects: **California, Los Angeles · Law**.

The Case of the Velvet Claws. Morrow, 1933

Eva Griffin and her lover have witnessed a murder, and she wants her name kept out of the press. When her husband is murdered, she and Perry are wanted by the police.

The Case of the Sulky Girl. Morrow, 1933

Mason's client is Frances Celane, a woman who lives under the power of her uncle Edward, who controls the family will. If Frances marries, she loses a million dollars, and when Edward dies, she is the most likely suspect.

Wills

The Case of the Curious Bride. Morrow, 1934

Greg Moxley married and conned Rhoda Lorton out of her fortune only to die in a plane crash. But when she remarries a very rich man, Moxley suddenly reappears, and the new bigamist bride needs a good lawyer.

The Case of the Howling Dog. Morrow, 1934

Mason finds himself caught between two feuding neighbors when his client, Arthur Cartright, wants Clinton Foley's dog to stop barking. Before he can settle the dispute, Mason has one strange will, one poisoned dog, and a dead woman.

Wills

The Case of the Lucky Legs. Morrow, 1934

When a scam orchestrated by movie promoter Frank Patton leaves him dead, the police are looking at Marjorie Clune and her lover as the suspects, and Mason has to defend them from the charges.

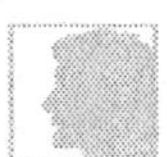

The Case of the Caretaker's Cat. Morrow, 1935

An odd will leaves the former caretaker, Charles Ashton, and his cat in luxury, but the grandson of the man who left the legacy has a vendetta against the cat. Mason needs to figure out how this all connects to the million-dollar estate.

Cats • Wills

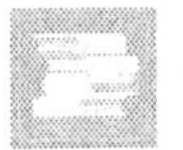

The Case of the Counterfeit Eye. Morrow, 1935

Mason's client is missing his glass eye, and when it is found in the hand of suicide and wealthy businessman Hartley Bassett, Mason thinks the scene is a setup.

The Case of the Sleepwalker's Niece. Morrow, 1936

Philip Reese is stabbed to death in his half-brother's home, and Mason must decide if a sleepwalking man is responsible for his actions, and for the bloody knife found under his pillow.

The Case of the Stuttering Bishop. Morrow, 1936

Julia Branner gave up her love child when millionaire Renwold Brownley would not let her marry his son. Now, with his son dead, the millionaire finds himself petitioned by a girl claiming to be his granddaughter, and her own supposed mother does not believe she is for real.

The Case of the Dangerous Dowager. Morrow, 1937

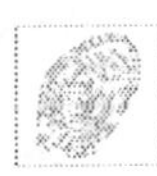

Mason takes the task of sailing out to a gambling ship and getting the IOUs signed by Matilda Benson's niece and discovers the ship's owner dead from a gunshot wound.

The Case of the Shoplifter's Shoe. Morrow, 1938

Sarah Breel is a compulsive shoplifter, and her niece, Virginia Trent, turns to Mason when some valuable diamonds left in her aunt's care go missing.

The Case of the Substitute Face. Morrow, 1938

Moms Newberry is worried that her husband Carl, newly rich, has squandered their new funds and placed their daughter Belle at risk, and she turns to Mason for help.

California, San Francisco • Shipboard

The Case of the Perjured Parrot. Morrow, 1939

The question for Mason on this case is whether wealthy Fremont Sabin died before he divorced his wife, or whether his estate passes to his son.

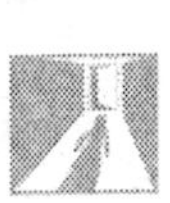

California, Grizzly Creek • Wills

The Case of the Rolling Bones. Morrow, 1939

Alden Leeds has escaped the sanitarium where his family confined him, only to have his fingerprints appear on the murder weapon when John Milicant, a blackmailer, is murdered.

The Case of the Baited Hook. Morrow, 1940

When Mason accepts half of a $10,000 retainer to represent a masked client, he ends up accused of murder by Hamilton Burger. His challenge is to determine if the masked woman is heiress Byrl Gailord or the pauper, Adelle Hastings.

The Case of the Silent Partner. Morrow, 1940

Mildreth Faulkner needs Mason's help when her competitor in the flower business buys into her family-owned business.

The Case of the Empty Tin. Morrow, 1941

When a tin can with a clue is discovered among Mrs. Florence Gentrie's preserves, the only thing missing is the corpse needed to show there was a murder.

The Case of the Haunted Husband. Morrow, 1941

When Stephanie Claire finds it necessary to fight off an attacker who picked her up hitchhiking, she wakes up behind the wheel of the car with the man nowhere to be found.

The Case of the Careless Kitten. Morrow, 1942

When banker Franklin Shore disappeared, it cut his brother Gerald off from the estate, and now Franklin has returned after a 10-year absence, creating even more confusion, and a murder.

The Case of the Drowning Duck. Morrow, 1942

Mason is hired to look into a 20-year-old murder when wealthy John Witherspoon is reluctant to have his daughter marry the killer's son.

The Case of the Buried Clock. Morrow, 1943

Jack Hardisty is under a cloud of suspicion for embezzling from his father-in-law, Vincent Blane's, bank, but his death casts a shadow over Jack's wife Millicent and brings Mason into the case.

The Case of the Drowsy Mosquito. Morrow, 1943

Mining prospector Salty Bowers needs Mason's protection when a series of arsenic poisonings may be a murder attempt.

The Case of the Black-Eyed Blonde. Morrow, 1944

Diana Regis hires Mason while sporting a black eye, given to her by her boss's son, and soon Mason has a dead body to explain.

The Case of the Crooked Candle. Morrow, 1944

When a man dies on a yacht, it leads Mason to a land acquisitions scheme that is dragging innocents into the court.

The Case of the Golddigger's Purse. Morrow, 1945

Harrison Faulkner has some rare fish, but when his fish are stolen and he tries to recapture them, he pays for the attempt with his life.

Fish, tropical

The Case of the Half-Wakened Wife. Morrow, 1945

Scott Shelby needs Mason to negotiate the sale of an island loaded with oil, but the lawyer ends up defending Shelby's wife from a murder charge when he is poisoned, shot, and drowned.

The Case of the Borrowed Brunette. Morrow, 1946

Eve Martell was told she could bring herself and a chaperone to a furnished apartment, but Eve's aunt also wants Mason when a dead man moves in as well.

The Case of the Fan-Dancer's Horse. Morrow, 1947

A car accident brings Mason in contact with a dancer who goes from missing her costume to missing a horse.

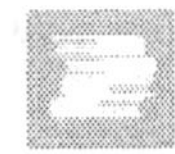

The Case of the Lazy Lover. Morrow, 1947

Mason receives two checks from Lola Allred, a woman who has fled with her daughter's boyfriend, a key witness in an important lawsuit, and now Mason needs to deal with her jilted husband.

The Case of the Lonely Heiress. Morrow, 1948

A Lonely Hearts magazine attracts Mason's attention when an heiress's letter leads to the corpse of a beautiful woman.

The Case of the Vagabond Virgin. Morrow, 1948

John Racer Addison finds himself on the hotseat when the help he provided to an 18-year-old runaway is twisted into a blackmail case that could end his business career.

The Case of the Cautious Coquette. Morrow, 1949

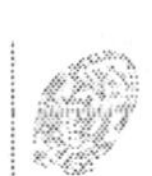

Mason is hired by the oft-married Lucille Barton, who wants Mason to get husband number two to continue alimony if she marries husband number three, while the gun she has for protection is used against husband number one.

The Case of the Dubious Bridegroom. Morrow, 1949

While Mason is hired to help Edward Garvin protect his wealth after his quickie Mexican divorce, Mason ends up defending him against a murder charge when Garvin's ex-wife is murdered.

The Case of the Negligent Nymph. Morrow, 1950

Mason's troubles begin when he becomes wanted for robbery after rescuing a nude woman from an island.

The Case of the One-Eyed Witness. Morrow, 1950

When an envelope full of money and a note are the only clues to their client, Mason and his crew find it difficult to even understand whether she is alive or dead.

The Case of the Angry Mourner. Morrow, 1951

Mason finds himself defending a mother and a daughter against the charges that one of them could have murdered playboy Arthur Cushing.

California, Bear Mountain

The Case of the Fiery Fingers. Morrow, 1951

Nellie Conway comes to Mason, and for one dollar, she gets to tell her tale of a man with an invalid wife who is planning murder. Mason has to go through two trials to clear this one up.

Louisiana, New Orleans

The Case of the Grinning Gorilla. Morrow, 1952

At a courthouse auction, Mason spends five dollars to buy the private personal belongings of a woman named Helen Cadmus. She was the secretary of millionaire Benjamin Addicks, and supposedly committed suicide on Addicks's yacht, but Mason finds his five dollar investment will lead to a dangerous investigation.

The Case of the Moth-Eaten Mink. Morrow, 1952

While dining out with Della Street, Mason decides to determine why a waitress would abandon her job and her mink coat.

The Case of the Green-Eyed Sister. Morrow, 1953

Sylvia Bain Atwood appeals to Mason for help when it appears the Bain oil money may be founded on the bank robbery profits of one J. J. Fritch. When Fritch threatens the Bains with exposure, he is dispatched, and Mason finds himself on the trail of a murderer.

The Case of the Hesitant Hostess. Morrow, 1953

Appointed by the court to defend indigent Albert Brogan, Mason feels confident he will win until his witness hightails it for Las Vegas, leaving him without a defense.

Nevada, Las Vegas

The Case of the Fugitive Nurse. Morrow, 1954

When Steffanie Malden's physician husband dies, she finds herself asked to account for the money he had reserved for his affair with the now-missing nurse, Gladys Foss, money that will be discovered missing and find Mason accused of embezzling.

The Case of the Restless Redhead. Morrow, 1954

Mason takes the case of Evelyn Bagby, a woman he thinks is innocent of murder despite the fact that she has the murder weapon and the dead woman's jewelry.

The Case of the Runaway Corpse. Morrow, 1954

Mason is hired to prove that Myrna Davenport's husband is trying to send her away for his attempted murder, but things get serious when he really does die.

California, Fresno

The Case of the Glamorous Ghost. Morrow, 1955

Amnesia has struck Mason's client Eleanor Corbin, found wandering in a park with jewels in her makeup case, and a dead husband.

The Case of the Nervous Accomplice. Morrow, 1955

Sybil Harlan's plan to place her husband in financial difficulty and drive him back into her arms proves faulty when her accomplice is murdered and she stands accused of the crime.

The Case of the Sun Bather's Diary. Morrow, 1955

Arlene Duvall is accused of spending the half million stolen by her father, and she needs Mason to protect her and clear her father's name.

The Case of the Demure Defendant. Morrow, 1956

Held for the murder of her uncle, Nadine Farr has confessed under the influence of a truth serum, and now she needs Mason to free her from the charge.

The Case of the Gilded Lily. Morrow, 1956

Paying the blackmailer to protect his wife Ann's reputation seemed like a good idea to Stewart Bedford, until his money is taken by the beautiful accomplice of the blackmailer, who is left dead, killed with Stewart's own gun.

Blackmail

The Case of the Terrified Typist. Morrow, 1956

Mason is disturbed when his temp, Mae Wallis, appears to be part of the scheme to steal diamonds from an importing company down the hall from his offices, and the attempt leads to the death of a diamond smuggler.

Jewels

The Case of the Daring Decoy. Morrow, 1957

Enticed to a hotel room where he meets a blonde with a gun who ends up dead, Jerry Conway is forced to concentrate on his own case and look away from the proxy fight to gain control of Texas Global.

The Case of the Lucky Loser. Morrow, 1957

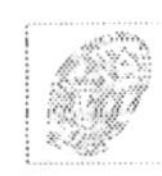

Mason is given a retainer by a client named Dorla Balfour who wants him to handle a case that has already been decided.

The Case of the Screaming Woman. Morrow, 1957

John Kirby has a story ready about a needy hitchhiker who can alibi him for the murder of Dr. Phineas Babb despite the evidence that places him at the scene of the murder.

The Case of the Calendar Girl. Morrow, 1958

Forced to go to the evil Meridith Borden for money, George Ansely is so upset he drives into the car of model Beatrice Cornell, and then he really needs Mason to sort out his wayward evening.

The Case of the Foot-Loose Doll. Morrow, 1958

Mildred Crest thinks she can rescue her life when she switches identities with a dead hitchhiker named Fern Driscoll, until the dead woman's past comes back to haunt her and she needs Mason's protection.

The Case of the Long-Legged Models. Morrow, 1958

Mason's client has an unusual problem. Stephanie Falkner has inherited her father's real estate, but he earned it gambling. Now that she is willing to sell to George Casselman, she needs Mason. Especially when Casselman becomes a corpse.

The Case of the Deadly Toy. Morrow, 1959

Divorce turns ugly when Mervin Selkirk's seven-year-old son Robert's custody is the cause, and his mistress Norda Allison begins to be blackmailed.

The Case of the Mythical Monkeys. Morrow, 1959

Forced to spend a night in a cabin with a man, Gladys Doyle wakes the next morning to find him gone and a corpse in his place.

The Case of the Singing Skirt. Morrow, 1959

When a customer in her gambling house kills his wife, Ellen Robb decides that her life as a come-on has ended and she wants Masons's help.

The Case of the Duplicate Daughter. Morrow, 1960

Muriell Gilman's father left the breakfast table and never returned, but he left her with a bloodstained workshop scattered with $100 bills.

The Case of the Shapely Shadow. Morrow, 1960

Three women wanted him, but now Morley Theilman is dead, and Mason must figure out who killed the golden goose.

The Case of the Waylaid Wolf. Morrow, 1960

When an heir to a fortune is murdered, Mason's pretty and poor client is the most likely suspect.

Wills

The Case of the Bigamous Spouse. Morrow, 1961

Gwynn Elston is a door-to-door encyclopedia salesperson who has seen a picture of her best friend's husband in another person's house.

The Case of the Spurious Spinster. Morrow, 1961

Susan Fisher has found something wrong with the books at the mining company owned by the spinster Amelia Corning, and Mason finds himself in the middle of the battle when the company's books are made public.

The Case of the Blonde Bonanza. Morrow, 1962

Mason has to figure out why the perfect figure of model Dianne Alder needed to be altered, and whether the issue of gaining weight would push her to murder Harrison Boring, the agent who signed her to the contract.

The Case of the Ice-Cold Hands. Morrow, 1962

Mason is asked to place a bet by a beautiful brunette, and left to explain to the police why he was using embezzled funds to bet on the ponies.

The Case of the Reluctant Model. Morrow, 1962

Collin Durant has labeled the Phellipe Feteet owned by millionaire Otto Olney a fake, and the resulting lawsuit leads to the death of a man connected to the witness needed by Mason for his court case.

Art

The Case of the Amorous Aunt. Morrow, 1963

A young couple comes to Mason with a story about their widowed, wealthy aunt, and the man who is stalking her.

The Case of the Mischievous Doll. Morrow, 1963

Although the law is trying Minerva Minden for the death of Dorrie Ambler, Mason is convinced the woman is still alive.

The Case of the Stepdaughter's Secret. Morrow, 1963

Harlow Bissenger Bancroft's wealth does not spare him from blackmail, but it is his wife who is accused of murdering the scoundrel and the one who needs Mason's help.

Blackmail

The Case of the Daring Divorcee. Morrow, 1964

Adelle Hastings shows up at the office one day with a tale of woe and in need of protection. But she disappears before Mason returns from lunch, and he then finds out that she is being threatened by her husband Garvin.

The Case of the Horrified Heirs. Morrow, 1964

When the life of elderly and ailing widow Lauretta Trent crosses the path of the young and not-so-rich widow, Virginia Baxter, Mason is left with a case of murder.

The Case of the Phantom Fortune. Morrow, 1964

This case kicks off when Mason is paid to attend a buffet and discovers his presence as a lawyer is needed when death strikes.

The Case of the Beautiful Beggar. Morrow, 1965

After her three-month cruise, Daphne Shelby's uncle warns her not to come home, but to get in touch with Mason instead.

The Case of the Troubled Trustee. Morrow, 1965

When a beautiful heiress finds her financial dealings in the hands of a young man, the mining stock that is at stake becomes a motive for murder.

The Case of the Worried Waitress. Morrow, 1966

Mason cannot even go out to eat without a waitress asking for help, so he leaves her a tip: one free consultation for a young woman in serious trouble.

The Case of the Queenly Contestant. Morrow, 1967

Mason's new client is trying to hide the fact that she won a beauty contest, and he needs to find out why.

The Case of the Careless Cupid. Morrow, 1968

The widow Anson feels she has a shadow, and considering that she is wealthy, Mason feels the source may be within her own family.

The Case of the Fabulous Fake. Morrow, 1969

Mason's client wants to disappear so badly that she will only identify herself by her measurements.

The Case of the Crimson Kiss. Morrow, 1971

A collection of the following stories: "The Case of the Crimson Kiss," a Perry Mason novelette, and four non-Mason stories.

Short stories

The Case of the Crying Swallow. Morrow, 1971

A collection of the following stories: "The Case of the Crying Swallow," a Perry Mason novelette, and three non-Mason stories.

Short stories

The Case of the Irate Witness. Morrow, 1972

A collection of the following stories: "The Case of the Irate Witness," a Perry Mason short story, and three non-Mason novelettes.

Short stories

The Case of the Fenced-In Woman. Morrow, 1972

Morley Eden has returned from vacation to discover an unknown woman has divided his house in half and has a restraining order keeping him out of her half.

The Case of the Postponed Murder. Morrow, 1973

When Sylvia Farr comes looking for her long-lost sister Mae, Mason is confused when he discovers this story may be better the other way around.

The Case of the Too Many Murders (by Thomas Chastain). Morrow, 1989

A wealthy businessman murders his dinner companion and then is murdered himself, and the accused is the man's widow who wants Mason to defend her against the charges.

Chastain, Thomas

The Case of the Burning Bequest (by Thomas Chastain). Morrow, 1990

When Anne Kimbro's stepmother is found stabbed with garden shears in the exact spot where Anne's mother was killed 20 years earlier, the case falls to Mason.

Chastain, Thomas

The Modern Practitioners

Frances Fyfield (pseud. of Frances Hegarty) ✍

Sarah Fortune

Working for a private firm in London, this lawyer is not your average solicitor. Her personal life is as complicated as her cases, and she is an intriguing character to read about. While trying to balance the important issues in her own personal life, she finds her professional career complicated by convoluted criminal cases that need her to act as a detective.

Readers may also enjoy P. D. James (Cordelia Gray), Lia Matera, and Julie Smith. **Traditional**. Series subject: **Law**.

Shadows on the Mirror. U.K.: Heinemann, 1989 (U.S.: Pocket, 1991)

Fortune is still suffering from the death of her unfaithful husband two years prior to this case, and she is battling her fatigue with the law and her multiple interests in men. The aggressive courtship of Charles Tysall is off putting, and turns dangerous when there appears to be a connection to Fortune and the body of woman found on the eastern shore.

England, London

Perfectly Pure and Good. U.K.: Bantam, 1994 (U.S.: Pantheon, 1994)

Fortune's mentor, Ernest Matthewson, has sent her to Merton to work on an estate problem and to recover from the aspects from the previous book. The members of the Pardoe family prove challenging and memories from Fortune's past continue to interfere in the present.

England, Norfolk, Merton

Staring at the Light. U.K.: Bantam, 2000 (U.S.: Viking, 2000)

Cannon Smith is trying to put his past as a bomb-maker away now that he has married Julie, but his evil twin, Johnny, will not let him rest. It falls to Fortune to protect them from Johnny, and she finds the twins dependency a major problem.

England, London

Frances Fyfield (pseud. of Frances Hegarty) ✍

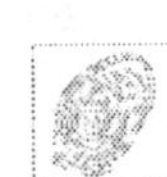

Helen West/Geoffrey Bailey

As Crown Prosecutor for London, Helen West teams with Detective Superintendent Geoffrey Bailey to solve crimes in modern English society. As exciting as the cases may be, the development of the relationship between these two principals is also part of the story. Fyfield is much more interested in the psychological reasons for crimes then in chasing clues. Readers may also enjoy Deborah Crombie, Elizabeth George, and Martha Grimes. **Traditional**. Series subjects: **Law · Teams**.

A Question of Guilt. U.K.: Heinemann, 1988 (U.S.: Pocket, 1989)

West is the prosecutor assigned to the case when Eileen Cartwright falls in love with her lawyer, Michael Bernard, and then arranges for the death of his wife Sylvia. When West finds herself in need of help, she receives it from Detective Superintendent Geoffrey Bailey, beginning an association that will last the series. Stanislaus Jaskowski is the fall guy, but will the Crown be able to prove anything against a clever murderer?

England, London

Trial by Fire. U.K.: Heinemann, 1990 (U.S.: *Not That Kind of Place.* Pocket, 1990)

Bailey has been assigned to Branston, and the community's movement towards upward mobility is confronted by the dead body of a woman killed during a crime of passion. When Bailey has to accuse Antony Sumner, a friend of a friend of Helen's, Helen is off the case and investigating on her own.

England, Branston

Deep Sleep. U.K.: Heinemann, 1991 (U.S.: Pocket, 1991)

Margaret Carlton, wife of the "Caring Chemist," Pip Carlton has died in her sleep, but West is convinced that things may not be as they seem. Bailey's investigation is complicated by the fact that his fellow officer, Duncan, is separated from Pip's assistant Kimberly, and as the case progresses, the pressures of the investigation will cause someone to kill again. DA

England, London

Shadow Play. U.K.: Bantam, 1993 (U.S.: Pantheon, 1993)

Mr. Logo is a menacing man who has been prosecuted for indecent assault several times, and West has failed to put him away each time. He is desperate to find his daughter who ran away, and when West gets involved in the personal life of Rose, her secretary, things begin to accelerate.

England, London

A Clear Conscience. U.K.: Bantam, 1994 (U.S.: Pantheon, 1994)

Feeling low about her career and her personal life, West hires a cleaning woman named Cath. When she discovers that Cath is being abused by her husband and that Cath's brother has been murdered, she finds a reason to become re-energized in the law.

England, London

Without Consent. U.K.: Penguin, 1996 (U.S.: Viking, 1997)

West finds her life complicated when she must try the rape case of D. S. Ryan. While the young officer maintains absolute silence on his guilt, the two detectives try to determine the truth.

England, London

Steve Martini ✍

Paul Madriani

Lawyer Madriani stars in a series of novels that may be more psychological thriller than detective fiction. They are included here to show the logical extension of the Perry Mason character into a modern setting. Unlike Mason, who remains static through the series, and rarely deals with personal issues, Madriani is a volatile character with many complications in his personal life. Readers may also enjoy Michael Connelly, J. A. Jance (J. P. Beaumont), John Sandford, and William G. Tapply. See the author's website at http://www.stevemartini.com. **Hard-boiled**. Series subject: **Law**.

Compelling Evidence. Putnam, 1992

Madriani has left his firm to strike out on his own after having an affair with the boss's wife. When Ben Potter's campaign for the U.S. Supreme Court is cut short by his suicide, the initial investigation begins to shift towards a murder probe. The most likely suspect is Talia Potter, and she wants Madriani to help her defense.

California

Prime Witness. Putnam, 1993

Madriani is made special prosecutor for the town of Davenport when a series of murders disrupts the fabric of the community. When the evidence points to a college security guard whose defense attorney is Adrian Chambers, a woman with a vendetta against Madriani, he knows the case will be personal.

California, Davenport • Serial killer

Undue Influence. Putnam, 1994

Paul's wife Nikki has died of cancer, and he is left to raise their daughter Sarah and look after Nikki's sister, Laurel Vega. Laurel is caught in a custody battle with her ex-husband Jack, and when Jack's new wife is found murdered, Laurel is the prime suspect.

The Judge. Putnam, 1996

Madriani is not one to sympathize with judges, but he does take the case of Judge Armando "the Coconut" Acosta, who has been caught in a sting and arrested for soliciting a prostitute. When the arresting officer is murdered, Madriani begins to think his initial instincts might have been correct and he should have kept his distance from this case.

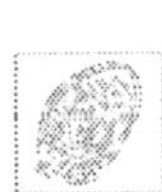

California, Capital City

The Attorney. Putnam, 2000

Having moved to San Diego, Madriani takes the case of Johan Hale who has just won the state lottery. Acting as the guardian for his eight-year-old granddaughter before the lottery, Hale finds himself under assault from his daughter and a fanatical feminist activist who want to convert his care into cold hard cash.

California, San Diego

The Jury. Putnam, 2001

Madriani is called upon to defend Dr. David Crone, a research physician whose assistant, Kalista Jordan, an African-American, has been murdered. Her dismembered body has been found and the evidence points to Madriani's client. Their research into mapping the human genome is so secret that it hinders Crone's defense. When something from the past points additional evidence towards Crone, Madriani begins to believe that his client may indeed be guilty.

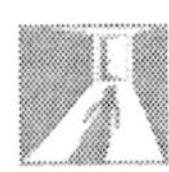

California, San Diego • Genome research

***The Arraignment.** Putnam, 2002

Lia Matera ✍

Laura Di Palma

Matera writes this series about San Francisco lawyer Laura Di Palma, a powerful defense attorney politely known as a shark. Her aggressive style is not typical of the traditional female lawyer, so she must deal with feminist issues as well as legal. Her cases may be recommended to traditional and hard-boiled mystery readers. Readers may also enjoy Frances Fyfield and Julie Smith. **Traditional/Hard-boiled**. Series subject: **Law**.

A Radical Departure. Bantam, 1988

Radical lawyer Julian Warneke has hired DiPalma to work in his office, and she is stunned when he is poisoned with hemlock at lunch. To her surprise, her own mother is an heir in the man's will, and she becomes motivated to discover the truth behind these circumstances.

California, San Francisco • Wills

The Smart Money. Bantam, 1988

DiPalma has moved back to her hometown to ruin the life of the man who ruined her: high school sweetheart Gary Gleason. She wants to take the job of public defender just to show that she can, and then leave town with him in her dust. However, things at home do not go smoothly, and when two murders occur, her job becomes more than a personal revenge fantasy.

California

The Good Fight. Simon & Schuster, 1990

DiPalma takes the case of her old friend Dan Crosetti, head of a political action center, who is accused of murdering the FBI plant inside his organization. As a consequence, DiPalma finds her personal and professional life in a turmoil, and her career as a lawyer is threatened.

California, San Francisco

A Hard Bargain. Simon & Schuster, 1992

DiPalma's been fired, so she goes on a retreat with her cousin Hal that is interrupted when P.I. and former lover, Sander Arkelett, shows up with a case. Karen McGuin has committed suicide with a gun left by her husband Ted, and the question is did he want her to die.

California, Dungeness

Face Value. Simon & Schuster, 1994

Now on her own, DiPalma decides to take the case of a former cult member who has turned on the cult's leader, Brother Mike. Forced to hit the streets as an investigator, DiPalma is shocked by the murder of six people, and the sexual exploitation of the cult's members, while she struggles to build a case against the cult's leader.

California, San Francisco • Cults • Washington, San Juan Island

Designer Crimes. Simon & Schuster, 1995

The last words of labor attorney Joceyln Kinsley are "designer crimes," uttered after being shot in her office while DiPalma was consulting her about suing her former boss, Steven Sayres. When the words lead DiPalma to a conspiracy that allows for hits on people disgruntled with their bosses or employees, DiPalma wonders who was the intended victim when Kinsely was hit.

California, San Francisco

Lia Matera ✍

Willa Jansson

Perhaps more humane than her counterpart Laura DiPalma, Lia Jansson is a Bay City lawyer with the heart of a liberal and the skills of a detective. Readers may also enjoy Frances Fyfield and Julie Smith. See the author's website at **Traditional**. Series subject: **Law**.

Where Lawyers Fear to Tread. Bantam, 1987

While attending school, Jansson becomes the editor-in-chief of the *Malhousie Law Review* when the current editor, Susan Green, is murdered. When she decides to probe into the murder, she is arrested, and her studies must be put aside to protect herself as well as catch a criminal.

California, San Francisco

Hidden Agenda. Bantam, 1988

The San Francisco office of Wailes, Roth, Fotheringham and Beck wants Jansson to come on board as an associate, an odd occurrence considering her leftist tendencies and their staunch Republican platform. When, on a retreat to the Mariposa Estates Hotel's Wilderness Conference Center, she is set up to take the fall for a murder, she scrambles to save her own neck.

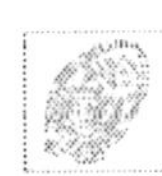

California, Yosemite

Prior Convictions. Simon & Schuster, 1991

When Jansson is asked to mediate a domestic violence case, she does not expect a tangled web of intrigue to complicate the case. Her client is Christine Rugieri, an ex-radical now living the contemporary life who is threatened by her first husband, Tom, who years ago went to prison based on her testimony.

California, San Francisco

Last Chants. Simon & Schuster, 1996

Having lost her job on her previous case, Jansson is now working for a law firm specializing in multimedia issues. But one day she sees a friend of her family named Arthur Kenna waving a gun in public, and through her own quick decision, ends up her friend's hostage. He claims the gun was pressed upon him by a stranger, but the police have a body that ties to the weapon, and they want Kenna as their suspect.

California, San Francisco

Star Witness. Simon & Schuster, 1997

A psychiatrist asks Jansson to defend his client Allen Miller, accused of murder. The weird part is that it seems probable that Jansson may be able to use the client's belief in his abduction by aliens as a credible defense.

California, Santa Cruz • UFOs

Havana Twist. Simon & Schuster, 1998

Jansson's mother has made an illegal trip to Cuba and then failed to return with her tourist group. Jansson drops everything and rushes to her mother's aide, discovering that trying to work within the system of this island nation is a challenge beyond her abilities. Can she trust her new found allies, or are they the CIA?

Cuba, Havana

Julie Smith ✍

Rebecca Schwartz

San Francisco lawyer Schwartz is a contemporary feminist lawyer. She earns her stripes as a detective in this series by sheer accident, but her plucky ability to persevere against all odds makes her an interesting character. Readers may also enjoy Frances Fyfield and Lia Matera. **Traditional**. Series subjects: **California, San Francisco • Law**.

Death Turns a Trick. Walker, 1982

Rebecca Schwartz has been playing piano in a feminist bordello, but when it is raided one night, she is arrested along with everyone at the house. When she is released, she returns home to discover the corpse of a part-time student and part-time prostitute named Kandi.

The Sourdough Wars. Walker, 1984

The making of sourdough bread is critical to many in the city, but few would have expected that the announcement of the sale of the sourdough starter created by the famous Martinelli family would lead to Peter Martinelli's death. Schwartz is compelled to discover if the dead man really did die from dough, and who will get the dough when all the issues are settled.

Cooking

Tourist Trap. Mysterious Press, 1986

Rob Burns, Schwartz's reporter boyfriend, is chosen by a serial killer as his conduit. The killer is targeting tourists to the Bay City, and as the clues are dropped, Schwartz too often finds herself at the scene of the crime.

Serial killer

Dead in the Water. Ivy, 1991

Marty Whitehead is Schwarz's friend who works at the Monterey Aquarium. When Schwartz goes to view the exhibits, she does not expect to see a woman's body in the kelp tank. The victim is Marty's boss, a woman who has been sleeping with Marty's husband.

Aquariums • California, Monetery

Other People's Skeletons. Ivy, 1993

Schwartz's law partner, Chris Nicholson, is accused of murder, but she cannot reveal to Schwartz what her alibi is. What Schwartz discovers is that her partner, the dead critic Jason McKendrick, and others all have deeply buried secrets that will confuse her on this case.

William G. Tapply ✍

Brady Coyne

On a normal day, Boston-based lawyer Coyne works with wills and deeds. But his high-powered cases often force him to become a detective, so Coyne often needs to act more like a private investigator than an attorney. His cases can be recommended to any hard-boiled mystery reader. Readers may also enjoy Jeremian Healy, Steve Martini, and Robert B. Parker. **Hard-boiled**. Series subject: **Law**.

Death at Charity's Point. Scribner, 1984

George Gresham is a shy, unassuming teacher who commits suicide, leaving a note in his pocket when he plunges off a cliff at Charity's Point. His mother, who carries a life insurance policy on her son, would like to prove that it was murder. Coyne probes into a family with a long history of violent deaths and discovers a connection to Vietnam.

Academia • Massachusetts, Boston

The Dutch Blue Error. Scribner, 1985

Daniel Sullivan has a stamp called the Dutch Blue Error, worth more than a million dollars. The problem is that the rare, one-of-a-kind stamp has supposedly been the stamp owned by Oliver Hazard Perry Weston, and now he wants Coyne to buy the second stamp to maintain the value of his stamp. When Sullivan ends up dead, and Coyne's assistant is accused of murder, he must act as a detective to clear up the mystery.

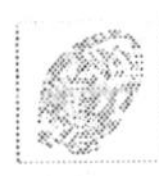

Massachusetts, Boston • Stamps

Follow the Sharks. Scribner, 1985

Eddie Donagan sells shoes at the mall and remembers a time when he was the best pitcher the Boston Red Sox had on their team. When his 12-year-old son is kidnapped, he turns to Coyne for help. Battling the mother of the child and the FBI were hard enough for Coyne, until a death mars the investigation and pushes him to test himself.

Baseball • Kidnapping • Massachusetts, Boston

The Marine Corpse. U.S.: Scribner, 1986 (U.K.: *A Rodent of Doubt.* Collins, 1987)

While author Stu Carver is undercover as a homeless man, his throat is cut and he is left for dead on the streets of Boston. Coyne, who had acted as Carver's agent, is hired by the man's uncle to probe into the death to discover if anyone had penetrated the disguise and killed the author for nefarious reasons.

Authors • Homeless • Massachusetts, Boston

Dead Meat. Scribner, 1987

If Coyne can combine fishing and work, he is happy. While in Maine to negotiate the sale of a lodge, he discovers that a Native American tribe would like to purchase the lodge because it sits on sacred ground. When a moose is killed with a bow and arrow and a man is killed by the same method and scalped, Coyne finds himself in the middle of a murder case with racial overtones.

Maine, Greenville · Native Americans

The Vulgar Boatman. Scribner, 1987

When Coyne and his girlfriend. Sylvie Szabo, travel to the Massachusetts North Shore, it is to visit with gubernatorial candidate Tom Baron. But Baron has a surprise: his teenage son is missing and the boy's girlfriend is dead. Coyne accepts an assignment that requires him to investigate and keep the case of out the papers.

Massachusetts, Windsor Harbor

A Void in Hearts. Scribner, 1988

Coyne is willing to listen to P.I. Les Katz's tale of how he cheated a client and blackmailed her husband. Coyne's advice to his client is to come clean, but when Katz is killed, Coyne finds the widow of the P.I is his new client.

Massachusetts, Boston

Dead Winter. Delacorte, 1989

Unitarian minister Desmond Winter's son is under a cloud of suspicion. Marc Winter is suspected of killing his wife Maggie, and Desmond wants Coyne to investigate. When one of his leads is also killed, Coyne knows he is hot on the trial of a killer.

Massachusetts, Newburyport

Client Privilege. Delacorte, 1990

Chester Popowski has received two things: a nomination to the federal bench, and a blackmail threat. He wants Coyne to solve his second problem, and when the blackmailer ends up dead, the cops want Coyne to solve their problem.

Massachusetts, Boston

The Spotted Cats. Delacorte, 1991

Coyne is summoned to Cape Cod and the home of his invalid friend and former big game hunter, Jeff Newton. The weekend turns bad when burglars steal seven gold pre-Columbian jaguars and leave Newton near death. When Coyne investigates, the trail leads to Montana and the perpetrators.

Massachusetts, Cape Cod · Montana, West Yellowstone

Tight Lines. Delacorte, 1992

When Susan Ames knows she is dying, she wants her lawyer Coyne to track down her only heir: her long-estranged daughter, Mary Ellen Ames. Five of her close friends do not know where Mary Ellen is until her body is found in her summer cottage, and then the suspects begin to die as well.

Massachusetts, Boston · New Hampshire, Teal Pond

The Snake Eater. Otto Penzler, 1993

Coyne takes the case of a small-town Vietnam Vet accused of growing marijuana, and is pleased when the case is dropped. Befriending Daniel McCloud, Coyne promotes a book idea to an agent, but the agent drops the idea. When Coyne begins to explore why everyone is backing away from McCloud, he wishes he had never taken the case.

Massachusetts, Wilson Falls

The Seventh Enemy. Otto Penzler, 1995

The star of Walt Kinnick's *Outdoors* is in town to testify against a gun-control bill, and to everyone's surprise, he changes his testimony and speaks in favor of the anti-gun measure. Someone is unhappy enough to try and kill him, and that means he needs to rely on his old pal, Coyne.

Fishing • Massachusetts, Boston

Close to the Bone. St. Martin's Press, 1996

Paul Cizek is Coyne's fishing buddy, and the criminal attorney Coyne leans on when his clients need a top-notch defense. Often able to free controversial clients, Cizek should be on top of his game, but depression leads him away from his wife and friends. When his fishing boat is found abandoned at sea, Coyne begins a search for his friend.

Massachusetts, Boston

Muscle Memory. St. Martin's Press, 1999

Coyne's latest client is former basketball star Mick Fallon, who is being divorced by his wife. When Coyne discovers that Fallon is deep in debt to the mob for gambling, he thinks he has heard the worst. Then Fallon's wife is murdered, and his client is suspect number one.

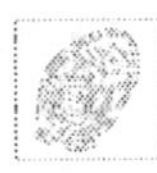

Massachusetts, Boston

Scar Tissue. St. Martin's Minotaur, 2000

Jacob Gold calls Coyne with the news that Gold's 15-year-old son Brian's body is missing from a fatal car accident that killed Brian's girlfriend Jenny. When the small-town police seem to resent his help, and things at the scene of the accident do not add up to a skilled observer, Coyne knows he may be on the trail of a mystery.

Massachusetts, Reddington

Past Tense. St. Martin's Minotaur, 2001

Coyne and his girlfriend Evie Banyon are having a tryst on Cape Cod when the body of Larry Scott is found in their cottage. Scott has been stalking Evie, and the cops think the two lovers may have done away with Scott. When Evie disappears, Coyne travels to the small town where Evie and Scott's troubles began, and that is when his troubles really begin.

Massachusetts, Cortland

First Light. Scribner, 2001

This novel was co-written with Philip R. Craig and also features Craig's series character J. W. Jackson, an ex-cop. Jack Bannerman, a Martha Vineyard's businessman with a missing wife, hires Jackson to find her. Coyne arrives in the resort community for a fishing tournament but is distracted when a nurse of a client also goes missing. As the two detectives investigate, the question becomes: Is a serial killer working this resort community?

Craig, Philip R. • Massachusetts, Martha's Vineyard • Serial killer • Wills

Judith Van Gieson ✍

Neil Hamel

Contemporary lawyers can find cases that need their detective skills as well as their legal skills, and in Albuquerque, New Mexico, Neil Hamel finds this to be true. Although she specializes in real estate and divorce, her office keeps attracting murder cases. Readers may also enjoy Jean Hager, Tony Hillerman, and Abigail Padgett. See the author's website at http://www.judithvangieson.com. **Traditional**. Series subject: **Law**.

North of the Border. Walker, 1988

Carl Roberts comes calling on his former lover, Hamel, with a tale of blackmail over an adopted baby from Mexico and how it may interfere with his campaign for public office. When Hamel travels to Mexico, she discovers a dead Mexican lawyer and a case that will threaten her before it is concluded.

Mexico, Juarez • New Mexico, Albuquerque

Raptor. Harper, 1990

Hamel inherits a free ride to Montana to see the rare gyrfalcon, but once there she and the birders are witness to a body falling off a cliff. When the leader of the birders, March Augusta, is accused of the crime, Hamel jumps to his defense.

Birds • Montana, Fire Pond

The Other Side of Death. Harper & Row, 1991

Lonnie Darmer, an old friend of Hamel's, is driven home from a party in a drunken stupor, and disappears the next day. When her body is found in an Anasazi ruin, the police rule suicide. But Hamel knows she was locked in a battle with her ex-husband over his latest construction project.

New Mexico, Santa Fe

The Wolf Path. Harper & Row, 1992

Not everyone is thrilled with Juan Sololobo's plan to reintroduce wolves into the high desert country of New Mexico, but when bandits release his wolf Sirius and it is accused of killing cattle, he is so mad he threatens a government official who ends up dead. Hamel believes that the wolf and the man are both innocent, and fights against the ranching community that wishes to keep things under control.

New Mexico, Soledad • Wolves

The Lies That Bind. Harper & Row, 1993

Martha Conover has been accused of killing Justine Virga with her automobile, three years to the day after Justine had killed Martha's grandson with her car. Despite the overwhelming evidence to the contrary, Hamel accepts her defense and begins a spirited search among the Latino community for a reason for Justine's death.

Hispanic-Americans • New Mexico, Albuquerque

Parrot Blues. Harper & Row, 1995

Parrot researcher Deborah Dumaine has been kidnapped along with her rare macaw named Perigee. Her husband, Terrance Lewellen, asks Hamel to find her, despite the fact that he was in a bitter divorce proceeding with the now-missing woman.

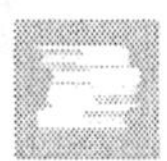

Birds • New Mexico, Albuquerque • Parrots

Hotshots. HarperCollins, 1996

A forest fire fighter named Joni Barker is accused of negligence in the fire that caused her death, and her parents ask Hamel to clear their daughter's name. Battling the Forest Service is as intense as battling an fire, and Hamel finds this case will lead her into unexplored territories.

Colorado, Oro • Forest fires • New Mexico, Albuquerque

Ditch Rider. HarperCollins, 1998

Settling into her new neighborhood, Hamel decides to defend 13-year-old Cheyanne Morales, a neighbor girl who has confessed to shooting a young gang member. While suspicious of the confession, Hamel discovers that her neighbors may seek their own justice, and she has a tension-filled neighborhood to deal with and a murderer to find.

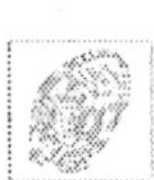

New Mexico, Albuquerque

Chapter 6

Private Detectives

The origins of private detectives as characters can be traced to the development of the Pinkerton Agency and its famous motto: "We never sleep." From the emblem of the omnipresent and constantly alert human eye comes the logical abbreviation of private investigator (P.I.) to private eye.

Ignoring some early forerunners, including Sherlock Holmes, it could be said that the fictional private detective as we know it developed within the pages of the very popular and proletarian pulp magazines of the 1920s. A story by John Carroll Daly in the December 1922, issue of *Black Mask* magazine, called "The False Burton Combs," is considered the first private eye short story. In the June 1, 1923, issue of *Black Mask*, a story by Daly called the "Knights of the Open Palm," introduced the private detective Race Williams. Following in the footsteps of Daly, and under the leadership of the magazine's editor, Joseph T. "Cap" Shaw, many authors began to develop similar characters. Other authors offered stories to such pulps as *Dime Detective*, *Thrilling Detective Stories*, *Detective Fiction Weekly*, and *Action Detective*.

Although Daly's short stories were the most popular features in *Black Mask*, as a novelist he was less successful than another *Black Mask* contributor, Dashiell Hammett, who used his own experiences as a Pinkerton agent to create a series of novels from his *Black Mask* works. These novels featured a nameless detective remembered as The Continental Op. But Hammett's crowning achievement was *The Maltese Falcon*, in which he created the archetypical private detective Sam Spade.

Following the same pattern and cobbling his own short stories as well, Raymond Chandler moved from the pages of *Black Mask* into novel format with his private detective, Phillip Marlowe. Hammett and Chandler popularized the private detective in novel format, legitimized it as a literary form, and raised the playing field for the practitioners.

After the Second World War, the popularity of the paperback format proved to be a springboard for the career of Mickey Spillane. His Mike Hammer novels galvanized the field with their surprising popularity, but proved to be less of a literary achievement than his predecessors. Almost a throwback to the days of the pulps, his character's excessive violence, mistreatment of women, and promotion of political points of view now unpopular make his works challenging to read today.

When Ross Macdonald's Lew Archer novels appeared on the bestseller lists in the late 1960s and early 1970s, they pushed Spillane's pulpy style of writing out of the way to make room for a more soft-boiled private detective and plots based on the psychology of the crime rather than the physiology of the detective. Macdonald's painfully developed family tragedies proved that there was more to private eye writing than just plot-driven violence. When Macdonald passed the torch, it was to other writers like Robert B. Parker, who studied Hammett and Chandler, and used the lessons to develop a contemporary private detective with modern sensibilities accompanied by the ability to stand tall in a fight.

In 1972, P. D. James wrote *An Unsuitable Job for a Woman,* featuring one of the first modern female private detectives. Although female detectives had been around as long as the men, they often were cast in the mold of the effervescent Honey West, an oversexed woman whose sole purpose seemed to be taking off her clothes at some point during her case. James's detective was a capable woman challenged to run an inquiry agency when it fell in her lap. In 1974, Maxine O'Callaghan's Delilah West appeared in a short story in Alfred Hitchcock's Mystery Magazine. In 1977, Marcia Muller created Sharon McCone, an American woman with a social conscience, but her work received little recognition upon publication. These two ground-breaking efforts bore full fruit in 1982 when Muller's second McCone adventure was published in the same year as Sue Grafton's *A is for Alibi* and Sara Paretsky's *Indemnity Only.* Whether in response to the increased awareness of women's roles in the mystery field, or serving as a catalyst for the advent of the woman character and writer, these female private detectives led a revolution that transformed the private detective novel and the rest of the mystery field.

The other development that transformed the private detective novel took place at roughly the same time. When Michael Z. Lewin was able to have his private detective set up shop in Indianapolis, it helped break the New York–Southern California regional grip on the fictional private detective.

In today's market, we have male and female private detectives in equal numbers, private detectives setting up shop in every region of the world, and novels whose first release is in the paperback format. Riding the most popular mystery fiction trend of the 1990s, the historical, we even have private detectives like Nate Heller by Max Allan Collins or Roman detectives created by Lindsay Davis and Stephen Saylor.

Repeatedly declared a dead art form, the private detective novel has proved to be quite resilient against any reports of its death. Its continuing popularity may be traced to its most basic component: the required feisty independence of the investigator. The vast majority of private detectives are "lone wolf" detectives, working without the support that backs up a police detective. Fiercely loyal to their clients, the private detective risks all even if the client proves unfaithful. Private detectives usually find themselves fighting corruption in society as well as trying to solve murders. Similar to the amateur, the private detective does what many readers wish they could do: confront authority, triumph over impossible odds, and right the wrongs of society. Since the mid-1970s, the private detective affords the modern reader all the same advantages that most of mystery fiction enjoys: diversity of characters, regionalism, and contemporary themes.

Private Detectives

The Historical Founding Members

Raymond Chandler ✍

Philip Marlowe

Raymond Chandler is credited with bringing a literary sensibility to the pulp writing of this early period by creating his P.I. Philip Marlowe. Chandler reveals little about the character's background, but reveals everything about the man's character through his actions. Cynical about the world, but dedicated to the cause of his client, the character of Marlowe helped to establish the code of the fictional private detective that includes battling to find the truth no matter what the odds. Chandler's use of the Los Angeles setting is another strength of this series. Robert B. Parker (see his own listing for his Spenser novels) completed the unfinished work of Chandler and then a novel of his own invention featuring Marlowe. **Traditional/ Hard-boiled**. Series subject: **California, Los Angeles**.

The Big Sleep. Knopf, 1939

When Marlowe is hired to investigate the gambling debts of General Sternwood's youngest daughter, Carmen, everyone thinks he is looking for Rusty Regan. Regan was married to the oldest Sternwood daughter, Vivian, and it is her connection to the hood Eddie Mars that starts Marlowe on the trail of drugs, pornography, and murder.

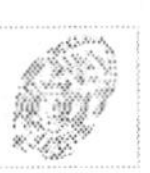

Farewell, My Lovely. Knopf, 1940

After Moose Malloy encourages Marlowe to search for his old girlfriend, Velma, Marlowe also finds himself encouraged to hunt for the missing woman by his cop pal Nulty. After crossing paths with a woman named Anne Riordan, who seems to know more about the case than he does, he also finds himself looking for Helen Grayle's missing jade and trying to solve the death of a man who worked to recover them.

The High Window. Knopf, 1942

Marlowe's client is the embittered widow of Jasper Murdoch, who believes her daughter-in-law Linda has stolen the priceless Brasher Doubloon. While working the case, a young P.I. stalks Marlowe. When the P.I. is killed, Marlowe suspects Morny, a Hollywood hood, who is married to Linda's roommate.

The Lady in the Lake. Knopf, 1943

Marlowe is hired by a perfume manufacturer who wants his wife, Crystal, found, but when Marlow ventures to their lake cabin, he finds the caretaker's dead wife. Both women disappeared on the same day and are connected to the death of a Bay City doctor's wife, all of which has interested a rogue cop in Marlowe's investigation.

The Little Sister. Houghton Mifflin, 1949 (Also published as *Marlowe.* Pocket, 1969)

Hired by Orfamay Quest to locate her brother Orrin, Marlowe instead locates a murder that leads to a plot used to blackmail a crook and his actress girlfriend. Feeling empathy for the actress, Marlowe gets himself hired to protect her from a blackmailer and a murderer.

The Long Goodbye. Houghton Mifflin, 1954

Marlowe's longstanding friendship with an alcoholic Englishman, Terry Lennox, leads to danger when Terry becomes a suspect in his wife's murder and then uses Marlowe to escape to Mexico to commit suicide. A second story deals with Marlowe babysitting the suicidal author Roger Wade and the complications arising from Roger's beautiful wife, Eileen. ED

Authors

Playback. Houghton Mifflin, 1958

Marlowe is hired by a lawyer to follow a girl arriving on the Super Chief. The trail leads to a motel in Esmeralda where Marlowe loses in a fight with a blackmailer, and Marlowe's sympathies turn to the woman when she is left with the dead body of her blackmailer.

Blackmail

Poodle Springs. Putnam, 1989

Based on four chapters left by Chandler, Robert B. Parker's story takes Marlowe from his marriage to Linda Loring and into the bigamist relationships of Lee Valentine. Hired by the hoods to rein in Valentine, Marlowe finds his romantic ideals may be interfering with his ability to investigate.

California · Parker, Robert B.

Perchance to Dream (by Robert B. Parker). Putnam, 1991

In a direct sequel to *The Big Sleep*, written by Robert B. Parker, Vivian's butler Norris has hired Marlowe to hunt for the escaped and very crazy Carmen Sternwood. Forming an uneasy alliance with hood Eddie Mars, Marlowe finds himself investigating the rich who use others for their personal pleasures.

Parker, Robert B.

Carroll John Daly ✍

Race Williams

Daly first appeared in the pages of the pulps with a character named Three-Gun Mack, but that P.I. was just the forerunner to his major character, Race Williams. Williams is a man of action, and is more likely to shoot suspects than to interview them. He is constantly threatened by the forces of evil, some of which take on a level of conspiracy similar to Dr. Fu Manchu. These novels lack all the sensibilities expected in a contemporary work, especially in the areas of character development and theme. But what they lack in those areas, they make up for in action, action, and more action. Daly's writing in both the short story format and the novels were extremely popular in their time. **Hard-boiled**.

The Snarl of the Beast. Clode, 1927

Race Williams is called to a secret rendezvous with a client who is living as an addict in a tenement. When he is attacked by the mysterious enemy known only as the Beast, he must determine why this supernatural evil presence has an interest in his client.

New York, New York

The Hidden Hand. Clode, 1929

Just hours after being approached about going to Florida to apprehend major crook McCleary, Race is almost assassinated. Then a mysterious fat man approaches him with a tale of a super crime god, the Hidden Hand. McCleary is just the first of four criminals Race hunts down in Florida before his final confrontation with the Hidden Hand.

Florida

The Tag Murders. Clode, 1930

Five underworld characters have been murdered and metal tags pinned to their corpses. Race is hired by Burton Jewelry, who has lost a client to the Tag Murderer, but when Race kills the Tag's chief assassin, he himself is marked for death. Sent to distract Race is The Flame, a woman who will complicate his life in this case and in others to follow.

New York, New York

Tainted Power. Clode, 1931

Minutes after Race witnesses an underworld rubout, the dead man's boss hires him to protect the boss at a rendezvous with The Flame. It seems that three different sets of crooks are negotiating for the Power, or control over all things criminal in New York.

New York, New York

The Third Murderer. Farrar, Straus, 1931

In short order Race punches out one of the racketeering Gordon brothers, gets involved in a rendezvous with The Flame, and is hired as a bodyguard for a client who wants to remain anonymous. The person the client wants protected is murdered, and The Flame manages to set a trap for Race on behalf of the Gordons.

New York, New York

The Amateur Murderer. Washburn, 1933

Race is asked to masquerade as Hulbert Clovelly, and represent him in the negotiations for the missing diamond that has brought a host of nefarious people to Baltimore in search of the jewel. When Race's focus shifts to protect Clovelly's innocent sister, a train ride to New City and a few gun battles later finds him up against the master criminal who plotted the entire enterprise.

Maryland, Baltimore • Railroads

Murder from the East. Stokes, 1935

Race is asked to join the team led by the General, which intends to battle the evil agents of the nation of Astran, which has been raiding U.S. secrets by torturing and murdering the families of government workers. The top agent for Astran is Count Jehdo, husband to The Flame, and Race finds his efforts complicated by his love for the mysterious Flame.

New York, New York

***Better Corpses.** Hale, 1940

The Adventures of Race Williams. Mysterious Press, 1989

A collection of the following stories: "City of Blood," "Corpse & Co.," "Dead Hands Reaching," "Just Another Stiff," and "Some Die Hard."

Short stories

Dashiell Hammett ✍

Nick Charles/Nora Charles

Based on his own experiences as a Pinkerton detective, Hammett created The Continental Op and Sam Spade before being seduced by Hollywood. His relationship with Lillian Hellman is the basis for the plucky couple Nick and Nora Charles, and this work comes out of his writing period when he was influenced by the movies. An aberration in Hammett's style, this novel features the retired P.I., Nick, teamed with his elegant and very rich wife, Nora, thus transforming Nick from a potential hard-boiled hero into a dilettante. This novel can be recommended to soft-boiled and traditional mystery readers. **Soft-boiled/Traditional**.

The Thin Man. Knopf, 1934

Nick is slumming in New York with Nora at Christmas time when a former client's daughter tries to involve him in the murder of her father's mistress. Her father, an eccentric professor, has gone into hiding to work on an experiment, and each family member seems to have their own reason to prevent Nick from figuring out the solution to this crime.

Humor · New York, New York · Teams

Dashiell Hammett ✍

The Continental Op

The anonymously named investigator, The Continental Op, was based on a co-worker of Hammett's during his days as a detective for the Pinkerton Detective Agency. Representing the omniscient way that truth and justice work in the real world of private detectives, the character moves through his cases with a quiet and faceless efficiency that eventually leads to the administration of justice. The Op short stories and novels are considered classics in the P.I. field. **Traditional/Hard-boiled**.

Red Harvest. Knopf, 1929

Old Elihu Willisson's crusading son is dead. Now he wants the Continental Op to clean up the mining town Elihu built from scratch before it was taken over by crooks. The Op is now ready to take on all the sins of Personville, and cleaning up the town becomes his priority.

Mining • Montana, Personville

The Dain Curse. Knopf, 1929

The Op is working through Continental for the insurance company of scientist Edgar Leggeet, who has had a diamond theft. But this opening gambit leads to three scenarios that trace the curse on Gabrielle Leggett. The first deals with the death of her parents, the second with the death of her cult leader, and the last with the death of her husband.

California, San Francisco

$106,000 Blood Money. Bestseller, 1943 (Also published as *Blood Money.* World, 1943; also published as *The Big Knockover.* Jonathan, 1943)

This story originally appeared in *Black Mask* magazine in two parts. The first was titled "The Big Knockover" and the second part was called "$106,000 Blood Money." The Op hunts down the mastermind behind a bank robbery in the first part, but only solves the bank robbery. In the second part, he uses a victim's brother as the bait to draw out the mastermind behind the robbery.

Short stories

The Continental Op. Bestseller, 1945

A collection of the following stories: "Death on Pine Street," "The Farewell Murder," "Fly Paper," and "Zigzags of Treachery."

Short stories

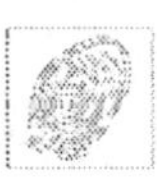

The Return of the Continental Op. Jonathan, 1945

A collection of the following stories: "Death & Company," "The Gutting of Couffignal," "One Hour," "The Tenth Clue," and "The Whosis Kid."

Short stories

Hammett Homicides. Bestseller, 1946

A collection of the following stories: "The Girl with the Silver Eyes," "The House in Turk Street," "The Main Death," and "Night Shots." Two non-Op stories are also included.

Short stories

Dead Yellow Woman. Jonathan, 1947

A collection of the following stories: "Dead Yellow Woman," "The Golden Horseshoe," "House Dick," and "Who Killed Bob Teal." Two non-Op stories are also included.

Short stories

Nightmare Town. Mercury, 1948

A collection of the following stories: "Corkscrew," and "The Scorched Face." Two non-Op stories are also included.

Short stories

The Creeping Siamese. Jonathan, 1950

A collection of short stories: "The Creeping Siamese" and "This King Business". Also includes four non-Op stories.

Short stories

Woman in the Dark. Jonathan, 1951

A collection of the following stories: "Arson Plus," "The Black Hat that Wasn't There," and "Slippery Fingers." Also includes four non-Op stories.

Short stories

The Big Knockover. U.S.: Random House, 1966 (U.K.: *The Dashiell Hammett Story Omnibus.* Cassell, 1966)

A collection of the following stories: "The Big Knockover," "Corkscrew," "Dead Yellow Women," "Fly Paper," "The Gatewood Caper," "The Gutting of Couffignal," "$106,000 Blood Money," "The Scorched Face," and "This King Business." Also includes one non-Op story.

Short stories

The Continental Op. Random House, 1974

A collection of the following stories: "The Farewell Murder," "The Girl with the Silver Eyes," "The Golden Horseshoe," "The House in Turk Street," "The Main Death," "The Tenth Clew," and "The Whosis Kid."

Short stories

Nightmare Town. Knopf, 1999

A collection of the following stories: "Death on Pine Street," "House Dick," "Night Shots," "One Hour," "Tom, Dick or Harry," "Who Killed Bob Teal?" "The Zigzags of Treachery." Also includes 13 non-Op stories.

Short stories

Dashiell Hammett ✍

Sam Spade

Hammett's novel featuring Spade can clearly be called one of the greatest mysteries ever written. It is the earliest example of how the private eye could also serve as a literary icon. Devilish in appearance, the key to Spade's appeal is the reader's inability to decide if this is a good man doing something bad or a bad man doing the inevitable. **Traditional/ Hard-boiled**.

The Maltese Falcon. Knopf, 1930

Sam Spade and his partner, Miles Archer, are approached by a seductive woman named Wonderly who needs protection from a man named Floyd Thursby. When Archer is murdered under mysterious circumstances while trying to protect her, Sam decides to avenge the death of his partner. He discovers that Wonderly is willing to lead Sam on the trail of a valuable, ancient, jeweled bird known as The Maltese Falcon.

Antiquities · California, San Francisco

The Adventures of Sam Spade and Other Stories. Bestseller, 1944 (Also published as *They Can Only Hang You Once.* Mercury, 1949; also published as *A Man Called Spade.* Dell, 1945)

A collection of the following stories: "The Assistant Murderer," "His Brother's Keeper," "The Judge Laughed Last," "A Man Called Spade," "Night Shade," "They Can Only Hang You Once," and "Too Many Have Lived."

Short stories

The Golden Agers and Beyond

Fredric Brown ✍

Ed Hunter/Am Hunter

Brown's novels follow the development of Ed Hunter from a young boy to a private detective under the tutelage of Am Hunter, his uncle and former carny man. One of the strengths of this series is its blend of light humor and mystery. Brown's experience as a science fiction writer brings some "woo-woo" elements to his detective series. See a website about the author at http://members.tripod.com/~gwillick/brown.html. **Soft-boiled/Traditional**. Series subjects: **Humor · Teams**.

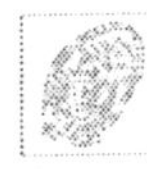

The Fabulous Clipjoint. Dutton, 1947

Ed Hunter's father, Wally, is murdered in a dark Chicago alley. That night, Ed flees to the carnival where his Uncle Am is working, and asks for his help in solving his father's murder. Suspicion falls on Wally's widow who is Ed's stepmother, and her daughter Gardie; and as the men push their investigation, they find themselves up against the Chicago underworld.

Illinois, Chicago

The Dead Ringer. Dutton, 1948

On a dark and stormy night while the carny is enjoying a successful run in Evansville, a naked midget is found with a knife thrower's weapon in his back. Suspicion falls on one of the posing girls, and Ed chases her while Am chases the murderer.

Circus · Indiana, Evansville

The Bloody Moonlight. Dutton, 1949 (Also published as: *Murder in the Moonlight.* Boardman, 1950)

Ed and Am are now working as P.I.s for the Starlock Agency in Chicago when Ed gets his first assignment—go to Tremont and find out if Justine Haberman's half-uncle is crazy or if he has a radio device that might be getting signals from a strange source. When Ed discovers a body he blames on a throat-slashing werewolf, suspicion falls on him, and he needs to work hard to clear his own name.

Illinois, Tremont

Compliments of a Fiend. Dutton, 1950

When Am disappears, the entire Starlock Agency leaps into action. An old text that mentions the Ambrose Collector sends Ed and Estelle Beck, a fellow rooming-house resident, after the murderer of another roomer, and on the trail of his uncle.

Illinois, Chicago

Death Has Many Doors. Dutton, 1951

The Hunter and Hunter Agency takes a protection case for Sally Doerr because Ed wants to know why she feels threatened by Martians. Staying overnight as a bodyguard leads to the discovery of her body, and Ed must scramble among her relatives to find the murderer.

Illinois, Chicago

The Late Lamented. Dutton, 1959

The receptionist from their old agency finds herself the key to the embezzlement of the city of Freeland's treasury, and Ed and Am leap to her defense.

Illinois, Chicago

Mrs. Murphy's Underpants. Dutton, 1963

Ed and Am are hired by the young son of Vincent Dolan when the boy overhears a plot to kill his father. The complication is that Vince is the man who rides herd over all of Chicago's bookies, and there are plenty of folks who would like to take him for a ride. As Ed and Am dig deeper into the case, they also discover that the threats may extend to others in the Dolan family.

Illinois, Chicago

Michael Collins (pseud. of Dennis Lynds) ✍

Dan Fortune

Following one of the early traditions of the eccentric detective, Collins created a one-armed P.I. whose physical limitations would make him unique in the hard-boiled world. Fortune's handicap links directly to his wild youth, and serves as a symbol of how this detective is isolated from a normal existence. Otherwise, as the series develops, the themes mature, as does the detective. **Hard-boiled**. Series subject: **Physically challenged**

Act of Fear. Dodd Mead, 1967

A New York patrolman is mugged and the crime takes on significance when Pete Vitanza hires Fortune to finds his friend, Jo-Jo Olsen, who went missing at the same time as the mugging. Pete takes a beating for hiring Fortune, and Fortune is warned off the case by the mob. However, a trip to Florida gives him the last clue he needs to discover who murdered a mobster's girl. ED

Florida, Spanish Beach • New York, New York

The Brass Rainbow. Dodd Mead, 1969

Sammy Weiss needs Fortune as an alibi when the small-time gambler gets into the big time—a man he threatened is found murdered. The police now want to know what Fortune is doing alibing a killer when he discovers a missing $25,000 that could provide the motive for murder.

New York, New York

Night of the Toads. Dodd Mead, 1970

Rey Vega is a big-time producer who wants to muscle in on the contract of Fortune's actress girlfriend, Marty. Fortune discovers that she is not alone in feeling the pressure and decides to save all the women under Vega's thumb.

New York, New York • Theater

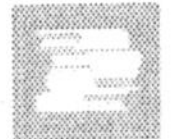

Walk a Black Wind. Dodd Mead, 1971

The day after a cocktail waitress is found murdered, a man who has only known her for two weeks offers Fortune a big fee to hunt for her killer. When it turns out that the dead girl was living under an assumed name and was the daughter of an upstate New York mayor, Fortune finds her death will take him in directions that he did not expect.

New York, New York

Shadow of a Tiger. Dodd Mead, 1972

The wife of a French pawnbroker seeks Fortune out to determine the truth behind her husband's death. Fortune finds that the pawnbroker was tied up and brutally beaten and his shop ransacked, yet $300 was left behind in the cash register. The crime has the earmarks of an inside job, and he must deal with a wide-ranging cast of characters before his investigation ends.

New York, New York

The Silent Scream. Dodd Mead, 1973

Mia Morgan gives Fortune a photograph of a blonde and tells him to find her without asking Mia any questions. The job proves easy, and the woman is identified as Diana Woods, with the only remaining question being what is the connection between the two women.

New York, New York

Blue Death. Dodd Mead, 1975

Leslie Carter's husband has failed to pay a debt, and she hires Fortune to deliver the money her husband owed to the International Metals and Refining Corporation. Fortune has difficulty until he hunts down Walter Berger, President of IMRC, and delivers the money, only to have the act lead to a death.

New York, New York

The Blood-Red Dream. Dodd Mead, 1976

Fortune is asked to locate Kate Vytautis's old grandfather. When it turns out that some Eastern European freedom fighters and a gang of urban militants are also interested in the old man, the case proves more difficult than Fortune had anticipated.

New York • New York

The Nightrunners. Dodd Mead, 1978

Bradley Kern could be the heir to a fortune from his father's chemical empire. However, he is in a Mexican jail waiting for his cousin Bill Kern to arrive with $8,000 bail money. When the compulsive gambler Kern takes off with the money, the family hires Fortune to spring their son.

Connecticut

The Slasher. Dodd Mead, 1980

Fortune hears from his old girlfriend Marty, whose husband's niece appears to be the tenth victim of the Canyon Slasher. Fortune goes to the West Coast where Marty and the girl's roommate have some doubts about laying this one at the doorstep of the serial killer.

California, Los Angeles • Serial killer

Freak. Dodd Mead, 1983

A note on the door claiming "freak, freak, freak" is the only clue that Ian Campbell finds after he returns from a two-month absence to finds his son and his son's wife missing and their assets liquidated. Suspicions about Ian Campbell's company and threats from two hoods convince Fortune that he is on the right track.

New Jersey, Chatham

Minnesota Strip. Fine. 1987

Jeanne-Marie, a Vietnamese refugee, is murdered walking the streets on New York's Minnesota Strip, and she was a woman that Fortune was hired to find. His client, Judy Lavelle, is also interested in Roy Carter, her boyfriend, and a man who was also hunting Jeanne-Marie. It is up to Fortune to figure out how white slavery and smuggling figures into this murder.

New York, New York • Prostitution

Red Rosa. Fine, 1988

Fortune's proximity to the death of an old bag woman interests him in her plight, and when he discovers she is the thrice-married former American Communist Party activist Rosa Gruenfeld, he knows her past may have led to her murder.

New York, New York

Castrato. Fine, 1989

After moving to California, Fortune's first case involves client Dianne Owen's search for the brother of her ex-husband Frank. The first body found has ties to the CIA and the Salvadoran rebels, and Fortune needs to figure out whether this is a domestic problem or an international one.

California, Santa Barbara

Chasing Eights. Fine, 1990

Jack Price believes he is suspect number one when one of the players in his weekly poker game is murdered. When he disappears, his wife's only recourse is to hire Fortune to find her husband. Over a 15-hour period, Fortune concludes the case by playing a cat-and-mouse game with Jack, his wife, and the underworld of Santa Barbara's Nighttown section.

California, Santa Barbara

The Irishman's Horse. Fine, 1991

Hired by the wife of a State Department executive when her husband disappears from the U.S. embassy in Guatemala, Fortune finds himself on the track of the mysterious Madrona, a man deep into gun and drug smuggling. A company fronting for the drug traffic becomes the hunting ground, and when one of its executives is murdered, Fortune knows he is on the right track.

Guatemala, Guatemala City

Cassandra in Red. Fine, 1992

Fortune is hired to look into the knifing of Cassandra Reilly. She was a homeless person whose background and education allowed her to be a spokesperson for Santa Barbara's underclass. Her outspoken nature is also the reason she was murdered.

California, Santa Barbara

Crime, Punishment and Resurrection. Fine, 1992

A collection of the following stories: "The Big Rock Candy Mountain," "Black in the Snow," "Crime and Punishment," "The Motive," "No One Likes to be Played for a Sucker," "The Oldest Killer," "Resurrection," "Who?," and "The Woman Who Ruined John Ireland."

Short stories

Fortune's World. Crippen & Landru, 2000

A collection of the following stories: "Angel Eyes," "Can Shoot," "The Chair," "Culture Clash," "A Death in Montecito," "Eighty Million Dead," "Family Values," "Killer's Mind," "Long Shot," "A Matter of Character," "Murder is Murder," "A Reason to Die," "Role Model," and "Scream All the Way."

Short stories

Thomas B. Dewey ✍

Mac

The Midwest is used to advantage by Dewey, whose Mac is similar to Ross Macdonald's Archer, in that the basis for many of the cases can be found in the rich and troubled past of the characters. As with many of the private detectives from this period, Mac is a relatively anonymous character. The focus of the series is on establishing truth and dealing with it in a compassionate way. The social significance of the plots is another strength of this series, and the writing is literary without being pretentious. **Traditional/Hard-boiled**.

Draw the Curtain Close. Jefferson, 1947 (Also published as *Dame In Danger*. Dell, 1958)

Mac is called to the estate of big-time hood Warfield, who wants Mac to guard Warfield's wife from some unspecified danger. Mac refuses. Warfield ships a package to his wife through Mac, and when the delivery person is murdered, Mac is drawn into protecting Cynthia Warfield from danger.

Illinois, Chicago

Every Bet's a Sure Thing. Simon & Schuster, 1953

When the International Agency's detective is spotted tailing Harriet Mitchell, he is killed, and Mac accepts the assignment of following the woman. Boarding her train, Mac soon finds himself tossed off, but his attachment to the woman's son keeps him on the case.

California, Los Angeles • Trains

Prey for Me. Simon & Schuster, 1954 (Also published as *The Case of the Murdered Model.* Avon, 1955)

The nude body of a woman with two names is found on a white shag rug, and in her directory she circled the names of a commercial photographer and Mac. Called in by his cop friend, Mac finds himself hired by the father of a department store heir and charged with clearing the boy's name.

Illinois, Chicago

The Mean Streets. Simon & Schuster, 1955

Mac goes undercover as a schoolteacher to investigate juvenile delinquency in the school district. His attention is drawn to Louis and Joey Arvin, who are involved with reefers and a mysterious Mr. Smith. Despite his doubts about his ability to work in this environment, he is able to take some steps to help the students.

Academia

The Brave, Bad Girls. Simon & Schuster, 1956

Sherry Turner is willing to pay Mac $200 just to have him see her home when she believes she is being followed by two men. Mac finds himself beaten and mistaken for a man named Kadek. When he is politely apologized to for taking an incorrect beating, his curiosity leads him to another woman with ties to this odd case.

Illinois, Chicago

You've Got Him Cold. Simon & Schuster, 1958

Charles Traven goes on a bender after an argument with his wife, and when he sneaks home in shame he finds her dead. He turns to Mac for help, but is slain by the police, and Mac feels obliged to investigate anyway.

Illinois, Chicago

The Case of the Chased and the Unchaste. Random House, 1959

Mac flies to L.A. to bodyguard a five-year-old girl whose father has been receiving threatening letters demanding money or else. A dysfunctional household helps provide plenty of suspects, and things heat up when a suspicious suicide may be a homicide.

California, Los Angeles

The Girl Who Wasn't There. Simon & Schuster, 1960 (Also published as *The Girl Who Never Was.* Mayflower, 1962)

Mac would like to help Virgie Henley when she believes her husband's year-old death was not an accident, but it is not until she is followed and threatened that he can get a clue to follow. She is able to identify her stalker, but a car bomb nearly ends Mac's life, and he wonders whether the danger lies in the past or the present.

Illinois, Chicago

How Hard to Kill. Simon & Schuster, 1962

When Cathy discovers her husband dead, she turns to Mac for help before calling the police. Under their suspicious scrutiny, Mac must explain away his personal relationship to Cathy and his potential as suspect number one.

Illinois, Chicago

A Sad Song Singing. Simon & Schuster, 1963

Cress has been left a suitcase by her musician lover, Richie Darden, and while he is out on the road she is being pursued by men who would kill her to get its contents. Turning to Mac for protection earns him a beating, but creates a determination to help this girl.

Illinois, Chicago

Don't Cry for Long. Simon & Schuster, 1964

Mac is on assignment at a political rally when he witnesses the death of Joe Flannery, bodyguard to Congressman Farnum's daughter, but he is able to prevent her kidnapping. Hired to protect the Congressman from a blackmailer, Mac finds he must bait a trap to bring the person to justice.

Blackmail • Illinois, Chicago

Portrait of a Dead Heiress. Simon & Schuster, 1965

The fiancé of heiress Lorrie King is convinced she did not commit suicide, so Peter Kramm hires Mac to work along side the cops who also have their suspicions. When Mac discovers her money is missing and she had a lover, he realizes he and his client are going to be surprised by what they discover.

Illinois, Chicago

Deadline. Simon & Schuster, 1966

Peter Davidian is going to die in the electric chair if Mac does not discover evidence to save his life. Travelling to the small Illinois town where the clues lie, Mac finds himself in a hostile environment with just four days to prevent an unjust execution.

Illinois, Wesley

Death and Taxes. Putnam, 1967

Marco Paul wants Mac to deliver a million dollars to Marco's daughter, but Paul is killed before he can reveal the location of the cash. With everyone assuming he knows where the money is, Mac finds himself on the run through Chicago's underworld, trying to stay one step ahead of those who would kill him to get to the cash.

Illinois, Chicago

The King Killers. U.S.: Putnam, 1968 (U.K.: *Death Turns Right.* Hale, 1969)

Nat Pines has sold a load of guns to the League of Good Government, and Mac is sent to collect the payment. However, the guns were no good, and Mac is left with a corpse in his apartment and a simple collection case that has turned sour.

Illinois, Chicago

The Love-Death Thing. Simon & Schuster, 1969

Bernard Reinhart hires Mac to go to Southern California and find his missing daughter, Dawn. Finding her is simple, but when he finds her working in a mob-controlled massage parlor, getting her to return proves to be a whole different thing.

California, Los Angeles

The Taurus Trip. Simon & Schuster, 1970

Relocated to California, Mac is hired to protect aging actor Peter Rinaldi when a threatening note to him leads to the death of Michele Armande, another aging actress. What is the secret held in the Hollywood film community that would threaten the lives of these elderly stars?

California, Los Angeles • Film

Stanley Ellin ✍

Murray Kirk

The Eighth Circle won the Edgar when it introduced P.I. Murray Kirk and became an instant classic in this genre. This single novel is an example of the meeting between the hard-boiled and noir, and puts into perspective the eternal question about the private eye. Is he a good man forced to do bad things because of the people he deals with, or is he a bad man able to survive as a bottomfeeder? **Hard-boiled.**

The Eighth Circle. Random House, 1958

Murray has fallen in love with Ruth, the fiancée of a cop named Arnold who is under indictment for perjury. Hired by Arnold's rather naïve lawyer to prove that Arnold is innocent, Murray may be more interested in making the cop look bad. ED

New York, New York

John Evans (pseud. of Howard Browne) ✍

Paul Pine

Evans, a former fiction editor and screenwriter, created a midwestern hero in Pine, a Chicagoland P.I. with a hard-boiled sensibility. Evan's work can be compared favorably with Thomas B. Dewey or Ross Macdonald. The early books in the series appeared under the pseudonym of Evans, and the later books under the author's real name. **Traditional/Hard-boiled**. Series subject: **Illinois, Chicago**.

Halo in Blood. Bobbs-Merrill, 1946

Pine is hired by John Sandmark to try and split up his daughter and her fiancé. The first night on the job leads to the fiancé's death, and Pine finds himself allied with nightclub owner, D'Allemand, who wants to find out who killed his shill. Falling for the client's daughter only complicates the case for Pine as he finds his clues lie out of state and in the past.

Halo for Satan. Bobbs-Merrill, 1948

Bishop McManus puts Pine on the trail of a manuscript that purports to be the testament of Jesus Christ in his own hand. When the man who has the manuscript disappears and a dead hood involves the underworld, Pine finds himself with three potential clients, all of whom want the sacred text.

Religion

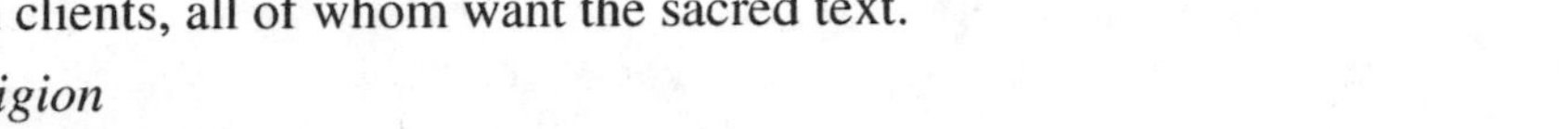

Halo in Brass. Bobbs-Merrill, 1949

The Fremonts want their daughter back, and Pine drives to Lincoln to begin his search. Discovering that another woman, Grace Rehak, left Lincoln at the same time, Pine must decide which woman he is searching for to discover the truth of either woman's whereabouts.

The Taste of Ashes (by Howard Browne). Simon & Schuster, 1957

Pod Hamp has made a threatening phone call to Serena Delastone about her daughter, Karen, and some letters and photos that should not be made public. Pine knows the first P.I. to work this case is dead and that the scandal of Edwin Delastone still hangs over this family.

Browne, Howard • Illinois, Olympia Heights

The Paper Gun (by Howard Browne). Dennis McMillan, 1985.

A collection of the following stories: "The Paper Gun," and "So Dark for April."

Browne, Howard • Short stories

A. A. Fair (pseud. of Erle Stanley Gardner) ✍

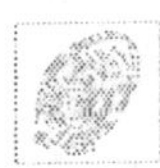

Bertha Cool/Donald Lam

A. A. Fair and Rex Stout both managed to create a blend of the eccentric detective and the hard-boiled P.I. But unlike Stout's eccentric great thinking detective, Nero Wolfe, who is treated with some respect, Bertha is not a very good detective. Her eccentricities make her a fun character, and a great foil for Lam, the traditional P.I. It is Lam's abilities that really make the series shine, and he should appeal to any hard-boiled mystery reader, while the battle of the sexes between the two could appeal to soft-boiled and traditional mystery readers. **Soft-boiled/Traditional/Hard-boiled**. Series subjects: **California, Los Angeles • Teams**.

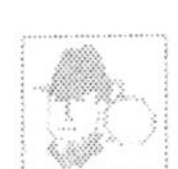

The Bigger They Come. U.S.: Morrow, 1939 (U.K.: *Lam to the Slaughter.* H. Hamilton, 1939)

On the very first day he is hired by Cool, Lam is sent to find Morgan Birks and serve him with a divorce decree. Morgan is a fugitive, and Lam finds that Morgan's wife, Sandra, and her best friend, Alma, want to assist him in his investigation. Ironically, Lam was disbarred for proving you can legally commit murder in California, and this case echoes those circumstances.

Turn on the Heat. Morrow, 1940

Lam is given the job of tracking down a woman missing since her marriage broke up in 1918, and he is warned off the case as soon as he reaches the town of Oakview. His investigation prompts the return of the missing Mrs. Lintig and the discovery of the whereabouts of her husband James. However, an interested female journalist is the one to discover the first body, and Lam needs to manipulate everyone to keep his client and himself out of jail.

California, Oakview

Gold Comes in Bricks. Morrow, 1940

Henry Ashbury's daughter Alta is being tapped for money and he hires Cool, who sends in Lam disguised as a physical trainer. Discovering that Alta is being blackmailed for an affair with a man who is accused of murdering his wife, Lam finds himself deep into a mining stock scam that has led to murder.

Blackmail

Spill the Jackpot! Morrow, 1941

Cool sends Lam after Corla Burke, a woman missing two days prior to her wedding date, and Lam falls for one of the suspects in the case. Helen Framley has been rigging slots, and it is her partner's murder that begins to draw Lam towards Corla's location.

Gambling · Nevada, Las Vegas

Double or Quits. Morrow, 1941

Lam goes to Dr. Hilton Devarest's home, where a jewel robbery has been committed, only to discover the doctor dead from carbon monoxide poisoning and the stolen jewels in the glove compartment of Devarest's car. A missing secretary is accused, but the chauffeur is an ex-con, and an adventurer who takes advantage of women is also present. Lam needs to scramble on this case as he is suspect number one.

Owls Don't Blink. Morrow, 1942

Cool and Lam go to New Orleans to meet a New York lawyer named Hale who wants to find a girl named Roberta Fenn who disappeared three years prior. Once found, the woman disappears again when a dead lawyer ends up in her apartment. A second woman, whose name has been borrowed by Fenn, is also hiding, and her husband wants an explanation. It is Lam's brains that keep the two detectives out of trouble and on the hunt.

Louisiana, New Orleans

Bats Fly at Dusk. Morrow, 1942

The connection between a secretary hit by a car and her dead boss's will are the issue when Cool is hired by a blind beggar with an interest in the girl. With Lam in the Navy, Cool is on her own, until she is jailed for her investigation, and Lam gets a 36-hour pass to save his boss.

Wills

Cats Prowl at Night. Morrow, 1943

Everett Bender comes to Cool with a wild tale of finances, former business partners, and greedy wives, but the case gets sidetracked when his maid is murdered and his wife is missing. Sued by the man's secretary, and without Lam because of his military service, Cool scrambles to stay one step ahead of the client and the cops.

Give 'Em the Ax. U.S.: Morrow, 1944 (U.K.: *An Axe to Grind.* Heinemann, 1951)

Despite his post-WWII trauma, Lam accepts the case of a woman named Georgia Rushe who believes her boss and lover, Ellery Crail, has mistakenly married a fortune-hunting woman named Irma. Knowing that Irma has a history of auto accident claims, Lam pushes in that area and discovers the murder of one of her victims. Chasing a master blackmailer keeps Lam on the scent of several cross-schemes.

Crows Can't Count. Morrow, 1946

Lam is hired by Harry Sharples to determine where a certain piece of antique jewelry has gone. It has left the possession of a ward and gone to a South American estate for which Sharples is the trustee. Discovering that a fellow trustee's murder may relate to the fact that he has the jewelry, Lam goes to South America to try to unravel this case of estates and emeralds.

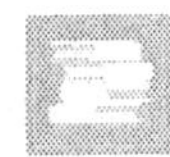

Colombia, Medellin • Jewels

Fools Die on Friday. Morrow, 1947

Secretary Carlotta Hanford wants Cool and Lam to keep her real estate boss, Gerald Baldwin, from being poisoned by his wife Daphne. When both husband and wife are poisoned, Daphne dies and Gerald recovers, and the police are suspicious that Lam may have had a hand in the evil deed.

Bedrooms Have Windows. Morrow, 1949

Lam is trapped in a murder/suicide that leaves him the fall guy, and he needs to trace client Lucille Hart to get the answers. When Lucille is strangled, the police figure Lam is the guilty party again, and police ally Sellers now treats Lam as a culprit rather than a friend.

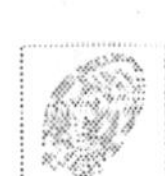

Top of the Heap. Morrow, 1952

Over Lam's objections, Cool orders him to alibi the very rich John Carver Billings and his involvement with mobster Gabby Garvanza's girlfriend, Maurine Auburn. With Garvanza dead and the involvement of a mining company's interest heating up the pot, Cool and Lam dissolve their association over the tempest.

California, San Francisco

Some Women Won't Wait. Morrow, 1953

Stephenson Bicknell wants a woman tailed to Hawaii, and both detectives reluctantly end up shipboard for the islands. Lam finds himself chasing one woman to get to another, only to discover that both woman are the victims of blackmail in paradise.

Blackmail • Hawaii, Honolulu • Shipboard

Beware the Curves. Morrow, 1956

Six years prior in Paris, writer John Dittmar Ansel was given an idea for a novel by a man named Karl, and now he wants to locate the man and clear the rights. Lam is suspicious of his client, and learns that Karl has been murdered. Wanting the reward money that is offered, Lam puts his brains to use to try and solve this mystery.

California, Susanville

You Can Die Laughing. Morrow, 1957

Texan oilman Lawton Corning is interested in the missing Yvonne Wells whose signature is crucial to a land deal Corning needs to close. With Yvonne's husband cooperating and his neighbor a key witness, Lam sets out on a trail of a possible murder tied to the ownership of the inherited land.

California, Banning

Some Slips Don't Show. Morrow, 1957

Barclay Fisher went to a convention where he was indiscreet, and now he wants the Cool-Lam agency to stop a possible blackmail attempt that would ruin his marriage. Lam feels the woman may be innocent, but her boyfriend the real culprit, and the pressure is turned up when his client is threatened with exposure.

Blackmail • California, San Francisco

The Count of Nine. Morrow, 1958

Wealthy adventurer Dan Crockett II has decided to throw a big party, and he needs the protection of the Cool-Lam Agency to keep gatecrashers from stealing his valuables. Cool blows the assignment, and Lam steps in to begin a search for the missing artifacts only to have a blowgun used against its owner.

Pass the Gravy. Morrow, 1959

Fifteen-year-old Sandy Eden wants the Cool-Lam agency to find her uncle Amos because her family benefits from the same trust fund that will pay Amos off if he makes it to his thirty-fifth birthday without being convicted of a major crime. Daphne Beckley wants to know if Amos has made her a widow, and trustee Jerome Campbell makes Lam suspicious that this case will turn to murder.

California, Bakersfield

Kept Women Can't Quit. Morrow, 1960

Sergeant Frank Sellers is angry with Lam when a suspect Lam represents in a huge armored car robbery investigation has only half of the money in his possession, claiming that the cops took the rest. Sellers needs the Cool-Lam agency to clear his own name, and the detectives decide they can work for their adversary.

Bachelors Get Lonely. Morrow, 1961

Montrose Carson suspects that someone in his office is leaking real estate secrets to his chief rival, and he wants the Cool-Lam agency to plug the leak. So Cool sets Lam up as one of Montrose's clients to try and attract the rival firm. The scam leads to Irene Addis, but Lam looks beyond the obvious and finds a Peeping Tom, a stripper, and murderer.

Shills Can't Cash Chips. U.S.: Morrow, 1961 (U.K.: *Stop at the Red Light.* Heinemann, 1959)

Consolidated Interinsurance needs to locate Vivian Deshler about an auto accident, and they hire Lam to trace her through Vivian's best friend, Doris Ashley. Dudley Bedford is Doris's boyfriend, and he tries to turn Lam and gain help scamming the insurance company. But when money schemes turn to murder, the police become interested in Lam's activities.

California, Colinda

Try Anything Once. Morrow, 1962.

Carleton Allen is upset that he took Sharon Baker to a motel. His indiscretion threatens him, but he is also upset because that night Ronley Fisher was murdered in a nearby motel pool. He wants Lam to check back in under his false name to lead the police away from him, and Lam refuses. But Cool says yes, and soon Lam is up to his neck in the police investigation.

Fish or Cut Bait. Morrow, 1963

Jarvis Archer wants his secretary followed to find out what is bothering her, and the Cool-Lam Agency goes on a 24-hour watch when the secretary reveals that she is the victim of a stalker. Lam's suspicions are focused on Archer, while Cool is suspicious of the victim, Marilyn Chelan.

Up for Grabs. Morrow, 1964

Homer Breckenridge of the All Purpose Insurance Company needs an investigator just like Lam to fly out to Tucson and look into Helmann Bruno's claim of whiplash injuries from an auto accident. At the Butte Valley Guest Ranch, all of its visitors have been tricked into accepting a vacation there by the insurance company, which hopes it can disclaim liabilities for their injuries.

Arizona, Tucson • Insurance

Cut Thin to Win. Morrow, 1965

Clayton Dawson has a daughter, Phyllis, who is involved with Sidney Elton, a man of whom her father does not approve. Phyllis may have been driving drunk and responsible for striking a woman. When Lam ends up a bagman on a payoff to the victim, he needs to clear himself of the charges.

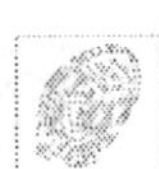

Widows Wear Weeds. Morrow, 1966

Nicholas Baffin is being blackmailed, and he figures that making a big show of paying off the amount through the Cool-Lam Agency will discourage the blackmailers from ever coming back. But the woman in the blackmail photos with Baffin disappears, and the blackmailers give up the photos without a fight. So Lam tries to investigate why this threat suddenly became meaningless.

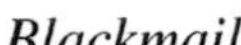
Blackmail

Traps Need Fresh Bait. Morrow, 1967

Barney Adams is an investigator for Continental Divide Insurance, and he is worried when an ad appears soliciting witnesses to an accident in which his company is involved. So Barney pays Lam to answer the ad and find out what is up with the other litigants in the accident.

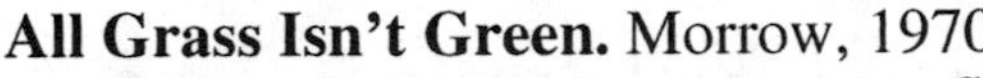
All Grass Isn't Green. Morrow, 1970

Milton Carling Calhoun wants to find novelist C. E. Hale, but when Lam tracks Hale down, someone has cleared out his apartment. The trail leads to a smuggling operation with connections to Mexican drugs, and eventually to a murder.

Brett Halliday (pseud. of Davis Dresser and House Name) ✍

Mike Shayne

The big redheaded detective from Miami was a hard-boiled operator whose adventures stretched over most of this period of the private eye development. Attended by his faithful secretary Lucy, and united with his best friends, newspaper reporter Tim Rourke and cop Will Gentry, he solves most of his cases in Miami. Eventually, the character became a house name at the publisher and the series was continued by other authors, but the stories and the character continue to be one of the best P.I.s in this period. See a Mike Shayne website at http://www.mikeshayne.com. **Hard-boiled**. Series subject: **Florida, Miami**.

Dividend on Death. Holt, 1939

Phyllis Brighton has been convinced she has an Electra complex and wants to kill her mother, so when Shayne arrives at the Brighton estate and finds the mother dead, he doctors the evidence to protect Phyllis. The family nurse is next to be killed, and Shayne has to pursue his case despite being wounded.

The Private Practice of Michael Shayne. Holt, 1940

Originally approached by lawyer and best friend Larry Kincaid to retrieve some information for Kincaid's client, Elliot Thomas, Shayne finds himself riding to the rescue of Phyllis Brighton again. The information was to clear Thomas, but Shayne feels set up when his gun is used to kill the lounge lizard enticing Phyllis into her bad ways.

The Uncomplaining Corpses. Holt, 1940

Arnold Thrip wants to hire Shayne to burgle his own house, but Shayne sends Joe Darnell in his place. Joe is murdered and so is Thrip's wife. The dead woman thought her husband wanted her money, but the dead woman's brother has just been released from prison, paroled from a murder charge.

Tickets to Death. Holt, 1941

Shayne misses an opportunity to gain information from a tipster when the tipster is murdered. He journeys to a small town, where counterfeit greyhound racing tickets are causing concern for the local paper, a gambler, and a nervous stockholder.

Florida, Cocopalm

Bodies Are Where You Find Them. Holt, 1941

It's election time in Miami Beach, and Shayne is backing Jim Marsh against Burt Stallings. When a girl with dirt on Stallings ends up dead in his bed, he hides the body, only to have it disappear. The corpse is Helen Stallings, Burt's daughter, and the heat is on to solve her murder.

The Corpse Came Calling. Dodd Mead, 1942 (Also published as *The Case of the Walking Corpse.* Handi-Books, 1943)

Shayne is visited by a dying New York P.I. who utters, "They didn't get . . ." and dies clutching part of a claim ticket. A visit from a beautiful woman who wants her husband murdered and two hoods looking for the claim ticket lead Shayne onto the trail of some German spies.

Espionage

Murder Wears a Mummer's Mask. Dodd Mead, 1943 (Also published as *In a Deadly Vein.* Dell, 1956)

Shayne and his wife Phyllis are on vacation when an actress in a big festival production spies her long-lost father. He has just hit a big gold strike, and soon he is murdered. Suspicion falls on the old man's partners, but then another actress is murdered.

Colorado, Central City · Theater

Blood on the Black Market. Dodd Mead, 1943 (Also published as *Heads You Lose.* Torquill, 1958)

Late one night Clem Wilson calls Shayne from his service station and tries to hire him, but is killed while on the phone. Evidence at the scene indicates someone is evading the WWII gas-rationing restrictions, and the most likely suspects are some gangsters connected to the dead man's AWOL son.

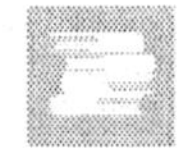

World War II

Michael Shayne's Long Chance. Dodd Mead, 1944

Plans to move to New York are held up when Shayne heads to New Orleans to find the drug-addicted daughter of a New York editor. When he rooms near Barbara Little and she ends up a corpse, he becomes suspect number one for the New Orleans cops.

Louisiana, New Orleans

Murder and the Married Virgin. Dodd Mead, 1944

Shayne believes the story of the lieutenant whose fiancée committed suicide on the eve of their wedding. He agrees to clear the name of the dead woman, who stood accused of stealing the Ghorski emerald from her employers, the Lomax family.

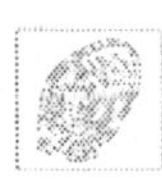

Jewels · Louisiana, New Orleans

Murder Is My Business. Dodd Mead, 1945

A young soldier, tied to a spy ring, is run over by Jefferson Towne, candidate for the mayor of El Paso. Shayne's evidence proves the soldier was dead before he was hit, but Towne wants nothing to do with Shayne, as he has had an association with the man's daughter.

Mexico, Juarez

Marked for Murder. Dodd Mead, 1945

Tim Rourke, Shayne's lifelong pal and a newspaperman, is using the power of the press to pressure a hood named Brenner who wants to open gambling casinos in Miami Beach. When Tim is shot, Shayne returns from his New Orleans exile to hunt for Tim's assassin.

Blood on Biscayne Bay. Ziff-Davis, 1946

Shayne takes care of a marker held on Christine Hudson by gambler Arnold Barbizon by force, rather than with the string of pearls she had provided to pay off her debts. This leads to the murder of Hudson's maid, Natalie, and the revelation that the string of pearls had a purpose.

Counterfeit Wife. Ziff-Davis, 1947

When he is jilted by his secretary Lucy, still in New Orleans, Shayne sells his ticket to that city to a man for $200. When the bills are part of a ransom, Shayne ends up with the man's suitcase containing the rest of the ransom, the man's big blonde accomplice, and a dead body in his apartment.

Blood on the Stars. Dodd Mead, 1948 (U.K.: *Murder is a Habit.* Jarrolds, 1951)

While the cops think Shayne is the most likely person to have stolen the rare ruby bracelet, the owner, Mark Dustin, thinks Shayne is the most likely person to recover it. When someone tries to murder Lucy and Mrs. Dustin takes a powder, Shayne knows he is deep into another mystery.

Michael Shayne's Triple Mystery. Ziff-Davis, 1948 (Also published as *Dead Man's Diary and Dinner at Dupre's.* Dell, 1950; *A Taste for Cognac.* Dell, 1951)

A collection of the following stories: "Dead Man's Diary," "Dinner at Dupre's," and "A Taste for Cognac."

Short stories

A Taste for Violence. Dodd Mead, 1949

When Shayne receives a letter from Charles Roche predicting Roche's death, Shayne and Lucy travel to Kentucky just in time to read about his death in the paper. Charles had just been about to take an active role in managing his father's mines, previously operated by a trust and managed by Seth Gerald. Perhaps the clue lies in the fact that Charles was prepared to settle with the miners who are striking against the mine.

Kentucky, Centerville • Mining

Call for Michael Shayne. Dodd Mead, 1949

Arthur Devlin wakes up next to a corpse 11 days after he was supposed to be sailing aboard The Belle of the Caribbean on vacation. The last thing he remembers is the bon voyage party, and he has no explanation for his current clothes, his beard, the corpse under his bed, and the $10,000 in his pockets. Recognized as Joey by a stranger, he turns to Shayne to unravel the mess.

Florida, Key West

This Is It, Michael Shayne. Dodd Mead, 1950

Shayne receives a message from reporter Sara Morton, and when he and Tim O'Rourke explore, they discover her body in her hotel room. Shayne seeks to discover what was behind the threatening notes sent to the woman prior to her death.

Framed in Blood. Dodd Mead, 1951

Bert Jackson is a newspaper reporter with an idea that could lead to blackmail, and when he tries to hire Shayne and Tim to run interference, he is tossed out of Shayne's office. When death strikes close to home, Shayne decides he will have to work on this case anyway.

Blackmail

What Really Happened. Dodd Mead, 1952

Four things happen in rapid succession: Shayne is warned to ignore any communications from Wanda Weatherly; Shelia Martin asks to see Shayne about Wanda; Tim Rourke's friend, Ralph Flannagan, is accused of trying to murder Wanda; and Shayne stumbles on Wanda's dead body.

When Dorinda Dances. Dodd Mead, 1951

When Dorinda dances, men drool, but the fact that someone thinks she is the daughter of Judge Lansdowne could lead to the end of her father's career.

One Night with Nora. U.S.: Torquil/Dodd Mead, 1953 (U.K.: *The Lady Came By Night.* Jarrolds, 1954)

Nora Carrol crawls into Shayne's bed one night until she realizes that he is not her husband Ralph. When she discovers she is off by one floor in the apartment building, it may be a good thing as Ralph is dead in the apartment above Shayne's bed.

She Woke to Darkness. Torquil/Dodd Mead, 1954

Brett Halliday is attending the Mystery Writers of America Edgar award banquet in New York when Elsie Murray, an aspiring writer, pushes an unwanted manuscript upon the author. When he discovers the writer has been murdered, he brings Shayne up from Miami to solve the crime.

Authors • New York, New York

Death Has Three Lives. Torquil/Dodd Mead, 1955

From out of Lucy's New Orleans's past steps Jack Bristow, shot by someone he thought he had murdered. While Shayne holds off the cops, Bristow escapes, and Shayne finds himself protecting Lucy from a charge of accessory to murder.

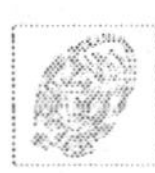

Stranger in Town. Torquil/Dodd Mead, 1955

Returning from vacation, Shayne stops at a bar in Brockton where a beautiful girl with amnesia intrigues him, and two hoods try to run him over with their car. Staying on to probe into the girl's secret, he leaves Lucy holding the fort in Miami against some hoods who may want to rub him out.

Florida, Brockton

The Blonde Cried Murder. Torquil/Dodd Mead, 1956

Things are hopping at the Hibiscus when a woman calls from a man's room to report a murder. While the house detective is finding no one home, Shayne is sitting in his office listening to the woman's story. Soon he is investigating the disappearance of her murdered brother's corpse.

Weep for a Blonde. Torquil/Dodd Mead, 1957

Richard Kane has become obsessed with the idea that his wife, Lydia, an old friend of Shayne's dead wife Phyllis, is romancing Shayne. Taking Lydia as a client makes sense until she is murdered and Shayne is left holding the bag.

Shoot the Works. Torquil/Dodd Mead, 1957

Mrs. James Wallace arrives home a day early from a New York trip to find her husband, Jim, dead in his bed. Shayne is asked to discover why two tickets to South America were next to Jim's packed suitcase, and who decided to kill the man.

Murder and the Wanton Bride. Torquil/Dodd Mead, 1958

Walter Carson is murdered late one night with an appointment card in his pocket indicating he was to meet with Shayne the next morning. Shayne protests his innocence until he returns to his office and finds a woman from the dead man's home town who is trying to shut down a scandal involving Carson and his wife.

Fit to Kill (by Robert Terrall). Torquil/Dodd Mead, 1958

Tim Rourke is in an unnamed Central American country when the police confiscate his notes and beat him. This leads him to help an American undergraduate named Carla Adams escape the country, but when she is arrested by customs officials at the airport, Tim needs his old friend Shayne's help because she has stowed uncut diamonds in his typewriter case.

Terrall, Robert

Date with a Dead Man. Torquil/Dodd Mead, 1959

Mrs. Groat is worried when her husband is missing just two weeks after he was one of two men rescued when a plane crashed in the Atlantic. An expansion of the previously collected short story "Dead Man's Diary."

Target: Mike Shayne (by Robert Terrall). Torquil/Dodd Mead, 1959

After 13 years in jail, Bram Clayton is a little surprised to have Miriam Moore waiting for him when he is released. But he is not surprised to hear that she wants his help in knocking over a Miami Beach gambling operation. Before he accepts the task, Clayton makes the mistake of trying to revenge himself on Shayne.

Terrall, Robert

Die Like a Dog (author unknown). Torquil/Dodd Mead, 1959

Henrietta Rogel is the sister of the recently dead millionaire, John Rogel, and when she believes the family pet went the way of her brother, she hires Shayne to keep herself from being the next victim.

Murder Takes No Holiday (by Robert Terrall). Torquil/Dodd Mead, 1960

Shayne just happens to be taking a three-week holiday in St. Albans to recover from injuries when Pete Malloy of the Internal Revenue Service asks him to look into the death of one of his informants there. The dead man had tried to finger Paul Slater, who may be involved in a smuggling operation.

Caribbean, St. Albans • Terrall, Robert

Dolls Are Deadly (by [Walter] Ryerson Johnson). Torquil/Dodd Mead, 1960

Shayne does not want mobster Henny Henlein's business, but when Henny receives a voodoo doll, he wants Shayne to try and find out why. While Mike is out fishing, Henny's body washes ashore, and the police want Shayne to explain the situation.

Johnson, (Walter) Ryerson • Religion

The Homicidal Virgin (author unknown). Torquil/Dodd Mead, 1960

Tim Rourke's paper asks Shayne to answer an ad they received for a soldier of fortune. When he pretends to be Mike Wayne and answers the ad placed by Jane Smith, Shayne discovers a 19-year-old girl who wants her stepfather murdered.

Killers from the Keys (by [Walter] Ryerson Johnson). Torquil/Dodd Mead, 1961

Esther "Sloe Burn" Piney is a stripper with a thing for a man she wants Shayne to locate, and Mrs. Steve Renshaw is a woman on the lookout for her husband, who is wanted by the mob in Chicago. When Shayne realizes they are the same man, he begins to search in earnest for a man sitting on $200,000.

Johnson, (Walter) Ryerson

Murder in Haste (by Robert Terrall). Torquil/Dodd Mead, 1961

Sam Harris, convicted for the murder of Rose Heminway's husband, sits in his cell waiting to be executed in five days. But his wife, Norma, has been busy trying to convince Rose that she might have been mistaken in her testimony. She hires Shayne to help her twist the case around and earn the release of her husband.

Terrall, Robert

The Careless Corpse (author unknown). Torquil/Dodd Mead, 1961

Julio Peralta's wife, Laura, is missing an emerald bracelet, and he needs Shayne to help locate it. When he goes to Miami Beach to investigate, the local cops arrest him, and Lucy is taken hostage in the office to keep Shayne off the case.

Pay-Off in Blood (author unknown). Torquil/Dodd Mead, 1962

Shayne agrees to ride shotgun for a doctor friend of Tim Rourke who is trying to make one last payment to a blackmailer. But when someone takes a photo of the exchange, and the good doctor is murdered, Shayne is suddenly on the track of a killer.

Blackmail

Murder by Proxy (author unknown). Torquil/Dodd Mead, 1962

Ellen is on her own in Miami, taking a separate vacation from her husband Herbert, and her sexuality interests other men on the Miami nightscene. When five days go by and Herbert arrives to find Ellen's room unused at the hotel, he sets Shayne on her trail.

Never Kill a Client (author unknown). Torquil/Dodd Mead, 1962

Shayne gets one half of a thousand-dollar bill in the mail and an airplane ticket to Los Angeles. He cannot find his client, Else Cornell, when he reaches the West Coast, but soon he discovers she holds a secret important to the Cubans, and they want it back.

California, Los Angeles • Espionage

Too Friendly, Too Dead (author unknown). Torquil/Dodd Mead, 1963

When Linda Fitzgilpin went to bed, her husband, Jerome, was in the bed next to her. But when she is awakened by a phone call telling her he is dead in Miami Beach, she hires Shayne to discover the truth behind his bizarre behavior.

The Corpse That Never Was (author unknown). Torquil/Dodd Mead, 1963

Late one night the couple who live above Lucy commit suicide, and Shayne discovers that the woman was Elsa Armbruster Nathan, heiress and daughter of Eli Nathan. Nathan hires Shayne to explain her living arrangements and discover her murderer.

The Body Came Back (author unknown). Torquil/Dodd Mead, 1963

Carla Andrews is in Miami because her daughter is going to marry a newly elected state senator, when Carla's long-lost husband appears at her hotel. She murders him and tricks Shayne into removing the body when she sets up her own daughter, and Shayne finds himself in the middle of a nightmare that has him accused of murder.

A Redhead for Mike Shayne (author unknown). Torquil/Dodd Mead, 1964

Shayne is staking out a liquor warehouse late one night when he is forced to kill one member of the gang. The Russian-made gun that the hood had intrigues Shayne, and he follows the gun on a trail of more death and intrigue.

Shoot to Kill (author unknown). Torquil/Dodd Mead, 1964

Shayne reluctantly agrees to speak to a wayward wife because her husband, Ralph Larson, is a good friend of Tim Rourke. Dorothy Larson's affair is over, but Ralph murders her boss anyway. However, to Shayne's surprise, the ruling is that the boss was dead before Ralph killed him.

Michael Shayne's 50th Case (author unknown). Torquil/Dodd Mead, 1964

Marvin Blake returns early from a convention to find Harry Wilsson sneaking out of his wife's bedroom, so Marvin leaves to attempt suicide. He ends up Shayne's client when he fails at his attempt, but his wife is murdered and he stands accused.

Florida, Sunray Beach

The Violent World of Michael Shayne (by Robert Terrall). Dell, 1965

Trina Hitchcock needs Shayne to help her when her father, U.S. Senator Emory Hitchcock, is being blackmailed by Sam Toby over his affair with Maggie Smith. Shayne has one night to end this when Toby, a powerful lobbyist, is to appear the next day at a committee hearing chaired by Hitchcock.

Blackmail · Terrall, Robert · Washington, D.C.

Nice Fillies Finish Last (by Robert Terrall). Dell, 1965

Joey Dolan has a tip on a horse for Tim Rourke, but when Tim and Shayne go to the rendezvous, no Joey. When Joey is found murdered, Rourke is the investigator until he is in so deep he needs to call on his buddy Shayne to help him out.

Terrall, Robert

Murder Spins the Wheel (by Robert Terrall). Dell, 1966

Shayne arrives at the estate of big-time bookie Harry Bass just in time to prevent his murder, but not in time to prevent the loss of $200,000. Bass thinks someone may be rigging college football games, and he wants Shayne to find out who.

Gambling · Terrall, Robert

Armed . . . Dangerous . . . (by Robert Terrall). Dell, 1966

Taken prisoner by street thief Francis McQuade, Michelle Guerin becomes a witness to his brutal murder of a diamond carrier. She thinks he would be a great addition to her gang, but her big surprise will come when she discovers he is Shayne, undercover.

New York, New York • Terrall, Robert

Mermaid on the Rocks (by Robert Terrall). Dell, 1967

Kitty Sims invites Shayne and Tim Rourke down to her Key Gaspar place when someone cuts her pet cat's throat. When they all go snorkeling, they discover someone has altered Kitty's tank and she nearly drowns. The key to the solution of the crimes lies in an old will left behind by a Prohibition-age mobster.

Florida, Key Gaspar • Terrall, Robert • Wills

Guilty As Hell (by Robert Terrall). Dell, 1967

Candida Morse is executive secretary for headhunter Hal Begley, and she is the power behind the throne in such extracurricular activities as industrial espionage. When the principals involved in this case of missing information gather on a Georgia marsh to do some duck hunting, Walter Langhorne is shot. Shayne, in the hunting party, becomes a detective as well.

Terrall, Robert

So Lush, So Deadly (by Robert Terrall). Dell, 1968

Dotty De Rham is sailing on her ocean-going yacht to Brazil for a carnival, but she is also fighting with her husband and flirting with her husband's friend, Paul Henry. When she writes a new will disinheriting her husband, the fuel hits the fire. When the ship docks in Miami, her parents hire Shayne to straighten out the mess.

Shipboard • Terrall, Robert • Wills

Violence Is Golden (by Robert Terrall). Dell, 1968

International drug pusher Adam is still mad about Shayne's interference in *Armed . . . Dangerous . . .*, so he sends a team of assassins to Miami to murder Shayne at a Dolphin's game. Interpol's Jules LeFevre is murdered after giving Shayne enough clues to send him on a Caribbean odyssey to take down Adam.

Caribbean, St. Albans • Terrall, Robert

Lady, Be Bad (by Robert Terrall). Dell, 1969

When someone as connected as Sam Rapp arrives in the state capital to lobby for a gambling bill, the other side needs someone just as hard hitting, so Shayne and Rourke fly to Tallahassee to testify against the bill. When a Tampa mobster sends a hit man to prevent his testimony, Shayne finds protecting himself is as vital as not letting the bill pass.

Florida, Tallahassee • Terrall, Robert

Six Seconds to Kill (by Robert Terrall). Dell, 1970

U.S. Attorney General Eliot Crowther is in Miami to accept an award. Meanwhile, a newspaper is revealing his ties to a Latin American dictator through his law firm, the same firm that falsely convicted Felix Steele of murder. Now Steele's wife is being set up as the fall guy for the assassination, and Shayne has to scramble to prevent two crimes.

Terrall, Robert

Fourth Down to Death (by Robert Terrall). Dell, 1970

Sid Zacharias owns the Miami football team, and when star quarterback Ronnie James is injured in a game, he is suspicious. He thinks that Joe Truck, the quarterback's blocker who failed to carry out his assignment, may be on the take to help lay bets on the game. Sid hires Shayne to compete head to head with an investigator from the commissioner's office.

Football · Sports · Terrall, Robert

Count Backwards to Zero (by Robert Terrall). Dell, 1971

Shayne is coming off a very tough case in Bermuda when he decides to catch a ride on the Queen Elizabeth back to Miami. Someone on board is worried by Shayne's presence, and that gains him a beating. Then, he receives a proposition from Anne Blagden, and suddenly he is guarding a mysterious Bentley with an important cargo.

Shipboard · Terrall, Robert

I Come to Kill You (by Robert Terrall). Dell, 1971

A drunk and desperate Shayne is trying to gamble enough to pay off loan shark Larry Zito, and then he gets involved in a petty holdup that put the cops on his trail. As his life spirals out of control, Shayne finds himself drawn deeper and deeper into Zito's operation.

Caribbean, St. Albans · Organized crime · Terrall, Robert

Caught Dead (by Robert Terrall). Dell, 1972

Tim Rourke is in Venezuela to cover the story of the ouster of strongman Guillermo Alvares when an old acquaintance, Paula Obregon, talks him into taking some loaded cigarettes to the dictator at La Vega prison. When Tim is forced to switch places with another reporter, and the cigarettes blow up half the prison, Tim needs his pal Shayne to fly down and bail him out of a terrible situation.

Terrall, Robert · Venezuela, Caracas

Kill All the Young Girls (by Robert Terrall). Dell, 1973

Larry Zion of Consolidated-Famous Pictures is run off the road by an ambitious actress who wants the lead in *The Buccaneer*, and Zion's family hires Shayne to protect him from any more attempts. Kate Thackera proves to be a handful for Shayne to control, but when her murder is tied to a takeover bankrolled by a skin magazine publisher, Shayne finds himself deep into a case with many twists and turns.

Film · Terrall, Robert

Blue Murder (by Robert Terrall). Dell, 1973

Senator Nick Tucker's wife, Gretchen, has left him, and the young man is looking to Shayne for help. Gretchen has a history of drug use, and she has been seen in public with hood Frankie Capp. But the anti-pornography senator is in for one more surprise: his wife may be starring in a porn film.

Terrall, Robert · Pornography

Last Seen Hitchhiking (by Robert Terrall). Dell, 1974

Meri Gillespie is hitchhiking, but what makes everyone interested in her is that she has a pre-Columbian funeral mask in her knapsack that belongs to her companion, Professor Samuel Holloway. Frieda Field, another P.I., has been hired to find the girl who may have fallen prey to a serial killer murdering girls, and eventually Shayne is drawn into the case.

Antiquities · Florida · Terrall, Robert

At the Point of a .38 (by Robert Terrall). Dell, 1974

Shayne is rolling up to a late-night radio station where Tim Rourke is doing an interview show when he witnesses a murder in the parking lot. This event hooks Shayne up with the Shin Bet, or Israeli counterintelligence, and sets him on the trail of murder, drug smuggling, and international terrorism.

Terrall, Robert · Terrorism

Million Dollar Handle (by Robert Terrall). Dell, 1976

Shayne is surprised to find himself being judged guilty when evidence surfaces that he was on the take from Miami's biggest dog track owner. But then Max Gray is murdered, and Shayne risks going to jail on an even greater charge.

Terrall, Robert

Win Some, Lose Some (by Robert Terrall). Dell, 1976

Werner, an out-of-work architect, hooks up with his girl, Pam, and a rogue cop named Downey to kidnap a loan shark for the ransom he could bring. But when Eddie Maye ends up dead, his widow hires Shayne to track down the kidnappers and avenge her husband's death.

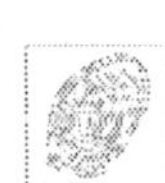

Kidnapping · Terrall, Robert

Jonathan Latimer ✍

Bill Crane

These novels were written in an era when alcoholism was socially acceptable as a comedic device, and Crane takes full advantage of this, claiming he can only solve a case when he is loaded. Employed by an agency headed by The Colonel, Crane is sent all over the country as an operative. These novels are reminiscent of the screwball comedy films of this period. **Soft-boiled/Traditional**. Series subject: **Humor**.

Murder in the Madhouse. Doubleday, 1935

Miss Van Kamp's strong box is missing, and with it the $400,000 in bonds plus the key to $800,000 more in her safe deposit box. The problem is that Miss Van Kamp herself is under lock and key, having been committed to a sanitarium. Sent to her aid is Crane, disguised as a patient.

Mentally challenged · New York

Headed for a Hearse. Doubleday, 1935 (Also published as *The Westland Case.* Sun Dial, 1938)

When Robert Westland, on death row in Illinois, receives a letter from an M. G. who can clear him, a team is assembled to reexamine his case. Using four key clues, Crane has four days to solve the locked-room murder of Robert's wife.

Illinois, Chicago · Locked room

The Lady in the Morgue. Doubleday, 1936

Crane is in Chicago by chance when a telegram from the Colonel sends him to the morgue to try to identify a female suicide with the phony name of Alice Ross. At the morgue, the body is snatched, the morgue attendant is murdered, and Crane is accused by the cops, and the mob, of having stolen the corpse.

Illinois, Chicago

The Dead Don't Care. Doubleday, 1938

Penn Essex has been receiving threatening notes from The Eye demanding $50,000 for an unspecified debt, and Crane is sent to Key Largo to determine what is going on. When some suspects are killed and the ransom disappears, Crane has to take to the high seas to catch a murderer.

Florida, Key Largo · Florida, Miami

Red Gardenias. Doubleday, 1939 (Also published as *Some Dames Are Deadly.* Jonathan, 1955)

Nine months prior, Richard March died of carbon monoxide poisoning, and then one month passed before John March went the same way. So washing machine king, Simeon March, hires Crane to come to the community of Marchton and ferret out the truth. Accompanied by the Colonel's niece, Ann Fortune, the two begin to act like Nick and Nora Charles.

Marchton

Ross Macdonald (pseud. of Ken Millar) ✍

Lew Archer

Ross Macdonald managed to rescue private eye writing from the 1950s pulp style of Spillane and place it on the *New York Times* Best Seller List by the late 1960s. Lew Archer is a master at exploring the histories of the characters who people his cases, and it is this style that has made this series famous. Some critics claim that Macdonald wrote the same book over and over, but a case can be made that he was exploring the effect of crime on the individual, rather than a puzzle-driven plot. See a Ross Macdonald website at http://www.januarymagazine.com/crfiction/rossintro.html. **Traditional/Hard-boiled**.

The Moving Target. Knopf, 1949 (Also published as *Harper.* Pocket, 1966)

The very cool Elaine Sampson hires Archer to locate her missing husband Ralph, an alcoholic millionaire prone to odd behavior. Archer's suspicions are that Ralph was kidnapped, and that is confirmed when a letter arrives demanding payment.

California, Los Angeles · Kidnapping

The Drowning Pool. Knopf, 1950

Archer is hired by Maude Slocum whose semi-professional actor and husband James has received notes mentioning her infidelity. They live in quiet desolation with Jane's rich mother, Olivia, who dolefully hands out an allowance to her son while their 16-year-old daughter, Cathy, lives in misery, a constant reminder of their growing hate for each other. When Olivia is found dead, Archer finds one lead heads him toward a gangster with designs on the Slocum's property.

California

The Way Some People Die. Knopf, 1951

Archer is hired by a concerned mother who wants her daughter, Galley Lawrence, found. Galley may have run off with a small-time hood named Joe Tarantine. Oddly, Joe's boss, a big-time hood named Dowser, wants Archer to find his employee.

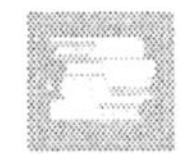

California, Los Angeles

The Ivory Grin. Knopf, 1952 (Also published as *Marked for Murder.* Pocket, 1953)

Archer accepts the task of following an African-American maid for her ex-employer, Una Larkin. This ties into the missing heir of an agricultural fortune, Charles Singleton.

California, Arroyo Beach • California, Bella City

Find a Victim. Knopf, 1954

While cruising on the highway one day, Archer passes the seriously wounded Tony Auista, a truck driver for the Meyer line. He tries to save the man's life by pulling into a trailer court for help. That trailer court will be the key as the now-dead man's girl, Anne Meyer, worked there.

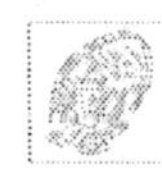

California, Las Cruces

The Name Is Archer. Bantam, 1955

A collection of the following stories: "The Bearded Lady," "Find the Woman," "Gone Girl," "Guilt-Edged Blonde," "The Sinister Habit," "The Suicide," and "Wild Goose Chase."

Short stories

The Barbarous Coast. Knopf, 1956

George Wall has wife problems that involve Bassett, the manager of an exclusive club, and Bassett wants to hire Archer to dispose of the pesky Wall. Helen Campbell has disappeared, and her departure may have been hastened by her connection to the murder of Gabrielle Torres, the daughter of a former boxer who now guards Bassett's club.

California, Los Angeles

The Doomsters. Knopf, 1958

Carl Hallman was sent to the state hospital by his brother, Jerry, cut off from communication with his wife, Mildred, and forced to make an escape just to hire

Archer. Carl is angry because he was sent to the hospital the day after his senator father was killed in a household accident. He suspects Jerry and his wife, Zinnie, are conspiring to hide their involvement in his father's death, and he wants Archer to prove it.

California, Purissima

The Galton Case. Knopf, 1959

Anthony Galton walked away from his family 20 years ago when they disapproved of Teddy, the pregnant woman he married, but now his 70-year-old mother, Maria, wants him to return and claim his part of the estate. Archer accepts the assignment, but discovers that the trail he will follow will confuse more than explain these complex relationships.

California, San Francisco • California, Santa Teresa

The Wycherly Woman. Knopf, 1961

When Homer Wycherly returns from a two-month cruise, he discovers his daughter, Phoebe, has dropped out of college, and he hires Archer to find out where she has gone. Homer wants Archer to avoid his angry ex-wife, Catherine, but she seems like fertile ground to hunt for Phoebe.

California, Boulder Beach

The Zebra-Striped Hearse. Knopf, 1962

Colonel Mark Blackwell divorced Pauline years ago and now he and his new wife, Isobel, are concerned about his daughter Harriet's upcoming marriage to painter Burke Damis. Because Damis's paintings are unknown to the art world and he has entered the country under another name, the family may have a right to be concerned.

Artists • California, Bel Air

The Chill. Knopf, 1964

Alex Kincaid had only one day to enjoy his marriage before his new bride, Dolly McGee, took off after a visit by a mysterious man with a grey beard. Her appearance in a postwedding news photo may be the clue that reveals a past Dolly worked hard to keep a mystery, and it becomes Archer's job to figure out what that could be.

California, Pacific Point

The Far Side of the Dollar. Knopf, 1965

Tommy Hillman has run away from the school that was to have controlled his difficult behavior, and his rich father, Ralph, is threatening to sue over the boy's escape. So Dr. Sponti turns to Archer to retrieve the boy. His investigation does reveal that perhaps the school is not a place anyone would wish to return to.

Academia • California, Laguna Perdida

Black Money. Knopf, 1966

Peter Jamieson's girl, Ginny Fablon, wants to dump him and marry a man named Francis Martel. He claims to be a French aristocrat, but even Ginny's mom knows that Francis is not who he claims to be. Competition for Archer comes from another P.I., and the evidence seems to indicate that Francis may be on the run from French agents.

California, Montevista

The Instant Enemy. Knopf, 1968

Sandy Sebastian's parents think her new love, Dave Spanner, is a wild man. That may be why she takes off from home in the middle of her senior year, and Archer needs to determine why she would want to tote her father's shotgun with her.

California, Los Angeles

The Goodbye Look. Knopf, 1969

Larry and Irene Chalmbers had a burglary when they were away in Palm Springs but the only thing taken was an old gold Florentine box that they kept in their safe. Hired by their lawyer, Archer is asked to retrieve the item and his suspicions fall on their servant or their son who is engaged to the lawyer's daughter.

California, Pacific Point

The Underground Man. Knopf, 1971

When a brush fire rages through Santa Teresa, Archer is asked to retrieve a young boy named Ronny from his Grandma Nell's house, where he has been taken for a visit by his father, Stanley. But Stanley is not where he should be, and wife Jean fears he is repeating the pattern established by his father when the man deserted Stanley's family.

California, Santa Teresa

Sleeping Beauty. Knopf, 1973

A savage oil spill off the coast of Pacific Point caused by the blowup of an oil platform owned by the Lennox family's firm finds Archer and Laurel Russo mourning together on the beach. Archer's attempts to interest her husband, Tom, in her ultimate fate pits the two men against each other.

California, Pacific Point · Environment

The Blue Hammer. Knopf, 1976

Jack and Ruth Biemeyer have had a painting stolen, and they hire Archer to retrieve the work, reputed to be by Richard Chantry. Chantry is a mystery himself, having disappeared from his Santa Teresa home in the mid-1950s. The model for the painting is an enigma as well, and as Archer probes, he finds no answers to the questions raised.

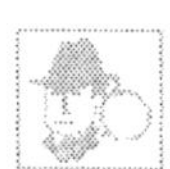

Art · California, Santa Teresa

Lew Archer, Private Investigator. Mysterious Press, 1977

A collection of the following stories: "The Bearded Lady," "Find the Woman," "Gone Girl," "Guilt-Edged Blonde," "Midnight Blue," "The Sinister Habit," "Sleeping Dog," "The Suicide," and "Wild Goose Chase."

Short stories

Strangers in Town. Crippen and Landru, 2001

A collection of the following stories: "The Angry Man," and "Strangers in Town." Also includes one non-Archer story.

Short stories

Mickey Spillane ✍

Mike Hammer

Mickey Spillane is the most popular mystery author of his period in terms of sales. His P.I., Mike Hammer, is a throwback to the pulp days, and an unacceptable investigator to some contemporary readers because of changes in sensibilities. However, *I, the Jury* remains one of the most surprising mystery novels of all time. **Hard-boiled**. Series subject: **New York, New York**.

I, the Jury. Dutton, 1947

Jack Williams lost an arm during the South Pacific campaign while saving Hammer's life, so when he is murdered by a vicious killer, Hammer is driven to find his murderer. All the attendees at a party at Jack's house that night are suspects, including the gangster Kalecki.

My Gun Is Quick. Dutton, 1950

Hammer befriends a hooker one night and lends her $150, but the next night Red is killed by a hit-and-run driver. Hammer believes it is murder, and he begins to shove his way into the underworld of New York call girls, on the prowl for a killer.

Vengeance Is Mine! Dutton, 1950

Hammer is found dead drunk next to the dead body of Chester Wheeler in a hotel room. Although Wheeler's death is ruled a suicide, Hammer's ticket is pulled, and he launches an investigation. Why does Hammer's gun have four bullets left out of six, if there is only one in Wheeler?

One Lonely Night. Dutton, 1951

Hammer is walking across a snow-covered and deserted New York bridge when a scared young girl seeks refuge with him. Hammer and the man chasing the girl draw on each other, and the girl dives off the bridge to an icy death. Before he dumps the body in after the girl, Hammer removes a Communist party membership card from the man's pockets, and this is the lead he will need to solve this mystery.

Communism · Espionage

The Big Kill. Dutton, 1951

When a small child's father is killed by some hoods, Hammer is left with the child. As Hammer begins to search for an explanation, he crosses paths with the D.A. who is examining a gambling syndicate.

Gambling

Kiss Me, Deadly. Dutton, 1952

On a deserted road returning from Albany, Hammer runs over a desperate Berga Torn. She is on the loose from an asylum, and she and Hammer are captured, tortured and left for dead. Learning that the late Berga was Mafia boss Carl Evello's girl gives Hammer a place to start when he begins to chase his tormentors.

Organized crime

The Girl Hunters. Dutton, 1962

For seven years Velma has been gone, sent to her death by Hammer when he assigned her to guard the jewels of a woman who lost her own life in a robbery. Hammer has descended into alcoholism and self-pity, but when a dying Richie Cole reveals that Velma is still alive, Hammer rehabilitates himself to begin a search.

The Snake. Dutton, 1964

Velma is almost lost again when she protects a young girl and two killers try to rub her out. Sue Devon needs protection as she believes her father killed her mother, and he is the former D.A. now running for governor of New York.

The Twisted Thing. Dutton, 1966

Ex-con Billy Parks calls on Hammer from Sidon when he is falsely accused of having kidnapped the son of Rudolph York, brilliant and wealthy scientist. Hammer manages to return the son but then loses the father, and his focus shifts to finding the murderers of the kidnapped boy's father.

Kidnapping • New York, Sidon

The Body Lovers. Dutton, 1967

Two women are found tortured and murdered, both wearing only exotic negligees, and Hammer finds himself on the trail of a serial killer. First Mitch Temple of *The News* is murdered, and then Hammer receives a tip that he will have to move fast to prevent Greta Service from becoming female victim number three.

Serial killer

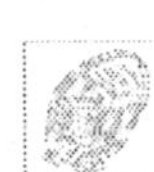

Survival . . . Zero! Dutton, 1970

Hammer is on the spot when Lippy Sullivan dies, tortured to death. His last words are, "for no reason." From the simple fact that Lippy was a pickpocket, Hammer builds a case that turns violent before it resolves itself.

The Killing Man. Dutton, 1989

Velda is beaten at her desk and the client is killed with Hammer's paper spike one day when he is away from the office. Now Hammer has to determine who Anthony Cica was, and why would someone want to do this to the man.

Black Alley. Dutton, 1996

Gut-shot and near death, Hammer bounces back to pursue $89 million worth of mob money. Along the way, he finally finds the time to propose to Velda.

Rex Stout ✍

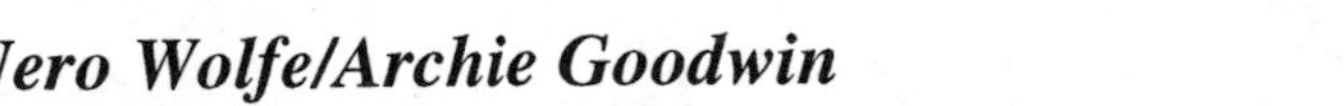

Nero Wolfe/Archie Goodwin

Stout's brilliant creation combined two types of detectives in one novel. Nero Wolfe is the great thinking eccentric detective who is overweight, grows orchids, and never leaves his brownstone in New York. His private eye is Archie Goodwin, who represents Wolfe on the streets and also serves as Wolfe's recording secretary.

The series character was maintained by Robert Goldsborough in the late 1980s and into the 1990s. These novels can be recommended to soft-boiled and traditional mystery readers. The website for The Wolfe Pack is http://members.tripod.com/nerowolfe. **Soft-boiled/ Traditional**. Series subjects: **New York, New York · Teams**.

Fer-de-Lance. Farrar, 1934 (Also published as *Meet Nero Wolfe.* Mercury, n.d.)

Wolfe reluctantly takes the case of the missing immigrant ironworker, Carol Maffei, when his sister claims he is missing. When the discovery is made that Maffei was connected to the death of a college president who was playing golf, Wolfe knows he is on the trail of a clever killer.

The League of Frightened Men. Farrar, 1935

Paul Chapin has lived his whole life with the crippling legacy of a hazing received at Harvard. The 30 students responsible formed the League of Atonement, but apparently this is not enough. Someone is killing the members, and the most likely suspect is Chapin until Wolfe enters the picture.

The Rubber Band. Farrar, 1936 (Also published as *To Kill Again.* Hillman, 1960)

Back in Silver City, Nevada, the life of a young Englishman was saved by The Rubber Band Gang, and as a reward he promised to share his wealth with them some day. Now, as the Marquis of Clivers, the man has returned as a diplomat to the United States, and the daughter of one of the gang members wants Wolfe to stake her claim.

The Red Box. Farrar, 1937 (Also published as *The Case of the Red Box.* Avon, 1958)

A fashion model eats one piece of candy and dies of poisoning, and some fellow orchid growers convince Wolfe to leave his brownstone to investigate. All that leads to is his being fired as a detective, and then another victim dies right in Wolfe's office. Now it is personal.

Too Many Cooks. Farrar, 1938

Believe it or not, Wolfe is in West Virginia at the Kanawha Spa, where he has joined the world's greatest chefs. One chef named Laszio had a bad reputation, and when he is murdered, the police suspect Wolfe's pal Jerome Berin, one of the Fifteen Masters on his first trip to the United States. Of course, Wolfe leaps to his defense.

Cooking · West Virginia, Marlin County

Some Buried Caesar. Farrar, 1939 (Also published as *The Red Bull.* Dell, 1945)

Fred Pratt, cafeteria magnate, has purchased the grand national champion bull, Hickory Caesar Grindon, and intends to have one hell of a barbecue. Instead, someone steps in on the bull's behalf and murders Fred, just as Wolfe and Goodwin are forced off the road by a flat tire on the way to display Wolfe's orchids. Knowing this is a case of murder, despite the fact that Fred's body was left to look like a victim of Caesar, the two detectives begin an investigation.

Cows · New York

Over My Dead Body. Farrar, 1940

Wolfe is not often surprised, but he is taken aback when the girl he adopted as an infant in Montenegro 20 years ago shows up on his doorstep needing help. She is accused of a jewel robbery, and then she stands accused of murder. Wolfe needs to set aside his personal feelings and solve this murder within his family.

Where There's a Will. Farrar, 1940

A contest of wills is a perfect hunting ground for Wolfe, so when a hunting accident proves to be the death of Noel Hawthorne, his three sisters are forced to turn to the great detective when it is proved to be a murder. The contested will leaves it all to the man's mistress, and the family intends to fight to the death over their shares.

Wills

Black Orchids. Farrar, 1942 (Also published as *The Case of the Black Orchids.* Avon, 1950; *Cordially Invited to Meet Death.* Jonathan, 1945; and *Invitation to Murder.* Avon, 1956)

A collection of the following stories: "Black Orchids," and "Cordially Invited to Meet Death."

Short stories

Not Quite Dead Enough. Farrar, 1944

A collection of the following stories: "Booby Trap," and "Not Quite Dead Enough."

Short stories

The Silent Speaker. Viking, 1946

At a gala event, Cheney Boone is prevented from speaking when someone uses a monkey wrench to cave in his skull. Wolfe manages to get hired by the industrialists to find a killer among them, but a beautiful blonde gets in the way. When a second murder occurs and the newspapers are having a heyday, he finally pulls all the clues together.

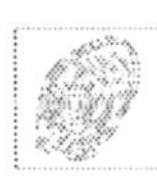

Too Many Women. Viking, 1947

Several months before Wolfe is consulted, an employee at an engineering firm dies, and rumors persist the he was murdered. Asked to investigate the death of Waldo Moore, Wolfe knows he needs a man on the scene. So, Goodwin goes undercover, and discovers that most of the women at the plant did not like Moore.

And Be a Villain. U.S.: Viking, 1948 (U.K.: *More Deaths Than One.* Collins, 1949)

The first meeting between Arnold Zeck, the Napoleon of crime, and Wolfe takes place after a guest on a radio show drinks the sponsor's product and dies. Wolfe gets hired by the sponsor, and finds himself face to face with a master blackmailer and a deadly threat.

Trouble in Triplicate. Viking, 1949

A collection of the following stories: "Before I Die," "Help Wanted, Male," and "Instead of Evidence."

Short stories

The Second Confession. Viking, 1949

For the second time, Wolfe goes up against Zeck. When he chases after a lawyer named Louis Rony, he is warned off by Zeck. His failure to listen costs him his orchid collection and almost kills his gardener, Theodore. The case also leaves Wolfe trying to explain how his car came to kill Rony.

Three Doors to Death. Viking, 1950 (Also published as *Door to Death.* Dell, 1951)

A collection of the following stories: "Door to Death," "Man Alive," and "Omit Flowers."

Short stories

In the Best Families. U.S.: Viking, 1950 (U.K.: *Even In the Best Families.* Collins, 1951)

The final confrontation with Zeck occurs in this book and it has a surprise: after a tear gas attack on his home, Wolfe goes into hiding without even telling Goodwin where he is. Then, to Goodwin's surprise, he is hired by Zeck himself to trail Barry Rackham, the husband of a wealthy and much older woman.

Curtains for Three. Viking, 1951

A collection of the following stories: "Bullet for One," "Disguise for Murder," and "The Gun with Wings."

Short stories

Murder by the Book. Viking, 1951

Joan Wellman's father knows his daughter was murdered, although she died in a hit-and-run accident. He talks Wolfe into taking the case, and they soon discover that author Baird Archer's book has just been rejected by Joan at her publishing company.

Authors • Publishing

Triple Jeopardy. Viking, 1952

A collection of the following stories: "The Cop-Killer," "Home to Roost," and "The Squirt and the Monkey."

Short stories

Prisoner's Base. U.S.: Viking, 1952 (U.K.: *Out Goes She.* Collins, 1953)

Goodwin brings Priscilla Eads home one night, hoping to keep her until her twenty-fifth birthday when she will be eligible to inherit $8 million. Wolfe balks, and out into the night goes Priscilla to meet her death. Goodwin takes a leave to solve her murder, and Wolfe decides he will go to work for Goodwin on this case.

Wills

The Golden Spiders. Viking, 1953

A kid on the streets who wipes windows for money sees a woman mouth the words, "Help, get a cop." He hires Wolfe for a mere pittance, and then is run down by the same car. Wolfe's ire is raised, and the capture of a murderer cannot be far off.

Three Men Out. Viking, 1954

A collection of the following stories: "Invitation to Murder," "This Won't Kill You," and "The Zero Clue."

Short stories

The Black Mountain. Viking, 1954

Only his heritage, and his loyalty to his friend Marko Vukcic, could get Wolfe across the Atlantic and behind the Iron Curtain. He and Marko are on a mission to help liberate their homeland of Montenegro from the Yugoslavian government, but Wolfe is sidetracked when it appears that he will also have to solve a murder on the journey.

Shipboard · Yugoslavia

Before Midnight. Viking, 1955

The partners in an ad agency are disturbed when their million dollar prize, with five anxious contestants, is left in limbo when the only partner who knew who won has been murdered. They come to Wolfe with their problems and expect him to solve it, without sending one of them to jail for murder.

Advertising

Three Witnesses. Viking, 1956

A collection of the following stories: "Die Like a Dog," "The Next Witness," and "When a Man Murders."

Short stories

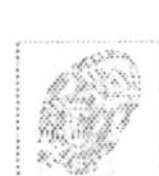

Might As Well Be Dead. Viking, 1956

James Herold is having second thoughts about banishing his son from his Nebraska home when the boy was accused of theft, a charge now found to be false. So he hires Wolfe to locate his son, and to their amazement, his son may be on trial for murder. However, Paul Hays will not talk about his past.

Three for the Chair. Viking, 1957

A collection of the following stories: "Immune to Murder," "Too Many Detectives," and "A Window for Death."

Short stories

If Death Ever Slept. Viking, 1957

Wolfe normally avoids domestic squabbles, but when Otis Jarrell offers him $10,000 to find out bad things about his daughter-in-law, Wolfe accepts. Goodwin is sent after the girl, and falls under her charms. When a corpse is found, it appears that Goodwin has made himself the most likely suspect.

And Four to Go. U.S.: Viking, 1958 (U.K.: *Crime and Again.* Collins, 1959)

A collection of the following stories: "Christmas Party," "Easter Parade," "Fourth of July Picnic," and "Murder is No Joke."

Short stories

Champagne for One. Viking, 1958

Goodwin is a slightly unwelcome guest at the annual dinner held to raise funds for Grantham House, a home for unwed mothers. When one of the attendees, and a former resident, drinks a glass of champagne and dies, Goodwin is convinced he should have seen who committed the evil deed.

Plot It Yourself. U.S.: Viking, 1959 (U.K.: *Murder in Style.* Collins, 1960)

Wolfe has august company when two novelists, a playwright, and the heads of three publishing houses gather in his office to discuss an uncomfortable topic: plagiarism. When Wolfe agrees to look into the charges, his investigation uncovers the first body, and guarantees that this scheme will be a deadly time in the publishing industry.

Authors • Publishing

Three at Wolfe's Door. Viking, 1960

A collection of the following stories: "Method Three for Murder," "Poison a la Carte," and "The Rodeo Murder."

Short stories

Too Many Clients. Viking, 1960

Wolfe feels like he is ahead of the police in trying to solve the death of Thomas Yeager, vice-president at Continental Plastic Products, because the man had hired them to make sure he was not tailed to a particular address. Unfortunately, he dies at home before ever journeying out. Unfortunately, when Goodwin reports that to Wolfe, he learns the man who hired him was not Yeager.

The Final Deduction. Viking, 1961

Jimmy Vail has been kidnapped and held for ransom, and his wealthy wife, Althea, wants Wolfe to help get him returned. Despite thinking that the kidnapping is humbug, Wolfe and Goodwin get involved, and see their client's husband safely returned. However, people begin to die, and the case will just not go away.

Kidnapping

Gambit. Viking, 1962

Paul Jerin is able to play 12 chess games at once which is what he is accomplishing at The Gambit Club when he is poisoned with a cup of hot chocolate. The drink was brought to him by the industrialist Matthew Blount, a man who had objected to Paul's attentions to his daughter Sally. She brings Blount's case to Wolfe, and the great detective begins an investigation.

Homicide Trinity. Viking, 1962

A collection of the following stories: "Counterfeit for Murder," "Death of a Demon," and "Eeny Meeny Murder Mo."

Short stories

The Mother Hunt. Viking, 1963

Once again, misogynist Wolfe must battle his tendencies when a woman brings him a problem involving a baby left on her doorstep. This case gets so complicated Wolfe has to leave the brownstone, and Goodwin finds himself embroiled in the clue of the horsehair buttons.

Trio for Blunt Instruments. Viking, 1964

A collection of the following stories: "Blood Will Tell," "Kill Now—Pay Later," and "Murder is Corny."

Short stories

A Right to Die. Viking, 1964

Paul Wipple is an African-American whose son was to marry a white woman, until she is brutally murdered. When Dunbar Wipple, a civil rights worker, is arrested for the deed, Wolfe needs to seek clues to free the husband and find the killer.

African-Americans · Race

The Doorbell Rang. Viking, 1965

Taking on the FBI may seem overwhelming, but Wolfe has a client named Rachel Bruner who has some things in her possession the bureau would just as soon keep secret. Then a writer doing an article on the FBI is murdered, and Wolfe seeks to stop the government-sponsored corruption.

Federal Bureau of Investigation

Death of a Doxy. Viking, 1966

Wolfe is caught between his loyalty and his greed when Orrie Cather, one of his own detectives, is arrested for the murder of Isabel Kerr. She was his mistress, but was also being kept by the wealthy Avery Ballou, who will pay Wolfe a great deal of money to find her murderer as long as his name is kept out of the papers.

The Father Hunt. Viking, 1968

Amy Denovo is sitting on a quarter of a million dollars left to her by her father. She wants Goodwin to find out who and where her father is, but Wolfe gets involved when it appears the girl's mother might have been murdered.

Death of a Dude. Viking, 1969

Goodwin is on Lily Rowan's dude ranch in Montana when the foreman, Harvey Greve, is arrested for murdering one of the guests who might have gotten his daughter pregnant. With Goodwin having trouble solving the murder by rifle shot, Wolfe makes a tremendous decision: he leaves New York for the Wild West.

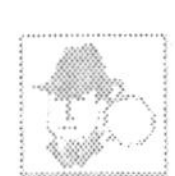

Montana, Lame Horse

Please Pass the Guilt. Viking, 1973

Set during the Mets' run for the pennant, this Wolfe case is a baffling one, which forces him to decide who was the intended victim as well as the murderer. An airline executive named Peter Odell is blown to bits by one of many bombs going off in New York that summer, but he was in the office of Amory Browning at the time of the explosion. So, who was supposed to be killed, and who did the killing?

A Family Affair. Viking, 1975

When a waiter who lives near Goodwin is killed, Wolfe's investigation leads towards Watergate's legacy. Then, a witness is blown up in the brownstone, and Wolfe takes this case so personally he actually leaves the brownstone.

Death Times Three. Bantam, 1985

A collection of the following stories: "Assault on a Brownstone," "Bitter End," and "Frame-Up for Murder."

Short stories

Murder in E Minor (by Robert Goldsborough). Bantam, 1986

Two years after his retirement, Wolfe is coaxed out of his doldrums when Maria Radovich calls with a tale of woe. Her uncle, Milan Stevens, conductor of the New York Symphony, has received threats, and Wolfe is willing to take the case because he knew Milan when he was a freedom fighter.

Goldsborough, Robert · Music

Death on Deadline (by Robert Goldsborough). Bantam, 1987

Harriet Haverhill's *Gazette* is threatened with a takeover by the British scandal monger, Ian MacLaren. Wolfe takes an interest in the paper's fate, and places a full page ad in the paper resisting the takeover. A murder follows, and the great detective needs to reactivate his skills.

Goldsborough, Robert · Newspapers

The Bloodied Ivy (by Robert Goldsborough). Bantam, 1988

Hale Markham dies on the campus of Prescott University, and president of the university, Walter Willis Courtland, pays a call on the brownstone. When Goodwin goes to the campus to begin an investigation, he finds himself arrested. Once again, for the sake of his employee, Wolfe must abandon the brownstone and venture out into the world.

Academia · Goldsborough, Robert · New York, Poughkeepsie

The Last Coincidence (by Robert Goldsborough). Bantam, 1989

Lily Rowan's niece, Noreen James, is murdered, and the fault seems to lie with her playboy boyfriend, Sparky Linville. Lily would really like Wolfe's help, but as Goodwin's investigation progresses and two different people confess to the crime, so would Goodwin.

Goldsborough, Robert

Fade to Black (by Robert Goldsborough). Bantam, 1990

When two competing ad agencies produce the same style ads for their clients, a murder occurs. The opportunity to investigate this case is almost enough for Wolfe, but he prefers a paying client as well.

Advertising · Goldsborough, Robert

Silver Spire (by Robert Goldsborough). Bantam, 1992

Reverend Barnabas Bay has received threatening notes in his collection plates for the last six Sundays. As the master of the Tabernacle of the Silver Spire, he has received national attention as a televangelist, but now one of his people wants him to receive the attention of the great detective, Nero Wolfe.

Goldsborough, Robert · Religion

The Missing Chapter (by Robert Goldsborough). Bantam, 1994

With an echo of Goldsborough's situation, author Charles Childress has been keeping alive the character, Sergeant Barnstable, after the original author of the series dies. When Childress dies and his death is dismissed by the cops as a suicide, his publisher, Horace Vinson, comes to Wolfe with a plea for an investigation.

Authors • Goldsborough, Robert

Patricia Wentworth ✍

Maud Silver

A little old lady detective with a habit of knitting during her interviews, Miss Silver has decided that her pension could be supplemented by becoming a private investigator. Her abilities draw customers to her home. She certainly has no need to advertise, especially with so many customers recommended to her by her ally, Detective Frank Abbot. This is the private eye's answer to Miss Marple. **Soft-boiled/Traditional**. Series subject: **England**.

Grey Mask. U.K.: Hodder, 1928 (U.S.: Lippincott, 1929)

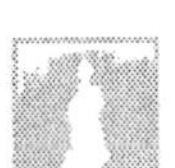

Charles Moray has spent four years trying to forget that he was jilted by Margaret Langton. But when he returns from years of travelling to resume his role as the head of his dead father's estate, he makes a startling discovery. Peeking through a keyhole in his father's house, he seeks a masked man and a gang of conspirators trying to gain the estate of a young woman, who appears to be the long-lost Margaret. He turns to Miss Silver for the help he needs to solve this mystery.

The Case Is Closed. U.K.: Hodder, 1937 (U.S.: Lippincott, 1937)

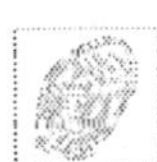

Geoffrey Grey has been serving one year of his life sentence for murdering his uncle. His wife Marion, and his cousin Hilary believe he is innocent, and when they uncover a witness, they proceed with an investigation. However, Hilary's ex-fiancé believes that they all will be better off if they get Miss Silver on the case.

Lonesome Road. U.K.: Hodder, 1939 (U.S.: Lippincott, 1939)

Rachel Traherne has great wealth, and with that responsibility has come three attempts on her life. She turns to Miss Silver to determine who is trying to kill her, and the detective moves into Whincliff Edge to be on the scene as action develops.

Danger Point. U.K.: Hodder, 1942 (U.S.: *In the Balance*. Lippincott, 1941)

Miss Silver is returning to London by train when she encounters Lisle Jerningham. She detects that the girl is troubled, and as she probes she hears the tale of a woman who is afraid her husband is trying to kill her.

The Chinese Shawl. U.K.: Hodder, 1943 (U.S.: Lippincott, 1943)

During WWII, Laura Fane comes of age and comes into her inheritance. Her cousin Tanis Lyle invites her to his estate, The Priory, for a house party that includes Miss Silver as one of the guests. When Laura falls for a wounded pilot instead of her needy cousin, things heat up and Tanis is killed, leaving Miss Silver with a crime to detect.

World War II

Miss Silver Intervenes. U.K.: Hodder, 1944 (U.S.: *Miss Silver Deals in Death.* Lippincott, 1943)

Giles Armitage has disappeared, believed lost in a shipwreck, until the day that he is reunited with his fiancée, Meade Underwood. His memory is lost, and she nurses him, until he is accused of murder when a woman from his past, Carola Roland, is found murdered. Meade turns to Miss Silver for help.

Amnesia · England, London

The Clock Strikes Twelve. Lippincott, 1944

The Paradine family has gathered for New Year's Eve, and James Paradine, the patriarch, knows that one of the members of his family has stolen his company's valuable blueprints. His intentions to reveal the thief are cut short by his murder, and Miss Silver is left to sort through the family to find the killer.

England, Birleton · Holidays · New Year's Eve

The Key. Lippincott, 1944

Major Garth Albany is furloughed to the village of Bourne during WWII, and he is reunited with a woman from his past who is devoted to him. Janice Meade and Albany are on the spot when a church organist is found dead, and the verdict is suicide. But a missing church key and other clues leave Scotland Yard unsatisfied, and when Miss Silver arrives to help, the investigation begins to move forward.

England, Bourne · Music · Religion

She Came Back. U.S.: Lippincott, 1945 (U.K.: *The Traveller Returns.* Hodder, 1948)

Anne Jocelyn has spent the last three years in Occupied France, and when she is able to return to England, it is only to discover her own tomb in the family cemetery. Her husband rebuffs her attempts to begin their marriage again, but she is made welcome by Lyndall Armitage despite the fact that Anne's husband appears to now want to live with Lyndall. When a murder occurs, it will take Miss Silver's sleuthing to discover the truth.

World War II

Pilgrim's Rest. Lippincott, 1946 (Also published as *Dark Threat.* Popular Library, 1951)

Judy Elliot had been warned not to go to Pilgrim's Rest, but she accepted a position as a housemaid anyway. When a death occurs, and she is terrorized by a killer, she turns to the old woman who claims to be a private detective, Miss Silver.

England, Holt St. Agnes

Latter End. Lippincott, 1947

A fortune teller warns Lois Latter that she will be poisoned. Perhaps the reason lies in the fact that everyone at Latter End hates her because of her scheming ways. When she is poisoned, her husband James hires Miss Silver to get to the truth.

Wicked Uncle. U.S.: Lippincott, 1947 (U.K.: *Spotlight.* Hodder, 1949)

Gregory Porlock has plans of his own when he invites a strange combination of people to his house for a weekend party. However, when it appears that blackmail is the underlying reason for the gathering, someone sticks a knife in Gregory. This leaves Miss Silver with a house full of suspects and a murder case to solve.

Blackmail

The Case of William Smith. Lippincott, 1948

William Smith has lost his memory in World War II, but his skill at making wooden toy animals has landed him a position at Tattercombe's Toy Bazaar. When he falls in love with the shop's new assistant, Katharine Eversley, some strange accidents begin to occur as she tries to uncover his true identity. Seeking advice from Abbott, Smith is directed to Miss Silver for the answers he needs.

Amnesia • England, London

Eternity Ring. Lippincott, 1948

While Abbot is visiting family, he hears of a woman named Mary Stokes who witnessed a murder for which the local police have no corpse. Seeing how troubled the woman is, he asks Miss Silver to investigate. When it is discovered that a woman named Louise Rogers is missing and fits Mary's description, the case begins to heat up.

England, Deeping

Miss Silver Comes to Stay. Lippincott, 1949

The very rich, and very eligible, James Lessiter has returned to his ancestral home in Melling. Everyone in town knows that local girl Rietta Cray still carries a torch for Lessiter, but no one expects to find him dead and the clues pointing towards her. Miss Silver may be the only neutral person and the only defender of a woman accused of murder.

England, Melling

The Catherine Wheel. Lippincott, 1949

Mischievous old Jacob Travener, who has lived off the proceeds of his ancestor's smuggling operations, is now getting ready to write his will and to divide the booty. He invites eight cousins to the Catherine Wheel Inn for speculation purposes. However, nine show up, and one is murdered, and Miss Silver is left to chase a killer amongst the greedy heirs.

Wills

The Brading Collection. Lippincott, 1950 (Also published as *Mr. Brading's Collection.* Severn, 1987)

If Lewis Brading had listened to the advice given to him by Miss Silver, he might still be alive. Instead he is found dead among his famous collection in a stronghold at a country club, and suspicion has fallen on his secretary, James Moberly, the only other person with access to the collection.

England, Ledstow • Jewels

Through the Wall. Lippincott, 1950

When her uncle, Martin Brand dies, he passes his fortune on to his relatively estranged niece, Marion Brand. When she arrives at the family home to live among her relatives, she finds that there is resentment in the air. When she stands accused of a murder, the police ask for Miss Silver's help to clear her name.

Anna, Where Are You? Lippincott, 1951 (Also published as *Death at Deep End.* Pyramid, 1963)

Miss Silver is hired by Thomasina Elliot to find her missing friend, Anna Ball. Miss Silver assumes the position that Ball had held as the governess to the three Craddock children at Deepe House.

England, Linconshire, Deep End

The Ivory Dagger. Lippincott, 1951

From the collection of ivories hoarded by the rather mean-spirited Sir Herbert Whitall, a dagger held by Lila Dryden appears to be the weapon used to kill the man. When Lady Sybil Dryden hires Miss Silver to prove her niece innocent, the detective understands that many people held a grudge against Whitall, including Lila's former lover, Bill Waring.

Antiquities

The Watersplash. Lippincott, 1951

Two murders take place on a Friday, separated by one week, in the normally tranquil village of Greenings. When Miss Silver launches an investigation, she discovers that there was a common thread between the two victims that could lead to a case of blackmail gone horribly wrong.

Blackmail · England, Greenings

Ladies' Bane. Lippincott, 1952

The village of Bleake is dominated by the medieval manor house called Ladies' Bane, and despite its strange legacy, Geoffrey Trent wants to purchase the property. His wife Allegar, and her newly arrived sister, Ione Muir, feel this may not be the best choice. Miss Silver, who is on the scene to investigate Geoffrey's finances, is in place when a young ward named Margo is killed.

England, Bleake

Out of the Past. Lippincott, 1953

While on holiday on the Channel coast, Miss Silver is dragged into a murder investigation when the body of Alan Field is found in the Hardwick's beach house. He has just returned from South America after a three-year absence, and Miss Silver has plenty of suspects from which to select a murderer.

England, Channel Coast

Vanishing Point. Lippincott, 1953

Elderly women are disappearing, and Miss Silver has stepped in to try and solve the mystery. The village of Hazel Green is dominated by Lydia Crewe. Her autocratic nature and her bad treatment of her nieces leads Silver in one direction, while the nearby research station has a secret that may relate to the disappearance.

England, Hazel Green

The Benevent Treasure. Lippincott, 1954

It will take all of Miss Silver's skills to sort through the sad story brought to her by the young Candida Sayle. She believes that she is threatened by her two aunts over an inheritance. Could Aunt Olivia and Aunt Clara really be planning murder?

England, Retley

The Silent Pool. Lippincott, 1954

Retired actress Adriana Ford has asked Miss Silver for help. She has been the victim of some suspicious accidents recently, but Miss Silver's presence encourages her to rejoin society. Unfortunately, she is murdered during her own party, and Miss Silver goes on the hunt for a killer.

Poison in the Pen. Lippincott, 1955

Heiress Valentine Grey is celebrating her upcoming wedding when a second suicide mars the scene in Tilling Green. Miss Silver is there to investigate the reasons behind the deaths, and to protect the soon-to-be bride from danger.

England, Tilling Green • Weddings

The Listening Eye. Lippincott, 1955

Paulina Paine is deaf, but she is an expert lip-reader. When she oversees a conversation between two men at an art exhibition, she is so distressed by the words that she runs to Miss Silver for help.

Deaf • England, London

The Gazebo. Lippincott, 1956 (Also published as *The Summerhouse.* Pyramid, 1967)

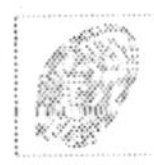

Althea Graham's mother has been found dead in the gazebo that graces the Graham family estate. With her death, Althea is free to marry her fiancé Nicholas Carey, but that freedom has brought them to the attention of Scotland Yard. They turn to Miss Silver to clear their names.

England, London

The Fingerprint. Lippincott, 1956

Georgiana Grey has lived under the care of her uncle, Jonathan Field, for her whole life, but her plans to inherit his fortune go awry when her distant relative, Miriam Field, moves in. Miriam charms Jonathan, and he believes the evidence that Georgiana is plotting against Miriam. When Jonathan is killed, the police believe that Georgiana may be the cause, and she needs Miss Silver's help.

The Alington Inheritance. Lippincott, 1958

Jenny Hill knows that she was to have inherited the Alington Estate according to the stories told to her by her now-dead guardian. Instead, she finds herself the governess of two young girls who live there now. However, someone does know the truth, and when she finds herself in danger, she turns to Miss Silver.

The Girl in the Cellar. U.K.: Hodder, 1961 (U.S.: Aeonian Press, 1976)

A woman without a memory finds herself with a dead body, and she needs Miss Silver to discover who she is, and whether or not she is a murderer.

The Modern Practitioners

Linda Barnes ✍

Carlotta Carlyle

Tall, red-haired and driving a cab, this Boston P.I. works in a contemporary American society that allows her to stretch her wings as an investigator. Her ward, Paoline, adds complications to her life, as does the occasional man who wanders into her world. Readers may also enjoy Sue Grafton, Jeremiah Healy, Sara Paretsky, and Robert B. Parker. See the author's website at http://www.lindabarnes.com. **Traditional**. Series subject: **Massachusetts, Boston**.

A Trouble of Fools. St. Martin's Press, 1987

Carlyle is trailing a drug dealer who is getting too close to her ward while she is also hired to find the missing brother of a little old lady with an unusually large amount of money. When the two cases begin to merge, Carlyle finds herself up against some IRA-connected cabbies and the Boston Mafia.

The Snake Tattoo. St. Martin's Press, 1989

Carlyle has two weeks to find a hooker with a snake tattoo or her ex-mentor Mooney will be up on brutality charges for attacking a high-ranking member of the Vietnamese community. Then a young suburbanite comes to her with a pathetic tale of his missing girlfriend, and suddenly Carlyle has two cases while she is also trying to remodel her bathroom.

Coyote. Delacorte, 1990

Carlyle is visited by a Spanish-speaking woman who wants her to retrieve her green card. The skittish woman bolts from Carlyle before the P.I. learns that the woman's name is Manuela Estefan, and that her green card was discovered on a body dumped in The Fens. Carlyle's friend, a policeman named Mooney, is able to tell Carlyle that the body was so mutilated they may not be able to identify it, but she can identify the second body when her client receives the same treatment.

Steel Guitar. Delacorte, 1991

Carlyle used to sing backup for blues singer Dee Willis, and the two women were close. So close that Dee ran off with Carlyle's husband, and the P.I. does not expect to see her former musical associate again. Years later, when someone steals Dee's music, surprisingly she turns to Carlyle for help.

Musicians

Snapshot. Delacorte, 1993

Carlyle has been receiving photos of a child in the mail, and the eerie action is explained when she learns that Emily Woodrow's child has died from a strain of leukemia with a very high recovery rate. While the mother is driven to find out why her child died, Carlyle's ward, Paolina, is taking dangerous chances to find her father. Carlyle agrees to help both women, and is driven down a strange path by the case.

Medical

Hardware. Delacorte, 1995

Carlyle is asked to help explain a recent series of attacks on Boston's cabbies, so she returns to her familiar haunts to help out her fellow drivers. Her involvement with Sam Gianelli is placed under strain when the case turns ugly, and she becomes involved with a strange computer geek named Frank.

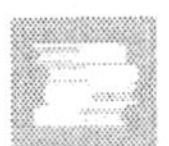

Cold Case. Delacorte, 1997

Twenty four years prior to this case, the famous writer, Thea Janis, disappeared at the age of 15, just after the release of her sensational debut novel. A man was convicted for her murder, but now a new manuscript has appeared that seems to imply that Thea may be writing again. It will be Carlyle's job to discover the truth.

Authors

Flashpoint. Hyperion, 1999

Carlyle accepts the task of making an elderly woman's apartment safe from burglars. Then, the woman is killed in her apartment, and Carlyle feels obligated to discover how this event occurred. Soon she finds herself involved with developers eager to pounce, and an arsonist that may try to end her investigation.

Richard Barre ✍

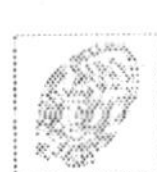

Wil Hardesty

If Raymond Chandler defined California as one of the premier regions for the private eye, it is contemporary authors like Barre who extend that definition into a new generation. Hardesty is a Vietnam vet who has turned to private investigating. Hardesty's joy of surfing has been spoiled by the death of his young son in a surfing accident, an accident that may have been his fault. Readers may also enjoy Robert Crais and Michael Connelly. **Traditional/Hard-boiled**.

The Innocents. Walker, 1995

Hardesty is still hauling himself up from the depths of hell after his son's death when he is dragged into a case involving seven dead children whose bones have just been exposed in the desert by a flood. A childhood prank, which led one of the young boys to swallow a commemorative metal, is the only piece of evidence left to identify any of the bodies. The boy's guilt-ridden father, trying to avoid publicity, hires Hardesty to try and locate the man who bought his son many years ago when the whole family was struggling in Mexico.

California, La Conchita · California, Los Angeles · Children at risk

Bearing Secrets. Walker, 1996

Despite surviving the radical battles of the 1970s, Max Pfeiffer is tainted by his association with the vicious murder of Angela DeBray and the national attention it attracted at the time. So when a plane is discovered at the bottom of a drought-lowered lake and it contains the long-missing ransom money, the FBI calls on Max and he commits suicide. Max's daughter hires Hardesty to prove her father's innocence in the old case.

California, San Francisco • California, Tahoe

The Ghosts of Morning. Berkley, 1998

When the mother of Hardesty's high school surfing buddy, Denny Van Zant, becomes convinced that someone knows her son did not die in Vietnam, she sends Hardesty to Hawaii to ransom Denny's location. Hardesty fails to deliver, and falls under the spell of Kordell Van Zant, Denny's very rich and powerful father. He struggles to understand the Van Zant family, and works out the demons left over from his Vietnam War service.

California, LaConchita • Hawaii, Hilo • Vietnamese Conflict

Blackheart Highway. Berkley, 1999

Hardesty is accompanying his current flame, Kari Thayer, while she is attending a broadcast journalists convention in Bakersfield when he is approached with a job offer. Twenty years prior to this book, country western singer Doc Whitney murdered his wife and two daughters, but parole has put him back on the streets. Lute DeVillbis, who used to wildcat with Doc's father, Gib, is afraid that Doc may believe that Lute murdered Gib, and want revenge.

California, Bakersfield • Music

Max Allan Collins ✍

Nate Heller

Using his Chicago P.I. Heller as a fly on the wall, Max Allan Collins examines real-life crimes and tries to explain them away. Heller is a hard-boiled womanizer with the capability to defend himself. Collins's attention to historical detail while being able to propel a plot is the strength of this series. Many actual important historical figures appear as characters in these novels. They can be recommended to any traditional or hard-boiled mystery reader. Readers may also enjoy Harold Adams, Philip Kerr, Ken Kuhlken, and Mickey Spillane. See the website for The Friends of Max Allan Collins at http://www.muscanet.com/~phoenix/index.html. **Traditional/Hard-boiled/Historical**. Series subject: **Historical (1900–1999)**.

True Detective. St. Martin's Press, 1983

As a cop, Heller was involved with an assassination attempt on the mobster Frank Nitti. He quit the force in disgust, and opened the A-1 Detective Agency. Now he finds himself hired to protect Chicago mayor Cermak from an assassination plot, while a beautiful actress hires him to find her brother. SH

Illinois, Chicago

True Crime. St. Martin's Press, 1984

Heller is involved in the capture and execution of John Dillinger, and then finds himself in northern Wisconsin when he becomes enmeshed in a plot to kidnap a prominent lawman. These events relate to the first book, and form the middle part of the Frank Nitti trilogy.

Illinois, Chicago • Wisconsin

The Million Dollar Wound. St. Martin's Press, 1986

During WWII, Heller and boxing buddy Barney Ross are sent to Guadacanal to fight the Japanese. A flashback tells us that Heller had been involved in a Hollywood union struggle in 1939, and the events after his service involve him in the murder of Estelle Carey. All three of these events tie into previous books and bring to closure the Frank Nitti trilogy.

California, Los Angeles • Film · Illinois, Chicago • Pacific Ocean, Guadacanal • World War II

Neon Mirage. St. Martin's Press, 1988

Heller is hired to protect Jim Ragan, proprietor of a wire service, but he fails at the task. His subsequent interest in Ragan's niece leads him to Las Vegas. There he witnesses the founding of the gambling empire, and he comes into contact with Bugsy Siegal and Virginia Hill.

Illinois, Chicago • Nevada, Las Vegas

Stolen Away. Bantam, 1991

This novel is split into two parts. The first part occurs in 1932, when Heller was a cop from Chicago assigned to the Lindbergh kidnapping in New Jersey. The second part takes place four years later, when the governor of New Jersey sends for Heller when he is considering a reprieve for Bruno Hauptmann, the man accused of kidnapping the Lindbergh baby. SH

Illinois, Chicago • Lindbergh kidnapping • New Jersey, Hopewell

Dying in the Post-War World. Foul Play, 1991

A collection of the following stories: "Dying in the Post-War World," "House Call," "Marble Mildred," "Private Consultation," "Scrap," and The Strawberry Teardrop."

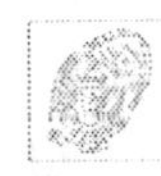

Short stories

Carnal Hours. Dutton, 1994

Heller is summoned to the Nassau home of Sir Harry Oakes one day prior to Oakes's horrifying death. After witnessing a less than stellar investigation, he leaves, only to be blackmailed back to the island by Oakes's daughter Nancy. Teamed with Erle Stanley Gardner, a reporter, and a dashing British spy named Ian Fleming, Heller tries to solve this mysterious case that the government wishes to blame on Nancy's husband.

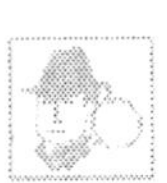

Caribbean, Bahamas • Oakes, Sir Harry

Blood and Thunder. Dutton, 1995

Heller is given the opportunity to fly to Louisiana with a bullet-proof vest for The Kingfish, Huey Long. The Kingfish keeps him around as a bodyguard, but Long is assassinated anyway. Heller makes it his mission to try to determine if the accused assassin, Dr. Carl Weiss, worked alone.

Long, Huey • Louisiana, Baton Rouge

Damned in Paradise. Dutton, 1996

Jumping back to when Heller was a Chicago cop, he finds himself on leave to take a job as special investigator for Clarence Darrow. Darrow is working on the second trial in the Thalia Massie rape case. Heller must deal with the racial overtones when five Asian men are charged with the ugly crime.

Darrow, Clarence · Hawaii · Race

Flying Blind. Dutton, 1998

Heller is hired to bodyguard the famous flyer, Amelia Earhart, while she is on a national tour in 1935, and the two become lovers. When Amelia and Fred Noonan take off on the last leg of her famous flight in 1937, Heller is well aware of the machinations of her publicity hungry husband, G. P. Putnam. When the government thinks Heller might be the man to find the missing flyer, he agrees and journeys to the South Pacific.

Earhart, Amelia · Pacific Ocean, Saipan

Majic Man. Dutton, 1999

In 1949, when James Forrestal, the nation's first Secretary of Defense, is being run out of office by President Truman and columnist Drew Pearson, Heller is providing personal service to the Forrestal family. He is intrigued when Pearson discloses the existence of the Majestic Twelve, and speaks of a saucer crash in the Nevada desert.

New Mexico, Roswell · Washington, D.C. · UFOs

Angel in Black. New American Library, 2001

In 1947, in a vacant lot on South Norton Avenue in Los Angeles, a woman's body is discovered cut in half. The first two people on the scene are Bill Fowley, a reporter for the Hearst paper who was chasing police calls, and his companion P.I. Nate Heller. Heller finds himself working for the Hearst paper, and feeding information to the lead investigator, L.A. detective Harry "the Hat" Hansen, to deflect suspicion from himself.

Black Dahlia case · California, Los Angeles · Short, Elizabeth

Chicago Confidential. New American Library, 2002

In 1950, Heller's agency is rocked when his partner Bill Drury agrees to cooperate with the hearings on organized crime being held by United States Senator Estes Kefauver. Heller's association with Jackie Payne, a mobster's girlfriend, finds him worrying about her abduction and fearing a hit man's assignment to get Drury.

Kefauver hearings · Organized crime

Robert Crais ✍

Elvis Cole

Beginning his life as a spirited wisecracker, Cole matures into a modern knight who is not shy about using force to right wrongs. Pairing Cole with a tough sidekick named Joe Pike, Crais continues to explore the American landscape, using Southern California in a similar fashion to Raymond Chandler. A love story that develops over the series also adds interest. These novels can be recommended to any hard-boiled mystery reader. Readers may also enjoy Richard Barre, Dennis Lehane, and Harlan Coben. See the author's website at http://www.robertcrais.com. **Hard-boiled**. Series subject: **California, Los Angeles**.

The Monkey's Raincoat. Bantam, 1987

Ellen Lang has been so smothered by her husband Mort, that when he deserts her, she is helpless. Cole is hired through Ellen's friend Janet Simon, but he is unable to return Mort to Ellen because his corpse is found in the trunk of his Cadillac. With a shady movie producer, some drug deals gone wrong, and a child in jeopardy, Cole has to balance all these elements to finds a murderer. AN MA

Stalking the Angel. Bantam, 1989

When the Hagakure manuscript, entrusted to American businessman Bradley Warren, is stolen from his home, it is an insult to his Japanese associates and a potentially huge financial loss. To the Japanese, the manuscript is sacred and Cole finds himself competing with them to recover the document. To Warren, money is sacred, and even after his daughter is kidnapped, he is not making Cole's job any easier.

Antiquities

Lullaby Town. Bantam, 1992

Big time Hollywood director Peter Alan Nelsen would like to see the boy he fathered with Karen Shipley years before he became movieland's wunderkind. So he hires Cole, who manages to follow the 10-year-old trail and locates Shipley in Connecticut. However, his investigation splits open Shipley's world, and threatens the life of the boy that Nelsen wishes to meet.

Connecticut, Chelan • Organized crime

Free Fall. Bantam, 1993

Jennifer Sheridan's boyfriend is LAPD officer Mark Thurman, a man under pressure as a member of the REACT team. His involvement in a sting operation has led to the death of a black man, but Cole discovers that the man's family has dropped its wrongful death suit. Jennifer wants her man back, but Cole's sympathies drift towards the family of the dead man as he battles politicians and gangs to find the truth.

Gangs • Police corruption

Voodoo River. Hyperion, 1995

Jodi Taylor, a rising television star, sends Cole to Louisiana to locate her birth parents, a simple enough task until Cole discovers that someone else has been there first. When the lousy P.I. Jimmie Ray Robenack is murdered for his efforts, Cole has to discover why Taylor's history is so threatening to a killer.

Louisiana, Baton Rouge

Sunset Express. Hyperion, 1996

When Susan Martin's body is found dumped inside some garbage bags, her wealthy husband Teddy blames it on a kidnapping gone wrong. LAPD officer

Angela Rossi finds a hammer with remnants of Susan on it, tossed in a bush outside the family estate, but the defense team feels the evidence is tainted so they hire Cole. Cole's investigation will force him to choose sides in a case with echoes of the O. J. Simpson murder trial.

Indigo Slam. Hyperion, 1997

Lucy Cheneir has come into Cole's life, and it is her advice that leads him to accepting a protective role over three kids lost in the witness protection program. Their father, already on the lam in the program, has angered the Feds and some Russian mobsters, and Cole must work to protect the children while keeping their father alive.

L.A. Requiem. Doubleday, 1999

Joe Pike and Cole have had a unique lifelong relationship, and for the first time in that relationship, it is Pike who needs Cole's help. When Pike was in the LAPD, an incident led to his leaving the force and scarred him forever. Currently, Pike is seeking to discover why his former lover, Karen Garcia, is missing and when the cops want to arrest him, his only hope is to go on the lam and rely on Cole as an investigator.

James Crumley

Milo Milodragovitch/C. W. Sughrue

Lost in the worst sensibilities of the 1970s, both of Crumley's P.I.s struggle with a world full of alcohol, drugs, and violence. Crumley follows in the literary tradition of Hammett, Chandler, and Macdonald, but adds a sense of weariness and hopelessness to the private eye legends. Readers may also enjoy Lawrence Block (Matthew Scudder) and James Lee Burke. **Hard-boiled**. Series subject: **The West**.

The Wrong Case. Random House, 1975

Milodragovitch's P.I. business is down the tubes, and he has taken to drink. When Helen Duffy arrives in his office from Iowa, looking for her missing brother Raymond, it sets Milodragovitch on a course that he hopes will keep him close to Helen.

Northwest State, Meriwether

The Last Good Kiss. Random House, 1978

Abraham Trehearne is a poet and an alcoholic, drinking his way through the American West. Sughrue is hired by Abraham's ex-wife to hunt down the man before he drinks himself to death. But Sughrue also becomes embroiled in Abraham's search for Betty Sue Flowers, a barmaid's daughter, who has left a trail of sad, sordid events through the West.

Authors

Dancing Bear. Random House, 1983

Milo has abandoned his own business and is working for Haliburton Security. He is tracked down by Sarah Weddington, and the large fee offered by the old woman tempts him to revive his career. But he soon finds himself in over his head when he confronts more guns and drugs than he would prefer.

Montana

The Mexican Tree Duck. Mysterious Press, 1993

Sarita Cisnerso Pines is missing, and the FBI is unable to satisfy her husband's need to find his wife. So he hires Sughrue to get the job done, and the P.I. finds himself competing with the agency and some rogues from South America also intent on finding the woman. Searching throughout the West, he needs to discover the meaning of the hollowed-out sculpture of a duck.

Bordersnakes. Mysterious Press, 1996

Both of the P.I.s are down on their luck. Sughrue has been gut-shot and left for dead in New Mexico. Milodragovitch is broke when someone takes over his legacy, and he is intent on revenge. The two team up in El Paso and begin a march across the West to satisfy their needs.

Teams

The Final Country. Mysterious Press, 2001

Milo has settled down in Texas after his last adventure to be near his girlfriend Betty. He is helping run a tavern that is a front for a money-laundering operation and tracking bail jumpers. When he witnesses the death of the bar owner, he finds himself tracking down the shooter, Enos Walker, to keep himself out of the frame. But women will be his downfall, especially when they try to put him right back in the frame for a murder. DA

Lindsey Davis ✍

Marcus Didius Falco

The closest thing ancient Rome has to a P.I. is private informer Marcus Didius Falco (see also Steven Saylor). Using the voice of a contemporary P.I. and humor, Falco takes the reader into the back streets of Rome and on grand adventures in the Empire. Readers should be aware that this series mixes humor with the historical. Readers may also enjoy Steven Saylor. See the author's website at http://www.lindseydavis.co.uk. **Soft-boiled/Traditional/Historical**. Series subjects: **Historical (0000–1000) · Humor · Italy, Rome (Ancient)**.

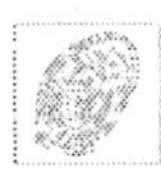

The Silver Pigs. U.K.: Sidgwick, 1989 (U.S.: Crown, 1989)

Falco's overseas experience in the Emperor's Army comes in handy when the private informer gets embroiled in the case of a Senator's niece whose bank box holds an illegally obtained silver pig mined in Britain. His attempts to help Sosia Camillus leads to her murder, so he is off to Britain to find the source of the wealth and the responsible murderer.

England (Ancient)

Shadows in Bronze. U.K.: Sidgwick, 1990 (U.S.: Crown, 1991)

Falco's triumph has led him to the position of imperial agent for Caesar Vepasian. Barnabas, the companion conspirator of Atius Pertinax from book one, seems to be on a campaign of assassination trying to seek revenge. Falco is sent to Croton and Neapolis, where, teamed with his allies Petronius Longus, nephew Larius, and Helena, he battles the conspiracy.

Venus in Copper. U.K.: Hutchinson, 1991 (U.S.: Crown, 1991)

Falco returns to private investigation work when the wealthy real estate developer Hortensius asks him to investigate the background of a woman named Severina. She is Hortensius's fiancée, but he believes she may be after his wealth. When Hortensius dies from poison, Falco realizes the developer's problems may be greater than the women in his life.

The Iron Hand of Mars. U.K.: Hutchinson, 1992 (U.S.: Crown, 1992)

To get him out of the way so that he can pursue Helena, Titus Caesar sends Falco to Roman Germany. Once there, the investigator discovers that the legion stationed there contains some individuals who carry an old grudge against him from his years in service.

Germany (Ancient)

Poseidon's Gold. U.K.: Hutchinson, 1993 (U.S.: Crown, 1994)

Falco returns from Germany to discover his apartment is occupied by squatters. A man appears making demands based on debts owed by Falco's brother Festus. When that man is found dead, Falco finds himself accused of murder.

Last Act in Palmyra. U.K.: Century, 1994 (U.S.: Mysterious, 1996)

Anacrites, Vespasian's chief spy, asks Falco to go to Petra on a mission, unaware that the man has set Falco up for a fall. Upon arrival in Petra with Helena, he discovers a dead playwright, and finds himself under suspicion from the local authorities.

Time to Depart. U.K.: Century, 1995 (U.S.: Mysterious, 1997)

Petronius Longus, captain of the watch, has finally captured Rome's top criminal, Balbinus. As he and Falco place him on a ship to send him into exile, they feel a sense of satisfaction. When those people who helped send the criminal abroad begin to die, they begin to believe their enemy may never have left the Empire.

A Dying Light in Corduba. U.K.: Century, 1996 (U.S.: Mysterious, 1998)

When a man is killed and the Chief of Spies is left for dead, the Emperor turns to Falco for an investigation. Distracted by the impending birth of his child, Falco's investigation flounders until a trip to Iberia begins to unravel the case.

Three Hands in the Fountain. U.K.: Century, 1997 (U.S.: Mysterious, 1999)

Falco and Petronius are present when a severed hand is found in a fountain. As they make some inquiries, they discover that body parts have been showing up in Rome during public festivals. The hunt leads to the 200 miles of aqueducts that snake through the city, and hide a serial killer.

Two For the Lions. U.K.: Century, 1998 (U.S.: Mysterious, 1999)

Forced to work under Chief Spy Anacrites, Falco makes plans to escape his overseer by becoming a census taker. However, his services as a detective are needed by a client whose relative has eloped, while someone murders a lion rather than a star gladiator.

One Virgin Too Many. U.K.: Century, 1999 (U.S.: Mysterious, 2000)

As Procurator of the Sacred Poultry, Falco is distracted when a young girl named Gaia wants his protection. When he discovers later that she has been selected to be a Vestal Virgin, he begins to understand why Titus Caesar wants him to find her.

Ode to a Banker. U.K.: Century, 2000 (U.S.: Mysterious, 2001)

Aurelius Chrysippus, patron saint to the struggling writer, has offered to publish Falco's poetry, a generous offer that leads the private informer into a murder investigation when he is a suspect in Chrysippus's death.

Authors

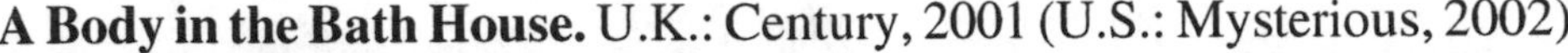

A Body in the Bath House. U.K.: Century, 2001 (U.S.: Mysterious, 2002)

When the mosaic floor of a bathhouse is removed, a body is discovered. Suspicion falls on two plasterers named Gloccus and Cotta, who have gone to Brtiannia to work on a project with big cost overruns that has drawn the attention of the Emperor. When Falco follows with his family in tow, he also has his sister's secret to protect.

Construction • England (Ancient)

***The Jupiter Myth.** Century, 2002

Loren D. Estleman ✍

Amos Walker

An anachronism, Amos Walker is the best modern representative of the great P.I.s who have come before. Estleman's skill as a writer and his respect for the genre allows him to use all the conventions of the private eye to his advantage. Walker's stomping grounds are Detroit, a city that goes through many changes during the run of this series. A reader with a sense of the history of the private investigator will love this series. Readers may also enjoy Robert B. Parker and Bill Pronzini. See the author's website at http://www. lorenestleman.com. **Traditional/Hard-boiled**. Series subject: **Michigan, Detroit**.

Motor City Blue. Houghton Mifflin, 1980

Ben Morningstar has a lot of problems being a retired crime boss but none as devastating as the fact that his ward, Marla Bernstein, is missing. Her trail leads to the world of pornography, drugs, and eventually murder. Walker receives some help from a hooker named Iris and deterrents from some of Detroit's underworld, but eventually he completes his assignment.

Organized crime

Angel Eyes. Houghton Mifflin, 1981

Dancer Ann Maringer has a strange request of Walker: to find her when she is missing. She leaves a huge ring as a retainer for Walker and agrees to meet him later, but she never makes the rendezvous. Walker finds himself fending off someone who wants the ring and trying to explain the dead body in Ann's apartment.

The Midnight Man. Houghton Mifflin, 1982

Because he owes him a favor, Walker feels obliged to help Sergeant Van Sturtevant investigate the shooting that left three cops dead and Sturtevant wounded. A radical group frees the person being held responsible for the crime spree, and Walker finds himself hunting the cop killer on the streets of Detroit.

The Glass Highway. Houghton Mifflin, 1983

Sandy Broderick anchors the news in Detroit, and he now wants to do something for his son, Bud, who he abandoned years ago. The boy has vanished, and the clues seem to indicate that Bud's involvement with an older woman named Paula Royce leads to the drug scene.

Sugartown. Houghton Mifflin, 1985

Nineteen years ago when Joseph Evancek was let go from his job, he killed his wife and daughter, then turned the gun on himself. His mother, just arrived from Poland, wants to know the fate of her grandson, and Walker is set on the trail. A second case, involving an expatriated Russian novelist, begins to merge with the first, with deadly results.

Every Brilliant Eye. Houghton Mifflin, 1986

Barry Stackpole and Walker have an association that started in Vietnam, and the loss of his legs and the pressures of his career as a reporter have set Barry to drinking. When someone also wants to kill the man, Walker believes the clues might lie in the book on Vietnam that Barry is writing.

Authors • Vietnamese Conflict

Lady Yesterday. Houghton Mifflin, 1987

From out of his past, Iris returns to Walker's life and gets him involved in her search for her real father. What should be a simple matter turns deadly when Iris begins to receive little message to stop the hunt. Walker, still in love and determined to be a hero, presses on towards the truth.

Downriver. Houghton Mifflin, 1988

DeVries has had a lot of time to think about the crime that sent him to jail. Free now, he searches for the $200,000 dollars taken in the armored car robbery that occurred during the 1967 Detroit riots. As the fall guy, he feels the money should be his, and he sets Walker on the trail of the thieves who have it.

General Murders. Houghton Mifflin, 1988

A collection of the following stories: "Blonde and Blue," "Bloody July," "Bodyguards Shoot Second," "Dead Soldier," "Eight Mile and Dequindre," "Fast Burns," "Greektown," "I'm in the Book," "The Prettiest Dead Girl in Detroit," and "Robber's Roost."

Short stories

Silent Thunder. Houghton Mifflin, 1989

A huge number of illegal weapons are seized from the home of Constance Thayer when she is arrested for the murder of her husband, Doyle. Her attorneys want to hire an investigator to find the evidence to get her released on the grounds of justifiable homicide. Walker goes to work, knowing it will be an uphill battle to convince a jury that the former porn star is innocent of the charges.

Sweet Women Lie. Houghton Mifflin, 1990

Gail Hope is a former movie star whose good looks always got her into trouble, and now she wants to pay to end her relationship with mobster Sam Lucy. She uses Walker as her bag man, and when he tries to deliver the money, he discovers his client has lied, Sam is in a coma, and the CIA is interested in what is in the bag.

Never Street. Mysterious Press, 1997

Gay Caitlan's theory is that her husband Neil is so obsessed with film noir that he has slipped into a personal noir nightmare. When Walker finds Gay's brother dead in a drug house full of equipment stolen from Neil's production company, he also finds that Neil's mistress is being followed to uncover the goods from the robbery. So the question is, who is Walker really after?

Michigan, Mackinac Island

The Witchfinder. Mysterious Press, 1998

Jay Bell Furlong is a world-famous architect, and he has made his wealth on the West Coast. He has returned to Detroit and needs Walker's help because his one true love affair was destroyed when he believed the evidence in a photograph that later proves to be doctored. When Walker strives to find the truth, he discovers that many people in Furlong's past had a reason to destroy him.

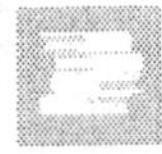

Architects

The Hours of the Virgin. Mysterious Press, 1999

The Hours of the Virgin is a section of the *Horae, or Book of Hours*, an ancient manuscript, which has gone missing. Offered a finder's fee by Harold Boyette, an independent consultant for the Detroit Institute of Art, Walker agrees to locate it. The prime suspect is Earl North, someone Walker is very familiar with because North murdered Walker's mentor when Walker was a young P.I.

Antiquities · Publishing

A Smile on the Face of the Tiger. Mysterious Press, 2000

Louise Starr returns to Walker's life, this time as a publisher interested in reprinting the works of paperback original writer Eugene Booth. Booth is one of the greats from the 1950s, but his career stalled after he wrote a novel about the race riots in Detroit in 1943. Walker's job is to find Booth and discover why he first accepted, and then returned, a check from Starr offered for reprint rights to his works.

Authors · Michigan

Sinister Heights. Mysterious Press, 2002

Walker is hired to hunt down the illegitimate heirs to some old Detroit auto money controlled by the estate of auto baron Leland Stutch. Walker's client is the 26-year-old widow, Rayellen Stutch, and she is worried about potential claims against the state and the moral obligation she has to share her wealth with Leland's heirs out of wedlock. When Walker begins to stir the pot, two deaths occur, one of which is personally devastating to Walker.

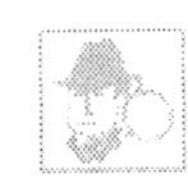

Automobile manufacturing

Sue Grafton ✍

Kinsey Millhone

The most popular of the female private detectives, Kinsey Millhone works out of her office in Santa Teresa, California. Her ability to work the mean streets while maintaining a perky personality appeals to a great number of readers and has made her the best-selling character of the 1990s. The good news for her fans is that she ages one year for every two books, so she should have a long and healthy career. Readers may also enjoy Linda Barnes, Marcia Muller, and Sara Paretsky. See the author's website at http://www.suegrafton.com. **Traditional**. Series subject: **California, Santa Teresa**.

"A" Is for Alibi. Holt, 1982

Millhone is hired by a recently released murderer who wants her name cleared. When Millhone begins to stir the ashes of an eight-year-old poisoning case, it adds elements of blackmail, sex, and money to what originally appeared to be an open-and-shut case.

California, Los Angeles

"B" Is for Burglar. Holt, 1985

Millhone is hired by Beverly to locate her missing sister, but when the police want to file a missing person report, Beverly gets shy. A coincidental murder and arson case next door to the missing sister's apartment sparks Millhone's interest, and soon the ties between the two cases grow stronger. AN SH

Florida

"C" Is for Corpse. Holt, 1986

Millhone, recovering from the broken arm received on her last case, is working out when she meets the very sad-looking Bobby. Broken in body and spirit by a car accident that killed his best friend, Bobby's mind only allows him to remember he was in trouble, and that the accident was a murder attempt. Millhone takes his case, and soon an even greater tragedy strikes her and Bobby. AN

"D" Is for Deadbeat. Holt, 1987

Millhone is handed a $25,000 cashier's check by a man who is not who he says he is, and when he dies, and the recipient of the check does not want it, Millhone is stuck. A legacy of alcohol abuse led the dead man to a case of vehicular manslaughter, and the check was to make up for the deaths.

"E" Is for Evidence. Holt, 1988

Millhone is set up to appear as an accomplice in an arson-for-profit scheme. Her supposed partner is Lance Wood, a wimp who inherited his family's business over all the other siblings' objections. Kinsey will take a bruising from a bomb in this one, but it will take more than that to keep her from restoring her honor.

"F" Is for Fugitive. Holt, 1989

Millhone is hired by the ancient father of an escaped convict whose life under an alias has just come to a crashing halt. Called to the oppressively small town of Floral Beach, Millhone takes up residency with the con's family in their depressing hotel. Her job, to clear the son, leads her down a dark path to the truth.

California, Floral Beach

"G" Is for Gumshoe. Holt, 1990

Millhone is handed a case involving a sickly daughter who needs someone to find her mother. At the same time, she discovers that someone has placed a contract on her own head. When she locates the missing mother, she finds a raving old woman with a cryptic story to tell. When her assassin finds her, he is a scary man who brings his son along on the kill. AN SII

California, Los Angeles • California, Mohave Desert

"H" Is for Homicide. Holt, 1991

Millhone's curiosity is piqued when one of California Fidelity's claims agents is murdered and she can trace an auto insurance fraud back to a claim he refused to handle. Bibianna Diaz becomes her contact and Millhone uses her to get to Raymond Maldonado, the leader of a Hispanic gang that regularly stages auto accidents to reap the benefits from the insurance settlements.

California, Los Angeles

"I" Is for Innocent. Holt, 1992

Her new office landlords hire Millhone to dig into an old murder. For six years, the law firm of Kingman and Ives has been interested in proving that Daniel Barney is guilty of shooting his estranged wife, Isabelle. Isabelle had three husbands, a slightly tainted business career, and her own alcoholism to distance her from her friends. Millhone's job is complicated by the fact that the murder weapon was stolen from a party where all the major suspects were present.

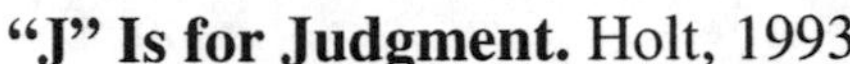

"J" Is for Judgment. Holt, 1993

Dana Jaffe has finally collected the half-million dollars owed her after the apparent suicide of her husband Wendell. Wendell was the mastermind of a Ponzi scheme that send his partner Carl Eckert to jail while Jaffe supposedly disappeared at sea. Mac Voorhis, Millhone's former boss at California Fidelity, now wants to hire Millhone to determine if a rumor that Jaffe is in Mexico has any truth to it.

California, Perdido • Mexico, Viento Negro

"K" Is for Killer. Holt, 1994

Janice Kepler's daughter is dead, but when someone delivers a pornographic tape of Lorna Kepler in her mother's mailbox, she hires Kinsey to research her daughter's death. When she probes into Lorna's life, she discovers the hooker's estate is $20,000 short and that the mob has an unusual interest in the investigation. SII

California, San Francisco • Pornography

"L" Is for Lawless. Holt, 1995

Henry Pitts has been Millhone's landlord forever, and she does him a favor by looking into the life of a recently deceased WWII veteran that he knew. His family cannot understand why he has no military service record. However, when the dead man's apartment is burglarized and an acquaintance of the old man is beaten, she knows someone else is interested in the same questions she is.

Texas, Dallas

"M" Is for Malice. Holt, 1996

With a $40 million dollar company driving their family, the Maleks should be content. But 18 years earlier, one of the Malek sons disappeared. The family thinks the four middle-aged sons should now be reunited, so they hire Millhone to carry out the task.

"N" Is for Noose. Holt, 1998

Tom Newquist has died, and his widow is not satisfied with the coroner's report. She knows that her husband has been wandering at night for the last six weeks, and that he was keeping some secret from her. She brings Millhone to her small town in the hopes that the private eye can find the answers.

California, Nota Lake

"O" Is for Outlaw. Holt, 1999

Millhone gets a call one day from a man who empties storage lockers that have been abandoned. He has the contents of one locker that contains information about Millhone. One item in the piles of stuff is a letter that reveals things about her past, and leads her to an old unsolved murder.

"P" Is for Peril. Putnam, 2001

Despite having abandoned his wife, Fiona Purcell, for a new wife, Crystal, who was a stripper, Dr. Dowan Purcell is still of interest to Fiona. So she hires Millhone to trace the doctor after he disappears, and the P.I. discovers links to a Medicare fraud investigation being conducted at the nursing home where the doctor works.

Nursing homes

"Q" Is for Quarry. Putnam, 2002

Sometimes the cops just cannot let go of an old case, and when two old cops want to clear an 18-year-old murder case, they hire Millhone. Sent to identify the victim, Millhone that finds her investigation awakens long-lost urges and the desire of a killer to kill again.

California, Quorum

Jeremiah Healy ✍

John Francis Cuddy

A knight errant for the modern world, Cuddy is affected by the death of his wife and visits her gravesite to talk to her about his cases and his life. When needed, he is not afraid to use violence to solve the cases he is on. Healy is a master at combining the toughness of the private eye with a true puzzle, so his novels can be recommended to both the traditional as well as the hard-boiled mystery reader. Readers may also enjoy Linda Barnes, Loren D. Estleman, Robert B. Parker, and William Tappley. **Traditional/Hard-boiled**. Series subject: **Massachusetts, Boston**.

Blunt Darts. Walker, 1984

Cuddy accepts a case involving the disappearance of a young runaway despite the fact that he is hired by the boy's grandmother and told to have no contact with the boy's father, a prominent judge. Of course, he is almost immediately warned off the case by the judge.

Cuddy believes the case will ultimately revolve around solving the reason for the disappearance of the judge's wife.

Massachusetts, Meade

The Staked Goat. U.S.: Harper, 1986 (U.K.: *The Tethered Goat.* Macmillan. 1986)

Cuddy gets a call from an old army buddy that includes a code implying danger, and Cuddy's task soon becomes hunting down the killer of his friend. At the same time, he is involved in an arson-for-profit scheme that threatens his own welfare, and leads to the murder of two innocents. SII

Pennsylvania, Pittsburg

So Like Sheep. Harper, 1987

Cuddy is asked by Boston homicide Lt. Murphy to explore a case involving a young black man accused of murdering his white girlfriend and admitting his guilt under hypnosis. Although no one else has any doubt, Cuddy discovers little inconsistencies in the case as he begins to explore.

Swan Dive. Harper, 1988

Cuddy gets hoodwinked into riding shotgun on an ugly divorce case when his old lawyer pal Chris calls for help. Roy seems to be in some coke-induced nightmare, while his wife Hannay struggles to save her child, Vickie. Then someone uses Roy's gun to kill a hooker and pushes Roy out of a window, and the police begin to suspect Cuddy may be the culprit.

Massachusetts, Peabody • Massachusetts, Swampscott

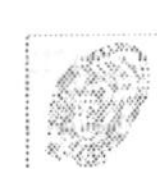

Yesterday's News. Harper, 1989

On the very same day that reporter Jane Rust hires Cuddy to investigate the death of her source, Jane is found a suicide in the tiny town of Nasharbor. The source, Charlie Coyne, was found stabbed behind the bar where he worked, and the police are reluctant to believe Coyne's testimony that a cop may be on the take from a porn ring.

Massachusetts, Nasharbor • Pornography

Right to Die. Pocket, 1991

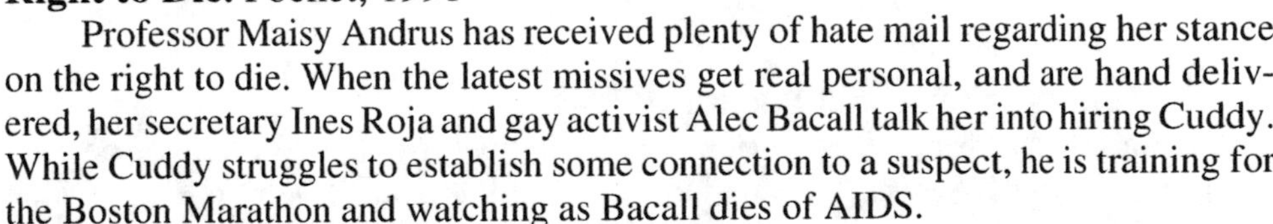

Professor Maisy Andrus has received plenty of hate mail regarding her stance on the right to die. When the latest missives get real personal, and are hand delivered, her secretary Ines Roja and gay activist Alec Bacall talk her into hiring Cuddy. While Cuddy struggles to establish some connection to a suspect, he is training for the Boston Marathon and watching as Bacall dies of AIDS.

Right to die

Shallow Graves. Pocket, 1992

Considering Cuddy was fired as an investigator from Empire Insurance, he has a right to be surprised when their death claims investigator, Harry Mullen, wants Cuddy to verify a half-million dollar claim on model Mau Tim Dani. Mau Tim was strangled in her apartment, and the police lay the crime off on a random burglary. Cuddy discovers that people in the modeling community may have had reasons to kill the model.

Models

Foursome. Pocket, 1993

Cuddy is called to the defense of the only remaining member of The Foursome when the other three are found slain with bolts from a crossbow. Steven Shea's weekend at his Maine house should have been a relaxing few days, but it is he who discovers the bodies of his wife Sandy and their best friends, Vivian and Hale Vandemeer. Cuddy, who does not like or believe his client, goes to work anyway and begins to unravel the truths behind the killings.

Maine, Marseilles Pond

Act of God. Pocket, 1994

Against his will, Cuddy takes on two clients for a joint case. Abraham Rivkind, co-owner of Value Furniture, is murdered in his store one night at closing time. His widow, Pearl, comes to Cuddy with William Proft in tow. Proft's sister was Rivkind's secretary, and she failed to return from her vacation right after the murders.

Rescue. Pocket, 1995

Cuddy rides to the rescue of Eddie Haldon, a boy scarred with a prominent birthmark, who casually asks him for help when they meet on the freeway during a car repair. When Eddie's companion, Melinda, is found dead, Cuddy launches a search to find the boy.

Florida, Mercy Key • New Hampshire, Elton

Invasion of Privacy. Pocket, 1996

Worried banker Olga Evorova wants Cuddy to look into the background of her fiancé, Andrew Dees. The search leads Cuddy to a mysterious condominium complex and the college records of a dead man. When things get dangerous, Cuddy goes on a thrilling hunt for a man with a serious plan.

Massachusetts, Plymouth Mills

The Only Good Lawyer. Pocket, 1998

The fact that he cannot abide his client is a problem for Cuddy, but no matter how he looks at the murder case swirling around Alan Spaeth, he is convinced the man is innocent. Knowing that the victim in the case was Spaeth's wife's lawyer, African-American Woodrow Wilson Gant, he realizes that his attempts to free Spaeth will be political and unpopular.

The Concise Cuddy. Crippen and Landru, 1998

A collection of the following stories: "The Bagged Man," "Battered Spouse," "Bertie's Moon," "Crossed Wires," "Deputy Down," "Double-Con," "Georgie-Boy," "One Eye Open," "St. Nick," "Someone to Turn Out the Lights," "A Soul to Tell," "Spin-a-Rama," "Summary Judgement," "The Three Muskateers," "Till Tuesday," "The Winfield Trade," and "Yellow Snow."

Short stories

Spiral. Pocket, 1999

Cuddy is in mourning, and he needs a fresh case to break him out of his funk. He goes to Fort Lauderdale when he hears from Colonel Nicholas Helides, a Vietnam vet and friend who has been struck down by a stroke. Helides needs Cuddy to locate his granddaughter

Veronica's killer. The reason for her death might lie in the fact that the very rich young girl, wrapped up in the world of rock and roll, was moving in dangerous circles.

Florida, Fort Lauderdale

P. D. James ✍

Cordelia Gray

The shy Cordelia Gray becomes the assistant to a private investigator in London, and then inherits his agency upon his death. Her dogged determination overcomes her own shortcomings as she proves to be a competent investigator. Gray is one of the first modern female private investigators along with Marcia Muller's Sharon McCone and Maxine O'Callaghan's Deliah West. Readers may also enjoy Antonia Fraser, Jennie Melville, and Dorothy L. Sayers. **Traditional**.

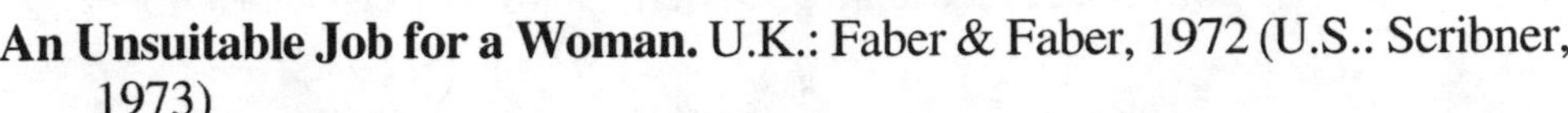

An Unsuitable Job for a Woman. U.K.: Faber & Faber, 1972 (U.S.: Scribner, 1973)

Cordelia Gray finds herself the owner of a detective agency when her partner and mentor, Bernie Pryde, commits suicide. She is determined to carry on and be successful, so she accepts a case offered by Sir Ronald Callender. He is interested in finding out why his son committed suicide.

England, Cambridge · England, Duxford · England, London

The Skull Beneath the Skin. U.K.: Faber & Faber, 1982 (U.S.: Scribner, 1982)

Sir George Ralston hires Gray to protect his wife, actress Clarissa Liele, from written death threats. On Courcy Island, owned by Ambrose Gorringe, there will be a production of *The Duchess of Malfi*, and Clarissa will be surrounded by a cast of characters that could potentially do her harm.

Actors · England, Courcy Island · Theater

Philip Kerr ✍

Bernard Gunther

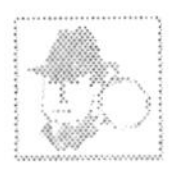

Kerr wrote a trilogy that covers the beginning, war years, and post-war years of Nazi Germany. His lead character is a world-weary P.I. named Gunther who becomes his eye on the times. This series captures European history with a master's touch, and could appeal to any reader who enjoys historical fiction. As a mystery, this series should be recommended to any hard-boiled mystery reader. Readers may also enjoy Max Allan Collins and Ken Kuhlken. See the author's website at http://www.philipkerr.co.uk. **Hard-boiled/Historical**. Series subjects: **Historical (1900–1999) · Nazi Germany · World War II**.

March Violets. Viking, 1989

In 1936 Berlin, the city is getting ready for the Olympics. A young couple named Greta and Paul have been shot and their safe robbed, and Gunther is hired to discover why. The real question is why does Greta's father's boss, Himmler, want to know what was in the safe.

Germany, Berlin

The Pale Criminal. Viking, 1990

In 1938, Gunther checks into the clinic of Dr. Kindermann, in search of clues to reveal why publishing dowager Frau Lange's son's revealing letters of homosexual love are now tools for a blackmailer. As he works, the Nazis take interest, and Gunther finds himself forced to rejoin the Kripo.

Germany, Berlin

A German Requiem. Viking, 1991

Moving from the Kripo to the SS, Gunther has been transferred to the Russian front and captured, then finally returned to Berlin. Returning to work as a P.I., he is sent to Vienna to prove that a former SS comrade is innocent of murdering an American Captain.

Austria, Vienna

Ken Kuhlken ✍

Thomas Hickey

Thomas Hickey suffers the driftlessness that was common as the Depression was winding down and America was preparing to fight a world war. His noir lifestyle makes him a perfect candidate to lead an investigation in the dark cases that come his way. Kuhlken is able to capture the 1940s in a way that should appeal to any historical fiction reader. Readers may also enjoy Harold Adams, Max Allan Collins, and Philip Kerr. See the author's website at http://www.kenkuhlken.net. **Hard-boiled/Historical**. Series subjects: **California, San Diego · Historical (1900–1999)**.

The Loud Adios. St. Martin's Press, 1991

Hickey owns a small potatoes agency with partner Leo Weiss. Then his wife runs off with his former partner in the music business, and he is drafted into the Army. While guarding the border, he is pushed into crossing the dangerous Tijuana border with a young soldier named Clifford Rose, on a mission to rescue Rose's sister Wendy. Hickey does not know the whole truth, and the sojourn into Mexico will prove very dangerous.

Mexico, Tijuana · World War II

The Venus Deal. St. Martin's Press, 1993

This prequel to the first book tells the story of Hickey and how he is struggling to hold together his marriage to Madeline for the sake of his daughter, Elizabeth. When he loses his lead singer at the club he manages, he and partner Leo Weiss go on a hunt for her.

Colorado, Denver

The Angel Gang. St. Martin's Press, 1994

Hickey is reluctant to leave his Tahoe cabin and his pregnant wife, Wendy, to take the arson-murder case involving Cynthia "Moon" Tucker Jones. The problem may lie in the fact that Cynthia was messing with small-time hood Johnny Sousa, the husband of her sister, Laurel.

Nevada, Tahoe

Dennis Lehane ✍

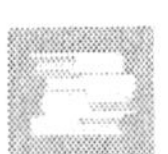

Patrick Kenzie/Angela Gennaro

The blue-collar neighborhoods of Boston are the stomping grounds of a hip male/female team that helped redefine the private eye in the 1990s. From the belfry of a church taken over for their office, the team handles everything thrown at them, and always ends up slightly bent but still standing. Readers may also enjoy Robert Crais, James Crumley, and S. J. Rozan. See the authors website at http://www.dennislehanebooks.com. **Hard-boiled**. Series subjects: **Massachusetts, Boston · Teams**.

A Drink Before the War. Harcourt Brace, 1994

When an African-American cleaning woman named Jenna Angeline goes missing with some important documents, Kenzie and Gennaro are hired by the politicians to retrieve the papers. She is killed before the P.I. team can find her, but her death does not end the case. Instead, the simple becomes the complex, and Kenzie and Gennaro find themselves up against a street gang and the government. SH

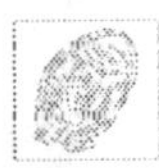

Politics

Darkness, Take My Hand. Morrow, 1996

Kenzie and Gennaro have been friends forever, growing up together in the blue-collar world of Dorchester. A series of killings stretch back over 20 years in the community, and Kenzie decides to find the murderer. His goal places himself and Gennaro in jeopardy and up against the mob.

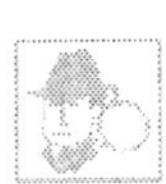

Massachusetts, Dorchester · Organized crime · Serial killer

Sacred. Morrow, 1997

Trevor Stone is dying, but his greatest concern is his missing daughter, Desiree. His first investigator has disappeared, so he turns to Kenzie and Gennaro to continue the case. As the two push their inquiries, they find themselves up against a cult and a bigger firm that may be covering up the truth.

Gone Baby Gone. Morrow, 1998

Helene McCready left the door unlocked one night, and now her daughter Amanda is missing from her bed. As time passes, the case grows cold for the police, and the media begins to lose interest. So, Helene and her family turn to the detective team to get on the trail of her four-year-old daughter. BA DI

Kidnapping

Prayers For Rain. Morrow, 1999

In six months, Karen Nichols is destroyed by a stalker, to the point where she takes a dive off the Boston's Custom House. Because he knew Karen, Kenzie seeks revenge, and he decides this is a perfect time to call in a favor from the estranged Gennaro who has quit the business.

Stalkers

Laura Lippman ✍

Tess Monaghan

Beginning her professional career as a newspaper reporter, Monaghan migrates to private eye status when she decides to start her own business after being laid off from her newspaper. Her cases show off the city of Baltimore, making the city's neighborhoods a character in the novels. Monaghan's extended family and complicated love life add flavor to the adventures. Readers may also enjoy Linda Barnes, Jan Burke, Sue Grafton, and Nancy Pickard. **Traditional**. Series subject: **Maryland, Baltimore**.

Baltimore Blues. Avon, 1997

Two years prior to this novel, Monaghan lost her job as a reporter for the *Baltimore Star*, so she is willing to take the money from her friend Darryl Paxton, a fellow rower. He wants his girlfriend Ava followed. Ava's affair with prominent but slightly sleazy attorney, Michael Abramowitz, is revealed by Monaghan's surveillance, and quickly Darryl is arrested for Michael's murder. Darryl's lawyer, rowing coach Tyner Gray, puts Monaghan on his staff to continue her investigation.

Charm City. Avon, 1997

Baltimore's big chance to nab an NBA team is threatened when the *Beacon-Light* runs a front-page story about the financial and moral instability of its potential owner, Wink Wynkowski. The paper hires Monaghan to investigate how her friend Feeney's story appeared, as the editor at the *Beacon* had cancelled the story as being too controversial. While the focus is shifting from the team to the owner, the controversy leads to an untimely death that embroils Monaghan in the center of the controversy. ED SH

Basketball

Butchers Hill. Avon, 1998

Years ago, Luther Beale shot an 11-year-old juvenile delinquent and became branded as the devil. Now, out of prison, he has hired brand-new P.I. Tess to find the children who were with Donnie Moore the night he died so that Luther can make restitution. When a strange missing persons case provides Monaghan with an African-American client who now owes her a favor, she compells the reluctant Jacqueline Weir into being her assistant, much needed as Baltimore's African-American community is not exactly opening its arms to the very white Monaghan's inquiries. AG AN

In Big Trouble. Avon, 1999

When an envelope arrives in the mail with a newspaper picture of her ex-boyfriend Crow, and the words "in big trouble," Monaghan is intrigued enough to contact his parents. Hired by them to find their missing son, Monaghan finds herself driving to Austin, Texas.

Crow has been gone for months, but he has made little impact on the music scene in Austin, and only a chance encounter with an old band mate leads her to a remote ranch and a dead body in San Antonio. AN SH

Texas, San Antonio

The Sugar House. Morrow, 2000

Ruthie Dembrow's brother accidentally killed a woman and went to prison for it, only to be killed in jail one month into his sentence. Ruthie wants to hire Monaghan to find out why, especially because no one knows who the girl was that her brother Henry murdered.

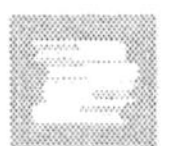

In a Strange City. Morrow, 2001

Tricked by a client into going to the annual appearance of The Visitor at Edgar Allan Poe's graveside, Monaghan is there when a second visitor appears. Someone shoots the false visitor, and Monaghan finds herself on an exploration of Poe's life and his influence on Baltimore while trying to protect a legend from being exploited.

Poe, Edgar Allan

Marcia Muller ✍

Sharon McCone

One of the pioneer contemporary female private eyes, McCone begins her career at All Souls Collective in San Francisco. Eventually, situations force her to branch out as an independent investigator. Her cases are always complex puzzles, and often concern a social issue. Her relationship with her co-workers, family, and her lovers also makes the series interesting. Readers may also enjoy Linda Barnes, Sue Grafton, and Sara Paretsky. See a fan's website at http://interbridge.com/marciamuller. **Traditional**. Series subject: **California, San Francisco**.

Edwin of the Iron Shoes. McKay, 1977

McCone has spent the last five months investigating the threats against a cooperative association of antique and junk dealers near the Civic Center, and it is common knowledge that any of the four agencies eager to purchase the cooperative's land could be the agents behind the trouble. When the head of the association, Joan Albritton, is murdered in her shop, McCone continues her investigation in the hope of helping the police solve the murder.

Antiquities

Ask the Cards a Question. St. Martin's Press, 1982

McCone is babysitting a suicidal friend, Linnea Carraway, in her apartment, when Molly Antonio, a tenant in the building, is killed. The investigation is headed by Greg Marcus, who is developing an interest in McCone as a person. His case is complicated by the strange characters that live in and around McCone's building, and he needs McCone's help to sort out the suspects.

The Cheshire Cat's Eye. St. Martin's Press, 1983

McCone responds to a cry for help and is shocked to discover her friend Jake Kaufmann dead in an old Victorian he was restoring. The conflict that set Jake up involves disagreements over how old homes should be restored, and a missing Tiffany lamp may be one of the major clues. Then, McCone is accused of the murder.

Antiquities

Games to Keep the Dark Away. St. Martin's Press, 1984

McCone is working for a recluse photographer, Abe Snelling, who wants her to find his missing roommate. Led to a small and failing town, Sharon finds the unfriendly residents difficult to interview. She is led to Tidepools, a hospice with a history of mysterious mercy killings.

Medical

Leave a Message for Willie. St. Martin's Press, 1984

McCone takes the case of Willie Whelan, the king of the flea markets (i.e., fence) when he thinks someone is following him. The murders of Jerry Levin, a man who recovers stolen Torahs, and Willie's girlfriend, Alida, clearly indicate that Willie did not tell McCone the truth about his case.

Double (with Bill Pronzini). St. Martin's Press, 1984

Told in alternating chapters by each author's P.I., this is a tale of the two characters meeting in San Diego at the National Society of Investigators annual convention. McCone's friend, hotel detective Elaine Picard, is pushed out of the tower of the Casa Del Rey Hotel, and when McCone presses her investigation, she ends up in jail and needs Nameless's help. He could use some help as well, as he is trying to trace a mother and child missing from the hotel.

California, San Diego • Pronzini, Bill

There's Nothing to Be Afraid Of. St. Martin's Press, 1985

McCone gets involved with some resettled Vietnamese who now occupy a hotel in San Francisco's Tenderloin district. Someone is trying to drive these people from their new home, and McCone's job is to find out who, especially after the body of Hoa Dinh turns up in the hotel's basement.

Hotels • Vietnamese-Americans

Eye of the Storm. Mysterious Press, 1988

McCone is making amends to her sister, Patsy, and niece, Kelley, for her inattention by taking a vacation to Appleby Island in the Sacremento Delta. Patsy is trying to restore a historic Victorian for a bed-and-breakfast, and someone is trying to stop the project. When a murder occurs, she must assemble the clues to protect her family.

California, Appleby Island • Hotels

There's Something in a Sunday. Mysterious Press, 1989

A routine surveillance job on Frank Wilkonson requested by Rudy Goldring turns to a mystery when McCone tries to report back to her client and finds him murdered. His veiled lies to her at the start of the case make her curious enough to probe into the man's family ties, and this leads her to Hollister, Wilkonson's home town, where she must select a murderer from among the wealthy or the homeless.

California, Hollister

The Shape of Dread. Mysterious Press, 1989

Two years prior, a stand-up comic named Tracey Kostakos was kidnapped and murdered by a parking valet at the Café Comedie, but now All Souls lawyers believe the truth may never have been told. They ask McCone to investigate this old case, and when she does, she turns up some discrepancies from the past, including some dark events in Tracey's life.

Trophies and Dead Things. Mysterious Press, 1990

Perry Hilderly is one of the four victims of a random series of street shootings. Because he is an All Souls client, they help clean up his affairs, only to discover a mysterious new will that disinherits his children and leaves his estate to four strangers. It becomes McCone's job to locate these benefactors and determine if any of them is a murderer.

Wills

Where Echoes Live. Mysterious Press, 1991

Former All Souls co-worker, Anna-Marie Altman, is now counsel for the California Coalition for Environmental Preservation, and she is investigating the intentions of the Transpacific Corporation to reopen a gold mine in the Tufa Lake region near the town of Promiseville. Anna-Marie is worried when the cabin she is sharing with her associate Ned Sanderman is broken into, when the original owner of the mine disappears, and when a body is found in the lake. She hires McCone to investigate the occurrences and fight against the giant corporation.

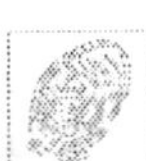

California, Promiseville • Mining

Pennies in a Dead Woman's Eyes. Mysterious Press, 1992

In 1956, Lis Benedict was convicted of murdering Cordelia McKittridge and is released in 1992. Jack Stuart, an All Souls lawyer, is the boyfriend of Judy Stameroff, Lis's daughter, and the two of them want to take Lis's case to the Historical Tribunal. McCone is not happy taking on an old case, but when it appears that Lis has been murdered, a historical case takes on contemporary meaning.

Wolf in the Shadows. Mysterious Press, 1993

Things at All Souls have changed, and McCone feels threatened by a possible premonition that will remove her from her investigative role. Then, her friend Hy Ripinsky disappears, leaving a trail of dangerous and threatening clues that sets McCone on his trail. AN

California, San Diego

Till the Butchers Cut Him Down. Mysterious Press, 1994

Cutting her ties to All Souls, McCone opens her own agency. Her first independent case comes from a man from her college days at Berkeley named T. J. Gordon. Gordon is a turnaround man who revives failing companies, but this ability also brings enemies. Gordon's problem is he feels threatened, and then he disappears, leaving McCone to chase him and bring him back from the dark side.

Nevada, Lost Hope • Pennsylvania, Monora

The McCone Files. Crippen and Landru, 1995

A collection of the following stories: "All the Lonely People," "Benny's Place," "The Broken Men," "Cache and Carry," "Deadly Fantasies," "Deceptions," "File Closed," "Final Resting Place," "The Last Open File," "The Lost Coast," "Merrill-Go-Round," "The Place that Time Forgot," "Silent Night," "Somewhere in the City," and "Wild Mustard."

Short stories

A Wild and Lonely Place. Mysterious Press, 1995

McCone likes the idea of a $1 million reward for the capture of the Diplo-Bomber, a terrorist who has been targeting the embassies of oil-rich nations. However, as she steps in to investigate a failed attempt to bomb the Azad consulate in San Francisco, her instincts point her towards the family that surrounds the counsel general, a Western-educated woman named Malika Hamid.

Caribbean, St. Maarten

The Broken Promise Land. Mysterious Press, 1996

McCone's sister Charlene is married to one of the top country western singers, Ricky Savage. But their marriage was already on the rocks when he begins to receive threats against himself and his family. Combining talents with Hy Ripinsky, McCone begins a personal investigation that proceeds despite Savage's uncooperative nature.

Musicians

Both Ends of the Night. Mysterious Press, 1997

Matty Wildress is McCone's former flight instructor, and she calls on her detective friend when her lover, John Seabrook, disappears and leaves his son, Zach, behind. John had wanted Matty to take his son and disappear as he did, but when Matty ignores the warning to compete in an air show, it has fatal consequences. McCone and Hy investigate to find Matty's murderer based on their own personal needs for revenge.

Airplanes • California, Los Alegres

While Other People Sleep. Mysterious Press, 1998

McCone's reputation is threatened when a mysterious imposter begins to pass out fake business cards that are duplicates of hers. What is more disturbing is that this doppelganger is using her physical similarity to McCone to become intimate with men. At the same time, McCone is investigating the lover of her office manager Ted Smalley, and as she finds herself prying into his personal life, she begins to understand how to deal with the invasion of her own.

A Walk Through Fire. Mysterious Press, 1999

Called to Hawaii, McCone's job is to investigate a series of accidents plaguing filmmaker Glenna Stanleigh as she tries to shoot her documentary. The film is focusing on the father of the film's backer, islander Peter Wellbright. As tensions mount between the native Hawaiians and the non-residents, McCone finds herself having to solve a murder as well.

Hawaii, Kauai

McCone and Friends. Crippen and Landru, 2000

This collection of stories features McCone and other characters from this long running series. A collection of the following stories: "The Holes in the System" (Kelleher); "If You Can't Take the Heat" (McCone); "Knives at Midnight" (McCone); "One Final Arrangement" (Savage); "Recycle" (Ripinsky); "Solo" (McCone); "Up at the Riverside" (Smalley); and "The Wall" (Kelleher).

Short stories

Listen to the Silence. Mysterious Press, 2000

McCone's father passes away and while celebrating his life with her family, her relatives discover a document that reveals a long-held secret that drives her from her mother's side. Her journey of discover leads her to her Shoshone roots, and puts her between contemporary Indians and a resort developer.

California, Alturas • Montana, Flathead Indian Reservation • Native Americans

Dead Midnight. Mysterious Press, 2002

Roger Nagasawa's parents believe the pressures of work drove their son to suicide, and taking their case reopens painful memories for McCone. The secret to Roger's death may lie within the financial machinations keeping the online magazine *InSite* afloat in cyberspace. Little does McCone know this case will take one more person out of her life and place her in jeopardy for the deed.

Oregon, Tillamock County • Publishing • Suicide • World Wide Web

Sara Paretsky ✍

V. I. Warshawski

Dramatic action and a hard-boiled edge highlight the cases of Chicago female P.I. Warshawski. V. I. is not the easiest person to like, and her prickly nature often sets her against her own support network. But that same personality quirk is the quality that makes her the determined detective that most of her clients need. An eye on social concerns highlights the series, and readers will find that Warshawski's cases are darker than those of Marcia Muller's Sharon McCone or Sue Grafton's Kinsey Millhone. Readers may also enjoy Lawrence Block (Matthew Scudder) and Jeremiah Healy. See the author's website at http://www.saraparetsky.com. **Hard-boiled**. Series subject: **Illinois, Chicago**.

Indemnity Only. Dial, 1982

Warshawski is hired by a man named Thayer to find out where Anita, his son Peter's girlfriend, has disappeared to. Anita's real name is revealed, and Thayer turns out to be an imposter. Things get even more complicated for the detective when she finds Peter dead, and soon the lesson becomes that children will suffer for the sins of their fathers.

Deadlock. Dial, 1984

Warshawski's cousin Boom Boom has a job in the Chicago shipyards with the Eudora Grain Company, where, after leaving a message for the detective, he is chewed up by the propellers of a grain carrier. Rumors of missing papers balanced against rumors of depression make Warshawski wonder: accident, suicide, or murder?

Ships

Killing Orders. Morrow, 1985

Warshawski's estranged aunt Rosa has fallen from the church's grace because of some phony securities found in the St. Albert Priory safe. Yet Rosa dismisses Warshawski almost immediately after hiring her. But the detective still finds a secret religious society mixed up with the North Shore's Catholic money, and she presses her case until her life is threatened.

Religion

Bitter Medicine. Morrow, 1987

Warshawski manages to get Consuelo Alvarado to a hospital when the 16-year-old goes into premature labor, but not soon enough to save her or the baby's life. Consuelo was the younger sister of Dr. Lotty Hershel's secretary, and soon Lottie loses her assistant, Dr. Malcolm Tregiere, to a brutal murder. Could the indifferent father of the baby be taking revenge, or is there some other sinister reason for these tragedies?

Blood Shot. U.S.: Delacorte, 1988 (U.K.: *Toxic Shock*. Gollancz, 1988)

Warshawski's mother protected Caroline Djiak from the neighbor's self-righteousness after Louise, an unwed teenager, gave birth to Caroline. Now Louise lies dying of a work-related kidney disease, and Caroline asks Warshawski to find out who her father was. Both Louise's disease and her past lead the detective to a chemical company in South Chicago owned by a rich industrialist who might be hiding the health problems caused by the plant. DA

Burn Marks. Delacorte, 1990

Warshawski's aunt Eleana is burned out of her SRO hotel. When the detective investigates the arson, she inadvertently earns the wrath of the supporters of a Hispanic candidate who is also an old acquaintance. Attempts are made on Warshawski's life, and the suspects seem to be involved in a Hispanic construction company working on the Dan Ryan Expressway.

Guardian Angel. Delacorte, 1992

Warshawski's dog is about to have puppies, and downstairs neighbor Contreras boots outs his alcoholic friend, Mitch Kruger, to make room. When Kruger's body is pulled from an industrial canal, Contreras wants Warshawski to find his killer. While she probes into the business of Diamond Head Motors, where the two friends work, she is startled to discover the trail leads back to a law firm owned by her ex-husband.

Tunnel Vision. Delacorte, 1994

Warshawski's current beau, Detective Sergeant Conrad Rawlings, has a sister named Camilla who wants the P.I. to do pro bono work by tracing the source of resistance to Camilla's all-female construction company and the low-income housing it promotes. Accepting the role reluctantly does not prevent Warshawski from asking for the same pro bono work from Dr. Lottie Herschel when she discovers a family of homeless people in her office building. Her ability to protect the family or discover the truth for Camilla becomes more complicated when a dead body is discovered in her office.

Homeless

Windy City Blues. Delacorte, 1995

A collection of the following stories: "At the Old Swimming Hole," "Grace Notes," "The Maltese Cat," "The Pietro Andormache," "Settled Score," "Skin Deep," "Strung Out," "The Takamoku Joseki," and "Three-Dot Po."

Short stories

Hard Time. Delacorte, 1999

Late one night, Warshawski is giving a lift home to her assistant Mary Louise and the assistant's ward, Emily, all of whom had attended the launch party at the Golden Glow for the latest movie featuring Lacy Dowell. Barely avoiding a body in the street and doing damage to her car, Warshawski is forced to discover who they almost hit. When the hit-and-run victim is identified as Nicola Aguinaldo, an escaped prisoner from the new and privatized prison in Coolis, Warshawski is shocked to be accused of her vehicular death by a rogue cop.

Illinois, Coolis · Prisons

Total Recall. Delacorte, 2001

A man named Paul Radbuka, who has recently recovered memories of the Holocaust and his connection to Lotty and her friend Max Loewenthal, is terrorizing Lotty. Part of this story ties to the Holocaust Asset Recovery Act, and Warshawski has an African-American client who has a claim against an insurance agency actively trying to block the passage of the Recovery Act in Illinois.

African-Americans · Holocaust · Race · World War II

Robert B. Parker ✍

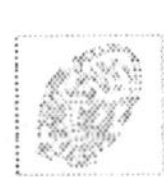

Spenser

Working out of Boston, this P.I. managed to become the most popular of the male P.I.s in the 1990s when the women private eye writers were dominant. Paired with his tough African-American enforcer Hawk, this duo combines interesting and tough methods to help their clients. Their appearances as TV characters did not hurt the popularity of this series. Readers may also enjoy Linda Barnes, Loren D. Estleman, Jeremiah Healy, and William Tappley. See at fan website for this author at http://www.linkingpage.com/spenser. **Hard-boiled**. Series subjects: **Massachusetts, Boston · Teams**.

The Godwulf Manuscript. Houghton Mifflin, 1974

When a university is missing an illuminated fourteenth-century Godwulf manuscript from its library, they ask Spenser to retrieve it. Suspicions fall on a radical student group, which gets one young man murdered and an innocent young girl needing Spenser's protection from a murder charge. As Spencer begins to dig, he is warned off by the mob, and he swiftly learns that the manuscript is the least of his problems.

Academia · Antiquities

God Save the Child. Houghton Mifflin, 1974

Before Spenser can get started finding Keith Bartlett, his family gets a ransom note drawn as a cartoon panel. After they pay the ransom, the release note, written in the form of a song, leads them to a stolen hearse with a jack-in-the-box inside the coffin. Spenser is pretty sure the kidnapping is a phony and he thinks even he would run away from this home.

Kidnapping

Mortal Stakes. Houghton Mifflin, 1975

Spenser gets to go behind the scenes at Boston's Fenway Park when the Red Sox suspect that their star pitcher may be throwing a game or two. What Spenser discovers on sidetrips to Illinois and New York is that Linda, the wife of pitcher Marty Robb, used to be a hooker in the Big Apple and even made a porn movie. A hood owns the gambling slips of a Boston broadcaster, the broadcaster knows the truth about Linda, and Spenser is the one who ends up defending her honor.

Baseball · Gambling

Promised Land. Houghton Mifflin, 1976

Spenser is hired by Harvey Shepard to locate his wife, Pam, and when Spenser travels to Cape Cod to get the details, he finds Harvey visiting with King Power's enforcer, an African-American named Hawk. Pam had a reputation around the Cape and the police are very interested in her disappearance, but Spenser has no difficulty finding her. The difficulty comes afterwards. ED

Massachusetts, Cape Cod

The Judas Goat. Houghton Mifflin, 1978

While on vacation in London, Hugh Dixon's family is blown up by a bomb, and after Hugh spends a year in the hospital, he is left without the use of his legs. He wants to seek his revenge and his instrument of revenge will be Spenser, who agrees to head to Europe to track the terrorists.

Canada, Montreal · Denmark, Copenhagen · England, London · Terrorists

Looking for Rachel Wallace. Delacorte, 1980

Hamilton Black Publishers is worried—Rachel Wallace's newest book is so controversial that the death threats aimed at the author must be taken seriously enough to hire Spenser to protect her. A macho wiseacre like Spenser does not endear himself to a feminist like Rachel, and they have a parting of the ways that leaves her free to be kidnapped. Spenser finds himself up against the radical right and a major snowstorm as he tries to locate the missing author before any damage can be done.

Authors · Kidnapping

Early Autumn. Delacorte, 1981

Custody battles can be ugly, so Spenser expects only the worst when he is hired by mother Patty Giacomin to steal her boy from the clutches of her husband, Mel. Mel gives the boy up easily, and Patty is so thrilled to have her son back that she asks Spenser to babysit the boy while she goes on a date. Taking the boy to his cabin in Maine, Spenser hopes to teach the boy to be survivor.

Maine, Kimball Lake

A Savage Place. Delacorte, 1981

Candy Sloan, reporter for television station KNBS in Los Angeles, has uncovered a scam whereby production companies pay off labor unions to ensure that their movies will be finished on time. When this knowledge causes her life to be threatened, she hires Spenser as a bodyguard. On unfamiliar territory, Spenser has to deal with the Hollywood insiders who make up the modern studio system.

California, Los Angeles • Film

Ceremony. Delacorte, 1982

Harry Kyle believes his little girl, April, has dropped out of high school to take up hooking, and through Susan he hires Spenser to find the girl and bring her home. Boston's Combat Zone becomes the logical hunting ground for April, and soon Spenser and his pal Hawk are drawn into the seamy world of sexual pleasure, which leads them to the lives of the rich and famous.

The Widening Gyre. Delacorte, 1983

Fearing that their opponent, Robert Browne, is connected to the mob, the campaign managers of Meade Alexander take the death threats they receive seriously enough to hire Spenser for protection. Things turn really nasty when the senatorial candidate reveals that he has received a videotape of his wife, Ronni, in bed with someone. The senator is willing to give up his run, but Spenser is willing to put even his personal life in jeopardy to spare his client that grief.

Politics

Valediction. Delacorte, 1984

Spenser needs some direction when Susan takes a job in San Francisco. Then his surrogate son, Paul Giacomin, provides him with a distraction when the girlfriend of one of the dancers in Paul's company disappears. Tommy Banks is the director of the company, and he is convinced that Sherry Spellman has been taken by the Reorganized Church of the Redemption.

Cults • Theater

A Catskill Eagle. Delacorte, 1985

When Hawk is jailed for murdering Emmett Colder, a security consultant for Russel Costigan, Spenser receives a plea for help from his estranged girlfriend, Susan. He leaps into the fray, freeing Hawk and going on the lam when it appears that Susan has disappeared into the warped world of Costigan.

California, San Francisco

Taming a Sea-Horse. Delacorte, 1986

The people Spenser helps never seem to forget him, so when madam Patricia Utley is worried about the same April Kyle that Spenser saved in *Ceremony*, she invites him to set off once again on the girl's trail. April has left Patricia's stable to work for Robert Rambeaux, a Juilliard student running his business on the side, and the man that she loves. However, when he cannot keep her, Spenser has to search for April one more time.

Pale Kings and Princes. Delacorte, 1987

Garrett Kingsley is angry when his reporter, Eric Valdez, is murdered while on the trail of a cocaine pipeline in Wheaton, so Kingsley hires Spenser to find out more than the Wheaton cops seem willing to reveal. Because Eric was castrated, local chief Bailey Rogers has dismissed this as a murder by a jealous lover. He might be right, as Valdez was sleeping with the chief's wife, and Spenser gets a big clue when another murder leads him down the right path.

Massachusetts, Wheaton

Crimson Joy. Delacorte, 1988

The Red Rose Killer is terrorizing all of Boston by killing black women and leaving behind a red rose. The police are terrorized themselves as the murderer claims to be a cop, and when they are frustrated by their inability to move fast enough, they hire Spenser and Hawk as vigilantes. Spenser's search becomes so successful that Susan receives a red rose.

Serial killer

Playmates. Putnam, 1989

Baron Morton is the chairman of the board of Taft University, and he knows that their basketball team is winning because of Dwayne Woodcock, the best power forward in the Big East Conference. The problem is that Dwayne is shaving points so that his team does not win by enough to cover the margin on the point spread, and the university needs someone to investigate the rumors that are reaching the public.

Academia • Basketball • Gambling • Sports

Stardust. Putnam, 1990

Susan is working as a consultant to the television show *Fifty Minutes* whose star, Jill Joyce, is suffering from harassment. Susan suggests that the producers hire Spenser for her protection. What Spenser discovers is that the star is unable to control her own emotions or her substance abuse, and when the woman's double is murdered, Spenser must attempt to defeat a very tricky opponent.

Television

Pastime. Putnam, 1991

Paul, rescued by Spenser once before, is pleading with Spenser to help his mother Patty, who has disappeared. Her involvement with Rich Beaumont may be just another in a series of bad relationships, but this one is really endangering her life.

Double Deuce. Putnam, 1992

Hawk has to call on the man he frequently works for when he is asked for help by the residents of a gang-plagued Boston housing project. The Double Deuce gang and its leader, Major Johnson, may be involved in the drive-by shooting of a teenage girl and her young daughter. Spencer deals with poverty and death in the inner city with his partner Hawk at his side.

Gangs

Paper Doll. Putnam, 1993

Spenser needs to discover if the random killing of Olivia Tripp was a street crime or something more, as her husband Loudon is thinking. When he investigates the family life of these aristocrats, he discovers that their public personas are very different from their private ones. Even with the landscape the unfamiliar South, Spenser is able to hunt for the truth among the remnants of a society trying to hold itself together.

South Carolina, Alton

Walking Shadow. Putnam, 1994

When the head of the Port City Theater Company believes he is being followed, he hires Spenser to discover the truth. There may be some truth in the paranoia, because one of the actors is murdered during the performance of the controversial play the company is producing. That is when Spenser's gifts are most needed to discover the truth, and he discovers he may be up against a Chinese-American mobster.

Massachusetts, Port City • Theater

Thin Air. Putnam, 1995

Not always on the best of terms with the police, Spenser finds he is twisted to their side when Lisa St. Claire, the new bride of a Boston detective, disappears. A woman with a past is both easy and hard to trace, and when Spenser finds himself in L.A. again, he knows he is on the trail to the truth.

California, Los Angeles • Massachusetts, Proctor

Chance. Putnam, 1996

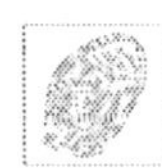

After helping the cops in the last book, Spenser finds himself helping the mob in his next case. Boston hood Julius Ventura wants Spenser to find his daughter's missing husband. Spenser and Hawk are willing to buy the cover story, but they are well aware that what really seems to be at stake is control of the mob in Boston.

Nevada, Las Vegas • Organized crime

Small Vices. Putnam, 1997

It might be easy to put away a kid like Ellis Alves for the murder of Melissa Henderson, especially if he is black and she is white. But his lawyer thinks the kid was framed, and he wants Spenser to prove it. When the detective gets to close to the truth, a hired assassin almost puts him in his grave, and the road to recovery must be followed before justice and revenge can be achieved.

New York, New York • Race

Sudden Mischief. Putnam, 1998

Susan's past haunts the detective when her ex-husband, Brad Sterling, organizes a fund-raiser called Galapalooza only to be accused of sexual harassment by one of his co-workers. With Brad deep in denial and debt from other marriages, Spenser finds his client unreliable, and when death interferes in the investigation, he finds a deadly twist to the case as well.

Hush Money. Putnam, 1999

The death of a young gay activist appears to be the stumbling block to tenure for Robinson Nevins, and he asks his friend Hawk to have Spenser investigate the allegations. He finds that tolerance on the academic campus is minimal, but he does not expect the intervention of a second deadly crime to lead Spenser to the truth.

Academia

Hugger Mugger. Putnam, 2000

The high-stakes world of horses pulls Spenser from his usual haunts to Georgia, when he accepts an assignment to guard the next triple-crown candidate, Hugger Mugger. Walter Clive, the horse's owner, has no confidence in the security firm in place, and that leaves Spenser as the odd man out. When one of Clive's daughters show a special interest in the P.I., he has to deal with his own emotions as well as the case.

Georgia, Lamarr • Horses

Potshot. Putnam, 2001

With a tip of the cowboy hat to the gunfight at the O.K. Corral and the movie *The Magnificent Seven*, Spenser travels to the small town of Potshot to help the beautiful blonde, Mary Lou Buckman, after her husband has been killed. Because Spenser finds himself up against a notorious gang of misfits led by The Preacher, he needs to gather his own clan. So familiar faces the Hawk, Chollo, Sapp, and Morris ride to the rescue of the damsel in distress.

Arizona, Potshot

Widows Walk. Putnam, 2002

Spenser is hired by former prosecutor Rita Fiore to defend Mary Smith from the charges of shooting her banker husband Nathan. As Spenser probes, and gets his usual help from his sidekick Hawk, a real estate scandal seems to be at the center of the storm and leads Spenser back to the bank where Smith worked.

Real estate

Bill Pronzini ✍

Nameless

This long-running series features the San Francisco P.I. without a name. Pronzini has long been considered one of the better writers in the field, and one of the series strengths is the inclusion of a play-fair puzzle in each. Nameless is given a host of personal demons to fight as well as interesting cases to solve over the course of the series. One of Nameless's cases is a joint venture with Colin Wilcox, while another is a joint venture with Marcia Muller, Pronzini's wife. Readers may also enjoy Lawrence Block (Matthew Scudder), Loren D. Estleman, and Jeremiah Healy. **Traditional/Hard-boiled**. Series subject: **California, San Francisco**.

The Snatch. Random House, 1971

Louis Martinetti and his partner-in-speculation, Allan Channing, are two wheeler-dealers used to calling the shots on big deals. But they find themselves on the other end when a kidnapper tricks a military prep school into handing over Louis's son, Gary.

Now they hire Nameless to carry the $300,000 ransom to the delivery point, which sets him up as the witness to the murder of kidnapper Paul Lockridge. When the boy is not released, Nameless must solve the murder of a kidnapper to find the boy.

Kidnapping

The Vanished. Random House, 1973

Elaine Kavanaugh has eagerly awaited the return from Germany of her fiancé, Roy Sands, who has just finished 20 years of service in the military. When he disappears just after his return to San Francisco, she turns to Nameless for help. A tie to another military man with a checkered background gives Nameless the clue he needs to pursue the missing man

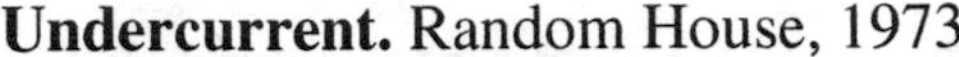

Undercurrent. Random House, 1973

After three months of marriage, Judith Page is convinced that the big deal her husband, Walter, is spending his weekends on may be another woman. When Nameless trails Walter to his murder, a big clue points to an old pulp writer named Russell Dancer, who also will need Nameless's help.

Authors · California, Cypress Bay

Blowback. Random House, 1977

When Nameless is waiting for the news about the lesion on his left lung, he accepts an invitation from old service buddy Harry Burroughs to travel up to Eden Lake in the Sierra Nevadas. But it becomes a working vacation when Nameless finds an odd mixture of men all fixated on Angela Jerrold, the wife of a guest, to whom Harry owes a lot of money. When an Oriental rug van goes into the lake with a driver who was murdered, Nameless has to determine how this new twist fits the tensions on the lake.

California, Eden Lake

Twospot (with Collin Wilcox). Putnam, 1978

Nameless is hired by Alex Cappellani, who is concerned that his mother may be romantically involved with a fortune hunter. But a related death in Hastings's territory (Collin Wilcox's character) involves him in Nameless's case, as told in alternating chapters by Wilcox.

Wilcox, Collin

Labyrinth. St. Martin's Press, 1980

Cop pal Eberhardt would really like to know why the dead girl found along the edge of Lake Merced had Nameless's card in her pocket, and Nameless would surely tell him if he knew. Haunted by the girl's death, he becomes embroiled in another case when Laura Nichols hires him to guard her wayward brother, Martin Talbot. When Talbot becomes the most likely suspect in Victor Carding's murder, Nameless is surprised to discover that the two deaths are related.

Hoodwink. St. Martin's Press, 1981

After Russel Dancer, from *Undercurrent*, invites Nameless to attend the first Western Pulp Con at a San Francisco hotel, the six members of the Pulpeteers are accused of having committed plagiarism 30 years ago. Soon, a locked-room mystery develops: Dancer, found with the dead body of Frank Colodny, is clutching the gun owned by Cybil Wade, the wife of Ivan Wade with whom Dancer fought.

Authors • Locked room

Scattershot. St. Martin's Press, 1982

During one week, Nameless has to find a missing socialite to server her with a summons, follow a man accused of infidelity by his wife, and guard some wedding gifts that prove to be the catalyst for a locked-room mystery.

Locked room

Dragonfire. St. Martin's Press, 1982

Nameless and his cop pal Eberhardt are relaxing at Eb's house when Eberhardt answers his doorbell and receives two bullets. When Nameless comes to the rescue, he is shot as well. Not as severely wounded as Eb, Nameless is able to rise from his hospital bed to hunt a killer, while Eberhardt lies dying in a hospital.

Casefile. St. Martin's Press, 1983

A collection of the following stories: "Booktaker," "Dead Man's Slough," "Death of a Nobody," "It's a Lousy World," "One of Those Cases," "Private Eye Blues," "The Pulp Connection," "Sin Island," "Where Have You Gone, Sam Spade?" and "Who's Calling."

Short stories

Bindlestiff. St. Martin's Press, 1983

A bindlestiff is a hobo and that is what Arleen Bradford believes her father to be when she hires Nameless to track him down. Despite the objections of another daughter named Hannah, Nameless begins his search for Charles Bradford in the Oroville hobo jungle, which leads him to the Roundhouse Museum and a reticent person named Dallmeyer who may hold the key to the mystery.

Homeless

Quicksilver. St. Martin's Press, 1984

Nameless is about to welcome his cop friend Eberhardt into his agency, but before that happens, he would like to clean up the case involving Haruko Gage. Gage designs wallpaper with her husband, Arthur, but lately she has been receiving jewelry through the mail as gifts from a secret admirer. Nameless does not expect this simple crime will lead him to the Yakuza, and a violent ritual murder.

Nightshades. St. Martin's Press, 1984

If Nameless can wrap up an insurance investigation quickly, he and friend Kerry Wade can enjoy a vacation together in the Musket Creek region of Northern California. But when the Northern Development Corporation wants to turn a sleepy ghost town of 16 citizens into a Disney-like theme park, the residents fight back. What should be a simple case soon turns into one of espionage, arson, and murder.

California, Musket Creek

Double (with Marcia Muller). St. Martin's Press, 1984

Told in alternating chapters by each author's P.I., this is a tale of the two characters meeting in San Diego at the National Society of Investigators annual convention. McCone's friend, hotel detective Elaine Picard, is pushed out of the tower of the Casa Del Rey Hotel, and when McCone presses her investigation she ends up in jail and needs Nameless's help. He could use some help as well, as he is trying to trace a mother and child missing from the hotel.

California, San Diego • Muller, Marcia

Bones. St. Martin's Press, 1985

Nameless's love of old pulps comes in handy when Michael Kiskadon asks him to investigate the suicide of pulp writer Harmon Crane. The death took place 35 years ago and is important to the client because Crane was his father. When an unexpected break occurs during an earthquake, Nameless is shocked by the revelations from a long-sealed tomb that will point to a murderer.

Authors

Deadfall. St. Martin's Press, 1986

Nameless thought he was out repossessing a car, but that case is forgotten when he is on the spot at the shooting of Leonard Purcell, who dies with the world "deadfall" on his lips. Tom Washburn hires Nameless to investigate the killing, which becomes more important when the detective discovers that Leonard's brother, Kenneth, died six months earlier in mysterious circumstances.

Shackles. St. Martin's Press, 1988

Taken prisoner by an unseen enemy from the past, Nameless is left to die shackled to a wall of a cabin in the mountains. His exploration of his own past and psyche while searching for clues he needs to determine who would do this him leave him scarred for life.

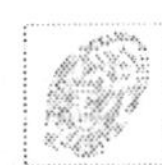

California, Deer Run

Jackpot. Delacorte, 1990

Allyn Burnett is concerned that her brother David's overdose of pills may not make much sense considering he just won $200,000 at a Lake Tahoe casino and had plans to wed Karen Salter. With David's roommate, Jerry Polhemus, behaving oddly, Nameless has a start on unraveling this sad tale.

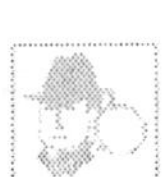

Breakdown. Delacorte, 1991

Thomas Lujack hires Nameless to clear him of the hit-and-run murder of Frank Hanauer, a partner with Thomas and Thomas's brother, Coleman, in a company called Containers, Inc. With just two witnesses to the accident, Nameless and Eberhardt begin an undercover investigation that seems to indicate that their client may not be all he claims to be.

Quarry. Delacorte, 1992

Nameless is hired by a crippled farmer in San Bernado who needs to find out why his daughter has suddenly returned to his farm. Nameless must find out whether Grady's fiancé is the cause of his daughter's problems, or whether a new relationship is driving her to despair.

California, San Bernado

Epitaphs. Delacorte, 1992

George Ferry's complaint that Gianna Fornessi, a tenant in the apartment building he manages in upscale North Beach, has stolen $2,000 leads to Nameless being hired by the girl's grandfather to protect her interests. Nameless discovers that George has dropped his claim after a beating, and Gianna disappears. When Nameless is the one to discover a body, he realizes his simple case is now a deadly one.

Demons. Delacorte, 1993

As an old friend, Nameless agrees to help Kay Runyon find the woman with whom her husband has become obsessed. Finding where Nedra Merchant lives is easy when Victor Runyon leads Nameless right to her house, but the case gets confused when a stranger seems to be as obsessed with Nedra as Victor is.

Hardcase. Delacorte, 1995

Finally united in marriage to his love Kerry, Nameless returns to work when Melanie Ann Aldrich asks him to discover her birth parents. When Nameless discovers her biological parents have a checkered past, she presses to meet her father anyway. However, Nameless's probing has uncovered some secrets that someone wishes to be kept secret, and a deadly confrontation is created.

Adoption · California, Marlin's Ferry

Spadework. Crippen and Landru, 1996

A collection of the following stories: "Ace in the Hole," "Bedeviled," "Bomb Scare," "Cat's Paw," "Here Comes Santa Claus," "Home is the Place Where," "Incident in a Neighborhood Tavern," "One Night at Dolores Park," "Skeleton Rattle Your Mouldy Leg," "Something Wrong," "Souls Burning," "Stakeout," "Twenty Miles from Paradise," "Worried Mother Job," and "Zero Tolerance."

Short stories

Sentinels. Carroll & Graf, 1996

Allison McDowell and her new boyfriend were driving home from Oregon when they disappeared off the highway, and Nameless has been hired by her mother to locate the young couple. Discovering that they were last seen in the town of Creekside, he discovers the little town is filled with the hostility of a vast conspiracy that impacted the young travelers.

California, Creekside · Cults · Oregon, Eugene

Illusions. Carroll & Graf, 1997

The most devastating death is a suicide, and when Nameless loses Eberhardt, he feels compelled to ask why. However, another case involving a Santa Fe businessman named Ira Erskine who wants his wife located distracts him until the simple case is twisted by a bizarre death.

California

Boobytrap. Carroll & Graf, 1998

Recently released from prison for setting boobytraps against his wife's lover, Donald Michael Latimer now intends to murder all those responsible for his incarceration. Nameless is one of those people, and he finds himself chasing the killer into a deadly retreat in the mountains. SH

California, Deep Mountain Lake

Crazybone. Carroll & Graf, 2000

Nameless needs to show why someone would fail to claim a $50,000 benefit from a life insurance payoff. The trail leads him to the gated community of Greenwood, where money fails to protect the inhabitants from death.

California, Greenwood

Bleeders. Carroll & Graf, 2002

Jay Cohalan thinks he has the perfect scheme planned with his girlfriend, Annette Byers, but Nameless foils their attempt to set up a phony blackmail attempt, and the P.I. ends up with the $75,000 in cash the couple had hoped to capture. When he tries to return the money to Cohalan's wife, Carolyn Dain, he finds her dead. Then, the murderer takes the money from Nameless while placing the barrel of a gun behind his ear and the detective must deal with the possibility of his own death.

Blackmail

S. J. Rozan ✍

Lydia Chin/Bill Smith

Stories in this unique series are told by two narrators: half of the books are narrated by Chinese-American Lydia Chin (the odd numbered books), and the other half are from Bill Smith's perspective (the even numbered books). One of the intriguing questions in the series is just what is the relationship between these two investigators? Using the greater New York landscape as a map, Rozan creates interesting puzzles from interesting perspectives, and has become one of the leading voices of the genre in the new millennium. Readers may enjoy Sue Grafton, Dennis Lehane, Sujata Massey, and Sara Paretsky. **Traditional**. Series subjects: **Asian-Americans · New York, New York · Teams**.

China Trade. St. Martin's Press, 1994

Chin is hired by the Chinatown Pride Museum when someone steals part of their porcelain collection. The porcelain has belonged to recluse collector Hamilton Blair, and it would be a great loss of face if the museum's loss would be made public. Teamed with her sometime-partner Smith, Chin begins to pry into a short list of suspects that includes some Chinese street gangs and some other porcelain collectors.

Antiquities · Gangs · Museums

Concourse. St. Martin's Press, 1995

Bobby Moran was Smith's mentor, so Smith is willing to go undercover as a security guard at the Bronx House for the Aged when one of Moran's security guards, Mike Downey, is killed while on duty. He has just begun his investigation when a second guard is killed. With Chin doing his legwork, Smith begins to discover a connection to the streetgang The Cobras, and their very scary leader, The Snake. SH

Gangs • Nursing homes

Mandarin Plain. St. Martin's Press, 1996

Chin is hired to deliver a $50,000 payoff for some stolen sketches that belong to fashion designer Genna Jing, but the buyoff goes bad when Chin is attacked and Smith misses the bad guys. When one of the suspects, producer Wayne Lewis, is found murdered, Chin and Smith pursue the evidence into the manufacturing end of the business and the illegal sweatshops that produce the product.

Fashion

No Colder Place. St. Martin's Press, 1997

While trying to build a 40-story apartment building in Manhattan, a construction company finds itself plagued by a series of accidents they suspect may be sabotage by one of their subcontractors. Smith finds himself working undercover as a bricklayer, while Chin works as a secretary in the construction trailer. When one of the accidents leads to murder, the two detectives find themselves with a more serious and dangerous case.

Construction

A Bitter Feast. St. Martin's Press, 1998

Chin finds herself hired by the lawyer of a new union in New York, the Chinese Restaurant Workers' Union, which believes that four of its members have gone missing. When her investigation pits her against other forces, including the NYPD and the Feds, she realizes that the issue may be much more involved than just the union's organizing.

Unions

Stone Quarry. St. Martin's Minotaur, 1999

Smith has owned a cabin in the woods for a retreat, but the sanctuary is invaded when his neighbor, Eva Colgate, asks him to locate some missing items that will reveal her long-held secrets. To his surprise, a second case develops when a dead hood is discovered in the basement of Tony Antonelli's bar. When Chin joins Smith in the woods, she discovers that she is truly a fish out of water.

New York, Schoharie

Reflecting the Sky. St. Martin's Minotaur, 2001

Chin's grandfather Gao hires her and Smith to travel to Hong Kong to deliver the ashes of a friend for burial, a communiqué from the dead man to his brother, and a valuable piece of jade the dead man bequeathed to a seven-year-old boy. When the boy is kidnapped, the two American investigators find themselves working the foreign streets to restore order. SH

Hong Kong • Jewels • Kidnapping • Wills

Winter and Night. St. Martin's Minotaur, 2002

Smith is summoned to a police station to bail out his 15-year-old nephew Gary Russell. Gary will not tell Bill what he is up to, and disappears that night from Bill's apartment. Feeling some guilt and a twinge of familial responsibility, Bill travels to the small New Jersey community of Warrenstown, where Gary had tried to make the high school football team and discovers a murder.

Football · New Jersey, Warrenstown · Sports

Steven Saylor ✍

Gordianus the Finder

The second of two Roman private detectives (see Lindsey Davis), Saylor has a much more serious approach to writing about the Roman period than Davis. Using the palette of ancient times to paint a solid mystery, Davis's novels could easily be read by any historical fiction reader. Readers may also enjoy Lindsey Davis and Sharan Newman. See the author's website at http://www.stevensaylor.com. **Traditional/ Historical**. Series subjects: **Historical (B.C.) · Italy, Rome (Ancient)**.

Roman Blood. St. Martin's Press, 1991

Cicero, a fresh, young lawyer in Rome, has taken over for Hortensius, a prominent defender, in the case of Sextus Roscius, accused of parricide. Seeking clues to Sextus's innocence, Cicero hires Gordianus to seek the truth. When the investigator discovers that the truth may lay at the feet of the emperor, things look grim.

Italy, Ameria (Ancient)

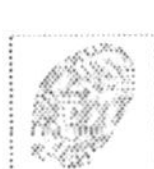

Arms of Nemesis. St. Martin's Press, 1992

The Spartacus slave revolt is in full swing when Marcus Crassus, the richest man in Rome, discovers that his overseer has been murdered. He hires Gordinaus to discover the murderer, and sets a deadline for the work after which 99 slaves will be killed.

Italy, Baiae (Ancient)

Catilina's Riddle. St. Martin's Press, 1993

When his benefactor, Lucius Claudius, leaves Gordianus a farm in the Etruscan countryside, he happily retires to the life of a gentleman farmer. However, Cicero is spying on his rival Catilina and he wants to use Gordianus's farm as a refuge for her, and a place where she can be observed. While Gordianus is making up his mind, a corpse appears as a warning to the detective, and he finds himself torn between the two camps as they go to war.

The Venus Throw. St. Martin's Press, 1995

While Rome is in turmoil, the Egyptian ambassador Dio asks Gordianus for protection, knowing that several Egyptian envoys have been recently murdered. With the ambassador dead before he can he launch an investigation, Gordianus finds himself embroiled in the internal affairs of those seeking power from the ruins of Rome.

A Murder on the Appian Way. St. Martin's Press, 1996

Turbulent times lead to the murder of Publius Clodius, a popular rival to Titus Milo, and the accusations between the warring camps lead to the destruction of the Senate House. Pompey seeks Gordianus's help in discovering the truth in an attempt to restore order to the city.

The House of the Vestals. St. Martin's Press, 1997

A collection of the following stories: "The Alexandrian Cat," "Death Wears a Mask," "The Disappearance of the Saturnalia Silver," "The House of the Vestals," "King Bee and Honey," "The Lemurs," "Little Caesar and the Pirates," "The Tale of the Treasure House," and "A Will is a Way."

Short stories

Rubicon. St. Martin's Press, 1999

Caesar has made his decision, crossed the Rubicon, and is marching on Rome. When Pompey decides to flee and leave the city of Rome vulnerable, he also leaves his cousin Numerius dead in the garden of Gordianus. Taking Gordianus's son-in-law Davus hostage, Pompey places Gordianus between the old guard and the new.

Last Seen In Massilia. St. Martin's Minotaur, 2000

With a civil war raging in Rome, Gordianus and son-in-law Davus rush to the city of Massilia in Gaul to hunt for Meto, Gordianus's son. While in the city, they see a woman fall to her death, and find themselves trying to solve two mysteries in a country where they do not belong.

France, Marseilles (Ancient)

A Mist of Prophecies. St. Martin's Minotaur, 2002

When the beautiful seer Cassandra dies in Gordianus's arms, she utters a dying clue pointing at a woman. The detective feels compelled to discover who was afraid of Cassandra's second sight.

Don Winslow ✍

Neal Carey

An apprentice P.I. who does not want to be one, Carey is one of the most unique characters in mystery fiction. His world-travelling adventures give a sweeping scope to these novels, while Carey's development as a character gives the series a pathos not always found in the P.I. canon. Readers may also enjoy Terence Faherty. See the author's website at http://www.donwinslow.com. **Traditional/Hard-boiled**.

A Cool Breeze on the Underground. St. Martin's Press, 1991

Carey is sent to London by the Friends of the Family, the investigative arm of the bank that employs his mentor Joe Graham. His task is to retrieve Allison Carey, the daughter of a powerful Senator who wishes to be Jimmy Carter's vice-president. Things do not go well for the apprentice detective and he finds himself at odds with his mentor.

England, London

The Trail to Buddha's Mirror. St. Martin's Press, 1992

Carey is sent to San Francisco to track down a Chinese artist who may have seduced a biologist into leaving his corporate job and defecting to the People's Republic of China. Carey pursues the two to Hong Kong and then into the homeland. Once there, he goes on a spiritual journey that leads to a solution that threatens to alter his life forever.

California, San Francisco • People's Republic of China

Way Down on the High Lonely. St. Martin's Press, 1993

After his China adventure is ended by his mentor Graham, Carey is sent to California to discover the whereabouts of the abducted two-year-old, Cody McCall. When he finds the trail leads to a white supremacy group working out of the Nevada desert, Carey must go undercover to recover the girl.

Children at risk • Cults • Nevada

A Long Walk Up the Water Slide. St. Martin's Press, 1994

Carey's new assignment is to baby-sit the precocious Polly Paget, a woman who has accused Jack Landis, the head of the Family Cable Network, of rape. Trying to clean up her act, while trying to keep all the wolves at bay, proves to be a challenge like no other for Carey.

Nevada, Las Vegas • Texas, Austin • Texas, San Antonio

While Drowning in the Desert. St. Martin's Press, 1996

Graham's latest assignment for Carey is a simple one: go to Las Vegas and take an old man back to his home in Palm Springs. But Carey finds the octogenarian Natty Silver a bit more than he can handle. While he chases the man around Vegas, the man tries to convince Carey that he is a witness to an arson fire and someone is trying to kill him.

Nevada, Las Vegas

Crime Specialist Detectives

Certain occupations lend themselves to aiding in criminal investigations while maintaining their status as private individuals. Occasionally these individuals will find their relationships with the professionals are cordial, and cooperation will be mutual in the investigation. On other occasions, they find themselves at odds with the investigation and sometime championing the causes of the weak and unrepresented.

The Historical Founding Members

Josephine Bell (pseud. of Doris Bell Collier Ball) ✍

Dr. David Wintringham

British writer Josephine Bell was one of the first mystery writers to feature a lead character in the medical profession. Her novels, based on her own experience as a physician, sometimes featured Dr. David Wintringham as the lead character, but she also wrote many non-series medical mysteries. Wintringham often found himself paired with Inspector Steven Mitchell of the Yard. Wintringham shares some of the characteristics of the great thinking detectives from the Golden Age. **Traditional**. Series subject: **Medical**.

Death on the Borough Council. Longmans, 1937

Councilor Hicks is interested in the doings at the local public library, where Harold Armitage is the chief librarian. Rumors have it that Harold's wife Caroline is having a liaison with Hicks, and when Hicks is found dead in Harold's office at the library, it draws the attention of visiting physician Wintringham.

England, Stepping • Libraries

Murder in Hospital. Longmans, 1937

At St. Edmund's Hospital, the body of Nurse Greenlow is found strangled with the strings of her nurse's cap and her body stuffed into a laundry basket. The hospital's work must go on, and the investigation has to take place in the hospital while its daily dramas occur. The investigation's lead falls to Wintringham, and he finds himself tracking down a murderer.

England, London

Fall Over Cliff. U.K.: Longmans, 1938 (U.S.: Macmillan, 1956)

Old. Mrs. Medlicott is dying from her second cerebral hemorrhage, and this means her estate will be divided among her relatives at her death. The problem is that over the years, some potential people who would benefit from the estate have fallen victim to various accidents. Wintringham is drawn into the case when a death occurs in his sphere, and he begins an investigation.

England • Wills

Death at Half-Term. U.K.: Longmans, 1939 (U.S.: *Curtain Call for a Corpse.* Macmillan, 1965)

The annual theatrical event at the school has fallen into the hands of the headmaster, who hires a troop of actors to replace the usual boys production. Alastair Wintringham attends the school, and it is good news that his famous uncle, the detective doctor, is going to be attending the performance as death is going to strike this school.

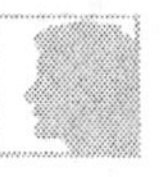

Academia • England • Theater

***From Natural Causes.** Longmans, 1939

***All Is Vanity.** Longmans, 1940

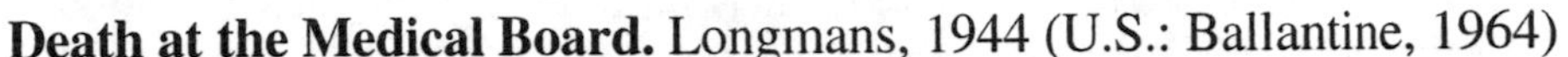

Death at the Medical Board. Longmans, 1944 (U.S.: Ballantine, 1964)

Dr. Rachel Williams is qualifying women for service during WWII when she crosses paths with a woman named Ursual Frinton. Her death during her interview process leads Williams to investigate her death, and she seeks out Wintringham's help as an ally.

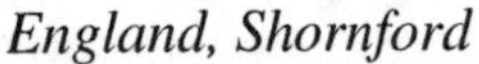

England, Shornford

Death in Clairvoyance. Longmans, 1949

Is it possible that Odette Hamilton could actually have foreseen a murder? Her vision of a man in a clown suit dying seems far-fetched, until a man in a clown suit actually dies. When Wintringham becomes involved, he must follow the truth, and not be swayed by the fantastic.

England, Summerton

The Summer School Mystery. Methuen, 1950

Falconbury School hosts music students each summer, and this particular summer Belinda Power's instrument shows up, but she does not. The mystery is solved when her body is found inside one of the orchestra's timpani. The local police ask Wintringham to investigate, and he begins to unravel the mystery.

Academia • England, Falconbury • Music

Bones in the Barrow. U.K.: Methuen, 1953 (U.S.: Macmillan, 1955)

On a commuter train one day, Terry Byrnes looks out the window and sees a murder. When no one believes him, the crime is forgotten. But Janet Lapthorn is concerned because Felicity Hilton is missing, and her husband Alastair is lying about his wife's whereabouts. When some bones are discovered, the police need Wintringham's help.

England, London

The China Roundabout. U.K.: Hodder, 1956 (U.S.: *Murder on the Merry-Go-Round.* Ballantine, 1965)

Eileen Forrester and her mother arrive at her dead brother's boardinghouse after his death to clear out his things. The tenants are oddly attracted to a miniature merry-go-around that is missing, so Eileen turns to Wintringham for help.

England

The Seeing Eye. Hodder, 1958

A celebrated art critic dies in the Westminster Art Gallery, and the police believe he was killed during an attempted robbery. But when Wintringham begins to investigate, he finds this case has more suspects than he needs.

Art • England, Westminster

Doris Miles Disney ✍

Jefferson Dimarco

Claims adjuster Dimarco is the hero of these novels by Doris Miles Disney. He works for Commonwealth Insurance of Boston, and his entry into mystery cases comes through the investigations needed to discover the truth behind the claims made by their clients. Disney is the author of many types of mysteries, and her non-series titles should be explored as well. **Traditional**. Series subject: **Insurance investigation**.

***Dark Road.** Doubleday, 1946 (Also published as *Dead Stop.* Dell, 1956)

Family Skeleton. Doubleday, 1949

Uncle Joe Bowen is not liked by any of his family. When he dies by nefarious means at a family gathering, it sets family member against family member. When DiMarco enters the fray, he finds himself with plenty of suspects.

Connecticut

Straw Man. U.S.: Doubleday, 1951 (U.K.: *The Case of the Straw Man.* Foulsham, 1958)

Commonwealth Assurance has insured Lincoln Hunter for $100,000, and will have to pay off if he is executed for the crime he has been convicted of: murdering his pregnant girlfriend. The case is built on the fact that Hunter wanted to marry someone else, and it will be DiMarco's job to determine if their client is worthy of saving.

Connecticut

Trick or Treat. U.S.: Doubleday, 1955 (U.K.: *The Halloween Murder.* Foulsham, 1957)

Mike Monroe needs to divorce his wife Edna so he can marry his secretary, Linda Haines. While he is away in Texas at Halloween, a sheet-covered murderer guns down his wife. DiMarco finds that no one connected to the woman could have done the deed, and that makes him suspicious that one of them did.

Connecticut • Halloween • Holidays

Method in Madness. U.S.: Doubleday, 1957 (U.K.: *Quiet Violence.* Foulsham, 1959; also published as *Too Innocent to Kill.* Avon, 1959)

Phyllis Bingham wants to see her mother, who has been kept a prisoner in a mental institution for 14 years since the start of Phyllis's second marriage. Phyllis's stepfather, Norman Carroll, seem anxious to keep her away from the home, as do the staff. When Dimarco suggests an independent examination of the woman, it may place her in danger.

Connecticut • Mentally challenged

Did She Fall or Was She Pushed? Doubleday, 1959

A fall from a 40-foot cliff does not bring any sympathy for Bella Shankle. When DiMarco investigates her death, he discovers that she was unliked by everyone. But none hated her more than the relatives who were about to benefit from her death.

Rhode Island

Find the Woman. Doubleday, 1962

Dr. Ira Chandler's body is pulled from Moosehead Lake one night and the clues lead investigators to believe he was murdered. When DiMarco looks into it for the insurance company, he discovers that the good doctor had many female companions, and just before his death he withdrew a large amount of money that now seems to be missing.

Connecticut · Maine, Moosehead Lake

The Chandler Policy. Putnam, 1971

Hilda Nielsen meets Earl Chandler at a turnpike reststop and helps him escape from two men who he claims he witnessed murder someone, only to discover his dead corpse further on down the road. The case falls into DiMarco's lap when the man's widow is a beneficiary of the $100,000 policy.

Connecticut, Bradford

Kenneth Fearing ✍

George Stroud

Fearing's writing career centered around poetry, but with his one mystery novel, Fearing created a unique situation. His lead character defines the paranoid character within a mystery novel setting and provided the source for one of the great film noir releases. Perhaps more suspense than detection, the power of this novel is so strong that it deserves to be listed here. It can be recommended to any traditional mystery reader. See a website about the author at http://www.english.uiuc.edu/maps/poets/a_f/fearing/fearing.htm. **Traditional**.

The Big Clock. Harcourt Brace, 1946 (Also published as *No Way Out*. Perennial, 1987)

Janoth Enterprises is an all encompassing organization that rules its employee's lives. It publishes *Crimeways*, a true crime magazine, and one of its writers is George Stroud. He is at the organization's mercy when it asks him to investigate the murder of Pauline Delos, because Stroud knows he is the culprit.

New York, New York · Publishing

Hugh Pentecost (pseud. of Judson Philips) ✍

Pierre Chambrun

Running a hotel may seem like a big enough job, but when hotel security requires that a crime be solved, then hotel manager Chambrun must save the reputation of one of New York's finest hotels. His experience as a resistance fighter during WWII helps him handle all the situations that arise within the hotel's walls. His cases are narrated by Mark Haskell, the hotel's public relations director. **Traditional**. Series subjects: **Hotels · New York, New York**.

The Cannibal Who Overate. Dodd Mead, 1962

The Hotel Beaumont is hosting the rather nasty writer Aubrey Moon. When Chambrun discovers that someone would actually like to murder the man in his hotel, he sets out to prevent the crime.

Authors

The Shape of Fear. Dodd Mead, 1964

Michael "Digger" Sullivan, a race car driver, is found robbing a suite in the hotel. His recent release on a murder charge in France still casts doubts over his veracity, and Chambrun does not take kindly to nefarious activities in his hotel. When Murray Cardew, social butterfly, dies in the hotel, it may be linked to what he knew about this case.

The Evil That Men Do. Dodd Mead, 1966

Doris Standing checks into the hotel late one night under an assumed name and without any luggage. Chambrun knows that this will be trouble as she has a retinue of hangers-on who will make his life miserable. When Jeremy Slade is murdered in her room with her gun, things do not look so good for the famous woman with no friends.

The Golden Trap. Dodd Mead, 1967

George Lovelace is a former espionage agent, and he has retired to the hotel to live out his golden years. But someone is still after him, and a series of accidents happen around him that indicate he needs an ally. Lovelace asks Chambrun for his help, and the two begin to plan a trap for a secret enemy.

Espionage

The Gilded Nightmare. Dodd Mead, 1968

George Battle, who owns the hotel, orders Chambrun to take care of Charmian Zetterstrom. Chambrun knows of her dead husband from his Resistance days when Zetterstrom was a Nazi sympathizer, but as a rich expatriated American widow, Charmain brings her own brand of death to the hotel.

Girl Watcher's Funeral. Dodd Mead, 1969

Rich Greek tycoon Nikos Karado is murdered in the hotel just two days prior to the fashion show he was sponsoring to launch the career of young designer Max Lazar. Chambrun must shift among the many men and women of New York's fashion industry to find someone desperate to end a line by murder.

Fashion

The Deadly Joke. Dodd Mead, 1971

The hotel is hosting the kickoff of Douglas Maxwell's senatorial campaign. When he arrives without his pants, and is shot by an assassin, the hotel staff, press, and the gathered spectators are horrified. But Chambrun gets an even bigger shock when, half an hour later, Maxwell walks into his office as alive as the hotel manager.

Politics

Birthday, Deathday. Dodd Mead, 1972

General Ho Chang is a guest at Chamburn's hotel. He needs special security as the FBI and CIA both know that Neil Drury is stalking the general. Drury seeks revenge for the death of his family by Chang's revolutionaries, and he has disguised himself using plastic surgery to make it easy to get close to the General.

Walking Dead Man. Dodd Mead, 1973

In the hotel's penthouse, a man fires a shot at George Battle, the hotel's owner, and then flees after the attempted murder. Chambrun knows that on any other night, he would be sleeping in that bed, and begins a search for someone who would want to kill him.

Bargain with Death. Dodd Mead, 1974

J. W. Sassoon has been murdered in the hotel, and the oil industry is in a turmoil. Chambrun is as much interested in the tycoon's female companion as he is in the Arab diplomat worried about some papers that Sassoon was carrying. When the dead man's son goes missing, the case becomes an even more desperate search for a reason for the murder.

Oil

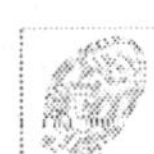

Time of Terror. Dodd Mead, 1975

Colonel Coriander of the Army for Justice has taken over the fifteenth floor of the hotel and is making demands of Chambrun. As hostages, he holds the children and governess of the British Ambassador, and Chambrun knows he has to be delicate in his negotiations or his hotel will be blown to bits.

Hostages • Terrorism

The Fourteen Dilemma. Dodd Mead, 1976

Winning the lottery should be a godsend to the Watson family, but it becomes a tragedy. As a part of their winnings, George, wife Helen, and 12-year-old Marilyn check into the Beaumont. Marilyn is handicapped, and a parent's worst nightmare comes true when someone takes advantage of her and kills her.

Children at risk • Physically challenged

Death After Breakfast. Dodd Mead, 1978

Chambrun is the rock upon which the Beaumont rests, and when he disappears one day, the staff is incapable of functioning. Then, Mark Haskell discovers the corpse of Laura Kauffman, one of New York's famous swingers, in her suite at the hotel.

Random Killer. Dodd Mead, 1979

Breakfast had been ordered for two in the suite held by TV personality Geoffrey Hammond, but when the waiter returned for the used dishes, he discovered that the man was dead, strangled with picture wire. Chambrun's forces jumped into action, but everyone is surprised when a few hours later, another guest is discovered in the same condition.

Beware Young Lovers. Dodd Mead, 1980

Hollywood glamour queen and famous lover Sharon Brand is a guest in the hotel to prepare for an appearance on the *Dick Thomas Show*. Three years prior, one of her young lovers disappeared, and this time around one of her lovers is murdered. For Chambrun and the police, the question becomes one of identifying who the real target is in the case.

Television

Murder in Luxury. Dodd Mead, 1981

Valerie Summers seeks refuge in the hotel when a dead man is found in her apartment. The police think she picked the professional crook up in a bar for sex, but she is claiming she was at the theater, alone. When a second murder strikes near her, and this time it takes place in the hotel, she now has Chambrun on her case.

With Intent to Kill. Dodd Mead, 1982

A teenaged boy is found floating in the hotel's pool, shot in the face. As additional murders begin to occur on the hotel's grounds, Chambrun begins to fear that he has an insider working the hotel and using it as a stalking ground.

Serial killer

Murder in High Places. Dodd Mead, 1983

Larry Welch, sitting on top of the most controversial story in his journalistic career, seeks refuge in the hotel. Chambrun is stressed by the request, and dismayed when his long-time secretary is kidnapped as a result of his decision to aid the reporter.

Kidnapping

Remember to Kill Me. Dodd Mead, 1984.

When a free rock concert in Central Park turns violent, some Central American terrorists take the opportunity to seize part of the hotel and demand the release of their fellow terrorists. How does this relate to the near-fatal shooting of the famous international beauty, Victoria Haven, that takes place on the hotel roof outside the penthouse?

Terrorism

Murder Round the Clock. Dodd Mead, 1985

A collection of the following stories: "Chambrun and the Double Event," "Chambrun and the Electronic Ear," "Chambrun and the Melting Swan," "Chambrun and the Obvious Clue," "Chambrun Gets the Message," "The Masked Crusader," "Murder Deluxe," "Pierre Chambrun and the Black Dogs," "Pierre Chambrun and the Last Fling," "Pierre Chambrun and the Sad Song," "Pierre Chambrun and the War for Peace," "Pierre Chambrun Defends Himself," and "Pierre Chambrun's Dilemma."

Short stories

Nightmare Time. Dodd Mead, 1986

Chambrun is left in charge of Guy Willis when the boy's parents leave him alone in their hotel room while they go to the bar for a late night drink. When the Air Force major and his wife fail to reappear, Chambrun has to decide if the hotel holds a clue to their whereabouts, or are they victims of an international espionage act.

Espionage

Murder Goes Round and Round. Dodd Mead, 1988

The hotel has a club, and it is featuring Toby March, an entertainer who impersonates various jazz stars. But after a performance one night, both March and his business partner Frank Pasqua disappear, leaving behind ruined hotel rooms. After a body is discovered in the basement of the hotel, Chambrun himself is shot while trying to conduct the investigation.

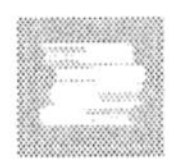

Music

The Modern Practitioners

Nevada Barr ✍

Anna Pigeon

Today, writers always look for a hook, and for Barr it was to use her experience as a park ranger to create a unique setting for each of her novels about Park Ranger Anna Pigeon. Pigeon is a federal law enforcement officer. As she travels about the country, transferred from one national park to another, she finds a death to investigate at each stop. Readers may also enjoy Jean Hager and Tony Hillerman. See the author's website at http://www.nevadabarr.com. **Traditional**.

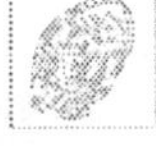

Track of the Cat. Putnam, 1993

When assigned to the Guadalupe Mountains to search for mountain lions, Pigeon is unprepared when one of her fellow rangers, Sheila Drury, appears to be killed by one of the creatures. But Pigeon has suspicions, and when another ranger disappears and she herself is threatened, she knows a more human killer is on the loose. AG AN

Texas, Guadalupe Mountains

A Superior Death. Putnam, 1994

Assigned to Michigan's Upper Peninsula park, famous for its isolated beauty and shipwreck diving sites, Pigeon discovers that a diver's death may be connected to a sunken cargo ship.

Michigan, Isle Royale National Park • Underwater

Ill Wind. Putnam, 1995

Something is amiss in the isolated communities near Mesa Verde, including the death of an asthmatic child and a fellow park ranger that had been friendly to

Pigeon. Within the mystical surroundings of the ancient ruins, Pigeon finds herself on the trail of a modern menace.

Colorado, Mesa Verde

Firestorm. Putnam, 1996

The Jackknife fire is tearing through Northern California, and Pigeon has been assigned medical and security duties at the base camp. As the disaster winds down, she and the remaining San Juan crew are caught in a firestorm, and one member of the team is murdered under cover of the winds and heat.

California, Lassen Volcanic National Park • Forest fires

Endangered Species. Putnam, 1997

On the isolated island in the park, Pigeon is the lone ranger among the fire crew present when a small plane crashes on the island. When the investigation of the crash begins to call into question the crew's integrity, Pigeon finds herself chasing a murderer and the honor of the service.

Georgia, Cumberland Island National Seashore

Blind Descent. Putnam, 1998

Only 90 miles out of 300 miles of the famous caverns are mapped, so its dangers outweigh its beauty at times. When a fellow ranger is injured, Pigeon must control her fears and descend into Lechuguilla, where small decisions will become a matter of life and death.

Caves • New Mexico, Carlsbad Caverns National Park

Liberty Falling. Putnam, 1999

Pigeon is in New York to nurse a sick sister, and seeks accommodations on Liberty Island, home of the famous statue. Among the crumbling ruins of the historic buildings that include Ellis Island, a danger exists for women, and Pigeon is almost a victim herself.

New York, New York • Statue of Liberty

Deep South. Putnam, 2000

Pigeon is the first ranger on the Natchez Trace Parkway, and because of that, she is meeting some resistance to her authority from the communities. When a prom night turns to disaster and leaves a 17-year-old dead girl named Danielle Posey on the Trace, the body is disfigured by a KKK sheet and a noose. Although both Danielle and her boyfriend are white, the visages of an old racial lifestyle still exist, and Pigeon finds this a most troubling case to solve. BA

Mississippi, Natchez Trace Parkway • Race

Blood Lure. Putnam, 2001

Pigeon is working on a wildlife management exercise involving bears and DNA in Glacier National Park when the party is attacked by a bear and a young man named Rory disappears. Later, a mutilated body is discovered. It is Rory's stepmother, and when the evidence shows this corpse was killed by a human, Pigeon is on the trail of another murderer.

Bears • Montana, Waterton-Glacier National Park

Hunting Season. Putnam, 2002

Sent to work at the Mt. Locust plantation on the Natchez Trace, Pigeon discovers a man's nude body in one of the mansion's bedrooms. When the dead man, Doyce Barnett, is identified as the brother of a candidate for sheriff, the case begins to get complicated. While local sheriff Clintus Jones proves helpful, Pigeon finds herself up against some local poachers and an undertaker who wants to bury more than dead bodies.

Hotels · Mississippi, Mt. Locust · Mississippi, Port Gibson · Natchez Trace National Park

Jan Burke ✍

Irene Kelly

As a news reporter, Irene Kelly crosses paths with all the wrong people while covering the crime beat in Southern California. Allied with a homicide detective (and sometime lover) named Frank Harriman, she finds herself walking a deadly beat that causes her personal suffering. Readers may also enjoy Barbara D'Amato, Laura Lippman, and Mary Willis Walker. See the author's website at http://www.janburke.com. **Traditional/Hard-boiled**. Series subjects: **California, Las Piernas · Reporters**.

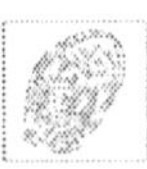

Goodnight, Irene. Simon & Schuster, 1993

When her mentor, O'Connor, dies in a bomb explosion, his former co-worker, Kelly is almost killed in a hail of bullets. Knowing that someone thinks she knows more about O'Connor's case than she does, she sets out on a path of discovery to try and save her own life. Her investigation leads to an old crime, and the state of Arizona, before she can uncover the truth.

Arizona, Phoenix

Sweet Dreams, Irene. Simon & Schuster, 1994

Two District Attorney candidates are squaring off at election time, and the campaign turns nasty when one of the candidates, Mont Montgomery, accuses the son of Brian Henderson of being a satanic cult member. Working with Frank Harriman, Kelly knows she is on a serious course when a human heart is left on her doorstep.

Cults · Elections

Dear Irene. Simon & Schuster, 1995

Someone hiding behind the name Thanatos is sending Kelly disturbing fan mail. After first ignoring the missives, Kelly becomes aware that they are clues to the work of a serial killer that is using her as a conduit.

Serial killer

Remember Me, Irene. Simon & Schuster, 1996

A chance encounter with a homeless man reunited Kelly with Lucas Monroe, a mathematician who has fallen on hard times. When Kelly gets a cryptic message from the man and learns of charges of blackmail, she launches an investigation. Her probing leads to a corrupt land development enterprise, and to someone willing to commit murder to protect their holdings.

Hocus. Simon & Schuster, 1996

Frank is kidnapped and the demands from Hocus, the terrorist group, come to Irene with a three-day deadline. When her own investigation stumbles and the police are ineffectual, she has to charge herself up to prevent her personal feelings from interfering with her prowess as a detective.

Kidnapping

Liar. Simon & Schuster, 1998

Kelly is devastated by the news that her aunt Mary Kelly, from whom she was estranged, has been murdered, and even more shocked to discover that she may be considered suspect number one. She begins a desperate search for her aunt's son Travis, made difficult by the fact that so little is known about this part of her family. As she probes into her family's secrets, she finds herself being drawn toward the boy and in need of a new suspect.

California, Los Alamitos

Bones. Simon & Schuster, 1999

Nick Parrish is facing the death penalty, and he wants to trade his life for a secret: where the police can find the body of Julia Sayre. Kelly is a part of the team assigned to cover the mission, and she finds the undue attention levied upon her by Parrish very uncomfortable. She will become more uncomfortable when it becomes apparent she is part of his escape plan. ED

California, Sierra Nevada Mountains

Flight. Simon & Schuster, 2001

Irene steps aside when her husband, Las Piernas Detective Frank Harriman, steps forward as the lead character. Ten years after a messy case involving police corruption, a plane has been found in the mountains. In the plane are the remains of Philip Lefebvre, a police officer whose reputation was tarnished by the murder investigation of businessman Trent Randolph. This discovery may mean that Lefebvre did not sell out to mobster Whitey Dane, and that the real killer is still on the loose.

California, Los Alamitos

Barbara D'Amato ✍

Cat Marsala

Freelance reporter Cat Marsala works the streets of Chicago, Illinois. Her cases usually revolve around a contemporary social issue. Strengths of this series are the believability of the plots and the growth of the character over the series. Cat's relationship with Chief of Detectives Harold McCoo sometimes gives the reporter access to those special places needed to be a good detective. These cases can be recommended to traditional mystery readers, and may appeal to the hard-boiled reader as well. Readers may also enjoy Jan Burke, Laura

Lippman, and Mary Willis Walker. See the author's website at http://www.barbaradamato.com. **Traditional/Hard-boiled**. Series subjects: **Illinois, Chicago · Reporters**.

Hardball. Scribner, 1990

At a symposium regarding the decriminalization of certain drugs, a bomb goes off that executes Louise Sugarman, leader of a pro-use group called Common Sense. Marsala had been sitting next to the advocate when the bomb exploded, and after regaining consciousness in the hospital, she finds herself without a memory. As her mind recovers, she becomes a greater and greater threat to uncover the killer.

Hard Tack. Scribner, 1991

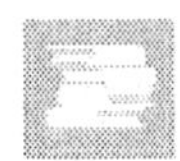

Invited to spend the Fourth of July sailing on Lake Michigan aboard the sloop Easy Girl owned by millionaire furniture manufacturer Will Honeywell and his wife Belinda, Marsala accepts despite that fact that she hates sailing and cannot swim. When financier Chuck Kroop's throat is cut in a room accessible to no one, with witnesses to prove it, Marsala has an at-sea locked-room puzzle to solve.

Lake Michigan · Locked room · Shipboard

Hard Luck. Scribner, 1992

A rush assignment on the state lottery leads Marsala to interview Jack Sligh, the advertising manager for the lottery. He drops a hint that he might have insider information for an exposé, and when Marsala returns to interview him, she's just in time to see him fall to his death. Compulsive gambling may have led to an impulsive murder as Marsala probes the world of big-time finances in state-run lotteries.

Gambling · Lotteries

Hard Women. Scribner, 1993

When Marsala picked Sandra Love out of Women's Court to produce a documentary about life on Chicago's streets, she did not intend to gain a roommate. Sandra's murder makes Marsala think that she was getting too close to the truth about prostitution in Chicago.

Prostitution

Hard Case. Scribner, 1994

Dr. Hannah Grant welcomes Marsala to her trauma center when the reporter decides to do a feature on the daily drama of life and death in an inner-city hospital emergency room. To her surprise, Hannah is murdered in the staff lounge, and Marsala believes it was an inside job.

Medical

Hard Christmas. Scribner, 1995

Looking for a softer story for the holidays, Marsala is happy to travel to Michigan at the invitation of Henry DeGraaf, president of the West Michigan Evergreen Growers Association. A story on growing Christmas trees should be pastoral, but when tensions inside the DeGraaf household leads to murder, Marsala is on the scene to launch an investigation.

Christmas · Holidays · Michigan, Holland

Hard Bargain. Scribner, 1997

When Officer Shelly Daniello is accused of a wrongful killing, she needs Marsala's help. Shelly was forced to kill her brother-in-law in self-defense during a domestic violence case, but the facts do not agree with her version of the crime. Between election-year campaigning and a media frenzy around the case, Marsala finds herself embroiled in a very sensitive case.

Hard Evidence. Scribner, 1999

Bringing home a bone for her dog Dapper should be an innocent gesture of good will, but when her significant other, Dr. Sam Davidian, recognizes the bone as human, Marsala needs to trace its origin. She begins at the exotic food emporium, Spenser and Angelotti, where she purchased it, and the business and the city decide to give her a fixed amount of time to solve the crime and prevent a panic amongst its customers.

Food

Hard Road. Scribner, 2001

In Chicago's Grant Park, Marsala and her nephew Jeremy witness a murder during the centennial celebration of the publication of *The Wizard of Oz*. Believing that her own brother Barry may be the murderer, Marsala sets out on her own mission to clear his name and end the threat to her own life.

Authors · Wizard of Oz

Janet Evanovich ✍

Stephanie Plum

Not everyone who loses their job would want to be a bounty hunter, but Plum does. And when she does, the wild humor that is the specialty of this series becomes evident. Allied with her pal Ranger and sometimes friend Morelli, she grows into a fairly good detective, even willing to use her own Grandmother for her schemes. These comic novels can be recommended to any traditional mystery reader. Readers may also enjoy Sparkle Hayter and Joan Hess. See the author's website at http://www.evanovich.com. **Traditional**. Series subjects: **Bounty hunters · Humor · New Jersey, Trenton**.

One for the Money. Scribner, 1994

Out of a job and out of money, Plum turns to her cousin Vinnie, the bail bondsman, for a job in a field she knows nothing about. However, her first assignment proves challenging when she goes after Joe Morelli, a former vice cop on the run from a murder charge, and the man who took her virginity. DI

Two for the Dough. Scribner, 1996

With a little more confidence and some idea of how the game is played, Plum is ready to go after her second man. This time Vinnie assigns her to the case of Kenny Mancuso, a man accused of shooting his best friend.

Three to Get Deadly. Scribner, 1997

Plum's third assignment is to find Uncle Mo Besemier, the kindly old candy-store owner who has jumped his bail. With little at stake, one of the big questions is why would

Uncle Mo skip? However, as she moves around the old man's neighborhood among the drug dealers and scammers, she realizes there may be more to his story than meets the eye.

Four to Score. St. Martin's Press, 1998

Plum has a challenge from a rival bounty hunter when Joyce Barnhardt takes up the chase for Maxine Nowicki. Maxine has jumped bail on charges of extortion, and the people who might help locate her are turning up dead. When threats are made against Plum as well, the case turns personal just as Plum is forced to move in with Joe Morelli.

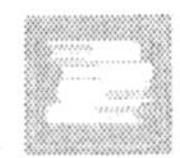

High Five. St. Martin's Press, 1999

With business slow on the bounty-hunting side of her life, Plum decides to take a job with Ranger doing the nasty things he does to survive. When this bothers her lover Joe, she begins to lose out on the personal end of things as well. Then her cheapskate Uncle Fred disappears, leaving behind some photographs that point to a disturbing past, and soon she finds the Mafia is interested in her activities.

Hot Six. St. Martin's Press, 2000

Plum teams with her vice cop friend Morelli, to hunt for a special killer: the son of international black market arms dealer, Alexander Ramos, has been murdered. The problem for Plum is that a videotape makes it appear that the number one suspect is her long time mentor, Ranger. When Ranger goes underground, it is up to his protégé to hunt him down.

Seven Up. St. Martin's Press, 2001

The elderly mobster, Eddie DeChooch, has jumped on a cigarette smuggling charge, and the job of hunting him down falls to Plum. Her chase is complicated when two former high school mates who are involved also disappear, but maybe not by choice.

Hard Eight. St. Martin's Press, 2002

Plum is on the trail of a mother named Evelyn Soder and her daughter, Mary, who have skipped on the woman's ex-husband. Evelyn's ex wanted to collect on a child custody bond that threatens a family friend, but Plum also needs to figure out why her investigation has brought threats from the mobbed up Eddie Abruzzi. Using her usual band of fellow travelers, including Ranger, she pushes her investigation despite the threats.

Children at risk

Antonia Fraser

Jemima Shore

British author Fraser created Jemina Shore, a tough and modern television investigative reporter. However, the cases reflect everything learned from the Golden Age plotters, and develop some strong storylines. Readers may also enjoy Amanda Cross. **Traditional**. Series subject: **Reporters**.

Quiet As a Nun. U.K.: Weidenfeld, 1977 (U.S.: Viking, 1977)

Sister Roseabelle Mary Powerstock of the Blessed Eleanor's Convent, known as Sister Miriam, takes her own life at the convent, and the Reverend Mother Ancilla asks Jemima to look into the cause. The reason: the dead nun had left a note saying Jemima would know the cause.

England, Sussex, Churne · Religion

The Wild Island. U.K.: Weidenfeld, 1978 (U.S.: Norton, 1978)

Jemima is in Scotland for the Highland holiday when she becomes embroiled in the troubles of the Beauregard family. Her host is dead, and Jemima finds suspects amongst the dashing war hero, the old priest, and the family servant.

Scotland, Inverness

A Splash of Red. U.K.: Weidenfeld, 1981 (U.S.: Norton, 1982)

Just like Agatha Christie, Chloe Fontaine, the novelist, has disappeared. Unlike Christie, this time it appears not to be by choice, and among the clutter the novelist left behind, Jemima hopes to find a clue to the reason.

Authors · England, London

Cool Repentance. U.K.: Weidenfeld, 1982 (U.S.: Norton, 1983)

Christobel, the mysterious actress, had abandoned all she knew to conduct a wild affair. Returning to her home, she wished only to return to her previous life and resume her career. But someone has other plans, and Jemima is around to investigate why.

Actors · England, Larminster · Theater

Jemima Shore Investigates. Methuen, 1983

A collection of the following stories from the TV series: "The Case of the Dancing Duchess" by Frances Heasman from a story by Simon Brett; "The Damask Collection" by Frances Heasman from a story by Peter Draper; "Death a la Carte" by John Burke from a story by Tim Aspinall; "A Greek Bearing Gifts" by John Burke from a story by Anthony Skene; "A Little Bit of Wildlife" by Frances Heasman from a story by Pauline Macaulay; "A Model Murder" by John Burke from a story by Dave Humphries; and "Promising Death" by Frances Heasman from a story by Simon Brett.

England · Short stories

Oxford Blood. U.K.: Weidenfeld, 1985 (U.S.: Norton, 1985)

Golden Lads and Girls is a television program produced by Megalith Television, and Jemima is hired to do an episode on Lord Saffron, the wealthy son of a former foreign secretary. Jemima's investigative radar comes alive when she discovers the confession of a former nurse who claims to have switched babies at birth. When an undergraduate at Oxford dies, it becomes a case of murder.

England, Oxford · Television

Jemima Shore's First Case. U.K.: Weidenfeld, 1986 (U.S.: Norton, 1987)

A collection of the following stories: "The Case of the Parr Children," "The Girl Who Wanted to See Venice," "Jemima Shore's First Case," "Swimming Will Be the Death of You," and "Your Appointment is Cancelled." Also includes eight non-Shore stories.

England · Short stories

Your Royal Hostage. U.K.: Weidenfeld, 1987 (U.S.: Atheneum, 1988)

On the eve of her wedding to Prince Ferdinand, Princess Amy is kidnapped by animal rights extremists. Freelancing as an investigator for American television, Jemima knows her detecting skills will bring in a great story.

England, London · Kidnapping · Reporters · Terrorism

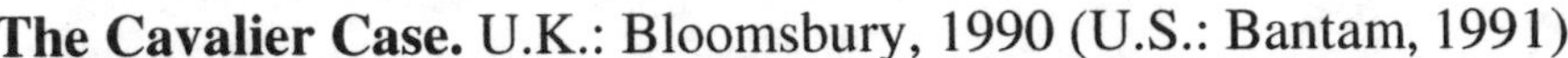

The Cavalier Case. U.K.: Bloomsbury, 1990 (U.S.: Bantam, 1991)

With echoes of *Laura*, the painting of Decimus Meredith, seventeenth-century Cavalier poet, solider and Viscount of Lackland, haunts Jemima. Stories of the Viscount's appearance may be tied into the plans by the current lord, Dan Meredith, to turn Lackland Court into an exclusive country club. When a servant dies, Jemima's story turns to murder.

England, Taynforshire

Jemima Shore at the Sunny Grave and Other Stories. Bloomsbury, 1991

A collection of the following stories: "Cry by Night," "The Blude-Red Wine," "Getting to Know You," "Jemima Shore at the Sunny Grave," and "The Tragedy of Sir Patrick Spens." Also contains four non-Shore stories.

Short stories

Political Death. Heinemann, 1994

With her own program called *Jemima Shore Investigates*, Jemima has decided to do a feature on aging. When Lady Imogene Swain decides to tell all about her 30-year-old affair with the current Foreign Secretary, Burgo Smyth, it includes details about the Faber Affair, and the case of a missing journalist.

England, London

Jean Hager

Molly Bearpaw

As an investigator for the Native American Advocacy League, Molly Bearpaw works the Oklahoma landscape trying to aid Cherokee Indians who need help. Although some credit can be given to Tony Hillerman for leading the way, authors like Hager who followed his lead are enriching the genre with mysteries set in America's Southwest. Her cases can be recommended to any traditional mystery reader. Readers may also enjoy Nevada Barr, Tony Hillerman, and Abigail Padgett. See a website about the author at http://title3.sde.state.ok.us/literatureanda/jean.htm. **Traditional**. Series subjects: **Native Americans · Oklahoma, Cherokee Nation Reservation.**

Ravenmocker. Mysterious Press, 1992

Bearpaw decides to probe into the death of Abner Mouse, who died of botulism in the Country Haven nursing home. His son, Woodrow, believes that a Ravenmocker, or Cherokee witch, is to blame for his father's death, but Bearpaw finds that there are plenty of human reasons as well.

The Redbird's Cry. Mysterious Press, 1994

When prominent lawyer Tom Battle is killed with a poisoned dart inside the Cherokee National Museum, the investigation falls on Bearpaw's shoulders. Suspects can be found among the True Echota Band, a splinter group in conflict with the Cherokee Nation, and Bearpaw is aided in her investigation by Deputy Kennedy.

Seven Black Stones. Mysterious Press, 1995

Controversy is raging in the Cherokee Nation when a bingo hall is built to attract revenue. The first death, by carbon monoxide poisoning, befalls Ed Whitekiller, and seven black stones are found near his body. When the second death also comes with the same sign, Bearpaw knows she has a determined killer on the loose.

The Spirit Caller. Mysterious Press, 1997

Bearpaw's assistant, Natalie's aunt, Talia Wind, has been murdered in the Tahlequah's Native American Research Library. To complicate matters, the library was previously the jail, and most folks believe it to be haunted. As the case becomes more complicated, her personal life becomes so as well, when her long estranged father returns.

Sparkle Hayter ✍

Robin Hudson

Generation-X readers will take a shine to TV reporter Hudson. Based on Hayter's own experiences as a reporter and as a stand-up comedian, Hudson's cases also include humor. These contemporary tales of modern urban life tell us much about American society while they entertain us as mystery fiction. Readers may also enjoy Simon Brett (Charlie Paris) and Antonia Fraser. **Traditional**. Series subjects: **Humor · New York, New York · Reporters**.

What's a Girl Gotta Do? Soho, 1994

Hudson's life is rapidly falling apart, as her husband has left her for another woman, and she has been demoted at the All News Network. When she attends a party armed with a tire iron because of the dangers of the neighborhood, she finds herself accused of murder when a blackmailer is killed—with a tire iron.

Blackmail

Nice Girls Finish Last. Viking, 1996

When her gynecologist, Herman Kanengiser, is shot in his office, Hudson's reporter instincts take her to an S&M club run by Mistress Anya, head of the Marquis de Sade Society. As she formulates her report, she must also deal with the fact that someone is shooting at her fellow reporters.

Revenge of the Cootie Girls. Viking, 1997

It's Girls Night Out, and it's Halloween. Hudson travels out into the night with her pals, comic Tamayo, rising star Clair, bald Sally, and her latest crew member, the out-of-towner Kathy Loblaws. When Kathy calls from a strange man's closet and asks for help, Hudson and her friends have one night to straighten out a case of murder.

Halloween · Holidays

The Last Manly Man. Morrow, 1998

Things are going well for Hudson in both her professional and personal life. Then she decides to pursue a story about a new male drug called Adam One, and she finds herself engulfed in a strange murder investigation that puts her within the macho male world.

Medical

The Chelsea Girl Murders. Morrow, 2000

Forced to move to the Chelsea Hotel when her apartment building burns, Hudson takes her cat and the clothes on her back. Surprised and suspicious when one of her neighbors at the Chelsea commits suicide, she launches an investigation and finds herself deep into the sordid world of arranged marriages.

Hotels

Mary Willis Walker ✍

Molly Cates

Forced to discover the truth behind the assignments she receives as a freelance crime reporter, Cates acts as detective to ferret out the truth. Her cases could also be categorized as suspense, as they always carry an elevated air of tension. Readers may also enjoy Jan Burke, Barbara D'Amato, and John Sandford. **Traditional/Hard-boiled**. Series subject: **Texas, Austin**.

The Red Scream. Doubleday, 1994

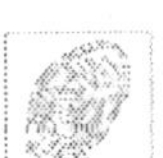

Cates's new book on serial killer Louie Bonk is doing well, but Bonk is heading for an execution. Her goal is to have one last interview, but she is finding roadblocks in her way, especially when she begins to believe that the only capital offense that Bonk was convicted for may have been committed by another. ED

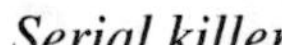

Serial killer

Under the Beetle's Cellar. Doubleday, 1995

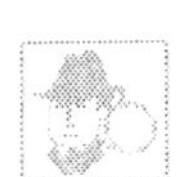

When a schoolbus full of children is kidnapped by a cult of religious fanatics, it is 46 days of tension and pain for the families. Cates decides to delve into the background of the cult's leader, Samuel Mordecai. Her investigation leads her back to the leader, and into the role of mediator. MA

Cults • Kidnapping

All the Dead Lie Down. Doubleday, 1998

Twenty years prior to this day, Cates's father committed suicide. Her attempts to prove otherwise estranged her from her own family, but now new evidence has surfaced, and she has launched a new attempt to clear his name.

Ex-Cop Detectives

The number of professional investigators who have retired from active duty but are willing to be dragged back into an investigation seems endless. Being stripped of their badges, their support organizations, and the funds to investigate are minor inconveniences to a determined ex-professional, now perhaps more properly labeled an amateur. But it is their previous experiences that make these ex-detectives such proficient investigators, despite giving up their guns.

The Historical Founding Members

Agatha Christie ✍

Hercule Poirot

The eccentric Belgian detective, Hercule Poirot, is an archetype in the mystery field. After his retirement from the Belgian police force, he becomes a sort of travelling private detective who acts just like a great thinking detective. Some of his early cases find him paired with Captain Hastings, and in the last few novels, we find him operating in association with mystery novelist, Ariadne Oliver. See the Agatha Christie Society website at http://christie.mysterynet.com/society. **Soft-boiled/Traditional**.

The Mysterious Affair at Styles. Lane, 1920

Poirot is involved in the troubles at Styles Court when the mistress of the manor house, Mrs. Cavendish, decides to marry her companion's distant cousin, Alfred Inglethrop. When this seems to send a once-contented family into a stew about the status of future inheritance, it brings into question whether the two Cavendish brothers might have poisoned their stepmother.

England, Essex, Styles

The Murder on the Links. U.K.: Lane, 1923 (U.S.: Dodd Mead, 1923)

Poirot is summoned to France by South American millionaire, Paul Renauld, but by the time he arrives, the man is dead. His widow tells Poirot that four masked men were demanding a secret from her husband, and it is his job to figure out who and what caused this deadly deed.

France, Merlinville-sur-Mer

Poirot Investigates. U.K.: Lane, 1924 (U.S.: Dodd Mead, 1925)

A collection of the following stories: "The Adventure of the Cheap Flat," "The Adventure of the Egyptian Tomb," "The Adventure of the Italian Nobleman," "The Adventure of 'The Western Star'," "The Case of the Missing Will," "The Chocolate Box," "The Disappearance of Mr. Davenheim," "The Jewel Robbery at the Grand Metropolitan," "The Kidnapped Prime Minister," "The Lost Mine," "The Million-Dollar Bond Robbery," "The Mystery of Hunter's Lodge," "The Tragedy at Marsdon Manor," and "The Veiled Lady."

Short stories

The Murder of Roger Ackroyd. U.K.: Collins, 1926 (U.S.: Dodd Mead, 1926)

In the village of King's Abbot, rumors are flying that some recent deaths may be murder. Mrs. Ferrars has put off Roger Ackroyd for one year while she mourns her dead husband, and then she is found dead. When Poirot arrives to investigate, his case will become one of the all-time classics in the mystery field.

England, King's Abbot

The Big Four. U.K.: Collins, 1927 (U.S.: Dodd Mead, 1927)

Poirot is warned that there is a criminal conspiracy taking place that involves The Big Four: a French scientist, an American millionaire, a brilliant Chinese gentleman, and a master of disguise.

England, London

The Mystery of the Blue Train. U.K.: Collins, 1928 (U.S.: Dodd Mead, 1928)

The Blue Train runs to the Riviera, and on the train is Katherine Grey, a newly rich woman seeking adventure. Also on the train is Ruth Kettering, a rich woman fleeing her husband, and the detective Poirot. These principals will meet when a woman dies and a detective is needed.

France • Railroads

Peril at End House. U.K.: Collins, 1932 (U.S.: Dodd Mead, 1932)

Nick Buckley is the new mistress of End House, and someone has tried four times to end her reign there. When Poirot's services are requested, it is to solve an attempt that was successful.

England, St. Loo

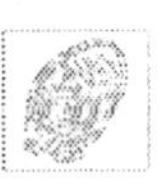

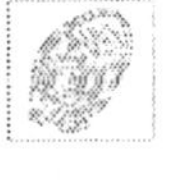

Lord Edgware Dies. U.K.: Collins, 1933 (U.S.: *Thirteen at Dinner.* Dodd Mead, 1933)

Poirot finds it difficult to be sympathetic when actress Jane Wilkinson asks him to investigate the death of her husband. Previously, the woman had asked him to dispatch her husband, George Alfred St. Vincent Marsh, fourth baron of Edgware.

England, London

Murder on the Orient Express. U.K.: Collins, 1934 (U.S.: *Murder in the Calais Coach.* Dodd Mead, 1934)

While travelling on the famous railway, Poirot is snowbound with the rest of his fellow travelers. When an American named Rachett is found dead, Poirot has plenty of time to discover a murderer among the people on the stranded railcar.

Railroads

Three Act Tragedy. U.K.: Collins, 1935 (U.S.: *Murder in Three Acts.* Dodd Mead, 1934)

The vicar, Stephen Babbington, drops dead from a poisoned cocktail at a party conducted by retired actor, Charles Cartwright. Remarkably, the death is declared a natural one, or so it is believed until a psychiatrist who attended the same party dies in the same fashion a few weeks later.

England • Theater

Death in the Clouds. U.K.: Collins, 1935 (U.S.: *Death in the Air.* Dodd Mead, 1935)

On a flight from Paris to Croydon, a passenger on the airplane is murdered when a small dart using poison from a South American tribe is delivered by blow pipe. All 13 people on the plane are suspects, but one of them is the detective Poirot.

Airplanes

The ABC Murders. U.K.: Collins, 1936 (U.S.: Dodd Mead, 1936; also published as *The Alphabet Murders.* Pocket, 1966)

Poirot finds himself up against a killer who murders people randomly, until you take into account the alphabetical order of their names and home towns.

England • Serial killer

Cards on the Table. U.K.: Collins, 1936 (U.S.: Dodd Mead, 1937)

When Poirot is invited to play a game of bridge, he is startled to discover his host, Mr. Shaitana, is dead. Perhaps this should not be a surprise as his host had paired four famous detectives with four people who may have got away with murder.

Bridge • England, London

Murder in Mesopotamia. U.K.: Collins, 1936 (U.S.: Dodd Mead, 1936)

Poirot is on the spot when an archaeologist's wife acts strangely on a dig in Mesopotamia. A nurse who is assigned to help the woman begins to suspect that the woman's behavior is being dictated by something exterior rather than interior. With the great detective's help, the pair begin to help the woman overcome her fears.

Archeology • Iraq, Hassanieh

Death on the Nile. U.K.: Collins, 1937 (U.S.: Dodd Mead, 1938)

Poirot takes a cruise on the Nile, and a young bride named Linnet Doyle is murdered. Working with her husband Simon and a boat full of suspects, Poirot works his usual magic to discover the means and motive for this cruel crime.

Egypt • Shipboard

Dumb Witness. U.K.: Collins, 1937 (U.S.: *Poirot Loses a Client.* Dodd Mead, 1937)

Emily Arundell has been dead for awhile, but her letter arrives on Poirot's doorstep warning him of the threats against her life. As he investigates, he discovers that relatives who expected her will to be drawn in a particular direction are worrying the surprised heir who benefited from the changes.

England, Market Basing • Wills

Murder in the Mews. U.K.: Collins, 1937 (U.S.: *Dead Man's Mirror.* Dodd Mead, 1937)

A collection of the following stories: "Dead Man's Mirror," "The Incredible Theft," "Murder in the Mews," and "Triangle at Rhodes." Some editions do not contain all of these stories.

Short stories

Appointment with Death. U.K.: Collins, 1938 (U.S.: Dodd Mead, 1938)

On a holiday tour of the Holy Land, an irritating old woman who brutally abused her family is murdered. For Poirot, the question becomes which family member was finally pushed to the limit.

Israel, Jerusalem

Hercule Poirot's Christmas. U.K.: Collins, 1939 (U.S.: *Murder For Christmas.* Dodd Mead, 1939; also published as *A Holiday For Murder.* Avon, 1947)

Simeon Lee's plan to reunite his family at Christmas turns into a nightmare when the cruel, rich old man is found in his locked bedroom with his throat cut. Poirot is asked to sort among the family members who might have returned to reap a revenge.

Christmas • England, Longdale, Addlesfield • Holidays • Locked room

The Regatta Mystery and Other Stories. Dodd Mead, 1939

A collection of the following stories: "The Dream," "How Does Your Garden Grow," "The Mystery of the Bagdad Chest," "Problem at Sea," and "Yellow Iris." Also contains four non-Poirot stories.

Short stories

Sad Cypress. U.K.: Collins, 1940 (U.S.: Dodd Mead, 1940)

Elinor Carlisle is being charged with murdering her fiancé's girlfriend, Mary Gerrard, by morphine poisoning, and the evidence is ironclad. That is, until Poirot decides to listen to her plight and takes her case. His reason: the case against her is too perfect.

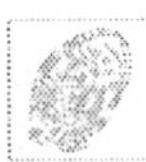

England, Hunterbury

One, Two, Buckle My Shoe. U.K.: Collins, 1940 (U.S.: *The Patriotic Murders.* Dodd Mead, 1941; *An Overdose of Death.* Dell, 1953)

Dr. Morley, a dentist, is found shot in the temple, and the police believe that he may have committed suicide. Then, one of his patients dies, and the case becomes more mysterious. As Poirot investigates, he discovers that the dentist had some odd co-workers and some prominent patients, all of whom could have a reason to dispatch the doctor.

Dentist • England, London

Evil Under the Sun. U.K.: Collins, 1941 (U.S.: Dodd Mead, 1941)

Arlena Marshall is the kind of woman other women hate and all men wish to know. Her arrival at the Jolly Roger Hotel on Smuggler's Island causes a stir, and leads to her being strangled. One of the hotel's guests is Poirot, and that means all the guests will have to account for their actions before they can leave.

England, Smuggler's Island • Hotels

Murder in Retrospect. U.S.: Dodd Mead, 1942 (U.K.: *Five Little Pigs.* U.K.: Collins, 1943)

Caroline Crale has spent 16 years in jail for murdering her husband, the famous painter Amyas Crale. Now, her daughter has asked Poirot to clear her mother's name.

Artists • England

The Hollow. U.K.: Collins, 1946 (U.S.: Dodd Mead, 1946; also published as *Murder After Hours.* Dell, 1954)

The simple facts are that Gerda Christow was found with a gun in her hand, standing over her husband's dead body at their estate, The Hollow. But when Poirot begins to probe into the details, he discovers that other women may have had an equal motive for murdering the roguish man.

England

The Labours of Hercules. U.K.: Collins, 1947 (U.S.: Dodd Mead, 1947)

A collection of the following stories: "The Apples of the Hesperides," "The Arcadian Deer," "The Augean Stables," "The Capture of Cerberus," "The Cretan Bull," "The Erymanthian Boar," "The Flock of Geryon," "The Girdle of Hyppolita," "The Horses of Diomedes," "The Lernean Hydra," "The Nemean Lion," and "The Stymphalean Birds."

Short stories

Taken at the Flood. U.K.: Collins, 1948 (U.S.: *There Is a Tide.* Dodd Mead, 1948)

Gordon Cloade has died, leaving his estate to his bride of two weeks, and disenfranchising the family who had been dependent on his generosity. When a mysterious stranger in the village dies, Poirot becomes involved in an investigation that will try to sort out this family squabble.

England, Warmsley Vale

The Under Dog and Other Stories. Dodd Mead, 1951

A collection of the following stories: "The Adventure of the Clapham Cook," "The Affair at the Victory Ball," "The Cornish Mystery," "The King of Clubs," "The Lemesurier Inheritance," "The Market Basing Mystery," "The Plymouth Express," "The Submarine Plans," and "The Under Dog."

Short stories

Mrs. McGinty's Dead. U.K.: Collins, 1952 (U.S.: Dodd Mead, 1952; also published as *Blood Will Tell.* Detective Book Club, 1952)

The guest of a widow and charwoman is accused of her murder, and sentenced to prison. Retired Superintendent Spence brings the case to Poirot, because he is convinced that the man is innocent.

England, Kilchester

After the Funeral. U.K.: Collins, 1953 (U.S.: *Funerals Are Fatal.* Dodd Mead, 1953)

The Abernethie family barely recovers from one death when another occurs. After a third, the family needs a detective like Poirot to discover who is a killer among those at Enderby Hall.

England, Lytchett St. Mary

Hickory Dickory Dock. U.K.: Collins, 1955 (U.S.: *Hickory Dickory Death.* Dodd Mead, 1955)

When Poirot's secretary, Miss Lemon, is upset, he delves into her concern over her sister. She is a matron at the Hostel for Youth, where petty thefts have plagued the institution. Poirot discovers that a quick confession is not going to explain all the necessary things needed to end his investigation.

England, London • Hostels

Dead Man's Folly. U.K.: Collins, 1956 (U.S.: Dodd Mead, 1956)

Poirot is invited to the home of Sir George Stubbs where a murder game is to be played. However, when the girl who was to play the corpse actually becomes a corpse, Poirot finds himself required to investigate for real. A disappearance, and another death, make this mystery game deadly.

England, Devonshire, Nassecombe • Mystery games

Cat Among the Pigeons. U.K.: Collins, 1959 (U.S.: Dodd Mead, 1960)

Things are not as they should be at Meadowbank School when a body is discovered in the sports complex. How this incident will relate to the troubles in the Middle Eastern country of Ramat, and how it will involve the detective Poirot, is the key to this novel.

Academia • England • Ramat

The Adventure of the Christmas Pudding and a Selection of Entrees. U.K.: Collins, 1960

A collection of the following stories: "The Adventure of the Christmas Pudding," "The Dream," "Four-and-Twenty-Blackbirds," "The Mystery of the Spanish Chest," and "The Under Dog." Also contains one non-Poirot story.

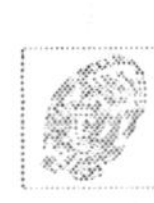

Short stories

Double Sin and Other Stories. Dodd Mead, 1961

A collection of the following stories: "The Double Clue," "Double Sin," "The Theft of the Royal Ruby," and "Wasp's Nest." Also contains four non-Poirot stories.

Short stories

The Clocks. U.K.: Collins, 1963 (U.S.: Dodd Mead, 1964)

Shelia Webb is hired to be a secretary, but when she arrives at her new assignment, she discovers a corpse. When the owner of the home, the blind Millicent Pebmarsh, returns home, she denies ever requesting a secretary. To everyone's surprise, including detective Poirot's, four clocks have been added to her home, each set to a specific time.

England, London

Third Girl. U.K.: Collins, 1966 (U.S.: Dodd Mead, 1967)

Norma Restarick startles Poirot one day by declaring that she may have committed a murder. After she disappears, Poirot's task becomes tracing her by finding a recent murder that would fit her circumstances.

England, London

Hallowe'en Party. U.K.: Collins, 1969 (U.S.: Dodd Mead, 1969)

As the village prepares for its festive Halloween celebration, a 13-year-old girl named Joyce insists that she has seen a murder being committed. When no one pays any attention to the girl, she is killed by the end of Halloween day. Poirot must plunge into this tragedy and try to locate a double murderer desperate to keep his or her identity a secret.

England, Woodleigh Common • Halloween • Holidays

Elephants Can Remember. U.K.: Collins, 1972 (U.S.: Dodd Mead, 1972)

Ariadne Oliver has an interesting problem for which she can use Poirot's help. Fifteen years prior, General and Lady Ravenscroft committed suicide, and Miss Oliver has been asked to determine who killed who in the suicide pact.

England, London

Curtain. U.K.: Collins, 1975 (U.S.: Dodd Mead, 1975)

Poirot makes a visit to the spot where his investigations began. At Styles Court, he becomes convinced that someone in the house has been involved in five murders, and will commit another. He calls his old pal Hastings in to help him investigate.

England, Essex, Styles

Black Coffee (by Charles Osborne). St. Martin's Press, 1998

In the spring of 1934, Poirot and Hastings go to Surrey to help Sir Claud Amory, whose formula is crucial to the defense of Great Britain. When they arrive, the inventor is dead, and the formula is missing. This is a novelization of one of Christie's plays.

Espionage • England, Surrey • Historical (1900–1999) • Osborne, Charles

Michael Innes (pseud. of John Innes Mackintosh Stewart) ✍

John Appleby

British writer Innes followed in the footsteps of Dorothy L. Sayers in his use of language and literary allusions, with erudite stories featuring the detective John Appleby. Appleby makes personal progress through the ranks of Scotland Yard until he is appointed commissioner of the Metropolitan Police in London, while solving many cases that take place within the circles of Oxford, often aided by his wife, Lady Judith. **Traditional**.

Death at the President's Lodging. U.K.: Gollancz, 1936 (U.S.: *Seven Suspects.* Dodd Mead, 1937)

President Josiah Umpleby of St. Anthony's College has been murdered, and the fact that the man was unpopular leaves the inspector with many suspects.

Academia • England

Hamlet, Revenge! U.K.: Gollancz, 1937 (U.S.: Dodd Mead, 1937)

The Duchess of Horton wants to include a performance of *Hamlet* as a part of her house party. But as others prepare to play their roles, someone is sending threatening messages using obscure Shakespearean quotes. When Lord Auldearn is murdered, Appleby is sent in.

England, Scamnum • Shakespeare, William • Theater

Lament for a Maker. U.K.: Gollancz, 1938 (U.S.: Dodd Mead, 1938)

The laird of Kinkeig, Ronald Guthrie, has taken his own life. Knowing that he was one of the most disliked men in the country, some believe his death may have been murder, and Appleby needs to sort out the various Highland tales to find the truth.

Scotland, Kinkeig

Stop Press. U.K.: Gollancz, 1939 (U.S.: *The Spider Strikes.* Dodd Mead, 1939)

Richard Eliot is the author of a series of novels featuring the hero, The Spider. When his character seems to take life, and begins to act out scenes only contemplated by Eliot but never published, Appleby finds himself chasing a literary character.

Authors · England, Rust

There Came Both Mist and Snow. U.K.: Gollancz, 1940 (U.S.: *A Comedy of Terrors.* Dodd Mead, 1940)

Appleby is on the spot when Wilfred Foxcroft is shot at the annual Christmas gathering of the Roper family. The family had hoped to end a long-standing quarrel, entertain its guests, and enjoy the new hobby of target shooting.

England, Basil

The Secret Vanguard. U.K.: Gollancz, 1940 (U.S.: Dodd Mead, 1941)

An odd coincidence links two events in separate areas. Appleby travels from London to Scotland to hunt the killer of the quiet poet, Philip Ploss, and the connection to the adventures of Shelia Grant, who appears caught in a spy thriller.

Authors · England, London · Scotland

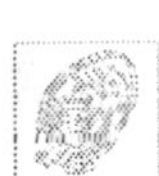

Appleby on Ararat. U.K.: Gollancz, 1941 (U.S.: Dodd Mead, 1941)

Torpedoed and abandoned on an island, the passengers of a ship that had been sailing for Australia are distressed to discover that one of their fellow travelers has committed a murder. Luckily, one of the shipwrecked is Appleby of the Yard.

Shipboard · Pacific Ocean

***The Daffodil Affair.** U.K.: Gollancz, 1942 (U.S.: Dodd Mead, 1942)

The Weight of the Evidence. Dodd Mead, 1943

Biochemistry professor Pluckrose dies in the courtyard of Nesfield University, struck down by a meteorite while lounging on the quadrangle called Wool Court. Except, when Appleby arrives to investigate, he discovers that things are not that simple.

Academia · England, Nesfield Court

Appleby's End. U.K.: Gollancz, 1945 (U.S.: Dodd Mead, 1945)

On a trip, Appleby encounters Everard Raven and his cousin Judith. A series of adventures throws the travelers together and it involves the family legacy of writer Ranulph Raven. The discovery of Heyhoe's head at Long Dream Manor pits Appleby against a murderer, leads to the capture of a murderer, and the selection of a wife for the detective.

Authors · England, Appleby's End

A Night of Errors. Dodd Mead, 1947

An ancient family curse has followed the Dromio family: each generation has produced a set of triplets. When the blessed event occurs to Sir Romeo Dromio, he murders two of the boys, leaving Oliver to grow up and establish the family fortune. When Oliver is burnt to death like his long-lost siblings, Appleby needs to find a murderer within a murderous family.

England, Sherris Magna

Operation Pax. U.K.: Gollancz, 1951 (U.S.: *The Paper Thunderbolts.* Dodd Mead, 1951)

Routh is a small-time operator who stumbles onto a conspiracy of major proportions. He is the key to allowing Appleby a chance to break a post-war organization that has nefarious plans for England.

Bibliomystery • England, Oxford

A Private View. U.K.: Gollancz, 1952 (U.S.: *One Man Show.* Dodd Mead, 1953; also published as *Murder Is an Art.* Avon, 1959)

A new young painter, Gavin Limbert, is murdered just prior to his exhibition, and when Appleby is persuaded to attend the opening, he is the last person to see the painting, The Fifth and Sixth Day of Creation, that goes missing.

Art • England, London

Appleby Talking. U.K.: Gollancz, 1954 (U.S.: *Dead Man's Shoes.* Dodd Mead, 1954)

A collection of the following stories: "Appleby's First Case," "The Bandertree Case," "The Cave of Belarius," "The Clancarron Ball," "The Clock-Face Case," "Dead Man's Shoes," "A Derby Horse," "A Dog's Life," "Eye Witness," "The Flight of Patroclus," "The Furies," "Imperious Caesar," "The Key," "Lesson in Anatomy," "The Lion and the Unicorn," "Miss Geach," "A Nice Cup of Tea," "Pokerwork," "The Sands of Thyme," "The Spendlove Papers," "Tragedy of a Handkerchief," "William the Conqueror," and "The X-Plan."

Short stories

Appleby Talks Again. U.K.: Gollancz, 1956 (U.S.: Dodd Mead, 1957)

A collection of the following stories: "Bear's Box," "Dangerfield's Diary," "Enigma Jones," "The Exile," "False Colours," "The Four Seasons," "Grey's Ghost," "The Heritage Portrait," "Here is the News," "The Lombard Books," "A Matter of Goblins," "The Mouse-Trap," "Murder on the 7.16," "The Reprisal," "The Ribbon," "Tom, Dick and Harry," "A Very Odd Case," and "Was He Morton?"

Short stories

Appleby Plays Chicken. U.K.: Gollancz, 1957 (U.S.: *Death on a Quiet Day.* Dodd Mead, 1957)

When David Henchman decides to escape the over-zealous attentions of his fellow Oxford students by taking a hike in the woods, he discovers a corpse with a bullet in its head. Volunteering to be Appleby's assistant leads this young man on a wild adventure in the moors.

England, Dartmoor

***The Long Farewell.** U.K.: Gollancz, 1958 (U.S.: Dodd Mead, 1958)

Hare Sitting Up. U.K.: Gollancz, 1959 (U.S.: Dodd Mead, 1959)

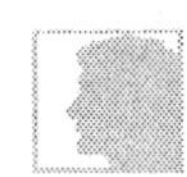

Bacteriologist Howard Juniper creates a dangerous secret in his laboratory that could hold the fate of the world. When he goes missing, Appleby traces him from a preparatory school owned by his twin brother to an island off the coast of Scotland.

Scotland, Ardray Island

Silence Observed. U.K.: Gollancz, 1961 (U.S.: Dodd Mead, 1961)

Charles Gribble announces that a forgery is discovered within the prestigious art world of London, and he interests Appleby in the case because this is a forgery of a forgery. But then Gribble's art dealer is dead, and Appleby finds himself investigating for the Yard.

Art • England, London

A Connoisseur's Case. U.K.: Gollancz, 1962 (U.S.: *The Crabtree Affair.* Dodd Mead, 1962)

Appleby has a nice conversation with Seth Crabtree, a carpenter recently retired from Spokane in America, and thinks his day is done. When the man is found murdered in the canal, he must investigate.

England, Pryde Park

The Bloody Wood. U.K.: Gollancz, 1966 (U.S.: Dodd Mead, 1966)

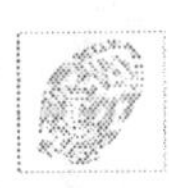

Grace Martineau is about to die and leave no heir to take up occupancy at Charne House. When she gathers her closest friends and relations around her to make a decision, it leads to someone taking things into their own hands.

England, Charne

Appleby at Allington. U.K.: Gollancz, 1968 (U.S.: *Death by Water.* Dodd Mead, 1968)

On a visit to Allington Park, where a celebration has created a festival grounds, Appleby discovers the body of a man in a gazebo. While the community tries to celebrate and ignore death, the retired inspector's investigation progresses.

England, Allington

A Family Affair. U.K.: Gollancz, 1969 (U.S.: *Picture of Guilt.* Dodd Mead, 1969)

Time has passed, but each art theft had been carried out with deliberate craft and intention. When Appleby begins to detect a pattern that no one else sees, it sets him on the trail of a brilliant and clever art thief.

Art • England, Oxford

Death at the Chase. U.K.: Gollancz, 1970 (U.S.: Dodd Mead, 1970)

Appleby is not impressed when Martyn Ashmore insists that once a year someone tries to kill him. That is, until Appleby witnesses this year's attempt. Does the answer lie in the fact that the attempt is made on the anniversary of Ashmore's torture while a Resistance fighter against the Nazis?

England, Ashmore Chase

An Awkward Lie. U.K.: Gollancz, 1971 (U.S.: Dodd Mead, 1971)

Appleby's son, Bobby, is having an early round of golf when he discovers a body in a sand trap. When a beautiful woman offers to watch the body, he beetles off to find the police. Of course, when they all return, there is no body or woman. Bobby, following in the steps of his famous father, decides to try an investigation.

England, Linger

The Open House. U.K.: Gollancz, 1972 (U.S.: Dodd Mead, 1972)

In one short night, Appleby's car breaks down and he approaches a mansion for help. Every window suddenly fills with light, and when the door opens, he finds a dinner laid out for one. Haunted by a woman in white, he must investigate on this strange night when he is the guest for murder.

England, Ledward

Appleby's Answer. U.K.: Gollancz, 1973 (U.S.: Dodd Mead, 1973)

Miss Priscilla Pringle is a well-known writer of detective stories that center around religion, so it is logical that she is intrigued when the last rector of Long Canings dies under mysterious circumstances. Asked by a mysterious stranger to devise a plot that he might wish to use for a real murder, she is fortunate to find the retired Appleby nearby for help.

Authors · England, Long Canings · Religion

Appleby's Other Story. U.K.: Gollancz, 1974 (U.S.: Dodd Mead, 1974)

Maurice Tytherton is shot to death in the night, and the next morning Colonel Pride, the Chief Constable, is bringing Appleby to Elvedon Court on a case of some missing pictures. When the death is discovered, the retired Appleby needs to polish up his skills on a murder investigation that points at a wayward son and a suspicious art dealer.

England, Elvedon Court

The Appleby File. U.K.: Gollancz, 1975 (U.S.: Dodd Mead, 1976)

A collection of the following stories: "The Ascham," "Beggar with Skull," "The Body in the Glen," "Cold Blood," "The Conversation Piece," "The Coy Mistress," "Death by Water," "Death in the Sun," "The Exploding Battleship," "The Fisherman," "The Memorial Service," "Poltergeist," "A Question of Confidence," "The Thirteenth Priest Hole," and "Two on a Tower."

Short stories

The Gay Phoenix. U.K.: Gollancz, 1976 (U.S.: Dodd Mead, 1977)

When the opportunity arose, Arthur Povey seized the moment and assumed the identity of his dead brother, Charles. Charles's financial empire falls under Arthur's control, but soon he falls victim to a blackmail scheme that puts his disguise in jeopardy. His curious neighbor, the retired Appleby, finds himself drawn into the plot.

Blackmail · England

The Ampersand Papers. U.K.: Gollancz, 1978 (U.S.: Dodd Mead, 1979)

While walking on the beach one day, Appleby is almost struck by a body when it falls from the North Tower of Treskinnick Castle, home to Lord Ampersand. The body is Dr. Sutch, an archivist, and the question becomes: was he pushed?

England, Cornwall

Sheiks and Adders. U.K.: Gollancz, 1982 (U.S.: Dodd Mead, 1983)

Duplication of costumes is not a wanted thing at a country fete, but Appleby is disturbed when he and his friend Pride both arrive dressed as Robin Hood. But his fate is much better than the duplicate sheiks, one of whom ends up dead on the archery fields.

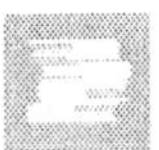

England, Drool Court

Appleby and Honeybath. U.K.: Gollancz, 1983 (U.S.: Dodd Mead, 1983)

Charles Honeybath is exploring the library of Terence Grinton when he discovers a body resting in a chair. When he returns with Appleby, the body is gone and the investigation is launched.

England, Grinton Hall

Carson's Conspiracy. U.K.: Gollancz, 1984 (U.S.: Dodd Mead, 1984)

Carl Carson's wife has an imaginary son named Robin, and he is making his plans to escape from this embarrassing situation, by faking the kidnapping of his fake son. But Carson's neighbor is Appleby, and that means if something suspicious is happening, his detective nose is in the air.

England, Garford House

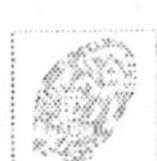

Appleby and the Ospreys. U.K.: Gollancz, 1986 (U.S.: Dodd Mead, 1987)

Clusters would be a great country house, if it was not plagued by bats. However, when Lord Osprey is murdered with an oriental dagger in his library, Appleby is on the scene to try and discover where Lord Osprey has hidden his antique coin collection.

England, Clusters

The Golden Agers and Beyond

Jane Langton ✍

Homer Kelly

Retired from his police career as a Lieutenant Detective, Kelly is a New England resident and Emersonian scholar. He exhibits the sensibilities of the New England area through his personality and his actions. He finds himself using his detective skills to solve many crimes, and his wife Mary is a great sidekick. **Traditional**.

The Transcendental Murder. Harper & Row, 1964 (Also published as *The Minuteman Murder.* Dell, 1976)

When two prominent citizens are murdered, Kelly is assigned the case. He receives surprisingly good help from a resident of Concord named Mary Morgan, and the two begin a match made in heaven.

Massachusetts, Concord

Dark Nantucket Noon. Harper & Row, 1975

The poet, Katherine Clark, is in Nantucket to view the eclipse, and when she is found kneeling next to a dead woman, her only defense is that the moon did it. As the case develops, it is discovered that the victim is Helen Green, wife of novelist Joe Green, and Katherine's former lover.

Massachusetts, Nantucket

The Memorial Hall Murder. Harper, 1978

Kelly has been asked to serve as a visiting professor at Harvard, and he is present when someone bombs Memorial Hall. A rehearsal of Handel's *Messiah* had been in progress, and the director, Hamilton Dow, is missing after the explosion. Because his reputation precedes him, Kelly is asked by the university to conduct an investigation.

Academia · Christmas · Holidays · Massachusetts, Boston · Music

Natural Enemy. Ticknor and Fields, 1982

Langton decides to reveal the murderer early in this title and focus on the why in this case. Kelly's nephew is concerned that since the death of Edward Herron, Buddy Whipple has moved in on Edward's daughters, Barbara and Virginia. So Kelly moves into the household to be on hand for any more suspicious behaviors.

Massachusetts, Walden Pond

Emily Dickinson Is Dead. St. Martin's Press, 1984

Amherst is hosting the Emily Dickinson Centennial Symposium, and the gathering has placed many competing and jealous Dickinson scholars in close proximity. When the beautiful Alison Groves, targeted to model Dickinson's clothes, disappears, Kelly finds himself back on the job. When an overweight scholar named Winifred Gaw is found dead in Dickinson's bed, Kelly finds himself on the trail of a murderer.

Academia · Massachusetts, Amherst · Poetry

Good and Dead. St. Martin's Press, 1986

Kelly finds himself in the Old West Church, trying to determine if the number of congregation members who are dying are being aided by a human hand.

Massachusetts, Nashoba · Religion

Murder at the Gardner. St. Martin's Press, 1988

Titus Moon has asked Kelly to attend the board meeting of the Isabella Stewart Gardner Museum to help end a threat to that institution. The requirement that the collection stays exactly the same and never changes has placed pressure on all, and the decision to sell the collection looms when someone begins to move paintings. Soon, all this tension produces a murder.

Art · Massachusetts, Boston · Museums

The Dante Game. Viking, 1991

Kelly has joined the faculty of the American School for Florentine Studies, but trouble continues to follow him. A maid and her lover, are found dead, and the clue left on their bodies refers to Dante's *The Divine Comedy*. Meanwhile, threats arise from a drug dealer, who feels the Pope is his problem and may use drastic means to eliminate the problem.

Italy, Florence

God in Concord. Viking, 1992

Kelly is aghast at the shopping mall planned for Walden Pond, and worried when the residents of the Pond View Retirement trailer park start dying. His attempt to rouse the alarm falls on deaf ears, and his attention is distracted by a young Thoreau scholar from India who has fallen in love and almost loses his life.

Massachusetts, Concord

Divine Inspiration. Viking, 1993

A fire at the Church of the Commonwealth killed the church sexton and destroyed the old organ. A new organ is being installed, and master organist Alan Starr is busy tuning the instrument when he discovers a 14-month old child abandoned at the church. Kelly and Starr discover that the baby's father is dead and the mother is missing, so they begin a search for the missing woman.

Massachusetts, Boston · Organs · Religion

The Shortest Day. Viking, 1995

The annual Christmas revels are being held in Memorial Hall at Harvard, and Kelly's wife, Mary, is one of the chorus singers. However, Sarah Bailey, the stage director, is worried that someone may be trying to kill her chorus, and she wants Kelly to help her find a murderer.

Christmas · Holidays · Massachusetts, Cambridge · Music

Dead As a Dodo. Viking, 1996

Kelly is at Oxford and interested in the contents of the Oxford University Museum. When a security guard dies in a fall from the museum's roof, Kelly must assume the role of detective again. When the death of a priest seems a suicide, and a cryptic note is left as a clue, Kelly must use the contents of the museum to discover a murderer.

England, Oxford · Museums

The Face on the Wall. Viking, 1998

Is there magical realism in the air, or is it just the human element? Kelly's niece Annie Swann, a children's book editor, has built a new home with a blank wall on which she would like to paint a mural. As she adds her own fairy tales, a face continually appears among her efforts. She asks her uncle to determine if an abused child is speaking to her through her art.

Art · Massachusetts, Concord

The Thief of Venice. Viking, 1999

Kelly is attending a rare books conference and staying with Sam Bell, a man who has examined some ancient relics that he believes may be fakes. The relics are in the care of the Procurator of Saint Mark, and when Lucia Costanza's husband is murdered and she disappears, the history of these relics may be the cause for a death in the present.

Bibliomystery · Italy, Venice

Murder at Monticello. Penguin, 2001

The Kellys have been invited to participate in the two hundredth anniversary of the election of Thomas Jefferson to be held at Monticello. Fern Fisher, Kelly's former student, is trying to write a book to restore some honor to the President's memory when she is attacked by a man named Tom Dean, who would like to do the opposite. When evidence mounts that Dean may be the serial killer, Kelly plays detective.

Virginia, Charlottesville · Monticello · Serial killer

The Escher Twist. Viking, 2002

When their close friend, Leonard Sheldrake, falls madly in love with a mysterious woman named Frieda, who he met at an Escher exhibition in Cambridge, the married couple agrees to hunt for her when she disappears. As the plucky couple tries to find the missing woman, they also stumble upon death.

Escher, Maurits · Massachusetts, Cambridge

Lawrence Sanders ✍

Edward X. Delaney

A retired chief of police, the tough ex-cop known as "Iron Balls" still battles to stop evil in his world. **Hard-boiled**. Series subject: **New York, New York**.

The Anderson Tapes. Putnam, 1970

When Duke Anderson decides to rob an entire building over the Labor Day weekend, his caper is documented by the transcripts from the bugging devices used to document his labors. Other accounts, such as eyewitness reports, court records, and testimony from the pen fill out the book, including the reports of a cop named Edward X. Delaney.

Holidays · Labor Day

The First Deadly Sin. Putnam, 1973

Celia Montfort is a compelling woman with a command over Daniel Blank, a man wounded by a recent divorce. When her manipulations turn him into a killing machine, his efforts garner the attention of the 251st Precinct commander, Delaney. As his own wife's life slips away from a mysterious disease, Delaney hunts for a serial killer.

Serial killer

The Second Deadly Sin. Putnam, 1977

Victor Maitland is one of those enigmas of fame: revered for his work and hated for his personal life. When his body is found stabbed to death in his studio, his death leaves the police department in turmoil. Desperate to close the case, the police call Delaney out of retirement to find a killer.

Art

The Third Deadly Sin. Putnam, 1981

A rare killer is loose in New York: a female serial killer. She wears a different disguise each time, but always a gold charm bracelet with the words "why not." Once again, the police are baffled by the random nature of the crimes, and call Delaney out of retirement.

Serial killer

The Fourth Deadly Sin. Putnam, 1985

Psychiatrist Simon Ellerbee has been murdered and the police are stymied by the case. When Delaney comes out of retirement to help, he is able to convince the dead man's widow to open his files and release the names of his six most violent cases, any of which could be the murderer.

Psychiatry

The Modern Practitioners

Lawrence Block ✍

Matt Scudder

Retired from the police force and troubled by alcoholism, Block's Scudder is one of the most dramatic of the recovering cops. Acting as a private detective, Scudder works the underbelly of New York, and the city comes alive in the hands of this author. Readers may also enjoy James Crumley, Loren D. Estleman, and Robert B. Parker. See the author's website at http://www.lawrenceblock.com. **Hard-boiled**. Series subject: **New York, New York**.

The Sins of the Fathers. Dell, 1976

Cale Hanniford asks Scudder to dig deeper into the facts behind the death of his daughter, Wendy, which has sent a minister's son to jail and to his eventual suicide. Now Cale believes his daughter may have been a prostitute, and he hires Scudder to dig into her background.

In the Midst of Death. Dell, 1976

When Jerry Broadfield is freed after being the star witness in a police corruption case, he seeks out Scudder because call girl Portia has been murdered, and he is the suspect. She had been trying to sue Jerry, but he claims he is innocent of her death.

Time to Murder and Create. Dell, 1977

Spinner has an envelope full of evidence on someone that is so sensitive he will not even clue in Scudder as to the contents, but he does arrange it so that Scudder receives the stuff when he is murdered. Now that makes Scudder the target for everyone who wants its contents.

A Stab in the Dark. Arbor House, 1981

Nine years ago Barbara Ettinger was murdered by the Icepick Prowler. Now her father comes to Scudder because he believes the serial killer that operated so many years ago is not the Louis Pinell just arrested for those crimes. So, Scudder sets out on a nine-year-old trail to find the real murderer.

Serial killer

Eight Million Ways to Die. Arbor House, 1982

Scudder intercedes between a prostitute and her pimp when the woman wants to leave her profession. Later Scudder is hired by the same pimp when the woman is found murdered. SH

When the Sacred Ginmill Closes. Arbor House, 1986

Beginning in 1975, when Scudder was still a heavy drinker, he witnesses a stickup in his favorite after-hours joint. He considers being a bounty hunter, and then is distracted when a drinking buddy falls under a shadow when his wife is murdered. The third aspect of this case evolves when his buddy's doctored bar books are stolen and held for ransom.

Alcoholism

Out on the Cutting Edge. Morrow, 1989

Paula Hoeldtke's father hires Scudder to find her—the actress seems to have had little success in the theater but much better luck at disappearing. While he hunts for someone known as The Butcher Boy, he must deal with his own alcoholism.

Alcoholism • Serial killer

A Ticket to the Boneyard. Morrow, 1990

Scudder is nearly helpless when a serial killer named James Leo Motley sets out to murder all of Scudder's women to avenge what he believes are Scudder's past sins against him. Scudder knows that the last name on the killer's list is his.

Serial killer

A Dance at the Slaughterhouse. Morrow, 1991

The cable television producer may have orchestrated the rape and death of his wife, so the dead woman's brother hires Scudder to prove him guilty. A snuff film death holds a major clue that will connect both murders and help Scudder and his girlfriend Elaine solve the cast. ED

Pornography

A Walk Among the Tombstones. Morrow, 1992

Kenan Khoury is a heroin dealer who ignored the advice of his wife's kidnappers. Now he wants Scudder to avenge her death, and Scudder must use his girlfriend, Elaine, and a host of streetwise New Yorkers to trace the villains.

The Devil Knows You're Dead. Morrow, 1993

Attorney Glenn Holtzmann is gunned down at a phone on Eleventh Avenue, and his death is blamed on a streetperson caught with the cartridge from the gun used in his murder.

When Scudder is not convinced, his exploration of the crime leads him into Hell's Kitchen and the darker side of New York. SH

A Long Line of Dead Men. Morrow, 1994

A tontine is a secret club, and in this book it consists of 30 men who gather once a year to celebrate their lives. This activity turns deadly when someone appears to be killing the members one at a time. Scudder is hired to look into the lives of these men for the clue that will lead to the person who feels driven to strike against all of them.

Even the Wicked. Morrow, 1997

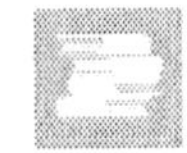

Scudder's defense lawyer friend discovers himself on the list of The Will. The Will is a serial killer who announces his victims in advance, and seeks to avenge himself on victims who seem to need to be killed. When Scudder's protection is broken and the lawyer is killed, Scudder sets off after the serial killer.

Serial killer

Everybody Dies. Morrow, 1998

When Scudder decides to help his connected pal Mick Ballou from Hell's Kitchen, he discovers that this assignment may be harder then he anticipated. When two of Ballou's numbers runners are murdered, Scudder finds himself searching through the unique environs of New York for clues as to who is trying to shut down Ballou.

Organized crime

Hope to Die. Morrow, 2001

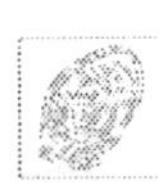

Scudder and his paramour Elaine have just been with the lawyer, Byrne Hollander, and his wife, Susan, when the the Hollanders are murdered in their home. The investigation into their deaths comes to a quick conclusion when the two perpetrators are found dead. But Scudder is hired to discover if a third party was involved in this crime, and as he pursuses his investigation, he begins to believe that there may be a mastermind behind it.

John T. Lescroart ✍

Dismas Hardy

Once a cop, and once a lawyer, Dismas is in conflict with himself as much as he is in conflict with the bad guys. Set in San Francisco, Lescroat uses his character's Irish background to the maximum. He bounces from various legal jobs, trying to find himself and protect the innocent. Readers may also enjoy Terence Faherty and Don Winslow. See the author's website at http://www.johnlescroart.com. **Hard-boiled**. Series subject: **California, San Francisco**.

Dead Irish. Fine, 1989

Tending bar for his friend, Moses McGuire, is how Hardy is coping when he gets the news that Moses's brother-in-law, Eddie Cochran, has committed suicide.

As Hardy begins an investigation, he discovers Eddie's connection to the drug market, but then the family's problems begin to surface as well and lead his investigation in another direction.

The Vig. Fine, 1990

Hardy receives a warning from Rusty Ingraham, a former co-worker in the San Francisco D.A.'s office. Louis Baker is being released from prison, and he is going to kill both of the attorneys. When Ingraham disappears from his boat, the warning may not have been effective. But then Hardy finds a connection to a loan shark named Johnny LaGuardia, and things may not be as they first seemed.

Hard Evidence. Fine, 1993

Recently married, and now a father, Hardy has returned to the D.A.'s office. When he is helping his friend Pico and the Aquarium with beached sharks, they have to gut one and discover the hand of a Silicon Valley billionaire whose body will shortly wash ashore. Hardy becomes the prosecutor when a Japanese call girl is charged with the crime.

Law

The Thirteenth Juror. Fine, 1994

Hardy has now switched to defense attorney work. His first case finds him defending Jennifer Witt against the charge of murdering her husband and son. His only defense against the hopeless evidence is to prove something was wrong with the husband, and when he discovers that he was a wife beater, a gleam of hope begins in the case.

Law

The Mercy Rule. Delacorte Press, 1998

Hardy accepts the case of Graham Russo, a former baseball player, whose long-suffering father, Sal, might have been helped along by his son when he dies of a lethal morphine injection. Although Graham has administered other shots, he claims he was not home the night his father died.

Law

Nothing But the Truth. Delacorte Press, 1999

Hardy's wife Franny is arrested for failing to reveal what she knows about a man who has disappeared. The man is accused of murdering his wife, and Hardy knows that her evidence is the man's only defense and the only hope for getting Franny out of jail. When the secret stays safe from even her husband, Hardy's job of finding his client becomes even harder.

Law

The Hearing. Dutton, 2001

Hardy reluctantly accepts the defense of junkie Cole Burgess, found with the dead body of SFPD homicide lieutenant Abe Gliskey. When D.A. Sharron Pratt decides this case can restore her sagging political fortunes, Hardy finds himself embroiled in controversy and conspiracy.

Law

The Oath. Dutton, 2002

When some suspicious deaths, tied to an HMO, are linked to Hardy's client, Dr. Eric Kensing, Hardy finds himself defending the man whose wife was having an affair with the dead man. As the investigation is pursued by Hardy's friend, Lt. Abe Glitsky, Hardy follows clues that lead him in a direction away from his client and towards a murderer.

HMOs · Law · Medical

Rogue Detectives

Mystery fiction authors have had a little fun twisting the natural order of things by creating rogues who must function as detectives. Sometimes they do it for their own roguishness, sometimes for pure profit, and other times they are defending their own names. But whatever their motivations, it is always interesting when someone sets a thief to catch a thief.

The Historical Founding Members

Jack Boyle ✍

Boston Blackie

Following in the footsteps of Raffles, Boyle produced one set of short stories. Boyle created a safecracker detective, giving the world an early example of how a rogue can have a heart of gold when it comes to murder. These tales were used to create media versions of this detective, insuring Boston Blackie's importance as a benchmark figure amongst the rogues. See a fan website at http://www.thrillingdetective.com/boston.html. **Traditional**.

Boston Blackie. Fly, 1919

A series of short stories that the author originally wrote for *Redbook* magazine were slightly revised and given the appearance of a novel when this book was first published. It features the criminal adventures of this distinguish crook and his devoted wife Mary.

California, San Francisco

E. W. Hornung ✍

A. J. Raffles

It may not be wise to invite England's greatest cricket player over for the weekend, because by night A. J. Raffles is also England's greatest thief. As with all the rogues, once confronted with a crime not of his own making, Raffles is also a fine detective. His constant companion is Bunny Manders, the only one who knows his secret. After the first four books, the series was continued by Barry Perowne (pseud. of Philip Atkey). After Perowne, there was one contribution each from David Fletcher and Peter Tremayne. The early novels are marred by the prejudices of their time, so reader beware. **Traditional**.

The Amateur Cracksman. U.K.: Methuen, 1899 (U.S.: Scribner, 1899; also published as *Raffles, the Amateur Cracksman.* Nash, 1906)

A collection of the following stories: "A Costume Piece," "Gentlemen and Layers," "The Gift of the Emperor," "The Ides of March," "Le Premier Pas," "Nine Points of the Law," "The Return March," and "Wilful Murder."

Short stories

The Black Mask. U.K.: Richards, 1901 (U.S.: *Raffles, Further Adventures of the Amateur Cracksman.* Scribner, 1901)

A collection of the following stories: "The Fate of Faustina," "A Jubilee Present," "The Knees of the Gods," "The Last Laugh," "No Sinecure," "An Old Flame," "To Catch a Thief," and "The Wrong House."

Short stories

A Thief in the Night. U.K.: Chatto, 1905 (U.S.: Scribner, 1905)

A collection of the following stories: "A Bad Night," "The Chest of Silver," "The Criminologist's Club," "The Field of Philippi," "The Last Word," "Out of Paradise," "The Raffles Relics," "The Rest Cure," "The Spoils of Sacrilege," and "A Trap to Catch a Cracksman."

Short stories

Mr. Justice Raffles. U.K.: Smith & Elder, 1909 (U.S.: Scribner, 1909)

Teddy Garland is the wicket-keeper for Cambridge, and a friend of Raffles, who is desperate to pay his debts prior to a big cricket match. He owes a money-lender named Dan Levy, who is also an acquaintance of Raffles. So Raffles tries to work his magic, only to have Teddy disappear.

England, London

Raffles After Dark (by Barry Perowne). U.K.: Cassell, 1933 (U.S.: *The Return of Raffles: Further Adventures of the Amateur Cracksmans.* Day, 1933)

Raffles and Bunny have returned to England after a two-year hiatus from their illegal activities, but very shortly they are right back at it. Visiting Prior's Acre and Sir Harmon Rand, the two become involved in a case that will lead to the rich man's death and an investigation that pits them against Scotland Yard.

England · Perowne, Barry

***Raffles in Pursuit** (by Barry Perowne). Cassell, 1934

***Raffles Under Sentence** (by Barry Perowne). Cassell, 1936

***She Married Raffles** (by Barry Perowne). Cassell, 1936

***Raffles vs. Sexton Blake** (by Barry Perowne). Amalgamated Press, 1937

Raffles' Crime in Gibraltar (by Barry Perowne). U.K.: Amalgamated Press, 1937 (U.S.: *They Hang Them in Gibraltar.* Hillman-Curl, 1939)

In Gibraltar, Detective Marius has been stabbed and Inspector Sacarello has been strangled, and the logical suspect is Raffles. He is on a mission to connect their deaths to his failed attempt to burglarize the American scientist Andrew Payne Hulburd.

Gibraltar · Perowne, Barry

***The A.R.P. Mystery** (by Barry Perowne). Amalgamated Press, 1939

Raffles and the Key Man (by Barry Perowne). Lippincott, 1940

Raffles is a talented cracksman, but he is no match for a master criminal like The Key Man. When his friend Eliot Lang is endangered by a relationship with The Key Man, it is Raffles who rides to the rescue.

England · Perowne, Barry

Raffles Revisited (by Barry Perowne). Harper & Row, 1974

A collection of the following stories: "The Birthday Diamond," "Bo-Peep in the Suburbs," "The Coffee Queen Affair," "The Darmoor Hostage," "The Doctor's Defense," "An Error in Curfew," "The Gentle Wrecker," "The Governor of Gibraltar," "The Grace-and-Favor Crime," "Kismet and the Dancing Boy," "Man's Meanest Crime," "Princess Amen," "The Riddle of Dinah Raffles," and "Six Golden Nymphs."

England · Perowne, Barry · Short stories

Raffles of the Albany (by Barry Perowne). U.K.: H. Hamilton, 1976 (U.S.: St. Martin's Press, 1977)

A collection of the following stories: "Adventure of the Dancing Girls," "The Baffling of Oom Paul," "The Baskerville March," "Carriages for Buckingham Palace," "Cocaine and the Thief with Trembling Hands," "Dinah Raffles and Oscar Wilde," "John L. Sullivan Obliges," "Raffles and the Automobile Gang," "Stealing the Venetian Horses," "Tusitala and the Money-Belt," and "The Victory March."

England · Historical (1900–1999) · Perowne, Barry · Short stories

Raffles (by David Fletcher). U.K.: Macmillan, 1977 (U.S.: Putnam, 1977)

Raffles returns to his ways in this modern adaptation of the cracksman.

England · Fletcher, David · Historical (1900–1999) · Short stories

Raffles of the M.C.C. (by Barry Perowne). U.K.: Macmillan, 1979 (U.S.: St. Martin's Press, 1979)

A collection of the following stories: "Bevercombe's Benefit March," "Black Mask and the Firefly," "Detectives Operate in This Store," "The Graves of Academe," "The Hermit of Fleet Street," "Lord's and the Dangerous Game," "Madame Blavatsky's Teacups," "The Ordeal of Dinah Raffles," "The Roskelly Injunction," "The Tongues of Deceit," and "A Venus at Lord's."

Historical (1900–1999) · Short stories

The Return of Raffles (by Peter Tremayne). U.K.: Magnum, 1981 (U.S.: Severn House, 1991)

Raffles is turned by his own government and forced to use his talents to help his country. It seems an indiscreet monarch has written some letters, and only Raffles can recover them and prevent an international crisis.

England · Historical (1900–1999) · Tremayne, Peter

The Complete Short Stories of Raffles—the Amateur Cracksman (by Barry Perowne). Souvenir Press, 1984

A collection of the following stories: "A Bad Night," "The Chest of Silver," "A Costume Piece," "The Criminologists' Club," "The Fate of Faustina," "The Field of Philippi," "Gentleman and Players," "The Gift of the Emperor," "The Ides of March," "A Jubilee Present," "The Knees of the Gods," "The Last Laugh," "The Last Word," "Nine Points of the Law," "No Sinecure," "An Old Friend," "Out of Paradise," "Le Premier Pas," "The Raffles Relics," "The Rest Cure," "The Return Match," "The Spoils of Sacrilege," "To Catch a Thief," "A Trap to Catch a Cracksman," "Wilful Murder," and "The Wrong House."

England · Short stories

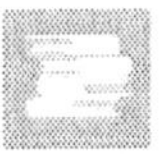

The Golden Agers and Beyond

Leslie Charteris ✍

The Saint (Simon Templar)

Simon Templar, known by his calling card featuring the stick figure that represents The Saint, is a modern day Robin Hood. His early adventures pit him against Scotland Yard, while later in the series he moves to New York. All of the later materials are novelizations by other authors from alternative sources. See at website about the author at http://www.saint.org. **Traditional**.

Meet the Tiger. U.K.: Ward, 1928 (U.S.: Doubleday, 1929; also published as *Crooked Gold.* Amalgamated, 1929; also published as *The Saint Meets the Tiger.* Sun Dial, 1940)

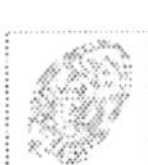

At the age of 27, the mysterious Simon Templar, still able to hide his secret identity as The Saint, settles into the sleepy little village of Baycombe. But after only three days there, his presence brings an assassin, and soon he is off on his first adventure in the murky world of crime, capers, and espionage.

England, Baycombe

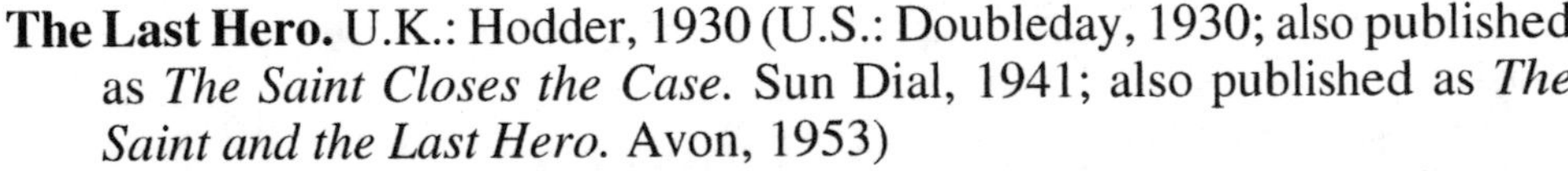

The Last Hero. U.K.: Hodder, 1930 (U.S.: Doubleday, 1930; also published as *The Saint Closes the Case.* Sun Dial, 1941; also published as *The Saint and the Last Hero.* Avon, 1953)

International arms dealer, Rayt Marius, is trying to get a new weapon from the English to sell to the evil Prince Rudolf. Of course, Templar and his merry band are trying to prevent that sale.

Espionage · England

Enter the Saint. U.K.: Hodder, 1930 (U.S.: Doubleday, 1931)

A collection of the following stories: "The Lawless Lady," "The Man Who was Clever," and "The Policeman with Wings."

Short stories

Knight Templar. U.K.: Hodder, 1930 (U.S.: *The Avenging Saint.* Doubleday, 1931)

Templar is returning to England to revenge the death of a friend. The Millionaire Without A Country, or Dr. Rayt Marius, returns to challenge the Saint in another combat that pits the fate of his homeland against the interest of the power-hungry Marius.

England

Featuring the Saint. U.K.: Hodder, 1931 (U.S.: Bonded, 1945; also published as *Featuring the Saint.* Avon, 1958 [two of the stories]).

A collection of the following stories: "The Logical Adventure," "The Man Who Could Not Die," and "The Wonderful War."

Short stories

Alias the Saint. U.K.: Hodder, 1931 (U.S.: Bonded, 1945 or Avon, 1957 [each contains only two stories]).

A collection of the following stories: "The Impossible Crime," "The National Debt," and "The Story of a Dead Man."

England • Short stories

She Was a Lady. U.K.: Hodder, 1931 (U.S.: *Angels of Doom.* Doubleday, 1932; also published as *The Saint Meets His Match.* Bonded, 1945)

Jill Trelawney has come to London to conduct her business and hopes she can stay clear of The Saint. She advertises herself as The Angel of Doom, and tries to build a mystique that will equal Templar's own reputation, all based on her need to avenge her father's ill-timed death caused by a police accusation.

England

The Holy Terror. U.K.: Hodder, 1932 (U.S.: *The Saint vs. Scotland Yard.* Doubleday, 1932)

A collection of the following stories: "Inland Revenue," "The Melancholy Journey of Mr. Teal," and "The Million Pound Day."

England • Short stories

Getaway. U.K.: Hodder, 1932 (U.S.: Doubleday, 1933; also published as *Saint's Getaway.* Sun Dial, 1943)

Templar has fled England to Austria, and he is in search of Dr. Stanislau Leberwurst, a master of marine engineering. He captures his quarry, but loses him to murder, and the search is on for the big secret carried by the wayward scientist. As his paths cross with the evil Prince Rudolf, a question of a diamond comes up.

Austria, Innsbruck • Jewels

Once More the Saint. U.K.: Hodder, 1933 (U.S.: *The Saint and Mr. Teal.* Doubleday, 1933)

A collection of the following stories: "The Death Penalty," "The Gold Standard," and "The Man from St. Louis."

Short stories

The Brighter Buccaneer. U.K.: Hodder, 1933 (U.S.: Doubleday, 1933; also published as *The Saint—The Brighter Buccaneer.* Avon, 1957 [does not contain all the stories])

A collection of the following stories: "The Appalling Politician," "The Bad Baron," "The Blind Spot," "The Brain Workers," "The Brass Buddha," "The Export Trade," "The Five Thousand Pound Kiss," "The Green Goods Man," "The New Swindle," "The Owners' Handicap," "The Perfect Crime," "The Tough Egg," "The Unblemished Bootlegger," "The Unpopular Landlord," and "The Unusual Ending."

Short stories

The Misfortunes of Mr. Teal. U.K.: Hodder, 1934 (U.S.: Doubleday, 1934; also published as *The Saint in England.* Sun Dial, 1941; also published in *The Saint in London.* U.K.: Hodder, 1952)

A collection of the following stories: "The Art of Alibi," "The Higher Finance," and "The Simon Templar Foundation."

Short stories

Boodle. U.K.: Hodder, 1934 (U.S.: *The Saint Intervenes.* Doubleday, 1934)

A collection of the following stories: "The Art Photographer," "The Damsel in Distress," "The Ingenuous Colonel," "The Loving Brothers," "The Man Who Liked Toys," "The Mixture as Before," "The Newdick Helicopter," "The Noble Sportsman," "The Prince of Cherkessia," "The Sleepless Knight," "The Tall Timber," "The Treasure of Turk's Lane," "The Uncritical Publisher," and "The Unfortunate Financier."

Short stories

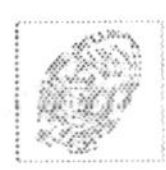

The Saint Goes On. U.K.: Hodder, 1934 (U.S.: Doubleday, 1935)

A collection of the following stories: "The Case of the Frightened Innkeeper," "The Elusive Ellshaw," and "The High Fence."

Short stories

The Saint in New York. U.K.: Hodder, 1935 (U.S.: Doubleday, 1935)

The Saint has come across the ocean to attempt to clean up the organized crime scene in New York. Whether he will be successful against Mr. Big will be dependent on his allies and on his adapting to a new country.

New York, New York

Saint Overboard. U.K.: Hodder, 1936 (U.S.: Doubleday, 1936)

On a foggy night onboard his ship The Corsair, Templar pulls Loretta Page out of the sea after shots have been fired, and men in an outboard come looking for her. From her he hears the story of the Lutine, and the sunken treasure that still lies aboard her.

Diving · Shipboard

The Ace of Knaves. U.K.: Hodder, 1937 (U.S.: Doubleday, 1937; also published as *The Saint in Action.* Sun Dial, 1938; also published as *The Saint: Ace of Knaves.* Avon, 1955)

A collection of the following stories: "The Beauty Specialist," "The Spanish War," and "The Unlicensed Victuallers."

Short stories

Thieves' Picnic. U.K.: Hodder, 1937 (U.S.: Doubleday, 1937; also published as *The Saint Bids Diamonds.* Triangle, 1942; also published as *The Saint at a Thieves' Picnic.* Avon , 1951)

The Saint, cruising through the countryside of Spain one day, rescues the helpless Joris Vanlinden from a beating, and inherits his attractive young niece, Christine, as well. He has been cheated by his boss, Reuben Graner, not a good thing when you are involved in jewel thefts. But now, he has the Saint on his side.

Spain, Santa Cruz

Prelude for War. U.K.: Hodder, 1938 (U.S.: Doubleday, 1938; also published as *The Saint Plays with Fire.* Triangle, 1942)

On a drive one night, Templar and Patricia Holm are out for a drive when they come across a house fire, and as Templar attempts to rescue Johnny Kennet, he discovers the man was locked into his room so that escape was not an option. He sticks with this troubled lad, eager to find a murderer.

England

Follow the Saint. Doubleday, 1938

A collection of the following stories: "The Affair at Hogsbotham," "The Invisible Millionaire," and "The Miracle Tea Party."

Short stories

The Happy Highwayman. U.K.: Hodder, 1939 (U.S.: Doubleday, 1939; also published as *The Saint—The Happy Highwayman.* Avon, 1955 [does not contain all the stories])

A collection of the following stories: "The Benevolent Burglary," "The Charitable Countess," "The Man Who Liked Ants," "The Man Who Was Lucky," "The Mug's Game," "The Smart Detective," "The Star Producers," "The Well-Meaning Mayor," and "The Wicked Cousin."

Short stories

The Saint in Miami. Doubleday, 1940

Going to Miami to help Justine Gilbeck, the Saint arrives only to discover she and her father are both missing. When a offshore tanker explodes, it is just one step in the adventures of The Saint as he tries to recover his missing charges.

Florida, Miami

The Saint Goes West. U.K.: Hodder, 1942 (U.S.: Doubleday, 1942)

A collection of the following stories: "Arizona," "Hollywood," and "Palm Springs."

Short stories

The Saint Steps In. Doubleday, 1943

It is not unheard of that a woman would approach The Saint in a bar, but this woman is a damsel in distress. Madeline Gray's story involves being warned off a meeting with Imberline of the War Products Board, to whom she wishes to introduce her father's invention, a synthetic rubber that could help the American war effort. Someone does not like this idea, or her father, and works their magic against their efforts while cloaked in the mantle of wartime patriotism.

New York, New York · Washington, D.C. · World War II

The Saint on Guard. Doubleday, 1945

A collection of the following stories: "The Black Market," and "The Sizzling Saboteur."

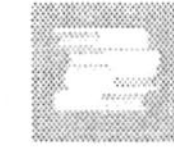

Short stories

The Saint Sees It Through. Doubleday, 1946

The Saint is in New York, on the trail of Dr. Ernst Zellermann, a phony psychiatrist. At a New York club, he makes an association with Avalon Dexter, and from there springs an adventure that leads The Saint on a chase after a blackmailer.

Blackmail · New York, New York

Call for the Saint. U.K.: Hodder, 1948 (U.S.: Doubleday, 1948)

A collection of the following stories: "The King of the Beggars," and "The Masked Angel."

Short stories

Saint Errant. Doubleday, 1948

A collection of the following stories: "Dawn," "Emily," "Iris," "Jeannine," "Judith," "Lida," "Lucia," "Luclla," and "Teresa."

Short stories

The Saint in Europe. Doubleday, 1953

A collection of the following stories: "The Angel's Eye," "The Covetous Headsman," "The Golden Journey," "The Latin Touch," "The Loaded Tourist," "The Rhine Maiden," and "The Spanish Cow."

Short stories

The Saint on the Spanish Main. Doubleday, 1955

A collection of the following stories: "The Arrow of God," "The Black Commissar," "The Effete Angler," "The Old Treasure Story," "The Questing Tycoon," and "The Unkind Philanthropist."

Short stories

The Saint Around the World. Doubleday, 1957

A collection of the following stories: "The Lovelorn Sheikh," "The Patient Playboy," "The Pluperfect Lady," "The Reluctant Nudist," "The Sporting Chance," and "The Talented Husband."

Short stories

Thanks to the Saint. Doubleday, 1957

A collection of the following stories: "The Bunco Artists," "The Careful Terrorist," "The Good Medicine," "The Happy Suicide," "The Perfect Sucker," and "The Unescapable Word."

Short stories

Senor Saint. Doubleday, 1958.

A collection of the following stories: "The Golden Frog," "The Pearls of Peace," "The Revolution Racket," and "The Romantic Matron."

Short stories

The Saint to the Rescue. Doubleday, 1959

A collection of the following stories: "The Element of Doubt," "The Ever-Loving Spouse," "The Fruitful Land," "The Gentle Ladies," "The Percentage Player," and "The Water Merchant."

Short stories

Trust the Saint. U.K.: Hodder, 1962 (U.S.: Doubleday , 1962)

A collection of the following stories: "The Bigger Game," "The Cleaner Cure," "The Convenient Monster," "The Helpful Pirate," "The Intemperate Reformer," and "The Uncured Ham."

Short stories

The Saint in the Sun. Doubleday, 1963

A collection of the following stories: "The Better Mousetrap," "The Fast Women," "The Hopeless Heiress," "The Jolly Undertaker," "The Prodigal Miser," "The Russian Prisoner," and "The Ugly Impresario."

Short stories

Vendetta for the Saint. Doubleday, 1964.

While dining, Templar overhears an English tourist address a man as Dion Cartelli, and almost get beaten for his troubles. The next day the man is dead, and the Saint is taking on the Italian Mob to get his satisfaction.

Italy, Sicily • Organized crime

The Saint on TV (by Fleming Lee). U.K.: Hodder, 1968 (U.S.: Doubleday, 1968)

A collection of the following stories: "The Death Game," and "The Power Artist." Both of these stories were adapted by Lee from teleplays.

Lee, Fleming • Short stories

The Saint Returns (by Fleming Lee). Doubleday, 1968.

A collection of the following stories: "The Dizzy Daughter," and "The Gadget Lovers." Both of these stories were adapted by Fleming from teleplays.

Lee, Fleming • Short stories

The Saint and the Fiction Makers (by Fleming Lee). Doubleday, 1968

Templar has the job of protecting thriller author Amos Klein, and then S.W.O.R.D. kidnaps him. Templar has to scramble just like one of the heroes the kidnapped author writes about. Based on one of the TV show episodes.

Authors · England · Lee, Fleming

The Saint Abroad (by Fleming Lee). Doubleday, 1969.

A collection of the following stories: "The Art Collectors," and "The Persistent Patriots."

Lee, Fleming · Short stories

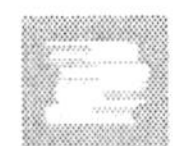

The Saint and the People Importers (by Fleming Lee). U.K.: Hodder, 1971 (U.S.: Doubleday, 1971)

Templar is upset when a Pakistani who works at his favorite restaurant is crucified. He launches an investigation that reveals someone is trading in people, and he means to shut them down.

England · Lee, Fleming

The Saint in Pursuit. Doubleday, 1970

Vicky Kinian's father disappeared in Lisbon in 1944, and when he sends a letter to his daughter asking her to come to Lisbon, there are many people who would be interested in what he is doing now. This novel is based on a comic strip featuring The Saint.

Portugal, Lisbon

Catch the Saint (by Fleming Lee). U.K.: Hodder, 1975 (U.S.: Doubleday, 1975)

A collection of the following stories: "The Adoring Socialite," and "The Masterpiece Merchant."

Lee, Fleming · Short stories

The Saint and the Hapsburg Necklace (by Christopher Short). U.K.: Hodder, 1976 (U.S.: Doubleday, 1976)

Vienna is the stalking grounds at the eve of WWII, when Templar tries to keep some diamonds out of Nazi hands.

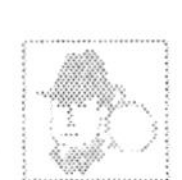

Austria, Vienna · Historical (1900–1999) · Short, Christopher

Leslie Charteris' Send for the Saint. Doubleday, 1978

A collection of the following stories: "The Midas Double," and "The Pawn Gambit."

Short stories

The Saint in Trouble (by Graham Weaver). Coronet, 1978 (U.S.: Doubleday, 1978)

A collection of the following stories: "The Imprudent Professor," and "The Red Sabbath."

Short stories · Weaver, Graham

The Saint: Good As Gold. Walter J. Black, 1978

A collection of the following stories: "The Imprudent Professor," "The Midas Double," "The Pawn Gambit," and "The Red Sabbath."

Short stories

The Saint and the Templar Treasure (by Graham Weaver). U.K.: Hodder, 1979 (U.S.: Doubleday, 1979)

Taking two hitchhikers to their destination in the French countryside leads Templar to a case of arson. As he stays on to help, it changes to a case of murder.

France · Weaver, Graham

Count on the Saint. U.K.: Hodder, 1980 (U.S.: Doubleday, 1980)

A collection of the following stories: "The Pastor's Problem," and "The Unsaintly Santa."

Short stories

The Fantastic Saint. Doubleday, 1982

A collection of the following stories: "The Convenient Monster," "The Darker Drink," "The Gold Standard," "The Man Who Liked Ants," "The Newdick Helicopter," and "The Questing Tycoon."

Short stories

Leslie Charteris' Salvage for the Saint. U.K.: Hodder, 1983 (U.S.: Doubleday, 1983)

Arabella Tatenor's husband is blown up on his boat, and she turns to Templar for help. All he can tell her is her husband might have been crook.

England

The Saint: Five Complete Novels. Avenel, 1983

A collection of the following noveles: *The Avenging Saint*; *The Lawless Lady*; *The Man Who was Clever*; *The Saint Closes the Case*; and *The Saint vs. Scotland Yard.*

The First Saint Omnibus: an Anthology of Saintly Adventures. Dorset, 1990

A collection of the following stories: "The Affair of Hogsbotham," "The Appalling Politician," "The Death Penalty," "The High Fence," "The Man Who Was Clever," "The Million Pound Day," "The Simon Templar Foundation," "The Sleepless Knight," "The Story of a Dead Man," "The Unblemished Bootlegger," "The Unfortunate Financier," "The Unlicensed Victuallers," and "The Wonderful War."

Short stories

John D. MacDonald ✍

Travis McGee

From his houseboat in Florida, this rogue makes a living recovering stolen property. Perhaps more suspense thriller than traditional detective, he still represents an interesting extension of the slightly off-center detective hero. The adventures of McGee also afforded

MacDonald a platform for his pithy comments on contemporary society. See a fan's website at http://members.bellatlantic.net/~mwarble/slipf18/home.htm. **Hard-boiled**.

The Deep Blue Goodbye. Gold Medal, 1964

Cathy Kerr steps onboard McGee's boat with a story about her father's hidden contraband and how Junior Allen had stolen it from her. McGee can keep a cut if he can figure out what made Junior Allen rich and take it away from him.

Florida, Lauderdale

Nightmare in Pink. Gold Medal, 1964

Nina Gibson lives in New York, and her life is invaded by McGee when her fiancé Howard Plummer dies and she comes into some money. But the money may have been obtained by illegal means, and some others just might want it back. A girl like Nina needs a knight errant to protect her interests, and that could be McGee.

New York, New York

A Purple Place for Dying. Gold Medal, 1964

Mona Yeoman has brought McGee to the wild West with a tale of how her father's estate, left to her, has been plundered by her father's best friend and the man she married, Jasper Yeoman. However, before McGee has all the details, someone kills Mona. Without a client, McGee could go home, but he knows that somewhere out there is the money.

West

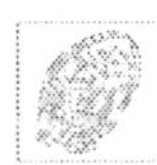

The Quick Red Fox. Gold Medal, 1964

Actress Lysa Dean needs McGee's help when she is sent blackmail photos from a party she attended with nine other men and women. McGee knows the first job is to find the other nine, but he is equally disturbed at the sadistic tone of the note accompanying the photos. He should be worried, as his witnesses are beginning to die, and there are threats to his ally, Dana Holtzer, Dean's aide.

Blackmail • California • Florida

Bright Orange for the Shroud. Gold Medal, 1965

Arthur Wilkinson comes to McGee with a tale of woe that leads right back to his relationship with Wilma Ferners. To keep up with the her needs and desires, he gets himself involved with a syndicate that includes large amounts of cash and men willing to take it from each other.

Florida

A Deadly Shade of Gold. Gold Medal, 1965

Twenty eight idols from Central America used to be in Sam Taggart's possession, but he comes to McGee with none left in his possession. Before he can tell McGee everything, his throat is cut. Teamed with a woman named Nora Gardino, who wants revenge, McGee finds himself in Mexico and on the trail of some illegally obtained antiquities.

Antiquities • California, Buena Villas • Mexico, Puerto Altamura

Darker Than Amber. Gold Medal, 1966

McGee is trolling for fish one night when a woman is thrown from a bridge and snagged by his line. The lovely Eurasian beauty would prefer to remain anonymous, but when her attackers return, she needs McGee to be her savior.

Florida · Shipboard

One Fearful Yellow Eye. Gold Medal, 1966

Glory Doyle Geis has called McGee in Florida and managed to get him to fly to Chicago. Her husband, Dr. Fortner Geis has died, but prior to his death he converted his entire estate into cash and squirreled it away from everyone. Now all the survivors are suspicious of each other, and with the IRS, they would like to locate the money.

Illinois, Chicago

The Girl in the Plain Brown Wrapper. Gold Medal, 1968

Helena Pearson knew she was in trouble, and her letter and check arrive on The Busted Flush after she is dead. Five years prior, McGee has done a salvage job for her husband Mick. Now his job is to find out why Maurie, Mick and Helena's daughter, is trying to commit suicide.

Florida, Fort Courtney

Pale Gray for Guilt. Gold Medal, 1968

When the owner of a marina refuses to sell to the developers of an industrial complex destined to occupy the space, he falls victim to a mysterious accident. Tush Bannon was McGee's friend, and the knight errant decides to avenge his death.

Florida, Broward Beach

Dress Her in Indigo. Gold Medal, 1969

T. Harlan Bowie's wife has died and his daughter Bix has fled that reality by going to Mexico with some friends rather than attend her senior year at Wellesley. He needs McGee's help when he discovers she had cleared her bank account just before she was killed in an auto accident. So with Meyer's help, McGee journeys to this foreign land and into a strange and dangerous area rife with adventure.

Mexico, Oaxaca

The Long Lavender Look. Gold Medal, 1970

McGee's famed Rolls Royce, Miss Agnes, goes for a dip in a canal one night when he swerves to avoid a woman. When someone takes a potshot at him and Meyer, McGee knows he has another damsel in distress. What he does not expect is to be arrested for murder.

Florida, Cypress County

A Tan and Sandy Silence. Gold Medal, 1972

Mary Broll is an old friend, but when her husband comes hunting for her, convinced she is onboard The Busted Flush, McGee finds himself in danger. His search for the woman leads to a Caribbean island and a strange and tangled case.

Caribbean, Granada

The Scarlet Ruse. Gold Medal, 1973

Stamp trading can be a lucrative business, but when Hersh Fedderman takes some money to buy some rare stamps, he is left with fakes. He needs McGee's help because the money came from mobster Frank Sprenger.

Florida, Miami · Organized crime · Stamps

The Turquoise Lament. Lippincott, 1973

Pidge Brindle has known McGee her whole life, and she turns to him with a special problem. Either she is going crazy, or her husband Howie is trying to kill her. After McGee investigates and gives the all clear, they sail away. Then McGee begins to worry about the salvage information the girl owns, and the millions of dollars that she may know about.

Hawaii, Honolulu

The Dreadful Lemon Sky. Lippincott, 1974

McGee is asked to hold a box containing more than $100,000 in cash by Carrie Milligan. When Carrie is found dead a few weeks later, struck by a truck on a lonely country road, McGee begins a search to find her killer.

Florida, Bayside

The Empty Copper Sea. Lippincott, 1978

Hub Lawless is believed drowned, and the fault lies with Van Harder, the boat's skipper. His friendship with McGee brings the detective onto the case, where McGee discovers a large insurance policy on the victim and a wife who insists her husband is dead, but not drowned.

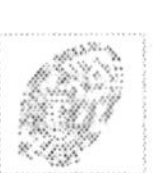

Florida, Timber Bay

The Green Ripper. Lippincott, 1979

McGee has found the woman of his dreams in the lovely Greta. But when she is murdered, his revenge drives him to take action. The key to her murder may lie within the Church of the Apocrypha. So, McGee joins and begins a plan that will lead him to a killer.

California, Ukiah · Cults

Free Fall in Crimson. Harper & Row, 1981

Two years earlier, Ellis Esterland, already terminally ill, was beaten to death on a Florida highway with his daughter, who would die a few weeks later. This left the rich man's estate to his estranged widow Josie. Esterland's son Ron hires McGee to investigate the crime, feeling that he should have received the money. Traveling to the Western coast of Florida, McGee finds himself enmeshed in a controversy that includes an odd filmmaker and some hot-air balloons.

Film · Florida · Wills

Cinnamon Skin. Harper & Row, 1982

Meyer lends his boat to his niece, Norma, and her husband, Evan Lawrence. When the ship is blown up and a Chilean terrorist takes credit, McGee wonders if the cause is drugs. Meyer's efforts in Santiago prior to the terrorist act may hold the key, and he and McGee begin a journey to hunt down a killer who tried to make it personal.

Florida, Lauderdale • Mexico • Terrorism

The Lonely Silver Rain. Knopf, 1985

What is the reason behind the cat-shaped pipe cleaners someone is depositing on The Busted Flush? How do these clues tie into what appears to be a campaign to assassinate McGee? The case begins with a simple search for a missing yacht, and leads McGee into a reassessment of his entire life.

Florida, Lauderdale • Mexico

Anthony Morton (pseud. of John Creasey) ✍

John Mannering (The Baron [aka The Blue Mask])

John Mannering, a Mayfair bachelor and man-about-town, has a secret identity as The Baron, a master cracksman. Eventually, John Mannering gives up his evil ways to become an antiques dealer and consultant to Scotland Yard. From his shop, Quinns in Bond Street, he ventures forth to solve crimes, most of which involve very expensive jewels. Eventually, he marries Lorna Fauntley Mannering, a famous portrait artist. His moniker is The Baron, but for some strange reason his early American cases referred to him as The Blue Mask. **Traditional**.

Meet the Baron. U.K.: Harrap, 1937 (U.S.: *The Man in the Blue Mask.* Lippincott, 1937)

In this first book, Mannering's reputation as a gentleman is so strong, he ends up deputized to search for himself by Inspector William Bristow. However, the reality is that he is a broken-hearted man, having to give up his love when his income is not sufficient. The Baron manages to discover a route to financial worth, and his sparring with the police begins, as well as his relationship with Lorna Fauntley.

England • Jewels

The Baron Returns. U.K.: Harrap, 1937 (U.S.: *The Return of the Blue Mask.* Lippincott, 1937)

The Baron is in the process of burglarizing the home of Gus Teevens in search of a diamond taken as payment for a questionable debt. Then, as the alarm is sounded, he meets a mysterious woman who will turn this attempt at simple burglary into an adventure.

England, Wimbledon • Jewels

The Baron at Bay. U.K.: Low, 1938 (U.S.: *Blue Mask at Bay.* Lippincott, 1938)

The Baron wishes to get his hands on the Five Jewels of Castilla. The problem is that other crooks are in possession of the treasures, and they vow to either keep their jewels or end the Baron's career. The first of the five jewels falls easily into his hands, but the adventure that begins leads to danger as he tries to recover the other four.

England, London • Jewels

The Baron Again. U.K.: Low, 1938 (U.S.: *Salute Blue Mask.* Lippincott, 1938)

Mannering is attempting to give up his life of crime as The Baron, and things have been quite good for six months. But when American jewel collector Henry Fallon's hotel suite is burglarized, it draws attention back to The Baron when an appeal is printed in the newspaper for his help. The appeal is from the fiancé of debutant Marion Delray, and The Baron returns to action to help right a wrong.

England, London · Jewels

Alias the Baron. U.K.: Low, 1939 (U.S.: *Alias Blue Mask.* Lippincott, 1939)

The Baron has gone legitimate, and his purchase of the famous Dellamont Emeralds in Paris makes him feel good. But his good mood changes quickly when he finds himself the victim of a burglary, and when the burglar is a blue-masked robber disguised as The Baron.

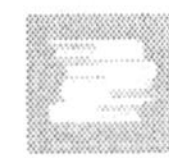

England, London · Jewels

The Baron at Large. U.K.: Low, 1939 (U.S.: *Challenge Blue Mask!* Lippincott, 1939)

The Baron is asked to take part in a historic occasion: the uniting of the Kallinov collection, owned by Lord Sharron, and the famous Gloria diamond, held by The Baron. The weekend at Beverly Towers starts pleasantly enough, but when a burglar takes place, The Baron must use his skills to recover the stolen goods.

England · Jewels

Call for the Baron. U.K.: Low, 1940 (U.S.: *Blue Mask Victorious.* Lippincott, 1940)

The Baron is asked to solve a series of thefts at an English country mansion where quite soon a summit meeting is to be held between American and British diplomats. When a robbery takes place, the police look at The Baron as the most likely suspect. Guarding the secret files of the diplomats and his own honor prove a tough task for the detective.

England, Hampshire · Espionage

***Versus the Baron.** U.K.: Low, 1940 (U.S.: *Blue Mask Strikes Again.* Lippincott, 1940)

***The Baron Comes Back.** Low, 1943

A Case for the Baron. U.K.: Low, 1945 (U.S.: Duell, 1949)

As World War II winds down, Scotland Yard is concerned that underground groups are turning to criminal ways for the profits available in weary and war-torn nations. They turn to The Baron when a series of deaths are tied to a gang of smugglers. When deaths occur in London, The Baron finds himself personally threatened by the desperate gangs who will stop at nothing to preserve their share of the new world order.

England, London · World War II

***Reward for the Baron.** Low, 1945

Career for the Baron. U.K.: Low, 1946 (U.S.: Duell, 1950)

Lorna has put up with enough adventure in her short life with The Baron, and she urges him to buy Quinn's antiques and jewelry shop when it comes up for sale. The death of old Quinn has left the place in the hands of his young nephew, and this place could lend an air of legitimacy to The Baron's life. But when murder intervenes, and a young couple's happiness is at stake, The Baron finds himself manipulating events to solve a crime.

England, London

The Baron and the Beggar. U.K.: Low, 1947 (U.S.: Duell, 1950)

The Adalgo diamond, whose history includes being stolen from the collection of the King of Spain, ends up in the window of Quinn's, The Baron's store. When a beggar shows more than normal interest in the item, it begins a mystery that leads The Baron down a dark path to murder.

Diamonds • England, London

A Rope for the Baron. U.K.: Low, 1948 (U.S.: Duell, 1949)

Despite warnings not to proceed, The Baron journeys to Hallen House on the moors, and visits with the eerie occupants. When he discovers that he will not be allowed to leave, his talents allow him to escape but put him in the spotlight for danger when a death points back to him.

England, Cornwellin • Jewels

***Blame the Baron.** U.K.: Low, 1949 (U.S.: Duell, 1951)

Books for the Baron. U.K.: Low, 1949 (U.S.: Duell, 1952)

Gloria Lithom believes her late father was murdered, and because of some of the bizarre occurances around the Lithom estate, The Baron is inclined to agree. The mystery seems to revolve around the late Earl of Lithom's book collection, and the mysterious stain on the carpet in the library.

Bibliomystery • England

Cry for the Baron. U.K.: Low, 1950 (U.S.: Walker, 1970)

The Diamond of Tears is a jewel whose possession ultimately leads the owner to death. So far, there have been four, and when Jacob Bernstein becomes the fifth, the case revolves around to The Baron.

England, London • Jewels

Trap the Baron. U.K.: Low, 1950 (U.S.: Walker, 1971)

A mysterious late-night phone call to The Baron from a man asks him if he buys jewels, but provides no details until a beautiful woman arrives at his doorstep with a tale of stolen jewels. Mrs. Courtney cannot go to the police, yet she needs a detective to recover her property. Oddly, the panicky man calls again, and the trail leads to an apartment with yet another beautiful woman who will lead The Baron in the direction he needs to go.

England, London • Jewels

***Attack the Baron.** Low, 1951

Shadow the Baron. Low, 1951

Scotland Yard asks The Baron to help track down the famous jewel thief, The Shadow. What The Baron fails to anticipate is that as he seeks to find The Shadow, the criminal might decide to seek him.

London, England

***Warn the Baron.** Low, 1952

The Baron Goes East. Low, 1953

The Baron is the one who sold the diamonds to Wannamaker, and now that they have been stolen, he would like to discover who did the deed. The cause could lie within an attempt to manipulate the money market, or it could just be the work of some gangsters.

Diamonds · England, London · Jewels

The Baron in France. U.K.: Hodder, 1953 (U.S.: Walker, 1976)

Jewel dealer Bernard Dale has been murdered, and his collection of the Gramercy jewels have been stolen. When Dale's roommate, Tony Bennett, is falsely accused of having committed the murder and stolen the jewels, The Baron leaps to his defense.

France, Chalon · Jewels

Danger for the Baron. U.K.: Hodder, 1953 (U.S.: Walker, 1974)

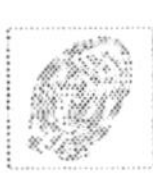

Five thousand pounds is a goodly fee, and The Baron is willing to seek the commission despite the fact that his client remains a mystery. But when the rendezvous fails to materialize, The Baron finds himself accused of murder. By seeking the missing jewels, The Baron hopes also to be led to a killer.

England, London · England, Surrey, North Guildford · Jewels

***The Baron Goes Fast.** U.K.: Hodder, 1954 (U.S.: Walker, 1972)

Nest-Egg for the Baron. U.K.: Hodder, 1954 (U.S.: *Deaf, Dumb, and Blonde*. Doubleday, 1961)

The Baron is interested in buying the wonderful offerings placed before him by the rather strange hunchback, Pendexter Smith. However, he does not want to take them from the old man's niece, a beautiful deaf and dumb girl named Miranda Smith. When the old man is dead, and violence threatens all associated with the jewels, The Baron is called to action.

England, London · Jewels

Help from the Baron. U.K.: Hodder, 1955 (U.S.: Walker, 1977)

Four years prior to the start of this case, the Fiora jewels were stolen from their owner, who was left dead. Now, on her twenty-first birthday, the body of Francesca Lisle is fished from the Thames, adorned with one of the missing pieces of jewelry.

Because he knew the dead woman, and because he always has an eye out for hot jewelry, The Baron launches an investigation.

England, London • Jewels

Hide the Baron. U.K.: Hodder, 1956 (U.S.: Walker, 1978)

When millionaire recluse, Jimmy Garfield, finds himself attacked, he passes an object hidden in his wheelchair to his employee, Joanna Woburn. His instructions are for her to deliver the item to The Baron, and this begins a case for the reluctant rogue. Ownership of the item now makes The Baron, and Joanna, the new targets for those who would like to get their hands on it.

England, London

Frame the Baron. U.K.: Hodder, 1957 (U.S.: *The Double Frame.* Doubleday, 1961)

The Baron becomes involved in a case of thieves who have fallen out. Brought into the mess by Della Gill, who wants to protect her brother Max, The Baron finds himself chasing a murderer among thieves.

England, London

Red Eye for the Baron. U.K.: Hodder, 1958 (U.S.: *Blood Red.* Doubleday, 1960)

Millionaire Theodorus Wray drops in at Quinn's in search of a pink diamond called the Red Eye of Love for his fiancée, Rosamund Morrel. He seems legitimate, but what has The Baron worried is that Mickey Odell, known as a swindler, is hovering around the American. When death strikes, it is up to The Baron to sort out the difference between love and greed.

England, London • Diamonds

Black for the Baron. U.K.: Hodder, 1959 (U.S.: *If Anything Happens to Hester.* Doubleday, 1962)

The Baron is contacted when the parents of Hester Vane are concerned about her welfare. After providing her parents no concern for 21 years, one day she steals some money from them and disappears with a middle-aged man. When the man is murdered, they need The Baron to find her and restore order.

England

Salute for the Baron. U.K.: Hodder, 1960 (U.S.: Walker, 1973)

The Old World Gallery has had a theft, and the accusations fall on their youngest employee, Kath Abbott. Her family knows The Baron, and he is capable of handling her case. He becomes concerned when the case escalates to one of arson, and then murder.

England, London

A Branch for the Baron. U.K.: Hodder, 1961 (U.S.: *The Baron Branches Out.* Scribner, 1967)

Changes are good, and The Baron has two to deal with. He wants to open an American branch of Quinns in Boston, and he wants to move to Harden Court in Louisburg Square. However, a hidden staircase in his new home contains a dead body, and the current owner has disappeared. When he is arrested for murder, his American plans are set aside.

England, Tewkesbury • Massachusetts, Boston

Bad for the Baron. U.K.: Hodder, 1962 (U.S.: *The Baron and the Stolen Legacy.* Scribner, 1967)

Brixton Jail has a new resident, and it is The Baron. After he has been asked to evaluate a collection, and after declaring them fakes, he is found to have the valuable jewels in his safe, and the owner dead outside his shop. From his jail cell, The Baron is forced to orchestrate his own defense using his wife and friends.

England, London · Jewels

A Sword for the Baron. U.K.: Hodder, 1963 (U.S.: *The Baron and the Mogul Swords.* Scribner, 1966)

For The Baron, it seems like a simple assignment: the richest man in England, Lord Gentian, wants to find a match to his Mogul Victory Sword. By the time The Baron has finished his work, he finds himself deeply involved in a question of inheritance and murder.

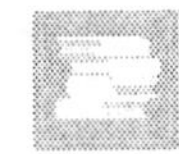

Antiquities · England, London

The Baron on Board. U.K.: Hodder, 1964 (U.S.: Walker, 1968)

Toji is a jewel expert from Thailand who is coming to London to have The Baron evaluate a collection in his possession. When a woman intercepts Toji at the airport and steals his collection, leaving the Thai dead, The Baron finds her trail leads to a cruise ship. Gaining passage on the ship, The Baron finds his prey dead and his list of suspects the entire list of passengers onboard.

England, London · Jewels · Shipboard

The Baron and the Chinese Puzzle. U.K.: Hodder, 1965 (U.S.: Scribner, 1966)

An invitation is extended to The Baron to fly to Hong Kong for the exhibition of the rare Li Chin treasures. Almost prevented from arriving, The Baron finds that the exhibition is a political hot potato between the two Chinese nations and a desirable prize for potential thieves.

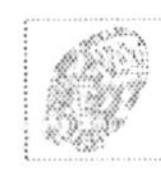

Hong Kong

Sport for the Baron. U.K.: Hodder, 1966 (U.S.: Walter, 1969)

The Baron has a client from Australia named Nathaniel Brutus, and he wants to buy a collection of jewels at auction. However, when the jewels are sold to another bidder, The Baron finds himself tied to his clients and on his way to Australia.

Australia, Baratta · England, London · Jewels

Affair for the Baron. U.K.: Hodder, 1967 (U.S.: Walker, 1968)

Two men are inexplicably drawn together by their association with Ethel Alundo. One is Mario Ballas, now collecting art after retiring from a career in crime, while the other is Professor Alundo, a leading pacifist. When a third man, The Baron, is drawn into their world, it leads the detective to America and the Hemisfair in San Antonio, in pursuit of the secret that Ethel holds over these two disparate men.

Illinois, Chicago · Texas, San Antonio

The Baron and the Missing Old Masters. U.K.: Hodder, 1968 (U.S.: Walker, 1969)

The Baron is asked to evaluate the paintings in the collection of 77-year-old Eliza Doze, and the simple assignment turns sour when things are not what they seem in Wiltshire. Blackmail is rampant in the countryside, and it almost costs a young girl her life. Then, someone tries to kill The Baron when he launches an investigation.

Blackmail • England, Wiltshire, Salisbury

The Baron and the Unfinished Portrait. U.K.: Hodder, 1969 (U.S.: Walker, 1970)

The Baron's wife, Lorna Mannering, has been commissioned to paint the portrait of Lady Vandemeyer. When she discovers that the model for the portrait is not the Lady, Lorna's maid is murdered in Lorna's place. The Baron goes undercover into the Cornelius Vandemeyer household to try and seek the answers needed to protect his wife.

Artists • England, London

Last Laugh for the Baron. U.K.: Hodder, 1970 (U.S.: Walker, 1971)

Josh Larraby, who works at Quinn's with The Baron, answers the phone one day and hears a plea, "But they're trying to kill me!" The single phone call leads to a trail of intrigue that distracts the business of Quinn's, but it gives The Baron a chance to exercise his detective skills once again.

England, London • Jewels

The Baron Goes A-Buying. U.K.: Hodder, 1971 (U.S.: Walker, 1972)

The Baron hires ex-Scotland Yard superintendent William Bristow to work at Quinns, but during his first day at work the two men are threatened by the Black Knight, a ex-con who wishes revenge on the two men who sent him over. When The Baron is accused of murder, he needs to rely on a man who may be able to work outside of the law as well as he worked within.

England, London

The Baron and the Arrogant Artist. U.K.: Hodder, 1972 (U.S.: Walker, 1973)

Tom Forrester, whose personality prevents The Baron from providing the assistance needed to boost the young artist's career, is almost killed. Despite his reluctance, The Baron takes up his case and finds himself implicated in a jewel theft and running to save his own reputation.

Artists • England, London

Burgle the Baron. U.K.: Hodder, 1973 (U.S.: Walker, 1974)

When asked by the Japanese government to evaluate the famous Jimmu Tenno Treasure, The Baron is please to comply. To his displeasure, he finds that Quinns is vulnerable to a thief, and soon he is on the trail of the items left in his care.

England, London

The Baron-King Maker. U.K.: Hodder, 1975 (U.S.: Walker, 1975)

Two things keep The Baron busy during this caper. He has been asked to protect the royal treasures of Taria by the country's prince, when a cache of silver is stolen from his own shop while he is distracted.

England, London • Jewels

Love for the Baron. Hodder, 1979

The law firm of Harcourt, Pace and Pace appeals to The Baron to evaluate the Peek Collection, a gathering of antiquities whose ownership is now in question after the death of the owner, Ezra Peek. To complicate matters, and despite his long relationship with his wife Lorna, The Baron finds himself attracted to the man's widow, Lucille.

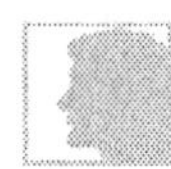

Antiquities · England, London

The Modern Practitioners

Harold Adams ✍

Carl Wilcox

Depression-era South Dakota is the landscape that Adams uses when he sets his roguish house painter on his adventures. Wilcox is the kind of criminal who originated in the great police departments: the concept was to set a thief to catch one. His appeal to women is legendary. Readers may also enjoy Max Allan Collins and Ken Kuhlken. **Traditional**. Series subject: **Historical (1900–1999)**.

Murder. Charter, 1981

Fin Larson has a young daughter to watch, and that brings him into contact with Carl Wilcox, a known rogue. Wilcox, with his ex-con status and his fame as a womanizer, makes him the odd man out in the small town. When Larson is murdered, and left in the fair barn that Wilcox has been hired to clean, he is on the spot to begin a little detective work and clear his own name.

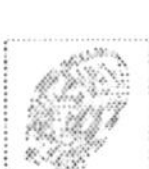

South Dakota, Corden

Paint the Town Red. Charter, 1982

Eleonore Matthews is the women who orginally got Wilcox sent up the river, and he should know enough to stay away from her. But when she arrives in Corden on the trail of some mob money, followed by the mob and the G-men, it places Wilcox right in the path of danger.

South Dakota, Corden

The Missing Moon. Charter 1983

The countryside's best moonshiner is out of action when he is arrested for the murder of Kate Bonney. Despite being found asleep next to the victim, the old man is claiming he is innocent, and Wilcox has a tendency to believe his story.

South Dakota, Lake Kampie

The Naked Liar. Mysterious Press, 1985

It should be no surprise that Wilcox's sympathies lie with the attractive widow, Trixie Cook, when her husband Bernie is murdered. The town of Corden is so small that when the two big city toughs show up, along with the widow's attractive sister Rita, Wilcox knows he has a complicated case to handle.

South Dakota, Aquatown

The Fourth Widow. Mysterious Press, 1986

Wilcox does not like the fact that the police are looking sideways at him because a body has been found behind his family's hotel. Orrie Buford, the substitute cop in charge in Corden, wants to nail Wilcox for the crime. Wilcox's mission becomes solving the murder of Flory Fancett, and clearing his own name.

South Dakota, Corden

The Barbed Wire Noose. Mysterious Press, 1987

When the town's only cop is ill, Mayor Syvertson asks Wilcox to step in and play detective. The case involves the death of Foote, found hung from a barbed-wire noose. Part of his mission is to determine if there is any connection to the death of Azalea Foote who died with her baby in a fire 10 years earlier.

South Dakota, Corden

The Man Who Met the Train. Mysterious Press, 1988

Ellsworth Ellison is a genius hiding in the town of Toqueville, until one night he walks in front of a train and ends his life. He had been working for a South Dakota judge, and after his death, his widow also goes to work for the judge. When Winnie Ellison is killed in an auto accident, the judge hires Wilcox to investigate the cause, while the town's banker hires Wilcox to look into the first death.

South Dakota, Toqueville

The Man Who Missed the Party. Mysterious Press, 1989

Despite his reputation, people keep giving Wilcox responsibilities, and this time he must take over the family hotel in Corden when his father suffers a stroke. The hotel is hosting the tenth reunion of the undefeated Corden High School football team, and when its star quarterback, Harmon Turner, is found murdered in the hotel, Wilcox must be a detective again.

South Dakota, Corden

The Man Who Was Taller Than God. Walker, 1992

In the town of Hope to paint signs, Wilcox is available to be a detective again when the body of Felton Edwards is discovered in a sand pit outside of town. Edwards was a famous womanizer, and as Wilcox probes into his life, he finds himself traveling to another small town to find the source for his murder.

South Dakota, Edenberg • South Dakota, Hope

A Perfectly Proper Murder. Walker, 1993

Wilcox has chosen to paint signs in Podunkville, but his timing is not so good. When his Model T is used as part of a murder, leaving the wealthy Basil Ecke dead, the local constable at first views him as the most likely suspect. Because there is a beautiful widow involved, Wilcox does not mind sticking around and investigating the murder of her husband.

South Dakota, Podunkville

A Way with Widows. Walker, 1994

Wilcox is faced with another case of the most likely suspect. Stella Feist is perhaps not the best candidate for conviction when she is accused of murdering her husband, Aaron. His body was found in the widow Darlene Singer's house where Singer's young daughter lived. But others in this small town also offer reasons to eliminate Aaron, and Wilcox must sift through them to find the killer.

North Dakota, Red Ford

The Ditched Blonde. Walker, 1995

Wilcox is once again sign painting in a small town when he hears of the death of a girl named Genevieve. Being pregnant in a small town is not a good thing, and the most likely suspect in her death is her boyfriend, Rex Tobler. Wilcox's probing brings more reasons to the surface, and disturbs the fragile calm of this small town.

South Dakota, Greenhill

Hatchet Job. Walker, 1996

The mayor of Mustard needs Wilcox's detective skills when Jackie Schoop Dupree is accused of murdering her husband. To complicate the case, her husband was a philanderer, but also the town cop. However, the murder did occur in the unfinished town hall, and political reasons may be as great a motive in his murder as any wanderings in Mustard's bedrooms.

South Dakota, Mustard

The Ice Pick Artist. Walker, 1997

Lilybell Fox is staying at the family hotel in Corden to research the background of the town's fathers when she is murdered in her bed. A hotel client named Murdoff had checked in and out that night, and is a lead suspect for Wilcox. To find her killer, Wilcox needs to take up her research and uproot some long-held secrets that hold a key to her murder.

South Dakota, Corden

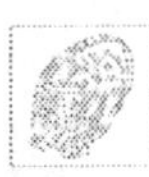

No Badge, No Gun. Walker, 1998

While painting signs in another small town, Wilcox is hired by Bjorn Bjornson to look into the rape and murder of Gwendolyn Westcott. His niece had liked older men, including her schoolteacher Chris Kilbride, but enough evidence could never be gathered to convict anyone of the crime, until Wilcox takes the case.

South Dakota, Jonesville

Lead So I Can Follow. Walker, 2000

Will marriage to Hazel spoil Carl Wilcox's status as a rogue? Perhaps not, because when they are canoeing on the St. Croix River on their honeymoon, they manage to get involved in a murder. The couple hears a scream and a gunshot, and discover a young man's body on some railroad tracks. A local femme fatale may be the cause when it is discovered the corpse was one of her suitors.

Minnesota, St. Croix River

Lawrence Block ✍

Bernie Rhodenbarr

At times a detective out of desperation, Bernie is an extension of the Raffles tradition in a modern American setting. He finds himself allied with a pet groomer named Carolyn Kaiser, and occasionally at odds with a slightly crooked cop named Kirschmann. Eventually trying to settle down to life as a used bookseller does not keep Rhodenbarr from being tempted by the dark side of burglary. Readers may also enjoy Simon Brett (Melita Pargeter) and Jonathan Gash. See the author's website at http://www.lawrenceblock.com. **Traditional**. Series subject: **New York, New York**.

Burglars Can't Be Choosers. Random House, 1977

Rhodenbarr could not pass up the easy money when he is offered the job of breaking into an apartment and stealing a blue leather box. All the set ups go well, and he is in the apartment doing the deed, when two cops show up. Now the set up is for Rhodenbarr, especially when he has to go on the lam when a dead body is discovered in the apartment with him.

The Burglar in the Closet. Random House, 1978

Craig Sheldrake has a problem only a burglar like Rhodenbarr could solve. When he divorced his wife Crystal, she kept the jewelry that Craig was using as a tax dodge. Now he wants his baubles back because he intends to marry his hygienist, and he wants Rhodenbarr to steal what he feels is rightfully his. When Rhodenbarr's attempt finds him on the spot for a murder, he once again is on the lam and trying to prove himself innocent of the deed.

The Burglar Who Liked to Quote Kipling. Random House, 1979

Rhodenbarr is given the opportunity to steal the only copy of a work by Rudyard Kipling for his client Whlekin. But when a Sikh shows up to steal it from the burglar, and the police show up on his doorstep blaming him for a murder, he knows he is deep into another case in which he needs to clear his own name.

Bibliomystery

The Burglar Who Studied Spinoza. Random House, 1980

This time Rhodenbarr's target is the coin collection of Herb Colcannon, and with Carolyn's help he is on site for the theft. But, he finds there is only one really expensive coin for the taking, and others are as interested in helping themselves to the single coin as he is.

Coins

The Burglar Who Painted Like Mondrian. Arbor House, 1983

Carolyn's cat, Archie Goodwin, has been catnapped, and she turns to her burglar associate Rhodenbarr for help. Already working his usual beat, Rhodenbarr finds that a priceless Mondrian painting may make a perfect ransom for a feline.

Cats

The Burglar Who Traded Ted Williams. Dutton, 1994

Rhodenbarr's attempts to go straight are sidetracked when demands from his landlord return him to a life of crime to finance his bookstore. When he burglarizes an apartment and discovers a dead man in the bathtub, Rhodenbarr also finds himself framed for a theft of a baseball collection that he never stole.

Baseball cards

The Burglar Who Thought He Was Bogart. Dutton, 1995

Of all the bookstores in the whole world, Ilona walks into Rhodenbarr's, and the two begin to have a strange romance tied to the Bogart film festival running in town. When Rhodenbarr simultaneously gets solicited by Hugo Candlemas to steal some documents, the two affairs merge into one. Following the movie Casablanca in style, Rhodenbarr finds himself placed between his duty and his love.

The Burglar in the Library. Dutton, 1997

Lettice Runcible has gone in a different direction from Rhodenbarr, and to survive his wounded heart, he sets up a romantic weekend at Cuttleford House, and brings along Carolyn and Raffles the cat. When he discovers a body in the library while trying to burgle its book collection, Rhodenbarr finds himself having to solve a countryhouse murder straight out of Christie.

Massachusetts, Williams Junction

The Burglar in the Rye. Dutton, 1999

Outraged that the life of his favorite author, Gulliver Fairborn, is going to be exposed to the world when Fairborn's agent, Anthea Landau, plans to auction his personal letters, Rhodenbarr accepts the charge from Fairborn's ex-lover, Alice Cottrell, to steal the letters. Instead, what he discovers is Landau's body, and once again the burglar detective needs to clear his own name.

Authors

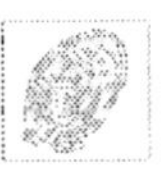

Simon Brett ✍

Melita Pargeter

Not all little-old-lady detectives have hearts of gold. Having been married to a gentleman crook, Pargeter knows how to maneuver through the criminal side of life to her advantage. This extension of Patricia Wentworth's Miss Silver is a humorous look at the roguish nature of the detective. Readers may also enjoy Lawrence Block (Bernie Rhodenbarr), Agatha Christie (Jane Marple), and Jonathan Gash. **Soft-boiled/ Traditional**.

A Nice Class of Corpse. U.K.: Macmillan, 1986 (U.S.: Scribner, 1987)

A relaxing time at the Deverux Hotel is threatened when one guest dies the same night Mrs. Pargeter arrives. With some of the insights provided by her late husband's activities, she launches an investigation to clear her own reputation.

England, Littlehampton

Mrs., Presumed Dead. U.K.: Macmillan, 1988 (U.S.: Scribner, 1989)

Mrs. Pargeter has moved in to Acapulco, one of six houses in the Smithy's Loam development just outside of London. When she is disturbed by her surroundings, she makes an attempt to contact the former owners. As she pursues Rod and Theresa Cotton, she makes discoveries that will disturb her.

England, Smithy's Loam

Mrs. Pargeter's Package. U.K.: Macmillan, 1990 (U.S.: Scribner, 1991)

A two-week holiday on Corfu seems like a good idea until Mrs. Pargeter agrees to carry a package for her travelling companion, Joyce Dover. What seems like an innocent gesture turns into a series of intrigues that require this little old lady to use all her detective skills.

Greece, Corfu, Agios Nikitas

Mrs. Pargeter's Pound of Flesh. U.K.: Macmillan, 1992 (U.S.: Scribner, 1993)

A few days with her friend Kim Thurrock at the Brotherton Hall health spa sounds like a lovely idea, until Mrs. Pargeter witnesses a body being taken away from the club. As she probes, she discovers that the spa is a front for some of her husband's former associates, and that she needs to expose their activities to save other lives.

England, London • Spas

Mrs. Pargeter's Plot. U.K.: Macmillan, 1996 (U.S.: Scribner, 1998)

Mrs. Pargeter is finally getting around to building the dream house she and her husband had planned outside of London. Her contractor, Concrete Jacket, is a former associate of her husband, and not always to be trusted. So, when she has a body in what was to be her wine cellar, she is ready to begin an investigation to clear her own name of any charges.

England, London

Mrs. Pargeter's Point of Honour. U.K.: Macmillan, 1998 (U.S.: Scribner, 1999)

Veronica Chastaigne is the widow of one of Mrs. Pargeter's husband's associates, and she is dying. Before she goes, she wants to return all the stolen art works in her home, and she wants Mrs. Pargeter to do the job. So, Mrs. Pargeter finds herself doing the reverse of the norm: defeating security systems so she can return items.

Art • England, London

Lee Child ✍

Jack Reacher

Reacher is a drifter, set loose upon the world by a series of circumstances that make him a wanderer who does not fear action. He is a survivor, using the skills he accumulated as a military policeman. But despite his loner ways, he steps in when he feels situations need to be corrected. He is a man not unwilling to use violence to adjust the balance of society. See the author's website at http://www.leechild.com. **Hard-boiled**.

Killing Floor. Putnam, 1997

When an unidentified man is found murdered in a small Georgia town, the most likely suspect is the drifter, Reacher. But within a few days, the local sheriff and his wife are murdered and a local bank executive disappears, and the focus shifts from Reacher as suspect to Reacher as detective. AN BA

Georgia, Margrave

Die Trying. Putnam, 1998

By random chance, Reacher is on the spot when some very bad people kidnap FBI agent Holly Johnson. The hunt for her is intense, because Holly's father is the Head of the Joint Chiefs of Staff. Unbeknown to Reacher, he may have to engineer their escape before his rescuers get him killed.

Illinois, Chicago · Kidnapping · Militia · Montana

Tripwire. Putnam, 1999

Digging swimming pools in Key West is not a romantic situation, but things get even hotter when a P.I. named Costello begins to probe into Reacher's background. When the P.I. ends up dead, and his fingerprints are removed, Reacher knows he needs to scramble to protect himself from an unseen enemy.

Florida, Key West · New York, New York

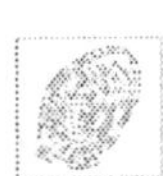

Running Blind. Putnam, 2000

When two Army females die after reporting sexual harassment and winning their cases, the FBI closes in on Reacher with an offer. He was the officer who investigated the cases originally, and he might be the agency's number one suspect. The murder method is bizarre, and the agency is having trouble deciding on the cause of death, when a third and fourth killing lead Reacher on a weary cross-country chase.

Serial killer

Echo Burning. Putnam, 2001

Sloop Greer is about to get out of jail, and his Mexican wife Carmen needs some protection because she believes her husband blames her for the jail term. Reacher, always able to get dragged into these dangerous situations, moves from being a hitchhiker to a bodyguard. When Sloop ends up murdered, Reacher needs to decide if he is protecting a woman in need or a murderer who set him up.

Texas, Echo

Without Fail. Putnam, 2002

Reacher is asked by M. E. Froelich to penetrate the defenses of the Secret Service around Vice-President-elect Brook Armstrong. What she fails to tell Reacher is that a renegade band of agents are trying to do the same thing. Teamed with his former colleague Frances Neagley, Reacher finds himself on the run again.

Secret Service • Vice-Presidents • Washington, D. C. • Wyoming

Jonathan Gash (pseud. of John Grant) ✍

Lovejoy

The world of antiques brings out the rogue in everyone, and no one is better able to manipulate things to his advantage than Lovejoy. His special talent as a divvie gives him a sixth sense about antiques and murder. He is also a rogue with women, but his charm seems to override his arrogance around the opposite sex. His appearances on television have increased his popularity. Readers may also enjoy Lawrence Block (Bernie Rhodenbarr) and Simon Brett (Melita Pargeter). See a fan website at http://www.frii.com/~saunders/gash.htm. **Traditional**. Series subject: **Antiquities**.

The Judas Pair. U.K.: Collins, 1977 (U.S.: Harper & Row, 1977)

The Judas Pair is a set of dueling pistols, the thirteenth made, that has been considered a myth among collectors. But when a customer offers Lovejoy 10,000 pounds for the set, he sets off on the trail. Unfortunately, someone will get killed for his efforts.

England

Gold from Gemini. U.K.: Collins, 1978 (U.S.: *Gold by Gemini.* Harper & Row, 1978)

Lovejoy sets out after some ancient Roman coins from the British territories that have been stolen from the local Castle museum. His search will take him into the countryside where death protects the old coins, and a trip to the Isle of Man is undertaken to attempt a recovery.

Coins • England, Isle of Man

The Grail Tree. U.K.: Collins, 1979 (U.S.: Harper & Row, 1980)

What more important item could a divvie chase than the Holy Grail? When the Reverend Henry Swan asked Lovejoy to authenticate the Grail, he refused. But after the dear Reverend is blown up on a boat, Lovejoy begins a search for the Grail, and the reason for the man's murder.

England, Buresford

Spend Game. U.K.: Collins, 1980 (U.S.: Ticknor, 1981)

Lovejoy and his companion, Sue, are on the scene when an acquaintance from the antiques world, Leckie, appears to drive over a cliff. Lovejoy decides to probe and does discover that there is more to this accident than first meets the eye. Leckie had some secrets, but he was not smart enough to use them to stay alive.

England

The Vatican Rip. U.K.: Collins, 1981 (U.S.: Ticknor, 1982)

To his great surprise, Lovejoy is sent after a prize that is held in the Vatican. Forced to learn Italian and travel abroad, the diviner needs all his skills to battle in a foreign country for the prize he seeks.

Italy, Rome • Vatican

Firefly Gadroon. U.K.: Collins, 1982 (U.S.: St. Martin's Press, 1984)

The Reverse Gadroon is a prize, and when Lovejoy finds himself bidding against a beautiful woman for the object, he is thrilled. But things turn ugly quickly, and once again Lovejoy finds himself on the chase.

England

The Sleepers of Erin. U.K.: Collins, 1983 (U.S.: Dutton, 1983)

Lovejoy is in church, but only to tryst with a woman. To his surprise, he interrupts a robbery and gets stabbed. To his greater surprise, he is accused of the crime and must work to clear his name of the charges.

England

The Gondola Scam. U.K.: Collins, 1984 (U.S.: St. Martin's Press, 1984)

Lovejoy has been charged with a unique task. He is asked to go to Venice and steal anything that is threatened with being covered by the waters, and to replace them with reproductions.

Italy, Venice

Pearlhanger. U.K.: Collins, 1985 (U.S.: St. Martin's Press, 1985)

Donna Vernon needs to finds her husband, and because Lovejoy is a divvie, she assumes he is up to the task. Never one to let down a lovely woman, he begins his chore, and discovers that this trail will lead to real pearls, fake pearls, and murder.

England • Jewels

Moonspender. U.K.: Collins, 1986 (U.S.: St. Martin's Press, 1987)

Lovejoy's special talents are called into action when he is asked to validate a Roman bronze figure discovered in his own hometown. Little does he realize that the controvery over this find will have him starring on national television.

England, East Anglia

The Tartan Ringers. U.K.: Collins, 1986 (U.S.: *The Tartan Sell.* St. Martin's Press, 1986)

Lovejoy is waiting for a delivery, only the driver is murdered and the item is stolen. What he thought was a fake turned out to be real, and he must travel to Scotland to recover the stolen property stolen from him.

Scotland

Jade Woman. U.K.: Collins, 1988 (U.S.: St. Martin's Press, 1989)

Forced to flee the country when all of his possessions are confiscated by the police, Lovejoy arranges a trip to the Far East. To his surprise, he is robbed of everything again, and now finds himself in a foreign land with no possessions or identity. Luckily for him, he still has his skills on which to trade.

Hong Kong

The Very Last Gambado. U.K.: Collins, 1989 (U.S.: St. Martin's Press, 1990)

A movie company in need of advice decides to employ the best when they hire Lovejoy to consult on a scripted robbery of the British Museum. Members of his own profession turn on him, and with the distraction comes an unusual and illegal assignment from the movie company.

England, London · Film · Museums

The Great California Game. U.K.: Century, 1991 (U.S.: St. Martin's Press, 1991)

Lovejoy finds himself in America, tending bar in New York and trying to survive. When his divvie skills are revealed, he finds an interesting job waiting for him. But when a fellow bartender is killed, he begins to have doubts about his assignment, and he takes off cross country to try to end the dirty deeds.

California, Malibu · New York, New York

The Lies of Fair Ladies. U.K.: Century, 1992 (U.S.: St. Martin's Press, 1992)

When accused of cleaning out a vacant house for its antiquities, Lovejoy knows this is the work of Prammie Joe, recently released from prison. However, he does not know that Joe is dead. With the help of his new assistant Luna, he begins to weasel his way into the scam that brought Joe to his end.

England

Paid and Loving Eyes. U.K.: Century, 1993 (U.S.: St. Martin's Press, 1993)

Lovejoy has been forced by his current status to take a driving job for Gaunt's Tryste Service, but it does bring him in touch with some lovely women. When this leads him to providing a service to local hood Big John Sheehan, he works his divvie magic. However, this may have led to some deaths, and Lovejoy finds himself in the middle of an international antiques scandal.

England · France, Paris · Switzerland, Zurich

The Sin Within Her Smile. U.K.: Century, 1993 (U.S.: Viking, 1993)

Lovejoy is sold at a charity auction to the highest bidder, a lovely woman with a wicked scheme. Soon he is on his way to Wales, in search of some Celtic gold finds, and accompanied by the mentally challenged people for whom the auction was held. His trip teaches him much about what the word normal actually means.

England, Wales · Mentally challenged

The Grace in Older Women. U.K.: Century, 1995 (U.S.: Viking, 1995)

Only Lovejoy could find himself investigating the arson and murder involved with a traveling Sex Museum owned by his friend Tyner. But he finds that a few carnival tricks of his own are what he needs to open the investigation up and discover the truth.

England

The Possessions of a Lady. U.K.: Century, 1996 (U.S.: Viking, 1996)

Lovejoy's business is going under, and he is desperately trying scams that include a dating service and selling fake Stone Age tools. But a note from Olga Maltravers Featherstone, containing the word *money*, sets him off on another adventure that will involve some illegal activities and murder.

England, London

The Rich and the Profane. U.K.: Macmillan, 1998 (U.S.: Viking, 1999)

The ancient Albansham Priory is in financial trouble, and what better consultant can there be than Lovejoy. However, Lovejoy tries to turn this to his advantage by breaking into the place with his friend Gesso. Gesso is caught, the painting he took disappears, and things are not going as planned in Lovejoy's life.

England

A Rag, a Bone, and a Hank of Hair. U.K.: Macmillan, 1999 (U.S.: Viking, 2000)

On a chance visit, Lovejoy learns that his fellow businessman Arthur Goldhorn is dead, and his wife and 15-year-old son are living on the streets. When he investigates, he finds their shop taken over by a German businessman with a dangerous background. More surprising, he discovers that the teenager has his capabilities.

England

***Every Last Cent.** Macmillan, 2001

Appendix

Bibliographies

Adey, Robert. *Locked Room Murders and Other Impossible Crimes: A Comprehensive Bibliography.* Revised and expanded ed. Crossover Press, 1991. 0962887005.

An outstanding example of a dedicated fan publishing his own notes for the edification of other fans.

Albert, Walter. *Detective and Mystery Fiction: An International Bibliography of Secondary Sources.* Brownstone Books, 1985. 094102802X.

The printed version of this bibliography attempts to guide the researcher to widely distributed information about the mystery.

Albert, Walter. *Detective And Mystery Fiction: An International Bibliography of Secondary Sources.* Locus Press, nd.

This CD-ROM version is an updated version able to be used on any PC or Apple with a CD-ROM drive and a standard web browser. It is a second edition, revised and expanded, from the original print work.

Barzun, Jacques, and Wendell Hertig Taylor. *A Catalogue of Crime: Being a Reader's Guide to the Literature Of Mystery, Detection, And Related Genres.* Harper and Row, 1989. 0060157968.

Get an arrogant and delightfully opinionated look at the mystery by reading the reviews of these experts.

Bleiler, Richard. *Reference Guide to Mystery And Detective Fiction.* Libraries Unlimited, 1999. 1563083809.

This work does a fine job of reviewing available reference sources for research in the genre.

Bourgeau, Art. *The Mystery Lover's Companion.* Crown, 1986. 0517556022.

Philadelphia bookstore owner Bourgeau lists his favorites.

Breen, Jon. L. *What About Murder? A Guide to Books About Mystery and Detective Fiction.* Scarecrow, 1981. 0-8108-1413-7.

Breen, Jon. L. *What About Murder? (1981–1991): A Guide to Books About Mystery and Detective Fiction* by Jon L. Breen. Scarecrow, 1993. 0-8108-2609-7.

If you want evaluations of books that talk about mysteries, Breen's annotated bibliography is the best place to go.

Contento, William G. *Mystery Fiction Miscellany: An Index.* Locus Press, 2000.

This CD-ROM combines Contento's *Index to Crime and Mystery Anthologies* with two works by Martin H. Greenberg, *Index to Ellery Queen Mystery Magazine* and *Mystery Short Fiction: 1990-2000.*

Contento, William G., and Martin H. Greenberg, ed. *Index to Crime and Mystery Anthologies.* G. K. Hall, 1991. 0816186294.

This book is a great place to check for hard-to-find mystery short stories. Check out the expanded coverage in the CD-ROM version called *Mystery Short Fiction Miscellany* listed below.

Cook, Michael L. *Monthly Murders: A Checklist and Chronological Listing of Fiction in the Digest-Size Mystery Magazines in the United States And England.* Greenwood Press, 1982. 0313231265.

This massive work attempts to list all the short stories in the field.

Cook, Michael L. *Mystery Fanfare: A Composite Annotated Index to Mystery and Related Fanzines, 1963–1981.* Bowling Green State University Popular Press, 1983. 0879722290.

Fans with a sense of dedication produce a lot of writings about the field, and dedicated bibliographer Cook indexed their work for this period.

Hagen, Ordean A. *Who Done It? A Guide to Detective, Mystery and Suspense Fiction.* R. R. Bowker, 1969.

The first book-length bibliography published in the field. Errors occurred, but it was the first major effort to list titles in the field.

Hubin, Allen J., ed. *Crime Fiction II: A Comprehensive Bibliography, 1749–1990.* Garland, 1994. 0-8240-6891-2. Two volumes.

The best list of published mysteries ever compiled. It is an indispensable to serious mystery researchers.

Hubin, Allen J., ed. *Crime Fiction III: A Comprehensive Bibliography, 1749–1995.* Locus Press, 1999.

The CD-ROM version of this work is an updated version able to be used on any PC or Apple with a CD-ROM drive and a standard web browser.

Machler, Tasha. *Murder by Category: A Subject Guide to Mystery Fiction.* Scarecrow, 1991. 0810824639.

Machler, a bookstore owner, organized some mysteries into about 100 subject categories.

Melvin, David Skene, and Ann Skene Melvin. *Crime, Detective, Espionage, Mystery, and Thriller Fiction and Film: A Comprehensive Bibliography of Critical Writing Through 1979.* Greenwood, 1980. 031322062X.

Gathering secondary source references into one index, the compilers of this work included English and non-English language sources.

Menendez, Albert J. *The Subject is Murder.* Garland, 1986. 0824086554.

Menendez, Albert J. *The Subject Is Murder: Volume 2.* Garland, 1990. 0824025806.

Volume One has 25 subject areas, while the second volume adds some old and some new categories while trying to organized the genre by subject.

Mundell, E. H., and G. Jay Rausch. *The Detective Short Story: A Bibliography and Index.* Kansas State University Library, 1974.

An expansion of the Queen title listed above, Mundell and Rausch updated the old work and included items overlooked by the Queens.

Pronzini, Bill, and Marcia Muller. *1001 Midnights: The Aficionado's Guide to Mystery and Detective Fiction.* Arbor House, 1986. 0877956227.

P.I. authors and married couple Pronzini and Muller put together this comprehensive list of best books in the field.

Queen, Ellery, ed. *The Detective Short Story: A Bibliography.* Little Brown, 1942.

The master mystery authors and publishers of *Ellery Queen Mystery Magazine* provided an early overview of the state of the art in the short story.

Queen, Ellery. *Queen's Quorum.* Little, Brown, 1951.

This history of the short story in the genre approaches the topic by listing the most important books published in the field.

Stiwell, Steven A., and Charles Montney, eds. *What Mystery Do I Read Next?: A Reader's Guide to Recent Mystery Fiction.* Gale Research, 1996. 0787615927.

This separate volume from their multi-genre title *What Do I Read Next?* tries to lead mystery reader's to potential novels with similar appeals.

Book Review Sources

Booklist

Each spring this magazine does a mystery issue that provides a great list of titles for selection purposes. It regularly reviews mysteries in a special review column.

Publishers Weekly.

Each fall this magazine does a Mystery Category Closeup that provides an overview of the mystery genre from the industry point of view. It regularly reviews mysteries in a special column.

Additional book review sources are listed in the Journals section below.

Conventions

Bouchercon, the World Mystery Convention, is held once a year in the fall. The convention is named for Anthony Boucher, a respected mystery reviewer and author. This fan's convention has grown in its 30-plus years to include authors, agents, publishers, and booksellers' concerns as well. Each Bouchercon maintains its own website.

Left Coast Crime Conference is held each spring in the western United States. The convention is similar to a Bouchercon, but its emphasis is to celebrate the authors of their region. Each Left Coast Conference maintains its own website.

Malice Domestic is a convention that was created to extend the work being done to elevate the status of women in the genre. Its goal is to celebrate the soft-boiled mystery, but traditional mystery readers will find that most of their authors are eligible for discussion at this convention. The convention is held each spring near the nation's capital. The convention's website is http://www.erols.com/malice.

Magna Cum Murder originated as an alumni activity for Ball State University. The convention has grown into a regional mystery convention that works very hard to bring two or three major international mystery stars each year. The convention's website is http://www.onlyinternet.net/secop/murder.html.

Encyclopedias

Barnett, Colleen A. *Mystery Women: An Encyclopedia of Leading Women Characters in Mystery Fiction, Volume 1: 1860–1979.* Ravenstone, 1997. 0938313290.

This work assembles the greats from the beginning of the genre to 1979.

DeAndrea, William L. *Encyclopedia Mysteriosa.* Prentice Hall, 1994. 0-671-85025-3.

The late mystery critic put this tome together to update or replace the *Encyclopedia Of Mystery And Detection*, but it may be limited by some factual errors and limited coverage. Both volumes should be kept. It did win the 1994 Edgar award for best reference book.

Green, Joseph, and Jim Finch. *Sleuths, Sidekicks And Stooges.* Scolar, 1997. 1859281923.

This enormous work organizes the genre by the characters. Its strength is that besides the lead characters, it gives equal tribute to the sidekick assistants and the authorities that the detective defies. Its weakness according to reviews is that some errors occur in the listings.

Herbert, Rosemary, ed. *The Oxford Companion to Crime & Mystery Writing.* Oxford University Press, 1999. 0195072391.

This work provides a comprehensive overview to the entire genre.

Murphy, Bruce F. *The Encyclopedia of Murder and Mystery.* St. Martin's Minotaur, 1999. 0312215541.

A personalized look at the genre.

Penzler, Otto, Chris Steinbrunner, and Marvin Lachman. *Detectionary: A Biographical Dictionary of Leading Characters in Mystery Fiction.* Overlook, 1977. 0879510412.

This dictionary format work is divided into four sections: detectives, rogues and helpers, cases, and movies.

St. James Guide to Crime and Mystery Writers. St. James Press, 1996. 0786710488.

The best single-volume reference work for fans and researchers.

Steinbrunner, Chris, Otto Penzler, Marv Lachman, and Charles Shibuk. *Encyclopedia of Mystery & Detection.* McGraw-Hill, 1976. 0070611211.

The first, and still the best, mainstream attempt to outline the genre for the average reader.

Wings, Robin, and Maureen Corrigan. *Mystery and Suspense Writers.* Charles Scribners Sons, 1998. 0684805219.

This two-volume work is a compilation of scholarly articles on the entire genre.

Filmography

Cameron, Ian. *A Pictorial History of Crime Films.* Hamlyn, 1975. 0600370224.
There is some text here, but the majority of this review is stills from all the great films.

Christopher, Nicholas. *Somewhere in the Night: Film Noir and the American City.* Free, 1997. 0684828030.
This study attempts to identify the chief characteristics shared by all the films in this sub-genre.

Crowther, Bruce. *Film Noir: Reflections in a Dark Mirror.* Continuum, 1989. 0826405045.
This work is a topical approach to the sub-genre and is heavily illustrated.

Everson, William K. *The Detective in Film.* Citadel, 1972. 0806502983.
This well-illustrated guide to the films features the greatest detectives filmed from 1903 to 1972.

Hardy, Phil, ed. *The BFI Companion to Crime.* University of California Press, 1997. 0520215389.
This British filmography offers a complete and detailed guide to crime on film.

Hirsch, Foster. *The Dark Side of the Screen: Film Noir.* Barnes, 1981. 049802234X.
A study of the participants and practioners in this sub-genre.

Martin, Richard. *Mean Streets and Raging Bulls: The Legacy of Film Noir in Contemporary American Cinema.* Scarecrow, 1997. 0810833379.
This study attempts to show how the sub-genre of film noir has influenced crime and mystery films since its heydays in the late 1940s and early 1950s.

Silver, Alain, and Elizabeth Ward. *Film Noir: An Encyclopedic Reference to the American Style.* 3rd ed. Overlook, 1992. 0879514795.
Each individual film listed has its production details listed with a brief summary of the plot.

Stephens, Michael L. *Film Noir: A Comprehensive Illustrated Reference to Movies, Terms and Persons.* McFarland, 1995. 0899508022.
This sub-genre receives a comprehensive treatment in an encyclopedia format that covers the directors, actors, films, plot devices, and themes.

Tuska, Jon. *The Detective in Hollywood.* Doubleday, 1978. 0385120931.
This is an overview with lots of pictures by renowned film critic, Tuska.

Guides

Benvenuti, Stefano, and Gianni Rizzoni. *The Whodunit: An Informal History of Detective Fiction.* Macmillan, 1979. 002509260X.
This historical guide was compiled by two Italian critics of the field.

Breen, Jon L. *Novel Verdicts: A Guide to Courtroom Fiction*, 2nd ed.. Scarecrow Press, 1999. 0-8108-3674-2. 0810817411.
Lifelong reader and review Breen has put together a comprehensive guide to this sub-genre.

Charles, John, with Joanna Morrison and Candace Clark. *The Mystery Readers' Advisory: The Librarian's Clues to Murder and Mayhem.* ALA, 2001. 083890811X.

This work introduces librarians to everything in this genre from collection development to programming and marketing tips.

Gorman, Ed, with Martin H. Greenberg, Larry Segriff and Jon L. Breen. *The Fine Art of Murder: The Mystery Reader's Indispensable Companion.* Carroll and Graf, 1993. 0-88184-972-3.

This Anthony Award-winning title is a cornucopia of mystery trivia for any fan, similar in style to the groundbreaking *Murder Ink.*

Grape, Jan, with Dean James and Ellen Nehr. *Deadly Women: The Woman Mystery Reader's Indispensable Companion.* Carroll & Graf, 1998. 0-7867-0468-3.

A compilation of articles by and about women in the mystery field. An absolutely delightful bedside book full of trivia.

Heising, Willetta L. *Detecting Men and Detecting Men Pocket Guide.* Purple Moon Press, 1998. 0-9644593-3-7 & 0-9644593-4-5.

Detecting Women 3 and Detecting Women 3 Pocket Guide. Purple Moon Press, 1999. 0-9644593-35-3.

These reader's guides and checklists feature more than 600 series by women and men. The pocket guides can be carried into a bookstore or library as a shopping guide.

Jakubowski, Maxim. *100 Great Detectives: Famous Mystery Writers Examine Their Favorite Fictional Investigators.* Carroll & Graf, 1991. 0881847291

Famous mystery writers examine their favorite mystery character in this guide edited by London bookstore owner Jakubowski.

Johnson Jarvis, Mary. *A Reader's Guide to the Suspense Novel.* G. K. Hall, 1997. 0-8161-1804-3.

King, Nina, and Robin Winks. *Crime of the Scene: A Mystery Novel Guide for the International Traveler.* St. Martin's Press, 1997. 0312151748.

There can be no better outline for travelers as they try to find books to match locations.

Lachman, Marvin. *A Reader's Guide to the American Novel of Detection.* G. K. Hall, 1993. 0-8161-1803-5.

Nichols, Victoria, and Susan Thompson. *Silk Stalkings: More Women Write of Murder.* Scarecrow Press, 1998. 0-810-83393-X.

A delightful spin through the accomplishments of women within the mystery genre, this book is the second edition of this guide.

Niebuhr, Gary Warren. *A Reader's Guide to the Private Eye Novel.* G. K. Hall, 1993. 0-8161-1802-7.

Oleksiw, Susan. *A Reader's Guide to the Classic British Mystery.* G. K. Hall, 1988. 0-8161-8787-3.

Ousby, Ian. *Guilty Parties: A Mystery Lover's Companion.* Thames & Hudson, 1997. 0500279780.

As much fun as *Murder Ink*, this fan-oriented review of mystery fiction is full of surprises and is wonderfully illustrated.

Penzler, Otto, ed. *The Great Detectives: A Host of the World's Most Celebrated Sleuths Are Unmasked by Their Authors.* Little Brown, 1978. 0316698830.

This work includes the words of the creators as they dissect their own creations.

Penzler, Otto. *The Private Lives of Private Eyes: Spies, Crime Fighters, and Other Good Guys.* Grosset and Dunlap, 1977. 0448143259.

Using the characters as the approach, famed bookstore owner and collector Penzler outlines the lives of these fictional people.

Siegel, Jeff. *The American Detective: An Illustrated History.* Taylor, 1993. 0878338292.

This colorful approach to the detective includes reproductions of book covers, as well as media stills and posters.

Stine, Kate, ed. *The Armchair Detective Book of Lists.* Mysterious Press, 1995. 0-89296-423-5.

A small book of lists full of the kind of trivia that mystery fans will just love to read.

Stone, Nancy-Stephanie. *A Reader's Guide to the Spy and Thriller Novel.* G. K. Hall, 1997. 0-8161-1800-0.

Each of the volumes in this series offers annotated titles in its area with special indexes to guide a reader through the genre.

Swanson, Jean and Dean James. *By a Woman's Hand: A Guide to Mystery Fiction by Women*, 2nd ed. Berkley, 1996. 0425154726.

An informal encyclopedic look at female authors who have made an impact on the genre.

Swanson, Jean, with Dean James and Anne Perry. *Killer Books: A Reader's Guide to Exploring the Popular World of Mystery and Suspense.* Berkley, 1998. 0425162184.

For the fan reader, this book is a marvelous overview of the field, including books, movies, and TV shows.

Vicarel, JoAnn. *A Reader's Guide to the Police Procedure.* G. K. Hall, 1995. 0-8161-1801-9.

Winn, Dilys. *Murder Ink: The Mystery Reader's Companion.* Workman, 1977. Second ed. issued in 1984 by Workman. 0894807684.

This classic volume represented one of the first fan-oriented publications in the field. It is full of trivia about the field. It was revised in 1984 in a second edition that was equal in fun and facts.

History and Criticism

Bailey, Frankie Y. *Out of the Woodpile: Black Characters in Crime and Detective Fiction.* Greenwood Press, 1991. 0313266719.

From slaves to assimilation, Bailey tries to trace the path of African-American characters in mysteries.

Ball, John. *The Mystery Story.* University of California, San Diego, 1976. 0891630198.
Examining every facet of the mystery story from origins, history, subgenres, authors, and characters, this work was produced as a companion to a reprint series the University was doing in the 1970s.

Binyon, T. J. *Murder Will Out: The Detective in Fiction.* Oxford, 1989. 019219223X
Tracing the history of mystery from Poe to the present, this work provides an overview of the development of the genre.

Bloom, Harold, ed. *Classic Crime and Suspense Writers.* Chelsea House, 1995. 0791022315.
This work contains excerpts from essays on Ambler, Buchan, Cain, Chandler, du Maurier, Fleming, Greene, Hammett, Hornung, John D. MacDonald, Ross Macdonald, Thompson, and Woolrich.

Bloom, Harold, ed. *Classic Mystery Writers.* Chelsea House, 1995. 0791022358.
This work contains excerpts from essays Berkeley/Iles, Chesterton, Christie, Collins, Crofts, Doyle, Freeman, Poe, Post, Rinehart, Sayers, Van Dine, and Wallace.

Bloom, Harold, ed. *Modern Crime and Suspense Writers.* Chelsea House, 1995. 0791022471.
This work studies Bloch, Condon, Dahl, Deighton, Ellroy, Harris, Highsmith, le Carre, Leonard, Ludlum, Parker, Spillane, and Vachss.

Bloom, Harold, ed. *Modern Mystery Writers.* Chelsea House, 1995. 0791023761.
This works studies Allingham, Blake, Brown, Carr, Crispin, Gardner, Himes, Innes, Marsh, Millar, Queen, Stout, and Tey.

Collins, Max Allan. *The History of Mystery.* Collectors Press, 2001. 1-888054-53-0.
An overview of the history of the genre supplemented with beautiful photographs.

Craig, Patricia, and Mary Cadogan. *The Lady Investigates: Women Detectives and Spies in Fiction.* Oxford, 1981. 0312464266.
The majority of this work is an analysis of women characters in the formative years of the mystery.

Davis, David Brion. *Homicide in American Fiction, 1798–1860.* Cornell, 1957.
This critical study looks at the formative fiction that led to the creation of the modern mystery.

Dove, George N. *The Reader and the Detective Story.* Bowling Green State University Popular Press, 1997. 0879727314.
This critical work takes the unique approach of tying the mystery to the process of reading and enjoying fiction.

Eames, Hugh. *Sleuths, Inc.: Studies of Problem Solvers.* Lippincott, 1978. 0397012942.
This work studies the contributions of Doyle, Simenon, Hammett, Ambler, and Chandler.

Haycraft, Howard. *The Art of the Mystery Story: A Collection of Critical Essays.* Carroll & Graf, 1946.
A collection of major essays created by practitioners in the field.

Haycraft, Howard. *Murder for Pleasure: The Life and Times of the Detective Story.* D. Appleton-Century, 1941.

This classic work of criticism and history was considered the standard by which all other criticism was measured for many years.

Klein, Kathleen Gregory. *Great Women Mystery Writers: Classic to Contemporary.* Greenwood, 1994. 0313287708.

Essays and bibliographies of major female contributors to the genre are provided by an impressive list of mystery fans and scholars.

Klein, Kathleen Gregory. *The Woman Detective: Gender and Genre.* University of Illinois, 1988. 0252015223.

A study of women's roles in the history of the genre.

Lachman, Marvin. *The American Regional Mystery.* Crossover, 2000. 096288703X.

A guide to the locations of mysteries set in the United States, with critical comments.

Landrum, Larry. *American Mystery Novels and Detective Novels: A Reference Guide.* Greenwood Press, 1999. 0313213879.

This book does a very through job of explaining the forces that created the mystery as a modern genre from its roots to the literary influences that shape it today.

Lehman, David. *The Perfect Murder: A Study in Detection.* University of Michigan, 1999. 0472085859.

This book examines the reason readers enjoy reading about murder. It is an enlarged and expanded update to the original 1989 edition.

Murch, A. E. *The Development of the Detective Novel.* Philosophical Library, 1958.

From its earliest ancestors through the Golden Age, this work attempts to trace the origins of the contemporary mystery.

Panek, Leroy Lad. *An Introduction to the Detective Story.* Bowling Green University Popular Press, 1987. 0879723777.

This overview of the history of the mystery looks at early contributors and then covers the various subgenres.

Panek, Leroy Lad. *Probable Cause: Crime Fiction in America.* Bowling Green University Popular Press, 1990. 0879724854.

Panek provides an overview of the first 100 years of crime fiction in America by putting together basic facts and observations that explain how the literature developed.

Schwartz, Saul. *The Detective Story: An Introduction to the Whodunit.* National Textbook, 1978. 0844256099.

A textbook for teaching the mystery.

Symons, Julian. *Bloody Murder: From the Detective Story to the Crime Novel.* Mysterious Press, 1992. 3rd ed. 0-89296-496-0.

The most respected contemporary analytical look at the detective story by the late British critic and writer of mystery fiction.

Symons, Julian. *Great Detectives: Seven Original Investigations.* Abrams, 1981. 0810909782

Symons has spent a lifetime studying the mystery novel and here he concentrates on seven of the best.

Thomson, H. Douglas. *Masters of Mystery: A Study of the Detective Story.* Collins, 1931.
This work may be the first attempt to create an overview of the field.

Walton, Priscilla L. and Manina Jones. *Detective Agency: Women Rewriting the Hard-Boiled Tradition.* University of California, 1999. 0520215079
A look at the effect on women in an area of the genre that traditionally was reserved for men.

Willett, Ralph. *The Naked City: Urban Crime Fiction in the USA.* Manchester University, 1996. 0719043018.
City by city, this guide provides an overview of crime-related fiction as it developed in urban America.

Winks, Robin W. *Detective Fiction: A Collection of Critical Essays.* Prentice Hall, 1980. 0132026899.
This collection contains most of the major essays on the field up until the publication of this work, including the famous Edmund Wilson essay, "Who cares who killed Roger Ackroyd?"

Winks, Robin W. *Modus Operandi: An Excursion Into Detective Fiction.* Godine, 1982. 0879234067.
A collection of contemporary criticism of the field by a historian and reviewer.

Mystery Bookstores

Mystery bookstores were a rarity until the 1980s when there was a boom in store openings. At the end of the 1990s, we witnessed the downside when independent mystery booksellers found themselves competing with large national chain bookstores and the Internet, and some went out of business. However, several fine mystery bookstores exist, and here is a list of some of the best.

Crime in Store (http://www.crimeinstore.co.uk)
32 Store Steet
London, WC1E 7BS
ENGLAND

Gaslight Books (www.gaslightbooks.com.au)
83 Wollongong St, Unit 10
PO Box 267
Fyshwick, ACT 2609
AUSTRALIA

The Mysterious Bookshop (http://www.mysteriousbookshop.com)
129 W 56th St
New York, NY 10019-3881
USA

The Poisoned Pen Mystery Bookstore (http://www.poisonedpen.com)
4014 N Goldwater Blvd., Ste 101
Scottsdale, AZ 85251-4335
USA

Sleuth of Baker Street (http://www.abebooks.com/home/sleuthbooks)
1600 Bayview Ave
Toronto, ON M4G 3B7
CANADA

Mystery Journals

Alfred Hitchcock Mystery Magazine
PO Box 54011
Boulder, CO 80322-4011
http://www.themysteryplace.com
$28 for 12 issues
Fiction, some reviews

Cads
9 Vicarage Hill
South Benfleet, Essex, England SS7 1PA
$9 per issue
Commentary and reviews.

Crime Factory
c/o Preston Lower Post Office
3 Gilbert Road
Preston, VIC 3072
AUSTRALIA
$38.50 (Australian) for four issues
http://www.crimefactory.net
News, interviews, articles, fiction and true crime articles about the Australian mystery scene.

Crime Time
Oldcastle Books Ltd.
PO Box 394
Harpenden, AL5 1XJ
ENGLAND
L30 for on year subscription
http://www.crimetime.co.uk
A solid and slick English magazine.

Deadly Pleasures
PO Box 839
Farmington, UT 84025-0839
$18 for 4 issues
http://www.deadlypleasures.com
Interviews, reviews.

The Drood Review
484 East Carmel Drive, #378
Carmel, IN 46032-2812
$20 per year for 6 issues
http://www.droodreview.com
Reviews.

Ellery Queen Mystery Magazine
PO Box 54625
Boulder, CO 80322-4625
$28 for 12 issues
http://www.themysteryplace.com
Fiction, some reviews.

Hardboiled
Gryphon Publications
PO Box 209
Brooklyn, NY 11228-0209
5 issues for $35
http://www.gryphonbooks.com
Fiction.

Murderous Intent
PO Box 5947
Vancouver, WA 98668-5947
$18 per year for 4 issues
Fiction.

Mystery & Detective Monthly
5601 North 40th Street
Tacoma, WA 98407
$30 per year, 11 issues
Letterzine.

Mystery News
262 Hawthorn Village Commons, #152
Vernon Hills, IL 60061
$20 per year for 6 issues
http://www.blackravenpress.com
Reviews.

Mystery Readers Journal
Part of members in the organization Mystery Readers International (see Organizations)

Mystery Review
PO Box 233
Colbourne, Ontario K0K 1SO CANADA
$21.50 for four issues
Commentary and reviews from Canada.

Mystery Scene
331 West 57th Street, Suite 148
New York, NY 10019-3101
$2 per year
http://www.mysteryscenemag.com
Commentary.

Over My Dead Body
PO Box 1778
Auburn, WA 98701-1778
$20 for 4 issues
http://www.overmydeadbody.com
Fact and fiction about the mystery.

Online Resources

General Guides to the Genre

ClueLass Home Page (http://www.cluelass.com)

Reviews

Mystery Guide (http://www.mysteryguide.com)

Mystery Reader (http://www.themysteryreader.com)

MysteryNet.com (http://www.mysterynet.com)

Mystery Listservs

Dorothy-l: http://www.dorothyl.com. A mailing list for mystery readers

Fiction-l: http://www.webrary.org/rs/flmenu.html. A mailing list for general readers' advisory questions including mystery fiction.

Rara-Avis: http://www.vex.net/-buff/rara-avis/. A mailing list for fans of the hard-boiled mystery novel.

Readers' Advisory Sites

Adult Reading Roundtable Mystery Genre Study (http://www.arrtreads.org)

Amazon.com Mystery and Thrillers page, including Otto Penzler's picks (http://www.amazon.com)

Awardweb (http://www.dpsir.fo.com/awardweb)

Barnes & Noble (http://www.barnesandnoble.com)

Bookbrowser (http://www.bookbrowser.com)

Genreflecting (http://genreflecting.com)

Publink.net (http://www.publink.net)

The Reader's Robot (http://www.tnrdlib.bc.ca/rr.html)

Organizations

Mystery Readers International (http://www.mysteryreaders.org)
PO Box 8116
Berkeley, CA 94707
$28 per year for a membership and subscription to *Mystery Readers Journal*, a thematic magazine that is worth the price of admission.

Mystery Writers of America (http://www.mysterywriters.net)
17 East 47th Street, 6th floor
New York, NY 10017
$80 per year for membership for professional writers and associates plus a subscription to *The Third Degree*, the group's official newsletter. Membership is also included in the regional MWA chapter. Membership includes the official Edgar Award program.

Private Eye Writers of America
4342H Forest DeVille Drive
St. Louis, MO 63129-1833
$50 per year for membership for professional writers and associates plus a subscription to *Reflections in a Private Eye*, the official newsletter.

Sisters in Crime (http://www.sistersincrime.org)
PO Box 442124
Lawrence, KS 66044
$35 per year membership for those who support women writers in the mystery field.

Publishers

Bookwire's index to publishers (http://www.bookwire.com/bookwire)

Independent Mystery Publishers (www.mysterypublishers.com)

Major Houses

Penguin: http://www.penguinputnam.com

Random House: http://www.randomhouse.com/BB/MOTI

St. Martin's Minotaur: http://www.minotaurbooks.com/

Soho Press: www.sohopress.com

Simon & Schuster: http://www.simonsays.com/email_update.cfm

Small Presses

Crippen & Landru Publishers: http://www.crippenlandru.com

The Do-Not Press: http://www.thedonotpress.co.uk

Five Star Press (PO Box 159. Thorndyke, ME 04986-0159, USA)

Intrigue Press: http://www.intriguepress.com

Dennis McMillan Publications: http://www.dennismcmillan.com

No Exit Press: http://www.noexit.co.uk

Perseverance Press/John Daniel & Co.: http://www.danielpublishing.com/perseverance

The Rue Morgue Press: http://www.ruemorguepress.com

Author Index

Title Index

Character Index

Subject Index

If any subject appears more than five times within a series, it is listed only once. Please check the series listing for exact titles.

Locations Index

This location index is provided with one caution. Mystery authors, for obvious reasons, occassionally feel more comfortable writing about a location that reflects reality but is disguised behind a pseudonym. Be aware that some of the locations listed below are listed under their name as presented in the work, including locations that are completely fictional. If any location appears more than five times within a series, it is listed only once. Please check the series listing for exact titles

United States

Undefined States